THE HUGUENOTS

AND

HENRY OF NAVARRE

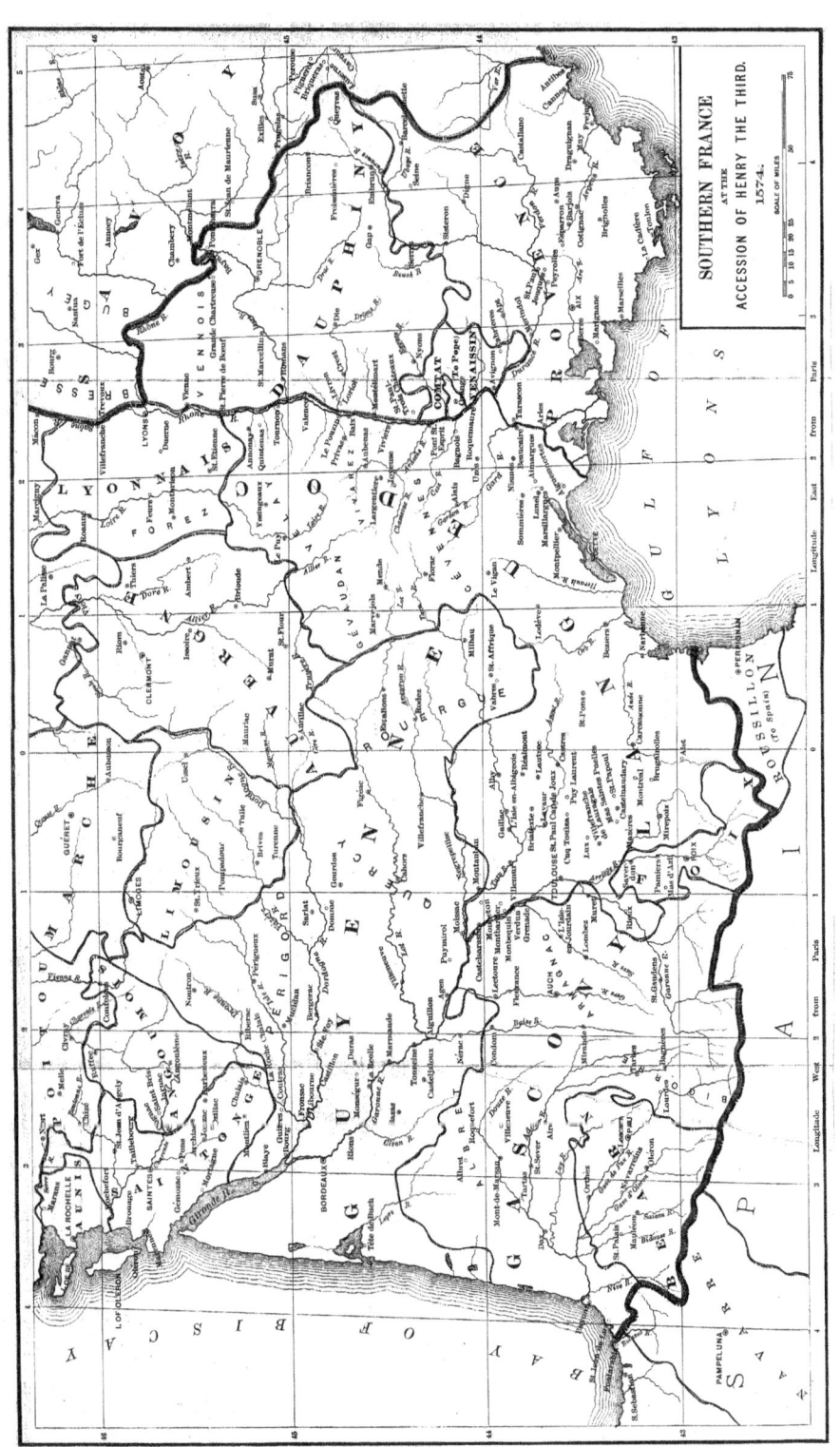

THE HUGUENOTS

AND

HENRY OF NAVARRE

BY

HENRY M. BAIRD

PROFESSOR IN THE UNIVERSITY OF THE CITY OF NEW YORK; AUTHOR OF THE HISTORY OF
THE RISE OF THE HUGUENOTS OF FRANCE

WITH MAPS

VOL. I.

Wipf & Stock
PUBLISHERS
Eugene, Oregon

Wipf and Stock Publishers
199 W 8th Ave, Suite 3
Eugene, OR 97401

The Huguenots and Henry of Navarre, Volume 1
By Baird, Henry M.
Softcover ISBN-13: 979-8-3852-0407-6
Hardcover ISBN-13: 979-8-3852-0408-3
eBook ISBN-13: 979-8-3852-0409-0
Publication date 9/26/2023
Previously published by , 1896

This edition is a scanned facsimile of the original edition published in 1896.

PREFACE.

In the History of the Rise of the Huguenots I attempted to trace the progress of the Protestant party in France from the feeble and obscure beginnings of the Reformation to the close of the reign of Charles the Ninth ; when, by reason of heroic struggles, and of the fortitude wherewith persecution and treachery had been endured, the Huguenots had gained an enviable place in the respect and admiration of Christendom. In the present work I have undertaken to portray the subsequent fortunes of the same valiant people, through a period not less critical and not less replete with varied and exciting incident, down to the formal recognition of their inalienable rights of conscience in a fundamental law of the kingdom, declared to be perpetual and irrevocable. As the Massacre of St. Bartholomew's Day constituted the most thrilling occurrence related in the former volumes, so in the volumes now offered to the public the promulgation of the Edict of Nantes is the event toward which the action throughout tends, and in relation to which even transactions of little weight in themselves assume importance. A conflict persistently maintained in vindication of an essential principle of morals is always a noble subject of contemplation. But when the matter at issue is nothing less than the claim to liberty of religious thought and expression, the assertion of the indefeasible title of all mankind to absolute freedom in the worship of Almighty God, the strife becomes invested with the highest interest; and the men who, for a long series of years, have stood forth as champions of a doctrine once ignored, or denied, receive the homage due to such as have benefited their race. The fact that their exertions were crowned with success adds lustre to their bravery and perseverance. Nor does it detract from the glory of their deeds or the interest of the recital that, possibly in a strange and wholly unlooked-for way, the general course of events was shaped to further their designs, so that the very steps taken by their opponents conduced marvellously to hasten the advance of the cause which those opponents sought to retard and overthrow.

During the greater part of the period of thirty-six years covered by these volumes (1574–1610), the history of the Huguenots was so closely interwoven with the general history of France that it would be impracticable to narrate the one without the other. The wars by which France was convulsed were waged for the purpose of constraining the Protestant minority in the kingdom to a conformity with the creed and rites approved by the Roman Catholic majority. The "Holy League" found the pretext for its existence in the popular belief that the ancestral religion was in danger of decline and ultimate ruin because of the lukewarmness of the reigning monarch and the heterodoxy of his prospective successor. The historian of the Huguenots is consequently compelled to be to some extent the historian of the war against the League. For the elected "Protector of the Churches" is the same Henry of Bourbon, King of Navarre, whose sword is to slay the hydra-headed monster of rebellion against the crown of France. More than this, the Huguenot noblemen and burgesses are the followers without whose support that sword would have been powerless to perform such prodigies of valor. The figure of Henry is not, it is true, the only heroic figure that comes upon the stage of action. His cousin Condé was even more devoted to Huguenot interests; and François de Châtillon, Count of Coligny, a worthy son of the famous admiral, bade fair, had not his life been cut short, to rival the fame, as he already emulated the manly courage and Christian virtues, of a father upon whose greatness the crime of Catharine de' Medici and the Guises had irrevocably set the seal of history. Yet the chivalrous form of Henry of Navarre is that of the chief actor upon whom the eye naturally and unavoidably rests, with the expectation that his words and his actions will exercise an influence leading if not decisive. Next in interest, therefore, to the edict by which he gave liberty of conscience and of worship to the Huguenots of France, stands the act of defection to the faith in which he had been reared—the Abjuration at Saint Denis, which must ever remain the great blot upon his fame as a man and a ruler, because based upon no conscientious convictions, but solely on motives of political expediency. To trace the decadence that led to an act as disastrous to public morality as disgraceful to the king himself must form a portion of my task in the following pages.

The marginal notes will, for the most part, furnish the necessary information regarding the authorities consulted. I have aimed to make conscientious use of every available source of accurate knowledge, whether Protestant or Roman Catholic. The extended historical works of De Thou and his continuator Rigault, of Agrippa d'Aubigné, of Jean de Serres, of Davila, of Benoist, and others, have afforded the means of comparison with the precious collection of fugitive papers and pamphlets contained in the "Mémoires de la Ligue," the "Mémoires de Nevers," and the "Archives curieuses" of Cimber and Danjou ; with the immensely extended correspondence of Duplessis Mornay ; with the Mémoires of Sully, and the less familiar Mémoires of Saint-Auban, Bouillon, Groulart, etc.; and with the letters of Hubert Languet, Busbecq, Pasquier, and other contemporaries. I have made constant use of the "Bulletin" of the French Protestant Historical Society, and the "France Protestante" of the brothers Haag, to both of which I expressed my indebtedness in the preface to my previous work. Without referring in detail to the collections of State Papers long known to the public, I desire to state the great benefit I have derived from the invaluable "Lettres missives de Henri IV," and from the despatches of the Florentine agents resident at the court of France (Petrucci, Alamanni, Cavriana, Rucellai, etc.), published under the title of "Négociations diplomatiques avec la Toscane ;" as well as from Professor A. Kluckhohn's collection of the letters of Frederick the Pious, and his monograph, "Zwei pfälzische Gesandschaftsberichte," in the Transactions of the Bavarian Royal Academy, and from the correspondence of the Guises with the ambassadors of Philip the Second and the Duke of Parma, edited by De Croze. Among the more recent contributions to historical science that have afforded me important assistance, I shall confine myself to a simple mention of Poirson, on the Reign of Henry the Fourth ; of Picot, on the States General ; of Anquez, on the Political Assemblies of the Huguenots ; of Mörikofer, on the Refugees in Switzerland ; of Professor Loutchitzky's "Documents inédits pour servir à l'histoire de la Réforme et de la Ligue ;" of M. Henri Fazy's "Genève, le Parti huguenot et le Traité de Soleure ;" of the

Mémoires of Gaches, on the Religious Wars at Castres and in Languedoc; of the Mémoires of La Huguerye; of Daval, on the History of the Reformation at Dieppe; of Count Delaborde, on François de Châtillon; of Read, on Daniel Chamier; of Stähelin, on the Abjuration of Henry the Fourth; and of Nicolas and Bourchenin, on the Protestant Académies, or Universities of France.

In the publication of the present volumes I carry out in part the plan I proposed for myself in the preface to the Rise of the Huguenots. Should they be received with the measure of favor extended, on both sides of the ocean, to that work, I hope at some future time to bring the historical series to its natural conclusion in a History of the Revocation of the Edict of Nantes, a theme to which new attention has been drawn by the commemoration, in many countries and in both hemispheres, of the Bicentenary of the promulgation of Louis the Fourteenth's proscriptive ordinance.

UNIVERSITY OF THE CITY OF NEW YORK,
August 24, 1886.

CONTENTS

OF

VOLUME FIRST.

BOOK I.

CHAPTER I.

1574–1576.

	Page
THE ACCESSION OF HENRY OF VALOIS, AND THE WAR AGAINST THE HUGUENOTS	3
Growth of the Huguenots in the Preceding Reigns	3
Catharine de' Medici's Letter	8
Mourning of "La Reine Blanche"	9
Henry's Anxiety	10
The Huguenots in Arms	11
Revival of Feudalism	12
Perplexity of the King of Poland	13
Escape from Cracow	14
Henry at Venice	14
Huguenot Leaders	15
The Prince of Condé	15
Losses in Normandy	16
Marshal Damville and the Parliament of Toulouse	17
Capture of Castres	17
First Siege of Livron	18
Condé's Declaration	19
Political Assembly at Milhau	21
Opposition to Alliance with the Politiques	22
The Alliance a Necessity	23
The Question of Religious Toleration	23
Henry's Tastes pacific	24
His first Intentions	25
Good Advice of the Emperor and the Doge	26

CONTENTS.

	Page
Of the Elector	26
And of the Prince of Orange	27
Special Instructions of Lord North	27
Intolerant Counsels of the Pope and the Queen Mother	28
Catharine's Influence	29
Damville's Interview at Turin	30
The Royal Council deliberates	31
Paul de Foix's Plea for Peace	31
Villequier's Reply	32
Henry resolves to Prepare for War	33
Official Declaration	35
Huguenot Operations	35
Montbrun's courageous Answer	36
Henry at Avignon	37
He joins the Flagellants	38
Death of the Cardinal of Lorraine	39
His Character	40
His Claim to have caused the Massacre	41
His Responsibility	41
The Huguenots of Livron	42
Capture of Fontenay and Lusignan	43
The Fairy Mélusine	44
Henry's Coronation and Marriage	45
His growing Devotion to Pleasure	47
His Lavishness and Penury	47
Conference of Nismes	47
Negotiations for Peace (April, 1575)	48
Beza's broad Statesmanship	49
Speech of Arènes	51
The Huguenot Demands	52
Surprise and Indignation	54
The Demand for Religious Liberty	55
Maximilian's Example	56
Catharine urges a better Offer	58
Punishment of the Authors of the Massacre demanded	59
Henry asseverates his Innocence	60
Coligny's Memory vindicated	60
Unpalatable Propositions	61
The Envoy of the Politiques derided	62
Henry offers unacceptable Terms	63
He substitutes better Conditions	63
End of the Negotiations	64
"The prodigious Demand for the Edict of January"	64
Intercessions of Foreign States	65
Treacherous Disguises	66
Capture of Montbrun (July, 1575)	67

CONTENTS. xiii

	Page
Henry is resolved that Montbrun shall die	68
Montbrun's Execution	69
Lesdiguières	69
Alençon's Escape and Proclamation (September, 1575)	70
The Huguenots duped	71
Catharine's Grief genuine	71
Wretched Condition of the Tiers État	72
"Le Manant paye tout"	74
Corruption of the Court	74
Puerile Extravagance and Lewdness	75
Henry and his Dogs	75
Foreign help for the Huguenots	77
Defeat of Thoré	79
A hollow Truce	80
Vain Efforts of the King to raise Money	81
Henry's whimsical Revenge	81
General Confusion	82
The Truce of Vivarais	82
The honorable Observance	85
Henry of Navarre escapes from Court	85
Entrance of the Germans into France	87
Excesses of the Reiters	88
Stout Demands of the Protestants	90
The Points which Catharine will not yield	91
Impatience of Henry and of the People	92
Edict of Pacification (Beaulieu, May, 1576)	93
Fourquevaulx's Description of the Condition of Languedoc	95

CHAPTER II.

1576–1577.

THE STATES GENERAL OF BLOIS AND THE SIXTH CIVIL WAR	97
Unpopularity of the "Paix de Monsieur"	97
Henry insists on carrying out the Provisions	98
Private Sentiments of the King	99
Alençon won from the Huguenots	100
Henry and Catharine indignant at the Guises	101
Royal Instructions to Montpensier	102
Humières resists the Edict at Péronne	103
The Origin of the League	104
Revival of the League after the Massacre	106
The Fraternities of Penitents contribute thereto	106
Manifesto of the League of Péronne	107

CONTENTS.

	Page
Oath of the League	107
Condé and Navarre	108
Caution of La Rochelle	108
Cardinal Bourbon and the Huguenots of Rouen	110
Threatening Indications	112
Extension of the League	114
A Roman Catholic Reaction	115
Suspicions of the Huguenots aroused	115
Henry's ignoble Pursuits	116
A Portrait of Henry of Valois	118
A Pasquinade against the King	118
Elections for the States General	119
Revolution in the Royal Policy	120
How to be accounted for	120
The Mémoire of Nicholas David	122
Was the Paper genuine?	126
Henry determines to become Head of the League	127
The King's "Little Council"	127
Henry's Letters of December 2, 1576	128
Opening of the States General (December 6)	128
Henry's Speech	129
Address of Chancellor Birague	130
Bold Demands of the States	131
Henry's Activity	133
His Vacillation	134
The Proscriptive Declaration (December 29, 1576)	134
Henry asks the Written Opinions of his Council	136
Candor of Morvilliers and Bellièvre	137
The Duke of Anjou entrapped	138
Politic Course of Guise and Montpensier	139
Deputies of the Three Orders before the King (January 17, 1577)	140
The Tiers État consents to the Repeal of the Edict	141
Huguenot Preparations	141
Envoys sent by the States to Henry of Navarre	142
Reply of the King of Navarre	144
Henry's Significant Assurance	145
Condé refuses to recognize the Delegates	146
His Protest	146
Marshal Damville's Reply to the States and to the King	147
Progress of Religious Toleration	148
Opposition to Signing the League in Paris	149
In Amiens and in Provins	149
Distress of the People	150
The Tiers État in Favor of Peace	151
Intercession of the Germans	152
The Protestant Counter-League	152

CONTENTS. XV

	Page
The King's Failure to obtain Funds	153
Fresh Consultation respecting the War	154
Nevers proposes a Crusade	154
Catharine speaks out for Peace	155
Henry declares his Change of Purpose	156
Catharine's Raillery	157
The Italian Comedians	157
The Sixth Civil War	158
Huguenot Reverses and bad Discipline	159
The Reformation and Democracy	159
Contrast with revived Feudalism	160
Misunderstanding between Damville and the Huguenots	161
Surprise of Montpellier	162
Charges against Damville	162
The Marshal's Reply	163
Navarre attempts to mediate	164
Thoré becomes Leader in Languedoc	164
End of the Sixth Civil War	165
Edict of Potiers (September, 1577)	165

CHAPTER III.

1577–1580.

THE CONFERENCE OF NÉRAC, AND THE SEVENTH CIVIL WAR	168
Contrast between the Edict of Poitiers and the Edict of January	168
The Situation accepted	169
Calumnies against the Huguenots	170
Accused of spreading the Plague	170
The Peace only partially observed	171
Ninth National Synod (Sainte Foy, 1578)	173
Dispute between Condé and the Consistory of La Rochelle	176
Degeneracy of Henry the Third	177
New Favorites and old Feudal Lords	178
Penury and Prodigality of the Court	180
The Provincial States protest	181
Debts of Henry of Guise	183
The Duke of Anjou	183
Singular Compact in the Comtât Venaissin	184
Papal Inconsistencies	185
The Conference of Nérac	187
"Langage de Canaan"	187
A Huguenot Retort	188
Henry of Navarre's Revenge	188
The Articles of Nérac	190

xvi   CONTENTS.

	Page
Henry the Third becomes Protector of Geneva	190
The King of France's Devotions	192
He institutes the "Ordre du Saint Esprit"	193
Popular Superstition	193
The People's Vengeance on the Lazy Priest	193
The Clergy reluctant to help the King	195
Tenth National Protestant Synod (1579)	196
Continuance of the Peace threatened	196
Preparations of the King of Navarre	198
Growing Discontent and Violent Measures	198
Outbreak of the Seventh Civil War (April, 1580)	200
The King of Navarre justifies his Course	200
Was the War unavoidable?	203
"La Guerre des Amoureux"	204
Most of the Huguenots take no Part	204
The Huguenots at Montaigu	205
Surprise of Cahors (May, 1580)	205
Ravages of the Plague in Paris	208
General Success of the Royal Arms	209
The Treaty of Fleix (November–December, 1580)	210
Conclusion of the Seventh Civil War	210

CHAPTER IV.

1580–1584.

THE UNCERTAIN PEACE, PROTESTANT FEDERATION AND THE PARISIAN LEAGUE

	Page
THE UNCERTAIN PEACE, PROTESTANT FEDERATION AND THE PARISIAN LEAGUE	212
Return of Comparative Quiet	212
Henry of Navarre's Justification	213
His own Court	214
Political Assembly of Montauban (April, 1581)	215
Checks upon the Authority of the "Protector of the Churches"	215
National Synod of La Rochelle (June, 1581)	217
Conflict of Civil and Ecclesiastical Authority	218
Ministerial Support	221
National Synod of Vitré (May, 1583)	222
Infractions of the Peace	223
The Duke of Mayenne in Dauphiny	224
St. Bartholomew's Massacre commemorated	225
Henry and his Mignons	226
Joyeuse and Épernon	226
The King attempts to remove Montmorency	227
The Nuns of Poissy	228
Infamy of the Royal Morals	229

CONTENTS.

	Page
Financial Embarrassment and Dangerous Expedients	230
Institution of the Fraternity of the Annunciation	231
The King's Waning Devotion	232
His Superstition	233
Discontent of the Guises	233
Conspiracy between the Guises, Savoy, and Spain	234
Doubtful Loyalty of Montmorency	235
Philip attempts to seduce the King of Navarre	235
Henry's Irresolution	236
He still leans to the Guises	237
Discourages the Advances of Navarre	237
The Affront to the King of Navarre	238
The Jesuits promote the League	241
Proposed Universal League among Protestants	243
The "Formula Concordiæ"	245
Scheme of Henry of Navarre	245
Mission of Ségur Pardaillan	247
The Envoy's Instructions	248
The Justification of the King of Navarre	250
His reply to the Threats of Henry III. (December, 1583)	251
Ségur's Mission misrepresented	252
Ungracious Letter of the German Princes (March, 1585)	253
The Scheme receives its Death-Blow	255
Henry's Disappointment	255
His tardy Reply to the Princes (February 15, 1589)	255
Contemporary View of Henry's Resources	257
The Protestant Cities and Regions	260
Death of the Duke of Anjou (June 10, 1584)	262
Disastrous Results of this Event	265
The Thought of a Huguenot King repulsive to the Roman Catholics	265
Authorship of the League	266
Philip the Second and the Jesuits	267
Henry of Valois recognizes Henry of Navarre as his Successor	268
Duplessis Mornay's sound Advice	270
Navarre is entreated to abjure Protestantism	271
His noble Reply	271
Reports of his "incorrigible Obstinacy"	271
Hostile Rumors	272
A pretended Protestant Confederacy	272
A clumsy Forgery	273
The League in Paris the Result of a systematic Plan	274
Scheme of Charles Hotman	275
The Council and the "Five"	275

Florimond de Ræmond's Account of the Huguenot Worship . . 277

xviii   CONTENTS.

CHAPTER V.

1584–1585.

	Page
THE HOLY LEAGUE AND THE EDICT OF NEMOURS	281
The King's cordial Hatred of the Huguenots	281
His Plan for the Extinction of Protestantism	282
Ambition of the Duke of Guise	283
Designs upon England	284
Dissension between the Conspirators	284
The Plot laid bare	285
Bernardino de Mendoza	286
The Huguenots and the Cities of Refuge	287
Reasons for the Retention of the Cities	288
The King reluctantly prolongs the Term of the Protestant Possession	290
The League circulates alarming Rumors	290
Narrative of Nicholas Poulain	291
Pretended Huguenot Conspiracy	292
Offer of the Sovereignty of the Netherlands to the King	294
A Royal Declaration against the League (November 11, 1584)	295
Conference of the League at Joinville (December, 1584)	296
Terms of the Alliance	297
Designs of Philip II.	298
Duplicity of the Duke of Guise	299
The Duke of Nevers resolves to consult the Pope	300
Gregory's Caution as to committing his Views to Paper	301
His Displeasure at the Duke's Pertinacity	302
Consecrated Rosaries in Place of Advice	303
Death of Pope Gregory	303
Sixtus V. censures the League	304
He bitterly condemns Gregory's Course	304
Ambition the Motive of the League	305
Unworthy Treatment of the Dutch Envoys	306
Mendoza tries to prevent an Audience	307
His reported Insolence	307
Magnanimous Reply ascribed to the King	308
Meanness of his real Speech	309
Insincerity of the King and Queen Mother	309
Failure of the Embassy	310
The Loss to France	310
Queen Elizabeth sends Earl Derby to France	311
Reported Atrocities of the English Persecution	312
New Edict against the League (March 28, 1585)	313
Declaration of Cardinal Bourbon (Péronne, March 31, 1585)	314
Henry of Valois publishes a Counter Declaration (April, 1585)	317
An undignified Answer	318

CONTENTS.

	Page
The King's spasmodic Activity	319
His Hatred of the Guises	320
The Guard of the "Forty-five"	321
His Unconcern	321
He desires to leave Matters of State to his Mother	322
General Success of the League	323
Philip the Second's Assurances	325
Henry of Valois writes to Henry of Navarre	326
He fails to call in his Assistance	326
Navarre's Offer declined	327
His Letters	327
The War to sift out true Frenchmen	328
Navarre's renewed Offers	328
Forcible Plea of the Bishop of Acqs	329
Remonstrances of Queen Elizabeth	330
And of the German Princes	331
The King's Evil Counsellors	331
His moral Turpitude	331
Navarre holds a Conference of Huguenot Chiefs	332
Advice of the Viscount of Turenne	333
Reply of Agrippa d'Aubigné	334
Henry of Navarre adopts D'Aubigné's View	335
Arrogance of the League	336
Its pretended Petition (June 9, 1585)	336
Insincerity of its Offer	337
Manifesto of Navarre, Bergerac (June 10, 1585)	337
Navarre challenges Guise	340
Favorable Impression produced	341
Guise declines the Challenge	341
Navarre's Willingness to be instructed arouses Suspicion	342
His Letter to the King (July 10, 1585)	343
The Conference of Nemours	344
Intolerant Edict of Nemours (July 18, 1585)	345
Conduct of the Guises approved	345
Practical Advantages secured by the League	346
The Guises renounce all Associations	346
The King orders Parliament to register the Edict	347

CHAPTER VI.

1585–1586.

PROSCRIPTION OF THE HUGUENOTS.—HENRY OF NAVARRE EXCOMMUNICATED BY THE POPE 349
A difficult Problem confronts the Huguenots 349
Joint Declaration of Navarre, Condé, and Montmorency . . . 350

CONTENTS.

	Page
Secret Correspondence of Henry of Navarre	352
Should Colonies be settled in France?	353
Contrast between the two Kings	353
Henry of Valois demands Money from the City of Paris and the Clergy	354
Who excuse themselves	355
Henry's significant Observation	355
The King of France and the Pope	356
Royal Embassy to seek Navarre's Conversion	356
His Readiness to submit to a Council	357
His Message to the Duke of Montpensier	358
Intrigue of Guise with the Spanish Ambassador	359
Margaret of Valois an Ally of the League	360
Guise impatient for the Excommunication of Henry of Navarre	361
Alliance with Montmorency essential to the Success of the League	362
Guise bids Mayenne avoid attacking Montmorency	363
Philip of Spain procrastinates	363
Protestation of Marshal Montmorency	364
Sixtus V. still opposes the League	365
He excommunicates and deposes the King of Navarre	366
Indignation and Ridicule in France	367
Navarre challenges the Pope to appear before a General Council	368
Hotman's "Brutum Fulmen"	369
Royal Declaration of October 7, 1585	370
Remonstrance of the Parliament of Paris	370
Forcible Plea for Liberty of Conscience	370
Crime of Proscription	371
Parliament's Opinion of the Papal Bull	372
Displeasure of Catharine de' Medici	373
The Printer punished	374
Henry of Navarre retaliates	374
The Enterprise of Angers	374
The Castle of Angers	374
A Plot to surprise it	375
The Castle in Huguenot Hands	377
Condé advances to Anjou	377
Peril and Escape of his Army	378
General Discouragement of the Huguenots	380
Numerous Apostacies	382
Flight into foreign Lands	382
The Huguenots in Savoy	383
A general Roll of the Protestants made	384
Perplexity of the Roman Catholic Bishops	385
A Confession of Faith imposed on Converts	386
Additional Guarantee of Sincerity	386
Pastoral Remonstrances	387
Jealousy among the Huguenot Leaders	387

CONTENTS. xxi

	Page
Henry of Navarre writes to the City of Paris	388
His Appeal to the Clergy	389
His Remonstrances addressed to the Nobles and Commons	390
Indecisive Warfare	391
The King's Levies in Germany and Switzerland	392
Guise's Anxiety lest Peace should ensue	392
His Entry into Paris (February, 1586)	393
Procrastination of the Duke of Mayenne	394
Huguenot Sarcasm	396
Condé returns to France (January, 1586)	396
Death of D'Andelot's Sons	397
Henry of Valois's Diversions	397
His injudicious financial Edicts	398
Intercession of the Protestant Cantons of Switzerland	399
Appeal of the German Princes	400
Conference of Montbéliard (March, 1586)	400
The Embassy reaches Paris	401
Speech of Duke Casimir's Envoy	402
The King's rough Answer	404
The Guises determined not to disarm	405
Conference of the League at Ourcamp	405
The League apprehensive	406
Conference between Catharine and Navarre, at Saint Bris (December, 1586)	407
Catharine refuses to grant religious Liberty	411
The Possibility of Navarre's Conversion	413
Huguenot Distrust of Garrisons	415
François de Châtillon and Milhau-en-Rouergue	415
Mutual Jealousy between Citizens and Soldiers	416
The Citizens become Masters of the Place	416
The " Citadel " demolished	417

CHAPTER VII.

1587.

THE BATTLE OF COUTRAS, AND THE ARMY OF THE REITERS	418
The War accomplishes nothing	418
Zeal of the League at Paris	419
Annoyance of the Duke of Guise	420
Huguenot Successes in Poitou	420
Lesdiguières in Dauphiny	420
Rout of Swiss Auxiliaries	422
Irresolution of the King	423
Parties at Court	423
The Queen Mother's Interview with Guise (May, 1587)	424

CONTENTS.

	Page
Meeting of the King and Guise (July, 1587)	425
The Duke's Debts	426
Joyeuse marches toward Guyenne	426
The Count of Soissons and the Prince of Conty join Navarre	428
Navarre marches toward the Dordogne	428
He takes position at Coutras	429
The Huguenot Line	430
Battle of Coutras (October 20, 1587)	431
Gabriel d'Amours offers Prayer	431
A Huguenot Battle Psalm	433
Rout and Death of Joyeuse	434
Navarre's Bravery	434
Prayer and Psalm after Battle	435
The first Pitched Battle gained by the Huguenots	436
The Fruits of Victory lost	437
Navarre's Justification	438
Queen Elizabeth renders Assistance	440
The Army of the Reiters	441
John Casimir's Compact	441
Baron Dohna	442
The Reiters enter Lorraine	442
Route taken by the Germans	444
They are joined by François de Châtillon	445
Want of Discipline and Losses	445
The Germans disregard Navarre's Orders, and push on to the Loire	446
They insist on going westward	447
Guise's Correspondence with the Spaniards	447
He attacks the Reiters at Vimory	449
He publishes glowing Accounts of his Victory	449
The Germans involved in increasing Difficulty	450
The Swiss send Deputies to the King	451
They determine to return to Switzerland	451
The Germans begin a Retreat	452
They are surprised by Guise at Auneau	453
Guise accuses the King of throwing Obstacles in his Way	453
The Reiters accept a Safe-conduct to Germany	454
Indignation of the League	455
Guise and Du Pont lay waste the County of Montbéliard	455
Magnanimity of François de Châtillon	457
His daring Retreat to Languedoc	457

MAP.

SOUTHERN FRANCE AT THE ACCESSION OF HENRY THE THIRD. 1574.

At end of volume.

BOOK FIRST.

FROM THE ACCESSION OF HENRY THE THIRD (1574) TO
THE BATTLE OF COUTRAS (1587).

BOOK FIRST.

FROM THE ACCESSION OF HENRY THE THIRD (1574) TO THE BATTLE OF COUTRAS (1587).

CHAPTER I.

THE ACCESSION OF HENRY OF VALOIS, AND THE WAR AGAINST THE HUGUENOTS.

AT the date of the accession of the last Valois to the throne of France, more than fifty years had elapsed since the first appearance of that religious and patriotic party whose adherents, after bearing the names of Lutherans, Christaudins, and Calvinists, had finally come to be commonly known as Huguenots. A movement begun in weakness had gained strength in face of formidable opposition. The short-lived favor of Francis the First was succeeded by persecution of the most cruel type. For nearly forty years the gallows, and the "estrapade" with its protracted torture, did their worst, but all in vain. During the short reign of Francis the Second the forces hitherto latent burst forth, and men discovered for the first time that the "new doctrines," as they were called, had enlisted under their banner not only the greater part of the intelligent classes of the population, but a considerable proportion of the nobility and gentry of the realm. It was not, however, until the beginning of the reign of Charles the Ninth that an opportunity was afforded to the Huguenots,

Growth of the Huguenots in the preceding reigns.

at the Colloquy of Poissy, to set forth before the king and his assembled court the true nature of their doctrines and purposes. All France, at this time, was inflamed with the desire to know for itself the merits of the new reformation. Whole provinces in the South seemed to have embraced Protestantism. The children of many districts "learned religion only in Calvin's catechism;" and vast congregations flocked to the Huguenot preaching. The ferment extended to Central France. The very ecclesiastics of the established church were affected. Bishops left their mitres, priests gave up their cures, monks threw off the cowl. Many of those who had not as yet taken any decided step were asking for more light upon the subject of their duty. When it was proposed to establish a Protestant theological school in Orleans, the canons of the church of the Holy Rood applauded the project and promised to come and listen to the lectures of the professors. Some parts of the North were not behind the fervid South in their excitement. In the great fair of Guibray, in Normandy, no wares sold more rapidly than the books and pamphlets wherein the doctrines of the Reformation were inculcated. A quarter of a century before (in 1534) the appearance of a placard against the papal mass, affixed to the door of the king's chamber, had created unparalleled consternation at court and throughout France. In his first transports of anger Francis even went to the length of abolishing the art of printing. When his inflamed passions had had time to cool down he still thought it incumbent upon him, as the Very Christian King, to appease Heaven for the sacrilege by a pompous procession, during the course of which six Lutherans were publicly burned to death on different squares of the capital. In the banquet held at its close, in the episcopal palace, he had professed such detestation for the Protestant doctrine as to boast that, if one of his arms were infected with the poison, he would cut it off, if his children were contaminated, he would immolate them. But now, in the first year of his grandson's reign, this very placard, whose original publication had cost the lives of printers and readers, was openly distributed by boys who with a loud voice made known the hand-bill by its striking title: "True Articles respecting the

Horrible, Great, and Insupportable Abuses of the Papal Mass." So much had the times changed.¹

In the very tribunals of law, accustomed to take cognizance of the Huguenots only when sentencing them to imprisonment or death, they now found advocates or apologists. The Bishop of Paris took occasion, in Parliament (1561), to allude to the friendly arbitration by means of which the Huguenots settled, in their church sessions and otherwise, the disputes arising between members of their own communion, and declared that it was an evidence of the impudence of the Reformers that they thus interfered with the prerogative of the royal courts. But his words were ably answered by the highest judicial officer of France, grave Chancellor L'Hospital. He marvelled, he said, at the effrontery and malice of those who blamed men for settling their disputes and controversies among friends. "As if," he added, with pardonable contempt for his reverend objector, "as if the whole system of law had not been enacted, and forms of trial had not been instituted for this very purpose—that men at variance with one another might be brought into concord, and induced to live lovingly together! Whoever he be that brings about this result deserves reward and not punishment."²

It was at this favorable conjuncture, and through the efforts of such enlightened men as Michel de l'Hospital, that the "Edict of January" (1562) was published. Based on equitable principles, this law recognized liberty of conscience as the right of all, and permitted the Huguenots to worship Almighty God, according to the rites of the Reformed religion, everywhere throughout France, outside of the walls of the towns and cities. If not a perfect law, it was so well adapted to the circumstances of the case that, perhaps, nothing better, short of absolute religious equality, could have been desired. Under this ordinance, well and faithfully executed, Roman Catholics and Protestants might have lived together long years, until the fuller development of the sense of natural justice should have

---

¹ MS. Geneva Library, published in Bulletin de la Société de l'histoire du Protestantisme français, xxviii. (1879) 457.

² Letter of Hubert Languet, Paris, July 13, 1561, Epistolæ secretæ, ii. 125, 126.

abrogated its provisions only to establish in their place a freedom having its sure sanction in universal charity.

Unhappily the age of brotherly love had not yet dawned. There were those who were not inclined to leave the Edict of January to mature its kindly fruits. Within six weeks the massacre of Vassy, perpetrated upon an unoffending congregation of Protestant worshippers in a Champagnese town (March, 1562), kindled a flame which burned with little intermission to the close of the reign of Charles the Ninth. To open warfare were added the further horrors of treacherous assassination. The massacre of St. Bartholomew's Day came as the sequel of three distinct civil wars, and as the precursor of two other wars, all instituted within the brief compass of a reign of little more than twelve years. It was a legacy of bloodshed and confusion that Charles left to his brother, Henry. Thirty thousand Huguenots may have fallen victims to the conspiracy of Catharine de' Medici, the Duke of Anjou, and the Guises; but the Huguenots were not all dead. For every one that had perished by sword there remained fifty of his comrades ready to maintain the cause whose interests he had fought to defend. Admiral Coligny was no more, and many other leaders had been assassinated with him; but the experience of the two years intervening between the massacre and the close of the reign of Charles proved conclusively that all the military genius of the Huguenots had not been buried in their graves. Many of the new commanders—some of them destined soon to distinguish themselves in the art of warfare—were very young. Henry, King of Navarre, was but twenty years of age. His cousin, Henry of Condé, was just a year older. François de Châtillon, Admiral Coligny's son, was a stripling of seventeen. François de la Noue was almost the only survivor of the older Huguenot chieftains of prominent rank. The mantle was certainly falling upon shoulders unaccustomed to bear such weighty responsibility; but the sequel would prove that the men whom circumstances, strange and unexpected, called to the front line of action were by no means unworthy to be trusted with its defence. The crisis was grave, the matters to be settled were of unsurpassed importance. Not the fortunes of the combatants alone were at stake, but the cause of religious liberty must be sustained. With what fluctuations of success and defeat that cause was prosecuted until the final enactment of the edict of Henry the Fourth, placing Protestantism under the ægis of the public law of the land, is the inquiry that furnishes the main theme of the present volumes.

On Sunday, the thirtieth of May, 1574, Charles the Ninth expired in the Castle of the Bois de Vincennes. Two weeks later, the messenger of Catharine de' Medici succeeded, by almost incredible diligence, in reaching Cracow, and brought to Henry of Valois the grateful intelligence that he had fallen heir to the crown of France.

The queen mother had promptly taken every step necessary to secure the peaceful succession of her favorite son. Unmoved by the approaching end of Charles, she had, on his death-bed, prudently procured from him, or in his name, letters patent conferring upon her the regency until Henry's return from Poland. With more composure than could have been expected from a mother in her fresh bereavement, she had authorized an examination of the late monarch's body, and the next day was careful to despatch letters to all the governors of France, assuring them that a sufficient natural cause had been found by the physicians for the fatal termination of his malady. She begged them to write to the new king, and inform him of their purpose to render him the same faithful service that they had displayed to his predecessors.

Nor were the Duke of Alençon and the King of Navarre overlooked, at a moment when maternal grief is wont to induce forgetfulness of everything save its own bitterness. The two state prisoners were summoned into Catharine's presence. They were told that their fate hung upon their submission. "Promise to make no attempt to escape from me, and I will leave Vincennes for Paris; otherwise I shall remain in the castle until my son's return from Poland." The youths not only yielded a most humble assent, but made no objection to signing letters addressed to the governors of all the provinces, commending the queen mother's course, and advocating a loyal recognition of her authority.[1] But on reaching the Louvre, the princes scarcely found their condition improved. Catharine kept her son and the King of Navarre within the castle, with guard upon guard. She had the chamber-windows grated like a prison, and stopped all the back passages into the town. "There is marvellous misliking at this dealing amongst all men," exclaims the indignant English ambassador. None the less did the queen mother maintain with effrontery to all with whom she conversed, that she would not have accepted the regency except at the request of the princes, and that whatever was done was done by their consent. At this very moment everybody knew that in truth Alençon did not dare to speak to anyone and no one dared speak to him. It was a curious commentary upon the queen's hypocritical assurances, that, directly after the audience at which she gave utterance to them, Alençon and Navarre sent a messenger to the favored Englishmen, to state that they had been constrained to use the speeches they had made. They desired Queen Elizabeth to continue her good friendship, and asked that she be informed when the Prince of Condé should be ready to start from Germany. Indeed, they entreated the prudent Queen of England to effect a landing on the coasts of Normandy, and entered into details of so perilous a character that the envoys deemed it the dictate of prudence not to commit them to paper.[2]

M. de Chemerault, Catharine's messenger to Poland, was entrusted with a long letter to the absent king. This production —no formal state paper, the work of the pen of her secretaries, but bearing on every line the impress of the queen mother's own mind—reveals the existence of a certain kind of grief, and of a cool calculation that seems never to have forsaken her. The grief is natural enough, but thoroughly selfish in its origin and manifestation, and quite

Catharine's letter to her son.

---

[1] Recueil des choses mémorables, 508 ; Jean de Serres, Commentarii de statu religionis et reipublicæ, pars v., Henrico tertio rege (Leyden, 1580), fols. 2, 3 ; Vincenzo Alamanni to Fr. de' Medici, Paris, June 2, 1574, Négociations diplomatiques avec la Toscane, iii. 931.

[2] "News from Paris," sent by Dr. Dale to Lord Burleigh, June 7, 1574 ; Dr. Dale to Smith and Walsingham, June 21 ; Dr. Dale to Lord Burleigh, same date. State Paper Office.

under the control of the writer's will. It is a piteous sorrow, she says, that has befallen a mother called so often to witness the successive deaths of her children. She has but one consolation—the hope of seeing Henry soon return to enjoy his new honors. She warns him that if she were to be called upon to lose him too, she would not consent to survive him. "In that case," she says, " I should cause myself to be buried alive with you!" She begs him to select the safest road returning —rather the way through the dominions of the Emperor and through Italy, than the way through the lands of the German princes, who have too many grounds of quarrel with France. She entreats him above all to make no delay in setting out, to accede to no requests from his Polish subjects who might wish to detain him until he had introduced order into the affairs of their country. At the same time she suggests, with her usual forethought, that it may be well to leave some one to govern temporarily in his place, in order that the crown of Poland may either be retained by him, or secured for his younger brother, or for the second of his own prospective sons. As for France, she counsels him to govern wisely and prudently, for the honor of God and the welfare of his subjects; to protect and reward the well-disposed, but to renounce faction, party spirit, and intimacies. " You are no longer *Monsieur* .... you are a *King* who must be served, revered, and loved by all." [1]

Meantime, while the parent who subscribed herself " your good and affectionate mother, if ever there was one on earth, Catharine," was pouring forth her measured grief and politic advice into the ears of her best loved son, the young wife of Charles the Ninth indulged in ostentatious manifestations of sorrow for the untimely death of a prince respecting whom the pope declared that his remarkable piety and singular virtue had been seen in the midst of the greatest dangers and the most trying emergencies.[2] In a dark

<small>Mourning of "La Reine Blanche."</small>

---

[1] Catharine to Henry III., Bois de Vincennes, May 31, 1574, Groen van Prinsterer, Archives de la maison d'Orange-Nassau, v. 13–16.

[2] "Cujus insignem pietatem, singularemque in maximis periculosissimisque ejus regni motibus difficillimisque temporibus virtutem perspexeramus." Gregory XIII. to Fred. de' Medici, June 11, 1574, Négociations avec la Toscane, iii. 932.

room whence every ray of the light of heaven was carefully excluded, Maximilian's daughter shut herself from the world for forty days to bewail her husband's death. The walls, the ceiling, the floor, were draped in black; the only light came from two small candles that rather revealed than dispelled the darkness. Elizabeth herself—"La reine blanche"[1]—was clad from head to foot in white, the immemorial badge of mourning of a widowed queen. Her ladies wore dresses of the same color, in startling contrast with the funeral garb of the gentlemen-in-waiting. "The mixture of black and white, with the faces pale as death in the deep gloom," says one that witnessed the scene, "produced a very touching and painful sight."[2]

The announcement of his brother's fatal illness had created in Henry of Anjou a restless and expectant condition of mind which he could not conceal from the eyes of his attendants; the tidings of that brother's death occasioned a joy that gleamed in every feature. How to get back to France as speedily as possible, was the problem which he set about solving with the help of the little company of his countrymen that formed the inner circle of his confidants. All were agreed that no time must be lost. Delay might be disastrous to the claims of the absent prince upon his ancestral throne. There was a powerful party that alleged that Henry's acceptance of the Polish crown involved a virtual renunciation of the French crown in favor of his brother, the Duke of Alençon. True, Alençon was in safe custody, and had paid for his cowardice by the sacrifice of his accomplices. So far so good.

Henry's anxiety.

---

[1] The name was derived from Queen Blanche, mother of Saint Louis, a model ruler, according to Étienne Pasquier, "laquelle s'y comporta avec telle sagesse, que tout ainsi que les Empereurs de Rome se faisoient appeller Augustes en commemoration de l'heur qui s'estoit trouvé au grand Empereur Auguste, aussi toutes les Roynes Meres anciennement, apres le decés des Roys leurs maris vouloient estre nommees Roynes Blanches, par une honorable memoire tiree du bon gouvernement de cette sage Princesse." Recherches de la France, chap. 18, book 2, p. 142.

[2] "Il che faceva, con la mistione del color nero e bianco, e con le faccie loro del color della morte in questa obscurità grandissima, un molto acerbo e doloroso spettacolo a riguardare." Alamanni to the Grand Duke, June 14, 1574, Négociations avec la Toscane, iv. 12.

"If ever I felt joy," Henry had written to one of his intimate friends, "it was when I learned that La Mole and Coconnas were well caged, but I shall never be fully satisfied till they dance with the rope about their necks."[1] But the further wish, which he had confined himself to hinting—that the same fate might also overtake others, doubtless referring to the King of Navarre, the Prince of Condé, and above all, the Duke of Alençon—had not been fulfilled. Alençon still lived, and might at any moment be supported as a candidate for the crown, if not by French arms, at least by the arms of the troublesome neighbors and allies of France. Indeed, no sooner had William of Orange heard that Charles was dead than he wrote that it was now time that the German princes should put forth every exertion to secure the crown for the Duke of Alençon.[2]

The ambition of his brother was not the only, nor, perhaps, the chief danger to be apprehended by Henry. All France was in commotion. The Huguenots were in arms. The bloody massacre of two years before, beginning in Paris, and repeating itself throughout the provinces, had not crushed them. The perfidy of the court had made them more wary, the evident determination of their enemies to compass their destruction had made them more resolute than ever to stand for their defence. Their recent struggle had been instituted rather with the desperation of men determined to sell their lives as dear as possible, than with any distinct hope of success; the favorable issue of many of their enterprises had converted the conflict into a war for the recovery of the rights pledged by solemn royal edicts. They were not crouching at the feet of a conqueror, and suing for their lives; but demanding liberty of religious worship in their sanctuaries, and satisfaction for the treachery practised upon their brethren in the

The Huguenots in arms.

---

[1] "Si jamais j'eus joye, c'a esté quand j'ay sçeu que La Mole et Coconas sont en caige, mais jusques à ce que le Seigneur qui les traictoit si doucement à la Rochelle ou un sien compaignon les hait fait dancer avecque la corde la [votte], je ne seray pas bien satisfait." Henry of Anjou to M. de Nancay, May 16, 1574, Groen van Prinsterer, iv. 375.

[2] "Et seroit maintenant temps que les Princes d'Allemaigne fissent tout debvoir possible pour faire donner la Couronne au Duc d'Alençon." Letter of the Prince of Orange, June, 1574, Groen van Prinsterer, v. 12.

faith. Either their demands must be granted, or their armed forces must be met in the field, and their strongholds carried at the point of the sword. And the problem was complicated by <small>Revival of feudalism.</small> the remarkable revival of the feudal spirit which the latter half of the sixteenth century was destined to witness—a revival which, if it obtained its full development only in the reign that was just beginning, must be regarded as deriving its first powerful impulse from the reign of Charles the Ninth. The king that undertook to wage war with a portion of his subjects, found himself compelled to purchase the support of the leading nobles in each province by the tacit acknowledgment of privileges which, when once conceded, assured to them a species of local independence. The vicious system of the transmission of civil and military offices from parent to child received a dangerous corroboration. The son was trained from his earliest days to regard the dignities and territorial authority of his father as his own just inheritance; and any attempt or threat of the crown to confer them upon another, no matter how much more competent he might be for the discharge of the functions connected therewith, was resented as an insult, and was sure to lead to open resistance. The great nobles were almost sovereign princes in their governments or provinces, the original gift of the ancestors of the reigning monarch;[1] they could be removed only by a war that might convulse the kingdom. And the consideration which they demanded from their lord paramount was exacted of them in turn by the members of the inferior nobility, to whom had been entrusted the administration of dioceses, cities, or castles.

---

[1] "Many of the greatest lords, some secretly, some openly, were alienated," says Davila, in speaking of this period; "and divers of those who had most experience in affairs, most authority with the people, and most reputation in war, were already (if I may use that word), *cantonized* in their several provinces and governments." Eng. trans. (book vi.), p. 203. Cf. Lestoile's designation, in 1583 (i. 162), of Montmorency, formerly Damville, as "gouverneur ou pour mieux dire *roy* de Languedoc." So, too (i. 63), when speaking of the refusal of the Baron de Ruffec, Governor of Angoulême, to admit Alençon (1575), despite repeated orders of the king and of Catharine de' Medici, "desquelles les gouverneurs faisoient fort peu d'estat en ce temps de' guerre, estans rois eux-mesmes."

Insubordination was rapidly becoming not the exception but the rule. Soon Henry the Third would have occasion to make the bitter remark: "See what civil wars come to! Formerly it would have puzzled a constable, a prince of the blood, to make a party in France; now the very varlets make one."[1] It was almost a necessary consequence of this relaxation of the bonds of the central government that disorder often ran riot, with few to stop its progress.[2]

Evidently Henry must lose no unnecessary time in returning to France, in accordance with the entreaties of his mother.

Perplexity of the King of Poland. But how should he accomplish his object, in view of the obstacles which the Poles would certainly interpose? The king's most candid and prudent advisers, Bellièvre and Pibrac, counselled him to adopt the manly course. Let him consult with his Polish nobles; let him establish order, and impart that confidence which Poland, so long a prey to discord and confusion, greatly needed; and then let him, with the consent of his subjects, and followed by their good wishes, revisit France. At the price of a delay which might, indeed, be tedious, and extend over months, but which would save him the loss of a crown for the acquisition of which much trouble and money had been expended not a year ago, Henry would render himself beloved, and gain a power that might be of great importance to his own ancestral dominions. On the other hand, Villequier, Souvré, and others—ministers of the king's pleasures—recommended an instant retreat from a region distasteful to Henry under any circumstances, and now doubly repulsive. Since this step could not be taken openly, let it be accomplished in secrecy. The disgrace sure to attach to the cowardly act was set forth by Pibrac, but all in vain. It was a part of the misfortune that always seemed to cling to the last Valois king of

---

[1] Lestoile (November, 1575), i. 62.
[2] The incident related by Claude Haton (ii. 770-773), although in some respects characteristic of the period, can scarcely be regarded as directly traceable to the source indicated in the text. The leader of the band of several hundred maranders who, for some days or weeks, struck terror into the inhabitants of the towns and villages of Brio, and killed, plundered, and ravished with little armed opposition, had raised his robber-soldiers under the warrant of forged letters of the king.

France that he gave a more ready hearing to bad than to good advice.¹

There is no need that the details of the precipitate and unkingly flight from Cracow to Vienna should here be repeated. Never did monarch begin his reign by a more inauspicious act, His escape from Cracow. or give clearer proof to the world that pusillanimity may easily coexist with exalted station. If the brilliancy of his entertainment by the emperor could have compensated for the ignominy of his own course, Henry might have recovered his self-respect when once he had gotten beyond the reach of his pursuers. But it may well be doubted whether all the imperial courtesies, accompanied by the suggestion that Henry should marry his brother's widow, were sufficient to obliterate from his mind the contrast between the circumstances attending his advent to Poland and those of his departure.

From Vienna the French king proceeded after a short stay to Venice, where he was received with every mark of profound Henry at Venice. respect, and entertained with a pomp that dazzled the eyes of all spectators. "As Venice surpasses all other cities of Italy," says a contemporary, "so during his sojourn of ten days did Venice seem to have outdone itself in the magnificence of its banquets and spectacles."² It was, however, but sorry fruit of so much splendor, if, as his own attendants asserted, Henry became, from the moment of his visit to the luxurious republic of the Adriatic, a changed person, appearing to have lost all manhood, and to have become weakly and effeminate.³ If Henry had been in haste to start for his native land, he now showed no disposition to hurry away from the enchantments of Italy. Accompanied by the Duke of Savoy, who had come to do him honor, he leisurely made his progress, stopping successively at Ferrara, at Mantua,

---

¹ De Thou, v. 55, 56 ; Jean de Serres, v. fols. 18-20.

² "Tanta conviviorum et spectaculorum magnificentia, ut Venetia, quæ omnes Italiæ urbes superat, seipsam tunc superasse omnino videatur." Jean de Serres, v. fol. 24.

³ Ibid., v. fol. 25. The lascivious displays to which Henry was treated were as unworthy of the doge who afforded them as they seem to have been enervating to the young prince by whom they were witnessed.

and at Turin. It was not until the second anniversary of the massacre of St. Bartholomew's day (the twenty-fourth of August, 1574), that he reached the capital of the Duke of Savoy, whose devoted services to the French monarch were amply rewarded by the impolitic cession of Pignerol and Savillian, with the Valley of Pérouse. These places had been left in the hands of the French, according to the terms of the Treaty of Cateau Cambrésis, as security for the restitution of those possessions of France which were still in the power of the Duke of Savoy. They were now given up without an equivalent, contrary to the advice of the best generals of France.[1]

It is time, however, that we should turn to the operations of the Huguenots during the months that elapsed between the death of Charles and the arrival of Henry in French territory. When the luckless "Enterprise of Saint Germain" came to an inglorious end, through the treachery or cowardice of Alençon, about three months before the conclusion of the last reign, the Prince of Condé, more fortunate than his cousin, the King of Navarre, succeeded in making good his escape from Picardy into Germany. The younger Montmorencies, the Sieurs de Thoré and Méru, joining him in his exile, added to his authority the prestige of the name of the oldest noble family in France. Condé, in view of the involuntary restraint of Alençon and Navarre, assumed the dignity of the first prince of the blood.

Huguenot leaders.

With the restless activity characteristic of that impetuous prince, Henry of Condé wrote or sent messengers in every direction, whence help for the persecuted Huguenots might be expected. Again and again, feeling the need of good advice, he begged the magistrates of Geneva to "lend" him Theodore Beza, their most prominent religious teacher, scarcely less highly valued as a prudent counsellor in political affairs than prized as a learned theologian and an eloquent preacher. In fact, so frequent and inconvenient did his calls become that at last even the self-denying Genevese grew tired, and suggested that Condé should henceforth obtain the desired counsel from the pen rather than from the lips of the

The Prince of Condé.

---

[1] De Thou, v. 100, 116-118 ; Jean de Serres, v. fol. 27.

reformer. On one occasion the prince came in person to Geneva, and there received a flattering welcome. The Council, whose notions of the sanctity of the Lord's Day seem to have been somewhat lax, among other tokens of good will, voted to "feast" Condé and his principal attendants; and the banquet, at which, we are told with great precision, six tables were spread, was set down for Sunday, the third of October.[1]

Thoré, by letters and messages, aroused the dormant energies of his brother, Marshal Damville, and impressed upon him the necessity of instituting a vigorous struggle to rescue from life-long imprisonment, if not from death, the captive head of the family, Marshal Montmorency, the Constable's oldest son.[2]

From Strasbourg and Basle, as from a centre, went forth the influences that for two years maintained the Huguenots in the field, enlisted in their behalf the sympathy and substantial support of the Protestant Princes of Germany, and finally secured very favorable terms of peace. The importance of the Protestant court on the banks of the Rhine may best be gauged by the care taken by Catharine de' Medici to maintain a body of salaried spies about Condé and his Huguenot companions, to keep her well informed respecting all their movements. She could scarcely have exhibited more solicitude to learn the secrets of a rival capital.[3]

The Huguenot arms fared differently in the North and in the South. Everything went ill with the Protestants in Normandy since the capture of Count Montgomery at the surrender of Domfront, three days before the decease of King Charles. In her glee at having finally gotten possession of the unfortunate knight who had been the instrument of the death of her husband, Catharine de' Medici did not wait for Henry's return from Poland, but hastened Montgom-

<small>Losses in Normandy.</small>

---

[1] Henri Fazy, Genève, le Parti Huguenot et le Traité de Soleure, 16, 28.
[2] Jean de Serres, v. fol. 8.
[3] " Neque obscuri rumores serebantur, Politicorum illorum non paucos primariæ notæ, Reginæ opere et artibus succenturiatos, ad Condæum in eum finem accedere, ut illius consilia explorarent." Jean de Serres, v. fols. 17, 18. Agrippa d' Aubigné (Hist. univ., ii. 176, 177) pretends to give the number of the paid spies kept by Catharine about her son Alençon and Navarre as exactly twenty-six.

ery's trial, and had the satisfaction of seeing him beheaded for treason on the Place de Grève, while Henry was still in Vienna.[1] Deprived of their leader, and overwhelmed by superior numbers, the Norman Huguenots lost one place after another. Saint-Lô was taken by assault, and two hundred men of its garrison were put to the edge of the sword; Carentan obtained honorable terms and surrendered without a blow.[2] It was otherwise in Languedoc and Dauphiny. Marshal Damville, Governor of Languedoc, although he apprehended that he might soon be compelled to make common cause with the Huguenots, at first merely concluded a truce with them; for, if he distrusted the Roman Catholic party, he had certainly no affection for the Protestants. Even the truce, however, displeased the bigots of Toulouse; especially as the truce was to be followed by a convocation of the three estates of the province at Montpellier. So the Parliament of Toulouse ventured upon the bold step of defying the marshal's authority by two public declarations. By the one the judges declared the truce to be null and void; while by the other they forbade all persons, of whatever rank or station, from attending an assembly called by the marshal without the king's permission, on pain of being declared rebels and transgressors of the laws of the realm.[3] It was not long, however, before the judges had more substantial reasons for solicitude in the capture of the important city of Castres, situated less than forty miles eastward of the seat of their parliament. Four times had the Protestant exiles from Castres sought to recover their homes from the hands of the enemy, and four times had they signally failed. Now, on the eve of a day of mournful associations for French Protestants (the twenty-third of August, 1574), a fifth attempt, planned and carried out with equal shrewdness and daring, proved altogether successful. The chronicler of the exploit has noted as worthy of everlasting remembrance the humble but glorious names of the thirteen braves, who, under the leader-

Marshal Damville and the Parliament of Toulouse.

Capture of Castres.

---

[1] Rise of the Huguenots, ii. 631-634. [2] De Thou, v. 63.
[3] Recueil des choses mémorables, 511; Jean de Serres, v. fols. 5, 6; De Thou, v. 65.

ship of the gallant Jean de Bouffard, Sieur de la Grange, forced their way in, through dangers that might well have appalled less determined men. It was one of the most glorious enterprises of a time abounding in venturesome undertakings.[1] In Dauphiny, where the experienced Huguenot Montbrun was confronted by the Roman Catholic Prince Dauphin, eldest son of the Duke of Bourbon-Montpensier,[2] success perched alternately on the one and the other standard. Here a town of small size and of no previous or subsequent importance suddenly acquired celebrity in consequence of the two sieges which it underwent. Livron, a place scarcely deserving a more pretentious designation than that of a simple village, was situated on the northern bank of the river Drôme near its confluence with the Rhône, not more than ten or twelve miles south of the episcopal city of Valence. Its very proximity to Valence,

First siege of Livron.

---

[1] See the long and interesting account in Jacques Gaches, "Mémoires sur les guerres de religion à Castres et dans le Languedoc" (first published by Charles Pradel in 1879), 174, etc. Among the most conspicuous of the thirteen were two brothers Jacques and Antoine Mascarenc, or Mascarene, one of whom may have been the progenitor of the Huguenot confessor and refugee for religion's sake, Jean Mascarene, whose story is told, and whose remarkable letters are printed, in the History of the Huguenot Emigration to America, by Charles W. Baird, ii. 124-127, and Appendix, 344-377.

[2] François de Bourbon, Prince Dauphin d'Auvergne (such was the territorial designation of the eldest son of the Duke of Montpensier), was a half-brother of the Princess Charlotte de Bourbon, whom, about a year subsequent to these occurrences (June 12, 1575), the Prince of Orange married after the divorce of the unhappy Anne of Saxony. (See Groen van Prinsterer, v. 312; Motley, Dutch Republic, iii. 21.) Charlotte had been secretly brought up by her mother, Jacqueline de Longwy, in the Protestant faith. This faith she never renounced. In 1559, an aunt having resigned in her favor the rich abbacy of Jouarre, Charlotte was forced to obey her father and enter the convent; not, however, before she had signed before a notary a protest against the act as one of constraint. The abbess embraced, in 1572, the first opportunity to escape from the convent and from France, taking refuge at the court of the elector palatine in Heidelberg. The elector refused to give her up to her father, unless the promise were first given that she should enjoy her religious liberty. De Thou, iv. 533, 534; Haag, La France protestante (2nd edit.), art. Bourbon-Montpensier, ii. 1088, 1089. Her brother became Duke of Montpensier on the death of his father (Louis), in September, 1582 (De Thou, vi. 205). He was, like his father, a devout Roman Catholic; but, unlike him, he was fair and conciliatory in his sentiments toward the Protestants. His son, Henry, died without male heirs in 1608.

while causing it to be overlooked by the Roman Catholics, added to its attractions for the adventurous Montbrun. This sagacious general, finding that Livron had become the refuge of many of the Huguenots of the neighborhood, labored to strengthen its weak fortifications, and worked to such good purpose that, when the Prince Dauphin undertook the siege, the Huguenots not only held their own, but sallying forth captured an ensign, spiked a large cannon brought to bear against their walls, and compelled the assailants to suspend for the time their offensive operations.[1] In the West of France tranquillity seemed for a time to be secured. A truce was effected by La Noue between the Roman Catholics and the Huguenots of Poitou, Saintonge, and Angoumois, according to the terms of which the Protestant garrisons were to receive a considerable monthly subsidy. It was stipulated that the truce should last for two months, by which time the return of Henry was expected; scarcely had a month elapsed when Catharine had set on foot a powerful army to overwhelm the Huguenots taken at unawares.[2] It was fortunate that the eye of La Noue had descried the danger from afar, and that he had adopted measures accordingly.

Meanwhile, before engaging in active hostilities, the Prince of Condé published to the world a statement of the causes which had led him to retire from the French court with a body of nobles and gentlemen of both religions. The "Declaration" was an impeachment of the house of Guise for all the high crimes and misdemeanors of which it had been

Condé's declaration.

---

[1] Recueil des choses mémorables, 512 ; De Thou, v. 65, 66 ; Jean de Serres, v. fol. 9. The first siege of Livron began June 23, and lasted only a few days.

[2] Recueil des choses mémorables, 514, 518 ; De Thou, v. 64, 69 ; Inventaire général de l'Histoire de France (Geneva, 1619), ii. 472. Although the name of Jean de Serres is upon the title-page of the "Inventaire," it must be remembered that Serres is the author of the work only so far as page 598 of the first volume (to the death of Charles VI.). The continuation was written by the inferior hand of Jean de Montlyard (Anquetil, Esprit de la Ligue, i. p. lxvi.), who drew, however, so largely upon the "Recueil," and the "Commentarii"—genuine works of Serres—that the "Inventaire," in the period now under consideration, is substantially the production of the voluminous and invaluable historian to whom we are so greatly indebted for our close knowledge of the events of the reigns of Charles IX. and Henry III.

guilty during the last fifteen years. Every feature of the course of the duke and his brothers was passed in review. The survey began with the abuse of their power over their nephew Francis the Second, to secure the total extinction of the royal family. It was God, not man, said Condé, that saved the Bourbons from destruction. Next came the massacre of Vassy, whereby Francis of Guise paved the way for every subsequent outrage. Four successive wars had been ended by as many edicts of pacification, each edict perfidiously violated at the instigation and by the acts of the Guises. The massacre of St. Bartholomew's day, not limited to the murder of Admiral Coligny nor confined to the capital, deluged the whole of France with innocent blood. It was a crime perpetrated in the king's name, after the commission of which letters, as from him, were despatched in every direction to princes and to commonwealths, letters infamous both for France and for Charles himself. The climax of crime was reached when the memory of Gaspard de Coligny was branded as that of a traitor, when Navarre and Condé were compelled to abjure the purer faith in which they had been educated, and when, afterward, they were forced against their will to take part at the siege of La Rochelle in a warfare against their fellow-believers. Before this city the Guises had, in fact, entered into a plot to assassinate Alençon, Navarre, and the writer himself—a plot that would have been carried into execution had not Anjou, the present King of Poland and the legitimate successor to the French crown, interfered to save him. At length, when Alençon found himself not only the object of the murderous attacks of the Guises, but defrauded of the position of lieutenant-general of the kingdom lawfully belonging to him on Anjou's departure, and treated with studied indignity, the duke resolved to withdraw from France and to seek refuge with old and tried allies of the realm. The plan having been discovered, Alençon had been thrown into confinement, as though he had plotted to take the life of his own brother, Charles the Ninth. Condé alone had succeeded, by the kind providence of the Almighty, in making his escape, and avoiding the still more terrible fate in preparation against himself. While distinctly recognizing Henry the Third as his rightful sovereign, the prince declared the demands of the Huguenots to be briefly comprehended in three: The provisional concession of universal religious liberty; the satisfaction of the honor of the victims of the massacre of St. Bartholomew's day; and the convocation of the states general of the kingdom in a free and legitimate manner. Such, with sundry complaints, somewhat stale it must be confessed, respecting the prevalence of immorality, blasphemy, and dissoluteness of dress, the oppressive taxation of the people, and kindred topics, constitute the chief contents of a paper which may well be regarded as the most authoritative declaration of the principles for which the Huguenots were in arms.[1]

At the very moment when the prince was giving to the world this public announcement of his designs, the Huguenots held in the city of Milhau-en-Rouergue a political assembly of more than ordinary importance. The South of France alone was directly represented—Languedoc, Dauphiny, and Guyenne; from the North and West no delegates were able to come on account of the desolations of war. In the deliberations now held, the terms of alliance with Marshal Damville were settled, subject only to the acceptance of the latter; while, on the other hand, the Prince of Condé was recognized as generalissimo, on condition that he should appear before the elector palatine, his son John Casimir, and the deputies of the churches, at the close of divine worship, and there take a solemn oath of fidelity to the Protestant cause. The prince was to promise in particular to live and die in the faith of the Reformed churches, and to exert all his powers for the defence of that faith and for the procuring of a public peace without religious distinctions. He was to engage never to lay down his arms without the consent of his co-religionists. He was to labor assiduously for the liberation of Alençon, Navarre, and Marshals Montmorency and Cossé, for the removal of foreigners from office, and for the appeasing of all controversies by the convocation of the states general.[2]

Political assembly at Milhau.

---

[1] Jean de Serres, v. fols. 11–14; Recueil des choses mémorables, 515. The latter gives the date, July 12, 1574.

[2] De Thou, v. 68; Recueil des choses mémorables, 516, 517; Jean de Serres,

It cannot be said that the new relations into which the Huguenots were on the point of entering were altogether satisfactory to the majority of the adherents of the party.

<small>Opposition to alliance with the Politiques.</small> The struggle which they had carried on with comparatively brief intermissions for the past fourteen years was a struggle not so much to defend civil rights as to maintain religious life. Reluctant as the Protestants had been to draw the sword in so holy a cause, they had been reconciled to this wretched necessity by the hope that they might be able to maintain, in the midst of the horrors of warfare and the temptations of the camp, a discipline so strict and exemplary as to elicit the approval of the most prejudiced of their opponents. For a time, under really devout and conscientious leaders, the Huguenot armies had in some measure realized this exalted ideal. The lapses from the religious and moral standard had, however, been deplorably numerous; and if it might still be asserted with truth that the Huguenot soldiers could generally be distinguished from the Roman Catholic troops by a higher tone of morals, by a closer adherence to truth, by an absence of profane oaths and blasphemous expressions, and by the fact that they were less addicted to the crying sin of the times, a foulness of speech and of writing almost beyond conception—if all this might be asserted with truth, yet it must be admitted that the contrast, altogether honorable to their faith, was attained only by the application of ecclesiastical laws and regulations whose severity the Roman Catholics derided as absurd and tyrannical. What, then, could be expected from an alliance with Damville and the Roman Catholics of his suite who made no pretence of affection for Protestantism? It is true that the marshal was to pledge his word not to introduce the Romish service into any town of which the Huguenots were masters; but could he promise that his soldiers would not introduce Roman Catholic manners and practices into Huguenot armies? Among warriors fighting under the same colors how could different standards of discipline be established for the different corps?

---

v. fols. 8, 14-17. In complaining of the unlawful participation of foreigners in the public administration, the Huguenots stated that they did not mean to include the queen mother.

Besides, the marshal himself was not above reproach, and his dissolute life, even if temporarily veiled by an appearance of decency and self-control, could not be forgotten by those acquainted with his past history.[1]

And yet we cannot be astonished, nor can we condemn with severity the Huguenot leaders if they accepted the proffered help of the great Montmorency of the South. Huguenot and Politique had a common enemy and, partly, common grievances. Both denied the legitimacy of the system under which France had been governed for many years; both demanded that foreigners be deprived of the undue share of the administration which they held, and that the will of the nation be consulted through the states general; both were indignant that a regent should pretend to detain in confinement the nearest princes of the blood and the noblest subjects of the crown. Those that are smarting under the same injuries readily join in measures for mutual defence, and often scan each other's character with less particularity than might really be advisable.

The alliance a necessity.

Meantime, while the confederates were justifying themselves by a public manifesto declaring their reasons and designs, and while the success of the Roman Catholic army under Montpensier in the West was balanced by the surprise of Castres, in the South, all France looked with eager anxiety for the young king's decision.

It was early in autumn (the sixth of September) when Henry reached Lyons. In the vicinity he had been met by his mother.[2] Now that he was once more on his native soil it was time that he should adopt some definite policy respecting the government of his ancestral kingdom. Peace or war, the toleration of dissent from the established Church, or the continuation of the old course of

The question of religious toleration.

---

[1] "Et ipso et ipsius comitatu nihil erat libidinosius neque effœminatius, ipse spurcis amoribus deditissimus," etc. Jean de Serres, v. fol. 37. I quite agree with Ranke (Civil Wars and Monarchy in France, Amer. ed. 291) that Jean de Serres, or Serranus, is probably the best authority for this period.

[2] "The king came to this town on the sixth, the queen mother, the Dukes of Alençon and Savoy being with him in the coach, and the King of Navarre

persecution; the liberation of Marshal Montmorency, or a relentless conflict with the younger sons of the late constable—with Thoré now engaged in collecting forces in Germany; above all, with Damville, the most powerful governor of Southern France, having under control the resources of the rich province of Languedoc from the gates of Toulouse to the banks of the river Rhône—such were the alternatives confronting the returning king, and between them he must make a prompt decision.

What Henry desired is not doubtful. The last Valois was no lover of warfare. Not that he was either deficient in a certain sort of bravery or altogether insensible to the attractions of military distinction. His campaign against the Huguenots had won him glory, when acting as his brother's lieutenant-general, and at the siege of La Rochelle he had exposed himself to danger to an extent that raised the apprehensions of his mother. Now, however, martial aspirations were altogether a thing of the past. His tastes were all pacific. If he had sighed when forsaking the delights of the French court and turning his reluctant steps toward the frozen north, his sojourn among the rough and uncultivated Poles had not tended to make Paris less dear. His escape from his late uncongenial surroundings appeared to be a true emancipation from bondage. Every stage in his homeward progress had confirmed these impressions. Vienna, Venice, Turin had only been stations on the way to the terrestrial paradise awaiting him in France. For its fruition, however, peace was an indispensable condition. War was too expensive. War would desolate the country, and render whole provinces incapable of furnishing their accustomed tribute. War swallowed up the treasure which royal luxury demanded for its own use. War distracted the minds of men from pleasure, the only proper pursuit of rational beings, and especially of kings and courtiers.

<small>*Henry's tastes pacific.*</small>

---

on horseback by the coach. The queen mother and most of the court went to meet him twelve leagues in his way. He keeps far greater state than has been used heretofore." Dr. Dale to Sir Thomas Smith and Francis Walsingham, Lyons, September 11, 1574. State Paper Office.

Accordingly, no sooner had Henry collected his thoughts and begun to realize the wonderful piece of good fortune that had befallen him in his accession to the throne, though only the fourth son and the sixth child of his father,[1] than he resolved to have peace at any cost. "Use every exertion," he had written to Catharine de' Medici, "to find the means of coming to an arrangement with the rebels, and, if possible, to quiet my kingdom."[2] In fact, if we may credit implicitly the king's own statements made in a very remarkable letter to Villeroy, written just ten years later, Henry had found time, on his journey, to reflect maturely upon the real wants of France, and had, from a consideration of these, and independently of his own personal preferences, reached the very same conclusions. It was with deep regret that he afterward recognized the mistake he had made in permitting himself to follow a different course. The pivotal point in his plan was the immediate convocation of the states general of the kingdom. This body would naturally devise the best measures for the interests of France entire, and its determinations would command obedience both from Huguenot and from Roman Catholic; or, if defied, could easily be enforced by royal authority. By the States, too, arrangements could be made for the payment of the debt, and for the thorough reform of the financial system. Finally, when the domestic affairs of the kingdom, both religious and civil, had been placed on a firm and equitable basis, Henry would himself demand of foreign nations so definite a settlement by treaty of their mutual relations as to preclude future interference in the concerns of France on the part of any of its neighbors.[3]

His first intentions.

---

[1] Besides Francis and Charles he had another elder brother, Louis, who died in infancy. His sisters, Elizabeth (Isabella), who married Philip the Second, and Claude, wife of Charles the Third, Duke of Lorraine, were also older than Henry.

[2] "Il Re ha scritto alla Regina, madre sua, che si faccia ogni opera, per trovar modi di accordarsi con li ribelli, e per quietare, si è possibile, questo regno." Alamanni to Grand Duke, Paris, August 5, 1574, Négociations diplomatiques avec la Toscane, iv. 18.

[3] Henry III. to Villeroy, Lyons, August 14, 1584, Groen van Prinsterer, Archives de la maison d'Orange-Nassau, Première série, Supplement, 233.

If, indeed, Henry really devised so wise a plan, his good resolutions ought to have been confirmed by the advice he received.

<small>Good advice of the emperor and doge,</small> At Vienna the emperor warned him that there is no sin so great as that of treating with violence the convictions of others. "Those who undertake to make themselves masters of men's consciences," Maximilian significantly added, "while they think to conquer heaven, often lose the earth."[1] So, too, at Venice the doge, Mocenigo, had not confined himself to congratulating Henry in the presence of the senate, upon his accession to the throne, and wishing him a happy return to his native land; he also added a suggestion to the effect that the most appropriate manner of restoring peace to France was to abolish the unfortunate memory of the crimes and errors committed on both sides, by an edict not more solemnly given than scrupulously observed by the king. This politic course, he said, would conduce both to the dignity and to the safety of the monarch himself. That was not all. When the public services of Henry's reception by the senate were over, and all witnesses were removed, Mocenigo proceeded to give the young king, in the name of the senate, the advice to apply his mind seriously to peace, and to disregard the warlike counsels given to Henry, as he had learned, by the papal legate.[2] Moreover, long before the king reached France, an envoy of the <small>Of the elector palatine,</small> elector palatine was in Paris on his way to meet Henry and inform him that unless certain conditions were granted—the liberation of marshals, the restoration of Damville, his brothers, and the Prince of Condé, to favor, etc.—it would be impossible to keep back the reiters; an invasion of France from the side of Germany was inevitable.[3] William of

---

[1] Recueil des choses mémorables, 523.

[2] This incident is vouched for by Jean de Serres, an unimpeachable authority. He states that he had the account directly from a very illustrious personage who was in Venice at the time and was acquainted with the most intimate affairs of state. Commentarii de statu rel. et reipubl., v. fol. 24. Agrippa d'Aubigné also (ii. 132) makes the doge give good counsel as to keeping faith with subjects.

[3] Alamanni to the Grand Duke, August 5, 1574, ubi supra. The elector palatine, had, in fact, given virtually this advice in the last days of Charles IX. "Le dit Sr. Electeur a mandé à S. M. par le dit Frégouse qu'il ne voit que

Orange joined in the advice so unanimously given by the most trusty allies of the king, and gave to the bearer of a letter congratulating Henry upon his accession special instructions to urge him to follow the promptings of a disposition kindly by nature, and, remembering that he was now the "father of his country," to use all clemency and tenderness toward his subjects. The prince even went so far as to hint that thus Henry might, in time, reach the Imperial dignity to which his ancestors and predecessors had so long aspired.[1] To these advocates of peace must be added Henry's late host, the Duke of Savoy, who was one of the most urgent.[2] Nor did Queen Elizabeth, slowly as she was apt to move in such matters, refrain from giving the young king some good advice. She sent Lord North on a special embassy to influence Henry to pacific and tolerant measures. "If he say"—so ran North's instructions—" it is not honorable for princes to capitulate with their subjects, or permit diversity of religion, or that large offers have been made to 'them of the religion' which they refuse to accept, he is to declare to him how much more honorable it would be for him to remit part of that worldly respect of honor for the benefit of his realm and of all Christendom, and to think that the true honor of a loving prince is to recover his subjects rather by mildness than the sword." And the queen not only fortified her position by historical examples, but boldly combated prevailing misapprehensions by asserting "that the permission of diversity of religion leads not to the unquietness that is pretended." She even defended the Huguenots from the charge of unreasonable suspicion, and frankly told Henry that "why they of the religion

And of the Prince of Orange.

Special instructions of Lord North.

---

deux moyens de bien composer toutes choses, sçavoir une liberté d'exercice de la religion généralement partout, et après qu'on sera retiré, chacun chez soy, une convocation d'Estats pour entendre les plaintes des subjects et les y pourvoir." La Huguerye to the Prince of Orange, May, 1574, Groen van Prinsterer, Archives de la maison d'Orange-Nassau, Supplement, 165*.

[1] Instruction accompanying a letter of the Prince of Orange to Henry III., September 27, 1574, Groen van Prinsterer, v. 61.

[2] "The Duke of Savoy is a great furtherer of the peace, and the queen mother and her chancellor the greatest persuaders to war." Dr. Dale to Smith and Walsingham, September 11, 1574, State Paper Office.

refuse without greater assurance such offers as he made to them, she takes to proceed for that the edicts of the late king were not as well observed as was his intention." [1] It was an excellent state paper. Dr. Dale declared to Walsingham that he never had seen a thing better done in his life than his penning of Lord North's instructions; significantly adding that, "if it would please the queen to work somewhat in deeds withal, it might work some good effect." [2]

Unfortunately, these were not Henry's only counsellors. Others beset his ears who were all for war; and these had both greater facilities for reaching him, and sufficiently specious reasons to allege. If the papal legate urged the old arguments against any compacts made with heretics, reminding Henry of the sanguinary precepts so often reiterated by Pius the Fifth, there were plenty besides to call his attention to the dishonor which, they said, would attach to a peace conceded by a sovereign to subjects in rebellion. Before Henry reached Lyons, it was known by well-informed diplomatists that Catharine de' Medici and Chancellor Birague, above all, were leaving no stone unturned to prevent the conclusion of peace with the Huguenots and Politiques. Nor were their motives obscure. The chancellor, as the author of the arrests of the marshals, had good reason to fear that, with the end of the war and the restoration of the Montmorencies to power, would come his own disgrace and fall. The queen mother, alarmed for her own ascendency, had again resigned herself to the direction of the Cardinal of Lorraine. It is quite true that the prelate avoided all parade of his influence, and employed the chancellor as the instrument of accomplishing his designs; but the latter never ventured to take a step without consulting him. As for Catharine, "she trusted the cardinal more than she trusted herself," and made little account of the general dissatisfaction created by her course. It was only a few days after the meeting of mother and son that the Florentine envoy wrote home that Henry professed to be desirous of doing everything

(marginal notes: Intolerant counsels of Pope and the queen mother.)

---

[1] Instructions to Lord North, in special embassage to the French king, October 5, 1574, State Paper Office.
[2] Dr. Dale to Walsingham, November 3, 1574, State Paper Office.

that Catharine might want. But to this statement he added another not less significant, which may serve to throw light on much of this unhappy king's subsequent mistakes and errors. "If he were disposed to do otherwise, I know not whither he could turn for counsel."[1]

An intelligent agent of Queen Elizabeth gave much the same account. The queen mother's authority he declared to be as ample as ever. Henry's travels had added little to his knowledge, and, though "more in show and countenance" than his late brother, he was in reality "far more simple" than Charles. The greatest matters of state were "carried away" by Catharine and Chancellor Birague, with Chiverny supporting whatever they chose to agree upon. The rest of the council, indeed, advocated peace, but these three were urgent for war, so that the poor king "floated between the storm and the rock." Though appalled by the present misery of himself and of his country, the queen mother's "pestiferous" advice had cast a spell over him.[2]

Catharine had not waited for Henry's arrival to begin to exert over him that nefarious influence of which it seemed fated that each of her sons successively should be the victim. Fearful of the effect of the tolerant counsels he had received from foreign princes, alarmed at the influence which Pibrac and other advocates of toleration among the French themselves were acquiring, apprehensive of a mutation amounting to little less than a revolution should her son return and repudiate the policy pursued by his mother during the regency, Catharine had despatched to Turin, Chiverny, Villequier, and others, agents well adapted to the work of prejudicing Henry's mind against the best class of his subjects.[3] And the task imposed upon them was not a difficult one. Henry had been nurtured in hatred and jealousy of the Montmorencies and of their cousins the Châtillons. He had been a boon com-

Catharine's influence.

---

[1] See the important letters of Alamanni to the Grand Duke, September 6, and September 18, 1574, Négociations avec la Toscane, iv. 18, 25.

[2] Thomas Wilkes to Walsingham, Lyons, November 4, 1547, State Paper Office.

[3] De Thou, v. (book 58) 98, 99.

panion of Henry of Guise. True, all three of the Châtillons—the married cardinal, the indomitable admiral, and the "fearless knight"—were in their graves. But the Montmorencies still lived. What Henry of Guise—the former comrade of Anjou's mad antics—was to prove himself to be, did not yet appear. A year's absence from France had not lifted Henry of Valois above the petty factions of the court. Besides, when his very mother had forgotten the sound advice she had given him only a few weeks before, was it astonishing that his majesty should take sides in a quarrel of which he ought to have been content to be the umpire? On the morrow of that Sunday on which his brother died, Catharine had written him, as we have seen, a letter full of maternal solicitude, and had begged him not to permit himself to be led by the passions of his servants. A few short weeks had passed, and the mother was advocating the very partisanship which she had previously condemned. Damville, ruler with almost viceregal powers of one of the fairest parts of the kingdom, had been urged to visit the king and by personal interview to seal the much desired pacification.[1] The marshal was not desirous of war, least of all of a war with the Huguenots for allies; and, in

Damville's interview at Turin.

the hope of securing the release of his elder brother, he consented to go to meet Henry at Turin. Before leaving Languedoc he did, indeed, use ordinary prudence by committing the reins of government to a faithful follower of his house, in preference to Joyeuse, a man of more than doubtful loyalty, whom the court had suggested as a proper depository of the trust. He had been equally careful to travel only by the sure roads, in order to avoid the possible pitfalls prepared by his enemies. But his reception by the king, when at last he reached his destination, scarcely rewarded him for the pains he had taken. While Henry professed an earnest desire for peace, he declared that it was below his dignity to treat respecting it with his own subjects; and his demeanor was in all respects so unsatisfactory, if not positively unfriendly, that the

---

[1] See Damville's message, received by Henry at Ferrara, and Henry's flattering reply conveying an invitation, as well as Duke Emmanuel Philibert's pledge of safety, in Jean de Serres, v. fol. 25.

marshal deemed it best to make a hasty retreat to his own government. It was fortunate for him, some said, that he discovered the preparations made to attack him on his return through the Alps, and was able to find a vessel sailing directly to a port of Languedoc.¹ The unsuccessful result of his visit to court decided the position of Damville. He threw in his lot with the Protestants, and signed the articles of agreement.

Still the court had not committed itself irrevocably to the policy of war. The question was first definitely submitted for discussion in the royal council and in the king's own presence, upon the arrival of Henry at Lyons. But the deliberation was rather for show than for real utility. Two champions had been selected, and to them the opportunity to speak was restricted. Paul de Foix was the spokesman for peace and toleration—Paul de Foix, said to be a scion of the noble house that once exercised sway over broad territories at the foot of the Pyrenees, and enjoying more substantial claims to consideration because he had been one of the bold advocates of milder measures in the famous " Mercuriale " of 1559, and because since then he had consistently followed the counsels of Chancellor Michel de l'Hospital.² His carefully prepared argument was worthy of its author and of the occasion. By unanswerable proofs he showed that a civil war—the most disastrous of all wars—was neither desirable nor necessary; that its success was more than doubtful. "Granting," said he, "that the Huguenots lack money, the sinews of war, how faithfully and well have they handled the little they have hitherto had. Besides, they have allies that will not desert them, and, as for themselves, they spare neither life nor property. They are men inured to the hardships of war, and bound together by the indissoluble chain of necessity. Among them reign order and discipline; licence and debauchery are unknown. In the armies of the king, on the contrary, what jealousy, what avarice, what ambition, what disunion prevail! Even the loss of a sanguinary battle, of two or three sanguinary battles, will not dishearten the Huguenots.

The royal council deliberates on peace or war.

Paul de Foix's plea for peace.

---

¹ Jean de Serres, v. fols. 26, 27, 28; De Thou, ubi supra.
² See his eulogy in the Mémoires de la vie de De Thou, liv. i. pp. 13-15.

Experience has taught that they are less sensible to the most cruel torture, to the most appalling dangers, than to the fear of the loss of liberty of conscience and the dread of incurring the contempt of their fellow-believers. Such a faction has never been so thoroughly extinguished but that from the ashes of those that were driven into banishment or butchered a new conflagration has arisen more terrible than the first. After all, what have the Protestants always demanded? Liberty of conscience. That was first provided for by the Edict of January, an edict too soon violated by an incident which, far from recalling to memory, I would that I could bury in eternal oblivion. Thence arose, not in a few provinces, but throughout the entire state and in every family, a most cruel and disastrous war." In glowing terms the orator proceeded to depict the horrors of which France had for ten or twelve years been the victim, horrors that culminated in a massacre on St. Bartholomew's day, which he preferred to regard as rather the result of necessity or chance than of premeditated design. He begged the king to wait for the coming of the deputies sent by the Protestants, and daily expected, and when they should have arrived to grant them those reasonable concessions with which they would be satisfied. "May your prudence, Sire, guard you against stumbling on the first step you take in ascending the throne of your ancestors."

To this harangue the champion of war made a brief and brutal reply. Affecting to disdain any attempt to refute the arguments brought forward by his opponent—he was no barrister, he said, but a man nurtured in arms, and knew better how to act than how to speak.—Villequier loudly asserted that to establish peace with heretics was to declare war with God, and to pronounce rebels those who had devoted their lives and means to so holy a war. The conflict had been well begun; a single blow would suffice to prostrate the enemy. Instead of waiting for the deputies to arrive, he counselled instant action. He bade Henry gather the laurels of which an untimely death had robbed his brother Charles, and, after two crowns so legitimately obtained, to earn the third crown now offered to him, by giving peace to the Church through

<small>Villequier's reply.</small>

the overthrow of the enemies of God. "Either your Majesty," said he, "must perish, with the entire State, or the Protestants must be utterly destroyed."

René de Villequier was as little a match for Paul de Foix in argument as in purity of morals, but the easy composure with which he had borne himself, and the sneer with which he treated the emotion betrayed by his predecessor, showed plainly enough that he understood full well that the king had already made up his mind. And, in truth, no sooner had Villequier ended, than Henry and his mother rose without giving any other member of the council an opportunity to express his sentiments. The next day the council was again assembled, but only to hear the announcement of the absurd determination which Henry had been persuaded to adopt. He would listen to the propositions of the Protestant delegates, should they come, but meantime he would prepare for war and prosecute it with vigor.[1]

Henry resolves to prepare for war.

After this there was evidently little prospect of peace. Henry, indeed, gave audience to the envoys of the elector palatine and other German princes whom Condé had interested in the cause of his fellow Huguenots, and heard their intercessions that the Protestants should have permission to exercise their religion and should have their property and dignities restored to them. But he replied that as his predecessors had always maintained the name and character of "Very Christian," he intended to live and die in the Catholic, Apostolic, and Roman religion, which

---

[1] I follow the detailed account given by De Thou, v. 105-115. Although Ranke seems to question whether any such consultation was held (Civil Wars and Monarchy in France, Amer. ed., 289), I deem the authority of De Thou conclusive. The future historian, then a young man, had just returned from an extensive and very instructive journey through Italy, in the suite of the veteran jurist and diplomatist, Foix, with whom he was in the most intimate relations. A very full account of the trip is given in the Mémoires de la vie de De Thou, liv. i., pp. 14-27. In this work, written, it is well known, by De Thou himself, he explicitly states (p. 27) that he was at court in Lyons when the discussion took place. "Il [De Thou] y resta quelque tems pour apprendre la résolution de la cour. On y délibera d'abord de la guerre contre les Protestans. De Foix, dans le Conseil, eut une dispute avec Villequier sur ce sujet; mais en secret cette guerre étoit résolue. De Thou disoit avoir vu de Foix en soupirer de regret," etc.

he expected to be accepted by all his subjects. He would, however, pardon the sins of the past, should the Huguenots restore to him the arms and the cities which they had appropriated, and return to the religion of the state; or, should they prefer so to do, he would freely permit them to leave the kingdom, taking their goods with them, and would provide them with letters to secure their safety.[1] To the Huguenots themselves that came from Provence and Dauphiny Henry gave a sharp answer, telling them that he would not speak of peace until his cities and castles should have been restored to his hands.[2]

The conclusions thus reached were set forth in official form. By letters patent of the tenth of September, Henry announced

---

[1] Lestoile, under date of September 10, 1574, i. 42. The documents published by Kluckhohn are of great interest. Henry, it appears, had written to the elector palatine from Cracow, soliciting his good offices in the discovery of the means of pacifying France (Letters of June 15, in Briefe Friedrich des Frommen, ii. 694, 695), and Frederick the Pious had accordingly despatched Dr. Weyer. The envoy made his way to Paris, but failed to obtain any satisfaction as to the plans of the government from the queen mother, who urged him to see the new king himself. Of the results of his interviews with the latter, whom he met coming from Turin to Lyons, Dr. Weyer has left us a full relation. (Published by Kluckhohn in his " Zwei pfälzische Gesandtschaftsberiche über den französichen Hof und die Hugenotten," Abhandlungen der kön. bayer. Akad. der Wissenschaften, xi. Bd. ii. Abth., Munich, 1870.) Henry did indeed declare to the ambassador that he did not intend to be the ' hangman ' of his subjects (" Ich will meiner underthonen henker nicht sein "), but he gave no assurances of toleration to be extended to the Huguenots. He even showed his annoyance at the elector's interference in their behalf in a letter to Frederick, of October 26 (Briefe, etc., ii. 727, 728). This drew forth a noble reply from the palatine (November 27, ibid., ii. 760–762). In the course of it he reminded Henry that in the promise of liberty of conscience which he made to the Protestants he granted them nothing at all, since he had no power over the souls of men, that power being reserved by God for Himself alone; while, as to the permission to retire to their houses and enjoy their temporal goods, the Huguenots derived no security therefrom, inasmuch as, not to speak of past massacres, even at the present moment the same humors and desires entertained by the royal council and the royal governors and officers, in every province and place, held them in fear and distrust. Besides, how could they subsist without worship of God, without baptism, without the sacrament of the Lord's Supper, without burial, without discipline?

[2] Alamanni to the Grand Duke, September 13, 1574, Négociations avec la Toscane, iv. 24.

his "paternal" purpose to pardon all his subjects who had borne arms against the will of their sovereign, or who, in disobedience to his commands, had left the kingdom. The single condition was that they should lay down their arms and return and live peaceably in their homes. Not a word was said about liberty of conscience or religious rights. It was not until about a month later (the thirteenth of October), that, finding that his first assurances had produced little effect, Henry wrote another letter, in which he promised the returning Huguenots that their consciences and religion should not be interfered with. Still there was no hint of the toleration of their worship, or of the convocation of a national council, or of the states general, for which they had called.[1] It was clear that Henry was determined upon a resort to the arbitrament of war. Catharine had persuaded herself and him that the campaign would be easy, short, and decisive.[2]

Official declaration.

It cannot be said that the Huguenots were unprepared for the issue. In Dauphiny and Vivarais they had not suspended their military operations. Insignificant towns were held by small garrisons at fearful odds. Le Pouzin, little more than a village, but advantageously situated on the western bank of the Rhône,[3] was bravely defended for ten days against an army of twelve, or, as others assert, of eighteen thousand men—French, Swiss, Germans, and Piedmontese—abundantly furnished with artillery, according to the ideas of the times, and fighting under the colors of the Prince Dauphin. The small Huguenot garrison first repulsed a general assault so decisively that all hope of taking the place save by the slower methods of a siege was abandoned; and when no longer able to maintain itself in the shattered walls against the enemy, ef-

Huguenot operations.

---

[1] Jean de Serres, v. fols. 29, 32 ; Recueil des choses mémorables, 521, 522 ; De Thou, v. 119.
[2] Jean de Serres, v. fol. 28.
[3] "The Protestants have fortified themselves in Livron, a strong place on the Rhône, and in Pouzin, upon the other side of the river, inaccessible but in one place, and that not above four men in front. They in Dauphiny have fortified themselves in the mountains very strongly." Dr. Dale to Smith and Walsingham, Lyons, September 29, 1574. State Paper Office.

fected a safe retreat by night to the neighboring city of Privas.¹ Brave Montbrun, who was in command, received calmly, almost defiantly, the king's summons to lay down his arms and retire to his home, if he wished to enjoy the benefits of the royal grace. He boldly vindicated the justice of his cause, and expressed his confident hope that God would not desert His own servants. "Whatever result, however, may follow," he added, "we shall put forth every endeavor, God willing, that the perfidious and degenerate Italians who abuse the royal and the French name may in deed acknowledge that they have to do with true Frenchmen, who regard a glorious death as the most excellent recompense of their faith and valor."²

<small>Montbrun's courageous answer.</small>

The final arrangements for an offensive and defensive alliance with Marshal Damville were effected not long after. In answer to a summons of the latter, the States of Languedoc convened in Montpellier, on the sixth of November. Of the twenty-three districts into which the extensive province was divided, the greater number were represented by Protestants, but not a few Roman Catholics were also there. Toulouse, however, sent no delegates. The union being formed, Marshal Damville was recognized as royal governor, and it was resolved, under his leadership, to make common cause against a common foe. In the long and not inappropriate declaration which the marshal thereupon published, only a single sentiment deserves especial notice, as indicative of the world's progress toward the recognition of the rights of man—"Religious controversy cannot be settled by arms, but by a free council, be it general or national."³ It was well understood by the whole nation that Damville repudiated the name of reli-

<small>Union with Damville.</small>

---

¹ De Thou, v. 110, gives a brief, Jean de Serres, v. fols. 29–31, a much more circumstantial account of this brilliant affair, which lasted from the 5th to the 15th of October.
² Jean de Serres, v. fol. 33.
³ "Perspiciens controversiam religionis non armis sed libero Concilio, sive generali sive nationali, componi posse." Jean de Serres, v. fols. 34–36. Of course, Damville, as a Montmorency, made much of the fact that he was "vere et genuine Gallus, et e primis Christianis et baronibus Franciæ."

gion, and styled himself "Liberator of the Commonwealth;" or, as others said, "Reformer of the King's Council."[1] Yet, for a time, the politic marshal seemed himself to have undergone a moral reformation which, he was acute enough to perceive, brought him into closer sympathy with the religious party whose interests he espoused.[2]

It was the middle of November when the king, instead of pressing on toward the capital whither the great interests of his kingdom called him, again turned southward to spend the season of Advent in the city of Avignon.

<small>Henry at Avignon.</small>

The finances of his state were in extreme confusion, the exchequer was empty, the very pages of the king, it was said, were driven to the necessity of pawning their cloaks to get food, and, but for a timely advance of five thousand francs which she obtained from a royal officer of the treasury, Catharine herself could not have provided for the wants of her own maids of honor.[3] None the less, however, did Henry and his court dismiss the wearisome consideration of the means of restoring prosperity to France, that they might engage in a form of devotion whose absurdity would create amusement did not its puerility awaken disgust. This most inconstant and profligate of princes was destined, at various stages of his reign, to hold forth hopes of a personal reformation of morals, only to disappoint his subjects by relapses into the most shameless debauchery. One of these spasmodic and short-lived changes was witnessed about this time. "At his being at Avignon," quaintly writes a correspondent of Lord Burleigh, "certain Jesuits came unto him, and persuaded him to leave that loose life of his, and to forsake such dames as he brought with him out of Venice, otherwise God would not prosper him. And hereupon he, being touched, hath confessed his sinful life to

---

[1] Alamanni to the Grand Duke, Lyons, November 9, 1574, Négociations avec la Toscane, iv. 29.

[2] "Inito fœdere, ipse quidem quasi sempiternum voluptati indixisset bellum, mulierculas amandat, severe autem interdicit suis ne secum habeant scorta, ne cui impune liceat blasphemare," etc. Jean de Serres, v. fol. 37.

[3] Lestoile, i. 47.

those Jesuits, with full purpose to live better, and so hath given himself to marry." [1]

But Henry's improvement in external morality was less striking and more transient than his newly conceived passion for the Flagellants. The "Flagellants" of the thirteenth, fourteenth, and fifteenth centuries, had been in turn held up for popular admiration by the clergy, anathematized by papal authority, and committed to the flames by the Inquisition. The superstition for which they had received such opposite treatment was subsequently discovered to be a profitable delusion, and under the name of "Penitents" the new flagellants were associated, with the Church's sanction, in confraternities which attracted, by reason of their singularity, not a little attention and surprise. It was in the papal city of Avignon that the Penitents first made their appearance on French soil. Clothed in long gowns reaching from head to foot, with no part of the face visible save the eyes, they paraded the streets, sometimes by day but more frequently by night, chanting lustily the mournful verses of the "Miserere." To express the idea of sorrow for sin more forcibly, each penitent was provided with a whip well knotted or furnished with metal points, by means of which he lashed the exposed back and shoulders of the brother whom he followed. It was a weird but loathsome spectacle, from which sensible men turned away with mingled shame and indignation. But Henry of Valois was both interested and pleased. The novel practice might prove a pleasant diversion, and if it could atone for moral delinquencies, the pain endured would be a cheap price to pay for the purchase of absolution. Was it not likely that the whip, in the hands of courtiers, would be more tolerable than the scourge of his own conscience? However this may be, the frivolous monarch no sooner saw the performance than he expressed a desire to take part in it. His example was at once followed by the courtiers. The king having become a member of that part of the confraternity which clothed itself in white—the "Blancs Battus"—

He joins the Flagellants.

---

[1] Thomas Wylson to Lord Burleigh, February 14, 1575; Wright, Queen Elizabeth and her Times, ii. 5.

Catharine made herself the patron of the "black penitents," and the Cardinal of Armagnac joined the "blue." It was not long before every seigneur or gentilhomme of the court was enrolled in one of the confraternities, whose cause he espoused with an ardor that would have done no discredit to the partisans of the factions of the circus in the imperial times of Rome or Constantinople.[1]

To one person the silly farce proved of tragic importance. Cardinal Charles, of Lorraine, had the imprudence to take a prominent part in the show, walking with bare, or nearly bare feet through the cold and wintry streets. The exposure brought on a fever to which he soon succumbed.[2] Whether the prelate died in the odor of sanctity, having discoursed, during his last hours, most learnedly and piously respecting religion—as his friends and adherents gave out—or passed away from the scene of his restless and nefarious activity after having spent whole days and nights, without sleep and uttering furious outcries—as his enemies asserted with equal positiveness—is a point which it is useless to discuss.[3]

Death of the Cardinal of Lorraine.

And so this bustling actor passed off the stage upon which he

---

[1] Lestoile, i. 47 ; Recueil des choses mémorables, 533 ; De Thou, v. 124. The Florentine envoy Alamanni, writing from Lyons, December 14, 1574, stands in admiration of the French king's piety : " È entrato in una compagnia di Battuti, che è in Avignone, e va agli uffizi sacri, vestito pare da Battuto, dando a ciascuno de' suoi popoli un ottimo esempio di sè, e monstrandosi in ogni cosa sua religioso e molto cattolico principe." Négociations diplomatiques avec la Toscane, iv. 33.

[2] If the date December 23, 1574, as given by Jean de Serres, were correct, Cardinal Lorraine would have died on the day of the month upon which his nephew, Henry of Guise, was murdered at Blois fourteen years later. But the true date was Sunday, December 26th. See Jean de Serres, v. fols. 45, 46 ;. Jehan de la Fosse, Journal d'un curé ligueur, 172; Lestoile, etc., ubi supra.

[3] Agrippa d'Aubigné, ii. 143 ; Recueil des choses mémorables, 535 ; Languet, Epistolæ secretæ, i. 68. As it his imprudent exposure did not sufficiently account for Lorraine's fatal illness, De Thou, Agrippa d'Aubigné, Olhagaray, and others discuss the absurd story of the cardinal's assassination by poison, administered, as some said, in a purse that was presented to him. For a contemporary account of his furious death and the fierce storm that raged throughout France at the time (" et l'appelle-t-on le vent du cardinal "), see Beza to Gabriel Schlusselberger, March 25, 1575 ; Berne MS., apud Bulletin de la Société de l'histoire du Prot. franç., xvi. (1867), 270.

had long played a leading part. Was it because the world had learned to know him so thoroughly, or because new characters so soon engrossed the undivided attention of the specta- *His character.* tors, that his removal produced less commotion, to use the expressive words of a contemporary, than would have fol- lowed the death of a simple village curate?[1] Of the person and work of Charles of Lorraine there is no need to speak at length. What he was is more clearly shown in the events of the quarter of a century preceding his death than could be set forth in any portrait, however skilfully delineated. That he was possessed of eminent abilities not even his enemies could deny. If neither profound nor learned, he was certainly shrewd, polished, versa- tile, and capable of turning to his own advantage every op- portunity that presented itself for acquiring distinction or for amassing wealth. With the help of others, cleverly appropri- ated, he had on more than one occasion contrived to present a good appearance both for scholarship and for eloquence. At the Colloquy of Poissy no orator upon the Roman Catholic side had acquitted himself so creditably; it had proved no difficult thing to persuade the multitudes that had not been present at the discussion that he had carried off the palm in a contest with the elegant and courtly Theodore Beza himself. He was the most plausible man in France. Until the refutation came, no one's assertions seemed more like the very truth than his. Presently, however, it was discovered that a man could be safe only when he believed just the opposite of what the cardinal said.[2] It made no matter whither he went; everywhere he practised the same arts of deception. What the Venetian am- bassador Suriano had depicted him as being in his earlier years,[3] he was to the very end of life. When the news of the Massacre of St. Bartholomew's Day reached Rome, the cardinal, who had not had the slightest knowledge of the impending blow, and had, of course, taken no part either in the plan or in the execu-

---

[1] Mémoires de Henry III., 12.

[2] The tree is known by its fruit—remarks Lestoile—and in his case the fruit was, according to the testimony of his own adherents, "que pour n'estre jamais trompé il faloit croire tousjours tout le contraire de ce qu'il vous disoit." Mémoires de Henry III., 11.

[3] See Rise of the Huguenots, i. 270.

tion, at once began to state that the destruction of the Huguenots was mainly due to his activity. The Tuscan agent at the French court visited Catharine de' Medici and informed her of the boast. Catharine was indignant at the unwarranted assumption. "The Cardinal of Lorraine," she said, "knew no more about the massacre than you did. But for me nothing would have been done. In consequence of certain advices I resolved upon it suddenly. Lorraine and the admiral are on a par for lies, inventions, and malignity."[1] "Perhaps it would be well, since he has an uneasy brain, to recall him to France," suggested Petrucci. "Oh, no!" Catharine promptly replied, "let us leave him there. If he were here, he would turn the world upside down."[2] Before the interview was over the queen and the ambassador showed that they were of one mind: this conduct of the cardinal was hateful in the extreme. "At Rome," said Petrucci, "he wishes to give the impression that, though absent, he governs the kingdom. In France, he pretends that he is the greatest favorite of the pope."[3]

His claim to have caused the massacre.

It is not possible to determine the precise share which belonged to the cardinal in the disasters of France during this eventful period. Other hands besides his were embrued in the blood of the persecuted reformers; other tongues were busy in defence of the sanguinary doctrine that heresy must be exterminated by exterminating its professors. Many a clergyman advocated the use of faggot and gallows, with no such attempts as Lorraine more than once put forth to shield himself from the imputation of inhumanity. And yet, despite his disclaimers at Saverne and elsewhere, the Huguenots held him, above all others, directly responsible for that relentless system of persecution which had its legitimate outcome in the civil wars that filled the latter half of

His responsibility.

---

[1] "Ella mi disce che non ne sapeva [sc. Lorraine] più che ne sapessi io, e che senza lei non se ne faceva altro; ma che per certi avvisi se ne risolve subito, e che Lorena e l'Ammiraglio andavono al pari di bugie e d'invenzioni e di malignità." Petrucci to Fr. de' Medici, September 29, 1572, Négociations diplomatiques de la France avec la Toscane, iii. 842.

[2] "Lasciamolo pure star là, perche quà metterebbe sotto sopra il mondo." Ibid., ubi supra. [3] Ibid., ubi supra.

the sixteenth century. In this estimate they were not alone. It will be remembered that a secretary of state, who had often met him at the council-board, and who belonged to the same religious communion, had long since associated his name with that of the bloodthirsty Diana of Poitiers, exclaiming, with reference to these two partners in infamy: "It were to be desired that this woman and the cardinal had never been born: for they two alone have been the spark that kindled our misfortunes."[1] Chary of his own life, Lorraine had been lavish of the lives of others;[2] consequently, few bewailed his loss.

Such a man, in an age much given to plain-speaking, was likely to be handled with uncomplimentary frankness. Ten years before the cardinal's death, the reformer Farel expressed, in his private correspondence, the estimate which his fellow Protestants had formed of their arch-persecutor. He described him as "the man who surpasses all other men on the face of the earth in wickedness and malice." And, more forcibly than politely, he declared it to be his opinion that the prelate had usual recourse for counsel and help, not to a single evil spirit—he was never without one or more imps ready to come to him at his call—but to the prince of fiends himself, from whom he received all aid and comfort in his efforts to serve Satan effectually and to destroy the whole work of God.[3]

Soon after the beginning of the new year the court left Avignon for the north. If the audacity of the Huguenots in taking Saint Gilles almost within hearing of the king,[4] and surprising Aigues-mortes before Henry had gotten well under way,[5] had been an annoyance, the rebuff he now received at Livron—"but a very little up-

The Huguenots of Livron.

---

[1] Claude de l'Aubespine. See Rise of the Huguenots, i. 271.

[2] Agrippa d'Aubigné, ii. 143. "Tres chiche et craintif de sa vie, prodigue de celle d'autrui, pour le seul but qu'il a eu en vivant, assavoir d'eslever sa race à une demesurée grandeur."

[3] Farel to Christopher Fabri, Neuchâtel, June 6, 1564, in the letters of the reformer appended to Fick's edition of "Du Vray Usage de la Croix," 315.

[4] Jean de Serres, v. fol. 47.

[5] The surprise of Aigues-mortes occurred January 12. The licence of the Protestant soldiers in plundering the place for the next seven days furnished a dangerous precedent, of which it would seem that advantage was soon taken. Jean de Serres, v. fols. 52, 53.

landish town"[1]—was still harder to be borne with equanimity. The Protestant inhabitants of Livron had again been forced to take refuge behind their strengthened works; they soon showed themselves true Huguenots, better acquainted with the art of defence than with the art of assault.[2] Henry was tempted to stop before the presumptuous town that had dared to deny admission to the royal troops. But his presence only incited the garrison to greater displays of courage. He was saluted at his approach by a discharge of artillery, and when the deafening report had ceased there succeeded a still more startling shout from the throats of hundreds of soldiers whom the Huguenot officers strove in vain to repress. "You will not butcher us in our beds, as you butchered the admiral!" was a cry that fell upon Henry's ears, mingled with other derisive words that told too clearly the depth of contempt to which the crown had fallen in the popular estimation.[3] A few days after the king's departure the siege of Livron was for a second time abandoned in disgust.

Meanwhile in the west the royal arms had purchased success at a heavy cost. The powerful army of the Duke of Montpensier captured the important city of Fontenay after a short but vigorous resistance; but the loss of the assailants in dead and wounded much exceeded that of the garrison. The castle of Lusignan was next attacked, but proved a more difficult place to master. The massive walls,

Capture of Fontenay and Lusignan.

---

[1] Dr. Dale to Lord Burleigh, Lyons, January 16, 1575, State Paper Office.

[2] "Monstrèrent bien qu'ils estoient vrais huguenos, qui sçavoient mieux le mestier de se deffendre que d'assaillir," Lestoile, i. 48. The second siege of Livron, begun December 17, 1574, and prosecuted with marked steadfastness of purpose by a powerful army under the direct command of Marshal de Bellegarde, is described at great length by Jean de Serres, v. fols. 42-52.

[3] "Hæc vero frequentius increbescebant: 'Haudquaquam nos in lecto, sicuti Amiralium, mactabis: educito in aciem cincinnatos illos tuos, veniant ad nostras uxores, et intelligent quam facilo sui copiam sint facturæ.'" Jean de Serres, v. fol. 55. This writer contrasts the unfortunate licence then prevalent with the strict discipline of the Protestant armies in the time of Coligny and Louis de Condé; when a disrespectful word respecting the king would have cost a soldier his life. The Recueil des choses mémorables, p. 538, and the Inventaire général, ii. 481, give a very similar form to the taunts of the Huguenot garrison: "Hau, massacreurs, vous ne nous poignarderez pas dedans nos licts, comme vous avez fait l'Amiral," etc. See De Thou, v. 122, 184.

which had defied for centuries the strength of successive assailants, were commonly reputed to be guarded by the spell of the most potent fairy of mediæval fable. The beautiful but unfortunate Melusine, fated by her mother's curse to assume the form of a serpent every Saturday until the Day of the last Judgment, unless she should find a husband too generous to pry into the awful secret of her life, had miraculously caused the fabric to arise for the abode of Raymondin, son of the Count of Forez. When her spouse broke his pledged faith, she fled from his embrace with a piercing wail, and, issuing from a window, was seen to fly through the air in monstrous shape. Thrice did she circle round the fated castle, then disappear forever from human sight. Only when Lusignan changed its masters, or when some member of the lordly family was about to die, did the occupants of the castle hear her piteous cry, repeated on three successive nights, sure presage of coming disaster.[1] This fortress had in the Middle Ages given title to a distinguished family. In the twelfth century Guy de Lusignan, after wearing the thorny crown of Jerusalem, had obtained the more substantial sovereignty of the kingdom of Cyprus. In the thirteenth century Hugues de Lusignan took part in the first crusade of Saint Louis and lost his life on the banks of the Nile. In the fourteenth century, Pierre de Lusignan was among the most strenuous advocates of the renewal of the effort to rescue the Holy Sepulchre from the hands of the infidel.[2] The fortress from which these stout warriors derived their name, although seized by the Huguenots in

The fairy Melusine.

---

[1] The story of the fairy is most fully told in the tale "Melusine," written by Jehan d'Arras for the delectation of the Count of Berry and Auvergne, in 1387, and recently edited afresh by M. Brunet (Paris, 1854). Brantôme vouches for the statement that divers washerwomen at the fountain below the tower had heard Melusine's cries, and that many soldiers and "men of honor" could testify to her loud lament when the castle was besieged. The name of Melusine is supposed to be an abbreviation of "Mère des Lusignans," "Mère Lusigne," or simple "Merlusine." The fairy had the credit of having built a number of other castles (among them Parthenay, Issoudun, and Soubise), from whose ruinous walls spectral apparitions or hideous cries issued from time to time.

[2] Michaud, Histoire des Croisades, ii. 439; iv. 125, 176; v. 184.

1569,[1] during the course of the third civil war, had the reputation of being nearly, if not quite impregnable. Besides, the garrison had the advantage of being commanded by René de Rohan, Sieur de Frontenay, who, on the approach of the royal army, threw himself into the place, with forty gentlemen and six hundred picked troops. Well did general and soldiers prove the wisdom of the movement and exhibit their own valor. One assault after another was bravely met and foiled. It was not until the siege had lasted nearly four months that the Huguenots could be brought to surrender Lusignan, and then they secured the most honorable terms. On the twenty-fifth of January, 1575, the small garrison that had so long held at bay a large army commanded by a prince of the blood, marched out with arms and baggage. The Protestants only lost twenty-five gentlemen and two hundred soldiers. Montpensier's loss was variously estimated at eight hundred or twelve hundred men. He satisfied his resentment against the castle that had so long detained him by razing the walls to the ground. Not even the famous "tour de Melusine" was spared.[2]

While his armies in Poitou and in Dauphiny were meeting with such indifferent success, Henry the Third was preparing to receive the rite of anointing and coronation at the hands of the Church. The ceremony took place, according to custom, in the city of Rheims. There, too, Henry was married to Louise de Vaudemont, a princess of the family of Lorraine. Neither event was altogether auspicious. Henry, whose mistake it was that he generally attended to secular affairs while he should have been absorbed in the offices of religion, and gave himself up to superstitious observances just as the claims of his kingdom were most imperative, exhibited the utmost irreverence when the time came for the acts that

Henry's coronation and marriage.

---

[1] Rise of the Huguenots, ii. 323. The castle of Lusignan, described by Froissard (Johnes's trans. i. 489) as "very grand and handsome," defied the arms of the Earl of Derby in his victorious expedition from Bordeaux soon after the battle of Crécy (ibid. i. 171).

[2] Recueil des choses mémorables, 524-527; Lestoile, i. 51; De Thou, v. 128-132; Agrippa d'Aubigné, ii. 147-157, whose account is very full, and who gives the text of the articles of capitulation.

were to set the approval of the Roman Catholic Church upon his succession to the throne. He slept instead of keeping vigil during the night preceding the coronation. He spent, in attending to his own attire and in inspecting the jewels to be worn by his bride, so large a portion of the day, that, contrary to all ecclesiastical precedent, the mass was necessarily deferred until afternoon, and the solemn Te Deum was either forgotten or purposely omitted. When the crown was placed upon his head, he interrupted the officiating prelate by impatient and ill-omened exclamations—that the crown hurt him, that it was slipping off. At the close of the service he had no time to permit the archbishop to divest him of garments consecrated by contact with the holy oil, but passed with perfect unconcern from the cathedral to the supper-room, and took part in the festivities dressed in his coronation robes.[1] The marriage of Henry with a princess of Lorraine, a relation of the Guises—a family already far too powerful in French affairs—was more inauspicious than the violation of churchly usage. Henry had broken off negotiations for the hand of a daughter of the good Gustavus Vasa, King of Sweden, to espouse a portionless girl belonging to a younger branch of a hated and dangerous race.[2] The match was unequal; the accession of power it was likely to bring to Henry of Guise and his brother could not be viewed by calm observers without serious apprehension. True, the restless Cardinal of Lorraine was dead, and it was not yet suspected that the eldest son of Francis of Guise had inherited the ambition both of his father and of his uncle. Yet it might have been supposed that the perils attaching to matrimonial al-

---

[1] For this last incident see Miss Freer, Henry III., ii. 17. Cf. also De Thou (who was an eye-witness of the coronation), v. 186, 187 ; Recueil des choses mémorables, 540 ; Lestoile, i. 51.

[2] Miss Freer, ubi supra, ii. 5, 6. According to the author of the Recueil des choses mémorables, 541, Catharine was a warm supporter of the Lorraine marriage alliance, by means of which she hoped to confirm her authority in France. And, indeed, Henry was profuse in his declarations to foreign ambassadors to that effect. "Elle me fit et elle me maria," he said. But common report made it quite otherwise, and the English envoy called attention to the king's own contradictory statements. See Dr. Dale's letters to Lord Burleigh, March 5 and 18, 1575, State Paper Office.

liances with any branch of the House of Lorraine would readily suggest themselves, in view of the troubles introduced by the marriage of Francis the Second and Mary of Scots. Meanwhile, for the present, the marriage made little change in Henry, unless it were that he became even more averse to serious occupations; more engrossed alternately in puerile devotion and frivolous pleasures, and more impecunious because of his lavish gifts.[1] During the whole of the Lenten season immediately following upon his coronation and marriage he went daily to mass and listened to sermon after sermon, each day in a new church. At the same time he resorted to every petty device to relieve his poverty. New taxes were imposed; new offices were put up for sale; money was raised by giving the privilege of cutting down two trees in every "arpent" of all the forests of France. One day Henry was reported not to have enough money to purchase a dinner, and the king actually sent to beg a loan from all the counsellors, advocates, and procureurs of the Parliament and Châtelet of Paris, obtaining from each a few hundred francs. Some days later the public, including the king's reluctant creditors, were treated to the information that Henry had turned the whole of this collection to account in the way of making a present of over fifty thousand livres to satisfy the rapacity of a single ravenous favorite.[2]

His growing devotion to pleasure.

His penury and lavishness.

The Huguenots, while ably conducting their military operations in Dauphiny and Languedoc, had been drawing more close the bands of their alliance with Damville and the Politiques. At a conference held in Nismes, about the beginning of the year, another perilous step was taken in the course to which the Protestants seemed driven, as by a fatal necessity, of establishing a commonwealth of their own, with its organized forms and its laws of action.

Conference of Huguenots and Politiques at Nismes.

---

[1] On his way from Avignon to Rheims, Henry was in such straits for money that he had to compel one "Ludovico da Diagetto, a Florentyne," much against his will, to loan him one hundred thousand francs, "or else the king could not have gone from Avignon to be sacred at Rheims, nor yet to be married." Thomas Wylson to Lord Burleigh, February 14, 157⅘, Wright, Queen Elizabeth and her Times, ii. 5. [2] Lestoile, i. 52.

The union was signed by Damville, in the name of the Roman Catholics, and by Viscount Paulin and Baron Terrides, on the part of the Protestants. The marshal engaged upon oath to abstain from every act contrary to the laws and statutes adopted by the allies, and promised, in any sudden emergency rendering it impossible to obtain their opinion, to obey implicitly the advice of the council with which he had been provided.[1]

Meantime, in the spring of 1575, negotiations were in progress at the French court which, although they have received scanty notice from historians, throw a brilliant light upon the purposes and the temper of the various parties in the State.[2]

From the pursuit of war or of pleasure the court now seemed disposed to turn its attention for a little while to the methods of obtaining the peace so ardently desired by the unfortunate classes of the population upon whom the burdens of the state rested most heavily. The queen mother, not many months since an advocate of war, had, with her usual variableness, veered round and become anxious for the restoration of peace. She had discovered to her great an-

Negotiations for peace. April, 1575.

---

[1] De Thou, v. 185; Jean de Serres, v. fols. 53, 54, where a portion, and Vaissète, Histoire du Languedoc, v. 241-244, where the whole of Damville's proclamation, dated January 12th, 1575, is given. It is interesting to note that as Marshal Damville had, from an enemy, become the leader of the Protestants of Languedoc, so the royal army with which the Protestants were confronted was commanded by the Duc d'Uzès, one of their best generals in former wars. In changing sides the duke was also accused of having developed a character for inhumanity previously unperceived in him. It was he that gave the disastrous example of mercilessly burning the gathered crops of the unhappy peasants of Languedoc. Jean de Serres, v. fols. 105, 113.

[2] The peace negotiations of 1575 are briefly described or referred to by Lestoile, i. 53; the Recueil des choses mémorables, 542-544; Inventaire général, ii. 483; De Thou, v. 186-188; Davila, 212; also by Agrippa d'Aubigné, ii. 173-175, whose sketch, if short, is very graphic. In comparison with these writers, however, Jean de Serres gives, in the concluding volume of his invaluable Commentarii de statu religionis et reipublicæ (v. fols. 63-101) a far more trustworthy and detailed account of this highly interesting episode in the history of the fifth civil war. In the Mémoires de Nevers (Paris, 1665), a work of almost equal rarity, the long report of the Protestant envoys themselves is inserted (i. 308-434), under the title "Negotiation de la paix faite par les deputez du Prince de Condé, en la présence du Roy Henry III. et de la Reine sa mère," etc. The two narratives supplement and corroborate each other.

noyance that her influence over the king was much diminished, and that "many things passed by her mill more than were wont." Besides, even her restless spirit was appalled by the indescribable jealousy and confusion reigning at court, and now she declared that she would have an end of the struggle with the Huguenots, cost what it might. In the words of an eyewitness of the deplorable scene: "They were all bent to preparations of war, but these domestic discords do tame them. It is a very hell among them, not one content or in quiet with another—not mother with son, nor brother with brother, nor mother with daughter."[1]

The king, too, professed a desire for reconciliation with his subjects of Southern France. He had gone so far as to permit both Damville and the Protestants to send deputies to the Prince of Condé at Basle, with the view of deliberating with him respecting the terms they ought jointly to insist upon.

On their way the deputies stopped at Geneva and, under pledge of strict secrecy, consulted the council of that faithful city respecting the propriety of their proposed demands, "for, gentlemen," said they, "the Protestants of Languedoc trust you as much as they trust themselves."[2] Nor was this all. The Prince of Condé sought and again secured permission that Theodore Beza should be present at the conference, and much did the reformer's sturdy good sense and clear perceptions contribute to the adoption of the manly course that was ultimately adopted. A statesman of large and liberal views, Beza, notwithstanding his long period of residence on the banks of the Leman, had not forgotten that he was the citizen of a larger commonwealth than the little republic of Geneva, or even the extensive kingdom of France. For him the whole of Christendom, at least the whole of that part of Christendom which had espoused the Reformation, constituted his greater country, whose interests were to be preferred far above the interests of any one city or state; while, as for Geneva,

Beza's broad statesmanship.

---

[1] Dale to Walsingham, two letters, both dated March 23, 1575, State Paper Office.

[2] "Parce que, disaient ils, ils se fient en Messieurs comme en eux mesmes." Fazy, Genève, le Parti Huguenot, etc. 25.

to her belonged, in the truest sense, the honor of being the holy city, with the high privilege of serving as the secure refuge of all that were persecuted in other parts for righteousness' sake. The broad policy of the reformer might make Beza a somewhat unsafe adviser for a place in itself so weak and so beset with enemies as Geneva;[1] it certainly adapted him in a singular degree to comprehend the larger diplomacy of European Protestantism. It commended him above all others to the sympathy and the esteem of so chivalrous a prince as Condé, with whom duty outweighed considerations of danger, and who always preferred a boldness that might be confounded with rashness to a prudence verging upon cowardice. So it was that, when at length the duties which twice called Beza to Basle in the spring of 1575 were fully discharged, and he was able to return to the scene of his accustomed labors, he was followed by letters from Condé to the magistrates of Geneva, full of expressions of thanks for having permitted their eminent theologian to take part in an enterprise so necessary for the glory of God and the quiet of poor France, wherein the Huguenots had need of the prudence which he so well displayed. "I assure you, gentlemen," said the grateful prince, in conclusion, "that besides the general esteem which his rare virtues have engraven on the hearts of all good men, I entertain a more special esteem for him on my own account, in accordance with which I shall make known to any person that may be so venturesome as to attack him, that he has assailed one of my greatest friends."[2]

---

[1] With all their deep reverence for his character and resplendent merits, the magistrates occasionally found it necessary to remonstrate with Beza for conduct which they deemed imprudent and likely to involve their city in trouble. It would appear, for example, that in December, 1574, some Huguenot exiles undertook a fruitless enterprise of a military character in the direction of Mâcon and Châlons. Discovering, upon the return of the refugees to Geneva, that Beza had been privy to the undertaking, the council commissioned the eminent Michel Roset kindly to set forth to him that he ought not to consent to such things, still less take part in them—" qu'il ne doit consentir à telles choses, moins s'en mesler." Fazy, 21. See, also, this author's valuable remarks, ibid. 11.

[2] "Qu'il se sera adressé à un de mes plus grands amis." Condé to the Council, Basle, June 22, 1575, MS. Geneva Archives, in Fazy, 135, 136.

At the conference the debate was long and earnest. What measure of religious liberty should be deemed sufficient? What satisfaction required for the late massacre? What security exacted to avoid the possibility of being cheated in the future as in the past? No wonder that the resolution was finally reached "to make good and stout demands on all these points, and to persist in them to the very end." For the Huguenots had excellent grounds of encouragement. Since the renewal of the war they had been almost uniformly victorious. "Never," wrote Beza, "even when we had large armies in the field, had we one-tenth part of the success which God has vouchsafed to us as against His enemies since the beginning of these last troubles."[1]

Early in the month of April the deputies from Languedoc, together with other delegates commissioned by Condé himself, found themselves in Paris. A few days later (on the eleventh of April) an audience was granted them at the Louvre. Henry of Valois was attended by his wife and mother, by his brother Alençon, by the King of Navarre, and by the members of the royal council, among whom figured Cardinal Bourbon, the Duke of Montpensier, Marshal Retz, Morvilliers, Sebastian de l'Aubespine, Bishop of Limoges, and others, drawn to the queen mother's apartments not merely by the duty of their office, but by curiosity to learn the conditions which the confederates would propose. One of the secretaries of state was present to make an official record of the proceedings.

In behalf of the little knot of envoys, some deputed by the prince, others by Damville, and still others by the Protestant churches—they may have been eight or ten in all—a former member of the Parliament of Paris, the courageous Sieur d' Arènes, was put forward to speak. Beauvoir la Nocle and such "fronts d' airain" as Yolet, Duchelar, and Clausonne stood by in silence. The long speech of Arènes was

Speech of d' Arènes.

---

[1] "Mais quant à nos frères des Eglises de France, la guerre va tousjours en avant, et vous puis dire que lorsque nous avons eu grosses armées, nous n'avions point la dixiesme partie de ce que Dieu a fait contre ses ennemys depuis les derniers troubles." Beza to Gabriel Schlusselberger Geneva, March 25, 1575, Bulletin de la Société de l'histoire du Protestantisme français, xvi. (1867) 269.

in every way worthy of a man distinguished alike for his eloquence and for his learning.¹ He expressed an earnest longing for peace, but warned the king that if France now presented the mournful spectacle of irreligion, discord, and insubordination to constituted authority, if the French name had come to be covered with opprobrium, as Henry might himself testify from his personal experience on his way to Poland, the cause was to be sought in no fatal conjunction of heavenly constellations or influences, but in the violation of "Piety and Justice"—his deceased brother's motto. The royal faith had been prostituted in the butchery of St. Bartholomew's Day, a butchery of which Charles the Ninth had proclaimed his detestation in public letters, but which he had been impotent to prevent; for young and reckless advisers, like those whom Rehoboam trusted, had prescribed remedies repudiated by older and wiser counsellors. To re-establish "Piety and Justice," those two pillars of the monarchy, was the object of the Prince of Condé and Marshal Damville in their present attempt.

Hereupon Arènes handed to the king a document in which the prince and the marshal had distinctly set forth their views. Henry, after assuring the envoys that he fully reciprocated the desire for peace so eloquently expressed by Arènes, bade them retire to the adjoining antechamber, and there await his answer to their demands.²

It was no ordinary letter that M. de Fizes, the secretary, now proceeded to read, nor was it altogether calculated to please the ears that listened. Condé and Damville began by the usual complimentary phrases, but soon came to sober and unpalatable truths. They assured Henry that both Protestants and Roman Catholics had been driven to take up arms by the same violence. As to the former, the chief cause of war was that they had not been suffered to enjoy the benefits of the Edict of January, so solemnly enacted and promulgated. Hence had arisen conflicts that culminated

<small>The Huguenot demands.</small>

---

¹ "Arennius, Condæi legatorum unus, vir cumprimis eruditus et eloquens." Jean de Serres, v. fol. 73.
² Négotiation de la paix, Mém. de Nevers, i. 308–313.

in the horrible massacre of St. Bartholomew's Day. As to the latter, the pernicious counsels which had been followed, and in accordance with which the first princes of the blood and the chief nobles were either to be executed or to be consigned to perpetual imprisonment, sufficiently explained their action. To put an end to this state of things, the prince and the marshal, in the name of their confederated followers, had reduced to writing their demands. The document that followed began by an article in which the king was requested to permit the free and public exercise of the Reformed religion throughout the entire extent of the French dominions, without distinction of persons or places, and including the celebration of Divine worship, prayers, the administration of the holy sacraments and of marriage, the visitation of the sick, the burial of the dead in the common cemeteries, schools, the printing and sale of books, the discipline of the Church, the holding of consistories, colloquies, and synods, collections for the poor, and, in general, all else necessary to the proper observance of the rites of the Reformed religion. So much for the first article. The remaining sixty-seven articles were not inferior in boldness. They stipulated for the right to build and own churches, for safe residence in every part of the kingdom, for the application of the tithes paid by Protestants to the support of their own ministers, for the re-establishment of the salutary ordinances of Jeanne d'Albret in the Kingdom of Navarre, and for the punishment of blasphemy. They did not, however, forget to suggest that the toleration sought for must not be extended to Epicureans and atheists, for these should be visited with all forms of punishment.

After providing for an equality in religion, the confederates proposed a plan for securing the impartial administration of justice. So far as possible the same number of judges ought to be appointed from both religions. But as that result could not at once be attained, a temporary expedient was recommended. It was proposed that the greater royal council be increased by adding to its members, on Condé's nomination, as many Protestants as it now contained Roman Catholics; and that forty judges chosen from this entire college and taken equally from the two religions should sit, one-half at Montpellier and one-half at Cadours, to entertain appeals from the parliaments. Among many other provisions all tending to the same end, we need only notice two demands—the one for the punishment of the perpetrators of the Paris massacre, as the most satisfactory proof of the king's detestation of that crime, and as the firmest basis of a lasting peace;[1] the other for the annulling of all sentences for religion's sake pronounced since the time of Henry the Second, and especially the sentences of Admiral Coligny and Count Montgomery. As a pledge for the execution of the edict of pacification, the confederates begged to be allowed not only to retain the cities now in their possession, but to add to this number two other cities in each province of the kingdom. There were other demands, of a scarcely less startling character, which must be passed over for the sake of brevity.[2]

When the articles had been read, the envoys were recalled into the royal presence. Neither Henry nor Catharine wore the benignant looks of a brief hour ago. "I am amazed," exclaimed the former, "at the new and strange contents of your articles, and that you have dared to bring them to me;[3] for you must have been present when they were concocted and have known what they were. This leads me to think that you do not by any means care so much for peace as you professed. Well! what else is there that you wish?" In vain did Arènes excuse himself and his comrades as ambassadors confined by their instructions to the tenor of the articles they had presented. Henry insisted that

Surprise and indignation of Henry and Catharine.

---

[1] The Southern Huguenots had been in favor of even stouter demands. "They of Languedoc would have had put in that the authors of the slaughter of Paris should be put in their hands to be executed, and the death of the admiral revenged; but this was thought by common assent to be an impossible thing, and therefore without purpose to be asked." R. Stafford to Burleigh, Basle, March 29, 1575. State Paper Office.

[2] Jean de Serres, v. fols. 65-73. The text of the Protestant articles is not given in the relation in the Mémoires de Nevers.

[3] "Lesquels il trouvoit fort estranges et s'esbahissoit comment nous les avions osé presenter." Mém. de Nevers, i. 313.

Arènes was a leader in the councils of the confederates.[1] The Huguenot turned to Catharine de' Medici to entreat her kind offices with her son, and she graciously promised to employ them, meanwhile protesting that she would be far from advising Henry to grant unreasonable demands. "I know full well," she added, "that your Huguenots are cats that always alight on their feet; but even had they fifty thousand men in the field, with the admiral alive and all their leaders at their head, they could not talk more arrogantly than they do now."[2]

Two days later, in a second audience, the king's ministers undertook to explain the reasons why Henry could not grant the first and chief article of the demands of the confederated Politiques and Huguenots. "The king, being a Roman Catholic," said Morvilliers, "wishes all his subjects to belong to that faith. It is only right that the Protestants should renounce a religion that has been the cause of tumults and discord." "The Protestants," replied Arènes, "will obey the king in everything, save in religion, where God prefers obedience rather than sacrifice. Events have proved our loyalty; for so often as King Charles accorded us religious liberty, we laid down our arms and restored the cities that had fallen into our hands. The charge of insubordination is a stale calumny, long since refuted. The Protestants, indeed, teach that, so far as religion is concerned, we must simply follow the voice of God. If, therefore, the authority of the Roman religion rest on an antiquity of five hundred, or even a thousand years—a thing utterly out of the question—we shall appeal to the authority of centuries much more remote. We shall turn back to the times of Christ and his apostles, upon whose teaching our religion is founded. Against the Truth there is no prescription of antiquity."[3] "We do not demand the actual exer-

The demand for religious liberty.

---

[1] "Que je sçai estre de leur conseil et des plus avant." Lestoile, i. 53.
[2] Ibid., ubi supra.
[3] "La coustume generale du royaume de France," said Arènes, "est que le seigneur ne prescrit point contre le vassal, ny le vassal contre le seigneur, et moins contre le roy. Donc à plus forte raison les hommes ne peuvent acquerir ny prescription ny possession contre le Roy des Rois, et Seigneur des Seigneurs, mesmement au droit de vassalité, qui est le droit de legitime ser-

cise of our religion all over France; for that we must abide a more opportune time. But there can be no firm concord where distinctions are made between citizens; for if the one class become more fierce and overbearing, the other will become more distrustful."

The arguments of Arènes were reinforced by those of Clausonne, who in the matter of toleration adduced the example of the Emperor Charles the Fifth, and showed that Henry's conscience could scarcely interfere with his grant of religious liberty to the Huguenots, in view of the engagements into which he had entered for the purpose of obtaining the crown of Poland. So, too, another ambassador, Beauvoir la Nocle, pointed to the liberality of the Emperor Maximilian who granted religious liberty in his hereditary dominions, and even in Vienna itself, upon receiving a payment of one hundred thousand crowns of gold. "Would to God, Sire," he added, turning to the king, "that we had paid you a million crowns at a time when we could have furnished them! We should have saved a far greater sum of money than that, and the lives of a hundred thousand of our brethren!"[1]

<small>Maximilian's example.</small>

Thus it was that, the Parisian Matins being yet recent, their scenes of carnage could not be effaced from the minds of the Protestants, whose delegates seemed forced as by some uncontrollable impulse, to call up the unwelcome apparition even in the presence of royalty itself. A little while after the occurrence of the episode that has just been narrated, another incident happened, no less striking in character. The Huguenot demand for the exercise of the Reformed worship everywhere throughout France was under consideration. Holy Baptism, the king was reminded, is a divine ordinance, administered in

---

vice que devons à Dieu, reglé par regle de fief, qui est sa volonté expresse, et non par nos inventions et traditions depuis survenues." Mém. de Nevers, i. 318.

[1] "Pleust à Dieu (dit-il) que nous en eussions baillé un million, Sire, du temps que nous le pouvions faire, pour espargner cent mil de nos freres, qu'on a depuis tuez et meurtriz pour la religion." Mém. de Nevers, i. 324. "At utinam tibi (inquit) Rex, C X M dependissemus, eo tempore quum nobis facultas præstandi erat. Longe majorem summam et C M fratrum necem redemissemus." Jean de Serres, v. fol. 82.

the Protestant churches only at public service and at the conclusion of the preaching. Great, therefore, said the deputies, are the dangers to which the infant children of the faithful are exposed, when they have to be taken long distances, often in the dead of winter or through inclement rains, to the "temple," that they may receive the sacred rite. Henry of Valois whose ignorance of the religious usages of a considerable body of his southern subjects was as profound as was his indifference to their interests, remembered only the easy method by which a similar difficulty could be met in the Church of Rome. "Comment," he asked in some astonishment, " comment ne les ondoyez-vous pas, comme icy?" The majority of the delegates, uninitiated into such refinements, in place of answering the king's question, were compelled to turn to one another and ask in some perplexity the meaning of the strange verb "ondoyer" which his majesty had been pleased to use; while M. de Beauvoir, for all reply, exclaimed in a tone loud enough to be heard in every part of the room: "We have been only too much deluged both with blood and with water"—"On ne nous a que trop 'ondoyés' en sang et en eau."[1]

The theme was undoubtedly an exciting one both for the king and for his mother; and presently Henry of Valois, warming with the debate, called for wine, and, when he had drunk it, urged the Huguenots to trust him. "If I be not compelled," he said, "I will give you peace and see that it be observed." "That," replied Beauvoir la Nocle, "will be very necessary; for hitherto your ministers have acted as if their instructions were simply to harry us by every means, in utter contempt for your edicts."

---

[1] Mémoires de Nevers, i. 325. Littré (Dictionnaire de la Langue française, s. v.) defines "ondoiement" as Baptism which is administered in case of necessity and in which the ceremonies of the church are omitted. Du Cange (Glossarium ad Scriptores Mediæ et Infimæ Latinitatis) gives the equivalent in the Latin of the thirteenth and subsequent centuries—"undeiare," "undaizare," and "undare;" and quotes certain letters that passed between French bishops respecting the validity of an "ondoiement" in which the application of water, possibly by a mother or by a layman, was accompanied simply by the formula, "In nomine Patris," etc. Among the instances cited is this one, from the fifteenth century: "La suppliant enfanta d'un fils, lequel, incontinent qu'il fut né, elle print et umdea."

Again the wily Queen Mother urged the envoys to produce their supplementary instructions. When they repeated that they had been entrusted with none, she informed them that they ought not to have come with conditions which they knew they could not obtain. To which they pertinently replied: "We came in answer to the repeated commands of the king to lay before him our complaints." When Henry again insisted that they should offer terms more in accordance with justice, since he was resolved not to concede these, Catharine exclaimed: "My son, dismiss these men. I believe that it is God's will that we make no peace with them, in order that they may pay the penalty they deserve. All foreign princes will learn the terms which you have offered and they have refused. All will aid you in inflicting punishment upon them." She added in a lower voice: "You know what they wrote to you. God favors kings. No one will approve this obstinacy of your subjects." "Not the Pope, nor the King of Spain," interjected Beauvoir. "Well," retorted Catharine, "will any Catholic prince regard the peace you demand as a just one?" "Yes," said Beauvoir, "the Emperor will." And so the discussion proceeded; the king vehemently protesting that should he make the concessions asked by the Huguenots, he would deeply offend the Papists, and the envoys as resolutely maintaining that, in the universal desire of the people for peace, even the holders of ecclesiastical benefices would gladly acquiesce.[1]

<small>Catharine urges the ambassadors to offer better terms.</small>

The question of "justice" was scarcely less knotty than the question of "piety." The Huguenots declared that, as matters now stood, there could be no expectation that their rights would be respected. "How can we hope for justice," said they, "at the hands of judges that hate us worse than they do Turks?"[2]

---

[1] Négotiation de la paix, Mém. de Nevers, i. 327; Jean de Serres, v. fol. 83.

[2] Two points in the demands of the confederates, it should be noted, failed to obtain the approval of the most candid and fair-minded among the Huguenots themselves. The first was a provision (in Article 25) for the relief of those Protestants who having bought judicial positions had, on account of their faith, been arbitrarily deprived of them; the second was the stipulation (in Article 26) that those ecclesiastics who, when embracing Protestantism, had

The most intense interest was manifest when the thirty-fourth article was reached, in which the Huguenots had called for the punishment of the authors of the massacre of St. Bartholomew's Day. The court was ready with an answer, and Morvilliers was its mouthpiece. "Great sins have been committed on both sides," he said, with an air of impartiality; "let them all be buried in oblivion.¹ It will be but a poor augury of a firm peace if we undertake to investigate and punish the many injuries inflicted upon each other by Catholics and Protestants." But Arènes repudiated the amnesty so suavely suggested. "This massacre was no sudden outburst of anger, but a premeditated plot; it was not a sudden attack, but a treacherous destruction of those who at the time of a feast suspected anything else rather than hostility. The Huguenots were slain when they had come to Paris by the king's express invitation. So were eight hundred slain at Lyons, after they had been summoned to the citadel, in accordance with the command of the king's governor. So were eighteen hundred butchered in Rouen. This blood cries aloud to God for vengeance. The king, to whom God has given supreme command next to Himself, cannot refuse to hear it nor excuse himself from inflicting condign punishment because of the multitude of culprits. The ancient Romans decimated whole legions. Those who think that no satisfaction ought to be exacted for this crime do the greatest indignity to the memory of King Charles and to the reputation of your Majesty and of the queen your mother. You yourself know, Sire, from

Punishment of the authors of the massacre demanded.

---

been permitted by Charles the Ninth, to resign their benefices in favor of their friends, in order, under their name, to enjoy the revenues of the same, should be enabled to carry out the arrangement. It was justly urged that the first demand gave countenance to the pernicious abuse of venality of judicial offices, and the second to the yet more reprehensible practice of simony. Morvilliers had good reason to tell the Huguenot envoy that the latter was a demand unworthy of the religion they professed. Jean de Serres, v. fols. 69, 86, 87.

¹ When a little while before, Catharine de' Medici said to one of the envoys, "Beauvoir, il faut oublier et ne parler plus des choses passées;" the latter aptly retorted, "Madame, il nous faudroit bailler quelque charme pour les nous faire oublier, les choses passées." Mémoires de Nevers, i. 326.

what occurred upon your journey to Poland, how strongly foreign princes detest so great a crime. Should a new edict forbid any investigation into the misdeeds committed at the time of the massacre, they will believe that the assurances given by your brother that he detested the crime were a mere pretence. The royal majesty ought to be clear not only of crime, but of the very suspicion of crime." To this one of the real authors of the massacre answered by asseverating his innocence. "That crime," said Henry, "occurred contrary to my will, and I detest it with all my heart. Nor can it be in any way imputed to my brother, King Charles." Catharine de' Medici was a little more guarded in her assertions. She granted that grave sins had been committed by her adherents, but she thought that the faults on the one side must be weighed against the faults on the other. The Huguenots, too, she said, had slain three or four hundred Roman Catholics at Nismes, and thrown the bodies into the wells. To which Clausonne replied that the slaughter at Nismes had been greatly exaggerated, and that it happened in time of war and contrary to the will and efforts of the magistracy. It were absurd to compare with this a massacre perpetrated in time of peace.[1]

Henry asseverates his innocence.

If the king and his mother had been reluctant to promise a judicial investigation for the purpose of discovering and punishing the authors of the massacre, they showed even more unwillingness to do justice to the memory of the great hero of the Huguenots. When the envoys pronounced Gaspard de Coligny worthy of everlasting praise, Henry remarked that they ought, as loyal subjects, to be more solicitous for the good name of King Charles than for that of the admiral. "The king, my brother, pronounced the admiral's sentence of condemnation with his own lips. If the admiral be declared innocent, it will redound to my brother's very great

Coligny's memory vindicated.

---

[1] Minor discrepancies in numbers between the accounts in Jean de Serres (v. fol. 89) and the Mémoires de Nevers (i. 341) need no special attention. If the queen mother exaggerated, the Huguenot envoy undoubtedly underrated the victims of the "Michelade" of 1567. They numbered not "seven or eight," nor "scarcely a score," but eighty souls. See the Rise of the Huguenots, ii. 224, 225.

ignominy." In vain did Arènes reply that the sentence was precipitate, and dictated by persons who had imposed upon Charles the Ninth; his royal auditors, and especially the queen mother, exhibited their extreme vexation in word and in look; none the less because the Huguenots would not hear of a pardon to be granted to the admiral's children—a pardon which would in itself have been an admission of guilt.[1]

These were not the only unpalatable propositions. Henry not unnaturally objected to the article by which he would be made to recognize everything done by Condé and Damville as having been done by dutiful subjects in his service; although the envoys had no difficulty in finding precedents for this somewhat inconsistent declaration in the pacificatory edicts of Charles the Ninth. He was still more incensed when mention was made of the states general, and it was proposed to reduce the taxes to the scale of the times of Louis the Twelfth. The demand of towns as pledges for the execution of the royal edict of peace met with no greater favor in Henry's eyes; even when he was reminded that, for lighter reasons than the Huguenots might allege, God had granted the Jews cities of refuge.[2] But the king was provoked above measure when his attention was called to the request of the Protestants that foreign princes—the Queen of England, the elector palatine, and the Duke of Savoy, not to speak of the Swiss cantons—should take part in the contract, and that a copy of it should be placed in their hands with all due solemnity. "What is the object of this demand?" said Henry with unusual irritation. "If the edict should be violated by me, what will these princes undertake to do against me? I have no authority over their dominions, nor have they any in turn over mine. Let them attend to their affairs, and command their subjects; I shall manage my own kingdom and my own people."[3]

Propositions unpalatable to the king.

---

[1] Négotiation de la paix, Mém. de Nevers, i. 354; Jean de Serres, v. fol. 94.
[2] Mém. de Nevers, i. 358-365; Jean de Serres, v. fols. 95, 96.
[3] Jean de Serres, v. fol. 08. "Sembla que le roy s'esmeut aucunement; demandant par deux ou trois, que luy feroient ceux-là, s'il contrevenoit à la paix? Qu'ils n'avoient que voir sur luy, ni à se mesler de ses affaires, non plus qu'il ne se mesloit en tel cas des leurs." Mém. de Nevers, i. 365.

Through the long discussion the envoys of Condé and of the Huguenots had, day after day, defended the articles entrusted to their charge, and, unwelcome at every point as were the terms proposed, the king and his court had listened with respectful attention. It was otherwise when Monsieur de Saux, the deputy of Marshal Damville, undertook to dilate upon the necessity of reforming the abuses of the Church. The drama had been serious enough, in places even pathetic; it now turned into a broad farce. It was one thing to listen to those brave, scarred Huguenots, whose right arms had often dealt on the battle-field blows as steady and crushing as the arguments that now dropped from their lips; it was quite another to sit quietly and hear a studied and insincere harangue on the trite subject of church reformation from the representative of one of the most dissolute of Roman Catholic noblemen. The orator had not advanced far before the company began to fidget and yawn. Old Cardinal Bourbon muttered some indignant exclamation. Then Catharine de' Medici, whom no one could surpass in bitter raillery, broke out upon the deputy of the Politiques. "Those are fine words, Saux! You want to make a speech, forsooth. As if you could instruct us! We know all that you know. We are of the same religion as you. We listen patiently to 'those of the religion,' because from them we can learn something; but can any one endure you with quietness?" In vain poor Saux endeavored to secure a hearing, demanding it in the name of Damville and his associates; as often as he opened his lips he was greeted by the jeers of the entire company.[1]

The envoy of the Politiques treated with derision.

---

[1] Jean de Serres, v. fol. 99; Mém. de Nevers, i. 368. It must be confessed that the envoys of the Politiques found themselves more than once in an embarrassing situation; especially when it appeared by the statement of one of their own number (in spite of Saux's denial) that they had not only approved but signed with their own hands the Huguenot " cahier," including, among other things, a stipulation for the liberty of nuns to marry. " What! " said Henry, who had an inherited taste for sarcasm. " You wish and demand, on the one hand, that the Catholic Church be reformed, and, on the other, that the nuns may be suffered to marry." And both the king and his mother laughed heartily at the discomfiture of the Politiques. Mém. de Nevers, i. 385.

About a fortnight had been spent in negotiation, profitless save as exhibiting the aims and temper of the parties. Both sides were quite ready to conclude a bargain; the difficulty was that they were too far apart in their views to give much hope of an amicable agreement.[1] At last on the twenty-third of April, the king offered his terms: The Protestants to have sixteen cities—eight in Languedoc, six in Guyenne, and two in Dauphiny—and, in turn, to restore to the king the cities now in their possession in the state in which they were before the war. The king to appoint four new judges in the Parliament of Paris and select sixteen from the existing body, who should together administer justice for the benefit of the Huguenots. So, also, at Montpellier. Elsewhere the Huguenots to have the right to challenge peremptorily four judges.[2] These conditions the Protestant envoys promptly declared to be inadmissible, Beauvoir la Nocle begging Henry to remember that the people must be satisfied. Thereupon the monarch deigned, the next day, to enlarge the terms. He consented that the Huguenots should enjoy liberty to reside unmolested in any part of the kingdom, and to worship in all places now in their possession, excepting the four cities of Montpellier, Castres, Aigues-mortes, and Beaucaire. Besides this, the same right was to be enjoyed by all noblemen holding fiefs of the first rank, for themselves and for all visitors; while nobles of inferior jurisdiction were allowed the same privilege for themselves and their families, but not in walled cities and their suburbs, especially cities belonging to the queen mother or to Anjou, nor within ten leagues of Paris or two leagues of the court.[3]

The king offers unacceptable terms.

He substitutes better terms.

---

[1] To Jean de Serres, v. fol. 99, the whole transaction was wonderfully like the haggling of shrewd hucksters, "making a small offer at first, then adding a little, asking, detaining, throwing in vague hints of threats, feigning to go away, returning."

[2] Jean de Serres, v. fol. 100; Mém. de Nevers, i. 368, 369.

[3] The written answer given by Henry to the Huguenot demands, article by article, was dated Paris, May 5, 1575. To this he appended, under date of May 18th, two short sentences slightly enlarging his concessions. The only additional point of importance was that the Protestants should have in each baili-

These were almost the concluding scenes of the negotiations. The envoys would neither accept nor refuse the proposals of the court. They could only promise to report the terms to those who had sent them. It was with reluctance that they obtained permission to withdraw from Paris. But, if the wrangle between Henry and Catharine, on the one hand, and the Huguenots and their allies, on the other, had proved fruitless of good so far as the immediate results aimed at were concerned, it had not been without its moral effect. It was something, within the very walls of the Louvre, and a stone's throw from the window from which Charles amused himself, less than three years before, with firing his arquebuse at the miserable Huguenots, as though they had been game—it was something, I say, for Huguenot envoys unblushingly to make "a strange and prodigious demand for the Edict of January." It was proof positive that the boy-king's advisers and instigators had failed to fulfil their part of the bargain; more than one Huguenot remained, if not to reproach, at least to require satisfaction for the crime perpetrated on that wretched Sunday of August. The Protestant ranks had been thinned by the assassin's dagger, but their spirit was not broken. They exacted neither more nor less than they had claimed as their right in previous negotiations. There were, indeed, those among them that doubted the expediency of insisting at this time so strenuously upon terms which they could scarcely hope by any possibility to obtain; but the judgment of the leaders was vindicated by the issue; the very rigidity of the conditions from which they declined to recede determined the wavering and strengthened the party.[1] Even La Rochelle, in the vicinity of which Huguenot arms had met with little success, holding scarcely

End of the negotiations.

The "prodigious" demand for the Edict of January.

---

wick of the kingdom an enclosed place, and that among these places should be one city in each of the ancient governments, to be selected by his majesty. The document in full is printed at the end of the narrative of the Huguenot envoys, Mém. de Nevers, i. 425-433.

[1] "Comme plusieurs interpretoient la dureté des articles avoir esté telle pour monstrer leur fermeté, et par là tirer à soi ceux qui marchandoient encores; comme il avint." Agrippa d'Aubigné, ii. 176.

an inch of ground on the mainland, and scantily supplied with bread, was now induced, through brave La Noue's persuasive words, to assume a bold front.[1] Just as the Huguenot envoys were on the point of returning to their homes, with the exception of Arènes and a companion, left behind to avoid the appearance of relinquishing all hope of peace, there appeared in Paris ambassadors from several foreign states, sent to enforce upon Henry the wholesome counsel that he should come to an understanding with his subjects and quench the flames of war. The Swiss legation was specially imposing, with a magistrate of Berne, not less eminent in station than distinguished for eloquence, at its head. Almost the same day came the ambassador of Duke Emmanuel Philibert, of Savoy. Both urged Henry to grant the petitions of his Protestants for religious liberty, and the Savoyard pointed as an example to the partial toleration he had accorded in his own dominions. Queen Elizabeth added her intercessions to those of the continental allies of France, using her ambassador, Dr. Dale, as her mouthpiece. All these efforts, however, proved as abortive as those of the Huguenots themselves.[2] Not long after, the Prince of Orange, to whom it would seem that Henry had himself sent an envoy, about the end of April, requesting his good offices in allaying the commotions in France, in turn despatched one Dr. Junius, Governor of Veere, to Paris, with instructions to gratify the king's laudable desire. Dr. Junius arrived too late to be of much service, for the Protestant deputies were gone. But he elicited at least a frank avowal from his majesty. "Thereupon," says the governor, "the king *ex tempore* gave me this answer . . . that he saw distinctly from the results that nothing has been gained by the attempt to take from the Protestants of his kingdom of France the exercise of their religion, and that he has consequently made up his mind to govern his subjects with all gentleness and fatherly af-

Marginal note: Intercessions of foreign states.

---

[1] Ibid., ubi supra.
[2] The Huguenot envoys give a very minute and circumstantial account of the Swiss and Savoyard efforts in their long narrative of their mission. "Négotiation de le paix," Mém. de Nevers, i. 388-424. See also Jean de Serres, v. fols. 102, 103 ; Agrippa d'Aubigné, ii. 175 ; De Thou, v. 188.

fection, and to give them reason to love and obey him." To all which, and to the king's request that he should labor with the Prince of Condé to bring him to his way of thinking, the worthy governor doubtless listened with courtesy and apparently with implicit confidence. None the less, however, did he express to Condé, with pardonable scepticism, his suspicion respecting peace negotiations, of whose progress the Pope was said to be kept advised, and which met with approval at Rome. The horrible acts were yet fresh in men's memories by which former edicts of pacification had been violated.[1]

Throughout the summer, uninterrupted by the progress of the fruitless negotiations to which we have been attending, the desolating plague of war continued its ravages. Not that the conflict was without its exciting adventures. In the struggle, which often narrowed itself down to an attempt to take city by city, treachery and stratagem had a rare opportunity for display. Many were the disguises adopted, many the cunning plans devised. Mont Saint Michel, commonly called "Mont Saint Michel au péril de la mer," in the extreme southwestern corner of Normandy, was a stronghold much coveted by the Huguenots of that province. The prospect of gaining those massive walls by open warfare was not encouraging. But a party of five-and-twenty Protestants, dressed in the rough garb of pilgrims, found ready admission at the gates. Slowly and with well-simulated devotion they climbed the six-score steps that led to the abbey church, situated on an eminence commanding the town. Here, after paying for a mass, and buying consecrated candles, they concluded the solemn farce by stabbing the priest when he turned to present the plate for their offerings, and made themselves masters of the holy place.[2]

Treacherous disguises.

But whatever military advantages the Huguenots obtained

---

[1] Dr. J. Junius to the Prince of Condé, June, 1575, Groen van Prinsterer, v. 237–243.

[2] De Thou, v. 192, 196; Lestoile, i. 56; Agrippa d'Aubigné, ii. 158–160; Claude Haton, ii. 895. The latter refers the incident to a date about two years later.

in various parts of the realm were more than outweighed by the death of "the brave Montbrun." This daring and energetic leader, the terror of the enemy in Dauphiny,[1] had just defeated a large body of Swiss auxiliaries, upon whom he inflicted a loss of eight or nine hundred men and eighteen ensigns, while that of the Huguenots scarcely amounted to half a dozen men. But his brilliant success in this and other engagements had made Montbrun and his soldiers more incautious than usual. They attacked a strong detachment of men-at-arms, and mistaking the confusion into which they threw the advance guard for a rout of the entire body, dispersed to gather the booty and offered a tempting opportunity to the Roman Catholics as they came up. Montbrun, who, too late, discovered the danger of his troops, and endeavored to rally them, was at one time enveloped by the enemy, but would have made good his escape had there not been a broad ditch in his way. Here his horse missed its footing, and in the fall the leader's thigh was broken. In this pitiable plight he surrendered his sword to a Roman Catholic captain, from whom he received the assurance that his life would be spared.[2]

Capture of Montbrun, July.

The king and his mother had other views. Henry, on receiving the grateful news of Montbrun's capture, promptly gave orders that the prisoner be taken to Grenoble and tried by the Parliament of Dauphiny on a charge of treason. Vain were the efforts of the Huguenots, equally vain the intercession of the Duke of Guise, who wished to have Montbrun exchanged for Besme, Coligny's murderer, recently fallen into Huguenot hands. Henry and Catharine de' Medici were determined that Montbrun should die. They urged the reluctant judges by reiterated commands; they overruled the objection that to put the prisoner to death would be to violate good faith and the laws of honorable warfare. Catharine had not forgotten the honest

---

[1] "Ex præcipuis ducibus Huguenotorum, qui multa fortiter et feliciter in his bellis civilibus fecit." Languet, Epistolæ secretæ, i. 114.
[2] Jean de Serres, v. fols. 106, seq.; Recueil des choses mémorables, 546, etc.; De Thou, v. 203; Agrippa d'Aubigné, ii. 137.

Frenchman's allusion to her " perfidious and degenerate " countrymen.[1]

As for Henry, an insult received at Montbrun's hands rankled in his breast and made forgiveness impossible. Some months before, the king had sent a message to him in a somewhat haughty tone, demanding the restoration of the royal baggage and certain prisoners taken by the Huguenots. " What is this! " exclaimed the general. " The king writes to me as a king, and as if I were bound to obey him! I want him to know that that would be very well in time of peace; I should then recognize his royal claim. But in time of war, when men are armed and in the saddle, all men are equal." On hearing this, we are told, Henry swore that Montbrun should repent his insolence. In his glee over the Huguenot's mishap he recalled the prophecy and broke out with the exclamation, " Montbrun will now see whether he is my equal."[2]

Henry resolute that Montbrun must die.

Under these circumstances there was little chance for a Huguenot, were he never so innocent, to be acquitted by a servile

---

[1] See above, page 36. Catharine and the knot of Italians whom she had gathered about her were very sensitive on the point of nationality. Lestoile (i. 57) tells us that, Tuesday, July 5, 1575, a captain La Vergerie was hung and quartered by order of Chancellor Birague and some maîtres de requêtes named by the queen mother, for merely saying, in a conversation respecting a quarrel between the University students and some Italians at Paris, that his friends ought to espouse the side of the former " et saccager et couper la gorge à tous ces b. d'Italiens qui estoient cause de la ruine de la France." The popular indignation vented itself in a multitude of sonnets and pasquinades against Catharine de' Medici.

[2] " Estant en Avignon, il [Henry III.] escrivit une lettre audit Monsieur de Montbrun, un peu brave, haute et digne d'un roy, sur quelques prisonniers qu'il avoit pris, et sur l'insolence faite. Il respondit (si) outrecuydemment que cela luy cousta la vie. ' Comment,' dit-il ; ' le Roy m'escrit comme Roy, et comme si je le devois reconnoistre ! Je veux qu'il sçache que cela seroit bon en temps de paix, et qu'alors je le reconnoistray pour tel ; mais en temps de guerre, qu'on a le bras armé, et le cul sur la selle, tout le monde est compagnon.' Telles paroles irriterent tellement le Roy, qu'il jura un bon coup, qu'il s'en repentiroit." Brantôme, Mestres de Camp Huguenots de l'Infanterie Francoise, Œuvres, xi. 151. Brantôme was at court when, over a year later, news came of Montbrun's capture. Henry, he tells us, was greatly pleased, and said : " Je sçavois bien qu 'il s'en repentiroit, et mourra ; et verra bien à cette heure s'il est mon compagnon." Ibid., p. 152.

parliament. Accordingly Montbrun was condemned to be beheaded as a rebel against the king and a disturber of the public peace. The execution was hastened lest natural death from the injury received should balk the malice of his relentless enemies. A contemporary, who may even have been an eye-witness, describes the closing scene in words eloquent from their unaffected simplicity. "He was dragged, half dead, from the prison, and was carried in a chair to the place of execution, exhibiting in his affliction an assured countenance; while the Parliament of Grenoble trembled and the entire city lamented. He had been enjoined not to say a word to the people, unless he wished to have his tongue cut off. Nevertheless he complained, in the presence of the whole parliament, of the wrong done to him, proving at great length his innocence and contemning the fury of his enemies who were attacking a man as good as dead. He showed that it was without cause that he was charged with being a rebel, since never had he had any design but to guarantee peaceable Frenchmen from the violence of strangers who abused the name and authority of the king. His death was constant and Christian. He was a gentleman held in high esteem, inasmuch as he was neither avaricious nor rapacious, but on the contrary devoted to religion, bold, moderate, upright; yet he was too indulgent to his soldiers, whose license and excesses gained him much ill-will and many enemies in Dauphiny. His death so irritated these soldiers that they ravaged after a strange fashion the environs of Grenoble." [1]

<small>Montbrun's execution.</small>

The death of so prominent and energetic a Huguenot captain was likely to embolden the Roman Catholic party, not only in Dauphiny but in the rest of the kingdom.[2] In reality it only transferred the supreme direction in warlike affairs to still more competent hands. The young lieutenant of Montbrun, who shortly succeeded him in command, was François de Bonne, better known from his territorial designation as Sieur

<small>Lesdiguières.</small>

---

[1] Recueil des choses mémorables, 547, 548. See Jean de Serres, Commentarii, v. fols. 113-115 (I need not remind the reader that the two accounts are from the same hand). Also De Thou, v. 203, 204; Davila, 212; Lestoile, ii. 58; Languet, i. 129; Inventaire général, ii. 485, 486.

[2] Languet, i. 114.

de Lesdiguières, a future marshal of Henry the Fourth. Although the resplendent military abilities of Lesdiguières had not yet had an opportunity for display, it was not long before the Roman Catholics discovered that they gained nothing by the exchange. Lesdiguières was as brave as his master in arms, and he was his master's superior in the skill and caution with which he sketched and executed his military plans. The discipline of the Huguenot army at once exhibited marked improvement.[1]

Meanwhile an event occurred elsewhere that checked the exultation of Henry, and threw his court into a paroxysm of confusion and alarm. The intelligence reached the Louvre that Alençon, the puny brother of the king, the disturber of well-laid schemes, had escaped from Paris, and was on his way to join the malcontents.[2] Under pretext of an amorous intrigue he had been allowed to visit a house in the suburbs; but one day while his escort patiently waited for his return at the front door of the residence of his mistress, the prince quietly took horse on the opposite side of the house and rode off southward at full speed. A day or two later, when quite beyond reach of his pursuers, he sat down and indited a manifesto, or at least published such a paper to the world, in which he declaimed with violence against his brother's favorites, and, while professing the intention to maintain the rights of the nobles and the clergy, promised to secure those of the people, and demanded the convocation of the states general. Nothing was more specious than were these assurances. The only difficulty was in the character of him that uttered them. Could the selfish boy, who, tired of the monotony and insignificance of his position at court, fled

Alençon's escape from court and proclamation, September, 1575.

---

[1] Recueil, De Thou, etc., ubi supra.

[2] The king had, some weeks earlier, received warning of such a plan, and had brought the matter before the royal council; but Catharine expressed her incredulity, and advocated that Henry should rather assure himself of his brother by winning his heart. His Majesty was not pleased at this. "Well," quoth the king, "it is you, mother, that do hold him up by the chin, and without you he would not be so bold as he is; but I will have my reason of him." Memorandum, in Dr. Dale's handwriting, without date, but sent from Paris in the summer of 1575, State Paper Office.

to the arms of the Protestants and Politiques, be really in earnest? Strange as it may appear, many of the best citizens imagined it to be so. Both Huguenots and upright Roman Catholics, ignorant of Alençon's true nature, suffered themselves to be amused by a sheet of paper. Some ministers of religion went further, and, in the churches of La Rochelle and Montauban, public thanksgiving was made to God over the happy escape of the prince from imprisonment. At that very moment, we are told, Alençon was excusing himself at Rome and trying to persuade the Pope that he had taken the step only from necessity.

<small>The Huguenots duped.</small>

The time was to come when the instincts of Catharine's youngest son would be fully understood, the time when the pseudo-patriot would turn out to be an arrant coward, with no solicitude save for his own petty interests, with no aptitude except an inherited capacity of no stinted measure for dissimulation and deceit. When that time arrived it was not unnatural for the Huguenots to pass from credulous trust to the opposite extreme of unreasonable suspicion, nor was it strange that they came to believe the escape of Alençon from court to be but a subtle device of Catharine to lure the Protestants on to their ruin. The queen mother's agitation they insisted was assumed only for the moment; in her heart she rejoiced that Alençon would soon be at the head of the German army which Condé and Casimir were bringing, at so great a cost of trouble and treasure, to dictate peace at the gates of Paris. In truth, however, this conclusion was as ill-founded as the first hasty rejoicing was premature. Catharine's grief was sincere. The Florentine envoy was no heretic to be hoodwinked, and there was no profit to be derived from deceiving his master the Grand Duke of Tuscany. We may, therefore, conclude with safety that Catharine was altogether unprepared for Alençon's escape and, at first, utterly cast down by it. Alamanni declared that, on calling upon the queen mother, he found her marvellously depressed. He had never seen her so disheartened by any occurrence since his arrival in France. She spoke in few and broken words, as if fearing to touch the wound, and, almost with tears in her eyes and appar-

<small>Catharine's grief genuine.</small>

ently forgetful of her royal dignity, declared that she never would have thought such a thing possible.¹ Meantime the court did not waste its time in useless regrets. The union of Alençon with Damville and the Huguenots made a formidable combination. It was important to avoid driving the younger Montmorencies to extremities. So Marshal Francis, the head of the family, was formally liberated (on the second of October) from the imprisonment in which he had been languishing for over a year. After a few days more of hesitation, the king gave him audience, greeted him with warmth, and begged him to forget past injuries.²

Happy had been the lot of France if selfishness had been the supreme characteristic of Alençon alone. Unfortunately this weak prince was but a type of the nobleman of the period. In the incessant contests waged between the privileged classes, it was the wretched "tiers état" that was forced to bear the brunt of all the misfortunes befalling the land. "It will be found in the end," says the curé of Mériot, "that the seigneur will come to an agreement with the king, without giving himself any further solicitude for the

Wretched condition of the "tiers état."

---

¹ Alamanni to the Grand Duke, September 22, 1575, Négociations avec la Toscane, iv. 45. Dr. Dale says almost the same thing. "The king was very heavy and sorrowful and the queen mother as one dismayed. They spake both very lowly for their degree." Letter to Smith and Walsingham, September 28, 1575, State Paper Office. Recueil des choses mémorables, 550–553; Lestoile, i. 60; De Thou, v. 214, 215; La Fosse (Journal d'un curé ligueur), 174; Agrippa d'Aubigné, ii. 177, 178; Jean de Serres, v. fols. 116, seq.; Davila, 214. The correspondence of the English ambassador gives a vivid impression of the "marvellous perplexity" at Paris—the court amazed, the king tormenting himself upon his bed, the chancellor and others going home to utter laments over the untoward incident among their familiars, all men finding fault with the queen mother, because she was the let that Monsieur was not stayed, almost all the kings' followers booted in the court, and those that were not noted as not ready to do loyal service. The king knew not what to do, fearing that his troops would refuse to obey any of the generals that he might send to reduce Alençon by force of arms; fearing, also, that should he go in person, his troops would desert him. He concluded, however, promptly to send to his fugitive brother the plate, jewels, apparel, household stuff, and servants he had left behind him in his precipitate flight. Dr. Dale to Smith and Walsingham, September, 1575, State Paper Office.

² Alamanni to the Grand Duke, November, 1575, Négociations, iv. 47.

general weal, especially in what concerns the interest of the poor people of the towns and villages. Such is the condition of the princes of France that they always put forward the public welfare when they desire to avenge their quarrels upon each other, but they force the miserable commoner to endure the discomfort of the war, under the burden of which he is overwhelmed, and in return he gains nothing from the fine promises made by the princes. Instead of the relief which they promise the people, they open the door to all sorts of brigandage, to theft, robbery, and assassination. So it happened at this time, by reason of Alençon's declaration and protestation. In consequence of the prince's withdrawal from court, for the security, as was alleged, of his own person, the war was rendered worse by the half than it was in previous years for the poor laborers and villagers, by larceny, theft, extortion, rape, murder, and every other form of outrage, without rebuke or interposition of law or justice. And it cannot be otherwise; for, if one of the princes that are at war with each other were to undertake to punish the armed men of his party for the injuries they commit, instantly all his followers would leave him and go over to his enemy, and he would thus remain alone and without support." [1]

Claude Haton spoke only of what he had seen with his own eyes in the fertile province of Champagne. For had he not witnessed with indignation the perfect unconcern with which, for example, the Duke of Aumale, when on his way to join the Duke of Guise and help to repel the German reiters, had stopped in Provins and spent a day in playing tennis with the nobles of the place, while his followers scoured the neighborhood and devoured the scanty property of the villagers, depriving them even of the very necessaries of life?[2] But the curate's bitter words were equally true of a great part of France. The reckless prodigality of the upper and ruling classes was

---

[1] Mémoires de Claude Haton, ii. 782.

[2] Ibid., ii. 779. The reader curious to know the heart-rending details of popular suffering may study the document printed in the appendix to the same work (pages 1141-4), entitled "Remonstrances très humbles des villes de Troyes, Reins, Chaalons," etc.

every day increasing the load under which the peasantry staggered. Not a finger was raised to lighten the crushing burden. The scornful exclamation had passed into a proverb, "Le manant paye tout."[1] None dreamed that the rustic clown had a long memory, in which the full budget of his grievances, through the centuries, was faithfully stored up, and that he would one day importunately demand his reckoning at a time and in a manner very distasteful to his chronic debtor. "Le manant paye tout," said every member of the privileged orders, from the king down to the most insignificant baron who had contrived to avoid the forfeiture of his prescriptive rights, that would have resulted from engaging in the plebeian pursuits of trade or manual labor. In vain did the general distress call forth murmurs from all parts of the kingdom, cries to the effect that the king must do something to relieve the universal distress, loud protests from Roman Catholics that those under the protection of the Huguenots were better treated than the subjects of the king that had not taken up arms.[2] Never had the court been more thoughtless of the welfare of the nation, more wholly given up to riotous excess. Serious-minded men stood aghast, superstitious men thought they saw in the unbridled licentiousness of the times signs of the approaching end of all things. "It had seemed," said they, "in the time of Charles the Ninth, that the dissoluteness of the court could go to no greater lengths; but since the accession of Henry the Third, and especially since his marriage, it has passed all bounds and become so outrageous that all that was once practised under those ancient Roman emperors, masters of corruption and detestable lasciviousness, appears now to be revived. To specify would be to rehearse each most shameful statement contained in Suetonius, Herodian, Lampridius, and other similar historians of antiquity."[3]

Marginal notes: "Le manant paye tout." "Corruption of the court."

---

[1] Dialogue du maheustre et du manant, in Satyre Ménippée (Ratisbon, 1726), iii. 551.

[2] "Allegande che quelli che stanno sotto la protezione delli ugonotti sono meglio trattati." Alamanni to the Grand Duke, 1575, Négociations avec la Toscane, iv. 37.

[3] The language is substantially that of the author of the Recueil des choses mémorables (Dordrecht, 1598), 541.

A modern may well beg to be excused from giving a detailed account of enormities from a recital of which the chronicler of the sixteenth century drew back in horror; especially in view of the fact that the reference to the strange mixture of puerile extravagance, foul lewdness, and absurd devotion to which the king and his favorites were addicted is only germane to the theme of this history in so far as light may be thrown upon the motives of the policy exercised toward the Huguenots. Prudent counsellors had no standing with the young king. Their place had been usurped by the wild ministers to his pleasures. Among such bastard statesmen loud and angry disputes passed for an equivalent of rational discussion. Low broils and even assassination of rivals, whether in political or in amorous intrigue, abounded. M. du Gast, one of the chief participators in the bloody scenes of St. Bartholomew's Day, was found dead in his bed, six weeks after Alençon's escape. Although the instigator of the murder was shrewdly suspected, no attempt was made to discover and punish the culprit. None the less did the king indulge in extravagant displays of sorrow at the death of his favorite, bury him with great pomp by the grand altar in the church of Saint Germain l'Auxerrois, and assume the dead man's debts, said to amount to more than one hundred thousand francs.[1] A few days later, the monarch so recently plunged in grief was seen in his "coche," traversing the streets of Paris, in company with his young queen, visiting private houses and especially convents, and laying his hands on all the little dogs of a certain prized breed that he could find.[2] Great was the annoyance of the nuns and the ladies thus robbed of their pets; still greater the indignation of the more sober part of the population at the ridicule which was sure to attach to the royal name in the estimate of foreigners. For it was not a passing whim that led Henry to lavish upon his dogs the care that might advantageously have been expended upon his miserable subjects. Ten years later, when Chancellor Leoninus and his asso-

Puerile extravagance and lewdness.

Henry and his dogs.

---

[1] Lestoile (October 31, 1575), i. 61.
[2] Ibid. (November, 1575), i. 62.

ciates came to the Louvre, bringing with them a magnificent offer to Henry—nothing less than the sovereignty of the Low Countries, quite equal by themselves to a kingdom—even, as one diplomatist dryly remarks, to the kingdom of Poland [1]—the astonished envoys, at their solemn reception, found the monarch of France standing in the midst of his minions with "a little basket, full of puppies, suspended from his neck by a broad ribbon." [2] Devout Roman Catholics were still more shocked when they beheld Henry nonchalantly come up to the altar to receive the consecrated wafer, after having frolicked all through the service of the mass with his canine companions; while the sick who presented themselves to be touched for the king's evil scarcely ever saw him go through the mystic ceremonial without a dog resting upon his arms.[3]

Meanwhile, if Henry of Valois was sinking into effeminacy, surrounded by favorites who from men seemed to have been changed into women, in another part of France at least one of his subjects, laying aside the natural timidity of her sex, had seized the sword and was battling for her faith in right manly fashion. The virtuous Madeleine de Miraumont, sister of the Bishop of Le Puy, was a young widow of large possessions in Auvergne and as ardent a partisan of the reformed as her brother was of the papal cause. It was not a difficult matter for a woman of remarkable beauty, who betrayed no marked preference for any one of her many admirers, to gather about her a band of gallant young noblemen. When she took horse

---

[1] Morillon to Cardinal Granvelle, December 11, 1575, Groen van Prinsterer, v. 326.

[2] See the graphic account of the interview in Motley, United Netherlands, i. 96.

[3] "Il recevoit Dieu, qui sçait en quelle conscience! Car, ou tout affublé, ou tenant un chien, ou ayant folastré, tout durant la messe, quelquefois avec des chiens, il s'y présentoit hardiment. Aussi touchoit-il les escrouelles presque toujours chargé d'un chien sur un bras." Les mœurs, humeurs et comportemens de Henry de Valois (1589), Cimber et Danjou, Archives curieuses, xii. 468. Henry's irreverence on such occasions was of less importance if, as the writer of another libellous tract asserts, this monarch, in consequence of the fact that, at his anointing, the "sainte ampoule" was not "disposed" as usual, never acquired the inestimable prerogative of curing the king's evil. La vie et faits notables de Henry de Valois, Archives curieuses, xii. 432.

in person, armed cap-a-pie, full sixty knights gladly enrolled themselves under her banner, which, to use the expression of an appreciative historian, they esteemed to be no less the standard of love. With such a following, the exploits of the fair Amazon were as extraordinary as her warfare was novel. Not only did she repeatedly defeat superior forces of the enemy, but when besieged in her own castle by M. de Montal, royal lieutenant for Lower Auvergne, she boldly charged the Roman Catholics with scarce two score cavaliers, turning them into flight and mortally wounding their leader. No wonder that, in after times, as often as the Huguenot gentlemen from other parts of the kingdom would undertake in playful banter to reproach their comrades of Auvergne with having been soldiers of the Lady of Miraumont, the Auvergnese accepted the intended taunt as a compliment and bewailed the misfortune of those whom fortune had denied the privilege of so honorable a service.[1]

To add to the confusion reigning throughout France there came the report of the approach of foreign arms. The Prince of Condé had prevailed upon the elector palatine and his son again to give the Huguenots a much-needed support.[2] Duke John Casimir promised to enroll a considerable force, consisting of eight thousand reiters (two thousand in his own name and the rest in the name of Condé) and eight thousand Swiss foot soldiers. The invading army was to be provided with a supply of artillery, regarded, according to the notions of the sixteenth century, as quite sufficient—four large cannon, and twelve or fifteen field-pieces, and an abundant store of ammunition. On his side, the prince engaged that Marshal Damville would raise and bring from Languedoc a force of twelve thousand foot and two thousand horse. The treaty now signed included provisions to the effect that John Casimir should be consulted upon all questions of peace and war, and that the claims of his German troops for wages should

Foreign help for the Huguenots.

---

[1] Agrippa d'Aubigné, ii. 164.
[2] See Condé's long letter to John Casimir respecting the causes of the war, Jean de Serres, v. fols. 123-127.

be paid in full before their final discharge. It was also stipulated that John Casimir should sign the compact existing between Damville and the Protestants, and that an essential article of any future treaty of peace with the King of France should be that John Casimir be placed in command of the three bishoprics—Metz, Toul, and Verdun—as royal governor.[1]

It was always the misfortune of the Huguenots that their geographical distribution was such as to separate them from their allies by wide distances. Between the German frontier and the provinces in which the Protestants were numerous, intervened other provinces in which the Protestants had little or no foothold. In its consternation at the sudden flight of Alençon, the court had not forgotten to take measures for preventing that prince, so far as possible, from obtaining the support of the nobility, and had renewed its efforts to intercept any assistance from abroad. Unfortunately, the leaders of the Huguenot army of reinforcement made the capital mistake of dividing their troops. Since John Casimir was not yet ready to march with the main body, they permitted Thoré-Montmorency to lead a detachment to the help of his brother, Damville. Thoré's entire force consisted of only twelve or fifteen hundred German horse, with a few mounted French gentlemen, and five hundred arquebusiers. It was sheer madness to attempt, with such insignificant numbers, to penetrate so far through

---

[1] Recueil des choses mémorables, 554 ; Jean de Serres, v. fols. 127-129 ; De Thou, v. 217. See the text of the treaty, published for the first time in full, from that one of the two extant copies which was sent by the elector palatine to the magistrates of Geneva, by Henri Fazy, Genève, le Parti Huguenot et le Traité de Soleure, 146-157. The treaty is dated November 27, 1575 ; the elector palatine's letter four days later. The Duke of Aumale (Histoire des Princes de Condé, ii. 110), with true French pride, stigmatizes the agreement as odious, and its provisions as both absurd and impossible of execution. He hardly knows which to admire most—the extravagance of the palatine's claims, or the simplicity wherewith he seems to accept the chimerical engagements of his Huguenot allies. Without going to this length, we may certainly be permitted to deplore the necessity to which the French Protestants were driven by the fury of their enemies, of calling in, like their Roman Catholic fellow citizens, the help of foreign troops, and of exposing themselves to the taunt of caring less for the integrity of their country's territory than for their religious privileges.

a region in which defensible elevations abounded, which was intersected by rivers, and whose population was in arms to preclude the passage.[1] When to these difficulties was added the fact that, while the Germans had an inexperienced leader, and soon were mutinous for the payment of their wages, the court had collected a greatly superior force[2] to oppose their entrance, under such skilled captains as Henry of Guise, his brother, the Duke of Mayenne, Armand de Biron, and Philip Strozzi, no wonder that the expedition ended in disaster. After having suffered great annoyance from the skirmishing attacks of the enemy, Thoré was met and signally defeated, on the tenth of October, upon the banks of the Marne, not far from Château Thierry. It was with difficulty that the incompetent young man, with a handful of his reiters, succeeded in extricating himself from the meshes of his enemies and joining Alençon at La Châtre, after a break-neck ride of seventy leagues. On the other hand, Henry of Guise fought bravely, received a severe wound in the cheek, and fell to the ground half dead. The honorable scar (balafre) borne by him to the day of his death was the occasion of the epithet of "Le balafré," by which his followers gloried in designating him.[3] The loss on the Protestant side, if small in killed, was great in the number of wounded.

Defeat of Thoré.

---

[1] So it appeared to Hubert Languet, himself a Burgundian by birth, when he first heard of the design. "Via est adeo longa et adeo impedita montibus et fluminibus, ut putem pœne esse impossibile ut eo perveniant quo constituerunt, cum præsertim dicantur esse tantum duo millia et paucos pedites sint secum habituri et forte duces imperitos. Nam audio ipsorum ducem præcipuum fore Thoræum, filium connestabilis natu minimum." Epistolæ secretæ, i. (2) 124. It would appear, however, that Languet was misinformed respecting the route Thoré was to take, and supposed he would traverse Burgundy instead of Champagne.

[2] 10,000 to 12,000 foot, and 1,200 horse, besides the troops sent by the Dukes of Uzès and Montpensier.

[3] Lestoile (under date of October 11th), i. 61 ; Mémoires de Claude Haton, ii. 789; Agrippa d'Aubigné, ii. 179–183; Jean de Serres, v. fols. 140, 141 ; De Thou, v. 221, 222; Recueil des choses mémorables, 556. See also the account of the "Skirmish between the Reiters and Guise," sent by Dale to Burleigh, October 11, 1575, State Paper Office. Agrippa d'Aubigné devotes an entire chapter to this engagement, which he calls "Deffaitte de Dormans"—

Meanwhile, Catharine de' Medici had forgotten none of the arts by means of which she had, single-handed, more than once frustrated the well-devised counsels of statesmen and the carefully-laid schemes of war. In carrying into execution her intrigues she had never been sparing of time, fatigue, or exposure. She now left Henry to his puerile occupations and his dogs, while she posted to Touraine to confer with Alençon, and was rewarded by her success in patching up a hollow truce. It was to last about seven months,[1] and the conditions were very favorable to her youngest son—among other things, payment to the Germans, and the transfer of six places of security—Angoulême, Niort, Saumur, Bourges, and La Charité to the Duke of Alençon, and Mézières to the Prince of Condé.[2] But, after all, the truce amounted to little or nothing. Condé and John Casimir refused to ratify the arrangements, and neither the court nor Alençon took the trouble to observe it. As the queen-mother had had no other end in view than to prevent or delay the entrance of John Casimir into France, there remained nothing to be done for the present but to oppose him with an armed force of mercenary troops. For by December the army of John Casimir, which recognized the Prince of Condé's joint authority, had swollen in size, and included ten thousand horse, six thousand Swiss, two thousand lansquenets, and three thousand French arquebusiers. It was only waiting in the neighborhood of Saverne to receive tidings of the advance of Damville with troops and ready money.[3]

Hereupon Henry ordered a levy of six thousand Swiss and made arrangements for a suitable number of Germans. But a levy required money, and of money he had none. So the king

---

Dormans is ten or twelve miles east of Château Thierry—and remarks, somewhat hyperbolically, that the battle is "presque inconnue à tous ceux qui ont escrit, et de ceux qui l'ont veue estimée plus digne du nom de bataille que plusieurs à qui on a donné ce titre."

[1] November 22, 1575, to June 25, 1576.

[2] Recueil des choses mémorables, 558; De Thou, v. 222; Jean de Serres, v. fols. 143, 144; Davila, 216; Agrippa d'Aubigné, ii. 178, 179; "Accord between Monsieur and the Queen Mother," Magny, November 8, 1575, State Paper Office.

[3] Recueil des choses mémorables, 559.

betook himself to the Hôtel de Ville, and begged the city of Paris to furnish him with two hundred thousand livres wherewith to hire the troops that might defend the citizens against the dreaded Huguenots. But the prudent merchants of the capital were more suspicious of the king, who seemed to have instituted from close at hand an irreconcilable war against their purses,[1] than afraid of Condé and John Casimir, who were yet a good distance off. Instead of money came an answer in the form of a vexatious array of figures. The burghers broadly hinted that the king wanted their hard-earned gold for his favorites rather than for his armies, and they very distinctly pointed out the bottomless abyss of the king's prodigality, which no wealth of theirs could hope to fill. Paris had, in the past fifteen years, furnished the crown with thirty-six millions of livres, besides the sixty millions contributed by the clergy. What was there to show for an enormous expenditure which, rightly applied, might have secured the extension of the kingdom by lawful conquest? France had gained no honors; it had only incurred the ridicule of strangers. Other remarks there were, equally distasteful to the king, on the universal corruption of clergy and judiciary, and the wastefulness pervading every branch of the administration.[2] It is not surprising that Henry was provoked beyond endurance. He adopted, however, a strange method of revenge. Bringing the royal troops to the immediate vicinity, he posted Guise with his division at Saint Denis, Biron at Montmartre, Retz at Charenton, and so on, encircling the city in every direction, and compelled the citizens who had refused him ready money for his levies—or his favorites—to loosen their close-drawn purse-strings for the payment of the beleaguering forces.[3]

Vain efforts of the king to raise money.

Henry's whimsical revenge.

---

[1] "Ita peroratio semper de pecunia erat et Parisiorum crumenis bellum indicebatur." Jean de Serres, v. fol. 165.

[2] Recueil des choses mémorables, 560; Jean de Serres, v. fols. 153, 158; Agrippa d'Aubigné, ii. 217-219; De Thou, v. 223, 224.

[3] The incident is detailed by Jean de Serres, v. 159; Recueil des choses mémorables, 561, and Inventaire général, ii. 491. It is not mentioned by De Thou.

Never had France presented a scene of greater inconsistencies and more widespread confusion than it did about this time. Everywhere deceit and contradictory purposes seemed to reign. The king had made a truce, and was preparing for war. Alençon chose almost the same moment for the publication of the armistice in his court and for the confirmation of the agreements entered into by Condé with John Casimir;[1] and, while he assured the Pope of his unimpeachable orthodoxy and upright intentions, was begging the Protestant city of La Rochelle to furnish him money, and asseverating his purpose to espouse the quarrels of the Reformed Church of France.[2] Meanwhile, this excellent prince and worthy son of Catharine de' Medici took possession of such of the cities pledged to him as consented to admit his troops, and accepted the substitutes offered for the other cities whose audacious governors defiantly refused to obey the king's commands, troubling himself little about the failure of the court to fulfil its engagement to entrust Mézières to the Prince of Condé.[3]

General confusion.

In fact, the only compact about whose honest observance any solicitude was exhibited was an agreement made, not by kings or princes, but by the untitled inhabitants of a small province. The people of Vivarais—that fragment of Languedoc, on the right bank of the Rhône, of which Viviers was the most considerable town—were wearied of the relentless progress of a conflict raging at their very hearths. Here had the misery of the civil war become most conspicuous because the drama was seen enacted on so contracted a stage. There were two governors of Languedoc, both claiming royal appointment: the Protestants respected the authority of Marshal Damville, the Roman Catholics the authority of the Duc d'Uzès. Under the governor of Languedoc, the Protestants

The truce of Vivarais.

---

[1] The truce was proclaimed in Alençon's court, December 23, 1575, according to De Thou, v. 227, 228. Alençon confirmed Condé's engagements, December 22, 1575, according to Jean de Serres, v. fol. 152, 153.

[2] The self-reliant and prudent city reluctantly made Alençon a present of 10,000 francs. Lestoile, 63 ; De Thou, v. 228, 229.

[3] Ibid., v. 227, 228.

obeyed two lieutenants, Pierregourde and Cugières, governors of the upper and lower divisions of Vivarais respectively; while the Roman Catholics recognized Du Bourg as governor of the whole district. Each party had its own provincial estates. Some of the towns held for the Protestants, some for the Roman Catholics. Four thousand soldiers, living in idleness, not only consumed the scanty resources of the inhabitants, but inflicted on them a thousand insolences such as troops are wont to indulge in when unrestrained by strict discipline. Agriculture and trade were suspended. Townsmen and villagers alike groaned under their burdens, while the military leaders alone made light of grievances in which they found a source of profit for themselves. Under these circumstances the people took the matter into their own hands. Men of both religious communions, deputed by the two provincial estates, came together, and, after mature deliberation, entered into a compact for mutual protection. The document setting forth this agreement is so singular, and has been so little noticed by historians, that its contents must be alluded to. It began by a joint profession of loyalty. Both parties declared that they persevered constantly in their obedience to Henry, and recognized as his representatives, the Roman Catholics the Duc d'Uzès, the Protestants Marshal Damville. They maintained that their sole aim in taking the present step was to ward off disaster from their common country. The Protestants, in particular, solemnly affirmed that, in the new league into which dire necessity had driven them to enter, they had no intention of forsaking the common alliance of the Reformed Churches of France. After this preamble the terms of the truce were given. "All hostile attempts, either by open force of arms or by secret counsels, shall henceforth cease within the bounds of Vivarais. No one, whether native-born or stranger, shall be exposed to any danger. No injury shall be done by any one, whosoever he be, to agriculture or commerce, to persons or property. No hostile attack shall be made against the cities; there shall be no hostile gatherings, no inroads into the country. Discord having been allayed, there shall be free intercourse between the towns and the country. Whoever shall do otherwise, shall be held an enemy, and shall be punished as a plunderer and a disturber of the public peace, according to the severity of the laws, with the unanimous consent of all the orders." There were other provisions, respecting the remission of unpaid taxes, the release of prisoners, the restoration of cattle, and the diminution of garrisons. The treaty was to be submitted for approval by both sides to the governors whom they recognized, and indeed to the king himself; but, even should it ultimately be found impossible to secure their sanction, no recourse was to be had to arms until the expiration of at least a month's interval after due notice of the failure. As to any nobles or cities that might decline to endorse the compact, both Protestants and Roman Catholics agreed to proceed against them in arms, as enemies of their common country and unworthy of the common alliance.[1]

Great as was the delight of the wretched burghers and peasants of Vivarais; equally great was the indignation of the king, of both governors, in fact of every captain and scheming public man interested in the war. Even some of the neighboring Protestant churches complained of the irregularity of the action of their brethren, in thus providing for their own safety. As for the royalists, they saw in the movement a dangerous innovation, the introduction of an "imperium in imperio," threatening the royal authority. It was from such beginnings, forsooth, that the Swiss cantons had thrown off the yoke of their princes, claimed popular liberty, and founded commonwealths of their own. There was an end to all possibility of carrying on war, if money could be refused by the people. Meanwhile the truce of Vivarais bore wholesome fruit in the relief of the impoverished inhabitants, now freed from the presence of the greater part of the late garrisons, and in the revival of trade and husbandry.[2]

If the compact between the Protestants and the Roman Catholics had been remarkable for its origin, it was still more notable for the honorable observance of its conditions. Geydan, a neigh-

---

[1] Jean de Serres, v. fols. 167–170; De Thou, v. 304, 305.
[2] Jean de Serres, ubi supra.

boring Huguenot captain of great activity, much given to bold enterprises, conceived the notion of taking advantage of the security felt by the Roman Catholic garrison of Viviers, and made a sudden and successful attack upon it. The Roman Catholics at once carried to the Protestants their complaints because of this infraction of the treaty. The Protestants disclaimed all complicity in a movement which had originated beyond the boundaries of the province, but promised to execute their engagements to the letter. They summoned Geydan to surrender his prize and withdraw from Vivarais; and, when he returned an insolent answer and vindicated his action as legitimate, they promptly began preparations, in conjunction with the Roman Catholics, to expel him by force. Happily, however, Geydan was persuaded by his friends to recede from his position, and the town of Viviers was restored to the Roman Catholics. It was, indeed, a signal instance of good faith in a perfidious age.[1]

The honorable observance.

Henry of Navarre chose this time of general confusion to make his escape. For nearly four years had he been detained at the royal court. Ever since his bloody nuptials he had been, to all appearance, a sufficiently devout Roman Catholic. Yet, if he occasionally attended mass and exhibited no very great desire again to listen to Huguenot preaching, he was as loose in his ideas of morality as most of the young nobles of the day. In ignoble rivalry with Alençon and Guise for the good graces of Madame de Sauve, the Bearnese seemed utterly to have forgotten the quarrel of the religion of his mother, and of his own childhood, as well as the interests of the party of which he was the natural head. "The King of Navarre was never so merry nor so much made of," wrote the English ambassador, just after Alençon's stealthy withdrawal from Paris.[2] His neglect of his Huguenot comrades in arms was, however, more apparent than real. He was only abiding

The king of Navarre escapes from court.

---

[1] Jean de Serres (who gives the date of the restoration as February 27, 1576), v. fols. 172, 173; Recueil des choses mémorables, 565, 566; De Thou, v. 306, 307.

[2] Dale to Burleigh, September 28, 1575, State Paper Office.

the time to break his prison bars and seek more congenial associations. The opportunity he sought at last arrived. Henry of Navarre had prudently dissembled his indignation at the humiliating position he was forced to occupy at court. Little fear was entertained that he might venture on the dangerous attempt to make his way to his distant friends. He was therefore permitted to indulge in his favorite pastime of the chase with the less suspicion, because, as he customarily resorted in the direction of Senlis and Chantilly, places north of Paris, the capital lay between him and the only practicable line of flight. Of the freedom thus obtained he made good use. Early in February, 1576, having contrived to rid himself of those who had been placed about him to watch his movements, he suddenly started with a few trusty horsemen, and making a wide circuit to avoid Paris, crossed the Seine near Poissy. So prompt had been his actions that, before his enemies were fully aware of his design, he was beyond pursuit. Avoiding the highways on which he might have been stopped, he reached the city of Alençon, and thence made his way with little delay to Saumur and placed the Loire between himself and the court.[1] Once safe and within easy distance of his Protestant allies, Henry, who had thus far been taciturn beyond his wont, raised his eyes to heaven and exclaimed: "Praised be God who has delivered me! They killed the queen, my mother, in Paris. There, too, they slew the admiral and all my best servants, and they intended to do the same by me. Never shall I return unless I be dragged thither." And then, resuming his usual cheery tone, he assured his suite, with a good-natured laugh, that he had left in Paris only

---

[1] Dale to the secretaries, February 6, 1576, State Paper Office. Agrippa d'Aubigné, who both planned and accompanied Henry's flight, gives by far the fullest account in his Histoire universelle, ii. 183-189, supplemented by his Mémoires, 482, 483. See also Mémoires de Sully, chap. vii.; Davila, 217, 218; Jean de Serres, v. fol. 166; Recueil de choses mémorables, 564, 565; De Thou, v. 304. Alamanni's letter announcing to the Tuscan court the escape of Navarre "yesterday" (Négociations avec la Toscane, iv. 46) must have been dated February 4th, and not 1st. The account of a recent writer (Miss Freer, Henry III., ii. 83), who makes Henry, in his escape, first cross the Seine and subsequently flee to La Fère and thence to Vendôme, is singularly involved.

two things that he regretted—the mass and the queen his wife—the latter he would have again, the former he would try to do without.[1] The King of Navarre had not waited to reach the Loire before renouncing the outward profession of the faith that had been forced upon him. At Alençon he stood godfather for a Protestant child,[2] and the little court of Henry at Saumur and Thouars resounded once more with the sermons of Huguenot preachers. If Henry himself and his chief adherents showed little evidence of fervent religious feeling, and were not seen at the solemn celebration of the Lord's Supper, according to the rites of the Reformed Church, the reason may be found with quite as great probability in the worldly engrossments of the king himself as in any alleged intrigue of the Duke of Alençon to prevent Navarre from supplanting him in the esteem of the Huguenot party.[3]

Meantime the auxiliaries whom the Prince of Condé had been at such pains to collect were steadily making their way into the heart of the kingdom, in perfect contempt for the truce concluded between Catharine de' Medici and her youngest son, and giving not the slightest heed to the letters that Alençon pretended to despatch for the purpose of preventing their march. The expedition, John Casimir informed the king, in most polite terms, was not intended against his Majesty's person. "It is directed," said he, "against the murderers and persecutors of our true religion, and in general against those who create commotion and work

Entrance of the Germans into France.

---

[1] Lestoile, i. 66.

[2] Ibid., i. 66; Agrippa d'Aubigné, ii. 188. The latter mentions the coincidence that, at the Huguenot *prêche*, on the morrow after Henry's arrival, the 21st Psalm was sung in regular course, much to the king's surprise, beginning with the lines,

Seigneur, le Roy s'esjouira
D'avoir eu delivrance.

[3] See the tempting offers of the younger brother of the King of France to secure as an irrevocable appanage the whole of Guyenne, with ample securities, Agrippa d'Aubigné, ii. 190. Agrippa asserts that only two gentlemen of the court, including himself, presented themselves at the Holy Communion. Compare the passage just cited of his Histoire universelle with his Mémoires, p. 483.

folly in your kingdom."[1] The forces under the joint command of the prince and Duke John Casimir had become a formidable army. Henry in vain attempted to hinder its advance by promising the leaders a good and stable peace, and the German reiters a handsome sum of money in the way of wages, while endeavoring to secure the recall of the Swiss by their own cantons. Condé, John Casimir, and the Germans rejected his offers, and, though Berne consented to issue a summons to its subjects to return, the mercenaries paid no attention to the order. The Germans entered France through the upper part of Champagne, and passing by Langres, penetrated into Burgundy and Bourbonnois. Everywhere their course was marked with bloodshed and pillage. The environs of Langres were laid waste; the movable goods of the poor peasants were heaped up in the wagons which the reiters insisted on taking with them wherever they themselves went; the villages were then set on fire. Near Dijon they captured the venerable abbey of Citeaux, the original home of the monks hence called Cistercians, and in a few hours had stripped the monastery of everything valuable that had not previously been carried away for safety to Dijon. At Citeaux the reiters had defied the express commands of the Prince of Condé, with whom the monks had entered into a compact and from whom they had obtained a promise of immunity; at Nuits, a small town but a few miles farther on, they acted with equal insolence and with more flagrant inhumanity. The place had the temerity to deny admission to the invaders, but had yielded after a brief cannonade. Duke John Casimir promised the inhabitants that their lives should be spared and their property respected, and Condé not only ratified the terms of surrender but introduced a small body of nobles and of his own troops to preclude the danger he apprehended from the Germans. Even then the reiters rose in open meeting and demanded the pillage of Nuits as their due. When it was refused by the prince, they attacked and dispersed or killed the guard which

<small>Excesses of the reiters.</small>

---

[1] John Casimir to Henry III., Heidelberg, November 17, 1575, Kluckhohn, Briefe Friedrich des Frommen, iii. 913.

he had set, and then ruthlessly put to the sword every man, woman, and child that came in their way. The town was thoroughly sacked.¹ It was a butchery, the report of which carried terror far in advance of the army which it disgraced. A little later the reiters again became clamorous for money, and threatened Condé that unless their demands were met they would elect a new leader.²

At length the invading army and the forces commanded by the Duke of Alençon effected a junction, and the latter was proclaimed general-in-chief of the combined troops. His united army, reviewed on the plain of Soze, numbered thirty thousand men.³ Catharine, at no time idle since the escape of Alençon from court, now saw that no time must be lost in breaking the force of the great preparations of the Huguenots. Henry trembled for his sluggish repose. Paris, whose citizens would have preferred to see their king in arms rather than engaged in processions to supplicate Heaven for the restoration of peace,⁴ trembled for its walls. The tortuous paths of diplomacy must again be tried, and this time with more real earnestness. Another year of war had proved how fruitless the attempt was likely to be to coerce the Huguenots into submission. Not only were they as strong as ever, but a large army of strangers had entered France, and the king was powerless to check or to expel them. The treasury was empty; the taxes were wrung from the impoverished people with extreme difficulty. Henry was resolved to have peace at any cost. True, he would put on

---

¹ John Casimir to Frederick the Pious, Argilly, January 26, 1576, Kluckhohn, Briefe, etc., iii. 943; Jean de Serres, v. fols. 163, 164; De Thou, v. 303, 304; Recueil des choses mémorables, 563.
² Recueil, ubi supra.
³ Recueil des choses mémorables, 566; Jean de Serres, v. fols. 174, 175; De Thou, v. 307; Wilkes to Burleigh, Vichy, February 13, 1576, State Paper Office.
⁴ "The people of France," says Claude Haton, "would have been more grateful to the king had he gone to the war in person than it was when it saw him go or heard that he went in the procession; for his presence in the war would have been worth a thousand men. But he would not hear of such a thing, and he had greatly changed since he became king," etc., Mémoires, ii. 825.

a bold face, and scout the terms they suggested as absurd; but he had no serious intention of holding out.

From Moulins the confederates sent their demands to the king. The Protestants made about the same requests as they had made a year before, with a special provision that the tithes they paid should go to the support of their own ministers. The count palatine would have had them stipulate that the churches should be used in common by the Roman Catholics and the Protestants. The King of Navarre set forth his claims to a restitution of his rights, to the dower of Margaret of Valois, and to possible support in reconquering his kingdom beyond the Pyrenees.[1] The Duke of Alençon's chief aim was to secure for himself an appanage worthy of his rank. Duke John Casimir sought to be put in possession of the "Three Bishoprics"—Metz, Toul, and Verdun—as royal governor; and the Protestants supported him in the application. The three fortresses would be substantial guarantees of the stability of the coming peace.

The stout demands of the Protestants.

I may be excused from entering with detail into the story of negotiations in which " the ingenuity of a single woman proved more than a match for the calm judgment of the most illustrious men, supported by the weapons of powerful armies."[2] There were the usual eloquent pleas for toleration, and the usual inconsistencies in urging them. There was also a full proportion of sensible suggestions, which, had they been acted upon, might have changed the history of France for the next three centuries. Again the Sieur d' Arènes spoke eloquently and forcibly. " A single religion in a state is, indeed, desirable; but, when a religion cannot be exterminated without public offence, prudent men agree that it must be tolerated until the minds of men be

---

[1] The remarks of Jean de Serres (v. fol. 185) respecting the surprise generally felt at the character of the King of Navarre's first demands are worthy of notice : "Hæc erant Navarræi postulata longe diversa quam et rumor disseminasset et complures rerum aulicarum non imperiti arbitrarentur, qui nervosiora et magis virilia expectabant a Navarræo."

[2] "Mulieris versutia plus potuit quam clarissimorum virorum sobrium consilium, ingentibus etiam viribus armatum." Jean de Serres, v. fol. 175. The course of this protracted and important negotiation is traced at great length by this author, v. fols. 175-202.

changed by a Power superior to the power of man."¹ Beutrich, the envoy of John Casimir, declared that the Protestant religion not only exacts obedience to legitimate authority, but seeks to restore to the king the authority usurped by the Roman Pontiffs. And he added, in explanation of the demand for the three cities for his master: "We distrust, Sire, not you, but the counsellors about you, who, because the lion's tail is not long enough, would add the wolf's."² Count Ventadour, brother-in-law of Marshal Damville, and an ally whose accession to the ranks of the confederates had added great moral weight, proposed, through a special embassy, that only two religions should be authorized, while all others should be proscribed as before. And he advocated several reforms, including regular meetings of the states general every two years, the application of one-fourth of all ecclesiastical revenues to the support of hospitals, and the abolition of the system of purchase of judicial offices. " For," said he, " what has been purchased at wholesale will infallibly be sold again at retail."³ The negotiations had also their ludicrous side. The Protestant envoys were still so deceived regarding the character of Alençon and the attitude of Catharine de' Medici toward him, that they exhibited an anxiety, amounting almost to apprehension, lest the poor prince's rights should be overlooked; and Catharine assured the envoys, with becoming gravity, that she would pledge her word that Alençon should be satisfied.⁴ It may be affirmed with safety that rarely did Catharine keep her word so well as in the present instance.

One point after another was conceded by the court at the urgent pressure of the confederates, till it seemed that everything would be yielded. But there were two petitions Catharine would not concede. One respected the tithes: she was resolute that the Huguenots should not be relieved of their financial embarrassments. The other was the confiding of Metz, Toul, and Verdun to Duke John Casimir: the Huguenots could not be suffered to obtain such security against future assaults, or the favorable edict now to

_{The two points which Catharine will not yield.}

---

¹ Jean de Serres, v. fol. 179.
³ Ibid., v. fol. 187.
² Ibid., v. fols. 183, 184.
⁴ Ibid., v. fols. 188, 189.

be put forth might in very deed become irrevocable, not from the unwillingness, but from the inability of the king to repeal it. Every art of diplomacy was, therefore, employed to persuade the envoys to recede from their position. Nor was the effort in vain. The envoys were finally induced to write a letter to the Duke, begging him to renounce his claim, on the ground that otherwise the treaty would fail, and France would again be plunged in the horrors of civil war. Reluctantly, and only, it would seem, because of his excessive sensitiveness to the unjust aspersion of his motives—as though he were in quest of private gain rather than the general good of his co-religionists—did John Casimir consent to receive the promises which took the place of the "Three Bishoprics."[1]

<small>Henry's impatience and that of the people.</small> The queen mother's shrewdness had won the day, not without the assistance of that bevy of court beauties on whose charms she was wont on such occasions to place great dependence.[2] Even thus, however, she had had difficulty in restraining Henry's eagerness. He would have the peace, he exclaimed, if it cost him half his kingdom.[3] As for the people, its impatience knew no bounds. Between the Roman Catholic and the Huguenot armies the unhappy inhabitants of the towns and villages had little chance of saving any of their scanty possessions. The Huguenot leaders levied large sums of money on the provinces of Central France, which were reluctantly paid to secure immunity from invasion. Auvergne was assessed one hundred and fifty thousand livres, Berry, forty thousand; the single city of Dijon is reported to have paid two hundred thousand livres, and Nevers thirty thousand. The Roman Catholic troopers, on the plea that they were unpaid, indulged in the usual excesses, not against those

---

[1] Jean de Serres, v. fol. 201. According to Hubert Languet, who appears to have been well informed, the King of France, finding that John Casimir could not be moved from his position, resorted to the Swiss Protestant Cantons. He begged them to use their intercessions with the elector palatine to induce him to overcome his son's obstinate determination, the only remaining impediment to the conclusion of peace. The scheme succeeded but too well. Epistolæ secretæ, i. 186.

[2] Jean de Serres, v. fol. 201.   [3] Lestoile, i. 67, 68.

who opposed them, but against the villages that had espoused the defence of the king—"pillaging, robbing, ravaging, plundering, killing, burning, violating, exacting ransoms." The poor people was devoured by both sides. If there was an abundance of thieves in the one party, there was no lack of robbers in the other.[1] The Protestant army was not far from Paris; the exaggerated fears of the terrified inhabitants made it even nearer than it really was. " They of the faubourgs generally," wrote an eye-witness, " remove their goods into this town with such diligence that a man can scant enter the gates for the press of people, carriage, and cattle." [2]

In the beginning of May the peace that marked the conclusion of the Fifth Religious War was given to the world in a royal edict of pacification, known as the "Edict of Beaulieu," from the spot where it was concluded, a village near Loches, in Touraine. The chief points in the " Paix de Monsieur," as the accommodation was popularly called, were these: Henry ordained entire oblivion of the past. He granted to the Protestants universal freedom of worship throughout France, without exception of time or place, unless the particular lord should object to its exercise upon his lands.[3] The Protestants were, moreover, guaranteed the liberty to instruct their children, to administer the sacraments, to celebrate marriage, to establish schools, and convene consistories and synods, the latter in the presence of a royal officer. They were promised admission to offices and the establishment of "chambres mi-parties" in each of the parliaments of the kingdom, wherein cases affecting them should be tried by an equal number of judges of the two religions. Henry declared his intention to assemble the states general at Blois within six months. He disowned all participation in the horrors of the massacre of St. Bartholomew's day, repealed the sentences pronounced against Admiral Coligny and other Huguenot leaders, and approved of the acts performed and the alliances entered into by

The Edict of Pacification May, 1576.

---

[1] Lestoile, i. 68. See Claude Haton, ii. 849.
[2] "News from France," inclosed in Dale's letter to Burleigh, April 17, 1576, State Paper Office.
[3] Paris alone was excepted.

the Protestants. In token of sincerity he conceded to them eight cities in pledge.¹ The Huguenot leaders were not forgotten. The Prince of Condé was appointed governor of Picardy, with the city of Péronne as his residence. His brother, the Marquis of Conty, received a military command. Duke John Casimir was promised a large annual subsidy and a force commensurate with his rank. As to Alençon, the prince about whom the Huguenot envoys had displayed so much anxiety, and for whom they had had so much misplaced sympathy, the queen mother was as good as her word. If the youth was not satisfied with the magnificent appanage that was granted him—the rich provinces of Berry, Touraine, and Anjou, together with the annual revenue of one hundred thousand crowns of gold—he must indeed have been a difficult person to please.²

In the general exultation over the return of peace and the concession of a larger religious liberty than had ever before been granted to them, the Huguenots may be pardoned for making little account of the mode in which their recent ally, the youngest Valois, had contrived to secure a lion's share of the real fruits of the war. They had yet to discover respecting the "Paix de Monsieur," that if the most specious pacification, it was also the least useful of all compacts to the adherents of the Reformed faith.³

---

¹ These were: In Languedoc, Beaucaire and Aigues-mortes; in Guyenne, Périgueux and Mas de Verdun; in Dauphiny, Nyons and Serres; in Auvergne, Issoire; and in Provence, Seine-la-grand-tour.

² The text of the edict of pacification is given in full in the Mémoires de Nevers, i. 117-135, and Haag, France protestante, x. 127-141. See also Recueil des choses mémorables, 569, 570, Agrippa d'Aubigné, ii. 214, etc., Davila, 219, 220, etc. Jean de Serres, gives a Latin summary of the edict, v. fols. 202-207. His invaluable Commentarii de statu religionis et reipublicæ (1580), I regret to say, end at this point. Nor does the circumstance that the works of this writer have been honored with a special mention in the "Index Librorum Prohibitorum" (I have before me the edition of Rome, 1841), in company with much other good literature, fully reconcile me to the necessity of henceforth threading the intricate maze of the events of the period now under consideration deprived of the assistance of a well-informed, clear-sighted, and conscientious guide.

³ " La paix la plus specieuse et la moins utile aux Refformez." Agrippa d'Aubigné, ii. 194.

The scene of the struggle in which the Huguenots found themselves plunged upon the return of Henry the Third from Poland was restricted so much to Languedoc that the condition of that extensive province is a matter of more than ordinary interest to him that would understand the ensuing events. We are fortunately in possession of a curious report made by M. de Fourquevaulx, governor of Narbonne, an upright and well-informed man, respecting that important portion of Languedoc which was comprised in the two "sénéchaussées" of Toulouse and Lauragais. The document, which is in the form of a series of answers to questions propounded to the writer in a letter of Charles the Ninth, despatched in the course of the preceding autumn, is dated on the twenty-third of January, 1574. (It is inserted among the "preuves" of Dom Vaissete's Histoire de Languedoc, v. 224–239.) Replying to an inquiry respecting the Roman Catholic ecclesiastics, Fourquevaulx stated that the bishops, archbishops, and other prelates of the two sénéchaussées, with a single exception, made it a rule to reside in their dioceses as little as possible. Motives of convenience, or expense, or proximity to hunting-grounds, or pleasure determined the place of their abode; for it would be a miracle were one of them found possessed of but a single prelature. It was fifty-seven years since Narbonne had laid eyes upon her archbishop. It was about as long since the archbishop of Toulouse had been at his see for over a week at a time. The suffragan bishops acquitted themselves little or no better. The bishop of St. Papoul was in Rome, the bishop of Lavaur in Paris, the bishop of Montauban at court; the bishop of Comminges (St. Bertrand de Comminges) was the solitary instance of an ecclesiastic of this dignity abiding by his own fold, doing the office of a good pastor and teaching his flock by precept and example. In the whole province of Languedoc there were twenty-two archbishoprics and bishoprics. Of these, four—Alais, Lodève, Nismes, and Uzès—were in the power of the Huguenots. The holders of fourteen of the remaining eighteen were absentees. At least one of the four who resided in their dioceses led a life that scandalized rather than edified the people under his charge. Following the example of their superiors, the abbots, priors, and curates shunned residence on a great variety of excuses, putting their benefices in charge of men of no account, some of whom dared not remain through fear of the Huguenots, while others could not, because their churches or monasteries had been burned during the wars or were occupied by soldiers. Consequently the people were left without religious instruction, the treasure of the district went abroad, almsgiving ceased, the ecclesiastical edifices not already destroyed went to ruin. Holy orders were conferred without discrimination, the sacraments administered without reverence or devotion, by priests and vicars unable to comprehend what they said or did. As the result, the laity held the sacraments and those that administered them in equal contempt.

In reply to the question, "whether the ecclesiastics enjoyed their possessions or were disturbed in them," Fourquevaulx gave a sorry exhibit of the number of towns and villages that were in the hands of the Protestants and from which no income could be expected. If the dioceses of Rieux and Comminges were exclusively held by Roman Catholics, it was otherwise with the diocese of Lavaur, where out of eight considerable towns (villes maîtresses), including Lavaur itself in the number, the enemy held five, and all the four-score smaller places, castles and villages.

Nor was the picture brighter when the governor of Narbonne came to describe the nobles, and their dealings with one another and with the people. The common opinion was that, had the Roman Catholic nobles chosen to exert themselves, the civil wars would long since have been over. But those who styled themselves Catholic played into the hands of those who belonged to the other party. "The one set of nobles hold the lamb, the others flay it; the rebels plunder (font les voleurs), and the Catholics find purchasers for them." Greed ruled both parties. Of the Huguenots, the governor of Narbonne, who had, some time since, violently expelled them from the city, draws no flattering portrait. "Little mention is made among the rebels of living as Christians; for it is only in name that they embrace their religion. They blaspheme, they plunder, they indulge in lewdness, they kill in combat and in cold blood, and do everything the Gospel forbids; alleging in justification that war permits them to act thus, especially against 'idolaters' as they style the Catholics." As to the latter, with them, too, everything was perverted.

Between the two religions the numerical disparity was great. Nine-tenths of the people were Roman Catholics, disposed to live and die in obedience to the king. From these must be excepted men of the long robe (of the legal profession), the bourgeoisie, the tradespeople, the men who had tasted of letters, and the young men who were friends of liberty. Little reliance could be reposed even upon those that had not openly gone over to Protestantism. So, too, such of the artisans as were of a somewhat sprightly turn of mind were either declared Calvinists or suspected to be such. The most trustworthy Catholics were "the simple folk and good peasants."

The statements of Fourquevaulx respecting the non-residence of the episcopate of Languedoc are illustrated by the circumstance that the Acts of the Council of the ecclesiastical province of Narbonne, which opened December 10, 1551, show that not a single bishop was present at its sessions. The absent prelates were represented by vicars. (Histoire de Languedoc, v. 169.)

CHAPTER II.

THE STATES-GENERAL OF BLOIS, AND THE SIXTH CIVIL WAR.

However grateful may have been the return of peace to the inhabitants of those extensive regions of France that had suffered most severely from the ravages of war, never had an edict of pacification been published whose concessions were so offensive to the enemies of the Huguenots as those of the "Paix de Monsieur." A toleration coextensive with the limits of the kingdom was guaranteed to the Protestant worship by a solemn law declared to be perpetual and irrevocable. To the heretics lately in arms, to heretics supposed to have been all but annihilated in the Parisian matins, to heretics stripped of their property by judicial process, not only was restitution promised, but courts were to be granted in each of the parliaments of France, from which impartial decisions might henceforth be expected. No wonder that monks stormed from the pulpits, that bigoted judges protested against the innovation. When the queen mother, accompanied by her daughter, the Queen of Navarre, proceeded to the great church of Sens and requested that the canons be assembled and a Te Deum be sung in gratitude for the return of peace, an old ecclesiastic, the spokesman of the clergy, replied, "Madam, according to what I hear of the terms upon which the peace has been concluded, it is the Huguenots that ought to sing the 'Te Deum laudamus' and not the Catholics. It would be more becoming for us to chant, 'Requiem æternam dona nobis, Domine.'"[1] The chapter of Notre Dame in Paris was not less insolent to the king himself; for the members refused to ring their bells and to sing the church's jubilant hymn, proposing to

Unpopularity of the "Paix de Monsieur."

---

[1] Mémoires de Claude Haton, ii. 833.

substitute in its place the psalm, "Circumdederunt me viri mendaces," with the appropriate introit, "Circumdederunt me dolores mortis." Henry was compelled to wait a whole day and then employ his own singers to perform the task declined by the canons of the cathedral. The latter paid for their disobedience by a fine imposed upon them by the parliament; but this did not daunt the people of Paris, who stoutly refused to light the customary bonfires in the streets or indulge in any outward demonstration of joy.[1] The king, however, made show of a firm determination to carry the edict into effect. On the fourteenth of May he proceeded to parliament, accompanied by the princes of the blood, and not only ordered the registration of the edict, but swore to its observance and directed all that were present to take a similar oath. About three weeks later he again met the judges, and commanded them to acknowledge the erection of the "chambre mi-partie," an institution so odious that only the royal presence deterred parliament from rejecting it.[2] Even then the refractory counsellors resolutely refused to recognize the appointment of that eloquent and learned Huguenot, the Sieur d' Arènes, whom the king had named as presiding judge of the mixed tribunal. He gained his seat only after repeated orders and threats from the king and his mother, and through the personal insistence of Chancellor Birague and other members of the royal council.[3]

Henry insists on carrying out the provisions.

The peace, thus declared and established with all the forms calculated to give it effect, was in reality little more than a hol-

---

[1] La Huguerye to the Prince of Orange, May 19, 1576, Groen van Prinsterer, Archives, Supplement, 188*. Mém. de Claude Haton, ii. 848. Mém. d'un curé ligueur (Jehan de la Fosse), 175, 176.

[2] June 7, Lestoile, i. 72. "It was much to be noted," wrote Dr. Dale to Lord Burleigh, May 11, 1576, "that the king caused the Duke of Guise, the Duke of Maine, the Duke d'Aumale, and the Marshal de Retz to be at the publication of the peace, and to swear to it, although it was very coldly done on the part of the Guises. They had the oath ministered unto them, and were willed to hold up their hand, which is the manner of taking an oath in this country." State Paper Office.

[3] Lestoile (under dates of July 16 and 30), i. 72, 73, 75. See, however, Davila, 220, and Claude Haton, ii. 866.

low truce. It was absurd to suppose that either Henry or his mother had any serious intention of maintaining a compact so honorable for the king's revolted subjects, so dishonorable for the king himself.[1] Henry had not disguised, during the negotiations of the past year, his indignation at the boldness of the Protestants. In the execution of the unfortunate Montbrun he had obtained revenge for the insult received from one Huguenot leader who, with fatal boldness of speech, had laid claim to equality with his monarch in time of war. Would his majesty be likely to forget the wound his self-respect had received from the whole body of the Huguenots when they compelled him to accept peace on terms dictated by them?[2] Precisely how he would obtain release from the humiliating engagements he had entered into—substituting another "perpetual and irrevocable edict" of more agreeable character for the "perpetual and irrevocable edict" which he had just promulgated[3]—it is by no means certain that as yet he imagined. Yet, even from the first, it is not improbable that he foresaw the useful end to which the states general, so anxiously and urgently demanded by the Huguenots, might be turned. In case, as was likely to be the issue, the enemies of the reformers should secure a clear majority in the great national convocation, Henry could as easily retract his engagements with his subjects as Francis the First had dispensed with the humiliating terms of his release from captivity under the Treaty of Madrid. Only, the grandson must be as careful as had been his grandfather to secure all the advantages afforded by his breach of faith before publishing to the world that his promises were null and void because of the force employed by his opponents. Some of these advantages had already been gained. The Duke

Private sentiments of the king.

---

[1] In fact Henry did not hesitate so to inform Duplessis Mornay, in August, 1583. He told him, without any apparent shame, " qu'il n'eut jamais voulloir de tenir la paix de 76, mais qu'aussi ne le cela il poinct, pour la façon dont elle avoit esté faicte." Mémoires de Duplessis Mornay, ii. 374.

[2] See Ranke's remarks, p. 293.

[3] The edict of pacification of 1576 and that of 1577 were declared, each, to be " cettuy nostre édit perpetuel et irrevocable." Texts in Mémoires de Nevers, i. 117, 291.

of Alençon, who now assumed the title of Duke of Anjou, was effectually weaned from the Huguenot party. He had sided with the Protestants only from motives of self-interest. As to any real affection for them or for their doctrine, those who knew him well asserted that they had heard him say frequently that "in his heart he hated the Protestants as he hated the devil."[1] Moreover, his sister, the Queen of Navarre, a pretty keen judge of character, described him to the life when she made the unamiable remark that "if all treachery were to be banished from the face of the earth, Alençon would be able to repeople it."[2] Now that the duke had been gratified with an establishment rivalling in splendor that of the king himself,[3] he was at no pains to conceal his perfect indifference to the fate of his late associates in arms. He not only forbade the Huguenots of Provins and Troyes to hold public services for the preaching of the Gospel, but used the most opprobrious language respecting them. "That Protestant canaille," he said, "is not worth the drowning."[4] "One needs only to know the Huguenots to hate them. I have never known any man of worth among them except François de la Noue."[5]

Not only had the king's younger brother been detached from the party of the "malcontents," but the German reiters in the service of the Protestants had been induced to leave the interior of the country. Thus the capital was freed from the dangerous proximity of the turbulent and unruly followers of John

Alençon won from the Huguenots.

---

[1] "Je sçay pour luy avoir ouy dire plusieurs fois, qu'il les haït comme le diable dans le coeur." The words are those of the King of Navarre to Sully. Mémoires de Sully, c. xv. (i. 102).

[2] Agrippa d'Aubigné, ii. 412: "Que si toute l'infidelité estoit bannie de la terre, son frère la pourroit repeupler."

[3] See "Estat des gages des seigneurs, gentilshommes, et autres officiers de la maison de Monseigneur Fils de France, Frere unique du Roy." This document, signed by the duke at Bourges, August 5, 1576, and occupying twenty-three folio pages of the Mémoires de Nevers, i. 577-599, is of interest in more points than one. It disposed of the sum (immense for the time) of 263,710 livres in annual salaries, apportioned among about 1,600 persons. The duke had the plentiful supply of fifteen almoners and seven chaplains, but only a single preacher. The chamberlains numbered 108, and the gentlemen of the bedchamber, 148.

[4] Mém. de Claude Haton, ii. 859.   [5] Agrippa d'Aubigné, ii. 233.

Casimir; and if, according to the statement of a resident diplomatist, the Germans, while waiting on the borders for the first instalment of the promised payment, daily inflicted damage to the extent of twenty thousand crowns upon their unwilling hosts,[1] there was at least this consolation, that the court was undisturbed by their violence in its continual round of pleasure.

Whatever Henry's ulterior designs might be, he was not yet ready for a renewal of the war with the Huguenots, and he was therefore resolved that no one should by ill-timed zeal precipitate the outbreak of the conflict. The lavish concessions of the edict of pacification fostered the rapid institution of the Roman Catholic associations of which I shall soon have occasion to speak. But the rumors of these events that reached the king's ears, instead of producing gratification, greatly disquieted him. It was reported that the Guises were secretly instigating the people of Burgundy and Champagne, as well as the inhabitants of the strongly papal provinces of Normandy and Picardy, to refuse a recognition of the right of worship accorded to the Protestants.[2] Neither Catharine de' Medici nor her son attempted to conceal their irritation. To Henry of Guise and his brother the Duke of Mayenne they gave on one occasion such open marks of displeasure as to attract the notice of the entire court. On the next day, indeed, a reconciliation was effected through the instrumentality of the Cardinal of Este; but the king insisted that the Guises should solemnly subscribe certain articles pledging their faith that they would enter into no league with any persons to contravene the terms of the peace. It is almost

Henry and Catharine indignant at the Guises.

---

[1] "E ogni giorno fanno danno per circa venti mila scudi." Saracini to the Grand Duke, July, 1576, Négociations avec la Toscane, iv. 75, 76. See, also, Languet's letter of August 16, in which he observes: "Ita tandem fiet ut istis militum direptionibus Gallia non solum ad egestatem, sed etiam ad vastitatem redigatur." Epistolæ secretæ, i. 215. John Casimir's reiters were said to bring with them from France four thousand wagons laden with the spoil of the miserable peasants. The animals at their command proving too few to draw the booty, the German captains compelled their chaplains to dismount and put into the service the horses they rode on. Languet, letter of September 8, ibid., i. 223.

[2] See Dale's letter of May 23, 1576, State Paper Office.

needless to say that the Lorraine princes displayed extreme repugnance to the assumption of this obligation, protesting that the death of their father and their own wounds received in the king's service were sufficient evidence of the devotion of the House of Guise to the interests of the French crown.[1] A few weeks later (on the thirty-first of August) Henry took vigorous measures to put an end to the formation of Roman Catholic associations in Brittany. The letter of instructions which he wrote to the Duke of Montpensier, governor of the province, leaves no room to doubt that even so late as the end of summer, the king was heartily opposed to the fanatical counsels which he afterward thought it advisable to adopt. He ordered the duke to undertake the justification of the course taken by the crown as a course dictated by necessity, and dwelt much upon the labor and trouble cheerfully undertaken by his mother in order to put an end to a war that must, if continued, entail the ruin of the kingdom. More than this, he warned the three orders of Brittany that whoever, without the express permission or command of the sovereign, should venture to form a league with any other persons, whomsoever, would render himself liable to the charge of treason. He declared his own great displeasure at the formation of the leagues in question, and ordered his mis-

Royal instructions to Montpensier.

---

[1] The incident is referred to both by Lestoile, under date of August 2, 1576 (i. 75), and by Saracini, in his letter to the Grand Duke of August 5 (Négociations avec la Toscane, iv. 77, 78). This seems to be the same matter to which Dale refers. Learning that Guise was holding an animated discussion, lasting nearly two hours, in the king's outer chamber with a gentleman from Picardy, the queen mother, after repeatedly sending " to see whether they were through," at length lost patience, and, coming out, boldly charged the duke that "he would never leave to trouble the peace of the realm," and called him into the royal cabinet where the dispute began afresh. The accusation was precisely that by which Chancellor l'Hospital had aroused Cardinal Lorraine's anger at Moulins ten years before (Rise of the Huguenots, ii. 186). The duke was very "malapert" with Catharine. He declared "that he had never done anything but for the king's service," and that if he and his friends were to forsake Henry, as others had done, his majesty "should have no man with him." As this was understood to be a thrust at Catharine's youngest son, she was naturally very angry. Dale to the Secretaries, July 28, 1576, State Paper Office.

guided subjects, with all the power and authority God had conferred upon him, instantly to abandon these "sinister" associations, whatever oath they might have taken, since no oath could be of force in opposition to the oath that bound them to their king and sovereign lord. By such impotent remonstrances did Henry oppose, or pretend to oppose, the progress of that portentous movement before which, when once it should have developed its full strength, his own authority was destined to meet a disgraceful fall.[1]

The earliest symptoms of resistance to the royal commands were shown on the northern borders. The edict accorded to the Prince of Condé the government of Picardy, with Péronne as his residence. Religious zeal and private feud conspired to nullify the concession. The governor of Péronne was Jacques d'Humières, the head of the most illustrious noble house of Picardy, a determined enemy of Protestantism. He was, moreover, a personal foe of the Montmorencies; for M. de Thoré had successfully asserted in the courts of law his claim to a great part of the property of his deceased wife, an heiress of the family of Humières. The governor found no difficulty in enlisting in his support many gentlemen of the neighborhood. Soon a league was formed the object of which was ostensibly the prevention of the spread of Protestant influence in Picardy. One hundred and fifty persons, writes a contemporary Italian diplomatist, took part. Among them were dependants of the dukes of Guise and Aumale. They took pains to inform the king that they and the whole nobility of the region believed themselves to be doing his majesty a most grateful service in preventing a place of such importance from falling into the hands of his enemies, his majesty's commands to the contrary notwithstanding.[2]

Not a little obscurity invests the origin of the formidable association which, under the name of the League, was, during

---

[1] "Instruction baillée par le Roy à Monsieur le duc de Montpensier, gouverneur de Bretagne, pour s'opposer aux ligues et associations qui se faisoient contre l'Estat." Mémoires de Nevers, i. 110–114.

[2] Alamanni to the Grand Duke, June 11, 1576, Négociations avec la Toscane, iv. 72.

the next quarter of a century, to measure its strength against that of the king, and to shake the very foundations of the throne. The combination of extreme men among the Roman Catholics for the protection of the supposed interests of their faith was not a new thing. Nothing was more natural than concerted action for such an end. When Jacques Lefèvre, in the very dawn of the Reformation, descried with prophetic eye the rapid progress of the purer doctrines, and gave expression to his expectation that "the inventions set up by the hand of man would speedily be cast down," the monk who heard him replied, without one moment's hesitation, with the threat of a "crusade" to be preached by himself and by his brother ecclesiastics. He did not even forget to add the doom of the monarch who might dare to espouse the side of heresy.[1] Accordingly, with the first reluctant concession of a limited toleration to Protestantism—with the first edict of the crown that seemed to admit that Protestantism had the barest right to live—came symptoms of the active principle that would permit no terms to be made with dissent from the established church, or with dissenters. Submission or death, was the only choice offered by the clergy to "those of the new religion." The Roman pontiff never tired of reiterating the necessity of enforcing this alternative, both in his letters to the kings of France and in his communications with such other persons as might be supposed to have an influence in shaping the policy of the government. Monks and parish priests repeated the cruel lessons to the people from ten thousand pulpits, from the steps of ten thousand altars, and doubtless dropped hints, not obscure, of possible co-operation between the more zealous of their followers. How early the idea of a union of the "better Catholics" for the defence of their imperilled faith took definite form, and became a practical reality, is uncertain. It could not, however, have been long after the publication of the edict of Amboise (1563). The provisions of that edict, far short as they came of the privileges granted by the January edict of the previous year, savored, in the opinion of the ecclesiastics and

The origin of the League.

---

[1] See the Rise of the Huguenots, i. 76.

their faction, as truly, if not as strongly, of impious connivance with the crime of heresy. Hence the "Fraternities of the Holy Ghost," that made their appearance in Burgundy, within a year or two after the conclusion of the first peace, having it for their avowed object to wage perpetual war against the Huguenots.¹ Hence, too, "the Christian and Royal League," of Champagne, a few years later, for the maintenance of the true Catholic and Roman Church of God—an association which, like its predecessors, aroused the jealousy and incurred the condemnation of the monarch.²

In its germ, therefore, the League had a domestic origin. It sprang from the suggestions of the French clergy. There seems to be no necessity for seeking its source outside of the kingdom. Yet the fact cannot be overlooked that the name and authority of the king of Spain begin very early to be associated with the patronage and growth of the institution. Philip the Second was so much in the mouth of Jean Begat, the councillor in the Parliament of Dijon to whom the Burgundian confraternities owed their institution, as to excite general astonishment and indignation that he was permitted to make such insolent reference to a king dangerous to France from the very proximity of his dominions. And certainly Philip and his minister, Cardinal Granvelle, were not slow to perceive the immense advantage that might accrue from the impression now beginning to gain ground, that his Catholic majesty was the natural defender of the orthodox faith, a faith to which Charles the Ninth and his mother were represented as lukewarm. It was not without significance that the cardinal was said to have caused the intolerant address of Jean Begat, in which he tried to prove the existence of two religions in France an insult to God and dangerous to public tranquillity, to be printed and published at Antwerp.³

With the massacre of Saint Bartholomew's day, and the sup-

---

[1] "Ineuntur . . . sodalitates quas Sancti Spiritus confraternitates vocant, de sempiterno adversus Huguenotos bello indicendo." Jean de Serres (edit. of 1571), iii. 53.

[2] See the Rise of the Huguenots, ii. 179, 180, 246.

[3] Jean de Serres, ubi supra. and De Thou, iii. 502, who is here, as in many other places, greatly indebted to this excellent author.

posed annihilation of the Huguenots throughout France, the Roman Catholic associations fell into neglect and were abandoned. There seemed to be no foe against whom to defend the faith. But the fourth, and especially the fifth, religious war roughly awakened the zealots from their dream of fancied security. And now a pacification had come conceding everything to the detested heretics— a peace which could artfully be represented as even more favorable to the Huguenots than to the followers of the king. For were not the most humiliating distinctions made between the two parties? Was not provision made for the prompt payment of the reiters of the Prince of Condé, while the king's reiters bade fair to wait long for their wages? Were not the Huguenot peasantry declared exempt of all impositions levied during the war, while the Roman Catholics were compelled to pay up all arrears even so far back as four years?"[1]

Revival of the League after the massacre.

To the facility with which associations were henceforth formed Henry the Third had unconsciously contributed greatly, by the favor he had in the past shown to the religious fraternities. The fantastic superstition of the Penitents, clad in white, blue, or black, furnished the pretext for meetings having quite another object than self-humiliation. Under the skilful guidance of ghostly advisers, the farce became sober earnest, and, in the end, the lash that had been so lightly laid upon the king's shoulders, became a very scourge, drawing forth from the miserable monarch real sighs and tears. The zealots, whom the devotional meetings of the fraternity permitted to assemble without exciting suspicion, soon passed from lamentations over the sins and misery of the age to a free discussion of political measures and a censure of the government. From this to a regular organization, for purposes of active warfare in the interest of shrewd leaders, the step was short and easy.[2]

The fraternities of Penitents contribute to the revival.

---

[1] " Et qui plus est, quand ce vient au traité de paix, ceux qui ont suivy leur party, sont declarez exempts de toutes impositions faites durant la guerre, et les nostres sont contraints de payer les arrerages jusqu'à quatre années." Letter of Montluc, Bishop of Valence, remonstrating against a renewal of the war, Mémoires de Nevers, i. 472.   [2] Davila, 221.

"The Prelates, Lords, Gentlemen, Captains, and Soldiers inhabiting the cities and flat country of Picardy"—so they styled themselves—set forth a manifesto and an oath. In the former they justified their action by alleging that their enemies had "hitherto had no other end in view than to establish errors and heresies in this kingdom, from all time very Christian and Catholic, to annihilate the ancient religion, to exterminate those who make inviolable profession of it, to undermine gradually the power and authority of the king, to change his state in everything and everywhere, and to introduce another and novel form of government." After these general grounds for their "common accord and holy union," the writers proceeded to state its particular occasion to be the information, obtained from some of the gentlemen and soldiers of Condé's suite, of that prince's intention, so soon as the city of Péronne should be entrusted to his hands, to make it the Protestant capital, with prospective results of ruin, not only to the province of Picardy, but to Paris itself. Against such disaster they expressed the hope that they might receive the help of all the princes, prelates, and noblemen of the realm, in view of the fact that the "rebels" had plotted the death of their majesties and of the Duke of Anjou, the annihilation of the holy faith, and the ruin of the French people. A holy and Christian union and perfect intelligence and co-operation between all the good, faithful, and loyal subjects of the king, was declared to be the true and only means reserved by God for the restoration of religion and of the realm. The document contained other provisions for securing the efficiency and extension of the league; but these need not detain us.

Manifesto of the League of Péronne.

The oath accompanying the manifesto became the form which, with slight modifications, was adopted by every similar association throughout France. Three objects were set forth as the great ends contemplated: To reestablish the Roman Catholic and Apostolic Church; to preserve Henry, by the grace of God, third of the name, and his successors, very Christian kings, in the state, splendor, authority, service, duty, and obedience due to him by his subjects, as contained in the articles that should be presented to him at the

Oath of the League.

states; and to restore to the provinces of the realm their ancient rights and liberties such as they were in the time of Clovis, the first Christian king. To this and to promises of faithful and unswerving obedience to the constituted head of the League every member gave in his adhesion by calling on the name of God his Creator, by laying his hand upon the Gospel, and by invoking the pains of excommunication and everlasting damnation in case of disobedience.[1]

Such were the beginnings of the new association that was within a few months to spread over a great part of France, and for which its friends prepared the way by assurances boldly given that although the king was compelled to disavow and condemn it, he secretly wished the project good success.

Meanwhile the Prince of Condé in vain demanded the fulfilment of the stipulations of the treaty made in his favor. Obtaining, however, the promise of the towns of Saint Jean d'Angély and Cognac, in Poitou, in lieu of unattainable Péronne, he secured possession of them by a prompt and sudden movement, to the surprise and possibly to the regret of those who had desired merely to quiet his importunity.[2] Henry of Navarre, equally cautious with his cousin not to trust his person to the doubtful faith of his late enemies, preferred La Rochelle to the allurements of the royal court. But the independent and pardonably suspicious character of the inhabitants again manifested itself. They neither would admit him with his Roman Catholic suite (for they recognized among his followers some who had played a bloody part in the Parisian matins),[3] nor would they allow him to sit on a dais, which they maintained to be the prerogative of the sovereign alone. But when the Roman Catholics had been left outside of the walls, when Henry and his sister

Condé and Navarre.

Caution of La Rochelle.

---

[1] The manifesto of the League of Péronne is given by Agrippa d'Aubigné, ii. 223-228. The oath may be found ibidem, ii. 228-230; in the Recueil des choses mémorables, 579-581; in Davila, 222, 223; and, with some errors of transcription, in Loutchitzky, Documents inédits pour servir à l'histoire de la Réforme et de la Ligue, 39-42.

[2] Davila, etc.

[3] "Gens qui avoient joué du cousteau à la S. Barthelemi."

Catharine had made all due public recognition of their fault in attending the papal mass, under compulsion, and had shown much sadness of countenance and shed tears, we are told that even the unimpressionable Rochellese received the culprit with something approaching their former good-will.[1]

None the less, however, did La Rochelle, a few months later, take alarm when Condé made himself master of the neighboring port of Brouage. A serious division of sentiment arose in the city, and the prince, who had been invited to enter the Huguenot capital in the same quiet manner as the King of Navarre, was soon after requested to defer his coming until a more propitious time. When at last he was again requested to visit La Rochelle, he came (on the fourth of December) only to accuse the mayor and his party of a treacherous scheme to betray the city to the king upon a guarantee that its municipal privileges should be formally acknowledged and its anomalous claim of a virtual independence receive the express sanction of his majesty. It would seem probable that the prince and the sturdy champions of La Rochelle were equally in the wrong, and that the treason of the mayor was as much a creation of the imagination as were the alleged ambitious designs of Condé. At any rate, it was fortunate that the rapid approach of more real dangers proved sufficient to dissipate suspicions on both sides that may have been groundless, and to unite the Rochellese and the Bourbons in a common struggle for the defence of their faith.[2]

---

[1] Agrippa d'Aubigné, ii. 219 ; Mémoires de Sully, chap. vii. Letters of Henry of Navarre to the "maire, échevins et pairs de La Rochelle,' Niort, June 16, and Surgères, June 26, 1576, in Dussieux, Lettres intimes de Henri IV. (Paris, 1876), 39, 41, 42, and in Arcère, Histoire de La Rochelle, ii. 18. In the second communication, he assures the Rochellese that he desires no solemn entry as governor and royal lieutenant-general, and does not aim at establishing any one else as governor, but wishes to come in simply with his household attendants, according to the list that he has handed in, and bringing with him no suspected persons.

[2] The view of the quarrel taken by De Thou, v. 326-8, and by Agrippa d'Aubigné, ii. 231, 232, is very favorable to the prince. See also Languet's letter of February 3, 1577, Epistolæ secretæ, i. 277. Arcère gives, ii. 22-29, from La Popelinière, a representation more creditable to the citizens.

An incident that occurred in Rouen about this time revealed very clearly the spirit animating the clergy and no inconsiderable part of the Roman Catholics of France. At the conclusion of the peace, the Parliament of Normandy, having received explicit orders from the court to abstain from remonstrances, had entered the edict upon its registers and had solemnly sworn its observance. This was on the twenty-second of May. "Nothing," dryly observes the historian of the parliament, "was more frequent at the time than oaths." At heart all the judges were beside themselves with indignation at the very thought of harboring Protestant worship inside of the walls of a city that prided itself upon its orthodoxy. However, old Cardinal Bourbon, Archbishop of Rouen, in response to an appeal addressed to him to use all his influence with the king for the purpose of inducing his Majesty to remove the hated "prêche," sent comforting messages to his flock. "After I have accompanied his majesty on his contemplated visit to the sea-ports of Normandy, I shall come to Rouen and spend some time there, expelling the heretics and taking all necessary steps."[1] A few days later, the prelate repeated these assurances, and promised the canons, when they came to meet him at the abbey of Jumiéges, that he would soon be at his archiepiscopal see and try every means to put an end to the preaching which had been introduced into the city.[2] A fortnight passed and the pledge was redeemed. One July day the Huguenots were peaceably assembled in the place of worship assigned to them in accordance with the recent treaty, when the news reached them that a pompous procession was approaching. It was the cardinal archbishop, accompanied by Claude de Sainctes, Bishop of Evreux, and an ample train of canons and other ecclesiastical dignitaries, and preceded by the great cross of the cathedral. It was not strange that the Huguenot minister thought it advisable to consult his own safety in prompt flight. As for the laity, having no time to

Marginal note: Cardinal Bourbon and the Huguenots of Rouen.

---

[1] "Pour en expulser les héréticques et faire ce qui sera nécessaire." Reg. capit. ecclesiæ Rothom., June 26, 1576, apud Floquet, Histoire du parlement de Normandie, iii. 164.

[2] Reg. capit. ecclesiæ Rothom., July 11, 1576, ibid., iii. 165.

withdraw, they waited in some trepidation to see what the result would be. Happily it fared better with them than it had fared, fourteen years before, with the Huguenot worshippers of Vassy. Cardinal Bourbon was not famous as a preacher, but on this occasion he took the pulpit and delivered a long sermon not much to the taste of his unwilling hearers. It cannot be said that the discourse contained anything novel, but its statements were strange enough in such a place. The speaker mingled invitations with threats. He assured the Protestants that he reached forth his arms to receive them into his embrace. He ridiculed the idea that the truth had not been known, and that there had been no church, for fifteen hundred years and over, nor, indeed, until the reformers made their appearance, some sixty years since. If we may credit the doctor of theology to whom we are indebted for the preservation of Cardinal Bourbon's first and greatest oratorical effort, the results were so striking that they might have turned a head less well balanced. That very day the cathedral was thronged by a pious crowd, which, as counted by a knight of the Holy Sepulchre, numbered about twenty-one thousand persons. The church, we are told, seemed to be the city and only home of all —so empty were the streets. It was a kind of new creation for the city of Rouen, and it sealed the fate of the Huguenot preaching in the Norman capital. Forty of the Protestant worshippers of the morning congregation were heard to declare that they had done forever with the Reformed worship.[1]

Such was the story of what the cardinal was accustomed to call his " inspiration "—an act which the Huguenots denounced as a flagrant outrage and an insolent defiance of the royal authority, an act which the cardinal's admirers applauded as a justifiable assertion of his duty as a shepherd toward his erring flock.[2] As for the king, when informed of the prelate's exploit,

---

[1] " La saincte et très chrestienne résolution de Monseigneur l'illustrissime et révérendissime Cardinal de Bourbon, pour maintenir la religion catholique et l'église romaine. Par T. J. B. (Berson) Parisien, docteur en théologie et frère mineur." Paris, 1586. Archives curieuses, xi. 63–87. See, also, Lestoile, ii. 73 ; Agrippa d'Aubigné, ii. 230.

[2] Claude Haton tells us that the cardinal, when forbidding the Protestants

he did not pause in his right royal pastime of frolicking with his dogs. One feature of the incident, however, struck him as sufficiently singular to merit a jest. When informed how the cardinal had succeeded in scattering the Huguenots of Rouen by means of his cross, Henry quietly observed: "I wish that it were as easy to put to flight the rest of the Huguenots, even if the basin of holy water and all had to be brought into requisition."[1]

This incident was a straw that indicated the drift of things. That an archbishop should thus dare to violate decency and brave the indignation of a little knot of Protestant worshippers, <small>Threatening indications.</small> in an intensely Roman Catholic city, by an unseemly interruption of a solemn religious service, was not in itself a very singular circumstance. That his impudent and lawless act should remain unpunished, despite the complaints of those whom he had insulted and their partisans, was a more significant fact full of menace to the Huguenots. But Cardinal Bourbon's exploit did not stand alone. Other disquieting intelligence came from various quarters. It was esteemed good ground for suspicion that the king had sent Gondy, Bishop of Paris, to the papal court, and, through his instrumentality, had secured from the pontiff a bull authorizing a considerable alienation of church property. The concession, it was thought, looked to a speedy renewal of war.[2] The claims of the late ally of the Huguenots, Duke John Casimir, appeared to receive very little consideration, when once he had, by the promise of the payment of a part of what was owed him, been induced to remove his hungry reiters to the borders of the land.[3] More ominous infractions of the edict were the insults to which the

---

from assembling again for worship, asserted "that the right appertained to him, and not to the king, to preach or authorize preaching in his diocese." Mémoires, ii. 861.

[1] "À la charge qu'on y deust porter le benoistier et tout." Lestoile, i. 73.

[2] None the less did the bull excite the anger of the clergy and call forth an unusual amount of denunciation from the pulpits of Paris. The alienation permitted the sale of property producing an annual income of 50,000 crowns. Lestoile, under date of August 13, 1576, i. 75.

[3] Saracini to the Grand Duke, July, 1576, Négociations avec la Toscane, iv. 75, 76; De Thou, v. 322-4.

Protestants of Paris were exposed as they went to or returned from Noisy-le-sec, the place which had been grudgingly accorded them for their religious services. On two successive Sundays, the twenty-third and thirtieth of September, the Huguenot worshippers, as they neared the city or entered its streets, were greeted with a shower of stones. Swords were drawn, and some persons were killed and many wounded.[1] From other places where the edict permitted the Protestants to meet for worship their ministers were driven away. The "chambre mi-partie" was not established in most of the parliaments; in several of these courts of law the edict of pacification itself had not been recognized and published, and decisions contrary to its spirit and letter had been made.[2] As time advanced it became more and more clear that the states general, for the convocation of which the Huguenots had been so urgent, were to be employed as an instrument in their destruction. The representatives of the entire nation, it was distinctly announced by the enemies of toleration, would have the power to release the king from the engagements into which he had entered. That the coming assembly should contain a vast preponderance of those who favored a repeal of the royal edict, was the evident aim of the Guises and of all who sympathized with them. The marriage of the Duke of Aumale to the sister of the Marquis of Elbeuf furnished the occasion for a meeting of the different members of the powerful Lorraine family at Joinville; but it was matter of public notoriety that the gathering had more significance than its festive character imported, and that shrewd men there

---

[1] Lestoile, i. 78; Claude Haton, ii. 867. Noisy-le-sec was about two leagues distant from the walls of Paris, in an easterly direction; it is scarcely half that distance from the present walls, and gives its name to a neighboring outwork, one of the cordon of forts by which the capital is encircled. See, also, the letters of Dr. Dale, of October 2, 1576, and of Dr. Dale and Sir Amias Paulet (who came to succeed Dale as English ambassador at the French court), October 13, 1576, which show the gravity of the attack and the supineness of the Roman Catholic authorities. State Paper Office.

[2] See the summary as set forth by Casimir's envoy, Doctor Weyer, De Thou, v. 322-324, and Agrippa d'Aubigné, ii. 222. Among the places from which Protestant ministers were driven away, Lyons, Gien, Rouen, Metz, and Saint Lô were particularly mentioned.

discussed the means of collecting money and massing forces in view of the assembly of Blois.[1]

Meantime, in Poitou and other provinces similar associations to the League of Péronne were industriously formed. In Paris itself the agents endeavored to shelter themselves under the pretended favor of the king, and maintained that Christopher De Thou, the first president of parliament, was cognizant of Henry's secret intentions. But De Thou, if we may believe his son's representations, firmly and, for the time, successfully opposed the institution of the League in the capital.[2] Elsewhere the true and loyal servants of the king were less active or less able to cope with the nefarious scheme that seemed so suddenly to have sprung into existence. For to the energy of the Guises the far-reaching influence of a new and vigorous religious society had allied itself. The Jesuit fathers, if not the authors of the League, as some asserted, are credited with the doubtful honor of having been its chief promoters and preachers.[3] Where their own numbers were not sufficient to enable them to act directly, the Franciscan monks became their instruments in moving the people.

Extension of the League.

It was under such circumstances that the royal summons was issued (on the sixth of August) for the convocation of the states general at Blois, on the fifteenth of November following. While the Huguenots were industriously exerting themselves to restore their churches overthrown by war, while it was even asserted by men worthy of confidence that more than five hundred churches had been re-established, especially in Dauphiny and Languedoc, since the conclusion of peace, and that the number might be greatly increased but for the lack of ministers of the gospel [4] — the enemies of Protestantism were leaving no stone

---

[1] Saracini to the Grand Duke, September 22, 1576, Négociations avec la Toscane, iv. 82.

[2] De Thou, v. 316, 317.

[3] Agrippa d'Aubigné, ii. 223, 230.

[4] Languet, letters of August 16 and 26, 1576, Epistolæ secretæ, ii. 215, 218. The veteran diplomatist, although at this time writing from Ratisbon, kept himself admirably well informed respecting France. In fact, so much did he have to do with his countrymen, and especially the French ambassador, that he incurred the displeasure of some persons at the imperial court. He took pains

unturned to frustrate the reasonable hopes of the reformers. Protestant worship had not yet been instituted in the larger and more powerful cities of the realm. The plea for delay was that only by delay could dangerous tumults be avoided. The Protestants expected that the coming states would remedy the entire difficulty.[1] The papal party, on the contrary, were resolved that, so far from being admitted into the cities, Protestantism should not have a place anywhere within France. The intentions of the Guises became more and more evident. New articles of association between the Roman Catholics were concocted, and printed at court so secretly that a copy could hardly be secured by any one not belonging to the circle most interested in the proscriptive work. The very violence of the seditious pamphlets and broadsheets made the envoy Saracini doubt whether they were in reality the production of Guisard emissaries, and did not rather, as seemed more likely, emanate from the facile pen of unscrupulous Huguenots or scarcely less dangerous Roman Catholics of the faction of the "Politiques," being intended to generate suspicion and alarm in the ranks of the followers of the King of Navarre.[2] At least they pointed unmistakably to war, and tended to render the convocation of the states general a futile expedient, should indeed the states be convoked at all.

A Roman Catholic reaction.

If the Huguenots were suspicious of treachery where none was really plotted, their opponents could scarcely deny that few men had ever had so good reason as they for entertaining distrust. Calm men of affairs might weigh the motives of the king with moderation, and balancing Henry's known impecunious state against his hatred of Protestantism, might conclude that the preponderance of prob-

The suspicions of the Huguenots aroused.

---

however, to justify his course, first by alleging the necessity of gaining accurate information for his master, the Elector of Saxony, and, secondly, by acknowledging that he still retained such affection for his native land as to be eager to learn the events daily occurring there, and especially in a time of such mutation and uncertain hope of peace. Ibid., i. 228.

[1] Languet, ubi supra.

[2] "Per generare sospetto nella parte del re di Navara e di altri di quella fazione." Saracini to the Grand Duke, October 10 and November 5, 1576, Négociations avec la Toscane, iv. 83, 85, 86.

ability was in favor of the sincere purpose of the monarch to maintain the edict he had lately sworn to preserve inviolate. They might urge that no clearer proof could be found of the straits to which Henry was reduced than the fact that, when four months had passed since the restoration of peace, his German mercenaries still remained unpaid and could not therefore be disbanded; although their wages were running up at the rate of half a million francs a month, not to speak of the immense loss inflicted upon the country by their daily exactions. They might consequently scout the popular interpretation of the continued presence of the reiters as an evidence of the king's intention to overwhelm the Huguenots in due time.[1] But the King of Navarre, the Prince of Condé, and Marshal Damville, having had very large experience of Medicean arts, and being tolerably well instructed as to the necessity of caution, took quite another view of the situation, and, as the time approached for the meeting at Blois, sent a gentleman to wait upon the king and protest against the validity of the states general, in view of the retention of the German reiters.[2] And they very clearly announced their determination to stand upon their defence should any one attempt to deprive them and their allies of the rights and privileges tardily conceded to them in the late edict of pacification.[3]

Meanwhile, how was the fortunate youth occupied to whom, according to the law of primogeniture, the supreme power belonged; the last monarch of Valois race who, not content with one crown, still claimed, as his chosen device showed, the crown of Poland, not to speak of another crown which, his admirers said, awaited him in heaven?

Henry's ignoble pursuits.

What were the lofty pursuits of Henry, by the grace of God third of the name, on whose faithful observance of his oath or perjured violation of his edict the political and spiritual destinies of millions of anxious subjects seemed to depend? The sprightly diary of a well-informed contemporary informs

---

[1] Languet, letter of September 28, Epistolæ secretæ, i. 232, 233.
[2] Saracini, letter of October 30, Négociations avec la Toscane, iv. 84.
[3] Recueil des choses mémorables, 583, 584.

us with considerable detail. Had the pleasure-loving king applied himself to the search of the best methods for earning the contempt of all classes of the people, he could scarcely have discovered any course more appropriate than that which he adopted. One day he returns from Normandy to Paris, with the queen his wife, bringing a great quantity of apes, parrots, and little dogs, bought at Dieppe. A few weeks pass, and Henry is seen devoutly engaged in the effort to gain the advantages of the jubilee proclaimed by the pope. Attended by only two or three persons, he walks through the streets of his capital barefooted, holding a rosary of large beads in his hands, and mumbling the accustomed prayers. The people, who have recently had some experience of his devices for relieving a chronic depletion of purse, interpret this unkingly devotion as a new plan, suggested by the queen mother, to extract money from the pockets of the Parisians; but the Parisians only close their pockets the more resolutely, and write pasquinades in place of very loyal addresses. When not in the streets, Henry is in the congenial company of his favorites, to whom now the name of "mignons" begins to be opprobriously applied—men, if they deserve the name of men, as hateful to the outside world for their arrogance and for their effeminacy, as they were dear to his majesty for the fertility of their imagination in inventing new kinds of diversions—men for whom amusement has become the staple occupation of life—men that wear their hair, redolent of perfumes, and curled with consummate art, rising above their little velvet caps much like that of common women of doubtful reputation—men that encircle their necks with stiff-starched ruffs of linen a half-foot in length, above which their heads look for all the world like the head of Saint John the Baptist on a charger.[1] As for Henry himself, he does not show himself unworthy of his chosen associates. When the Protestants came to complain of the outrage to which their brethren in the faith, returning from worship, have been subjected at the very gates of Paris, they find the king riding on horseback, dressed as an Amazon, and learn that he is every

---

[1] Lestoile, i. 74.

day planning new dances and banquets, as if his realm were the most peaceful kingdom in the world.[1]

A portrait of Henry sent by an English ambassador to his royal mistress, about this same time, has been preserved. "The king is of good stature," he writes, "and has an indifferently good presence. The hair of his head is black and something long, but turned and rolled up, as I think, with some hot iron like a very roll round about his head, and from the roll to the crown is very smooth. His cap was black, with only one jewel, and so little that it covered little more than the crown of his head, and all the rest of his garments were also black." It may be remarked that the patriotic Englishman had evidently no intention to paint any member of the French court in too glowing colors. "There were besides," he gallantly wrote the virgin queen, "other ladies, young and old, fair and foul, to the number of nine or ten, but this I do assure your majesty of my faith that there is more beauty in your majesty's little finger than there is in any one lady that there was, or in them all."[2]

A portrait of Henry of Valois.

A year or two ago it was the Huguenot soldiers alone who from the walls of defiant Livron taunted Henry with his participation in the massacre of Saint Bartholomew's Day. Now Roman Catholic pens were busy deriding the unmanly king and his childish or womanish occupations. So Pasquin wrote his titles: "Henry, by the grace of his mother useless King of France and of Poland imaginary, Doorkeeper of the Louvre, Warden of Saint Germain l'Auxerrois, Buffoon of the Churches of Paris, Son-in-law of Colas, Starcher of his wife's collars, and Curler of her hair, Haberdasher of the Palace, . . . Superior of the Four Orders of Mendicant Friars, Conscript Father of the White Flagellants, and Protector of the Capuchins."[3]

A pasquinade against the king.

---

[1] Lestoile, i. 78.

[2] Sir John Smith to Queen Elizabeth, St. Die, December 16, 1576, State Paper Office.

[3] Journal du règne de Henry III. p. 19. "Colas" is, of course, the nickname of Henry's father-in-law, Nicholas de Vaudemont. A different reading makes Henry "*incert roi* de France."

Meanwhile the elections were in progress in every bailiwick and senéchaussée, and the three orders were busy with the preparation of the statement of their particular grievances. The time for the meeting of the states general was approaching, but long before it arrived the Huguenots discovered that the measure about which they had been so strenuous was likely to prove an occasion of oppression, if not of ruin. A representative body formed out of the most intelligent and upright men of the nation might initiate reforms of inestimable importance to the French people; but what could be expected from the delegates of such constituencies as most of the districts into which France was subdivided? Had Condé and his associates mistaken their strength, and imagined that the Protestants could command a numerical majority in any considerable portion of the country? Be this as it may, they soon awoke to the unpleasant truth that their enemies were fully resolved to make good use of the opportunity. Often in the local elections the Huguenots were practically excluded from a participation in the choice of deputies, by the selection of a time or place that precluded all voters but such as were Roman Catholics from making their appearance. If he presumed to come to the polls held in the parish church, and in connection with the service of the mass, the Huguenot gentleman or artisan might pay dearly for his temerity.[1] Sometimes the Protestant candidate if elected was arbitrarily set aside simply because of his religion.[2] In most cases, however, there was no need either of intimidation or of exclusion; the Roman Catholics, as at Provins, outnumbered the Protestant gentry in the ratio of ten to one. What use under such circumstances of much debate? The first and chief article in the documents drawn up to be sent to the states general was, of course, the article of religion. On this, indeed, there was, if we may believe Claude Haton, perfect agreement up to a certain point:

_{Elections for the states general of Blois.}

---

[1] Agrippa d'Aubigné, ii. 235. "Les convocations particulières n'ont esté convoquées qu'aux Messes et paroisses des Catholiques, et partant les Reformez privez de leurs voix aux elections, lesquelles leur ont esté à haute voix deffendues contre la liberté."

[2] *E.g.*, in the territory of Vendôme and at Etampes. Ibid., ubi supra.

every speaker was quite willing that there should henceforth be but one religion tolerated in France—provided only that the religion tolerated be that which the speaker professed.[1] In the end the Romish party was sure to carry the day and demand the exclusion of every religion but the "Catholic, Apostolic, and Roman," and the Protestants, at best, were allowed to append to the official document an article favoring the toleration of Protestantism, to which they subscribed their own names.[2]

Early in December the states general, originally summoned for the middle of the preceding month, convened in the ancient city of Blois. It was notorious that the Roman Catholic party had secured an overwhelming majority of the deputies. This information, and the fact of which it was a clear indication, that the large concessions to the Protestants made by the edict of pacification had awakened a powerful and unexpected Roman Catholic reaction, apparently produced a radical change in the king's plans. Early in the spring Henry had declared that he would have peace, even at the price of half his kingdom. In midsummer he had written energetically to denounce the formation of Roman Catholic associations in Brittany as closely akin to treason. About the same time he had insisted that the Guises should pledge themselves by oath to the maintenance of the peace. Now the same monarch became an advocate of the proscription of the Reformed faith, and was ready to repeal his own "perpetual and irrevocable edict," and engage in a course of action that could end only in open war!

Revolution in the royal policy.

This rapid and complete revolution has perplexed many students of the period under consideration; it ought not, however, to surprise any that have familiarized themselves with the characters of the king and his mother. The attempt to discover a well-defined and consistent plan, steadily pursued by Catharine de' Medici or by her son the reigning

How to be accounted for.

---

[1] "Sur lequel poinct chascun s'accordoit, pourveu que ce fust celle que chascun tenoit." Claude Haton, ii. 865.

[2] Claude Haton, ii. 862–66, gives an interesting account of the angry disputes (which came near having a bloody termination) at the meetings of the noblesse of the western part of Champagne held in the Gray Friars at Provins, September 17th and October 8th and 9th.

prince, will always prove abortive. Consistency of policy was the one element in which they were conspicuously deficient. For principle, political or moral, they cared nothing. Whether they had any real religious convictions was a question which contemporaries, even their most intimate associates, answered differently. It was currently reported that the mother was an atheist; many deemed the son, despite his fantastic devotions, to be little better. Both, it is true, had a desperate hatred of Protestantism; not, it would seem, because of its abstract tenets, but because Protestantism was the religion of free and untrammelled thought, the ally of liberty, the enemy of despotism. Because, also, Protestantism was the adversary of the papacy, which, in every concordat with civil powers, knew how to make its material support valuable. Both Catharine and Henry knew well enough that, while the loyalty of the Reformed was unimpeachable, their system of doctrine as well as of ecclesiastical government comported better with a monarchy under which the people had rights that were recognized, or even with a republican system like that of the cantons of Switzerland, than with an absolute and tyrannical régime. They knew equally well that the scheme of morality professed and advocated by the reformers was a severe censure upon the lax manners practised by the court with their full approval. But even Protestantism, although cordially detested, was not pursued with consistent enmity; for Protestantism might on occasion become serviceable. While, however, the queen and her son had no well-ordered political or moral plan, according to which their actions were shaped, there was, nevertheless, one point that was never lost sight of. Not for a moment did they forget their own personal advantage. To reach this haven they were willing to tack as often as the wind shifted, with little regard for the opinions of the world, with no solicitude for truth or honor. The pursuit of self-gratification, uninterruptedly and relentlessly maintained, constituted the only unity of their lives, and this fact explains much that otherwise would prove inexplicable. If, after heading for a while in the direction of toleration, Henry the Third was seen abruptly to veer toward proscription and inevitable war, the secret of his apparently contradictory manœuvres is to be found in the circumstance that in both cases he was only beating in the direction of a self-indulgence in comparison with which both toleration and proscription were in reality matters of supreme indifference to him.

It is of some interest and importance, however, to ascertain, if possible, any event that determined or confirmed the king's sudden change of attitude to the Huguenots, on the eve of the assembly of the states of Blois. One such event was perhaps found in the publication by the Protestants of a very startling document revealing alleged designs of the Guises upon the crown of France itself.[1]

One Nicholas David—so the story ran—a counsellor in the Parisian Parliament, but a man of as little reputation for ability as for probity, having thrown himself into the party of the League from motives of revenge, had accompanied the Bishop of Paris in his recent mission to Rome. On his return, David fell sick and died in the city of Lyons. In a trunk, opened after his death, was found the paper which the Huguenots took pains to publish to the world, under the title of "Extract of a secret council held at Rome shortly after the arrival of the Bishop of Paris." It contained a summary of the views and purposes of the Guisard party.

The shameful peace lately entered into, says the writer, demonstrates that, although the race of Hugh Capet has succeeded to the temporal administration of the kingdom of Charlemagne, it has not inherited the apostolic blessing conferred by the pope. On the contrary, Capet's rash usurpation of the crown has brought upon him and all his descendants a perpetual malediction, rendering him and his successors disloyal and disobedient to the Holy Church. To insure the ruin of that church, they have introduced the damnable error which the French style the "Liberty of the Gallican Church," which is nothing else than the refuge of

The Mémoire of Nicholas David.

---

[1] It is probable, though not certain, that the mémoire of David reached the king's eyes before the opening of the states general. The Protestant preface to the translation was dated, as mentioned below, November 15, and since the document was brief, this was likely also to be the date of publication. If so, it is quite likely that a copy was in Henry's hands within a week from that time.

the Waldenses, the Albigenses, the Poor Men of Lyons, the Lutherans, and at present the Calvinists. No wonder that the victories of the kings who for the last sixteen years have battled in defence of the faith have been fruitless. There will never be success so long as the crown remains in this line.

God has by this last peace prepared the way for the restoration of the crown to the true successors of Charlemagne, against whom, inasmuch as they were despoiled of their rights by force and violence, no prescription holds. The race of the Capets is clearly seen to be given over to a reprobate mind. Whereas some of its kings have been smitten with folly, and have been men stupid and of no account, the rest have been rejected of God and men, because of their heresy, and proscribed and cast forth from the holy communion of the Church. On the contrary, the scions of Charlemagne are green and flourishing, loving virtue, full of vigor in body and intellect, qualified to execute high and praiseworthy enterprises. Wars have served to exalt them in station, honor, and pre-eminence, but peace will reinstate them in their ancient inheritance, the kingdom, with the consent and by the choice of the whole people. Unquestionably, therefore, the favorable terms accorded to the heretics by the edict of pacification must be viewed as proceeding from God and not from men; in order that the honor of having overthrown heresy may remain to the only true God and to the benediction of His holy vicar.

To this end the inhabitants of all Catholic towns ought, through salutary preaching, to be stirred up to prevent, by force of arms, the introduction of the public services of the abominable sect of the Huguenots. Meantime the king should be urged to give himself no concern, but to commit all authority to the Duke of Guise, who may thus become the sole and absolute head of the leagues formed with the connivance of the king himself. By Guise's orders the parish priests, both in town and in country, will then draw up a complete roll of all men capable of bearing arms, and will issue to each of their male parishioners, at the confessional, directions respecting the arms with which they are to provide themselves, for service under captains to be assigned by Guise himself.

The states general are the pit into which the heretics will fall. To this meeting those deputies must be sent who are most trusted by his holiness because of the oath of fidelity they have given to him and because of their obligations to the Catholic King. The queen mother will induce her misguided son Anjou to attend the states, in company with his brother the reigning monarch; and the King of Navarre and the Prince of Condé are to be enticed to the same place and threatened with being declared rebels in case they do not come. To disarm their suspicions, Guise will for the time absent himself. As the time shall approach, the troops of the parishes must be reviewed and kept in readiness for a prompt march under command of their chosen captains.

When once the states shall have met, the members, from the highest to the lowest, shall bind themselves by a solemn oath to observe everything agreed upon by the body, and the pope will be called upon to give to its conclusions the full force of a Pragmatic Sanction, and make them as binding as the Concordats between the Holy See and the French kingdom. Next, the states shall declare all heretical princes of the blood to have forfeited their rights to the succession, and shall renew their oath of fidelity to the successor of Saint Peter and to the Catholic faith, as laid down in the decrees of the Council of Trent. The edicts of toleration shall be repealed, and the edicts ordering the extirpation of heresy shall be restored to full force, the king being expressly relieved of all his promises made to the heretics. In order to overthrow all opposition encountered in the prosecution of the good work from any rebellious princes, the king shall be petitioned by the states to appoint, as lieutenant-general, a competent and experienced prince, strong in body and in mind, able to undergo the toil and to take counsel of himself, a man who has never had part, communication, or alliance with heretics—in other words, to select the Duke of Guise, who alone possesses all the qualities required in a great captain worthy of such a trust.

Having thus seized the power, the states shall set forth to the king's brother the enormity of his offence in abandoning the king and joining the heretics, in declaring himself their head, in raising an army, and finally in constraining his majesty not only to give him an excessive and unreasonable appanage, but also to permit and authorize the practice of that abominable impiety of heresy. This crime being the highest kind of treason, divine and human, and not in the competence of the king to remit and pardon, the states shall demand the appointment of judges to take cognizance thereof, after the very holy and pious example of the Catholic King in the case of his only son and of himself.[1] The demand shall be enforced by the simultaneous appearance of a portion of the parish militia and other troops, by whom the arrest of the Duke of Anjou and of all his associates shall be effected. At the same time the remainder of the parish troops shall take the field and attack the heretics, putting them to the sword and selling their goods to defray the expenses of the war. The Duke of Guise, finding himself now at the head of a powerful army, shall enter the provinces held by the rebels, whom he will easily subdue, laying waste the country, and slaying all that offer resistance, without losing his time in sieges like that of La Rochelle.

Having gained so glorious and complete a victory, and thereby acquired the unbounded affection and favor of all the cities of the kingdom and of the noblesse, the Duke of Guise will provide for the exemplary punishment of the king's brother and his accomplices, and thereafter conclude the whole matter, with the consent of his holiness, by imprisoning the king and the queen in a monastery, as Pepin, his ancestor, did Childeric. Having thus reunited the temporal heritage of the crown to the apostolic benediction which he already possesses, for the advantage of all the future descendants of Charlemagne, he will cause the Holy See to be fully recognized by the states of the kingdom, without restriction or modification, by abolishing the privileges and liberties of the Gallican Church. This he will beforehand pledge himself on oath to do."

---

[1] "A l'exemple tressaint et pientissime du Roy Catholique en l'endroit de son propre fils unique, et de soy-mesme." The allusion is, of course, to Philip II. and Don Carlos.

[2] This document constitutes the first of the long series of important contemporary tracts reproduced in the invaluable collection gathered and saved from

I have not hesitated to insert this important document, somewhat abridged, but essentially in the words of the original paper. For important the document is, whether it be regarded as genuine or fabricated. The view given of the designs entertained by the Guises and their adherents may not be authentic, but, in the light of the history of France during the next thirteen years, it must be accepted as a truthful representation. If a Huguenot and not a Guisard hand was employed in drawing it up, the Huguenot writer betrays an admirable acquaintance with designs whose fulfilment was delayed, but not wholly defeated, by premature publicity. Under such circumstances, it is not easy, nor is it altogether essential, to ascertain the authorship. Yet there is much that seems to render it probable that the story of its discovery among Nicholas David's effects is no myth. The document first saw the light as a pamphlet, provided with a preface written by a Protestant, and dated at Lyons, on the fifteenth of November. A few days later it found its way to the Louvre, and was read by Henry with more incredulity than fear. It was believed to be a forgery, and this opinion the historian Davila adhered to many years after.[1] All authorities, indeed, agree that the king took alarm only when similar warnings of his peril reached him, a little later, from the French ambassador at Madrid. But the fact which Davila did not know—a fact which De Thou had from the lips of M. de St. Goard himself—is significant: the paper sent by the patriotic ambassador which produced such commotion at the French court was a copy of the same document as that found in David's trunk. It had been forwarded to Spain for the information of Philip the Second.[2]

The great reaction of public sentiment in condemnation of

Was the paper genuine?

---

oblivion by Simon Goulart, and published under the title of Mémoires de la Ligue sous Henri III. et Henri IV., Rois de France. The preface to the first of the six octavo volumes is dated 1587.

[1] Davila, 224, 225. See Recueil des choses mémorables, 581.

[2] De Thou, v. 341. Mr. Smedley, History of the Reformed Religion in France, ii. 152, has already insisted on this circumstance which he considers as establishing the authenticity of the mémoire of David.

the edict of toleration, the wonderful success of the projectors of the Roman Catholic leagues, the disquieting discovery of the grow-ing popularity of the Guises as champions of doctrinal orthodoxy and of the claims of the church—all conspired to determine Henry's course. He felt himself too weak to attempt to crush the ambitious duke and his allies by a direct assault. It was more prudent, and more congenial to his tastes, to disappoint their expectations by an indirect, but not less effectual movement. He had entered upon the peace because weary of war, and had made lavish concessions to the Huguenots whom he cordially detested. The peace, which he never intended honorably to respect, and the unwilling concessions his enemies had wrung from him, having bred a new and formidable party in the League, he did not hesitate to renounce the one and retract the other, in the hope of undoing the mischief he had wrought. He determined to become himself the head of the League, to constitute himself the chief whom some of the manifestoes of the associations obscurely designated, to write "Henry of Valois" in the space purposely left blank for the insertion, in due time, of the name of "Henry of Lorraine."

Henry determines to become head of the League.

On Sunday evening, the second day of December, that ardent Roman Catholic nobleman, Louis de Gonzagues, Duke of Nevers, reached Blois, expecting that the formal opening of the states general would take place on the morrow. He found that a "little council," as it was called, had that day been held in the royal apartments. There were present, besides the king and the queens, his wife and mother, the Duke of Anjou, Cardinal Bourbon, the Duke of Montpensier, the chancellor, and one or two others. The object was to consider "what steps the king ought to take to secure that there should be but one religion in his kingdom." Nevers informs us that the council was held expressly on that day in order that his majesty might begin the holy work before the arrival at court of the delegates of any province, through fear lest it should be said that they had incited him to it. The result of the deliberations was a decision that when the orders, each in its assembly, should proffer a request for the exclusive establishment of a single religion, the king should signify his acceptance

The king's "little council."

of the petition.[1] It would seem to have been upon this same day—no day of rest for Henry—that he sent out letters to the royal governors throughout France, enclosing certain articles respecting the associations which, said he, "I have ordered to be instituted in all the provinces of my realm." The governors were commanded to have copies of these articles promptly made, and to use great diligence that these copies should be signed and forwarded to the king, together with the lists of members, within a month or six weeks at the farthest, and before the close of the sessions of the states.[2] It was clear that Henry had little thought of maintaining his tolerant edict for the benefit of the Protestants.

Henry's letters of December 2d.

The formal opening of the states general took place in a spacious hall of the castle, with all the pomp craved by an age delighting in startling pageants. The assemblage itself outnumbered former gatherings of the kind; for since the famous States of Tours, not far from a century before, several new sénéchaussées had been created, each entitled to representation in all the three orders. Henry presided, seated on a throne of violet velvet sprinkled with the typical lilies wrought in gold. On his right sat Catharine de' Medici, now a portly dame of fifty-seven years, considerably changed from the proud princess who, on another December day, sixteen years ago, brought before a similar convocation at Orleans the boy-king Charles, in whose name she was to reign supreme. Yet the Florentine Grand Duke's daughter was still in the vigor of her womanhood, with eye keen and penetrating, with unbroken resolution, with brow betraying no indications of regret or remorse for the misdeeds of the past. Beyond her, in another arm-chair, was puny Alençon, the mis-called Hercules, scarred not in war, but by disease, to whose insignificance no change of name to Anjou, no extravagant appanage could lend dignity, the impersonation of Medicean treachery without

The states general opened. December 6th.

---

[1] "Journal de M. le duc de Nevers, pendant les Estats tenus à Blois, ès années 1576 et 1577." Mémoires de Nevers, i. 166.

[2] Text of the letter, dated Blois, December 2, 1576, in Mémoires de Claude Haton, ii. Appendix, 1154.

the shrewdness that had made the fortune of the great merchant house of Tuscany. Louise, the younger queen, occupied a place upon her husband's left. On either side of the hall the secular and ecclesiastical peers were arranged in order of dignity, while immediately in front of the monarch, sat the chancellor, the highest judicial officer of the crown.[1]

Henry opened the session by courteously raising his cap from his head and bowing to the assembled deputies, and then proceeded to address them with a grace peculiarly his own.[2] The speech was a model of temperateness and conciliation. He deplored the ruinous change that had come over a kingdom once the most flourishing in Christendom, and declared himself and his late brother absolved of all responsibility for disasters occurring during their childhood. He praised the queen his mother for the incredible toils and labors she had undergone to prevent those disasters, and asserted that to her, after God, was due the preservation of the realm. "All true lovers of France," said he, "are bound to give her immortal praise for the vigilant care, the magnanimity and prudence with which she held the helm, and piloted this kingdom through the boisterous waves and fierce winds of faction and division that assailed it on all sides." Coming next to speak of himself, Henry dwelt much upon the pacific intentions of his accession, and the intense sorrow it had caused him to see the misery entailed upon his subjects by war. "Often," he piously exclaimed, "have I been moved to pray to God that He would be pleased in His mercy to deliver my people speedily from their misfortunes, or, in this the flower of my age, to put an end to my reign and to my life, that I might close both with the reputation becoming a prince descended from a long line of magnanimous kings. Much rather this, than that I should be suffered by heaven to grow old, a witness of calamities which I could not remedy, or

Henry's speech.

---

[1] Boullée, Histoire complète des Etats-Généraux et autres assemblées représentatives de France, i. 279, etc.

[2] "En la première séance d'iceux, le Roy après avoir levé le bonnet et salué l'assemblée, commença avec une grace et action bien séante sa harangue sur la commisération des afflictions de son royaume." Recueil des choses mémorables, 584.

that the memory of my rule should be handed down to posterity as the example of an unfortunate reign." Recognizing a good peace to be the sole cure for prevailing evils, he conjured his hearers, by their love and fealty, to assist him in removing even the very roots of discord, and assured them that he knew both the reasons for which he had been placed in so exalted a position, and the solemn account he must one day render for his conduct at the divine tribunal. "I have no other object in view but the welfare of my subjects," said Henry. "For this I shall labor night and day. To accomplish this I will use all my intelligence, care, and toil, not sparing even my blood and my life, if need be. Moreover, be assured that I promise you, on the word of a king, that I shall cause to be kept and observed inviolably all the regulations and ordinances that may be made by me in this assembly, and that I shall neither give any dispensation to the contrary, nor permit those regulations and ordinances to be in any wise infringed." [1]

Of the speech of the chancellor, whom, according to custom, the king requested more fully to explain his intentions, little need be said. The speaker was not the grave Michel de l'Hospital, the stately jurist whose calm and persuasive voice had so often been raised to still the discordant waves of passion, the ardent patriot in whose breast even the greatest reverses and old age itself never quenched the spark of hope nor caused him to despair of the republic. L'Hospital had been dead these three years and more. In his place sat René de Birague, one of the brood of Italians that had come in to hasten the destruction of France, a foreigner of whom no friend ever had the effrontery to assert that he, like his immortal predecessor, "had the lilies of France graven upon his heart." One half of those present could not hear the harangue which he uttered with cracked voice; the other half were annoyed at his indiscriminate and blundering censures, or disgusted that a chancellor of France should be obliged to apologize

Chancellor Birague's address.

---

[1] Text of Henry's speech in Mémoires de Nevers, and Agrippa d'Aubigné, ii. 242-5 ; i. 440-3. Summaries in Recueil des choses mémorables, 584 ; De Thou, v. 334, 335; etc.

to the representatives of the nation for a want of familiarity with the duties of his office.[1]

Henry had won golden opinions, in contrast with his chancellor. However, it is always unsafe to accord much praise to royal eloquence. In the present case it was well understood that the fine phrases and highly edifying and patriotic sentiments, of which Henry was the mouthpiece, had been supplied to him by the facile pen of Jean de Morvilliers, Bishop of Orleans.[2] This circumstance may help to account for the tone of exalted self-devotion of an address to the composition of which Henry, in the midst of his "mignons" and dogs, might have found it an irksome task to apply himself. It may also explain the incongruity between Henry's ardent expressions of a desire for a good and stable peace, and his letter, but four days old, ordering associations to be formed in all the provinces, the only result of which must be the overthrow of the edict of May, and a new resort to arms.

If the king had counted upon the plausible words of his harangue to obliterate the memory of two years of financial and political misrule, and to inspire his subjects with confidence either in his integrity, or in his patriotism and prudence, he had certainly made a gross miscalculation. He had ostentatiously promised, on his kingly word, to maintain inviolate, and to cause to be respected, whatever ordinances might be made by himself in the present assembly; the deputies, with a dawning consciousness of the rights of the people as superior to the king, went a step farther. One of their very first conclusions was to request his majesty to appoint a certain number of judges, to whom the states would add delegates

Bold demands of the states.

---

[1] "Ce qui étoit honteux dans un premier magistrat comme lui." De Thou, v. 336. M. de Blanchefort, a deputy for the nobles of Nivernois, says: "Parlant de la Noblesse, il ne contenta pas tout le monde ; puis blasmant les méchans qui contreviennent aux ordonnances, il n'en fit aucune distinction . . . De ma part je n'ouys pleinement ce discours pour en bien juger, attendu que M. le chancellier estoit aucunement loin, et parce qu'il a la voix fort cassée." Mémoires de Nevers, i. 443, 444.

[2] Lestoile, i. 80 ; Mémoires de Nevers, ubi supra. De Thou (v. 334), is our authority for the last statement.

from each province of the kingdom. The joint commission thus constituted was to be invested with absolute power to pass upon all general or particular propositions made by the three orders; its decisions were to be executed as laws of the realm.[1] The king's astonishment at this suggestion, offered to him by the delegates with the tiers état at their head, had not subsided, when the Archbishop of Lyons, Pierre d'Espinac, presiding officer of the clergy, presented to the assembly an unsigned paper, found by him, he said, under the table at which he was seated. This turned out to be a petition to the king, requesting him to pledge himself to cause whatever resolutions might be unanimously adopted by the three orders to be forthwith recognized as of legal force, and binding himself, where the orders disagreed, to make no decision without the advice and consent of the queen mother, the princes of the blood, the peers of the realm, and twelve deputies of the states. It must be admitted that Henry answered with more calmness and discretion than might have been expected from him, a proposal that would, by a single dash of the pen, have changed the constitution of the kingdom, and effectually tied the hands of a monarch who claimed to be absolute in the exercise of his authority. However interesting and important in the civil history of France, these and other questions of constitutional law that came up in the States of Blois, must be dismissed, as irrelevant to the special subject of the present work. Yet this must be noticed in passing: the spirit of inquiry showed signs of having passed from the domain of religion into that of government. For half a century men had been questioning the authority of the established church, and requiring its advocates to substantiate its claims by an appeal to the Word of God as the ulti-

---

[1] De Thou, v. 336. It is worthy of notice that, after all, the tiers état, in this as in other respects, showed itself more moderate than the other orders; for it urged, until overborne by them, that the thirty-six commissioners that were to act with the royal council should have only a consultative voice. It also demanded that, in all cases affecting a single order, the twelve commissioners of that order should possess a single vote with weight equal to the vote of the commissioners of the other two orders put together. See Boullée, i. 286, 287.

mate and only proper criterion. Within the last few years daring thinkers had turned their attention to the foundations of civil government, and had begun to demand the reasons for the anomalies of its present constitution. The investigation augured trouble in future for the despotic possessors of thrones, inasmuch as those who pursued it were no longer exclusively adherents of the reformatory school in theology. If François Hotman, author of the treatise "Franco-Gallia,"[1] was a Huguenot, the famous Jean Bodin, the most learned expounder of the spirit of the French monarchy in the States of Blois, the writer whose great work on the "Republic" was soon to be the subject of the praise of all men, was undoubtedly a Roman Catholic.[2]

Meantime Henry did not suffer his new zeal to grow cold. If any credit were to be gained by the advocacy of a proscriptive policy, he was resolved not to lose the opportunity to acquire it. His very rivals in public esteem took alarm lest he should rob them of their sole chance of making a strong party in the state; and Guise, who had purposely remained away, hastened to Blois to look after his interests. The king would not suffer the states, strongly imbued as they were with the sentiments of the League, to express themselves as they had purposed doing. Discovering that the Baron de Sennecey,[3] whom the nobles had chosen to be the spokesman for their order, had omitted from the draft of his formal address to the crown any demand for the sole establishment of the Roman Catholic religion, Henry was very indignant at this exhibition of a natural fear lest war should inevitably be renewed. The nobleman must be gained over by friendship or by fear. In the end, the form of words he was to use, when

Henry's activity.

---

[1] See the Rise of the Huguenots, ii. 615.
[2] Von Polenz arrives at this conclusion after a long and exhaustive examination. Geschichte des französischen Calvinismus, iii. 364–372. Bodin's own command, in his will, that his body should be buried in the church of the Cordeliers at Laon, is a very clear indication that the great jurist was no Protestant. With good reason does Bayle, in his extended article on Bodin, style him " one of the most learned men in France in the sixteenth century."
[3] Otherwise written Sénecé and Sennesçay.

touching on the knotty question of religious toleration, was drawn up by Catharine de' Medici herself, and submitted for final correction to Henry himself, before Sennecey was permitted to speak.[1] At about the same time the king was writing to distant provinces, approving the articles of associations submitted to him, and granting to the confederates the dangerous authority to levy money to carry them into execution.[2]

There are extremes of vacillation that to men of ordinary steadfastness of purpose appear nearly if not quite incredible. Can it be believed that, by the time the fourth week of the assembly of the states was well begun, Henry was in the greatest perplexity as to what course it was best for him to pursue? Yet such, we are assured, on what appears to be unimpeachable authority, was the case. The three orders were ready for the declaration of "the one religion;" it was now the king who showed painful hesitation and real fear of the renewal of hostilities. "He seems inclined now to one side and now to the other," wrote the Florentine envoy in his confidential despatches to his master, even so late as the twenty-eighth day of December.[3] Yet three more days passed, and the same pen could write an account of very positive declarations on the part of Henry and his mother. The king had at last published in an open council his will to tolerate none but the Catholic religion in his dominions, asserting that he had always been devotedly attached to the faith, but had hitherto been prevented by certain good reasons from testifying his affection. Now, however, in view of the good intentions of his subjects, whose deeds, he promised himself, would be conformable to their professions, he was fully resolved, with the forces God had given him, to defend the true Christian League. Catharine de' Medici followed with

The king's vacillation.

Declaration of Henry and his mother—December 29th.

---

[1] The Duke of Nevers vouches for this singular circumstance in his diary, under the dates of December 12 and 14, 1576. Mémoires, i. 167.

[2] See the Articles of the League of Champagne and Brie, with Henry's indorsement, dated Blois, December 11, 1576. Ibid., i. 117.

[3] "Ed ora si mostra inclinato da una banda e ora dall' altra." Saracini to the Grand Duke, Blois, December 28, 1576, Négociations avec la Toscane, iv. 96.

similar utterances and still stronger excuses for past action or inaction, based upon the minority and the disunion of her sons. Seeing that these impediments had been removed, she would show herself most constant and obstinate in defending the Catholic religion, and in permitting no exercise whatever of the Huguenot worship.[1] The words had been received with such great delight that a league was formed which had already secured the subscriptions of the delegates of five provinces. Nay, the campaign against the heretics was at once mapped out—the Duke of Anjou to command the vanguard, Henry in person the "battle," or main body, Guise, Mayenne, Nevers and others, the rear. An irresistible force of ten thousand horse and thirty thousand foot would pour into Poitou, and carry discomfiture into the haunts of the Huguenots.[2]

It may have occurred to some who heard, as it occurs to those who now read, the story of these proceedings, that the word of a king who could, without a blush, explain to his hearers that he had made his edict of pacification "solely that he might have his brother again, and drive the reiters and other foreigners from his kingdom," and fell back upon the superior and binding force of his coronation oath to excuse all subsequent perjury, was not likely to be of much account. It really added little weight to his statement that he asseverated that "this was his final resolution," and that "he wished no advice on the subject," and with hypocritical cant expressed himself as "hoping that God would grant him help."[3]

Even now, however, the utter faithlessness of Henry, worthy son of his Italian mother, was fully understood by few, if by any, of those who thought they knew him best. If his royal council did not believe implicitly his extravagant assurances of piety, the majority of its members certainly had little suspicion that his policy was at present aimed solely at establish-

---

[1] Saracini to the Grand Duke, December 31, 1576, ibid., iv. 98. See, also, Journal de Nevers, under date of December 29, apud Mémoires, i. 168, 169; and Lestoile, i. 80, 81.

[2] Saracini, ubi supra, iv. 99.

[3] "Que c'estoit sa dernière résolution ; qu'il ne vouloit sur ce aucun advis; qu'il esperoit que Dieu l'aideroit." Mémoires de Nevers, ubi supra.

ing the royal authority at the expense both of the League and the Huguenots, and that possibly he loved the Roman Catholic association about as little as he did the "heretics" themselves.

<small>Henry asks the written opinions of his council.</small> The king, after declaring his purpose to tolerate no second religion in the realm, requested each member of his council to give him a written opinion concerning the best method of carrying this purpose into effect, either by peaceable means or, if the worst should come to pass, by war. The answers have come down to us.[1] Whoever will summon the patience to plod through this mass of neglected documents, not deterred by the inelegance and barrenness of style constituting their most striking characteristic, will find himself in the end amply rewarded for his pains. In only one point do all the opinions agree: violent Leaguer and friend of more pacific devices unite in desiring that the end may be compassed without a resort to arms, and suggest the propriety of first endeavoring to gain over Navarre, Condé, and Damville. If there be any difference, the conversion of the Montmorency to loyalty is regarded as the most important. In other respects the views of the writers, and their treatment of the question, differ widely.

Louis, Cardinal of Guise, last survivor of Duke Claude's six sons, abettor of the massacre of Vassy and author of the massacre of Sens—amiable prelate whose convivial habits had earned him the distinctive cognomen of "le cardinal des bouteilles"[2]— illustrated his reputation for dense ignorance respecting matters of church and state by making provision for the possibility of any Protestants desiring, "through a divine inspiration," to join the "Holy League."[3] Such persons ought to be welcomed

---

[1] They occupy one hundred and ten folio pages of the Mémoires de Nevers (i. 179–288), under the heading, "Advis donnez au roy, par escrit, par son commandement, par la reine sa mère, les princes et autres seigneurs et les principaux de son conseil, s'il estoit expédient pour le bien de son estat, de faire la guerre à ceux de la religion prétendue reformée, ou de traitter avec eux. Au mois de Janvier, 1577." The date of the answers that bear any particular date is January 2.

[2] See the Rise of the Huguenots, ii. 13, 46, 170.

[3] "Que si quelques uns de la nouvelle opinion, par une inspiration divine, se veulent liguer, s'unir et associer à la sainte ligue, les associez les y recevront," etc. Mémoires de Nevers, i. 246.

to every privilege of the association—that of contributing to its funds not being forgotten—on condition, of course, that they indulge in no act of their religious worship, public or private. Seeing that the Holy League was pretty well understood to have been founded expressly for the destruction of Protestantism, we must confess that the cardinal gave himself unnecessary trouble in providing for an improbable contingency.

In the midst of the lavish praise accorded to the king's most laudable plan of exterminating Protestantism, or at least that external practice of its rites without which Protestantism could not subsist, one or two things claim attention. Morvilliers and Bellièvre, two of the king's most experienced counsellors, did not hide their candid belief in the quixotic character of an enterprise whose justice they felt themselves, under the circumstances, precluded from discussing. Morvilliers dwelt much upon the proverbial fickleness of the French, ever ready to undertake, but disinclined to persevere in difficult labors. And coming to the money indispensably necessary for a fresh war, he exclaimed: "As to the means of providing it, I swear in good faith that I do not know them, although for ten years I have concerned myself with such thoughts, and perhaps as much as any man of my profession. I see the affairs in this kingdom in such confusion, the whole people so impoverished, that I know not what we can promise ourselves. Meantime, your majesty can expect help only from your subjects. You can hope for nothing from friends, from credit, or from the merchants."[1] Bellièvre was even more outspoken in his disapprobation of the mad venture upon which Henry seemed to be driven. "Sire," said he, "when I consider the resoluteness of your subjects, who, after having been beaten consecutively in two great battles, like those of Jarnac and Moncontour, and having lost the greater number of their military men, with their leader himself, a prince of your blood, and the bravest combatants ever in their ranks, nevertheless refused after such great punishment to abandon their obstinacy—when I consider, too, that it was not in the power of the late king, your brother, to make

Candor of Morvilliers and Bellièvre.

---

[1] Mémoires de Nevers, i. 265.

them consent to peace, save by granting them the exercise of their religion, I tremble so often as I think of the resolution adopted by your majesty to interdict that exercise. Your majesty knows that they showed a like stubbornness after the siege of La Rochelle, and that having scarcely any forces or places left them in the kingdom, they have not failed to continue in the same pertinacity until the present hour. Taking all this into view, Sire, I cannot easily persuade myself that they will change opinion, for all your declarations, nor that words, or even arms, will be potent enough to heal a disease so inveterate as that which has possession of their minds." If the war must come, however, Bellièvre was clear that its authors must be its supporters. "It seems," said he, "that these gentlemen of the states general who gave you the advice, and, as it were, compelled your majesty by their very pressing requests to break this last edict of pacification, are bound to guarantee in their own names the issue of it, and to furnish you with everything necessary for the successful prosecution of the war."[1]

The Duke of Anjou, now to all appearances fully reconciled to his brother, was persuaded to write a reply to Henry's request for counsel which not only breathed as much hostility to the Huguenots as did any of the other papers, but indulged in open contempt of the resources at their command. He advised Henry to remonstrate courteously with Navarre on his folly in undertaking to cope with a monarch that had a hundred times as much money at command and more than a hundred times the number of troops to draw upon. He advised that Damville be plied with arguments based upon loyalty and religion. "As to the Prince of Condé," said he, "inasmuch as he has less means than the King of Navarre, and is more obstinate, it seems to me that you ought to speak more roughly and make him feel the rod with which he will be beaten should he be so unfortunate as to oppose your will in anything."[2] Dull-witted Anjou did not awake, until it was too

The Duke of Anjou entrapped.

---

[1] Mémoires de Nevers, i. 285, 287.
[2] Ibid., i. 235. "Luy faire sentir les verges dont il seroit fouetté, s'il estoit si miserable de contrarier en quelque chose à vos volontez."

late, to a realization of the mortifying truth that his treacherous brother had had no other view in urging him to an expression of sentiments similar to his own for the time being, than to destroy any lingering confidence which the Huguenots might still have in the puny prince. Nor had Henry miscalculated.[1] Two members of the council proved themselves shrewd enough to avoid the trap laid for them. Greatly to the surprise, and not a little to the chagrin, of Henry, the Duke of Guise, arch-enemy of the Huguenots, replied to the royal summons in the briefest manner, and excused himself from giving advice in so momentous an affair, on the ground of his youth and inexperience. Since the king had insisted on acquiring all credit with the Roman Catholics as head of the League, Henry of Guise was resolved that Henry of Valois should also have all the odium with the Huguenots.[2] In fact, the only sentences in the whole note that could possibly be construed as advice were a plea for justice to the heretics in case they behaved themselves quietly. "It is true, Sire," said the duke, "that there is no one that does not say that, in order not to create distrust among your subjects belonging to the new religion, you ought to give them all the assurances they shall ask or be able to imagine, as, indeed, you promise them through the associations which it has pleased you to command to be formed in your kingdom. Wherefore, Sire, it appears to me that you ought not to fail in this matter in a single point; provided always that they remain quietly in their houses, without contravening your will or intention in any respect."[3] The young duke had never made a more politic stroke—not even when, in the midst of the massacre of Saint Bartholomew's

Politic course of Guise and Montpensier.

---

[1] "Mais ayant veu le changement du roy, il a pensé que sa Majesté l'a fait parler ainsi pour le mettre en mauvais ménage avec les Huguenots, et il en a esté fasché. Aussi estoit-ce le seul dessein de S. M." Journal du duc de Nevers, ibid., i. 178.

[2] The Duke of Nevers says in his diary (January 4): "Le roy s'est estonné des advis de Montpensier et de Guise, pour estre courts. Mais ils les ont ainsi faits, de peur que le roy ne les monstrast aux Huguenots, comme M. de Guise l'a dit à ma femme." Ibid., i. 169.

[3] Mémoires de Nevers, i. 247.

Day, he ostentatiously rescued some Huguenots from the death awaiting them in the bloody streets of Paris.[1] The Duke of Montpensier was equally prudent.

A fortnight passed, and the states, after despatching those embassies to the Huguenot leaders to whose fortunes I shall *Deputies of the three orders before the king — January 17.* soon have occasion to refer, were admitted to the royal presence, and addressed Henry through their chosen spokesmen. The Archbishop of Lyons, in behalf of the clergy, insisted much upon the religious question, urging that no other faith be tolerated in France than the ancestral faith of the Romish Church. Baron de Sennecey, for the nobles, followed much in the same strain, but urged that, when all exercise of the Protestant religion should have been removed, no inquisition be made into the tenets of the individual Huguenots, but that these be left undisturbed in their consciences, each being suffered to believe what he would, so long as no pernicious example were set to others. As for Versoris, deputed to speak for the tiers état, he had received strict instructions from his order to insert the words "without war" in the plea for the enforcement of religious uniformity. But the orator, noted though he was for his eloquence, lost his self-possession, became

---

[1] The Rise of the Huguenots, ii. 491, note. The writer of the pamphlet "Response aux Declarations et Protestations de Messieurs de Guise, faictes sous le nom de Monseigneur le Cardinal de Bourbon, pour justifier leur injuste prise des armes," published in 1585, asserts that the Guises are moved in their entire course not by religion but by ambition. In proof of this assertion, he lays stress upon the incident referred to in the text. "Et de fait fut par aucuns zelateurs Catholiques remarqué qu'à la S. Barthelemy, apres avoir induit le feu Roy Charles à se deffaire de ceux de la religion, ils se contentèrent de se depescher sous ceste ombre des ennemis particuliers de leur maison, et venger leurs querelles propres, et firent les doux et les pitoyables, en tous les lieux de leur authorité faisant proffit en toutes sortes de la rigueur et severité de ce prince, qui selon la vigueur de son esprit s'en sçent tres bien appercevoir." Mémoires de la Ligue, i. 92. It ought not to be forgotten, however, that other instances of Henry of Guise's humanity can be alleged which need not be interpreted as due to selfish motives. For example, at the capture of La Charité, when the Duke of Anjou would have violated the terms of the capitulation, Guise would not consent, and rescued the Huguenots. In Agrippa d'Aubigné's words, "Là parut le Duc de Guise conservateur de la foi et du droit des gens." Histoire universelle, ii. 282.

confused, and forgot—so he maintained—to introduce the important qualification of his demand.[1]

It was the seventeenth of January, 1577—just fifteen years from the day upon which Charles the Ninth signed the famous Edict of January, the charter of the Protestant liberties. The coincidence is startling, as indicative of the revulsion of the popular feeling from that which found expression in the states general of Orleans and Pontoise. The clergy, indeed, had learned nothing, forgotten nothing. But a radical change had come over the other orders of the state, since Rochefort and Admiral Coligny presented petitions for the concession of churches to the adherents of the purer faith, and the memorial ("cahier") of the third estate demanded the absolute repeal of all intolerant legislation, the cessation of all persecution, and declared that "the diversity of opinion entertained by the king's subjects proceeds from nothing else than the strong zeal and solicitude they have for the salvation of their souls."[2] Thus much had civil war accomplished. So completely had the disastrous and apparently unavoidable resort to arms stifled the spirit of inquiry, and sealed beyond question the religious condition of France.

Two days later the upper estates succeeded in bringing the tiers état to sanction the repeal of the edict of pacification.

The Tiers état consents to the repeal of the edict—January 19. But the majority was small, since it comprised the representatives of only seven out of the twelve governments of France, and the remaining five[3] were loud in their protest against the proposed action.

Huguenot preparations. Meantime, the Huguenots had not been idle. From the moment that they had descried the unmistakable portents of approaching danger, their leaders had been making those preparations which previous experience of like perils rendered to some extent natural to them. Towns were garrisoned and fortifications repaired; castles were manned and

---

[1] Recueil des choses mémorables, 587; Agrippa d'Aubigné, ii. 246-251 (where Sénnecey's speech is given at great length). Saracini, in his letter of January 23, makes Versoris utter the qualifying clause which we know from other sources that he omitted. Négociations avec la Toscane, iv. 104, 105.

[2] See the Rise of the Huguenots, i. 492.

[3] Namely: Burgundy, Brittany, Dauphiny, Lyonnais, and Guyenne. Re-

provisioned. The situation was tacitly accepted as all but open war. In fact, the promptness of the measures adopted amazed not only the king and the states, but even wary Catharine de' Medici herself.[1] Bent upon carrying out their determination to have but one religion in France, yet reluctant to plunge at once into a costly and sanguinary struggle so soon after the return of much-desired peace, the states general resolved to try again the paths of diplomacy. On what grounds, moral or probable, they imagined that the King of Navarre, the Prince of Condé, or even Marshal Damville could be induced to acquiesce in the proscription of the Protestant faith does not appear. Certain, however, it is that the states gravely made a selection of deputies, carefully drew up instructions for their guidance, and sent them out on their whimsical mission.[2]

The three orders were represented, in the delegation to the King of Navarre, by the Archbishop of Vienne, Chevalier Rubempré, and Monsieur Mesnaigier. Long and ably did they labor with the king, whom they found at Agen just returned from the siege of the town of Marmande. They told him of the regret the states experienced at his failure to come to Blois. They tried to persuade him that ancient and modern history alike teach that a diversity of religion is alone sufficient to unsettle a nation. "The states general," said they, "have, to their great sorrow, learned by experience that the toleration of the exercise of a religion contrary to the true religion, which is no other than the Catholic, Apostolic, and Roman Church, can but bring a perpetual war, and the final ruin of both parties." The states therefore begged the King of Navarre to acquiesce in the petition which they had made to his most Christian Majesty to suffer no other religion than the Roman Catholic throughout France.

Envoys sent by the states general to Henry of Navarre.

---

cueil des choses mémorables, 587, 588 ; De Thou, v. 343 ; Agrippa d'Aubigné, ii. 251, 252.   [1] Lestoile, i. 80, 81.

[2] The envoys were selected before the close of the old year. See Saracini to the Grand Duke, December 28, 1576, Négociations avec la Toscane, iv. 96. Their instructions were read January 2d, and adopted on the 4th of the same month, and the envoys started for Gascony on the 6th. Mémoires de Nevers, i. 452 ; De Thou, v. 344.

That the recent edict of pacification could not be executed was the point which the deputies next attempted to prove, by reference to the disturbances alleged to have resulted from it in various places, to the annoyances inflicted upon the "poor Catholics" residing in the neighborhood of the cities pledged to the Protestants, and to the disappointment connected with the "chambre mi-partie." A more serious matter was broached when the deputies came to defend the violation of the solemn oath given by the monarch to maintain the edict of 1576; and the ground was distinctly taken that the king cannot pledge his word to the prejudice of his entire state and of the ancient customs of the kingdom. Now, the profession of the Catholic religion, they argued, is not merely an ancient custom; it is the chief and fundamental law of the realm, and the essential form that gives to the kings of France the name and title of "Christian." The oath upon the crucifix taken by the king at his coronation, and by all royal officers at their assumption of office, is as unchangeable as the Salic law, being even more fundamental; and neither king nor officer can henceforth depart from it for any reason, occasion, or pretext whatsoever. That oath cannot be superseded by any edict, much less by such an edict as that now in question, the very reading of which proves that it was extorted by force and by the violence of the times. The deputies assured the King of Navarre, however, that they were expressly authorized to promise the adherents of the new opinion—"ceux de la nouvelle opinion"—that they would not be molested. In fact, the states—such was their "extreme desire to see a good and immortal peace" in France—had not only commissioned them to offer to take the necessary oath to maintain it, but to state that they would petition the king to take a like oath and to impose it upon all princes, lords, and gentlemen whom it might concern. Nothing seems to have been said respecting any means to be taken for rendering the new oath any more binding than the oath given to maintain the "perpetual and irrevocable" edict which it was now proposed to repudiate.[1]

---

[1] "Instruction des gens des trois estats du royaume de France. . . . baillée icelle instruction à Monsieur l'archevesque de Vienne, à Monsieur

Henry of Navarre listened respectfully to the message from Blois. He is even recorded to have shed tears as the eloquent Archbishop of Vienne hinted at the disasters likely to befall him, should he turn a deaf ear, as the archbishop suggested that possibly the states general might conclude to declare all that should hereafter take arms against the king or come to an understanding with foreigners incapable of holding office or of succeeding to any dignities and especially to the crown.[1] But his written reply, although perhaps more conciliatory than was required by the circumstances of the case, was a distinct declaration that Henry cast in his lot with the Protestants. Although he praised the states general for their zeal, Navarre frankly expressed his fear that their request for the toleration of but one religion would entail new disturbances more pregnant with disaster than any previous struggle; for now, the view having once been formally sanctioned that the king is powerless to plight his faith, no secure accommodation with the Huguenots could be made. Henceforth the struggle must go on to the bitter end. Besides, it is one thing to deprive men of what has been given them and quite another not to have granted it to them at first. If it cuts to the heart the Roman Catholics, who have always enjoyed unmolested exercise of their religion, merely to see the Protestants enjoy the right of worship, it will irritate the Protestants far more to attempt to rob them of the right so often and so long permitted. Moreover, be it remembered that the oftener and the more vigorously it has been undertaken to abolish the reformed faith in France, the greater has been the decadence of the Catholic Church and its ecclesiastical order. And, in fact, the experience of France has been but the counterpart of that of Hungary, Bohemia, Germany, Scot-

The King of Navarre's reply.

Rubempré, Chevallier de l'Ordre du Roy, et à Monsieur Mesnaigier, General des finances de Languedoc, envoyez vers le Roy de Navarre." Blois, January 4, 1577. Mémoires de Nevers, i. 445-452.

[1] "Que peut-estre ils concluront à declarer que tous les biens de ceux qui prendront les armes contre le roy à l'advenir, ou qui auront intelligence avec les estrangers, seront confisquez, et eux incapables de toutes successions, dignitez et offices, et mesmement de la couronne." Ibid., i. 457.

land, and other countries. Everywhere Protestantism has baffled the attempt to annihilate it. Even if this religion were an error and a heresy—which it is not—it ought to be and can be removed by no such political gathering as that of the states general, but rather by an œcumenical council, free and lawfully assembled, or by a national council, in which all sides will gain a hearing. To the particular request addressed to him by the states general that he should aid them in securing the exclusion of every form of worship except the Romish, and consequently that he should forsake the religion he now professes, Henry of Navarre makes the following reply, significant in the light of subsequent events : "I am accustomed to pray to God every day, and I pray to Him now, in accordance with my belief, that He may be pleased to confirm and assure me in the grace of holding it inviolable ; and that, if it be bad, He may be pleased to enlighten my understanding, to show me the good, and give me the will to follow and embrace it, and to live and die in it, and after expelling from my spirit all errors, to grant me the strength and the means to help in expelling it from this kingdom, and, if possible, from the whole world." [1]

Henry's significant assurance.

In striking contrast with Navarre's studied politeness and conciliatory words was the determined attitude of the Prince of

---

[1] "Et après avoir chassé de son esprit tous les erreurs, luy donner force et moyen pour l'aider à la chasser de ce royaume, et de tout le monde, s'il est possible." Response du roy de Navarre à l'instruction des deputez, Mémoires de Nevers, i. 453-457. Hereupon Mr. Browning (History of the Huguenots, ii. 68) aptly remarks : "This declaration is highly characteristic of the epoch. He was at the time in arms for liberty of conscience, and yet declared his readiness to become a persecutor, if a change took place in his opinions." —That the reader may fully understand the case, he ought to be put in possession of two additional facts : 1st. That Henry of Navarre took pains, in the course of his answer, to clear himself of all responsibility for the proscription of the Roman Catholic religion in the principality of Bearn by his mother, Jeanne d'Albret. 2d. That, although the Protestant ministers disapproved and erased from the draft of the answer the sentence in which the king alluded to a possible conversion to the Romish faith, Henry insisted upon reinserting the objectionable passage. Agrippa d'Aubigné, ii. 259. This historian adds that the archbishop made Navarre's submissive words even more humble in his report than they were in the written reply.

Condé. The two cousins were of different natures. It must, indeed, be remembered that, while Henry of Navarre was, as he never failed to remind the deputies of the states and all others with whom he had dealings, the "third personage in the kingdom,"[1] the other Henry stood too far removed to entertain any expectations of succeeding to the crown of France. But history will not permit us to forget the constancy of the prince and the moral weakness of the Navarrese king at the massacre of Saint Bartholomew's Day, when not the possible attainment of a crown, but preservation of life, was in question.[2] On the present occasion, while Navarre bandied compliments with the Archbishop of Vienne, Condé, at Saint Jean d'Angely, absolutely refused to recognize the Bishop of Autun and his companions coming in the name of the states. The letter of which they were the bearers was returned to them unopened. The prince declared to the envoys that he would rather be buried in the depths of the earth than yield consent to the pernicious projects of those who had allowed themselves to be bribed by the sworn enemies of the crown. He honored and loved the clergy, he would do everything in his power to maintain the noblesse, and he pitied the members of the third estate because of the ruin impending over their heads; for these pretended states general were going to cut their throats. But he refused to acknowledge the convocation at Blois as a body representing the three orders of the kingdom.[3] About the same time (on the twenty-third of January) Condé put forth a printed protest, at La Rochelle, against the action of the "suborned and corrupted states that have been held in Blois." In this document the attempted suppression of the reformed religion was described as a breach of the public faith and of sacred oaths, and attributed to the king's evil counsellors, pensioners of the King of Spain—the same unpatriotic men that sought to pro-

---

[1] "Ayant cet honneur d'estre la troisième personne de France." Responce du roy de Navarre, Mémoires de Nevers, i. 456. See Stähelin, Der Uebertritt König Heinrichs des Vierten, 57.

[2] Rise of the Huguenots, ii. 468, 469.

[3] Recueil des choses mémorables, 589; De Thou, v. 352, 353.

long their tenure of power by plunging their native land in discord and wretchedness, and by causing the monarch to reject the proffer of the protectorate of Flanders and Artois, and decline the gift of the seigniory of Genoa. Under these circumstances the prince announced his resumption of arms, "by command and under the authority of the King of Navarre, prince primate of France, protector of the Reformed Churches and the associated Catholics, and royal lieutenant in Guyenne." He swore not to lay down his arms until he had re-established the kingdom in its full splendor and dignity, restored liberty to the states and authority to the edicts, and delivered the poor people from the insupportable tributes invented by the Italians.[1]

If Marshal Damville's reply to the message of the states was less belligerent, his representations of the disastrous results likely to follow the repeal of the edict of pacification were equally strong. Both in his communication to the states and in a document written, soon after, in answer to an announcement from the king himself,[2] the marshal, while laying great stress on the piety of the Montmorencies as descendants of "the first Christian baron," frankly set forth his conviction that recent events in his own province of Languedoc had disproved the old fallacy that diversity of religious faith necessarily entails enmity. "Since the so happy peace granted by God and by his majesty—a peace supposed by everyone to be perpetual, the hearts of men, especially in this government, had rid themselves of the veil of passion, and had become convinced that it is easy for persons of two different religions to bear with each other in a friendly fashion as true compatriots."[3] And this fact the mar-

Marshal Damville's reply to the states and to the king.

---

[1] "Les Protestations de M. le Prince de Condé, estant lors à la Rochelle, apportés en ce lieu de Blois, le deuxième de Février." Mémoires de Nevers, i. 470, 471. Also in Agrippa d'Aubigné, ii. 236–8.

[2] For a summary of the former see Agrippa d'Aubigné, ii. 260, 261 ; for the text of the latter, "Instruction du Mareschal de Dampville au Sieur Doignon, chevalier de l'ordre du Roi, envoyé vers ledit mareschal en febvrier, 1577." J. Loutchitzky, Documents inédits pour servir à l'histoire de la Réforme et de la Ligue (1875), 56–60.

[3] "Avoient jugé et conneu quil est aise de se compatir amiablement en deux religions comme vrais compatriottes." Loutchitzky, 57.

shal established by a reference to the recent agreement entered into by the provincial states of Languedoc, meeting at Beziers, which had sworn, before Damville and Joyeuse, to live according to the provisions of the royal edict of pacification—an agreement all the more significant, because, of those that made it, more than two hundred were of the old faith, and not six were of the reformed religion.

Surely the idea of religious toleration had made good and substantial progress when a marshal of France, a son of the grim constable Anne de Montmorency, could feel it necessary to "discharge his conscience," as he affirmed, both to the states general and to his king, by the advocacy of such views. But Damville went further. He plainly told Henry the Third and the states that, though their desire for one single religion in France was good, the method proposed for the attainment of the end was bad. Ill-success in the past, he urged, has taught us this. "It is to be believed that this diversity of religion is a matter which God has to do with, and that He has reserved the cure of it to Himself alone. We must, therefore, resign everything to His providence and goodness, and heal this disease by the good and holy conduct of churchmen, or by a good council, which is the true remedy for religious maladies, without resorting to idle means and aggravating it still further by violence."[1]

Progress of religious toleration.

Meanwhile, the associations for the defence of the Roman Catholic faith had been spreading with more rapidity, now that the king had himself given them formal sanction and had empowered his own officers to engage in the work of obtaining signatures to the roll of their members.[2] Henry indeed seemed

---

[1] "Il a à croire que ceste diversité de relligion touche à Dieu et luy seul s'est retenu le remede dicelle," etc. Loutchitzky, 58.

[2] See the articles of several associations, *e.g.*, of Moulins (Bourbonnois), dated January 22, 1577; of Dijon (Burgundy); and of Troyes (Champagne) dated March 22, 1577, in Loutchitzky, Documents inédits pour servir à l'histoire de la Réforme et de la Ligue, 34, 35–37, 37–39. From the minutes of the council of the city of Toulouse, from December 23, 1576, to March 20, 1577, the gradual spread of the League by the confederation of other cities and districts —Verdun, Quercy, etc.—may be traced. Ibid., 25–29.

to count upon the troops which the associations could set on foot as an important element of his military forces, and his trusty counsellors were carefully considering whether these men could most advantageously be employed in the field or in defending their own homes.[1] Not everywhere, however, was it easy to disarm the apprehensions of the citizens, grown pardonably suspicious through their past experience. In Paris, when the copies of the manifesto of the League were carried around from house to house to receive the signatures of the burgesses, the best citizens either signed with restrictions or absolutely declined to have anything to do with the paper, and denounced it as a new device of oppression and extortion. As for the authorities of the city itself, upon whom Henry had called for a sum of money to pay five thousand foot and two thousand horse to be employed in this sacred cause, they positively refused to accede to his plan, denouncing it as an absurdity to hope in so summary a way to do away with a religion that had outstood sixteen years of war, and they prophesied that the League would prove a detriment rather than an advantage to the royal cause.[2] At Amiens the people repelled by force a troop of Picard gentry and soldiers, with M. d'Humières at their head, who wished to compel them to subscribe to the League. Afterwards Amiens sent deputies to Henry, offering the king six thousand livres to be exempted from signing the obnoxious compact ; and his majesty, who asked nothing better than such refusals if he might obtain such offers, readily consented.[3] In the little town of Provins, whither the king had sent M. de Rosne, the three orders of the bailiwick deliberated maturely upon the proposition submitted to them, and came to a very sensible conclusion. "The League," said they, "is a novelty. We have never seen or heard the like in France. Our deputies are yet at Blois, and whether they have accepted or refused the League we know not.

---

[1] The latter was the view of L'Aubespine, Bishop of Limoges. Mémoires de Nevers, i. 271.
[2] Lestoile, under date of February 1st, ii. 83 ; Agrippa d'Aubigné, ii. 253-56 : Saracini to the grand duke, January 30, 1577, Négociations avec la Toscane, iv. 107.   [3] Lestoile, February 15th, i. 83.

There is no need of our taking an oath to maintain the only religion practised in this region, nor of binding the three orders by their signatures to furnish the king with money which they have never refused to give him. We cannot sign the League without knowing what the other cities of France have done, and especially Paris, the capital of the realm and the nursing mother of kings."[1] Great was the disgust of the royal envoy, who had confidently expected to reap a rich harvest in the management of the funds to be raised by the poor inhabitants for the support of the new "crusade." But for want of a better way of venting his vexation, he confined himself, when next he desired to enter Provins, to climbing deliberately over the insignificant walls and making his way in, followed by his suite—a derisive act that called down upon his unfortunate head much impotent wrath.[2]

In point of fact the "Sacred League" was by no means in a very sound or healthy state. With all the efforts put forth in its behalf, the people, utterly exhausted by the weight of their present burdens, refused to bend their necks to the fresh yoke. What they longed for was peace—peace at any price. Everywhere throughout France despair seemed to have seized the laboring classes. In Poitou and Guyenne it assumed a startling shape. As the nobleman whom the king had sent to confer with Henry of Navarre was passing through the region, the peasants flocked by hundreds to the roadside. They threw themselves on their knees or prostrated themselves in the dust before him. "If the king intends to continue the war," they cried, "we very humbly beg him to be pleased to cut our throats at once and put us out of our misery."[3] The harmony of the deputies at Blois was

Distress of the people.

---

[1] Claude Haton's account is, as usual, long and circumstantial. Mémoires, ii. 881–887.

[2] The curate of Mériot saw in the contemptuous act of M. de Rosne nothing less than sheer treason, and the Provinois punsters of the day, playing upon his name, took occasion to predict the total ruin of the city, now that so great a river had come all the way from Lyons to overflow their fortifications. Ibid., ii. 888.

[3] "Si le roy vouloit continuer la guerre, qu'il lui pleust leur faire couper la gorge, sans tant les faire languir." Lestoile, i. 84. It is a suggestive com-

more apparent than real. The members of the third estate had never been fully reconciled to the ideas of the two upper orders. They grumbled at the blunder of Versoris in neglecting to follow his instructions. Not content with their first ineffectual attempts to induce the clergy and the nobles to unite with them in reopening the matter and seeking the re-enactment of the despised edict, they took advantage of the pacific report of the Duke of Montpensier to which reference will shortly be made. After thanking the duke for his humane and sensible advice, they left the church of Saint Sauveur and proceeded in a body to the hôtel de ville. Here they promptly took action, begging Henry to reunite his subjects peaceably, and, in proof of their assertion that this had been their original desire, appended to their petition a copy of their grossly misrepresented action of the fifteenth of January. In vain did the advocates of war place obstacles in the way, alleging, among other things, that the states general had lost too many members, by the return of deputies to their homes, to be competent to transact business; Jean Bodin was more than a match for the objectors in legal erudition, and proved that a quorum of two-thirds of a deliberative assembly was possessed of all the powers of the entire body. Moreover, drawing upon that favorite treasury of illustration, the laws and customs of the ancients, he showed that the Romans had not suffered war to be declared without the formal consent of the largest representation of the state, whereas they permitted the conclusion of peace in the easiest way. The end of the whole matter was that the third estate drew up and presented to the king, on the twenty-seventh of February, a petition wherein the policy of peace was distinctly and forcibly enunciated.[1]

The tiers état for peace.

---

mentary upon this touching incident that some of the king's counsellors deliberately recommended his laying waste the provinces of Guyenne and Languedoc, burning the crops, and reducing the inhabitants to the last straits, in order that the people in their despair might rise against Navarre and Damville! Saracini, in his letter of February 13, 1577, records both the fact that the diabolic counsel was given, and the fact that Henry (be it said to his honor) rejected it. Négociations avec la Toscane, iv. 109.

[1] Agrippa d'Aubigné, ii. 262, 263, states the facts at length, and inserts the whole of the petition.

Other causes contributed to dampen the warlike zeal which Henry and his mother had lately affected. Too much stress ought not perhaps to be laid upon the arguments of the Protestant deputies, of whom two bodies had for some weeks been at Blois, and who, although they took good care not to recognize the validity of the pretended states general, were unremitting in their efforts to further the interests of their brethren. A deeper impression was apparently made by the words of Duke John Casimir, in whose name Beutrich, a bold and experienced ambassador, again made his appearance. For the blunt envoy was not careful to measure his words according to the rule of over-mild and courteous diplomacy. He remonstrated against the bad faith of the French court, and asked what likelihood there was that promises which the exhausted condition of the kingdom had not permitted Henry to keep in time of peace would be fulfilled when he should once more plunge into a new and needless war. Not content with this, Casimir's ambassador presented to the king a document whereby he renounced, in his master's name, all the personal honors and privileges conferred upon the duke by the late treaty, and intimated that Casimir held himself relieved of any reciprocal obligations. In fact, while asking for his passports, Beutrich made no attempt to disguise his intention of crossing the Channel in furtherance of the projected Protestant counter-league.[1] The covert threat was not without effect; especially when Henry received from his own agents information that the duke had taken his defiant course in consequence of promises from Queen Elizabeth that he should be appointed to the command of all the troops hereafter brought into the field by the Protestant confederates.[2]

Intercession of the Germans.

The Protestant counter-league.

---

[1] De Thou, v. 358, 359; Recueil des choses mémorables, 591; Languet, i. 290. The text of Peter Beutrich's letter to Henry III., dated March 7, 1577, is given by Groen van Prinsterer, vi. 56. "Son excellence m'a commandé," he wrote, "de remettre entre les mains de V. M., avant mon départ de vostre cour, toutes les terres et estats desquels il vous a pleu le gratifier puis naguères." The reason assigned was the circulation of rumors, both in Germany and in France, that these personal advantages prevented him from a manly advocacy of the rights of the troops that had followed him into France.

[2] Gaspard de Schomberg to Henry III., April 8, 1577, Groen van Prinsterer,

But what influenced the king more than Huguenot remonstrances or German threats—more even than the poor success attending the studied misrepresentations of his tool Villequier with the Langrave of Hesse and the other princes beyond the Rhine[1]—was the impossibility his majesty encountered of extracting money from the already depleted purses of his subjects. That war cannot be carried on without the means for the purchase of military stores and for the payment of soldiers, was an axiom none could have been found bold enough to deny. That Henry even in time of peace was always in want of money was equally notorious. He was ready to borrow on the right and on the left, of his own subjects or of foreigners. His penury led him from time to time to have recourse to the most impolitic and ruinous expedients. In July, this same year, he signed an edict by which he authorized the sale to one person in every parish of the kingdom of perpetual exemption from the burdens of taxation, from all forms of "tailles," as well as from other "imposts."[2] Little cared this degenerate king for the next generation, foreseeing—if, indeed, he foresaw anything—that with him the race of Valois on the throne of France would become extinct. Happily there were in the states general men who did care. So when Henry, having lost all hope of procuring new taxes, desired the sanction of the states to a sale of a portion of the royal domain, the delegates of the people, with the unterrified Bodin again at their head, refused to permit the alienation of property which did not belong to any one man, but to the nation as such.[3] It was evident that the people had learned something; they would not pour their resources into the leaky treasury of a monarch whose prodigality predestined him to impoverish not only himself but his subjects.

The king fails to obtain funds.

---

ubi supra. The rumor of the Protestant counter-league, it was reported, dampened the zeal of many persons who were on the point of joining the Roman Catholic League. Mémoires de Henry III., 20, 21.

[1] See Von Polenz, iv. 91–102 ; De Thou, v. 360–64 ; Recueil des choses mémorables, 591, 592.

[2] Isambert, Recueil des anciennes lois françaises, xiv. 337, where the title of the edict alone is given.   [3] De Thou, v. 347, 348, 355.

Another royal council was held, ostensibly to obtain advice, in reality to obtain a pretext for undoing everything that had been done. The occasion was the return of the Duke of Montpensier from a mission to Henry of Navarre, more than ever convinced of the absurdity of a new attempt to crush the Huguenots. The three cardinals—Bourbon, Guise, and Este—with a few laymen, were still eager for the suppression of heresy by force of arms, if need be. The Duke of Nevers, always a fiery advocate of the Roman Catholic Church, distinguished himself for his urgency. "What will men think, Sire," said he, "but that your zeal toward God has grown cold, if you are seen to change your purpose without any new necessity. And as to the divine side of the matter, do what you can, and God will do the rest. So did your predecessor, Saint Louis, who when he had lost one battle in Holy Land, fighting against the enemies of God's name, did not lose courage, but returned thither again."

Fresh consultation about the war.

Nevers proposes a crusade.

But the partisans of pacific measures—Morvilliers, Cossé, Biron, Montpensier, and his son the Prince Dauphin, and others—were not less outspoken; especially as it was no secret that Catharine was now quite as resolved to have peace as she had been, a few weeks before, to have war. For had she not of late hinted that it might be well to allow a little latitude in religion, until such time as a general council might be convened —a tolerant suggestion which the amiable Cardinal of Bourbon met with the truculent remark that he would himself be happy to act as the hangman of his two Huguenot nephews.[1] Had she not by her intercessions with the king called down upon her head his hot displeasure? "This is the third time you have spoken to me of peace," he had said. "If you loved my interests you would not seek to persuade me. Do not speak to me again about the matter."[2] The queen-mother's speech on the present occasion deserves attention on many accounts.

"My son," said Catharine, who had listened impatiently to

---

[1] Diary of Nevers, under date of February 9, 1577; Mémoires, i. 172.

[2] This interesting incident is related by Saracini, in his letter of February 13, 1577; Négociations avec la Toscane, iv. 110.

Nevers' plea, "you know that I was among the first to advise you to permit but one religion in your realm, and that I told you that you must make use to this end of the states general which are here met. You know, moreover, what practices, what dealings, I have had with the deputies of the three orders; especially with the Archbishop of Lyons, who at first was opposed to action.[1] So, too, with many others of the church, the noblesse, and the tiers état, to whom, by your command, I spoke, and whom I brought to this resolution. And, to tell the truth, they could never have gone so far, but for your command, since most of them alleged that they had no such powers conferred upon them by their instructions. Thereby it may be seen that my intention has always been that there should be but one Catholic and Roman religion in your kingdom. Accordingly, the maintenance of that religion has been my aim ever since your brother's accession to the throne, sixteen years ago. This will enable me to speak with the greater boldness.

Catharine becomes an outspoken advocate of peace.

"I am a Catholic, and have as good a conscience as anyone else can have," the queen mother proceeded. "Many a time, during the reign of the late king, have I exposed my life against the Huguenots. That is not what I fear. I am ready to die, for I am fifty-eight years old, and I hope to go to paradise. What I do not desire is to outlive my children, which would give me a cruel death indeed.

"I feel compelled to say, however, that until you have the means of executing this resolution to tolerate but a single religion, you ought not to declare yourself. If your predecessors went on a crusade to Constantinople, it was because the kingdom was at peace. Had they been situated as you are, they would have done as you do. You see what the King of Spain has done to his subjects in Netherlands, to whom he has granted the exercise of their religion in Zealand, Friesland, and Holland. It would be no novel thing for you to permit the exercise of the 'religion' in places where you cannot prevent it. Foreign princes, and even the Pope, will rejoice at learning this

---

[1] "Qui du commencement n'y vouloit pas mordre."

declaration, and will be glad that matters have been settled without a resort to arms. As to myself, I do not wish to gain credit among the Catholics for having destroyed this kingdom. I have no object but to preserve it. In its destruction the destruction of religion also is involved. On the contrary, if this kingdom be preserved, religion will also be preserved.

"We have scant means for carrying on war; we have scarcely the means of subsistence. The Prince of Condé will take the cities and all the open country. Hitherto nothing has been able to resist him. So far as I am concerned, because of the interest I have in them, I crave not to see the state nor the person of the king thus endangered. There may be others who care nothing for the loss of this commonwealth, provided they can say, 'I have faithfully maintained the Catholic religion,' or who hope to profit by its overthrow. I have nothing to say about them; but, for myself, I do not desire to resemble them. I advise you, therefore, to preserve your kingdom and your own person also; hoping that God may so favor you as that some day you may succeed in uniting the two religions in one."[1]

Such was the speech of Catharine de' Medici, as it has been handed down to us by one who seems to have written it down afterward from memory. Insincere and unprincipled as was the woman that made it, false to her own conscience and to her God as was the tongue that uttered such professions of piety and devotion, while the hands were yet gory with the blood of ten thousands of murdered innocents, the address itself illustrates, better than any words of comment could illustrate, the singular character of that vacillating princess, with whose ambition and with whose fears the fates of the Huguenots were so closely linked.

Henry's speech was more brief, but clearly revealed that his mind was fully made up. "Gentlemen," said he, "everybody has seen how zealously I embraced what was for God's honor, and how ardently I desired to see but one religion in my kingdom. I have even sued, if so I must speak, for the support of the members of the three estates, who were but lukewarm, urging them to ask for a single

<small>Henry declares his change of purpose.</small>

---

[1] Journal de Nevers, Mémoires, i. 175, 176.

religion, in the belief that they would aid me in carrying out so holy a resolution. But the sight of the slender means they have given me has enlightened me as to the little hope there is that I shall be able to execute my first intention. However, as Monsieur de Nevers says, one may change one's opinions when there is occasion. For myself, I do not think I fail in my duty if I do not now declare that I will suffer only one religion in my realm, since I have not the means to execute such a declaration. I desire my intention to be known, so that it may not be misrepresented outside of the council. I regard myself as more attached than anyone else to my religion; though there are those who, in order to be called pillars of the church, say everything that comes into their heads. It is my will, therefore, that this article of religion be left till after the conclusion of all the rest."

Delay under the circumstances was equivalent to defeat. The council broke up. Catharine de' Medici did not disguise her satisfaction. She went out, making light of the discomfiture of the belligerent party, and exclaiming to poor Nevers, with her accustomed raillery: "How so, cousin, did you want to send us to Constantinople?" A jest that she laughingly repeated to all whom she met.[1]

<small>Catharine's raillery.</small>

The time for the "crusade" had not come, and certainly neither Catharine de' Medici nor Henry of Valois was exactly another Saint Louis. None the less, however, had the French court a war upon its hands that must drag its slow length along for the coming six months, and could not be dismissed with as little ceremony as the now hateful states general of Blois. Meantime, both the queen-mother and king were disposed not to forego their wonted delights. Henry had secured from Italy a company of comedians, known as "I Gelosi," men unsurpassed for skill in lewd song and play, actors whose indecencies had even incurred the reprehension of the Parliament of Paris.[2] He prided himself upon the ac-

<small>The Italian comedians.</small>

---

[1] "Comment, mon cousin, vous nous vouliez envoyer à Constantinople?" Journal de Nevers, Mémoires, i. 177.

[2] Mémoires de Henry III., 23.

quisition, we are informed, as much as upon the conquest of a new kingdom, and Catharine was almost equally delighted. So when Cardinal Bourbon tried to induce the king to forbid the performances during Lent, the queen mother requested the prelate to forbear any further attempts to persuade his majesty to renew "his devotions of Avignon where he never left the Jesuits for a single moment."[1]

The short conflict to which the designation of the sixth civil or religious war has been given presents fewer incidents of note than any of the preceding contests in which the Huguenots were forced to engage. Of the two great armies set on foot for their destruction, the eastern descended upon the city of La Charité, and aimed to cut off all possible communication between the Protestants and their former allies beyond the Rhine. The western army was intended to overwhelm Poitou and Saintonge, and to wrest La Rochelle itself from the hands of those who tightly held it as their best place of refuge on the coasts of the ocean. The command of the eastern army was confided to the Duke of Anjou, as nominal leader. For the young prince had now obtained, as the seal of reconciliation with his mother and his brother, the coveted rank and title of lieutenant-general of the kingdom. Under him served the Dukes of Guise, Aumale, and Nevers, with Biron in charge of the artillery, making up by their own military skill and experience for Anjou's incompetence. The fruits of the campaign were seen in the important captures of La Charité on the Loire, and of Issoire and Ambert, in Auvergne. Nor was the Duke of Mayenne, younger brother of Guise, less fortunate in the conduct of the western forces. Brouage, next to La Rochelle itself the most important maritime post of the Huguenots, and the Ile d'Oléron, were the rewards of his well-directed assaults and superior numbers. Everywhere the Protestants lost ground. Henry of Navarre accomplished little or nothing; his adventurous dash upon Marmande turned out disastrously. So uniform was the ill-success attending the efforts of the Huguenots, that they long remembered and dis-

The sixth civil war.

---

[1] Journal de Nevers, Mémoires, i. 173.

tinguished this as "the year of evil tidings"—"l'année des mauvaises nouvelles."[1]

Much of this ill-success was indeed the natural result of their own faults. Dissension and division were rife in their ranks. The old discipline had of late suffered a grievous decline. The Huguenot soldiers, to use Agrippa d'Aubigné's expressive words, from "reformed" had become "deformed."[2] In the King of Navarre's court there were open quarrels between Henry's Roman Catholic followers and his stanch Huguenot followers, and the latter were not a little disgusted, and in part alienated, as they noticed that the Bearnese was more anxious to make sure of the Roman Catholics, by the display of extraordinary favor, than to satisfy the just expectations of the Protestant noblemen who espoused his cause from affection.[3]

Huguenot ill-success and lack of discipline.

The most sensible loss sustained by the Huguenots was the withdrawal of Marshal Damville, who not long after his brave answer to the States of Blois renounced the alliance which for more than two years had subsisted between the Protestants of Languedoc and himself.

The disputes that led to this unhappy result would scarcely deserve special mention did they not obtain importance as bringing into prominence certain tendencies of the period and of the Huguenot party.

In its early stages, the Reformation had been accused of aiming at the subversion of the constituted order of government. A change of religion, said the Romish prelates, necessarily involves mutation in the state. Francis the First had been taught this as an axiomatic truth. Somewhat later, it was maintained, with more precision of calumny, that the Huguenots, full of admiration for Swiss institutions, would be content with nothing short of substitut-

The Reformation and democracy.

---

[1] Lestoile, i. 87.—On the campaign in the east, see Recueil des choses mémorables, 593; De Thou, v. 370-373; Claude Haton, ii. 889-894; Agrippa d'Aubigné, ii. 281-283. On the western operations, see Recueil, 593-596; De Thou, v. 382-391, etc.
[2] Agrippa d'Aubigné, ii. 273.
[3] Ibid., ii. 284, 285.

ing for the existing monarchical system an association of cantons modelled on the pattern of Berne and Zurich. No valid proof was brought to substantiate the charge, nor is there any reason to believe that the thought of revolution was ever entertained. Yet, while the loyalty of the French Protestants must be regarded as having been above just suspicion, it is equally certain that the religious doctrines they had espoused were adapted to awaken in the breast of the people the consciousness of innate and indefeasible rights. This consciousness was sure, ultimately, to overthrow the entire fabric of despotism, both in state and in church, involving in the general destruction the prescriptive claims of the privileged classes and much-prized exemptions from burdens of taxation and service. The Reformation knew not that it was laying the foundations of democracy, and would have resented the imputation as slanderous; none the less did the Reformation lead inevitably to a recognition of the natural claim of the humblest citizen to the equal protection of the law, and to a share in the government of the state. So far it was true that the Reformation tended of necessity to the development of democratical institutions.

There was another equally unmistakable tendency in the age—the tendency toward the revival of feudalism in France, to which allusion had already been made. If the unconscious aspirations of the Reformation could meet their fulfilment only in the political freedom and equality of the nineteenth century, the re-establishment of great feudal lords, with their inferior and dependent barons, in every part of the country, recalled the ideas of the Middle Ages, and aggravated the oppressive yoke resting upon the neck of the people. Manifestly the Reformation and feudalism were natural enemies, and must, sooner or later, come into collision. Marshal Damville had, indeed, become a confederate of the Protestants of the South, but the alliance was the fruit of political exigencies, and was too abnormal to last. The governor of Languedoc, little less than a king in his extensive province, could no more look with complacency upon the reformed churches, with their popular organization and well-graduated representative government, than the consistories and synods,

Contrast with revived feudalism.

provincial and national, of the Huguenots could heartily submit to the control of the dissolute and arbitrary Montmorency.

Misunderstandings and suspicions arose from the very first. Damville was an undisguised Roman Catholic, and made no pretence of sympathy with the religious views of his allies. He did, indeed, affect much interest in the relief by the tiers état, and proclaimed himself the "liberator of the commonwealth;" but he never forgot that he was descended from the "first Christian baron," or overlooked the wide gulf separating a nobleman of his rank from the plebeian inhabitants of the Huguenot towns and villages of Languedoc. On the other hand, the Huguenots felt by no means sure that the marshal's high birth could make him a judicious governor, or that a man noted for his lavishness of his own property would administer the common funds with strict integrity and in the most economical way. They insisted, therefore, that he should do nothing without consulting a council which they themselves had given him, and they kept strict watch over the treasury. As time advanced, the mutual distrust grew. It was currently reported among the Protestants that the marshal, anxious to enter again into the king's good graces, had lately sent his wife to court, and had easily obtained forgiveness, on the condition of breaking away from his allies and turning his arms against them. At first, however, few thought that Damville would carry his new plans into execution without giving formal notice of his intentions to his late associates.[1]

It is not unlikely that the Huguenots of Languedoc, and their brethren in other parts of France, were inclined to be too suspicious. Perhaps, however, an impartial observer will pardon them if, after the Parisian matins and some kindred surprises, a childlike trust in Roman Catholic allies was not a leading feature in their character. Be this as it may, it was not many days after Marshal Damville had despatched his trusty messenger to the king with a noble plea in favor of toleration [2] before

---

[1] Mémoires de Jacques Gaches, 239.   [2] Ante, p. 147.

he received the unwelcome intelligence that the Huguenot inhabitants of Montpellier had risen, one Sunday night, the seventeenth of February, had made themselves masters of the city, and had elected young François de Châtillon governor of the city and district.[1] The town of Lunel, with its neighbors, Aimargues and Marsilargues, Aiguesmortes and Alais, followed the example of Montpellier. What rendered the act more vexatious was that the marshal's wife was at Montpellier, and his children had been left at Alais, so that his whole family appeared to have been made prisoners. Ten days later, a political assembly of the Huguenots of lower Languedoc, meeting at Lunel, approved the coup-de-main, and gave the reasons of it in thirty formidable articles. The sum was that the provisions of the compact of union had been disregarded, the decisions of the council reversed or nullified, and the finances grossly mismanaged. Protestants had been neglected, and Roman Catholics placed in office. The marshal had held communications with Rome and Savoy which he had not made known to the Protestants. He had retained traitors in his employ, had shown too little displeasure at the invitations of the king and the states general, and too much sluggishness in making his preparations for a war seen to be imminent, as though he had no intention to oppose the suppression of Protestantism resolved upon at Blois. To close the list of Damville's iniquities, he was held responsible for the imprudent or insolent reply of certain Roman Catholics of the "union," when deliberating on the answer to be returned to the deputies from Blois. "We are all in the same boat,"[2] said the Protestant deputies. "Not so!" answered their Roman Catholic allies. "It is only 'those of the religion' that the king

Surprise of Montpellier and other places.

Charges against Damville.

---

[1] François de Coligny, Sieur de Châtillon, was born April 28, 1557, and was therefore at this time but twenty years of age. See the transcript of the entries of the births of the various members of the family (two generations) in the "livre d'heures" of the Princess of Orange, made by her father, Admiral Coligny, and her grandmother, Louise de Montmorency. Bulletin de la Société de l'histoire du Protestantisme français, ii. 5-7. See, also, Count Jules Delaborde's biography, "François de Chastillon" (Paris, 1886).

[2] "Que nous estions tous embarquez dans ung mesme navire."

and states mean to attack."[1] The Lunel assembly dictated the only conditions upon which the "union" could be continued. There must be a council at Montpellier or Nismes, and the marshal must obey its decisions. The council alone must give commissions and pay out money. The cities must all have Protestant governors, and the Protestant cities must have Protestant consuls in addition.

It must be confessed that the Huguenot demands were great, and that some of the complaints appeared at first sight weak or frivolous. The marshal's answer made the most of these advantages. He accused his late allies of ingratitude, and maintained that, but for his timely aid, their cause would have been desperate. He dwelt with great effect upon the proofs he had given of confidence in their devotion to him, and made a frank and plausible reply to each successive article of the indictment. Having disposed of the charges as best he might, it was now the marshal's turn to comment upon what he termed the insufferable insolence displayed by the allies, not only in rising for such insufficient reasons and taking his wife and children prisoners, but in demanding the establishment of a council with sovereign powers. "In a word," said Damville, "they intend to assume the chair of state, and will issue their commands to the gentlemen, captains and soldiers, for the maintenance of their authority—a procedure tending to a republic rather than to any other form of government."[2] It was not the only time that the proud son of the constable indulged in a fling at the assuming burghers. But his supreme indignation was reserved for the head of "a little syndic" who had been so presumptuous as to call upon the marshal to take an oath to observe the Protestant articles at his hands. "Everybody knows," said Damville, "that, excepting the king, there is no one in France that can administer the oath to me."

The marshal's reply.

---

[1] "N'en vouloient qu'à ceux de la Religion."

[2] "Somme ilz seront dans une chaize et commanderont les gentilzhommes, cappitaines et soldats pour le soustien de leur auctorité, tendant plustost à la republicque qu'à autre domination." Le discours faict par Mr. le Marechal de Damville sur la rupture de l'union en l'an 77 respondant à tous les articles de ceulx de la religion. French Nat. Libr., MSS. Brienne. (Loutchitzky, 85.)

Clearly a partnership in which the persons interested entertained such conflicting notions of their respective positions and rights must be dissolved straightway. And this, however much Henry of Navarre and other cool heads might deplore the result. For the Béarnais was both surprised and pained—so he sent word to the Huguenots of Languedoc—at the discord that had sprung up in that part of France which had hitherto been a pattern of union and the chief strength of the Protestant cause. Suspicion might well be directed against enemies, but ought not to be encouraged in the case of friends like Damville, whose course had been so honorable that he dared pledge his own integrity for him. And he begged the Huguenots, in God's name and for the general good, not utterly to alienate their late ally, and thus play into the hands of the enemy, who now rejoiced as though seeing signs of the coming overthrow of the Protestant side.[1]

Navarre attempts to mediate.

Meantime the Huguenots of Languedoc, having broken with Marshal Damville, turned their eyes toward his younger brother, Guillaume de Montmorency, better known by his territorial designation as Seigneur de Thoré. The choice was a judicious one, suggested or approved by La Noue and Turenne, whom the King of Navarre had sent in haste to prevent Languedoc from falling into the power of the enemy. Thus did France behold the strange spectacle of two brothers at the head of armies and disputing with each other the possession of the most important province of the south—of another Roman Catholic of a most ancient family styling him-

Thoré becomes Huguenot leader in Languedoc.

---

[1] The defection of Marshal Damville is briefly referred to by the historians of the period, *e.g.*, Agrippa d'Aubigné, ii. 273, etc., but much the most satisfactory view of it can be obtained from the important original documents in the National Library of France, and published by Professor Loutchitzky in his Documents inédits pour servir à l'histoire de la Réforme et de la Ligue (Paris, 1875), pages 60–91. These consist of (1) the reasons set forth by the Assembly of Lunel, February 27, for breaking the union with Marshal Damville and seizing the cities; (2) the articles to be presented to him as conditions for renewing the union, adopted by the assembly on the same date; (3) Marshal Damville's answer, February; and (4) Henry of Navarre's instructions to the Seigneur de Ségur sent to the Protestants of Languedoc, dated at Aiguillon, May 25, 1577.

self "general commandant for the protection and defence of his Majesty's subjects making profession of the Reformed religion in the land and government of Languedoc, under the authority of the King of Navarre and Monseigneur the Prince of Condé."[1] As for brave Châtillon, whom his youth alone precluded from receiving an appointment which might have seemed more appropriate for him than for his cousin, the rescue of Montpellier from the overwhelming forces of Marshal Bellegarde constituted for him a new title of distinction. His exploit in breaking through the enemy's lines and returning within little more than a fortnight with a relief of five thousand men was the concluding event of the war.[2]

The struggle in which, since his disappointment in obtaining funds for carrying it on, Henry had lost all interest, was terminated, after the usual delays and diplomatic intrigues, by the sixth edict of pacification, known as the Edict of Poitiers, in the month of September, 1577.

In this document the liberal concessions made by the preceding Edict of Beaulieu were much curtailed. The Protestants were suffered to dwell unmolested in every part of the kingdom, but the public exercise of their worship was restricted to certain places. First, all noblemen possessed of the right of "haute justice" were permitted to have Protestant worship, for themselves and for all that chose to attend, in such place as they might designate as their chief residence. Second, the same noblemen could have worship open to all comers upon any of their other lands, but only so long as they themselves were present. Third, noblemen

The Edict of Poitiers (September, 1577) concludes the sixth civil war.

---

[1] Thoré takes this designation (in addition to his customary titles of privy counsellor, etc.) in a very interesting commission issued by him at Nismes, July 7, 1577, appointing a captain to raise troops for the purpose of checking the bands of ruffians that were laying waste the Protestant towns and villages of the Cevennes. The document is published in the Bulletin de la Société de l'histoire du Protestantisme français, vii. (1859) 398, 399.

[2] A glowing account in Agrippa d'Aubigné, ii. 311–313. The historian claims for himself that, having been sent to sound the disposition of Damville, although too late to prevent the marshal's defection, he was in time to prevent him from carrying over with him to the royal side any Protestant cities as helps to a reconciliation with his former foes. Ibid., ii. 267-273.

of lower jurisdiction were allowed worship at their residences for themselves and their families only. Fourth, the Protestants were authorized to continue the exercise of their religion in all cities and boroughs where it had been publicly practised at the date of the signature of the edict. Fifth, Protestant worship was granted in the suburbs of some one town or village in each bailiwick and sénéchaussée of the kingdom. So much for the most essential matter of the celebration of the rites of religion. Paris was, of course, excepted, with its neighborhood to the distance of ten leagues in every direction. So, too, the court of the king must not be polluted by the preaching of Protestant doctrine, by whatever else it might be polluted. Here the limit was fixed at two leagues only. The provision for the protection of the Protestants in the courts of law was also narrowed down. Instead of a "chambre mi-partie," composed of an equal number of judges of the two religions, and established in each of the eight parliaments, there were to be only four mixed tribunals (there were to be no mixed tribunals in Paris, Rouen, Dijon, and Rennes), and, instead of one-half, two-thirds of the judges were to be Roman Catholics.[1] On the other hand, Protestants were guaranteed admission into the universities and schools, and their poor and sick were promised assistance, on the same terms as Roman Catholics. As in the preceding pacification, eight cities were intrusted to the Protestants as pledges for their safety. The King of Navarre, the Prince of Condé, and twenty Protestant gentlemen were to swear, singly

---

[1] Michelet is, therefore, quite wrong in saying (La Ligue et Henri IV., p. 85) that there was to be "à chaque parlement une chambre protestante." The courts established for the protection of the Protestants in the four parliaments named in the text were not to be composed of Protestants (see article 21); and Agrippa d'Aubigné is correct in his brief statement (ii. 327): "Les chambres mi-parties biffees pour Paris, Rouen, Dijon, et Rennes. Aux autres quatre parlements des chambres ordonnées avec un des presidents reformé et le tiers des conseillers de mesme." Von Polenz well remarks (iv. 126, note) the difficulty and ungrateful character of the task of describing the edicts of pacification; as well as the difficulty arising from the vagueness and positive errors of the statements even of contemporaries. The circumstance that the edicts were never fairly carried out makes them a very unsatisfactory topic of discussion.

and collectively, to restore these cities to the king at the expiration of six years from the date of the edict.¹ A secret treaty signed at Bergerac treated of the marriage of priests and monks, of marriage within the prohibited degrees of consanguinity, and of other matters which it was thought prudent not to bring prominently to the public notice.²

France was sick of war. Everywhere there were rejoicings. Condé and the Rochellois were not more delighted than were the Parisians and the Roman Catholics, who had feared that the Protestants might be still better treated in the edict.³ The King of France and the King of Navarre each styled the document "his own edict." ⁴ The poor people said little or nothing that contemporary chroniclers have thought it worth while to transmit to posterity, but doubtless thanked God devoutedly for a little rest from bloodshed and rapine. Even the priests were glad that the war was over. One of their number could not suppress the observation that, seeing the terms of the edict of pacification were so similar to those of its predecessor, it would have been far better not to renew the war.⁵ As to the League, the king thought that he had very cleverly given it a death-blow by enacting in the fifty-sixth article of his edict that " all leagues, associations, and confraternities made or to be made, on any pretext whatsoever, to the prejudice of the present edict, be annulled," and by strictly forbidding the enrolling of men and the levy of money. It remained to see how much vitality the proscribed institution might still possess.

---

[1] Six of the eight cities were the same as in the former list, but Montpellier was substituted for Beaucaire, and La Réolle for Issoire, Art. 59. Text in Du Mont, Corps diplomatique, v. 302–308 ; Mémoires de Nevers, i. 290–307 ; Isambert, Recueil des anciennes lois françaises, xiv. 330, etc.

[2] Du Mont, Corps diplomatique, v. 308, 311 ; Isambert. Haag, etc.

[3] Saracini to the grand duke, October 4, 1577, Négociations avec la Toscane, iv. 131.

[4] See, as to Henry III., Recueil des choses mémorables, 596, and De Thou, v. 393 ; as to Henry of Navarre, Agrippa d'Aubigné, ii. 328.

[5] Mémoires de Claude Haton, ii. 900.

CHAPTER III.

THE CONFERENCE OF NÉRAC, AND THE SEVENTH CIVIL WAR.

CONCLUSIONS based upon abstract justice and deductions from expediency are wont to differ widely from each other. Wise men cannot always come to an agreement in deciding the knotty question whether it be not often advisable, in war as in matters of law, to accept much less than one is entitled to, rather than, by obstinately insisting upon the concession of one's full rights, run the risk of losing everything. In the present instance, some of the Huguenots, with Theodore Beza in the number, significantly pointed to the absurdity of making a distinction of places and permitting the Protestants to meet for worship in one spot while excluding them from another, as though God ought not equally to be adored in every part of the kingdom.[1] But others, perhaps not less zealous but possibly more practical in their views, maintained that the Peace of Bergerac was as favorable a compact as could be hoped for in the circumstances.

Contrast between the Peace of Bergerac and the Edict of January. The edict of pacification did, indeed, restrict materially the toleration extended by the famous "Edict of January," 1562, and by the more recent Peace of Monsieur. The "Edict of January" excluded the Huguenot religious assemblies from the walled cities, but sanctioned them everywhere else. The Peace of Monsieur, apparently more lavish in its concessions, granted the Protestants permission to hold their services wherever they pleased, with the single exception of the capital and its suburbs to a distance of two leagues, and required only the consent of the feudal lord within whose territorial jurisdiction the place of meeting might

---

[1] De Félice, History of the Protestants of France, Amer. ed., p. 235.

fall.¹ But, in the tumult of excited passion surging through France, neither stipulation had been executed. It was clear to every eye that, for the present, neither could be honestly carried into effect. When men were engaged in a desperate struggle, with passions inflamed by the strife, the excesses, and the calumnies of the past fifteen years, it was futile to think of settling the mutual relations of the professors of the two creeds upon a permanent basis. By and by, with the return of calmness and reason, this might be done. For the moment it was enough if some temporary adjustment of differences might be effected, some "modus vivendi" settled upon, to serve as a bridge to span the chasm between the existing confusion and the stable ground of a true and abiding peace.

Whether the treaty just made would answer the purpose, remained to be seen. But whatever the result might be, certain it was, that it offered a better prospect than any of its predecessors. It did not, indeed, recognize the right of Protestantism to universal toleration; but this very circumstance, while disappointing the just claims of the Huguenots, disarmed, in some measure, the malice of their most inveterate enemies.

The situation accepted. Whatever might be said of the Peace of Monsieur, it could not be asserted by the priests that the Peace of Bergerac countenanced the spread of the Reformed faith through the whole of France. The royal edict merely accepted the situation of affairs as it was. It admitted the existence of a second form of Christianity without endorsing it. Protestantism might be an evil the prevalence of which was to be greatly deplored; but Protestantism, as a form of faith and as a power in the state, could not be ignored. If the masses of the people could be disabused of their prejudices, if they could be set well on the way to learn the lesson that a diversity of religious tenets need not necessarily tend to discord and confusion, there might be some hope that the new pacification might either be

---

¹ If I mistake not, this last provision more than countervailed the superior advantages held forth in the later arrangement. It was better to be put to the inconvenience of going outside of the city walls, than to be left to the mercy of a capricious or unfriendly nobleman. The Huguenots had good reason to still regard the "Edict of January" as the great charter of their rights.

of lasting duration or give place only to some more perfect and equitable reconciliation. Unfortunately this was the darkest point in the horizon. The people could not unlearn in an hour the pestilent lessons sedulously taught them these many years, and there were those who had no thought of permitting the process, had the people been ever so ready to enter upon it. The same accusations that had been sown broadcast from the pulpits and confessionals, and by means of the printed handbill and placard, in the hour of the birth of the Reformation, were still disseminated among those credulous enough to believe them. The Huguenot name was still a bugbear held up to frighten not only children, but full-grown men and women. It was boldly maintained that the new heretics were enemies of the human race. If they did not worship the devil and eat little children at their nocturnal orgies, as had been reported twenty years earlier, in the time of the affair of the Rue Saint Jacques, they were undoubtedly, said their enemies, the willing agents in the spread of the plague. In the course of the very year of the Peace of Bergerac, there appeared at Lyons a pamphlet purporting to give a truthful account of the scourge that had just visited that city. The author was an envenomed enemy of Protestantism, Claude de Rubys, a man who played an important part in bringing about the provincial massacre following the Parisian matins.[1] The story he told bears a singular resemblance to the unfortunate incident rendered famous by the most fascinating of Italian novelists, in his historical record of the origin of the "Colonna Infame" of Milan. The Huguenots, not unlike the victims of popular malice and ignorance at Milan, were represented by Rubys as spreading the contagion by means of "certain infected pastes" which they had imported from Italy concealed in packages of silk. Nor was this the first offence of the kind, if we credit the accuser; for

The Huguenots calumniated.

They are accused of spreading the plague.

---

[1] "Discours sur la contagion de peste qui a esté ceste presente année en la ville de Lyon. . . . A Lyon, 1577." Cimber et Danjou, Archives curieuses, ix. 237-262. The passage referred to in the text is on pages 257-259. Respecting Rubys, see the Rise of the Huguenots, ii. 504, 514.

the same accursed sect had introduced the plague in similar nauseous drugs thirteen years before (1564), when they wished to prevent the erection of a citadel at Lyons, and, therefore, to destroy the Roman Catholics. Only, in the last-mentioned instance, the poison had come from Basle hidden in bales of other merchandise, and it had been carried into the very houses in which King Charles the Ninth and the lords of his court were lodging. It was well for the Huguenots that they lived under more enlightened forms of law, and that French jurisprudence did not, like the statutes of Milan, tolerate the application of torture at the mere caprice of the most petty judge, with the view of extracting the truth from a witness whenever his first answers did not appear altogether probable. Otherwise, it is to be feared that history would be compelled on this page to record the name of many a Huguenot victim, torn with pincers, maimed of a hand, with arms and legs broken, and left to languish full six hours upon the wheel before so-called "justice" would suffer the executioner mercifully to cut the wretched man's throat; as history is compelled to record the names of a Mora, a Piazza, a Migliavacca, and other unfortunates who suffered such barbarities at the time of the great plague that raged in Milan in the summer of the year of grace 1630.[1]

The Prince of Condé had so warmly welcomed the peace that he had ordered the announcement of it to be made in his camp by torchlight the very evening on which the tidings reached him. But the words of the proclamation had no magical effect to quiet inflamed passions or compel obedience. In defiance to the royal edict, Marshal Biron laid violent hands upon Villeneuve d'Agenois and upon Agen itself, the virtual capital of Henry of Navarre. In Languedoc Marshal Damville treated with supreme disdain the provisions relative to the return of the fugitives. The Huguenots of Beziers, Carcassonne, Castelnaudary, and other

The peace only partially observed.

---

[1] Alessandro Manzoni's "Storia della Colonna Infame" is well supplemented by Pietro Vorri's "Osservazioni sulla tortura," in which (chapter vii.) there is a transcript of the singular inscription on the column erected at Milan in commemoration of the punishment of the supposed culprits.

cities, finding admission denied to them, took the field perforce, and kept up the forms, with something of the reality of war, in a time of nominal peace. It was a novel sight to see two companies of about four hundred men each living off the district which they laid under contribution, and occasionally taking prisoners the most violent of their enemies. Still more singular was the discipline and the spirit of equality that reigned. Purchasing a full quantity of cloth with the proceeds of their plunder, the whole troop arrayed itself in precisely the same dress, with a gold chain about the neck or a red cord on the cap for the sole mark to distinguish the leaders. All ate together at commons in the spacious market-houses, where the captain and the minister who served as chaplain sat at the head of the long and rambling tables, and two lieutenants sat at the foot. The rest of the officers were mingled with the simple privates. It was not so much the weak fortifications behind which they were entrenched as the report of their courage and the rumor that they stood in favor with Châtillon, that long secured these bands of Huguenot soldiers immunity from hostile assault.[1] In Dauphiny the state of confusion was not less marked. Here Lesdiguières was able so to impress upon the mind of the royal governor the dangers to which his co-religionists were exposed from the implacable resentment of their enemies, that he actually obtained from him an arrangement allowing the Huguenots, until such time as the edict of pacification should be put into complete execution, to retain possession of all the strongholds they had in Dauphiny, and to draw upon the king a monthly sum of two thousand crowns for the support of the garrisons.[2]

---

[1] "Tant y a," says Agrippa d'Aubigné (ii. 333), to whom we are indebted for the quaint account, "que cette petite guerre dura autant que la petite paix que nous traittons maintenant."

[2] De Thou, v. 530–536. The compact was made by Laurent de Maugiron, who had just obtained the post of governor of Dauphiny (left vacant by the death of M. de Gordes) through the influence of his son, the well-known favorite of Henry III. It was very displeasing to the queen mother, and no stone was left unturned to induce the Protestants of Dauphiny to renounce the advantages it conferred upon them.

THE CONFERENCE OF NÉRAC.

Meanwhile, not deterred by the troubled state of a great part of France, the Reformed Church convoked, at Sainte Foy la Grande,[1] its Ninth National Synod (February, 1578). It was the first time that the highest ecclesiastical court of the Huguenots had met since the massacre of St. Bartholomew's Day. For nearly six years the Protestants of France, proscribed, the objects alternately of secret conspiracy and assassination or of the most sanguinary of open wars, had scarcely enjoyed a moment's respite from the assaults of their enemies. Self-preservation had engrossed their thoughts and withdrawn their attention from the consideration of the discipline and doctrine of the church. It was now time that they should devote the first opportunity, snatched from the pursuit of war, to the pressing claims of their internal organization and the care of their most vital interests.

The acts of deliberative bodies, however important in their results, rarely afford in themselves matters of interest for the general reader. But there are some points in the transactions of the present synod that are too characteristic to be passed over in silence.

The Huguenots, faithful subjects of the crown of France in all civil relations, were ever loyal to a republican theory of ecclesiastical government that admitted no earthly hierarchy, and recognized no lordship but that of Jesus Christ, the supreme head of the Church. On the present occasion they took pains to enunciate, at the very beginning of their proceedings, the principle that "no province can lay claim to possess any superiority or pre-eminence over the rest, either in general or in particular."[2] As an intelligent understanding of the religion taught by the Holy Scriptures is the indispensable foundation of Protestantism, the synod insisted much upon the necessity of a suitable education of the young. It was made the special duty of each province to search out every method proper for the institution of schools where young men might be trained to serve

---

[1] On the river Dordogne, in the extreme eastern part of the present department of Gironde.
[2] Art. 1. Aymon, Tous les synodes, i. 126.

the church some day in the exercise of the functions of the holy ministry. Ministers of the gospel were themselves urged to a very faithful and skilful use of the catechism in the instruction of their flocks. And parents were warned against the perilous practice of sending their children to schools under priestly or monkish influence, or permitting them to become pages or servants in the families of great lords or other persons "of some religion opposed to our religion."[1]

The synod gave its attention both to public and to family worship, and endeavored to define the proper relation between the two methods of approaching the Almighty. It prescribed the character of the preaching that should obtain in the French Protestant churches. The minister, it said, ought to aim at expounding as much of the sacred text as possible, avoiding display and long digressions; he should not cite a multitude of passages, heaping one quotation upon another, nor bring forward a number of different interpretations; it is his duty to use great moderation in referring to the ancient Doctors of the Church, and, above all, to profane histories and other works, "in order to leave to Scripture all its authority."[2] On the other hand, that it might not detract from the importance of the religion of the home, the synod distinctly set the mark of its disapproval upon the custom of holding public services for daily prayer in the Protestant churches. The churches that had adopted the practice were exhorted to conform to the usage of those churches that had no custom of the kind. In taking this action the Synod of Sainte Foy was only confirming the decisions of the National Synod of Paris, in 1565, which had discouraged the holding of services in church upon certain other days besides those on which there was preaching, or daily, upon the ground that the custom was calculated to promote superstition and to create contempt of the preaching of God's Word, and tended greatly to interfere with the duty incumbent upon every head of a family to institute daily worship for the members of his own household.[3]

---

[1] Arts. 2, 7, 23.   [2] Art. 7.
[3] Compare Art. 11 of the Synod of Paris and Art. 12 of the Synod of Sainte Foy. Aymon, i. 65, 66, 128.

It seems to have been in view of the recent publication of the great Protestant epic of Du Bartas on the Wonderful Work of Creation,[1] that the synod, fearful lest the fashion of adapting the language and figures of paganism to scriptural events should gain the ascendancy in the literature of the Reformed churches, recorded its desire that "those that shall hereafter take pen in hand to write the stories of the sacred Scripture in verse shall be notified not to mingle therewith poetical fables, nor attribute to God the names of false divinities, nor add anything to or take anything from Scripture, but confine themselves to the strict terms of the sacred text."[2] Among the less important provisions were those that reiterated the importance of executing the church's decrees against "dissoluteness" in dress, and especially in the wearing of the hair, and forbade a minister of the Gospel from practising the art of medicine.[3] The experience of conflicts in which the Protestants had been forced to engage dictated the propriety of a declaration prohibiting the faithful, in any future war, from separating themselves from the union of the churches, and agreeing to any private peace, upon pain of ecclesiastical censure.[4] More important than all was the lively interest testified by the Synod of Sainte Foy in the projects which, under the zealous patronage of that old and tried friend of the Huguenots, Jean Casimir, had taken shape, in September, 1577, in a conference held at Frankfort on the Main, for the purpose of devising, in company with the representatives of the other Reformed churches of Christendom, a plan for the close and hearty union of all Protestantism, and for thus silencing the calumnious reports to which the divisions of Protestantism daily gave plausible grounds.[5]

The most difficult matter upon which the synod was called to

---

[1] "La Semaine," of Guillaume de Saluste, Seigneur du Bartas, first appeared at Paris, in 1578, and ran through seventeen editions within four years. In all there were not less than thirty editions published. Haag, France protestante (first ed.), ii. 131.
[2] Art. 20.   [3] Arts. 21, 22.   [4] Art. 26.
[5] "Projet de reunion entre toutes les Églises Réformées et Protestantes du Monde Chrétien," appended to the Acts of the Synod of Sainte Foy, Aymon, i. 131-133.

act was an appeal—apparently the first appeal brought before a national synod from an inferior ecclesiastical court. The Protestant vessels, hovering as was their wont about the shores of the Bay of Biscay, had succeeded in taking a prize upon the high seas, and had brought it into port. The act had been approved by the Prince of Condé. The Consistory of La Rochelle declared the seizure unlawful, as having been made since the edict of pacification, and requested the prince not to approach the Lord's Table. They maintained that the whole church, indeed the whole city of La Rochelle, was suffering in consequence of this violation of good faith, and was denounced as a refuge of pirates and brigands. The prince, on the contrary, defended himself upon the plea that the capture had been made before the expiration of the forty days allowed for the publication of the peace, and from the sworn enemies of the King of Navarre and himself. Moreover, he plainly intimated to the consistory that he regarded the whole transaction as belonging to the province of those "affairs of state" which, for some mysterious reason, political leaders and kings are accustomed to ask the rest of the world to believe lie beyond the range of conscience and the laws of ordinary morality. The Synod of Sainte Foy, while by no means sharing in this remarkable view of public ethics, and while distinctly approving the zeal of the church and Consistory of Rochelle in its courageous opposition to scandalous vice, expressed regret that, in a matter of such moment, more time had not been taken, with the view of removing all suspicion and animosity. At the same time, it begged the prince to take in good part the remonstrance of the consistory, dictated by justice and necessity, and founded upon the Word of God, to remove the occasion of stumbling, and become reconciled to the church. This being done, it decreed that his highness be received to partake of the holy communion with his brethren.[1]

Dispute between Condé and the Consistory of La Rochelle.

It is the misfortune of the historian of this period that he is

---

[1] For this entire affair, so creditable to the manly courage and Christian consistency and candor of the persons that took part in it, see the minute of February 14, 1578, Aymon, i. 133, 134.

so frequently compelled to turn aside from the more congenial task of chronicling the incidents affecting the progress of the Huguenots, either in their interior life or in their struggle for the acquisition of full religious liberty, and forced to touch upon the disgraceful manners and morals of a king who, in the expressive words of a bitter contemporary pamphleteer, of all the inheritance left him by his predecessors had retained only their vices.[1] The digression, however unwelcome, is extremely important; since without a clear understanding of the recklessness and extravagance of the monarch, and the consequent burden of crushing taxes and hopeless debt imposed upon the people, it would be impossible to comprehend the circumstances that modified, if they did not altogether shape, the course of the adherents of the Reformed faith in France.

Some writers have represented the conclusion of the peace of 1577 as coincident with a notable change in the character of Henry the Third. Doffing in an instant all martial aspirations and manly enterprises, this prince, we are assured, resigned himself henceforth to a life of sluggish ease, with an evident alacrity which some interpreted as arising from inordinate love of pleasure, while others ascribed its origin to excessive devotion. Sudden mutations of the kind here indicated, however, are apt to be more apparent than real. The phenomenon is generally due to the more favorable opportunity enjoyed by the observer for obtaining a correct estimate of the true state of the case, or to the new freedom of the person observed in displaying those tendencies of his nature which fear or policy has led him until now to conceal. In Henry the adage was fully verified, that no one ever becomes a villain at a single stroke. The prince, young though he was, who, five years before, had been a principal conspirator in devising and executing the cowardly assassination of Admiral Coligny, and had both instigated and profited by the subsequent massacre and pillage, was no novice in crime.

Degeneracy of Henry the Third.

---

[1] "Remonstrance à tous bons Chrestiens et fideles Catholiques à maintenir la saincte Union . . . contre les efforts du tyran," etc. Mémoires de la Ligue, iii. 553.

The period intervening between his departure for Poland and the conclusion of the sixth civil war was, indeed, a time of political commotion and of extreme anxiety to every patriotic soul. But it witnessed in Henry the gradual but sure descent to still lower depths of moral corruption, and was the natural precursor of a state of shameless vice that astonished and repelled an age of unparalleled depravity. It was that he might give loose reins to his passions that Henry had longed for peace, that he was determined to have it at any cost. And the moment that the edict of peace was signed and registered by his parliaments, he plunged into excesses such as the world had not dreamed of his being capable of committing. Now it was that the government of France fell into the hands of the personal favorites of the king. The road to distinction was found no longer to run through the battlefield or the honest and skilful administration of public trusts. The brave and successful general and the statesman of wisdom and tried integrity were thrust aside, to give place for the cunning ministers of the monarch's pleasures. To have invented a new form of diversion, to know a pastime that aroused the king's curiosity, to be able to recollect or invent at will the tales of amorous intrigue and court scandal that constituted Henry's choicest table-talk—these were sure passports to favor. By the side of the fortunate possessors of these rare accomplishments, even the representatives of the oldest and most powerful families of feudal France stood at the greatest disadvantage. The new favorite was secure in the consciousness of a hold upon the king which no mere scion of an illustrious stock could dispute. Here, indeed, was a danger threatening the peace of France more serious than any perils that might come from abroad. Henry brought himself into direct opposition to a tendency of the times that had assumed portentous dimensions. The new feudalism, since the beginning of the century, had, as we have seen, been entrenching itself in the great provincial governments. It was with extreme jealousy that the great nobles beheld the rise of new aspirants to honor and to the confidence of the sovereign, and they could not but band together to resist the counsels and influence of men whom they

The new favorites and the old feudal lords.

regarded as upstarts and usurpers. But when it came to distributing among the king's "mignons" the government of provinces regarded by the present holders as hereditary possessions, the old nobles rose in rebellion against so flagrant an outrage upon all right and decency. They could be dislodged, it was evident, only after a prolonged and desperate struggle. The king's attempt to weaken the exorbitant influence of the old nobility by robbing it of its immense territorial privileges, and to substitute for the representatives of the Montmorencies and other ancient families young noblemen of a comparatively obscure lineage, has been interpreted as a sagacious stroke of policy intended to exalt the monarchy by freeing it of its present entanglements. If the view be correct, it must be admitted that the brilliancy of the conception is all that entitles the plan to respect. Assuredly in the execution it resembles a senseless blunder. Without adding to the number of his friends and supporters, Henry aroused the hostility of a large and powerful class, not less formidable than the Huguenots of whom he had long been confessedly an implacable enemy.

Meanwhile, distrust and violence characterized the royal court. The king's inordinate gifts and extravagant favors, instead of contenting, only excited the cupidity and stimulated the envy of those who wished to engross for themselves the fruits of Henry's reckless prodigality. In every direction reigned jealousy and dissension. Henry discovered that not even the semi-regal appanage he had conferred upon his younger brother was sufficient to establish fraternal sentiments between them. The old sore of deadly hatred broke out afresh in February, 1578, when the Duke of Anjou again fled from the vicinity of the court, alleging the insecurity of his person from the malice of his royal brother. In imitation of the king and the duke, the favorites had their own quarrels, which they settled by open combat or by secret assassination. When an unlucky wound received in a duel or in the street laid the king's minion upon a bed of sickness, Henry did not fail to show his extreme friendship by waiting upon the sufferer, and performing the common offices of friendship, with little regard for his own dignity or the claims of his station. When one of the favorites died the corpse became the recipient of such costly honors as were customary only in the case of kings, or princes of the royal blood.[1]

<small>Penury and prodigality of the court.</small> Upon the unworthy objects of the king's favor the treasure of France was lavished without stint, but no treasure could ever have satisfied Henry's desire to enrich them, or their own thirst for wealth. The shrewd counsellors of his majesty might rack their brains to discover new taxes, the collectors of the royal revenues might exercise their ingenuity in devising methods to exact more money from the poor peasantry, the queen mother might use her influence with old creditors to secure an extension of the time of their loans [2] —all might look about for fresh financial aid from credulous bankers. Everybody was at his wits' end to replenish a treasury that was in so leaky a condition that, no matter what was poured in, there was never any reserve on hand. Prodigality and penury walked hand in hand. To celebrate the Duke of Anjou's capture of La Charité, in the course of the recent war, the king gave a grand banquet in his honor at Plessis-lès-Tours, at which all the ladies in attendance were dressed in green silk, a material so scarce as to cost the sum, enormous for the times, of sixty thousand francs. Not to be outdone, the queen mother followed with a still more exquisite and luxurious festival in her castle of Chenonceaux, at an expense of one hundred thousand livres.[3] But the money was all raised by borrowing from the king's most affluent subjects, and especially from the Italians, of whom it is significantly stated that they knew well how to reimburse themselves twice over.

---

[1] De Thou, v. 539–544. See, also, Lestoile, i. 98, 99, for Henry's absurd manifestations of sorrow at the death of Maugiron, Queylus, and Saint-Mégrin.

[2] So Catharine, in 1576, begged the ambassador Saracini to write to the Grand Duke of Tuscany, requesting him by no means to insist upon the repayment of the sum of 45,000 crowns which he had advanced. Yet in the very letter in which Saracini complies with the request he estimates the yearly income of the Duke of Anjou at 860,000 francs. Letter of August 14, 1576, Négociations avec la Toscane, iv. 79.

[3] "En ce beau banquet les plus belles et honnestes de la cour, estans à moitié nues, et ayans leurs cheveux espars comme espousées, furent employées à faire le service." Mémoires de Henri III. (Cologne, 1693), 21.

The resources of ecclesiastical patronage placed at the king's disposal by the Concordat were exhausted. Benefices had been sold, or given away as a recompense for real or pretended services, and without the slightest reference to the religious interests of the people, until the greater part were held by women and married gentlemen. The abuse, indeed, had gone to such a length that not infrequently the revenues of these churchly endowments were conferred, in consequence of the efforts of parents, upon their infant offspring yet unborn.[1]

*There was no way to raise money but by recourse to the provincial states and to the clergy. But the provincial states, instead of augmenting the contributions, loudly protested against the burdens already resting on the poor people's neck. The Guises, greatly displeased at the superior favor shown by the king to his minions, had retired in disgust from Paris to their home.[2] They now took their revenge by stirring up the spirit of discontent, and thus, while rendering the monarch unpopular, earned the reputation of being the true friends of the oppressed.[3] The States of Burgundy, meeting at Dijon, were induced, through their exertions, to send deputies to court, and demand the reduction of the taxes to the scale of the good old times of Louis the Twelfth. The demand was certainly unreasonable, since it took no account of the altered state of affairs in Europe, since the great influx of the precious metals from America, and the consequent rise of the price of all commodities, and ignored the great increase in the necessary expenses of war and of the civil administration. None the less was the cry a very popular one. It came also from the deputies of the States of Normandy; and here it was accompanied by a terrible indictment of the cruel system under which the wretched victims of op-

---

[1] "Jusques aux enfans ausquels lesdits bénéfices se trouvoient le plus souvent affectés, estans encores en la matrice de leurs mères." Lestoile, i. 97.

[2] Ibid., i. 100.

[3] See the very important letter of Saracini, July 7, 1578, Négociations avec la Toscane, iv. 175, 176. "Poi che con questa arte e invenzione per loro si acquistano la benevolenza de' popoli, e Sua Maestà il sollevamente e la ribellione."

pression were ground into the very dust. The representative of the three orders drew a vivid picture of the villagers, bareheaded and prostrate, half famished, without a shirt for the back or shoes on the feet, looking more like corpses dragged from their graves than like living men, and in their desperation raising their hands and their voices to ask what must be the term of patient submission to the intolerable load. "How long," said they, " shall the licentious soldier, with the knowledge and under the eyes of the officers of justice, after having devoured and dissipated our entire substance, and stolen and carried off our household stuff, insult with impunity our wives and daughters, and maltreat our children in our very presence? How long shall evil counsel persuade the king that he can endlessly and beyond all bounds levy taxes in defiance of the privileges and laws of this province, and without asking the consent of the people? How long shall flattery have such weight as to give him to understand that he is holden to no laws, and owes no respect to his coronation oath or to compacts made with his subjects, against the law of nations and the constitutions of the emperors? Will not the inventors of edicts pernicious to the king's estate and the public repose remember that God, who is superior to kings, can hurl them into the abyss, as He knows well how, when it pleases Him, to remove kingdoms and monarchies wherein iniquity abounds and justice is buried out of sight? according as He threatens in Hosea, chapter twelfth, 'Auferam regem, inquit, in indignatione mea.'"[1]

There was much sober sense in these complaints; there were hints of possible dangers impending over the monarchy which

---

[1] The sentences translated in the text are but a few of the striking passages occurring in Clerel's address, in behalf of the three orders of Normandy, to M. de Carouges. The address is appended to a letter purporting to give to a gentleman of Burgundy a detailed account of the proceedings of the provincial estates of Normandy, held at Rouen in November, 1578. Cimber et Danjou, Archives curieuses, ix. 263-283. Whether from modesty or from fear, Clerel resolutely refused to accede to the desire of his fellow deputies that he should put his burning words upon paper; so that the reporter was forced to draw upon his memory.

Henry would do well to heed. But in his anxiety for money—money which he must have from some source or other to lavish upon his dogs and his favorites—his ears were deaf to the growing murmurs of the people; or if he heard them at all, it was some consolation to him to know that his former boon companion—Henry of Guise—that insidious rival who was now bidding so high for popularity, was even more hopelessly embarrassed than his majesty. His debts already amounted to scarcely less than a million livres, and were rapidly increasing. In his frantic effort to diminish the crushing load, he had lately sold to a frugal German soldier of fortune one of his choicest possessions.[1]

The Duke of Guise's debts.

As if to aggravate the misery of the kingdom, the Duke of Anjou had assumed the support of the Dutch in their struggle against Philip the Second, arrogating to himself the high-sounding title of "Defender of the Liberty of the Netherlands."[2] Now it was a characteristic of the fortunes of this most unlucky of princes, that he never by any chance touched a thing but he spoiled it, or drew a person to his party without involving him in ruin. Under pretence of levying troops to serve in the Low Countries under his banner, great bands of "vagabonds, robbers, and murderers" now took the field in Champagne and pillaged on the right and on the left. The wretched villagers declared that the very Turks would not have treated them worse. "Were the Duke of Anjou," wrote one of the witnesses of these disorders, "to live a hundred years, he would never have so many happy days as he has had curses from the people of France. I pray God that he may not reap disaster for the imprecations which the desperate people of his nation have uttered against him by reason of the evil done by those who held the country under his authority."[3]

The Duke of Anjou.

---

[1] Gaspard de Schomberg, whom we shall meet later as one of the chief negotiators of the Edict of Nantes, purchased for 380,000 livres the duke's earldom of Nanteuil-le-Haudouin. Lestoile, under date of September 15, 1578, ii. 103.
[2] Motley, Dutch Republic, iii. 344.
[3] Mémoires de Claude Haton, ii. 937, etc., 961.

About this time an incident occurred that brings into strong relief the incongruities resulting unavoidably from the absurd attempt of the Roman pontiff to occupy at the same moment the two positions of head of the papal church and temporal prince of territories acknowledging his jurisdiction. With the return of peace to France in general, no peace had come to the Comtât Venaissin, where the reluctance of the vice-legate to make any concessions to Protestants threatened to postpone indefinitely the close of the war. At length, however, the Protestants and the Roman Catholics, tired of the endless confusion, came to a parley at Nismes, in November, 1578. Thoré and François de Coligny were the representatives of the Protestants, while Guillaume de Patris, the vice-legate's deputy, and the Cardinal of Armagnac appeared for the Roman Catholics. The agreement that was reached accorded to all persons complete religious liberty. No one was to be molested on account of any religious views he might hold. The Protestants were guaranteed the enjoyment of all the property, offices, or dignities of which they had been deprived. It was even stipulated that the inhabitants of Cabrières, and other victims of the murderous attacks which had rendered the names of the villages on the banks of the Durance famous for all time, should be regarded as included in the treaty, and permission was granted them to prosecute their claims for the restitution of their goods before referees appointed by both parties to arbitrate between them. Provision was made for an equitable sale of the property of any Protestants that might desire to emigrate, while those who preferred to remain were expressly exempted from the jurisdiction, both civil and criminal, of the pope's judges, as of persons of doubtful impartiality. Their cases of law were to be tried before the Chamber of Nismes, in the first instance, and by the "Chambre tri-partie" of Languedoc, on appeal, the judges in both chambers acting in the name of his holiness, and not in that of the King of France. But the most remarkable article of all was one in which it was conceded that, in case any Protestant should be disturbed in the enjoyment of his property situated in the Comtât, he might apply to any of the judges of the French

Singular compact in the Comtât Venaissin.

king, and, upon a simple requisition, be placed in possession of whatever lands belonging to a papal subject might lie within the bounds of the court's jurisdiction.[1] Strange as it may seem, this singular compact was ratified not only by the three estates of the Comtât and by Henry the Third, but even by the pope himself. For Gregory the Thirteenth published, on the seventh of February, 1579, a bull expressly approving all that had been done. Thus did the same pontiff that had exhibited extravagant glee at the news of the wholesale massacre of St. Bartholomew's Day, and authorized Vasari to paint its bloody scenes on the walls of the Vatican palace, with a record of the explicit approval of the pope, the same pontiff that had urged Charles the Ninth to pursue his pious work of murder even to the destruction of the last Huguenot in the realm, now suffer the claims of expediency to outweigh the demands of a consistent but sanguinary theory. Such were the results of the attempt of the Bishop of Rome to exercise, at one and the same time, a universal episcopate and a secular lordship. The pope, acting as the pretended vicegerent of God, might demand of the kings of the earth that they should wage unrelenting warfare against the enemies of the Almighty, and endeavor to frighten them into compliance by holding up the punishment incurred by Saul because he spared the Amalekites as a fearful warning against disobedience. But the pope, acting as master of a petty district, was careful not to put into practice the lessons

---

[1] This article is, however, as De Thou observes, only a repetition of the forty-fourth of the secret articles of Bergerac adopted in the previous year, wherein the King of France promised to any Protestants of the Comtât that might be hindered in the enjoyment of their property within that district, "leur pourvoir sur les biens que les autres sujets de ladite ville d'Avignon et Comtât ont ès terres et païs de son obéissance, par lettres de marque et represaille, lesquelles seront à cette fin adressées aux juges ausquels de droit la connoissance en appartient." Du Mont, Corps diplomatique, v. 311. It is interesting to notice that this singular feature in French jurisprudence was even perpetuated in the Edict of Nantes (1598). The fifty-first of the secret articles of Nantes directly refers to and confirms the forty-ninth (forty-fourth) secret article of 1577, and merely provides that no "letters of marque" shall be issued by way of reprisal, save by letters patent of the king, sealed with his great seal. Text in Weiss, Histoire des Refugiés Protestants de France, pièces justificatives, ii. 377, and Anquez, Histoire des Assemblées Politiques, 495.

he had given to others, and not only spared the lives of the "accursed heretics," but even gave guarantees of an extraordinary kind for the protection of their property. What would a scoffing world say respecting papal sincerity on discovering that, besides the sufficiently scandalous articles of the public compact, there was a secret article that bound the burgesses of Roman Catholic Avignon to pay yearly to the burgesses of Huguenot Orange the sum of six thousand crowns, partly as a compensation for the injuries the latter city had received, partly as relief in view of the garrison which Orange was compelled to maintain?[1]

Meanwhile the unsettled condition of Southern France, a region to which treaties the most solemnly drawn up seemed impotent to restore tranquillity, called for new efforts of diplomacy. These Catharine de' Medici, never more in her element than when engaged in a conflict of cajolery and intrigue, did not hesitate to put forth. She found a good pretext for a journey to Guyenne in the maternal duty of conducting Margaret of Valois to her husband, from whom she had been separated ever since Henry made his memorable escape from court. Although it may well be believed that the King of Navarre, to whom the morals of his frail spouse were no secret, had little disposition to take her back, the possible advantages to be derived from a conference were too obvious to permit him to decline the meeting. Mother-in-law and son now saw each other again, after an absence of more than three years (August, 1578). Both came well prepared for the encounter of shrewdness and wit. Henry brought his good native sense, his cheerful and light-hearted disposition, which often concealed sober truth under the guise of the flippant remark or scoffing jest. Catharine, in addition to a keen intellect, fertile in devices to suit every emergency, brought with her that galaxy of youthful beauty which she was accustomed to call her flying squadron, and upon the effectiveness of whose charms she counted scarcely less than upon the learning and persuasiveness of Pibrac and other clever diplomatists of her suite.

---

[1] De Thou, v. 544, 545.

Next to the conversion of Henry of Navarre to the Roman Catholic faith, the queen mother had nothing more at heart than to induce him to consent to the restoration of the cities held by the Huguenots as pledges before the expiration of the appointed term. She was as likely to fail of the one as of the other object. Henry, with all his profuse expressions of willingness to receive instruction, certainly had no intention of forsaking Protestantism again until he could secure some greater prize than Catharine could offer at the present time. As to the cities he was equally deaf to entreaty. It would be sheer madness to give up the only securities the Huguenots possessed for the execution of the treaty, when the frequent and persistent violations of its provisions demonstrated how little their late enemies were inclined to respect their own promises or to permit the king to keep his. Catharine and her nymphs forgot no art to break down the resolution of the outspoken and somewhat obstinate soldiers, who, having struck and borne hard blows in the fight to win liberty to worship God, were in no mood to throw away such advantages as they might possess in the not improbable contingency of a new war forced upon them by treacherous foes. Catharine and her maids of honor had spent hours in laboriously training their tongues to counterfeit the biblical phraseology in which they supposed these religious men by preference indulged—" consistorial " turns of expression, as the queen mother styled them. They could talk glibly of " the counsel of Gamaliel;" they could exclaim with mock fervor, " How beautiful are the feet of them that preach the gospel of peace!" They called the king with effusion, " the Lord's anointed, the image of the living God;" and had at their tongues' end various passages from St. Peter's epistles in favor of the powers that be. Their very ejaculations were scriptural: " The Lord judge betwixt me and thee!" "I call the everlasting God to witness." " Before God and His angels." It was all very well, only the pupils were too eager to display their proficiency in the lessons they conned, not without bursts of laughter, every evening in Catharine's bedchamber. They found that the " language of Canaan," as they called it, imposed upon no one;

least of all upon men who read more of the Bible every day of the week than these fine ladies had read in their entire lives.

One day M. de Pibrac was brought out to make an oration of the kind wherewith he had once cheated the credulous Poles. With consummate art he strove to convince the Huguenots of the beauty of such an implicit confidence in their king as the surrender of their cities of refuge would evidence. His illustrations were profuse, drawn from Muscovy, Turkey, Persia, and whatever other quarter might furnish examples of subjects that joyfully laid down their lives for their soverign. It was grand; it was pathetic. The ladies wiped their eyes, and Catharine dramatically cried : " Ah, my friends, let us give God the glory ! Let us cause the rod of iron to fall from His hands ! " But when she turned to the group of Huguenot veterans sitting calm and motionless before the orator, and triumphantly asked them, " What can you say in reply ? " the governor of Figéac, one M. La Meausse, upon whom she happened to rest her eyes, promptly answered : " I say, madam, that the gentleman over there has conned his lessons well ; but to pay for his studies with our throats is a thing of which we cannot understand the reasonableness." [1]

Henry of Navarre surprises Fleurance.

The discussions were long and lively. The negotiation dragged through some months. When it threatened to become monotonous, variety was occasionally supplied by messengers announcing some new act of treachery or of retaliation. One evening a month or two after Catharine's arrival, a grand ball was given in her honor in the city of Auch. Henry of Navarre, Viscount Turenne, and young Sully were among the dancers. The king's enjoyment of the festivities was, however, somewhat marred by a friend who came and whispered in his ear a piece of news just received. It was to the effect that La Réolle, an important place on the northern

---

[1] " Je dis, ma dame, que monsieur que voilà a bien estudié ; mais de paier ses estudes de nos gorges nous n'en pouvons comprendre la raison." Agrippa d'Aubigné, ii. 337. It must be admitted that La Meausse's retort well deserved an honorable place in the celebrated chapter of the " Confession catholique du Sieur de Sancy," entitled " de l'Impudence des Huguenots."

bank of the Garonne, and one of the cities pledged to the Protestants in the Edict of Poitiers, had been betrayed to the Roman Catholics by its Huguenot governor—an absurd old man who had fallen in love with one of the queen mother's maids. Concealing his vexation, Henry of Navarre managed to withdraw from the crowd, and, hastily gathering about him his most trusty companions, took horse that very hour. His band was not large, but it was well mounted, and, long before that October night was past, he had reached and taken by surprise the walled town of Fleurance, or Florence, twelve or fourteen miles farther down the Gers. The only loss of the Huguenots was of a favorite page of the king. The next morning, Catharine de' Medici, who had not missed the Huguenot party, was not a little astonished to hear of its exploit. "Ah!" she said, laughing and shaking her head, "I see that this is Navarre's revenge for La Réolle. He wished to pay me for what I have done, but I have made more than he has by the exchange"—or, in her own words, for which the English furnishes no exact equivalent, " Le roi de Navarre a voulu faire chou pour chou ; mais le mien est mieux pommé." [1]

The court, and the foreign diplomatists too, held up their hands in amazement at the " exorbitant " demands of the Huguenots, who went so far as to claim for Henry of Navarre perfect freedom in the government of the province of Guyenne, with no interference on the part of Marshal Biron.[2] But in

---

[1] Mémoires de Sully, i. 73 (chap. 10) ; Agrippa d'Aubigné, ii. 334, 335. The correspondence of Henry himself, contained in the first volume of Xivrey, Lettres missives de Henri IV., shows that the romantic adventure of the text occurred not in August, but in October, 1578, between the 17th and 28th. A brief note to M. de Batz, apparently written on the morning of the day of the attack upon Fleurance, proves that Henry had for some time contemplated the movement, and had carefully made his preparations for it. The note itself presents to view the most attractive side of the writer's character. "C'est merveille," he says, "que la diligence de vostre homme et la vostre. Tant pis que n'ayez praticqué personne du dedans à Florence, la meilleure place m'est trop chère du sang d'un de mes amis. Ceste mesme nuict je vous joindray et y seront les bons de mes braves. HENRY." Lettres missives, i. 202.

[2] Saracini to the grand duke, March 2, 1579, Négociations avec la Toscane, iv. 247.

the end the Huguenots carried most of their points. Catharine, it is said, saw the necessity of making friends of them in order to counterbalance the growing power of the Guises and of Spain. Another treaty was arranged in twenty-seven articles, embodying a more favorable interpretation of the preceding treaties, and granting the Protestants the right to build churches and raise funds for the support of their ministers. Instead of their being compelled to give up the places already held as a pledge for their security, the number of places was actually increased. Fourteen cities—three in Guyenne and the remainder in Languedoc—were intrusted to them to keep until the autumn of the same year; and Henry of Valois engaged to pay to them thirty-six thousand livres tournois monthly for the Huguenot garrisons, that so the inhabitants might be spared from the exactions of the soldiery.[1]

Results of the conference.

This was not the only instance in which the King of France was forced to make concessions. Much as Henry hated the Protestants, it was his lot to see his own real interests for the most part bound up with the fortunes of those whose religious views he had been taught to detest. The great errors of his reign are, with few exceptions, traceable to the neglect or violation of the self-evident necessity of making friends and allies of the Huguenots. In the matter of the city of Geneva, Henry found himself not a little embarrassed how to act. If he looked at the question from the religious side, the little republic on Lake Leman seemed to be the very embodiment of everything from which his soul revolted. The home of Calvin had lost, since the great reformer's death, none of its singular pre-eminence as the virtual capital of continental

Henry takes Geneva under his protection.

---

[1] Text in Du Mont, Corps diplomatique, v. 337-341. The articles of Nérac were signed by Catharine and Navarre in February, and were ratified by Henry III. March 19, 1579. The instructions given to royal commissioners now despatched throughout the kingdom, to inquire into and apply a remedy to the prevailing malversations and disorders, are printed in the Mémoires de Nevers, i. 605, etc. The cities of Bazas, Puymirol, and Figéac, in Guyenne, were to be held by the King of Navarre until the last day of August, and no longer; the cities of Revel, Briatexte, Alet, Sainte Agrève, Baix, Bagnols, Alais, Lunel, Sommières, Aimargues, and Gignac, in the province of Languedoc, were to be held a month longer. See article xvii.

Protestantism. Inferior to Calvin in intellectual endowments Beza might be, but he was more of a man of the world, and, with the reputation of elegant literary accomplishments and eloquence, he was regarded, both by friends and by foes, as having justly fallen heir to the marvellous influence of his great predecessor. The theological school under his care was the most celebrated institution of its kind. It was still from Geneva that France was supplied with those reformed preachers whose instructions had as magic an effect in nerving the arms of Huguenot soldiers to deeds of valor as in implanting heroic endurance in the hearts of weak women and children. Geneva, in short, was, in the eyes of the pope and of the fanatical clergy of France, the nest of heresy which it behooved the Very Christian kings and all other Roman Catholic princes, above everything else, to destroy. " It were to be desired," wrote Henry of Valois himself, three years later, " that the city of Geneva had long since been reduced to ashes, because of the seed of bad doctrine which it has scattered abroad through many parts of Christendom, whence have ensued infinite evils, ruins, and calamities, and more in my kingdom than in any other place." [1]

But from a political point of view the safety and independence of Geneva concerned the French crown intimately. Geneva in the hands of the Duke of Savoy would be a perpetual menace to the French frontier. The city held the key to the most practicable passage for the Swiss mercenaries upon whose aid the crown principally depended, now that the armed support of feudal dependants had become so insufficient and uncertain. Besides, the Swiss themselves recognized in Geneva an indispensable bulwark of their own cantons; and Roman Catholic Soleure, not less than Protestant Berne, stoutly refused to approve of any plan that did not include Geneva in the ancient alliance between the Swiss and the French monarchy. The king himself was forced to take the same ground. " Geneva," he wrote in the letter which has just been quoted, " is so situated that it could not be reduced to obedience by any prince

---

[1] Henry III. to Mandelot and Hautefort, March 13, 1582, in Henri Fazy, Genève, le Parti Huguenot et le Traité de Soleure, 122.

among my neighbors but that he would hold in subjection the Swiss confederates and place them at his mercy; for it would be in his power—if he held the Pas de l'Écluse, which he would incontinently fortify—to prevent my rendering aid to the Swiss in their need, or their coming to my succor and service when I might summon them."[1]

Long and anxiously did Henry debate the matter with himself, setting over against the advantages to be expected from the alliance the denunciations in which the preachers of the League would be sure to indulge of a king that made himself the champion of obstinate heretics. In the end, he concluded, on the eighth of May, 1579, the memorable treaty in accordance with which he formally took Geneva under his protection. His apprehensions were fully realized in the loud outcry raised by the parish priests and monks.[2] A king that threw the mantle of his guardianship around Geneva, a king whose brother was supposed by everyone to be as good as married to Queen Elizabeth,[3] could not expect to escape the censure of the bigoted.

For Henry the Third was now reaping, in merited distrust and contempt, the ordinary fruit of insincerity and duplicity; while so clumsy were his attempts to purchase the favor of the priesthood, and atone by his devotions for the baseness of a life more and more suspected of infamous excess, that he rarely failed to create opposition and hatred where he sought to conciliate friendship. The

The devotions of Henry of Valois.

---

[1] Henry III. to Mandelot and Hautefort, ubi supra, 122, 123. The preamble of the Treaty of Soleure itself sets forth the importance of Geneva—"pour estre icelle ville de Genève l'une des clefs et principal boulevart du pays desdictes villes, et qui peult tenir le passage libre et ouvert entre sadicte Majesté et lesdicts Seigneurs des Ligues." Ibid., 190.

[2] Traité perpetuel fait par Henri III., roi de France, avec les villes de Genève, Berne et Soleure. Du Mont, Corps diplomatique, v. 347-349; and Fazy, 190-206. De Thou, v. 619, 620. The Duke of Nevers defends Henry's catholicity in the transaction in his "Traité des causes et des raisons de la prise des armes," Mémoires, ii. 38. (Cimber et Danjou, xiii. 65.)

[3] In this same month the Florentine agent wrote to his master that the Duke of Alençon said: "Che era per la Dio grazia maritato; e che ne restava molto contento, poichè questo gli avveniva con satisfazione della Maestà del Re e della Regina sua madre." Saracini to grand duke, May 31, 1579; Négociations avec la Toscane, iv. 257.

priests laughed in their sleeves when he sent to Chartres for a shirt for himself, and a similar garment for his wife, upon which the Holy Virgin's blessing had been conferred,[1] and when, a few days later, the young queen herself went in pilgrimage to the same famous shrine to supplicate that Our Lady would deign to grant her the long-desired boon of a son to be heir to the kingdom.[2] The same ecclesiastics applauded when, on the first of January, 1579, the king instituted the new Order of the Holy Ghost (Ordre du Saint-Esprit); for, if one cause of the institution was the circumstance that the insignia of the Order of Saint Michael had been so lavishly conferred as to become "a collar for all manner of beasts,"[3] another was undoubtedly the desire to strengthen the hold of the Roman Catholic religion upon the courtiers by rigidly excluding all heretics from the circle of the king's favorites.[4] Yet even here Henry contrived to offend the clergy by proposing to assign to each member an income of ten thousand crowns a year to be taken from the revenues of the church—a plan to which Pope Gregory the Thirteenth refused his consent, and which called forth murmurs of disapprobation from the preachers.[5]

If the king's devotions were received with suspicion or derision by the people, it was certainly not because of any lack of superstition in the lower classes of society. A violent earthquake occurring about this time in Central France was at first believed by many to be the sign of the approaching end of the world. At once various pilgrimages were set on foot in town and in country. Among other public demonstrations, a notable procession took place in the city of Tours, under the auspices of the whole body of the clergy and the civil judges. The people were all there, says a contem-

Popular superstition.

---

[1] Lestoile, under date of January 23, 1579, i. 113.
[2] Saracini to grand duke, February 3, 1579, Négociations avec la Toscane, iv. 240.
[3] "Collier à toutes bestes," Lestoile, i. 110, 111.
[4] See "Les Cérémonies observées à l'institution de l'ordre du Saint-Esprit," apud Cimber et Danjou, Archives curieuses, ix. 289-302.
[5] One of them, Dr. Bruslart, was put in the Bastile. Journal d'un curé ligueur (Jehan de la Fosse), 152, 153.

porary chronicler, without exception of age or sex, and even to young children. All assembled in their parish churches, whence they proceeded to the great church of Saint Martin of Tours. Here the procession formed, with the priests carrying the bones of the patron saint and other relics held in scarcely less reverence, and marched out of the city. "In it," to use the words of the appreciative curé of Mériot, "there were more than three hundred persons with body, head, feet, and hands naked, having before them but a simple sheet or cloth to cover their parts of shame. Some, by way of penance, carried great bars of iron upon their shoulders, others thick pieces of wood. The priests all walked barefoot and very simply clad." This was in midwinter—the twenty-sixth of January.[1] So far from being likely to undervalue any sincere act of devotion, the people seemed sometimes to outdo even their priests in zeal. Of this the inhabitants of the village of Courlons, not far from Provins, gave a signal proof. Desirous of obtaining from heaven a cessation of the destructive frosts that threatened their vineyards, the peasants petitioned their priest to order a procession, after vespers, to a chapel in a remote part of his parish. The indolent curate granted the request, but substituted a somewhat nearer place of worship, to which, after vespers were said, he led the way with his vicar. But scarce was the procession out of the village, when the people, turning their backs upon their chief ecclesiastic, directed their steps toward the place which they had themselves originally chosen. In the quarrel that ensued the parish priest was severely handled for his laziness; indeed, a few of the more enthusiastic members of his flock at length lost all patience, and deliberately seizing him, carried him to the bank of the neighboring Yonne, and threw him into the stream, where he nearly lost his life.[2]

The summer of 1579 witnessed important convocations of both of the religions, now and long marshalled with so hostile a front in France. The Roman Catholic clergy, suspicious, not

---

[1] Mémoires de Claude Haton, ii. 973, 974.
[2] Ibid., ii. 977.

without fair reasons, of the intentions of the king in convening them, had absolutely declined to meet in the capital, and had made out a list of places, all of them, it was hoped, sufficiently removed from court influences to permit them to exercise some independence of action. They also insisted that no cardinal or archbishop should have a seat in the assembly, because these dignitaries had had too much to do with those previous levies made upon the church, in which great abuses had been experienced. The king selected Melun for the seat of the clergy's deliberations, whence he subsequently brought them to Paris. But in neither place did he find the members very tractable. They complained that not less than twenty-eight of the French bishoprics had been left vacant in order that laymen might enjoy the revenues. As to other ecclesiastical benefices, if we can place any reliance upon the statements made by the Bishop of Bazas in a remonstrance addressed to the monarch in the name of his order, France would seem to have bid fair soon to rival Germany and England in the secularization of the property of religious institutions. In certain families abbacies and benefices had come to be regarded as among the chattels which father handed down to son, and the royal council itself had lately adjudged a bishopric to a woman of rank. The clergy declared that the road to reform lay in the adoption of the decrees of the Council of Trent. Not content with this, they enraged the king by demanding the repeal of that profitable Concordat of Leo the Tenth and Francis the First which had thrown almost the whole patronage into the hands of the crown ;[1] while they infuriated the people by deliberately resolving that the clergy had already paid enough of the state's debts, in accordance with the contracts of Poissy (1561).[2] When the news of the refusal to assist the king in his desperate straits reached the populace of Paris, the tiers état, having no mind to receive upon its neck the burden which the priests coolly proposed to transfer thither from their own shoulders, nearly brought on a riot in the streets of the capital. It was averted by the prompt and somewhat arbitrary action of the Parliament

Reluctance of the clergy to help the king.

---

[1] See the Rise of the Huguenots, i. 35–41. [2] Ibid., i. 543.

of Paris in summoning to its bar all the members of the convocation then within reach, and threatening with arrest any who should attempt to flee. In the end, Henry secured a renewal of the ecclesiastical tithes for the term of ten years, and thus appeased the people.[1]

While the convocation protracted its sessions through the summer and autumn, the Tenth National Synod of the Reformed Churches met at Figéac in Quercy on the second of August, and adjourned six days later. Its deliberations, however, except so far as they respected the constant solicitude of the Huguenots for the thorough education of candidates for the sacred ministry, and the effort to secure regular yearly meetings of the highest ecclesiastical court of the Reformed Church, contained little of permanent interest. How ineffectual any provision for periodical sessions of the national synods must prove, in the unsettled condition of France, appears from the circumstance that the plan was defeated from the very first by the outbreak of the war of which I must soon speak.[2]

Tenth National Synod, Figéac, 1579.

The preludes of these new hostilities now claim our attention. The Treaty of Nérac, we have seen, had conceded to the Huguenots fourteen places in Guyenne and Languedoc as security for the faithful fulfilment of the promises made to them. These places, unlike those granted by the peace of Poitiers and Bergerac, were to be restored at the end of six months. By that time it was presumed that tranquillity might be completely established. As the term approached, the question as to the conduct of the Huguenots became more and more difficult. Clearly the object for which the cities had been put in their custody was not

Preludes of new hostilities.

---

[1] Saracini to the grand duke, October 5, 1579, Négociations avec la Toscane, iv. 269; Mémoires de Claude Haton, ii. 980–983; De Thou, v. 616–619; also, see Ranke (Amer. edit.), 311.

[2] See the acts of the National Synod of Figéac, Aymon, i. 138–145. The numerous prescriptions regarding marriage, and the repeated prohibitions of dancing (a practice that would seem, from the thirty-second article of the succeeding Synod of La Rochelle, 1581, to have been rather increasing than diminishing), need not be inserted in these pages.

attained. The peace was no better observed since than before the convention of Nérac. In no province of the kingdom, in scarcely a point of the compact, was there an attempt to carry out the provisions conscientiously. Fresh places belonging to the Huguenots had been lawlessly captured by the court. Everywhere justice was denied to the Huguenots by the ordinary tribunals, while tedious delays had attended and, thus far, frustrated the institution of the "chambres tri-parties" which should have been erected for their special protection. Liberty of worship was denied to them; and if their children were sent to the schools to which they were guaranteed admission on equal terms with the children of Roman Catholics, they found the doors closed to them unless they would consent to abjure the faith of their parents. The peace was only an "appearance," an "imagination," a "fantasy," an exemplification of hope long deferred.[1] Almost at the very moment when their national synod was calmly deliberating upon matters of doctrine and practice at Figéac, the Huguenots had called at Montauban, scarcely more than fifty miles distant, one of their national political assemblies, to consult respecting the grave crisis in their affairs. The deputies were much excited. There were not wanting those that counselled an instant rising in arms, should the king attempt to recover by force the towns intrusted to the Protestants. But the majority was more temperate, and agreed that the King of Navarre be requested to resort to war only in case fresh remonstrances addressed to the crown failed to bring redress of Protestant grievances. All were of one mind regarding the impossibility of restoring the pledged cities. The court wits, never loath to make the Protestant ministers of the gospel responsible for any unpopular advice, would have it that the preachers had persuaded the Huguenot chiefs to this course of action by reminding them of the old maxim that it is the worst of symptoms when the sick man no longer retains the food he requires for his nourishment.[2]

---

[1] Anquez, Histoire des assemblées politiques des réformés de France, 28, 29.
[2] "Dicono che i loro ministri o predicatori li abbiano dissuasi, adducendo che era pessimo segno nell' infermo, quando non mostrava vista di ritenere

In vain did the king send Damville, who, since the death of his excellent brother François, in May, 1579, had succeeded to the honored name of Montmorency. Henry of Navarre came to meet him at Mazères, on the borders of the old principality of Foix, but in view of the little attention paid by the Roman Catholics to the prescriptions of the recent treaties, declined to surrender the small security which the Protestants still held against the sudden attacks of their enemies. Indeed, convinced that the outbreak of war could not long be postponed, the King of Navarre took measures to render the conflict prompt and decisive. With this end in view, he broke a number of gold coins in equal pieces, and gave or sent a fragment to François de Coligny in Languedoc, to Lesdiguières in Dauphiny, and to other Protestant chieftains in the provinces, bidding them to receive and act without hesitation upon any command respecting the time and manner of conducting hostilities that might hereafter be brought from him by messengers accredited by the possession of the fragments of the corresponding coins.[1]

The expected signal was not long deferred. In times of intense feeling even a slight provocation suffices to fire the train long since laid, and, when once the explosion has taken place, it becomes difficult, if not impossible, to apportion with accuracy the amount of responsibility belonging to the respective parties. The Huguenots had given the King of France many occasions for entertaining anger. The important city of Mende, capital of the district of Gévaudan, had been surprised by a Huguenot partisan leader on Christmas night, and, although the King of Navarre promptly disowned the act, the place had not been re-

---

quel cibo che doveva sostentarlo." Saracini to the grand duke, August 16, 1579, Négociations avec la Toscane, iv. 263.

[1] De Thou, v. 612, 613, is to be corrected by the more exact researches of the industrious Benedictine author of the ponderous Histoire général de Languedoc, v. 643. The meeting of Mazères was not, as the French translator of De Thou makes it, an assembly of the Protestant churches, and it took place in December, not a month earlier. The incident of the distribution of the broken coins occurred not at Mazères, as De Thou relates, but at a political assembly of the Huguenots held in Montauban, in January or February, 1580. Agrippa d'Aubigné's account, ii. 338, 339 (liv. iv. c. 3), is accurate.

stored to the royal officers. Moreover, the Prince of Condé, tired of his retreat at Saint Jean d'Angely, had by a bold movement thrown himself into La Fère, and thus secured at least a small part of Picardy—that refractory province with the titular government of which he had so long been forced to remain content. Great had been the indignation of the French king on hearing of the audacious blow struck by the younger Bourbon, and he had scarcely been prevented from proceeding at once to open hostilities by the entreaties of his mother, re-enforced by the plausible justification of the culprit and the intercession of the King of Navarre. Indeed, the latter, not without reason, gave Henry to understand that nothing could have occurred more likely to prove advantageous to the lasting interests of the crown than his cousin's presence in the heart of that very province where, four years before, had been laid the first foundations of the pernicious Catholic League.[1] But, more than anything else, the King of France and his counsellors resented the persistent refusal of the Huguenots to restore the fourteen cities of security placed in their hands for six months only, in accordance with the articles of Nérac. On the other hand, the Huguenots declared that, to their great regret, it was impossible for them to satisfy the king's requisition without exposing themselves to manifest ruin; for they had gathered none of those fruits of quiet and safety of which the cities pledged to them were intended to be the earnest. "Inasmuch," said they, "as these cities have been intrusted to the guardianship of men that are no other than your very faithful and natural French subjects, your majesty ought not to take the matter to heart as though they were kept back by Spaniards,

---

[1] "Prévoyant qu'en ceste province, en laquelle se sont jectez les premiers fondemens de ligue, il pourroit advenir par leur accroissement beaucoup de désordre à l'Estat, je m'asseure, Monseigneur, que pour en arrester le cours, rien ne pourroit tant servir que la presence de mon dict cousin." Henry of Navarre to Henry III., Nérac, January 24, 1580, Lettres missives, viii. (Supplement) 158. It is not a little significant of the real position of Catharine de' Medici, as still swaying the destinies of France, that in a letter to her, of the same date and on the same topic, the King of Navarre inadvertently uses the expression "voz edictz, Madame." Ibid., viii. 159.

Englishmen, or other foreigners. And in acting as we have done, it is our belief that we have not failed of keeping our engagements, since these were conditioned upon your majesty's promise to carry your edict into operation." [1]

In the war that ensued the King of Navarre took the initiative. The fifteenth of April was appointed as the time for a general rising, and for a few days before this date the Bearnese and his cousin were busy preparing and despatching letters intended to vindicate their course in the eyes of the world.[2]

A long "declaration" published by the King of Navarre on this occasion merits more than a passing notice; for it sets in a clear light the intolerable grievances to which the Protestant churches, of whom he claimed to be the "protector," were subjected.

<small>Justification of the King of Navarre.</small>

The Huguenots, said Henry, have not taken arms against the person of their monarch, but have risen simply because, by reason of continual infractions, the royal edict of pacification has become illusory, and their condition worse than that of the Jews in any land on the face of the globe, worse, indeed, than that to which, as Protestants, they would be reduced in Mohammedan Turkey or in the most barbarous of empires. In the matter of public worship, the edict grants them a place for their services in every bailiwick and sénéchaussée; but, despite frequent petitions, the provision remains unexecuted in most instances. No places have been assigned in the four bailiwicks of Champagne, none in Picardy, Anjou, Touraine, and other provinces. In some cases the Huguenots have been silenced by threats of massacre should they persevere in their demands.

---

[1] "V. M., Monseigneur, ne le doibt prendre à desplaisir, comme sy elles estoient detenues par Espaignols, Anglois ou aultres estrangers, et en cela ne pensons non plus avoir manqué à nostre foy lyée à la precedente promesse d'effectuer vostre edict, ainsi qu'elle est contenue aux articles de la conference." Henry of Navarre to Henry III., Mazères, January 10, 1580, Lettres missives, viii. (Supplement) 153.

[2] See the letter of Condé to Lord Burleigh, from La Fère, April 12, 1580, printed by the editors of the Journal of Lestoile (Collection Michaud et Poujoulat), i. 122, 123; and the letters of Henry of Navarre to the Earl of Sussex (April 13), to the Noblesse of France (April 15), and to Henry III. (April 20) in Lettres missives, i. 287-298.

Where their enemies have deigned to concede a place for the Protestant "prêche," it has been purposely selected because of its inconvenient situation. In the Pays de Caux, it is Cany—a village that has not a single Protestant inhabitant; for Meaux, it is Moissard—a village five leagues distant, deep in the forest of Crécy; for Rouen, Caen, and Bourges, it is some hamlet so remote as to preclude the attendance of the aged, as well as of the women and the children; as for Metz, the perils of floods are added to the other difficulties. In short, if, after long and vexatious delays, a place has been grudgingly granted, the choice has always fallen upon some sorry and distant village, near to a seditious population ready to massacre the poor Huguenots, on some river to drown them, or in recesses of the forests where their throats may be cut.[1] Under these circumstances the worshippers are forced to fall back upon those churches that may be established, not without hinderances of every imaginable kind, in the houses of such nobles as, under the edict, enjoy the right to hold religious services on their estates.

Nor are these the only annoyances to which the Huguenots are exposed. They are pestered by the curates and the vicars to bring their children to be baptized, to take, when near their end, the sacraments of the Roman Catholic Church, to contribute to the repair of ecclesiastical buildings. If advocates in Parliament or Châtelet, they are compelled to pay for masses and aid the religious fraternities. In almost every city they must drape their houses at the feast of Corpus Christi. The preachers are permitted to indulge in violent and seditious counsels to their hearers, whom they assure that fresh massacres are necessary, that the Huguenots must be exterminated, that such acts of blood are an agreeable sacrifice to God. No burial-grounds are granted according to the prescriptions of the edict. The bodies of the dead already buried are unearthed. So unjust are the officers of the law, that even where the mixed chambers are established,

---

[1] "On a tousjours choisi quelque mauvais village écarté, près des séditieux pour massacrer les pauvres gens, sur quelque rivière pour les noyer, ou dedans les bois et forests pour leur couper la gorge."

the Roman Catholics who constitute two-thirds of the court uniformly outvote the Protestant one-third. Cities that held for the Huguenots in the late war have, from revenge, been deprived of the exercise of justice. Protestants are excluded from office; their widows and orphan children can obtain no satisfaction for the murder of the dearest of relations. "In the city of Orleans, where by massacre, fire, and the greatest and most barbarous of cruelties one of the finest and most flourishing churches that ever existed in France has been reduced to ruin, the enemy still has his foot so firmly upon the throats of those who, through weakness or fear, have returned to the Romish religion, that they dare not say a word, or have a single religious book in their possession." The Protestants are caught and treated like brigands; their cities are the objects of lawless attack; their property is pillaged; their women are shamefully insulted. As to their cities of refuge, they contented themselves with the eight that were intrusted to their keeping for six years, and the fourteen that they were to restore in six months. But none of the engagements made with them have been kept. Excluded from some of the cities to which they sought to return, any Huguenots that have borne arms are in perpetual danger. Leagues, fraternities, processions, intimidate them and remind them of possible massacres awaiting them in the future.

Such was the picture drawn by Henry of Navarre of the injuries done to his fellow Huguenots—injuries to which they could no longer submit without the prospect of entire ruin. His own private wrongs and the wrongs of his cousin, the Prince of Condé, in the retention of cities belonging to them of right, and in the exclusion of the prince from his government of Picardy, were set forth in detail, but the particulars need not be repeated here.[1]

---

[1] "Declaration et protestation du roy de Navarre, sur les justes occasions qui l'ont meu de prendre les armes, pour la defense et tuition des Eglises reformées de France. Imprimé nouvellement, 1580." The document is given in full in Cimber et Danjou, x. 1-52. A counter declaration of Henry III., intended to weaken the King of Navarre, and promising protection to all Protestants that might remain quietly at home, was issued June 3, 1580. Text in Isambert, Recueil des anciennes lois françaises, xiv. 478.

Were these complaints well grounded? There seems to be no reason to doubt it. Was the oppression of the Protestants so remediless as to make a resort to arms unavoidable? Here opinions differed widely. The Huguenot nobles, with brave Châtillon among them, declared it impossible longer to maintain the forms of a peace that secured none of the rights so solemnly pledged by royal edicts, secret articles, and supplementary compacts. No sooner had the messengers of Henry of Navarre arrived, bringing with them the broken coins that were to accredit them, than they leaped into the saddle and hastened to the scene of action. Not so the ministers of the gospel, not so the people. Above all, the great province of Languedoc showed marked reluctance. Tired of conflicts, from the blasting effects of which they had not yet recovered, the cities—Nismes, Montpellier, and other places scarcely less important—positively declined to take up again the weapons of civil war; and it was not until more than three months had elapsed that "the city of antiquities" overcame its scruples. Aigues-mortes, Lunel, and Sommières were for a time the only towns of the lower part of the province whose Protestant population forsook their peaceful pursuits. La Rochelle and her old champion, François de la Noue, he of the Iron Arm, openly expressed their detestation of the war so lightly begun by the King of Navarre, and denounced it as unjust.[1] There were, indeed, not wanting those who denied that, so far as the Bearnese was concerned, the outbreak of hostilities had any other than personal motives.

It is no part of my province to describe at length the circumstances that had transformed the peculiarly strong tie of fraternal affection once subsisting between Margaret of Valois and Henry the Third into intense hatred. It is enough for the purposes of this history to say that the fair but frail Queen of Navarre was fully resolved to condone all the moral delinquencies of her husband, could she but move him to renew the struggle against her brother. If we may credit the gossip of contemporaries only too likely to be well informed, she did not

---

[1] Lestoile, i. 128; Agrippa d'Aubigné, ii. 348; De Thou, vi. 14.

even disdain to call in the assistance of her own rivals in the affections of her husband, and to employ timid Mademoiselle La Fosseuse, scarcely more than a child in years, to help in involving the wretched kingdom in new broils.' Be this as it may, there can unfortunately be no doubt respecting the loose morals which the unlucky bride of Saint Bartholomew's Day brought with her from the Louvre and made a current feature of the court at the foot of the Pyrenees, once distinguished by the virtues of Queen Jeanne d'Albret. Whether justly or not, the seventh civil war in which the Huguenots became involved received the sobriquet of "La Guerre des Amoureux"—"the Lovers' War."[2]

The conflict was fortunately of comparatively short duration, being well likened by a contemporary to a fire kindled in straw, so suddenly did it burst forth into flame, so uncertain was its progress, so completely did it die out at last. The better part of the Huguenots had remained peaceably at home, and the leaders had, consequently, at their disposal only the feebler portion of those who might have followed them in a war respecting whose necessity and justice there was less doubt.[3] In some places, too, the Huguenots who took part

Most of the Huguenots take no part.

---

[1] "Cela fit que pour lui remettre la guerre sur les bras, à quelque pris que ce fust, cette femme artificieuse se servit de l'amour de son mari envers Foçeuse, jeune fille de quatorze ans, et du nom de Montmorenci . . . fille craintive pour son age." Agrippa d'Aubigné, ii. 345 (liv. iv. c. 5). This chapter has a painful interest for the student of the public morals.

[2] Ibid., ii. 346 : " Ainsi fut resolue la guerre, qui pour les raisons susdits fut nommée la guerre des Amoureux." Henri Martin, Histoire de France, x. 600, is justifiably severe in criticising the blunder of a modern writer of some pretensions : "M. Capefigue, avec sa légèreté ordinaire, impute à Anquetil d'avoir inventé le nom de 'Guerre des amoureux,' aux temps des marquis de Louis XV. Il est fâcheux que M. Capefigue n'ait pas mieux lu les historiens de l'époque dont il écrivoit l'histoire."

[3] Lestoile's remarks (i. 128) are striking enough to be quoted : "Ceste petite guerre fust un petit feu de paille allumé et esteint aussi soudain, la meilleure et plus forte partie de ceux de la religion n'aiant bougé de leurs maisons, et y aians esté conservé soubs l'auctorité du Roy. Le reste qui ne remua qu'à regret et par force (et par l'artifice, comme on disoit, de la roine-mère, que vouloit ung peu exercer son gendre ; qui l'avoit trop proumené à son gré), fust incontinent appaisé, et aussi tost que le Roy voulust, lequel aiant en cest

committed for a while the military blunder of following timid counsels. So the Poitevin nobles who made themselves masters of Montaigu attempted to carry on a mode of warfare that honorably respected the rights of peasants and non-combatants, and found, at the end of six weeks, that for their pains they had not become forty strong. But when, altering their tactics, they boldly struck in one direction after another, penetrating by their raids even to Pirmil (or Pillemil), in the very suburbs of Nantes, the capital of Brittany—when, in short, "they exchanged their ruinous discretion for an insolent and needful rashness," their numbers grew so rapidly that in ten days they counted fourteen hundred followers.[1]

In the absence of any signal battle, the most noteworthy incident of the war was the assault and capture of Cahors. This town, skirted on three sides by the river Lot, is situated about as far to the north of Montauban as Toulouse is to the south. It had been given, together with the province of Quercy, of which it was the capital, in dower to the Queen of Navarre, despite the altogether politic custom that limited the marriage settlements of female members of the royal family to donations of money, and avoided the alienation of the territorial rights of the crown. But Margaret had never been placed in the actual possession of Cahors, and the unwillingness of Henry of Valois to fulfil his engagements constituted another of the causes of the inveterate hatred entertained by that relentless princess against her brother. It was not difficult for her to induce her husband to espouse her quarrel. The King of Navarre, disgusted that two-thirds of the Huguenots should have declined to heed his

Henry of Navarre surprises Cahors.

---

endroit une intention couverte, contraire à celle de sa mère, les faisoit crier et taire comme il lui plaisoit." See the Mémoires de Gaches, 283, 284, as to the divided counsels of the Protestants of Languedoc.

[1] The graphic account of Agrippa d'Aubigné (Hist. univ., ii. 346-349), who was an active participant in this adventurous campaign, calls forth a well-merited eulogium of the gallant Huguenot's book from the pen of M. Henri Martin, in his great history, x. 600, 601: "C'est presque toujours dans ce beau livre qu'il faut chercher les traits charactéristiques qui mettent en lumière la vraie physionomie du temps."

summons to war, and anxious at last to strike some blow by which he might win the martial distinction for which he had begun more than ever to thirst, gathered a force and undertook an attack which was condemned in advance by his most judicious advisers as rash and foolhardy. The issue, however, justified his boldness. The garrison of Cahors was, indeed, fully as strong as the following of the Bearnese; the city boasted, in the person of Monsieur de Vezins, a governor as distinguished for his bravery and good conduct as he had showed himself eight years before illustrious for his magnanimity toward the personal enemy whom, at much pains, he rescued from butchery in the Parisian matins.[1] The burgesses of Cahors, especially such as had participated in a local massacre of the small body of Protestants nearly twenty years before,[2] were violently opposed to Huguenot domination, and were quite ready to fight against it. But Henry of Navarre was rapid in his movements. At the very instant that he was reported to be at Montauban, engaged in earnest discussion of new terms of peace, he presented himself at the walls of Cahors, and found the garrison unsuspicious of the intended attack. The king was so fortunate as to make his attack under cover of an extraordinarily severe storm. The very explosion of the petards[3] by which an opening was effected through the gates defending one of the bridges

---

[1] The Rise of the Huguenots, ii. 480, 481.

[2] The French translator of De Thou, in undertaking to correct the historian's statement, himself blunders; for the massacre referred to was not connected with the events of St. Bartholomew's Day, as he erroneously supposes, but occurred on Sunday, November 16, 1561; see Languet's letter of December 11, 1561, Epistolæ secretæ, ii. 185, and Histoire ecclésiastique des églises reformées, i. 536-538. About forty-two Protestants were murdered. De Thou gives an account of the occurrence (iii. book 32, 284, 285,) evidently based upon the Histoire ecclésiastique, but misplaces it.

[3] This new implement of warfare was so strange as to lead the historian De Thou to describe it at considerable length (vi. 5), and it has been asserted that the pétard was first used at the siege of Cahors. But Jacques Gaches, in his "Mémoires sur les guerres de religion à Castres et dans le Languedoc," 245, 246, claims that the first pétard ever used in his native province was employed, with terrific effect, three years earlier, at the attack made by a Huguenot band under Jacques and Antoine Mascarene, upon Lisle-sur-Tarn, May 23, 1577. It was, he tells us, " un reveille-matin diabolique."

across the Lot was mistaken by many of the inhabitants for a succession of claps of thunder. But when once the entrance had been gained into the interior of the city, the Huguenots found enemies not inferior to themselves in courage and resolution. Had not brave Vezins been mortally wounded early in the struggle, it is probable that the final issue might have proved quite different. Henry and his companions exhibited prodigies of valor. They wrested the ground inch by inch from the besieged. They entrenched themselves in the streets, and laid siege to the public buildings in which large bodies of the enemy had shut themselves up. They went out boldly to meet and repulse such fresh troops as came to the relief of the town. At length, after a combat lasting for several days, Cahors belonged to the King of Navarre. It had cost him the lives of some of his best officers and men, but the exploit was the greatest triumph he had yet won. If the declaration of a friend, that the surprise of Cahors, lasting six days and six nights, was the most honorable of the century,[1] be regarded as too strong a panegyric, it must be conceded that few pitched battles have ever more firmly established the reputation of a military leader for skill and personal courage. The effect was great and instantaneous. Henry of Valois was beside himself with rage, most of all against his sister by whose machinations he had been deluded into supposing that nothing was farther from the thoughts of her husband, now deep in deliberations for peace, than so daring a hostile movement. As for the city of Toulouse and the whole region, the inhabitants gave themselves over for lost, and expected nothing less than that their fair fields would become a prey to the victorious Huguenots.[2]

---

[1] Agrippa d'Aubigné, ii. 350. This writer exaggerates the duration of the struggle, while Davila, 379, 380, who makes it last but three days, understates it. M. Berger de Xivrey, who gives a letter of Henry written before the smoke of battle was well over (Lettres missives, i. 302, 303), shows from Faurin's journal, that it extended four days, from Saturday, May 28th, to Tuesday, May 31st, inclusive. See also Lestoile, i. 124; Sully, i. 76, etc.; De Thou, vi. (book 72) 5, 6.

[2] An interesting letter of Montmorency (Damville) to the king, written from Pezenas, June 12, 1580, gives a vivid impression of the amazement and consternation of the Roman Catholic party at this brilliant affair. All efforts to

When experienced generals surveyed the whole field of operations in Southern France, and reflected upon the straits to which the royal troops were reduced through lack of that money which Henry of Valois chose to expend upon his pleasures rather than in carrying on the war, they trembled for the future. It seemed, indeed, as if the misery of France could go to no farther length. In addition to the curse of war, heaven had sent another scourge not less difficult to bear. The plague, which so frequently made its appearance about this time, raged in different parts of the kingdom, but had chosen Paris for its especial seat. The number of victims for the year was, as usual, variously estimated. A newsletter carried it as high as one hundred and twenty to one hundred and forty thousand persons. A more moderate and probably more correct account made it reach the figure of thirty thousand for the capital and its suburbs. All that could leave deserted the doomed city. For the space of six months the profitable stream of strangers from all parts of Christendom which was wont to pour in altogether failed. The poverty-stricken artisans, cut off from their ordinary means of gaining a livelihood, were likely to die of hunger A sight never before seen attracted the notice of the curious—numbers of workmen, upon whom time hung heavily because they had absolutely nothing to do, playing at games of quoits on the Pont Notre Dame and in other places most noted for the busy transactions of commerce.[1]

Ravages of the plague.

Despite, however, the brilliant success of the King of Na-

---

relieve Cahors were futile. "Tousjours ce a esté en vain, et ceste ladite ville prise, perdue, saccagée et ruynée. Elle est de si grande importance que encores qu'elle ne soit en ce gouvernement, ains en celle de Mr. de Mar. de Biron, la ville de Thoulouse, du ressort de laquelle elle est, et tout ce quartier là en [est] devenu si effrayé qu'ilz pensent que tout est perdu et en proye." Loutchitzky, Documents inédits, 135.

[1] Lestoile (under date of July, 1580), i. 125. See, too, Mémoires de Claude Haton, ii. 1013; and "Copie d'une missive envoyée de Paris à Lyon, par un Quidam à son bon amy, contenant nouvelle de la santé et du nombre des morts de la contagion, audict lieu et cité de Paris. A Lyon, 1580," reprinted in Cimber et Danjou, Archives curieuses, ix. 321–326. Haton notes, two years later (ii. 1081), that in a certain village near Provins almost one-half of the population had died of the plague.

varre's attack upon Cahors, and notwithstanding the inroads of destructive pestilence, the affairs of the Protestants did not prosper. The king's counter declaration, of the third of June, wherein he professed his firm purpose to maintain his edicts, and promised protection to all Protestants that should remain quietly in their homes, had its desired effect of weakening those that had taken arms under Henry of Navarre.[1] Moreover, each of the three armies set on foot by the king obtained great advantages. The army which was intrusted to Marshal Biron reduced a number of Huguenot strongholds in Guyenne, and surprised the town of Mont de Marsan, a place of importance belonging to the King of Navarre. The second army, under Charles, Duke of Mayenne, was so fortunate as to check the progress of Lesdiguières in Dauphiny, and to take by assault the town of Mure (in the present department of Isère), the sole remaining place in Lesdiguières's possession. The third army, under command of the newly created Marshal Matignon, after a vigorous siege, reduced La Fère, in Picardy, in the absence of the Prince of Condé, who had gone to Germany in the vain hope of obtaining fresh assistance from the Protestant princes of the empire.[2]

Success of the royal arms.

In these circumstances there was little to encourage the King of Navarre to continue the war he had so rashly begun, and in the prosecution of which he had met with little support from his fellow Huguenots. It was time that the voice of those that insisted upon peace should make itself heard. The result was a conference held at Fleix, a castle of Périgord, conveniently situated between the territories held by the contending parties. The King of France, himself by no means averse to peace, welcomed the suggestions

Peace conference at Fleix.

---

[1] Supra, p. 202, note.
[2] See a sketch of these military operations in De Thou, vi. (book 72) 11, etc. I cannot forbear expressing my profound astonishment at M. Drion's remark (Histoire chronologique, i. 152) : "C'est en vain que le roi de France oppose trois armées, commandées par ses mignons, aux Huguenots, victorieux sur tous les points." De Thou (vi. 20) characterizes the struggle in these few words: "Les armes des Protestants ayant été malheureuses presque partout." Moreover, what does M. Drion mean by the term "mignons," as applied to Marshals Biron and Matignon, and the Duke of Mayenne, Guise's brother ?

of his brother Anjou. This fickle prince had been, in connection with Margaret of Valois, a principal instigator of the needless war. Now that his mind had become inflamed with the desire to obtain a crown in the Netherlands, he was even more anxious to allay than he had been to promote civil discord in his native land. He came in person to Fleix, to hasten the deliberations which, so far as the royal side was concerned, were entrusted to the Duke of Montpensier, to M. de Bellièvre, and to Marshal Cossé.

The treaty of Fleix, which was the issue of the conference, was, in the main, little more than a re-affirmation of the treaty of Poitiers, as modified by the secret articles of Bergerac and the provisions agreed upon at Nérac. If adding oath to oath could effect anything in the way of securing the perpetuity of the compact between the crown and its Huguenot subjects, then certainly this treaty, containing detailed prescriptions that all the most important personages of the realm should swear to observe it, from the reigning monarch, his mother, and his brother, the King of Navarre and the Prince of Condé, through all the gradations of dignity down to the seneschals, the provosts and maires of towns and cities, would have stood a fair chance of enduring for all time. And if threats directed against the partisans of unlawful associations and fraternities could avail in opposition to the active efforts of secret conspirators, the "Holy League" must have died beyond the possibility of future resurrection. And if words and assurances were sufficient to meet the case of the distressed Huguenots, their chronic complaints seemed likely to be silenced for many a year to come. They were guaranteed the liberty to reside anywhere in France without molestation. The Romish clergy were enjoined from indulging in discourses from the pulpit tending to create sedition and disturbance. Nowhere were Protestants to be compelled to contribute to the expense of repairing churches belonging to an opposite faith, or when ill, to listen to the exhortations of ecclesiastics whom they detested. The Gordian knot of the tapestry and decorations on Corpus Christi day and other great festivals of the Church of Rome was cut by an article limiting the obligation of the Huguenot householder to a passive consent should the public authorities choose to place the hated emblems of joy upon the front of his residence.¹ The rights of the Protestants to certain places for public worship, to convenient grounds for the burial of their dead, and to impartial courts of justice, were solemnly re-affirmed. Even in the matter of the cities of refuge little change was made. The cities temporarily intrusted to the Huguenots by the articles of Nérac were to be restored to the king—those in Guyenne, within two months, those in Languedoc thirty days later. In case of the other towns, which the King of Navarre engaged to give up at the expiration of the stipulated term of six years, no modification of the existing agreement was made save the substitution of Figéac and Monségur for La Réolle.²

---

[1] "Et ne seront contraints tendre et parer le devant de leurs maisons aux jours et fêtes ordonnez pour ce faire : mais seulement souffrir qu'ils soient tendus et parez par l'autorité des officiers des lieux."

[2] The articles of Fleix, described in the title as "le lieu de Flex près de la ville de Sainte-Foy," are given in Du Mont, Corps diplomatique, v. 381-4, in Benoist, Histoire de l'Edit de Nantes, i. (preuves) 54, etc. The first forty-six articles were signed by Anjou and Navarre, at Fleix, November 26, 1580, and the forty-seventh article at Coutras, December 16. Henry III. ratified them by his signature, at Blois, ten days later.

CHAPTER IV.

THE UNCERTAIN PEACE, PROTESTANT FEDERATION AND THE PARISIAN LEAGUE.

<small>Comparative quiet returns.</small> For nearly eighteen years had France been a prey to civil contention. For so long a time the Protestants had stood with arms in their hands for the defence of the lives of their wives and children, and had struggled to win a boon more precious than any human life—the undisputed right to worship God according to the prescriptions of a Word regarded by them as of supreme authority. There had, indeed, been intervals of nominal peace, but they had been brief, treacherous, and often more dangerous than the periods of open hostilities. The fitful dream had generally been disturbed by rude alarms of coming war, by portents of approaching disaster, or by tidings of murderous assaults actually perpetrated upon unoffending men and women engaged in divine service. The hope of quiet and of justice at the hands of the king and his ministers had been so frequently disappointed as almost to give place to a settled feeling of despair. Now, at last, the prospect seemed to brighten. Peace was secured for a time. Neither party would be likely to disturb it. The monarch's Roman Catholic advisers had learned from the incidents of the past few years that it was vain to expect the extermination of a religious party that had long since taken form and consistency, and had been welded together by the very force of the hard blows received—a party that was even beginning to accept as a badge of honor the designation first given as a term of insult, and whose members were proud to designate themselves as Huguenots because the name recalled glorious scenes in their heroic and protracted struggle.[1] The Protestants, on their

---

[1] One of the earliest evidences of attachment to the name once strongly repudiated is found in a letter of Henry of Navarre, July 24, 1580, wherein he

part, had about reached the conviction that any attempt to secure universal toleration for their religion was, under the present circumstances, a hopeless undertaking. Moreover, they were thoroughly exhausted by the expense and fatigue of war. There were, indeed, complaints against the precipitancy of the King of Navarre in concluding a struggle which he had as precipitately begun. But Henry had much to say in his own justification. If he had acted in the matter with the co-operation of merely a few deputies from the Protestants of Southwestern France, it was because his associates in Dauphiny and Lower Languedoc, as well as in the north of the kingdom, had neglected to send envoys after receiving timely notice, or had been prevented by the dangers of the way. As to the treaty itself, so far from being ruinous, it was the very salvation of the Protestant churches. "This peace," he wrote to his old friend and counsellor the reformer Beza, "is not to our disadvantage. It ought to be received and welcomed by all for the re-establishment of our religion. I have been warned by many of our ministers that it would be better for us to return again to the fires of persecution, which would tend more to our upbuilding, than that through a continuance of war we should see all piety and discipline trampled under foot. We should, they say, have been satisfied with far less than the terms conceded to us rather than not secure peace."[1]

[side note: Henry of Navarre's justification.]

True, the objection was in everyone's mouth, in answer to the complaints of the Bearnese prince, that his own court afforded the most signal instances of irregularity, and that a reformation of manners and morals could begin nowhere more appropriately than in his own life. The candid reformer to whom he

---

recommends a Protestant gentlemen as one "that is a very zealous servant of mine and an old Huguenot—qui m'est fort affectionné serviteur et ancient huguenot." Lettres missives, i. 309.

[1] Ceste paix n'est point desavantageuse ; il est besoing que chascun la reçoive et embrasse pour le restablissement de nostre religion ; estant adverty de plusieurs de nos ministres, qu'il vaudroit mieulx retourner encore aux feux qui servoient plus à edification, que, par une continuation de guerre, voir toute pieté et discipline mise dessoubs les pieds," etc. Henry of Navarre to Beza, end of November, 1580. Lettres missives, i. 330–333.

had written appears not to have been slow in calling his attention to this important fact; for although his letter does not seem to have been preserved, we have Henry's reply to it, and can form a tolerably correct idea of the wholesome but unpalatable truths it contained. However, it was a part of the easy good nature of the King of Navarre that he rarely resented sound advice, even (as, it must reluctantly be admitted, was generally the case) when he took good care not to act upon it. In the present instance his amiable and flattering assurances to Calvin's successor were characteristic enough to deserve a place here. "I beg you," he said, "to notify me on all occasions, and to speak to me frankly and freely. If I do not profit, as I should, by the holy admonitions given to me, at least you will know that I do not reject them." As to his household, Navarre confessed, in the same letter, that, like everything else, it shared in "the perversity of the times," and he declared that it was one of his objects in securing peace that he might be able to give his attention to setting it right. It is almost needless to say that this seems to have been the last the king thought of the worthy reformer's suggestion.[1] The court of Henry remained about what it had been. Henry himself was neither more nor less addicted to the pursuit of pleasure and to the gallantry that had for some time been nearly as much in fashion in Nérac as in Paris.

His own court.

For almost five years from the conclusion of the treaty of Fleix the Huguenots enjoyed an immunity from open attacks on the part of their enemies, which, if it did not constitute so profound a peace as the remarks of the historian De Thou would lead the casual reader to imagine,[2] yet presented a de-

---

[1] Letter of Henry of Navarre to Beza, February 1, 1581, Lettres missives, i. 351–354. Both from this letter and from that quoted above it is clear that Navarre highly valued the reformer's friendship, and earnestly desired his good offices with the French Protestants as well as with the count palatine and others. In the postscript he wrote: "Je vous prie m'aimer tousjours, vous asseurant que ne sçauriez despartir de vostre amitié à prince qui en soit moings ingrat, et continuer vos bonnes admonitions comme si vous estiés mon père."

[2] "L'édit ayant donc été publié, la France jouit pendant près de cinq ans d'une paix profonde, soit parce que la guerre étrangère avoit détourné la cause

cided contrast to their previous condition. Into the causes of this calm and of the political movement tending to a new and more dangerous outbreak, which took place under cover of peace, we must presently inquire. Meanwhile, it will be well to glance for a moment at the internal concerns of the Huguenots.

The fair promises of the monarch, even with the guarantee of the great seal of state affixed to them, did not throw the veterans of so many years off their guard, or induce them to relax their preparations for the possible contingency of renewed hostilities. It was among the first steps of the King of Navarre to convene at Montauban, in April and May, 1581, one of those political assemblies of the Protestants of France, which, indeed, must be carefully distinguished from their ecclesiastical bodies or synods, but which became more and more important, as time elapsed, in determining their religious as well as their civil interests. The Assembly of Montauban had been summoned without the consent of the King of France ; but Henry the Third through M. de Bellièvre, a member of his privy council, as well as by letter, gave his approval of the meeting, upon the condition that its energies should be directed to a firm establishment of peace. Nor did the assembly decline the condition. It is certainly significant of the situation of the Huguenots at this time, that the thirty-four deputies of whom the body was composed were not chosen, according to custom, by the provincial political assemblies, but by the provincial synods, and that nearly one-third of the whole number were ministers of the gospel. Nor is it less worthy of notice that the assembly betrayed, in respect to the King of Navarre, a certain degree of distrust, by confirming and elaborating a system of checks upon his authority. The "Protector of the Churches"—for so was he officially designated—was provided with a body of four "ordinary" counsellors, each of whom was to be selected and supported by a well-defined constituency. If he thought fit to add two more counsellors, these were likewise

---

de nos maux, soit parce que la cour n'étoit occupée que de ses plaisirs." De Thou, vi. (book 72) 116.

to be chosen by the churches.¹ Thus were the Protestants not only to enjoy the best means of information respecting the conduct of affairs, but by their representatives to exercise an important influence in shaping the course of events. The prudent men who devised the scheme were pardonable if they remembered that Henry of Navarre not only had shown unmistakable evidence of a self-will that might some day give trouble to his associates in arms, but had once changed his religion. It is possible, moreover, that the ease with which he could, on occasion, publish to the world his willingness to be "instructed," in case he were in error in matters of religion, had not altogether escaped the notice of shrewd men, victims of repeated acts of treachery, in whose characters a consequent suspiciousness was perhaps a venial fault.

In the Assembly of Montauban the Huguenots adopted a form of oath by which Henry of Navarre and his namesake Condé, as well as the deputies of the churches, while professing their loyalty and subjection to the king, bound themselves to remain united "not only in the same doctrine and ecclesiastical discipline, conformably to the general confession of faith of the churches long since published, but also in all that might depend upon their mutual and lawful preservation." They promised, moreover, to do nothing save by command of the King of Navarre, with the counsel and advice of the churches, "so as to refer all matters to the authority that is due to him and to the common consent of all." In signal contrast with the fearful imprecations of excommunication and eternal damnation contained in the oath of the "Holy League," the Protestant oath confined itself to the simple declaration: ".Those that shall do otherwise will be disavowed." ²

---

¹ Anquez, 30–33. As indicative of the distribution of the Protestants in France, I notice that the first counsellor was to be elected by those of Languedoc, the second by Dauphiny and Provence; while Brittany, Touraine, Maine, Vendômois, La Rochelle, Poitou, Saintonge, Aunis, and Angoumois united in choosing the third, and fourteen provinces of the north, east, and centre of the kingdom joined in the selection of the fourth. The two additional counsellors were to represent Guyenne alone.

² "Formulaire du serment d'union adopté par l'assemblée de Montauban, Mai, 1581." Anquez, App., 452, 453.

A few weeks only had elapsed since the adjournment of the Political Assembly of Montauban when the Eleventh National Synod met in the city of La Rochelle. If that nation is happy whose annals are brief and monotonous, this ecclesiastical gathering, in whose minutes no record occurs of serious differences of opinion and no hints are given of acrimonious debate, must be regarded as indicating a goodly prevalence of harmony and concord.[1] The deputies reported, and praised God for the fact, that there was no one in the churches they represented that rejected or combated the doctrines of the Confession of Faith. The canons adopted were few and of slight importance. The change that has come over public opinion respecting the wisdom of church laws regulating the style of dress in which a member can innocently indulge may lead some readers to condemn as puerile the detailed prohibition not only of immodest apparel, but of such garments as "bear marks of a too ostentatious and indecent novelty."[2] Others may be amused at the evident futility of the ban laid by successive synods upon the irrepressible and ever-increasing tendency even of the Protestants of France to indulge in the frivolous diversion of the dance. But every candid and impartial person must look with admiration at the clauses which in simple language provide for the careful preservation of the records of the memorable events in the fortunes of the churches since the first of the cruel wars waged against them, and not less at the provisions that exhibit the interest felt in the promotion of sound and thorough education by enjoining upon every "colloque" or presbytery to maintain at least one "poor scholar" during his studies for the sacred ministry.[3] Rarely has a persecuted people, long harassed by the enemies of its faith, made

---

[1] The only thing approaching asperity is a memorandum of the surprise of the synod that the deputies from Dauphiny, Provence, Forêt, and Auvergne, having all failed to be present, "have not even had the civility to make any excuse by letters."

[2] "Ceux qui ont quelques marques notoires d'impudicité, de dissolution ou de nouveauté trop fastueuse et indecente, comme sont les Fards, Plissures, Houpes, Lardoires, Guiquerolets, Seins ouverts, Vertugalins, et autres choses semblables."

[3] Aymon, Tous les Synodes, i. 146-154.

greater sacrifices to secure for itself the unspeakable blessing of competent religious instructors.

<small>Conflict between the civil and ecclesiastical authorities.</small>
It must not be supposed that the strenuous discipline laid down by the synods was enforced without opposition, nor that there was an entire absence of conflict between the civil and ecclesiastical authorities within the bosom of the Huguenot party itself. In Montauban itself, pre-eminently a Protestant city, the municipal records show that the ministers and the consuls had, this very year, a decided struggle in which both parties insisted strenuously upon their rights. The ministers from the pulpit denounced a book printed in Montauban as unsound in its teachings, and bade the faithful neither to purchase nor to read it. The consuls, doubtless upon the complaint of the printer, declared the act of the ministers illegal and in direct violation of the fourteenth article of the treaty of pacification, which confided the duty of superintending the matter of printing simply to the magistrates. It would appear that the consuls found other grounds of complaint besides this. The ministers had taken occasion to denounce in round terms the prevalent extravagance in clothing and headdress; and when called upon to justify their conduct had appealed to the canons of the National Synod of La Rochelle. Thereupon the consuls commanded that the ministers be summoned, censured, and forbidden from henceforth encroaching upon the functions of the civil magistrates. Moreover, they were to be required to produce the record of the action of the synod, in order that, after an inspection thereof, "the magistrates and the church might keep step together and not infringe on each other's rights." What further came of this particular dispute does not appear.[1]

It is certain, however, that the ministers never renounced, in

---

[1] "Les articles du cinode" were to be exhibited "pour veoir si les retranchemens des chevelures et abilhemens y est contenu" and "pour veoir ce qu'a esté arreste par iceluy sur la police ecclesiasticque, afin que les Magistratz et l'Eglise marchent de mesme pied, sans entreprendre rien l'ung sur l'autre." Déliberations du conseil de la ville de Montauban, October 28, 30, 31, et Novembre 7, 1581, in Loutchitzky, Documents inédits pour servir à l'histoire de la Réforme et de la Ligue, 177–180.

favor of the civil authorities, the right, believed by them to be inherent in the consistory, or church session, of exercising a wholesome restraint over the tendency of the gentler sex to indulge in sinful conformity to the frivolous pomps and vanities of the world. It made little difference who the culprit was; the noble fared no better than the peasant. Three years later a notable struggle took place, in which the parties were no other than Charlotte Arbaleste, the pious wife of Henry of Navarre's learned and trusty counsellor, Duplessis Mornay, on the one side, and the distinguished Huguenot pastor of Montauban, Michel Bérauld, on the other.

The divine was the same who was elected moderator of the Thirteenth National Synod of the French Protestant Church, at Montauban, in 1594, the first ecclesiastical convocation of the kind held during the reign of Henry the Fourth.[1] But long before that time he had come to be regarded as the leading theologian of the southern part of the kingdom. Catharine de' Medici, being at Nérac in 1579, expressed some curiosity to see him, and, when Bérauld was presented to her, informed him that she was delighted to find him quite different in appearance from what she had been led to expect. She had been told, she said, that his face was black and hideous as that of a devil, and that he and his colleagues were denounced as the accursed cause of all the disorder reigning in the province. To which the intrepid Huguenot, without changing countenance, replied: "Madam, I am such in body and in looks as it has pleased God to make me—not hideous nor terrible, as I have been pictured to your majesty. And since you have done me this honor to send for me, I have not been willing to fail in my duty, being quite ready to answer the calumnious reports set in circulation by my enemies against my colleagues and myself, who pray to God night and day for the health and prosperity of your majesties, and who in our churches preach only the respect and obedience that is due to them, according to God's command."[2]

It so happened that Michel Bérauld had felt himself called upon, shortly before the coming of the family of Duplessis

---

[1] Aymon, Tous les Synodes, i. 173.
[2] Mémoires de Jacques Gaches, 264, 265.

Mornay to Montauban, to denounce from the pulpit the fantastic mode of wearing the hair lately introduced by the ladies, and, in particular, the extravagant use of an elaborate head-dress, much in vogue elsewhere, wherein a frame-work of wire was employed for the purpose of giving greater effect. Some ladies had even been excluded from the Lord's Supper because they would not take an oath never again to indulge in such finery, nor to permit their daughters to commit the like indiscretion. It may well be imagined that the arrival of so prominent a family as that of Duplessis Mornay, known to dress according to the prevailing fashion, was looked upon with some interest by the female population of Montauban. But Bérauld was equal to the emergency. In fact, not only did he refuse to furnish to Madame Duplessis and her household the "marreaux" with which, according to a usage long observed in the Huguenot churches, every communicant was required to provide himself before approaching the holy table,[1] but he induced the consistory of his church to make a formal demand that the lady should "remove her hair." Charlotte Arbaleste, however, was as determined as her husband, and scarcely less ready with her pen. Accordingly she declined to accede to the summons, alleging that her attire was no novelty. She had worn it without reproach for the past fifteen years. During this time she had resided within the bounds of many of the chief churches of Germany, England, and the Netherlands, as well as of France. She favored her opponents, moreover, with a long and detailed confession of her faith, and a protest wherein she dwelt much

---

[1] The "marreaux" or "méreaux" (sometimes called "marrons") were tokens distributed a few days in advance of the celebration of the Lord's Supper to all who, in view of their correctness of belief and consistency of life, were regarded as prepared worthily to commune. They were usually round pieces of metal, almost always of lead, much resembling small medals or coins, and generally bore, on the one side, the initial or abbreviated name of the church by which they were given and a chalice, and, on the other, a reference to some verse of the Holy Bible. A number of marreaux have been described, and a few reproduced by wood-cuts, in the Bulletin de la Société de l'histoire du Protestantisme français. See i. 139, etc., ii. 13, xxxii. 182. Apparently the oldest of the extant marreaux do not go back of the seventeenth century; many of them belong to the period of the "Desert."

upon the danger of imitating the Church of Rome by teaching for doctrines the commandments of men, triumphantly calling attention to the circumstance that in no passage of Holy Scripture could any reference be found to wire, the fruitful source of the present dispute. But neither Madame Duplessis Mornay's cogent arguments nor the moderate advice of such distinguished fellow-ministers as La Roche Chandieu and Serres could bend Bérauld's inflexible views of a pastor's duty to his flock. The practical solution of the trouble was found in the step taken by Madame Duplessis Mornay of going, two days before Easter Sunday, to a town, three leagues distant from Montauban, where the Huguenot minister believed, with her, that the mode of wearing the hair is not an essential of religion.[1]

In the church of Cuq-Toulza a somewhat similar commotion had a different result. In this case the bone of contention was not a lady's coiffure, but the no less obnoxious farthingale. Here, too, the offender belonged not only to the higher ranks of society, but to the most pious portion of the community. The family of "Madonne" de Lamy had been one of the mainstays of Protestantism in the district, and among its earliest adherents. None the less did M. de Rogier, when he undertook a crusade against the current infractions of church discipline, call for exemplary censure of the objectionable article of apparel. In the end, after a valiant defence of her rights, "Madonne" de Lamy, less courageous, or less sure of support, than Madame Duplessis Mornay, saw herself compelled to yield the point, and the farthingale was consigned to merited obscurity.[2]

More frequently, however, the complaints came from the other side. Repeatedly the municipal records attest that the ministers of Montauban called attention to the fact that their salaries, very modest in amount at best, were many months in arrears.[3] At length they inform us that Monsieur Bérauld, minister of the Word of God, at the

Ministerial support.

---

[1] See the long account of this incident in a fragment published in the Mémoires de Duplessis Mornay, ii. 487-514.

[2] Notice sur l'Église réformée de Cuq-Toulza, in Bulletin, xxxi. (1882) 123. Cuq-Toulza is a small town forty miles southeast of Montauban.

[3] *E. g.*, under the dates of September 13, 1585, and April 17, 1586, Loutchitzky, 183, 187.

consistory meeting, on Wednesday last, reproached the church for its ingratitude in not paying him his salary, and took formal leave. The consistory offered to pay him, but the indignant pastor persisted in his determination. It fared no better with the council of the King of Navarre, which represented to him, but in vain, the scandal which his abrupt departure would cause. Finally, the municipal council of thirty took the decisive step of deputing Monsieur de Noalhons, one of the consuls, with three other persons of influence. They were commissioned to wait upon Monsieur Bérauld and beg him not to abandon his flock, nor to deprive it of the spiritual nourishment he had been wont to give to it. If he should still persist, they were to draw up a protest, with all due formality, and strive in every way to detain him.[1] He must certainly have been of a very obdurate disposition whom such manifold supplications could not move.

Once more a National Synod of the Protestants was held in the city of Vitré, in Brittany (May, 1583). The only important fruit of its deliberations was that the Reformed Churches of France and the Netherlands were drawn more closely together by the institution of a system of mutual recognition and representation. In token of perfect accord, the members of the synod signed their names to the copy of the Confession of Faith and the Discipline of the Low Countries which was submitted to them, and the Dutch delegates in turn subscribed the formularies of the French Churches.[2]

---

[1] Délibérations du conseil, etc., June 1, 1586, Loutchitzky, 188, 189. Michel Bérauld was no common man. He was of the best representatives of that part of the Huguenots that would be satisfied with nothing short of the most complete recognition of their religious rights. It has been truly said of him that, from 1583 forward, scarcely an event of importance occurred in which he did not take part. He remained in Montauban as pastor, and, from the date of the foundation of the Académie of that city (1600), as theological professor, till his death (1611), an event which was regarded as a public bereavement. He enjoyed, with the celebrated Daniel Chamier alone, the signal distinction of having been called to be moderator of not less than three National Synods—Montauban (1594), Montpellier (1598), and La Rochelle (1607). See Haag, La France protestante, i. 304–311 ; Aymon, Tous les Synodes, i. 173, 213, 296.

[2] Aymon, i. 157.

It was the last time for many a year that the Huguenots were destined to meet to deliberate respecting questions of doctrine and practice. The succeeding eleven years were to be a blank in their ecclesiastical annals. The clouds of war were already gathering, and the times would soon call, not for synods, but for military councils hastily summoned to devise measures of common self-defence.

If, since the convention signed at Fleix, the Huguenots had not been the object of a general war, it was, nevertheless, only too true that they were still disquieted by the vexatious neglect of the king and his ministers to execute the articles of peace. The clergy begrudged the Protestants even the common rights of humanity, and found in the lowest class of the population a willing ally. The curé of Saint Barthélemi grumbled that the edict of pacification went to the length of permitting the heretics to have ministers of their own faith to accompany criminals to the place of execution.[1] No wonder, then, that priests similarly inclined interposed every obstacle to the equitable execution of the compact of Fleix. The abbé de la Trinité instigated the royal council, upon a frivolous pretext, to prevent the services of Protestant worship from being held in Vendôme, an original fief of Henry of Navarre, from which his branch of the Bourbon family derived its designation.[2] Enterprises were set on foot, with the connivance, in some cases, of royal judges, to surprise the places left by the edict in Protestant hands. In Picardy no Protestant worship was tolerated. Where places of worship were granted, the same ingenuity was exhibited as of old to render the concession nugatory. For the Protestants of Lyons and Rouen the most useless of conceivable places were assigned, at the distance of a dozen leagues, in the heart of the forests, and where there were no Protestants in the neighborhood. With malicious perversity Roman Catholic magistrates interfered with the execution of wills drawn up for the benefit of the Protestant poor and

---

[1] Journal d'un curé ligueur (Jehan de la Fosse), 186.
[2] "Ma principalle maison et celle dont je suis extraict." Henry of Navarre to Henry III., June 19, 1581, Lettres missives, i. 374, 375.

sick. These unfortunates were thus deprived of the help offered them by their compassionate fellow-believers, while, at the same time, they were refused admission to the public hospitals and poor-houses on the score of their religion. For the burial of the Protestant dead no cemeteries were provided. The Huguenot fugitives of many towns and villages of Languedoc dared not approach their former homes, now pillaged or in ruins. In Dauphiny, when the Huguenots, yielding to Navarre's persuasions, admitted the Duke of Mayenne, that nobleman paid no respect to the stipulations of the edict, but proceeded at once to destroy the fortifications of Livron, Loriol, and other towns which had stoutly defended themselves in the past wars.[1] In Guyenne the Roman Catholics even seized the important city of Périgueux, one of the places of surety accorded to the Protestants by the peace of 1576, and confirmed to them by subsequent treaties, and refused to restore it to the proper owners.[2]

The Duke of Mayenne in Dauphiny.

Such complaints and others not very different in character

---

[1] We learn from the MS. Journal of Lesdiguières, first published by Professor Loutchitzky, that the Protestants of Dauphiny complained that the treaty of Fleix was made without their knowledge and approval, and sent first to the Duke of Anjou, and then to the king, to request that Gap and Livron be given them as places of safety, in lieu of Serres and Nyons, assigned by the treaty of 1577. The king refused to make the substitution, and sent Mayenne with an army to reduce the Protestant Dauphinese. A part of the Protestant noblesse dishonorably submitted, and, at length, Lesdiguières, after having stood out for a time, also consented to the peace, upon the engagement of Mayenne to execute "the edict and the declarations following thereupon." When Mayenne subsequently proceeded to dismantle Livron and put garrisons under governors that favored the League in Embrun and other towns, in distinct violation of the edict, he justified his perfidy by interpreting the "declarations" in question to mean, not the declarations of Nèrac and Fleix, but certain commands in writing to act after this fashion which he alleged that he had received from the king. See the interesting documents in Loutchitzky, 113–126.

[2] The king, indeed, offered in lieu the insignificant "bicoque" of Puymirol, near Agen, and 50,000 crowns, payable in instalments within two years, but Henry of Navarre denied that this was any adequate reparation of so signal an outrage. The correspondence of Navarre with Henry III., M. de Bellièvre, Marshal Montmorency, and Marshal Matignon, from June to December, 1581, is my authority for the statements of the text. See Lettres missives, i. 374–459.

continued to be made to the king for several years in the formal papers drawn up by the political assemblies of the Huguenots, and by the mouth of envoys sent to court for the purpose of securing the royal attention.[1] And it cannot be said that, so far as verbal or written assurances went, they were altogether fruitless. The declarations of the king that he intended to have his compacts with his Huguenot subjects executed to the letter, and that all violations of them should be punished, would have been eminently satisfactory, had any vigorous steps been taken to give the declarations effect. As it was, at the very moment the monarch was threatening to prosecute any persons that should stir up strife, the priests and monks were preaching against the Protestants, and no attempt was made by the government to hinder them. In fact, the means were adopted best calculated to keep up the memory of the most savage cruelties which that or any other age ever witnessed. "Upon Saint Bartholomew's Day," wrote William Cecil, from Paris, in 1583, "we had here solemn processions and other tokens of triumphs and joy, in remembrance of the slaughter committed this time eleven years past. But I doubt they will not so triumph at the Day of Judgment."[2]

Commemoration of Saint Bartholomew's Day.

It is time, however, that we should again glance at the political events which were only too soon to precipitate the kingdom into a new and sanguinary struggle, with religion for the convenient pretext. Again are we compelled to look at the condition of the court, and to view the despicable personage to whose feeble hands, by the strange order of things, the destiny of France was intrusted. The contemplation is, certainly, not a pleasant one, and we shall not dwell, beyond the absolute requirements of the case, upon a scene better calculated to create astonishment and inspire disgust than gratify a laudable curiosity. The wild freaks of insanity are at all times repulsive to the intelligent spectator; but the mad antics of a youth upon whom, for his own misfortune, and the misfortune of millions

---

[1] Mémoires de Duplessis Mornay, ii. 320, etc.

[2] William Cecil to Lord Burleigh, Paris, August 25, 1583. Ellis, Original Letters, Second Series, iii. 23.

Vol. I.—15

of his fellow-men, the happiness of an entire country is dependent constitute a theme which the sensitive would be particularly glad to pass over in silence.

With Henry of Valois everything was going from bad to worse. His recklessness no longer knew any bounds. Nothing was bought at too high a price that contributed to the monarch's own enjoyment, or to the advancement of those whom he had selected to be the purveyors of his pleasures. All France was impoverished to provide for the support of the royal minions. Even death did not lighten the burden resting on the poor people; for a deceased favorite, however humble in his origin, must be honored with funeral obsequies so grand and sumptuous that a former generation would have regarded them as too extravagant for a member of the royal house itself. Anne de Joyeuse and Jean Louis de la Valette were the minions upon whom Henry had fixed his principal affection, and with regard to whom he seemed only to have one remaining solicitude—lest he should not succeed in apportioning lands, revenues, and dignities in exactly equal measure to each. In his infatuation for these striplings, he rated his good fortune above that of Alexander the Great because he had found such excellent friends. They were the two pillars upon which the prosperity of France was to rest.[1] There had been, indeed, a great disparity between the favorites; for while La Valette, the grandson of a notary, had begun life in obscurity, the possessor of an income of barely four hundred crowns, Joyeuse was at least the scion of a race that had achieved some distinction and boasted noble extraction. With regard to both, however, their royal admirer could not rest content until he had by letters patent assigned them a rank superior to that of any others of his subjects, of however ancient a pedigree, save only the princess of the blood and the members of the houses of Savoy, Lorraine, Cleves, and Orleans-Longueville. Anne de Joyeuse, from a simple count, found himself transformed into a duke and a peer of France; while, a few months later, the same honor was conferred upon his rival

Henry III. and his minions.

Joyeuse and Epernon.

---

[1] Busbecq to the Emperor, May 2, 1583. Epistolæ, fol. 35.

THE UNCERTAIN PEACE.

in the king's affections. In order to provide the latter with an estate appropriate to his rank, the king himself purchased for him the title to an important fief, and young La Valette appears in history henceforth as the Duke of Épernon. To bind his favorites still closer to himself in the bonds of extraordinary intimacy, Henry resolved to provide them with brides from the same family from which he had taken his own wife. Joyeuse was married to Margaret, daughter of the Duke of Vaudemont, the queen's younger sister. The monarch bestowed upon her a dowry of 300,000 crowns, just as if she had been a king's daughter, and made a present of an equal amount of money to the fortunate bridegroom. The banquets, jousts, and other festivities in honor of the marriage cost France the round sum of over a million crowns. The queen's remaining sister, Christine, was not yet marriageable, but she was betrothed to Épernon, and her dowry of 300,000 crowns was at once paid to him. It was more difficult to find provinces of the kingdom whose control might be intrusted to the upstart grandees. A royal command was likely to be of little avail in such case, and might meet with a positive refusal. It seemed more advisable to purchase the consent of the present holder than to undertake to compel his acquiescence in the transfer. Épernon had cast longing eyes upon the important province of Guyenne, and the king offered Henry of Navarre the sum of two hundred thousand crowns to relinquish it. But the Béarnais would hear of no smaller price than a million francs, to which extravagant figure his debts appear to have amounted, and so the negotiation fell through.[1] For Joyeuse his royal master resolved to make provision from the still more extensive province of Languedoc. In vain, however, did he order the old constable's son to resign his office in favor of Joyeuse, offering him the government of the Île de France instead. Montmorency absolutely refuse to make the exchange, and took such prompt measures to defend his rights that the king dared not wage war

The king attempts to remove Marshal Montmorency.

---

[1] "Ha risposto volerlo fare, sempre vogli pagare li suoi debiti, che sono circa un milione di franchi." Renieri to the grand duke, Paris, July 30, 1582, Négociations avec la Toscane, iv. 421.

with him "lest worse might befall him."[1] And when, a year or more later, Joyeuse undertook to stir up a revolt in Languedoc so as to gain a foothold there, the full anger of the descendant of the first Christian of France burst out. Having taken at Clermont a number of Joyeuse's partisans with arms in their hands, he put them all to death. He was about to do the same to other rebels against his authority captured at Lodève, when he received a message from the king declaring his displeasure that the cities of his realm should be sacked simply because of a quarrel between two of his marshals, and confirming Montmorency as governor of Languedoc.[2] To so low an ebb had the royal authority fallen; and so much was gained by resolute rebellion. In other undertakings, however, Henry was more successful. The necessitous Duke of Mayenne was easily prevailed on to sell the admiralty to Joyeuse for one hundred and twenty thousand crowns, two-thirds of the purchase money being paid down and good security given for the balance; and for eight thousand crowns, a minor favorite, Alphonso the Corsican, obtained the post of colonel of the Italian infantry. In short, the king exhibited himself, in the eyes of an astonished world, in the capacity of a shrewd broker, driving bargains for the purchase of the offices of state once bestowed as rewards of merito-

---

[1] Lestoile (May, 1583), i. 162, 163.
[2] Lestoile (October, 1584), i. 179. The disgraceful dissensions of the court had their parallel in the cloister. Sir Edward Stafford, in his letter of December 13, 1583 (Murdin State Papers, 384), gives us an amusing description of a "battell" that took place among the nuns of Poissy, in whose refectory the famous colloquy had been held more than a score of years before. On the death of the abbess, seventy-five of the sisters voted for an old woman as her successor, the other twenty-five for Madame du Perron, sister of Marshal Retz. Thereupon, Catharine de' Medici went to Poissy to persuade the nuns to receive the last-named lady; but the nuns barred the entrance, and the queen mother's servants were compelled to dig under the wall to get the gate open. Shutting themselves in their rooms, the nuns informed Catharine from the windows that they would starve "afore theie would loose their accustomed liberties." The next day they fell upon Madame du Perron, and beat her until she could no longer stand, as the author of their "harme." The king's guards had to arrest two or three of the "heddyest" of the nuns and put them in other religious houses before the commotion could be quelled.

rious services, and paying the purchase money out of his own pocket.¹

<small>Infamy of the royal morals.</small> There is another side of the royal character and life at which fortunately we are not compelled here to look. Rumors were afloat of excesses too gross to be put upon paper— stories were told of unnatural crime with too much circumstantial detail to be rejected as apocryphal. Prudent men abstained from saying more than that if the king was childless, it was the direct result of his lewd practices. The Florentine agent wrote in his secret despatches to his own government: "I shall describe to you by word of mouth the king's mode of the life, albeit his majesty asserts his intention to change it. Anyone that understands what it is must doubt whether God will delay overmuch to take vengeance."² A few months later he writes that the prince, whom he contemptuously designates, from the strange mixture of religious performances with his orgies, as "the bishop"—"il vescovo"— seems no longer to have a concern for anything, and gives everyone the impression that, inasmuch as he has no children, he is quite willing that the kingdom should come to an end with his life.³ Now and then a wit, more audacious than the rest of his kind, ventured to hint even to the king himself what the world thought of the moral atmosphere surrounding the throne; as when, on one occasion, Henry having remarked to his companions after dinner that he had always heard it said that, whenever the royal court stopped for ten days or a fortnight in any place where the plague was raging, the pestilence was sure to disappear, Rucellai promptly rejoined: "Yes, Sire, one devil drives the other away."⁴

What with an effeminate king who shunned everything

---

¹ Albertani to the grand duke, May 1, 1582. Négociations avec la Toscane, 442, 443.

² "Chi la sa, dubita che Dio tardi troppo a risentirsene." The same to the same, July 15 and 22, 1582, ibid., iv. 443, 444.

³ Ibid., iv. 456.

⁴ Henry felt the home-thrust, for he afterward expressed his wonder that he had not incontinently thrown Rucellai out of the window. Ibid., iv. 541.

manly, who cared more for the dogs in the basket which he carried suspended from a ribbon about his neck than for his unhappy subjects, and could never wring money fast enough from those unhappy subjects to bestow upon his insatiate favorites, France was wretched enough. When his resources ran low, when financiers stood aghast, and even Catharine de' Medici was driven almost to despair; when the tried counsellors of the crown attempted to resist the creation of new offices entailing fresh burdens for the people, Henry took the matter into his own hands. One day he went to parliament, and, utterly disregarding the remonstrance of the judges, compelled that venerable body to register not less than twenty-seven edicts whose obnoxious character it had pointed out.[1] And so the load of taxation went on receiving almost daily additions to its weight, despite the fact that the king himself received but a small part of what was drawn from the purses of the unfortunate tax-payers. It was the English ambassador's opinion, "that there were so many officers in France, that what sum soever the king received, either Taille, 'Demayne,' or any way else, the officers being paid, there came to the king, of every French crown that was received for him, but seven 'sous,' which is not above two groats of our money."[2] The people might murmur, but no account was made of the discontent; the people was a beast that had lost its teeth and its claws.[3] In place, however, of blind devotion to its king, once a proud distinction of the tiers état, there was now in men's hearts a deep-set hatred of a prince whose sympathies could not be touched by the sight of the general distress. When Henry and his wife were seen making pilgrimages to Our Lady of Chartres, and the faithful throughout France were exhorted to join in the processions set on foot in every city, to supplicate heaven for the boon of an heir to the throne, the miserable victims of royal prodigality were more inclined to invoke

Financial embarrassment and dangerous expedients.

---

[1] De Thou, vi. (liv. 74) 130.
[2] Sir Edward Stafford to the secretary, December 22, 1583. Murdin State Papers, 387, 388.
[3] Lestoile, i. 154.

curses than blessings upon the head of their king, and desired rather the extinction than the preservation of his race.[1] The sovereign, as though deaf to the popular murmurs, continued his untimely efforts to induce his subjects, instead of suing for relief from existing taxes, to consent to assume new obligations. Commissioners were sent out with this object in view, but they soon returned reporting the entire failure of the effort. No money could be raised without the immediate prospect of open resistance and bloodshed. "If," said the people, "the king were in pressing need, we should know our duty and do it; but his majesty asks for money only that he may, as is his wont, enrich a few young men by his ill-timed liberality. The demand is out of all reason."[2]

Meanwhile, this spendthrift king, this inventor of orgies too foul for pen to describe, had his moods of devotion, and continued to practise ceremonials for the most part as puerile, and frequently leading to as lavish an expenditure of the hard earnings of the people, as his unmanly amusements. Early in 1583 a new order of penitents was instituted, under the express sanction of Henry III. It took the name of the Fraternity of "the Annunciation," and on the day upon which the Roman Catholic Church celebrated that event (the twenty-fifth of March) a grand procession was held, through a pouring rain, in the streets of Paris, much to the disgust of the intelligent men and women of the capital. The procession was repeated on Good Friday, but, for greater respectability, by torchlight. The Parisians, who had heard of the king's affection for the Flagellants of Avignon eight or nine years before, now for the first time had the opportunity of witnessing the strange rites of these devotees, and the more singular conduct of a monarch who did not hesitate to put off his ordinary garb in order to assume the rough sack worn by the penitents, and to go on foot carrying the great cross. There was no doubt as to the orthodoxy of the statutes of the order;

Institution of the Fraternity of the Annunciation.

---

[1] Mémoires de Claude Haton, ii. 1080.
[2] Busbecq to the Emperor Rudolph II., March 20, 1583. Epistolæ, fols. 28, 129.

for among the grounds assigned for the adoption of the name of the Annunciation of the Virgin was this: "The third reason has been our common hope of one day seeing in this kingdom, through the ardent requests of the very holy Virgin, all the heresies, errors, and false opinions that ravage and trouble it overturned and destroyed, according as the Church has been wont to sing in her lauds: 'Gaude, Maria virgo; cunctas hæreses sola interemisti in universo mundo.'"[1] None the less did many of the clergy, despite the expressed approval of pope and nuncio, denounce from the pulpit a new superstition under the cloak of which courtiers attempted to screen shameful excesses from popular scrutiny and reprobation. Even Catharine de' Medici, who had once given her sanction to the Flagellants of Avignon, was alarmed when she heard from many quarters the prophecy that Henry was about to exchange his crown for a cowl, and violently reproached the Jesuit Auger, whom she held responsible for having induced her son to neglect the affairs of state, and from a king become a monk. The very lackeys that followed their masters to court caught the infection of the general contempt for the new devotion, and set on foot in the courtyard of the Louvre a mimic procession of penitents; for which insult Henry, when he heard of it, ordered eighty of the culprits to be flogged in good earnest. Evidently the monarch's great device for winning the reputation of sanctity had proved a complete failure. The people preferred to judge of his character from the reported incidents of his daily life rather than from the hypocritical displays of his assumed devotions.[2] However, for a time Henry kept up

The king's waning devotion,

---

[1] "Les statuts de la congrégation des penitens de l'Annonciation de Nostre Dame." Reprinted in Cimber et Danjou, Archives curieuses, x. 443. Beside a very full confession of faith, the statutes contain a pledge on the part of each member, if possible, to attend mass daily, and to repeat, on getting out of bed and on going to bed, three pater-nosters and three ave-marias, kneeling and kissing the ground at each repetition. I find only one act of benevolence inculcated: Every year, at the beginning of Lent, the rector was empowered to make an inquiry for poor young girls of marriageable age. On Lady's Day the members of the fraternity were to contribute toward their dowry, and husbands were to be found for them after Easter.

[2] See De Thou, vi. 294, 295; Lestoile, i. 159, 160; Jehan de la Fosse, 194;

the farce—wore the penitent's dress, partook of the holy communion every fortnight, fumbled with a necklace of ebony with death's heads in ivory, frequented the Capuchins' church, sang daily for two or three hours with the monks, dismissed his musicians, refused to have dancing at court, and excited general wonder by the practice of his self-imposed austerities. Nevertheless, it was not many months before his devotion, as observed by the attentive eyes of foreign diplomatic agents, had sensibly diminished, and he had returned again to his old pleasures.[1] Meantime, superstitious fears never relinquished their hold upon

and superstition. the king, prone, like his mother, to place implicit confidence in signs and portents. One night he had a remarkable dream. He fancied that he was attacked, torn in pieces, and devoured by the lions, bears, and other wild animals, of which he kept a number in the Louvre for use in mock combats. On awaking, Henry was so impressed with the idea that some disaster impended over him, that he sent and had the entire collection of beasts shot by his arquebusiers.[2]

An enemy more to be dreaded than any that his imagination could conjure up was stealthily gathering its forces and preparing a blow which the king would prove impotent to parry. The ambitious family of Lorraine had never lost its

Discontent of the Guises. longing for the power of which it had enjoyed a brief taste during the reign of Francis the Second. Henry of Guise and his brothers, the Cardinal and the Duke of Mayenne, had inherited the traditions of their father and of

---

Busbecq, fols. 36-39; Busini to the grand duke, March 31, 1583, Négociations avec la Toscane, iv. 459. Friar Maurice Poncet, who distinguished himself by his denunciations, made bold to style the king's institution, in his sermons, "confrairie des hipocrites et athéistes." Lestoile, ubi supra.

[1] The bulletins of the king's spiritual health, as despatched to the Grand Duke of Tuscany by his agent about this time, are sufficiently grotesque. According to Busini (letter of June 27, 1583), it was the nuncio that advised Henry to renounce the penitent's dress. The record closes, at the end of a little over a half-year, with the discouraging entry that the king is well enough in body, it is true, but "sendo ritornato a suoi soliti piaceri, sendo declinato assai dalla devozione." Letter of October 13, 1583, Négociations avec la Toscane, iv. 475.

[2] Lestoile, January 21, 1583, i. 156.

the Cardinal Charles of Lorraine. They could scarcely be expected to submit with good grace to the eclipse of their greatness through the sudden elevation of such upstarts as Joyeuse and Épernon. An excuse for resistance to the royal plans must be found, and the search was neither long nor difficult. In the good old days of their absolute authority under the name of their nephew Francis, the elder Guises had certainly never exhibited over-much solicitude for the welfare of the oppressed people; indeed, the great demand of the people had been for an accounting on the part of this grasping family for the immense sums of money that had passed through their hands. As to religion, Duke Francis and his brother Charles had assured the Duke of Würtemberg, at the conference of Saverne, of their virtual agreement with the doctrinal views of the German Reformers, and the churchman had volunteered the statement that in default of a red gown he would willingly wear a black one. Now, however, it was very convenient to assume the attitude of defenders of the faith, and to simulate a deep solicitude for the woes of a nation staggering under a load of inordinate taxation. At the very same moment, however, the members of this highly patriotic family were in close communication with the King of Spain and the Duke of Alva, the more or less openly declared enemies of France, and were plotting to open the gates of the kingdom and allow a foreigner to invade the soil for which they professed so much interest. Such conspiracies can rarely be kept secret, and it was not long before vague intimations reached the king. The first authoritative statements came to him through a messenger sent by Henry of Navarre. The partisans of the League were to rise in Champagne and Burgundy, so soon as the Duke of Savoy should make his appearance on the frontier. Meanwhile Charles Emmanuel was providing stores of ammunition and massing his forces in Bresse, whence, as from a centre, he might conveniently strike a decisive blow either northward or southward. Nor had the emissaries of Philip and the Duke of Savoy been idle in France itself. The Duke of Montmorency, disgusted with the policy of the king, angry at the preference given to per-

Conspiracy between the Guises, Savoy, and Spain.

sonal favorites over the representatives of the oldest families of the kingdom, especially indignant that Henry should persist, as he believed that Henry still persisted, in the intention of giving the province of Languedoc to Joyeuse, had lent a willing ear to those that suggested a practical method of revenge. He was to await the invader at Pont Saint Esprit on the Rhône, and to be aided by the Spanish king and the Duke of Savoy, from whom he had already received pecuniary help. Philip, who, when the occasion offered, knew well enough how to subordinate religion to policy, had even approached the King of Navarre, and endeavored to seduce him from his loyalty by flattering offers. The Bearnese, falling in with the customs of the insincere diplomacy of the period, had for some time been maintaining negotiations with the occupant of the Escorial, which were purposely invested with an air of close secrecy. Neither of the parties, bitter and irreconcilable enemies as they were at heart, had any other intention than to outwit the other; but Philip could scarcely have been aware of the fact that Henry of Bourbon from time to time transmitted to the King of France a full account of what had been said and done.[1] Of late the Spaniard had made more definite and tempting offers. "If your master will consent," said the plenipotentiaries of Philip to Duplessis Mornay, Navarre's representative, "the King of Spain will furnish him with the means to make war against Henry of Valois, and will continue his support until he shall have placed the crown of France upon his head. But your master must make up his mind at once; our king has other customers in France who are ready to strike a bargain with him."[2]

Disloyalty of the Marshal Montmorency.

Philip attempts to seduce the King of Navarre.

---

[1] Duplessis Mornay reported to the King of Navarre the substance of an interview with Henry III., in which he had said: "Qu'on lui avoit dict que vous traictiez avec le roy d'Espaigne, par certaines personnes interposees: ce qui estoit vrai; mais que sa majesté se pouvoit ressouvenir qu'elle l'avoit trouvé bon, et que de fois à aultre on l'avoit advertie de ce qui s'y estoit passé." Duplessis to the King of Navarre, February 20, 1584, Mémoires, ii. 527.

[2] "Particulierement que vous ne lui voulliez celer que, depuis peu, vous auroit esté declaré, de la part du roy d'Espaigne, que, si vous voulliez, on vous don-

The tidings of such serious designs upon the peace and integrity of his kingdom, and even upon the possession of the crown itself, made for the moment an impression upon the mind of the king and of Catharine de' Medici. It seemed at one time as if the feeble and irresolute prince would awake from his dream of securing peace at any price, and adopt decisive measures that might forestall all future attempts of his insidious enemies. He authorized levies of troops in Switzerland, and sent powder and gensdarmes to Lyons, the most vulnerable point of his territory—precautions that evidently excited the suspicions of the Guises lest their plans were discovered. He went further, and calling to him the Dukes of Nevers and of Mayenne, one Saturday, in the Tuileries, consulted them as to how conspirators should be handled. "The ambassador of Venice," said he, "came to see me this afternoon. I am greatly indebted to the Venetians because of the excellent reception they gave me on my return from Poland, and now they ask my opinion in respect to a matter in which I should wish to give them sound advice. They have discovered a conspiracy of some of the chief senators against the state. The truth of the matter is ascertained beyond a question, but they know not how to manage it. What think you?" Mayenne and Nevers were, doubtless, not slow in discovering an analogy between the case of the inculpated

Henry's irresolution.

---

neroit le moyen de lui faire la guerre, et qu'on le vous continueroit jusques à vous mettre la couronne sur la teste. Mais qu'il estoit temps de vous ressoudre, sinon qu'il avoit son marchand prest en France. Et lui dis que ces propos m'avoient esté tenues à moi mesmes." Ibid., ubi supra. "Les négociateurs du roi d'Espagne sur les difficultés que je leur faisois traitant avec eux, me dirent en partant, ' He bien vous refusez ce parti, nos marchands sont prêts,' entendant ceux de Guise." Note of Duplessis Mornay to De Thou, v. (liv. 79) 378. The offers were made through the Viscount of Chaux and one Undiano, his brother-in-law. What Henry III. asserted of the readiness of Guise to join forces with Navarre, or with any other Protestant, inside or outside of the kingdom, "provided only he were promised friendship and help for his establishment," was equally true of Philip II.'s disposition. "The alliances which he sought with those whom he condemned most before men as the favorers of heresy are unknown to those alone who do not wish to know." Declaration of the king against the Dukes of Mayenne and Aumale, Blois, February, 1589, Isambert, xiv. 638.

Venetians and their own. Very naturally they recommended mature deliberation and the fullest information before any step should be taken. The apprehension aroused by the king's interrogatory was not lessened when, on leaving his presence, Nevers ascertained by careful inquiry from the ambassadors of the Italian states, and from the envoy of Venice in particular, that there was not the slightest basis of truth for the alleged plot against the doge.[1] Yet, after all, Henry stopped short of any manly resolution such as the occasion and his own peril demanded. It is true that he thanked his cousin of Navarre heartily for his expedition in acquainting him with the conspiracy, and repeated his declarations of good will to his Protestant subjects. "I shall maintain peace with them; I shall show that I am well disposed to them," said he to Duplessis Mornay. Nor did he decline Navarre's offices in seeking to win Marshal Montmorency back to his duty. It was impossible, however, in a day to remove the impressions sedulously fostered by his most intimate counsellors through long years. He still thought, because thus he had been instructed to think, that the only perils to which he was exposed came from the dreaded Huguenots. The Guises might be troublesome at times, but they certainly meant no great injury.[2] As for the League, had he not first absorbed it by proclaiming himself its head, and then ordered it out of existence by expressly stipulating, in the edict of pacification of 1577, that all such associations should forthwith cease? In his present frame of mind, it was to no purpose that Henry of Navarre might offer him his sword, as he had offered it, months before, to attack Philip the Second in the very heart of Spain, as a diversion to further the attempt of Anjou in the Low Countries.[3] It was equally useless to try to persuade him that the patriotism of the Protestants was beyond question, or, to use their own words, that there was

<small>Henry still leans to the Guises,</small>

<small>and discourages Navarre's advances.</small>

---

[1] Duplessis Mornay to the King of Navarre, March 9, 1584, Mémoires, ii. 546.

[2] De Thou, vi. 211, 391.

[3] Justification des actions du roy de Navarre (July 6, 1583), Mémoires de Duplessis Mornay, ii. 301.

not a Frenchman in France more French than were the Huguenots.¹ Only the stern logic of subsequent events could convince him that his life-long views were altogether false.

Yet the loyalty of the King of Navarre, the head of the Huguenots, had recently been put to a severe test. For much less important grounds had a constable of Bourbon, early in the century, renounced his allegiance to Francis the First, and gone over to the side of the enemies of his country. When the emissaries of Philip came to the friends of Henry of Navarre with the offer of two hundred thousand ducats to be paid to him upon his promise to wage war against the King of France, and with the promise of four hundred thousand more when four cities should have been captured, and six hundred thousand for every year the war might last²—when, I say, these tempting inducements were held forth to the owner of the little kingdom at the foot of the Pyrenees, he was still smarting from a recent and cruel affront.

The affront to the King of Navarre.

"Never was Africa so fruitful of novelties but that France to-day surpasses it." Thus wrote an ambassador to his imperial master.³ The incident that elicited the remark was the strange treatment just received by Margaret of Navarre at the hands of her brother the king. The bride of Saint Bartholomew's Day had apparently resolved that all the infamy should not fall to the share of the male members of the house of Valois, and had made her married life as notorious for its irregularities as her nuptials had been distinguished by bloody massacre. For many years brother and sister had cordially hated one another. Now there was new cause of hostility. Henry had written to his favorite Joyeuse at Rome, detailing with malicious particularity the story of his sister's most recent lapses

---

¹ "Il est assés évident qu'il n'y a François plus François en France qu' eulx." Raisons pour induire le roy à accorder la prolongation des places, etc. (August 12, 1583). Ibid., ii. 362.

² Agrippa d'Aubigné's figures (Histoire universelle, ii. 457) differ somewhat from those of Sully, i. c. 18; while Duplessis Mornay (in his note to De Thou, ubi supra) makes the immediate offer to have been 300,000 crowns, with 100,000 crowns monthly.

³ Busbecq to the emperor, September 20, 1583. Epistola 24.

from virtue ; and Margaret, hearing of the contents of the royal letters, had been so audacious as to send a body of armed men to waylay the bearer, whom they wounded and robbed of his bundle of despatches.[1] Incensed beyond measure at the insult to his authority, Henry resorted to a measure of retaliation as coarse as it was cowardly. At a public ball in the Louvre, where, in the absence of the queens, his wife and his mother, Margaret of Navarre occupied the first rank in honor, the king approached her, and without a word of warning began to recount, in the hearing of the assembled crowd of courtiers and ladies, the shameful course of her recent amours. He gave the names of her numerous lovers, and described their unlawful visits with such minuteness as might have been expected only from an eye-witness. He even charged her with having recently given birth to a child, the fruit of adulterous connection with the grand equerry of the Duke of Anjou ; and concluded the taunting speech by ordering her to free the court of her contaminating presence by leaving Paris on the morrow. Nor was this all. When the Queen of Navarre had hastily started, with such escort as she could obtain, in the direction of Gascony, she was overtaken, at the distance of a few miles from the capital, between Palaiseau and Sainte Claire, by a troop of arquebusiers under command of a captain of the king's guard. The very litter in which Margaret travelled was stopped, and the queen was roughly ordered to unmask, while some of her companions were arrested and taken to Ferrières and even to the Bastile, there to be subjected to a judicial examination.[2]

It had long been well known that between Henry of Navarre and his wife little love was lost ; none the less, however, did the prince feel himself called upon to demand an explanation of the insult offered to his house, and a reparation of his

---

[1] The story is detailed in Miss Freer's Henry the Third, ii. 334, etc., at greater length than is here necessary. The scandalous life of Margaret of Navarre is told, and exaggerated, in Le Divorce Satyrique, ou Les Amours de la Reyne Marguerite, Mémoires de Henry III., 187, etc.

[2] Busbecq, ubi supra ; Busini to the grand duke, August 22, 1583, Négociations avec la Toscane, iv. 468 ; Lestoile, i. 164 ; Négotiation de M. Duplessis vers le roy Henry III., Aoust, 1583, Mémoires de Duplessis Mornay, ii. 364, etc.

honor. But no satisfactory answer could the king give. In fact, heartily sorry and somewhat ashamed of the length to which his passion had carried him, he assured Duplessis Mornay and Agrippa d'Aubigné, Navarre's envoys, that he had since learned the falsity of the charges made against his sister. But when the Huguenot gentlemen insisted upon some positive atonement in place of dilatory promises and vague generalities, and called his attention to the fact that he had done either too much or too little—too much, if his sister were innocent, too little, if she were guilty—they found that they had to deal with a monarch whose ideas were those of an eastern tyrant rather than the sentiments of a Christian and magnanimous ruler. How, they asked, shall it be said that the King of Navarre has received his wife, taking her at the hands of her brother thus foully smirched — "tout barbouillée?" "How?" he responded. "As the sister of a king." "Yes, but a just king," was their quiet retort. And when Agrippa d'Aubigné, in his excitement, accounting delay the equivalent of a denial of justice, proposed, on his master's behalf, to renounce the honor of the king's alliance and friendship, the latter exclaimed: "Go home and tell your master, since thus you dare to style him, that should he take that course, I shall place upon his shoulders a load under which the shoulders of the Grand Seignior himself would bend. Tell him that, and be off; he needs such men as you." "Yes, sire," the intrepid Huguenot answered, "he has been brought up and has grown under the load with which you threaten him. If you do him justice, he will do homage to your majesty for his life, his lands, and the men he has gained; but his honor, sire, he will enslave neither to you nor to living prince, so long as he has a bit of a sword in his grasp." [1]

While maintaining, despite affront and neglect, unswerving loyalty to their sovereign, and turning a deaf ear to the seduc-

---

[1] Agrippa d'Aubigné, Histoire universelle, ii. 415; Mémoires, 493, 494; Confession catholique de Sancy, 421; Négotiation de M. Duplessis, Mémoires, ii. 371, 372. See, also, Harangue au roi Henri III., faite par M. de Pibrac pour le roi de Navarre, etc., Cimber et Danjou, Archives curieuses, x. 187-200.

tions of the Spanish king, the Huguenots were not neglectful of the means of self-defence. Peace, indeed, prevailed, and the rights of the professors of the purer faith were, within certain circumscribed limits, recognized by royal edicts having every sanction known by the law. But no prudent man could help foreseeing trouble in the near future. Protestantism had to do in France, as elsewhere, with an undying enemy. The king might seek peace through love for quiet and repose; Catharine de' Medici might deprecate a renewal of hostilities as unlikely to result in any accession to her influence in the state; the great majority of the nation might denounce war as the certain precursor of ruin to countless homes; but the Roman Catholic clergy remained unmoved in its fixed determination to suffer no lasting agreement to subsist with the heretics who despised its authority and refused obedience to its commands. In the recent introduction of the Society of Jesus this intolerant spirit had received a marked accession of strength, for, if the last to enter the kingdom, the Jesuits bade fair soon to outstrip all their ecclesiastical competitors in the race for wealth and power.[1] The League was by no means dead, whatever the king might say or think. The thought of new wars, of fresh massacres, was never permitted to fade from the minds of devotees; it furnished the staple of countless sermons in every part of France. As for the Guises and their confederates, it was matter of public notoriety that a close correspondence was maintained between them and the courts of Spain and Rome, looking to the renewal of the strife with the Protestants under more favorable circumstances. The pope, moreover, through his nuncio, again applied, and with more

<small>The Jesuits and the League.</small>

---

[1] Jehan de la Fosse chronicles, in February, 1580, that this grasping order had involved itself in a quarrel with the curates of the capital by erecting a house near the Porte Saint Antoine, in which they installed some of their brethren, authorized by a pretended papal bull to administer the sacraments in any parish of the city. "Lesdicts Jésuites," he adds, "entrèrent en ceste ville comme pauvres, toutefois tost après devinrent riches." Journal d'un curé ligueur, 184. "Les Jésuites, qui sont les boutefeux de l'inquisition, croissent de jour en jour en auctorité." Raisons pour induire le roy à accorder la prolongation des places, etc. Mémoires de Duplessis Mornay, ii. 361.

urgency than had been displayed on any previous occasion, for the reception of the decrees of the Council of Trent. Although the project again failed (not so much because of any zeal of the king in defence of the liberties of the Gallican Church as because its success would be interpreted as a sure prelude of the introduction of the Inquisition, so held in horror that the very prospect would create fresh commotions), it was significant that the present moment should have been selected for the attempt.[1]

Under these circumstances it was not strange that Henry of Navarre should espouse the plan of uniting all the Protestant princes and states of Christendom in a confederation for mutual protection against the assaults of their common enemies. To this course he was perhaps the more encouraged by the knowledge of an incident of recent occurrence across the British Channel.

If Queen Elizabeth was generally cold and irresponsive, if in her island home she often seemed selfishly indifferent to the claims of the Protestants on the continent, exposed as they were to the rude buffetings of cruel fortune, there were those among her subjects, and even at her council-board, who more correctly estimated the services of what might properly be styled the advance-guard of the Reformation, and who sincerely desired that the heroism it displayed should be duly requited. When Geneva was again made the victim of Romish plots, when its revenues were diminished, and its very existence was imperilled, a chord of sympathy was touched which thrilled every truly patriotic soul in the great commonwealth of Reformed States. Then did the queen's best and most trusted advisers send forth an appeal to "the wealthier clergy and other godly, to contribute of that blessing that God hath bestowed upon them toward the relief of that poor afflicted

---

[1] Busbecq, under date of July 3, 1583, Epistola 21. "Cepandant, c'est de lors qu'on commence de plus belle à brasser avec le pape une ligue generale à l'extermination de tous ceulx de la relligion ; que le nonce faict plus grande instance qu'il n'avoit mesmes faict apres les massacres de la reception et publication du Concile de Trente et introduction de l'inquisition." Justification des actions du roy de Navarre (July 6, 1583), Mémoires de Duplessis Mornay, ii. 302. Cf., also, ii. 361.

town; which," said they, "in some part may seem to have deserved the fruits of Christian compassion, by former courtesies and favors shewed to sundry her majesty's subjects, in the time of the late persecution in Queen Mary's reign." The royal treasury could not be called upon, such were the drafts made upon the queen's resources by the troubles of Ireland; but Burleigh and Walsingham, Warwick and Leicester, with their associates, whose names are signed to the charitable appeal, felt themselves fully warranted in urging the English bishops to interest themselves in securing from their dioceses a generous assistance for the city of Calvin, and this, not merely as a Christian duty, but as a mark of personal respect. "So," wrote they to the Bishop of Chester, "shall you give us cause to think that you not only care, as in Christian compassion you are bound, to relieve the present distress of that poor town, which, through God's goodness, hath served in this latter age for a nursery unto God's church, but also to satisfy this our request."[1]

The idea of opposing the designs of the papacy, now supposed to have succeeded in banding all the forces of the Roman Catholic world for the destruction of Protestantism, by means of a universal league of the professors of the reformed doctrines was not a new one. We have seen that the National Synod of Sainte Foy, in 1578, had expressed its hearty approval of the conference held at Frankfort, during the course of the preceding autumn, under the patronage of a tried friend of the Huguenots, John Casimir, count palatine—a conference in which, to use the words of the official record of the synod, "there were proposed several very expedient means, and some very appropriate and effectual remedies, for uniting closely together the reformed churches of the Christian world, as well as for suppressing and putting an end to all the differences and contests which our enemies have called forth between them, and preventing a few fanatical and

Proposed Universal League among Protestants.

---

[1] Lords of the Council to the Bishop of Chester, Richmond, January 28, 158¾. Printed in Francis Peck's Desiderata Curiosa; or, a Collection of divers scarce and curious Pieces relating chiefly to Matters of English History (London, 1779), i. 132.

bigoted theologians from condemning, as they have threatened and declared their intention to condemn and anathematize, the largest and soundest part of the reformed churches which are at a distance."[1]

Nor would it seem that the Queen of England had at this time been less deeply impressed than Casimir himself with the importance of coming to the succor of the French and other Protestants menaced with destruction, for she sent to Heidelberg a special messenger, a member of her own privy council, the chief part of whose instructions was to express her majesty's vehement desire that a union might be formed between all those princes that had shaken off the papal yoke.[2]

These were, however, but vague desires and attempts, prosecuted with too ill-defined a plan to secure their end. Unfortunately, if a few of the German princes appreciated its importance, there were others—and they were among the most powerful—to whom the trifling differences of faith between Lutheran and Reformed seemed almost as momentous as the differences between the common creed of both and the doctrines of the Church of Rome. Although posted in the very forefront of the battle, and awaiting only the signal that should bring on a general engagement between the marshalled forces of the despotic system of the papacy and the champions of the Reformation, there were leaders upon the latter side who dared to insist upon settling the minor disputes subsisting in the Protestant ranks, even in face of the enemy—leaders who seemed not to dream that in so doing they were playing false to their principles and jeoparding the sacred cause of liberty and truth. Who shall say that with a different appreciation of the claims of loyalty to their allies, with a higher and more disinterested view of the mutual relations of the several divisions of the one great Protestant host,

---

[1] Aymon, Tous les synodes, i. 131. See supra, c. iii. p. 175.

[2] So the veteran diplomatist, Hubert Languet, had been informed by the Englishman. "Nondum satis intellexi quænam habeat mandata a sua regina, nisi quod in genere mihi dixit suam reginam valde cupere, ut ineatur concordia inter eos principes qui jugum pontificium excusserunt, eamque esse præcipuam causam suæ legationis." Letter from Frankfort, September 23, 1577, Epistolæ secretæ, i. 320.

the Elector of Saxony and the princes that sympathized with his narrow views might not have rendered the long struggle of the League an impossibility, by preventing Philip the Second from pouring into France the treasures of Spain and ravaging her fair territory by means of troops paid with Spanish gold? Who can even maintain confidently that such a Protestant confederation as that which they were ineffectually begged to join might not have forestalled the carnage and the unspeakable misery of a Thirty Years' War?

It was at the very moment when the minds of Queen Elizabeth and the French Huguenots had begun to turn to the importance, or, rather, the absolute necessity, of a good understanding among all the members of the Protestant family (1577), that the great champion of Lutheran orthodoxy, James Andreæ, with the aid of divers other theologians, completed, in the old Benedictine cloisters of Bergen, near Magdeburg, the famous "Formula of Concord"—"Formula Concordiæ." The document that had been so carefully and satisfactorily prepared to harmonize the views of both wings of the adherents of the Augsburg Confession, and unite "Lutherans" and "Philippists" in one common confession, proved the apple of discord for the greater Protestant world. The "formula" not only settled for Germany the doctrines of the ubiquity of Christ's body, and the presence of that body with the bread and wine in the Lord's Supper, but condemned in no measured terms the views of the rest of the Protestant world.[1] Such a work was well calculated to widen and render lasting the breach between the two confessions.

The "Formula Concordiæ."

Undismayed by this untoward incident, Henry of Navarre had resolved to convert into a reality the vision of a great Protestant union that had hitherto seemed to recede in proportion to the ardor with which it was pursued. If we may credit his own assurances, it had been his first intention, so soon as peace was once more firmly secured to the Huguenots, himself to undertake a journey that should

Scheme of Henry of Navarre.

---

[1] Such expressions as the following can scarcely be regarded as conciliatory:
"Prorsus rejicimus atque damnamus capernaiticam manducationem corporis

include a visit to the courts of all the monarchs and to the dominions of all the states making profession of the Protestant faith. He would have crossed to Great Britain and made the personal acquaintance of Queen Elizabeth and young James the Sixth of Scotland. Thence he would have pursued his way to the Netherlands, to Denmark, to Sweden, to Germany. Such a visit would have been fruitful of good, for it might have bound the Protestant princes in a friendship secured by Gordian knots.[1] Unable, on account of the continued state of disturbance prevailing in France, to engage in person in this important undertaking, the King of Navarre brought his proposal of a general Protestant union before the National Synod of Vitré (May, 1583), where the first steps toward a practical solution of the difficult problem were taken. It was an auspicious moment when the representatives of two independent churches of the Reformation—the churches of France and of the Netherlands—solemnly affixed their signatures to each other's Confession of Faith and Book of Discipline, in attestation of their perfect harmony.[2] By this synod the King of Navarre was unanimously begged to pursue the project which he had explained, and to employ as envoys to all the Protestant princes and states of Christendom men of authority, piety, and sound doctrine.[3] It would appear that the synod suggested as the most proper person for conducting this delicate mission the learned and versatile Duplessis Mornay, to whose rapid and animated pen we owe so large a portion of the striking correspondence of this period going under the name of his master, Henry of Navarre. It was, therefore, not without a tinge of disappointment that the churches and Duplessis Mornay himself saw the negotiation intrusted to Mon-

Mission of Ségur Pardaillan.

Christi, quam nobis Sacramentarii contra suæ conscientiæ testimonium post tot nostras protestationes malitiose affingunt, quasi videlicet doceamus," etc.

[1] Henry of Navarre to John III. of Sweden, July 15, 1583, Lettres missives, i. 532. See also his letter to the Elector Augustus of Saxony, ibid., i. 535.

[2] "Où nous eusmes cest heur de voir les Églises de Flandres, par l'envoy de leurs depputez, unies en doctrine et confession avec les nostres." Henry of Navarre to the churches (about the end of 1583). Lettres missives, i. 616.

[3] Ibid., ubi supra.

sieur de Ségur Pardaillan, who, as superintendent of the king's house and finances, at this time exercised a controlling influence in the management of affairs. The selection was regarded as injudicious by that portion of the Huguenots known as the "consistorial party"—men with whom the religious element greatly predominated over the political; men whom we must regard as the very heart of the movement, because their devotion to it depended not upon attachment to the person of their master, but upon their conscientious conviction of duty. Ségur was a man of restless activity, but impulsive and even violent in his conduct, and more likely to offend by his roughness than conciliate by his address.[1] Besides, he was not inaccessible to the approaches of flattery. On one occasion, after sturdily opposing the acceptance by the King of Navarre of an invitation of Henry the Third to visit the French court, Ségur disgusted his friends by as strongly advocating the journey. The change in his sentiments was the result of the attentions shown to him during a trip to Paris which he was induced to take. And he would probably have succeeded in persuading Henry to go, had not blunt Agrippa d'Aubigné interposed. Taking Ségur one day to a window of the castle of Nérac overlooking the waters of the Bayse, he quietly pointed to the precipitous rocks below, and told him: "I am commissioned by all the good people here to tell you that this is the leap you will have to take the day our master starts for the court of France." And when Ségur, surprised, as may be imagined, at such a suggestion, asked who would dare to make him take it, D'Aubigné, unabashed, replied: "I shall do it, and if I cannot do it alone, here are those that will assist me." Ségur turned his head only to see ten or twelve of the most determined Huguenot captains,

---

[1] The Life of Duplessis Mornay styles Ségur "homme violent, vehement et brusque de son naturel," and says that the churches desisted from the farther prosecution of the matter, "la voïans en main d'une personne turbulente, qui n'estoit pas pour la faire reussir, parcequ'il avoit en luy plus de zele que de science." Duplessis Mornay expresses himself in similar terms in a note to De Thou, vi. (liv. 79) 355, from which we learn the interesting fact that, although Ségur received the appointment as envoy, Duplessis Mornay drew up the greater part of the documentary papers—"j'en dressay néan moins toutes les dépêches."

who had drawn down their hats over their eyes, as, the faithful chronicler tells us, they were accustomed to do when anyone looked them too steadily in the face without knowing what was the matter in hand. Needless to say, Ségur did not further urge the journey of Navarre to Paris.[1]

Was it because of any mistakes on the part of the envoy that the mission of Ségur did not realize all the success that had been hoped for, or were the intrinsic difficulties of the case too great to be surmounted by even greater abilities than he possessed? I am inclined to believe the latter supposition to be correct. In justice to Ségur, it must be said that Henry of Navarre never seems to have entertained any sentiments but those of unlimited confidence in the sagacity and fidelity of his ambassador, and certainly his extant letters furnish ample testimony to the complete satisfaction of the monarch with the mode in which the instructions given were carried out.

The document embodying these instructions, and especially that part which refers to England, deserves more than a passing notice. It dwells at length upon the dangers to which the Protestants, not only of France, but of all Europe, are exposed.

The envoy's instructions. Since the scandalous attempt of the Duke of Anjou to become master of Antwerp, says the writer, the Huguenots have lost the last spark of hope based upon the promised succor of that prince. Indeed, the duke would have liked to sell to the Spaniards the places held by him in the Netherlands, and has sent Giulio Birago (Birague) to the pope to express his devotion to the Roman See, and request his holiness to bring about a marriage between him (Anjou) and a daughter of the King of Spain. His desire is to conquer a kingdom for himself in England. Great, therefore, is Queen Elizabeth's peril, especially from the quarter of Scotland, for whose youthful monarch she would do well, as speedily as possible, to provide a suitable marriage. No more appropriate bride could be found than the sister of the King of Navarre. Meanwhile Queen Elizabeth should exert her influence to incline the Protestant princes of Germany to favor an alliance of all the adherents of

---

[1] Mémoires de Théodore Agrippa d'Aubigné, 494.

the Reformation. These princes were formerly insensible, but have now awakened to the dangers threatening them from the direction of Austria. Besides, now that the Archbishop of Cologne has become a Protestant, they can control the future settlement of the empire, since they have four out of the seven electors on their side. The only obstacle to the alliance is the divergence of views between the Lutherans and the Reformed respecting the Lord's Supper. Let the decision of this question be referred to a general council or synod of the churches of the Reformation; and, until this be convened, let all unite in good friendship and silence useless contentions. The King of Denmark has already used his kind offices with the Elector of Saxony, his brother-in-law, and the elector has moderated his rigor toward those professing the views held by Calvin, and has begun to show less favor to certain theological doctors long acting as firebrands in Germany. Queen Elizabeth's influence would be great with the Saxon prince, and he would, doubtless, be ready to join her in a Protestant confederation, seeing the intrigues daily fomented against him by the Jesuits. An English nobleman of prominence, Philip Sidney, for example, ought to be despatched to Denmark and Germany. After this the princes, the imperial cities, and the Swiss, not to speak of the inhabitants of the Netherlands, could easily be persuaded to throw in their lot with England and Protestant France. In case of hostilities each state would be expected to contribute according to its means. The plan of a league sketched many years since, between Henry the Eighth, the queen's father, and the Protestant princes, might serve as a model for the new alliance. In this Henry Tudor offered to contribute to the common fund as much as should be given by any two of the electors. Queen Elizabeth, it is suggested, may deposit in Germany a sum of two or three hundred thousand crowns, to be employed in the defence of any part of the Protestant world that may be attacked. The King of Navarre will also send money to Germany, as well as a great quantity of jewellery, the avails of which can be used for the good cause.[1]

---

[1] "Instruction pour traicter avec la royne d'Angleterre et aultres princes estrangers protestans, baillée par le roy de Navarre au sieur de Ségur, y allant

Besides the document of which this summary of the most important part may suffice, Ségur was provided with a "justification" of the King of Navarre's actions in the past, and of the step now taken. The grievances of the Huguenots therein set forth are already in great part familiar to the reader. Especially does the writer emphasize the evidence of the existence of a general league for the extermination of all French Protestants, found in the urgency of the papal nuncio for the publication of the decrees of the Council of Trent and the introduction of the Inquisition, in the favor shown to the Jesuits, and in the systematic attempts to abase the King of Navarre and cut off his means of maintaining his authority.[1]

The "Justification" of the King of Navarre.

It must not, however, be supposed that in an age in which, if the means of communication were less direct than at present, and the channels of information, consequently, far more difficult, compensation was made by the extraordinary activity of salaried spies, the King of France could long remain ignorant of the undertaking of his cousin of Navarre. Nor was the latter much surprised to receive, within a few months, vigorous remonstrances from the court of Paris, with no obscure intimations that his boldness in undertaking to send out ambassadors was interpreted as an offence falling little short of the crime of treason.[2] But to complaints and threats, whether by letter or by voice of messenger, the Bearnese replied with right kingly dignity and honest pride. " Besides the fact," he wrote on one

---

de sa part en juillet 1583; dressée et minutée par M. Duplessis." Mémoires de Duplessis Mornay, ii. 272-294.

[1] "Justification des actions du roy de Navarre, baillée au sieur de Ségur, pour le mesme voyaige que dessus, le 6 juillet, 1583." Ibid., ii. 295-303.

[2] When Bellièvre, Henry III.'s envoy, urged the King of Navarre to take back Margaret of Valois, he refused to see her again until the French garrisons should have been withdrawn from ten leagues around Nérac (*i.e.*, from Agen, Condom, and Bazas), on the ground that he was menaced in his principal abode, and, to use Henry III.'s own words, "considérant le mescontentement que j'avois de la negociation de Ségur, il estime que je le tiens pour criminel de lèze majesté, et partant qu'il avoit d'autant plus à se garder et penser à la conservation de sa vie." Henry III. to Bellièvre, January 4, 1584, Lettres missives, i. 625.

occasion, " that Ségur has no commission whatever to say or do anything against your state and the obedience I owe to your majesty, I have always believed, monseigneur, that having been born in my own kingdom and sovereignty, and holding the title and right by succession to that kingdom of mine, which is one of the most ancient, and which I have lost, or more than three-fourths of it, for the service of your crown, I had not, nevertheless, forfeited the right and power to entertain friendship and alliance, like the other kings and princes of Christendom, for the good of my affairs and the union of the confessions of the religion I profess. Many of your subjects who are not of my rank are left unreproved for similar acts, or, at least, do not cease to treat with strangers respecting any matter it may seem good to them to treat of."[1]

Navarre's reply to the king's complaints and threats.

In similar terms was Chassincourt, a special envoy for the purpose, instructed to explain Ségur's mission. "The Dukes of Lorraine and Longueville," he was to say, "and even the seigneurs de la Marck, who have fiefs in French territory, are not found fault with because of their undertaking to send to foreign states; while the Dukes of Nemours and Guise are seen daily treating of their affairs in Italy, Savoy, and Scotland, without rebuke from their sovereign lord. Much more, on account of his rank, may the King of Navarre assume the right to act in like manner. But if it be against the plan proposed that objection is made, let it be remembered that the chief purpose is to invite all Protestant princes to a synod that shall adjust differences in the interpretation of the Holy Scriptures. This, which is a purely ecclesiastical matter, cannot be viewed as just ground of suspicion. Besides, the princes to be visited are old friends of France, of all men the least likely to disturb its peace. As to the fund of money which the King of Navarre is said to have intrusted to Ségur for deposit in Germany, he has long desired to place half a million of crowns in that country to draw against, and, as the French monarch is well aware, for lack of that sum he has been compelled more than once to renounce divers great enterprises. Such an arrangement is

---

[1] Henry of Navarre to Henry III., February 8, 1584, ibid., i. 637.

certainly unobjectionable, if the end contemplated be a good one. And the King of Navarre has ample ground of complaint that fault is found with his course in this regard, whereas none was found with the late Cardinal of Lorraine for the treasure he kept in Venice, or with the present members of the house of Guise who, as everybody knows, have a store of money in Germany. Yet the projects of the house in question ought, in the judgment of the wise, to be looked upon with far more mistrust, in their bearing upon the King of France and his estate, than those of the King of Navarre. The King of Navarre is naturally great only in the greatness of that estate, while the Guises can acquire greatness only from its ruin." [1]

However complete the vindication of Henry of Navarre, it cannot be denied that the mission of Ségur, purposely distorted in its aims and exaggerated in its importance by the enemies of the Huguenots, supplied a very convenient instrument to the advocates of the "Holy League" in their desperate effort to rally the fanatical portion of the Roman Catholic population to the defence of their church and the struggle to annihilate French Protestantism. Of this more will appear in the sequel.

Ségur's mission misrepresented.

Upon the incidents of the embassy of Ségur itself it is not necessary to dwell at length, especially since no practical results followed the protracted and wearisome negotiation. As might have been anticipated, the plan proposed by the King of Navarre met the hearty approval of the enlightened Walsingham and the warm concurrence of the Prince of Orange; while Frederick the Second of Denmark, John Casimir in the Palatinate, and a few other princes were anxious to see it promptly carried into effect. There were those, however, even among the Protestant rulers of Germany, who, like the Elector John George of Brandenburg, if not positively hostile, were too lukewarm, in view of the ill-success of previous conferences for the settlement of theological differences, to lend it any hearty support. And there were others who, if they did not imitate the Elector of Saxony

---

[1] Instruction de ce que le sieur de Chassincourt dira au roy sur le voyaige du sieur de Ségur," etc., Dec. 25, 1583. Mémoires de Duplessis Mornay, ii. 398–401.

in positively refusing to grant Ségur an audience, were nevertheless resolved to have nothing to do with the Calvinists of France until these should have renounced their views regarding the Lord's Supper as a preliminary step toward rendering a union possible. The issue of the whole matter was that, after keeping Ségur waiting an entire year, the German Protestant princes of the more extreme type, on the first of March, 1585, addressed to the King of Navarre a reply to the letters and instructions laid before them by his representative. This extraordinary paper was signed by Augustus, Elector of Saxony, by John George, Elector of Brandenburg, by Joachim Frederick, Administrator of Magdeburg, by Philip Lewis, Count Palatine and Duke of Zweibrücken (Deuxponts), by Julius and William, Dukes of Brunswick-Lüneburg, by William, Duke of Würtemberg, and Ulrich, Duke of Mecklenburg—in short, by all the princes who had approved the "Formula Concordiæ" and enforced its adoption in their dominions. After a somewhat lame attempt to explain their long delay in answering the king's polite invitation, the German princes entered upon a discussion which, if in form it partook of the character of a request, was in reality nothing short of a lecture addressed to their royal correspondent. They conceded that the Swiss reformer Zwingle had, at the Colloquy of Marburg in 1529, retracted many of his errors; but he had to the end retained many traces of his original mistakes. As to Calvin and his followers, the German theologians had discovered in their works perversions of Scripture, and even blasphemies, so numerous, and errors of such magnitude respecting the person of Christ and kindred topics, that the strife about the Lord's Supper had almost fallen into oblivion. In reply to the suggestion made by the King of Navarre that Protestants ought to imitate the cunning of the papists, who suppress their mutual disputes in order that unitedly they may wage a more successful and ruinous war upon Luther and the rest of the reformers, the princes declare that the policy recommended is equally displeasing in God's sight and pernicious to the churches. Reconciliation of the kind indicated by the King of Navarre is wont to be of short duration. So the history of the past and present

Letter of the German Protestant princes.

experience combine in testifying. The princes themselves have found that the best way of promoting concord within the church is by explicitly rejecting and condemning erroneous views, and thus proving to all men that they have no intention that everybody should persist in his own view, cherish false doctrines in his own home, and cloak them from external observation with the mantle of concord. On the contrary, it is their desire that all submit themselves to God's Word, which alone is truth, and according to it believe, decide, and instruct others. The king's proposal that, in anticipation of the convening of a universal council, all disputes be left unsettled and the wrangles of theologians be checked, would, if put into execution, only inflame the righteous indignation of the preachers of the Word of God against princes who sought to transform them into dumb dogs that dare not bark at the wolves laying waste the fold of Christ.

So far from endeavoring to reduce to its smallest dimensions the difference of doctrine between Lutherans and Reformed, the princes seem intent rather to dwell with satisfaction on the impossibility of a reconciliation. For they take pains to recall the startling declaration of Theodore Beza, at the Colloquy of Poissy, "that the body of Jesus Christ is as far removed from the bread and wine as the highest heaven is from the earth," and, with a positiveness that would have seemed more suitable in the mouth of Cardinal Tournon and his brother prelates than in the mouth of Protestants, assert that it is clearer than the noonday sun that between Beza, Duplessis, and Ségur, on the one side, and themselves on the other, no agreement respecting the points at issue could be found. It was quite in keeping with the rest of the communication, that, at its close, the princes offered to the King of Navarre a copy of the Formula Concordiæ, which they evidently believed might, if he would take the trouble to read it and compare it with the Holy Scriptures, prove the means of his conversion. His subscription to the work of Andreæ and his associates, it was hinted, would give some hope of future peace to Christendom.[1]

---

[1] "Responsio Principum Electorum, etc., ad Regem Navarræ," apud G. von Polenz, iv. 402-405.

So ungracious an answer to the united efforts of Henry and his indefatigable envoy gave a death-blow to the scheme. Prot-estantism must go on suffering all the baleful results of disunion, because of the narrowness of theologians and the stubborn wilfulness of princes who would subordinate no doctrinal statement, however little it might affect the great and fundamental truths of Christianity, to the surpassing importance of a union demanded by the external relations of all the opponents of the Roman Catholic system. The Protestant counter-league must be abandoned as chimerical, because, forsooth, of the impracticability of persuading the inhabitants of France and England that the inhabitants of Germany were right in ascribing ubiquity to the material body of Christ.

The scheme receives its death-blow.

As for Henry of Navarre, he was in no great haste to acknowledge the receipt of the condescending epistle and the precious volume accompanying it. Not particularly drawn to literary pursuits or interested in doctrinal discussions, the king, who felt himself to be, more than any other man living, the champion of the faith, engaged in a desperate struggle, hand to hand, with an enemy that had already slain thousands of his fellow-believers, looked with pardonable disgust upon the theological treatise thrust into his hand on the eve of battle. He had asked bread, and his good and kind friends beyond the Rhine had offered him a stone. The soldier, abandoned at his post by the allies upon whose help he had a good right to count, postponed to some more convenient time and place, when the smoke of battle and the roar of cannon should have ceased, the reading of their polite invitation to be converted to their peculiar tenets.

Henry's disappointment.

Nearly four years later, after the stirring events which we shall soon be called to contemplate, after the King of France's craven submission to the dictation of the Guises and the League, after the revocatory edict of Nemours, after the victory of Coutras, and that long train of events which led to the assassinations in the castle of Blois, Henry of Navarre vouchsafed a reply to the German princes. It was dignified and courteous, betraying in every line, as do so

His tardy reply to the German princes.

many important state papers of the period, the masterly hand of Duplessis Mornay. While praising the zeal of the princes, it objected to the mode by which they strove for concord. There was much, Henry said, that he approved in the book which they had sent him; much also, however, that was obscure or could have been better expressed. There were many subtilties of expression and bitter phrases. He gave it as his opinion that more could be hoped from a general council than from condemnations of doctrine emanating from princes and therefore rather royal than theological in their nature. Meantime his own delay in subscribing the "Formula Concordiæ" would not surprise anyone, in view of the fact that such a devoted adherent of the Augsburg Confession as the King of Denmark had absolutely refused to affix his name to it; while it was known that of the theologians who had originally endorsed it some would now act quite differently were they called on to do so again. This, and a few sentences contrasting the asperity with which many of the Lutheran theologians attacked the "churches under the cross" with the kindliness and charity with which the French uniformly spoke of their German brethren, constituted the substance of the reply.[1]

Among the numerous documents connected with the negotiations just described there is one that deserves more than a passing notice, because of its bearing upon the remarkable man around whom cluster the most interesting events of the remainder of the sixteenth century. At a moment when Henry of Navarre is shortly to be called to enter the lists almost single-handed against the collected forces of Roman Catholic France, I make no excuse for pausing in the narrative of events to transfer to these pages the most essential particulars

---

[1] Letter of Henry of Navarre to the German princes, Feb. 15, 1589. Lettres missives, ii. 437-443. G. von Polenz has given (Geschichte des französischen Calvinismus, iv. 356-429) a long and exhaustive account of the attempt of the King of Navarre to secure union by the promotion of a Protestant counter-league. Compare the account in De Thou, vi. (liv. 79) 353-363. It may be noticed that in the interval between the letter of the German princes and Navarre's reply the Elector August of Saxony had died and had been succeeded by his son Christian, who was favorably disposed to the Reformed.

of a contemporary statement, drawn up for the purpose of enlightening Queen Elizabeth respecting the power and material resources of the prince who sought intimate alliance with her. Such being the avowed object of the writer, it will not surprise the reader that the account gives the most favorable view of the situation. In most points, however, it may be unreservedly accepted as accurate.

The King of Navarre, says this writer, stands in high reputation as the probable successor both of the King of France and of his brother, the Duke of Anjou, because the one has been so long married without having children and the other is not yet married. The Protestants, of whom he is the acknowledged head, have used the peace with so much moderation that they have caused the people to forget, to some extent, the wounds inflicted by war. Moreover, the nation has suffered so much, during the prevalence of the peace, either from the new taxes imposed by the king, or from the devouring of its means by the troops of his highness the duke, that the two brothers have succeeded to the hatred previously entertained against the Huguenots, and the King of Navarre has, after a fashion, inherited the kindly feeling in which they were held, inasmuch as there is found reason to complain of everybody save him. His popularity would increase still further could he draw near to the centre of the kingdom. On the contrary, the popularity of the Guises is waning. As evidence of this, it may be noted, they recently came to Paris well accompanied and in the midst of their friends, but never did they venture to speak a single earnest word in behalf of the reformation of the government. And yet this was the very time when iniquitous and burdensome edicts were issued, and when the authority of the parliaments was infringed. Yet the Guises bowed before Épernon and Joyeuse as reeds bow before a water-spaniel. They have put up with a thousand insults, in order to gain some vile advantage. They have begged for favor, basely accommodating themselves to all vices, to all enormities, to every kind of freak; acquiescing especially of late in that confraternity which the parliaments, the Sorbonne, the university, the convents, the preachers, all in general condemned and loudly and clearly denounced. Such conduct has shown everybody that theirs is only a mask of excellence, that they seek only to profit by the public calamities, and that, were they to be raised up to authority, the inn would indeed have changed its sign, but only to offer men still poorer wine to drink.

The King of Navarre's possessions are extensive. He holds in sovereignty a part of the old kingdom which gives him his title—Lower Navarre, in which lie all the passages leading from France into Spain, and Béarn, a district about two days' journey square, with such towns as Oléron, Pau, Lescars, Orthez, and Navarreins—territories that together can furnish three hundred horse and six thousand arquebusiers.[1] Besides these provinces, which he holds in his own right, he does homage to the King of France for the following fiefs: The County of Foix, stretching from the territory of Toulouse to the Spanish border, including the towns of Pamiers, Foix, Mazères, Saverdun, and Mas d'Azil, containing a population mostly Protestant, and capable of furnishing a body of six thousand arquebusiers. For this fief he is bound to the king only in the simple acknowledgment made by kissing the hand, and himself possesses every right of sovereignty covered by the term "régale." In like manner he holds of the king the County of Bigorre, with Tarbes for its capital, a large city but greatly injured in the course of the civil wars; the Viscounty of Marsan, with Mont de Marsan, Roquefort, and Villeneuve; the Duchy of Albret, reaching from Bayonne to Bordeaux and even beyond the Garonne and Dordogne, wherein are situated Albret, Tartas, Casteljaloux, Nérac, and other places of note; the County of Armagnac (upper and lower), with sixteen hundred noble fiefs holding it, and the archiepiscopal city of Auch, the episcopal cities of Condom and Lectoure, and the towns of

---

[1] It is characteristic of the Huguenot writer that, in the midst of this catalogue of possessions and warlike resources, he does not forget the new university and its theological students: "En ce dict pays y a une Université en la ville d'Orthés, bien pourveue de gens doctes, en laquelle il entretient tousjours 50 escoliers en theologie, chacung l'espace de dix ans, pour servir au ministere de l'Evangile."

L'Isle en Jourdain, Grenade, etc.; the County of Rouergue, with Rhodez, Milhau, and Vabres; the County of Périgord, with the important city of Perigueux; and the Viscounty of Limoges. In sum, with the exception of a very few cities, the lands of the King of Navarre extend all the way from the Spanish frontier to the river Dordogne, and from the Bay of Biscay eastward to Languedoc and Auvergne. Now, those who have read the histories of France and England, and especially the chronicles of Froissart, know what was the might of a Count of Foix, a Count of Armagnac, a Duke of Albret, in the times of Edward the Third, a period when these districts were not so rich and highly cultivated as they now are. Hence, they can conjecture the resources at the command of the prince who holds in his hands all their single possessions. Besides this, all the provinces referred to are subject to the King of Navarre in the further capacity of governor and lieutenant-general for the king in Guyenne. In each province there are certain gentlemen of note who, either with or without the title of governors, are charged with the duty of watching over the safety of the most important places. Of such, in the County of Foix, are the Viscount of Paillez and the Seigneur de Miossens, Grand Seneschal; and in Rouergue the four viscounts of Panat, Monclar, Bourniquet, and Paulin. In Limousin, it may be mentioned, is situated the Viscounty of Turenne, with its castle bearing the same name, strong in situation, surrounded by six or seven neighboring cities, and by a great number of castles of nobles capable of holding in subjection all Limousin and a part of Auvergne. In the absence of Viscount Turenne, Chouppes, who defended Lusignan after the massacre of Saint Bartholomew's Day, commands as his lieutenant. North of the Loire the King of Navarre has extensive possessions; for example, the Duchies of Vendôme and Beaumont, the County of Marle, the Viscounty of Châteauneuf, and the District of Thymerais. In these districts most of the nobles persist in the profession of the Protestant religion, although in the late wars they had no place of refuge in their vicinity, and all are devotedly attached to the King of Navarre. Each fief has its own governor appointed by him.

For the general administration of this wide domain, four courts—"chambres de comptes"—have been instituted: in Béarn, for the King of Navarre's sovereign possessions; at Nérac, for his lands held of the French crown between the Loire and the Pyrenees; at Vendôme, for those between the Seine and the Loire ; and at Fère in Picardy, for such as lie in that province and for his rich possessions in the Netherlands. Each court has its president and counsellors, and all the courts report to the privy council of the king, in which Grateins sits as his chancellor, Ségur as superintendent of the royal house and finances, together with Guitry, Duplessis, and other gentlemen "de robe courte." Besides which, the King of Navarre has a salaried counsellor in each of the three parliaments of Paris, Toulouse, and Bordeaux, within whose jurisdiction his possessions lie.

In addition to his own estates, many noblemen and cities give to the King of Navarre their support as acknowledged head and protector of the Protestants; while other cities, belonging to the French crown, are so mixed up with his patrimonial estates that they have always held for him—such, for instance, as Bazas, Puymirol, Montségur, and le Mas de Verdun.

The resources of the Protestants are at his command. These, in Lower Languedoc, hold Nismes, Montpellier, Aiguesmortes, Uzès, Lunel, Aimargues, Marsillargues, Bagnols, Sommières, and other towns. The Cévennes, Vivarais, Velay, and Gévaudan are theirs. Enjoying again the close friendship of Marshal Montmorency, to whom their own friendship is equally necessary, they can assure themselves, with the exception of two or three places, of all Languedoc, the richest and most important province of all France. These Protestants of Languedoc can bring into the field six thousand arquebusiers, but not more than four hundred horse, because their province is less provided with nobles than the other provinces. M. de Châtillon, a nobleman of high hopes, and son of the late Admiral Coligny, in conjunction with his brother, D'Andelot, has the conduct of the affairs of the Huguenots in Languedoc.

The Protestant cities and regions.

In Provence, the Protestant churches are visibly multiplying under protection of the peace; even in such places as Arles and Aix, with hostile prelates and parliaments, or Marseilles, where, four years ago, there was not an avowed Protestant, but now there are more than two hundred Protestant families. Although but one city—La Tour de Seine—was conceded to the Huguenots in this province by the edict of 1577, there are several other places devoted to the King of Navarre. Matters have gone badly in Dauphiny, chiefly through the bad faith of the Duke of Mayenne; yet the Protestants hold Nyons and Serres, by consent of the King of France, and some other cities covertly, while they have to fall back upon, in case of need, the active support of the principality of Orange, in their immediate vicinity. They can furnish four hundred mounted gentlemen who have served in all the past wars, and four thousand arquebusiers. In short, one could cross the entire breadth of France, from the Pyrenees to the borders of Savoy, and put up only in friendly places not more than three leagues apart, all of them either belonging to the patrimony of the King of Navarre or under his protection.

Going northward from the duchies and counties which are his by inheritance, we find between the Garonne and Dordogne the district known as "the two seas"—"les deux mers," with a population almost wholly Protestant, which has been known in four days to raise a force of four thousand arquebusiers—a district wherein are situated Bergerac, Sainte Foy, and Castillon, all of them commanding passages across the Dordogne. Beyond this, again, are the regions of Angoumois, Saintonge, Poitou, and Aunis, all of which will send out at least five hundred gentlemen of the Protestant religion and six thousand arquebusiers. Here it is that the Prince of Condé commands, with his residence at Saint Jean d'Angely, and supported by such Protestant nobles as the Count de La Rochefoucault and the barons of Montandre, Montguion, and Montlieu. North of the Loire, the Huguenot party is less conspicuous; but there is no province of the kingdom where it cannot boast a goodly number of adherents among the nobles and high gentry. In Brittany, for example, Rohan, Laval, and his brother Rieux are the most prominent leaders; in Normandy, young Count

Montgomery has succeeded to the rank of his father, the unfortunate instrument of the death of Henry the Second.[1]

<small>Death of the Duke of Anjou.</small> It is impossible to conjecture with any degree of accuracy how long the address of statesmen, and the known aversion of the Valois king for anything calculated to disturb his sluggish ease, might have postponed the fresh crusade against the Huguenots incessantly preached by priests and monks in almost every parish of the land, had not the outbreak of hostilities been precipitated by the decease of one of the most worthless of Frenchmen. For it was part of the miserable lot of the Duke of Alençon and Anjou that he was fated, after having been the bane of the land which had a thousand times been ashamed to confess having given him birth, to do more damage by the end of which he was guiltless than by the whole course of his perjured and contemptible existence. He had never, indeed, demonstrated by any labors performed the appositeness of his baptismal name of Hercules, but there was this much of resemblance between his exit from the world and that of the Grecian hero's Hebrew prototype, that he ended his career by effectually pulling down upon him the mighty fabric of the French state, and by slaying more unfortunates at his death than he had slain in his life.

The death of the Duke of Anjou, the king's brother, was the life of the League, and thus the prolific source of countless disasters for France.[2]

The fatal termination of the prince's lingering illness, which had for some time been looked for, came on Sunday, the tenth of June, 1584. It was just a month to a day before the pistol of the assassin, Balthazar Gérard, robbed the young Dutch republic of its founder and most brilliant and patriotic defender. In the case of the Duke of Anjou, his contemporaries char-

---

[1] "Discours envoyé à M. de Valsingham, secretaire d'estat d'Angleterre, pour induire la royne Elizabeth à embrasser l'union du roy de Navarre et des princes protestans d'Allemaigne," May, 1583, Mémoires de Duplessis Mornay, ii. 235-241; with the accompanying "Estat du roy de Navarre et de son parti en France," sent to Walsingham, ibid., ii. 241-256.

[2] "La mort du duc d'Anjou, frère du roy, est la vie de la Ligue." Recueil des choses mémorables, 602, margin.

itably expressed themselves as doubtful whether the catastrophe so fatal to France was the result of his excessive debauchery in the Low Countries, or of regrets for the overthrow of his ambitious designs, or of ordinary illness, or of some "bad morsel" administered to him, or of other strange and execrable devices, such as Salcède had many months before been accused of having attempted to practise.[1]

Less than three years had elapsed since the duke, then at the height of his hopes, flattered himself that he was the most fortunate of younger sons. Accepted suitor for the hand of Queen Elizabeth, and sovereign-elect of a good part of the Netherlands, there seemed to be no reason that the youngest Valois might not equal in prosperity, if he did not surpass, any other member of a family which had enjoyed more than its due share of royalty. Catharine de' Medici might henceforth lay aside as idle her superstitious fears based upon the prognostications of Nostradamus; for had she not seen all her sons become kings? But the promise of unmixed happiness had proved a phantom without reality or substance. The prospective bridegroom visited England and was greeted with loud acclamations, but in due time he returned to the mainland no nearer the accomplishment of his hopes than before he set out on his journey. The story of the prince's experiences as Duke of Brabant was no less unsatisfactory. The prudent Netherlanders had taken good care to restrict the authority of the sovereign they called in by very definite stipulations, and Anjou, though to Brabant had been added the County of Flanders, the Duchy of Guelders, and the Lordship of Friesland, found his influence upon the conduct of public affairs, and especially his control of the state's treasury, far different from what a "son of France" and a descendant of the autocratic Francis the First naturally claimed as his due. But when the faithless child of Catharine undertook to put into practice the lessons of perfidy he had learned from early infancy, he only succeeded in investing his name with a loathing not unmingled with contempt and ridicule. So far from making himself master of the hospitable city of

---

[1] Recueil des choses mémorables, ubi supra.

Antwerp, with Bruges, Dunkirk, Ghent, and other places of importance, and placing them in the hands of his French followers, it was but a few hours after the outbreak of the "French Fury" before the prince was a fugitive from the city he had attempted to betray, unable by his most audacious falsehoods to convince the world that he had acted otherwise than as the most untrustworthy and ungrateful of men.[1] Some five months later (June, 1583), he left the Netherlands never to return. At Château Thierry, on the banks of the Marne, fifty miles eastward from the capital, he breathed his last. From his bedside frequent bulletins had for weeks been sent out, giving an account of the slow but certain progress of his disease. The King of France, more than half glad at the prospect of being relieved of a troublesome brother, was secretly less anxious than the Guises, who saw in his death the removal of the greatest impediment in the way of enlisting the popular interest in the revival of the "Holy League." Henry of Navarre, more reticent and apparently engrossed in his own concerns, watched from afar the event that would bring him a step nearer to the throne of France. By a singular coincidence, the malady to which Anjou succumbed presented the same extraordinary symptoms as were seen in the last illness of his brother, Charles the Ninth. Great quantities of blood in the most corrupt state issued from every outlet of his body, and exuded from every pore. The strange phenomenon perplexed physicians and baffled the medical science of the day.[2] To complete the resemblance in the end of the two brothers, Francis of Anjou died a single day after the tenth anniversary of the death of Charles, on the same day of the week, and almost at the very same hour and minute.[3]

---

[1] Motley, Dutch Republic, iii. 561–580.

[2] Duplessis Mornay to the King of Navarre, Paris, May 2, 1584, Mémoires, ii. 594. Agrippa d'Aubigné, ii. 423: "Le sang, comme il estoit advenu au roi Charles, lui jaillissant par tous les pores."

[3] "Concessit fato die hujus mensis decimo, eodem pene tempore et momento quo superioribus annis frater ejus Carolus; eodem certe morbo, nimirum e pulmonis ulcere." Busbecq to the emperor, June 18, 1584, Epistola 38. Busini to the grand duke, June 11, Négociations avec la Toscane, iv. 511. De Thou, vi. (liv. 79) 378. It is worth while to note that the Gregorian Calendar

"It may be said with truth that the death of the Duke of Alençon was the ruin of France." Thus wrote the Florentine Cavriana four years later, looking back upon the desolations of civil war from the standpoint of the assassination of the Guises at Blois.[1] So, too, thought and wrote other dispassionate observers, the learned Pasquier among the number. Henry thought otherwise. Was he not well rid of a restless brother, who had long been disturbing his sluggish repose by erratic and ill-considered enterprises? Were not his resources greatly increased, now that the inordinately great appanage conceded to the duke, eight years before, was once more reunited to the possessions of the crown? Could the short-sighted king imagine that the turbulent youths with whom Anjou had consorted would now betake themselves to the Guises, and lend new strength to a formidable party inimical to the royal family? Or, that the material gain occasioned by the absorption of Anjou's territories would be far more than counterbalanced by the loss of a person next in the succession, whom fanatical hatred of Protestantism could not denounce as a heretic, and therefore incapable of mounting the throne of France?[2]

Disastrous results of Anjou's death.

The passions, as well as the events, of the age with which we are now concerned can be understood only so far as we succeed in transporting ourselves to it, and, for the time, assuming its ideas as our own. To us, who are accustomed to look on the State as entirely distinct from the Church; who, in repudiating the claim of the civil power to inquire into the conscientious belief of the individual man, have almost gone to the extreme of denying its right to

The thought of a Huguenot king repulsive to the Roman Catholics.

---

went into operation, so far as France was concerned, in December, 1582, the tenth day of that month being called the twentieth, and Christmas being celebrated on the fifteenth. De Thou, vi. (liv. 76) 218; Mémoires d'un curé ligueur (Jehan de la Fosse), 193 ; Journal du règne du roi Henri III., 62. Charles IX. died on Sunday, May 30, Old Style, or June 9, New Style, 1574.

[1] "Si può dire con ragione che la morte del duca di Alençon sia stato la rovina di Francia." Cavriana to Serguidi, Blois, December 31, 1588, Négociations avec la Toscane, iv. 850.

[2] See Étienne Pasquier's letter on the origin of the League, Œuvres (édit. Feugère), ii. 292 ; De Thou, vi. (liv. 80) 390.

strengthen the sanctions of its legislation, and guarantee the sacredness of testimony by a solemn appeal to the Creator of all things—to us, I say, it may seem almost incredible that the notion of the possibility that a heretic might one day sit on the throne of Clovis and Charlemagne should be so abhorrent to the sentiments of the masses of the French people as to make them an easy prey to the orators of the League. Yet it must be confessed, by every person who has familiarized himself with the pamphlet literature of the last quarter of the sixteenth century, that the apprehension was wide-spread, and, in many cases, based upon conscientious convictions. The "Most Christian King" a Huguenot, a Protestant, a heretic! The idea was preposterous. "We have seen in our own times that the heretics have, in pursuance of law, been confined in prison, condemned to death, ignominiously dragged in a filthy tumbrel to the public square, there to be burned alive, and, as an indication of horror for their deeds, reduced to ashes; and you dare to say that a heretic is the legitimate heir to the throne—a heretic who, according to law, ought to be consumed by fire! Is there any law that calls a criminal from execution to the sceptre? And your king, who is worse than a heretic and a relapsed heretic to boot, alone of his kind has this power! Though, as a relapsed person, he has voluntarily renounced his right to succeed even to his patrimonial estates, and has given himself over to the pains of execution! Yet you boast that he is the legitimate heir!" These were the words of zealous Roman Catholics; not phrases put in their mouths by their leaders, but the honest speech of their hearts.[1]

The question, however, as to the true authorship of the League, as it was now about to reappear in a new and more formidable shape, is not a simple one, nor is it probably possible to give a perfectly satisfactory answer. It is undoubtedly true that the League was not the creation of the Guises alone, nor indeed the creation of any other leaders.

The authorship of the League.

---

[1] The speech is that of the "manant" in a famous pamphlet entitled "Dialogue du Maheustre et du Manant," published ten years after this time, and therefore subsequently to the accession of Henry IV. Reprinted in the Ratisbon edition (1726) of the Satyre Menippée, iii. 379.

There is ample ground for the assertion that, even without them, there would have been found other noblemen of prominence only too willing to assume the direction of the movement.[1] Never could the secular clergy or the monastic orders have resigned themselves without a struggle to the loss of the hold of the Roman Catholic Church upon the State. If the aversion of the people for a Protestant prince as next heir to the throne of his " Very Christian Majesty " had seemed likely to prove too weak to answer their purpose, certainly the priests and monks of France would have discovered other instruments, perhaps nearly as serviceable, to give that aversion new strength and direct its manifestation. Yet the fact is undeniable that the popular hatred of Protestantism, fostered as it was by the seditious sermons of preachers in Lent and Advent, and by the more private influence of the clergy throughout the year, constituted only one of several factors entering into the complicated problem. Besides the more palpable agency of the princes of the house of Lorraine, there are traces more and more distinct of the insidious influence both of Philip the Second and of the Jesuits. All the personages in the drama now about to be enacted in France had for the motive which they gave out to the world the preservation of the Roman Catholic religion and the destruction of the Protestant faith. But it would be a serious mistake to suppose that this ostensible unity of purpose secured a perfect accord in their sentiments, or freed them from the jealousies that are wont to reign in the breasts of confederates in causes less abundantly provided with the insignia of religion and piety. When the King of Spain took the Guises into his pay, he took good care that the wages which he agreed to give them month by month, and never pretended to remit punctually, should not be large enough to enable them to crush their opponents and render them too independent of their

Philip the Second and the Jesuits.

---

[1] M. de Lezeau insists "que les princes lorrains n'ont esté que les accessoires de ce party, et que sans iceux on n'eust pas laissé de trouver d'autres chefs pour commander, estant une condition qui n'est toujours que trop affectée et recherchée." De la religion catholique en France, MS. first published in Cimber et Danjou, Archives curieuses, xiv. 86, 89.

employer. Fifty thousand crowns every thirty days, and this promised only for six months, was certainly a paltry allowance for the maintenance of an army in the field. It was sufficient, however, to encourage the Guises to borrow on the right hand and on the left, and involve themselves in hopeless bankruptcy.[1] On the other hand, the Guises had their own plans, quite irrespective of the interests of Philip; and even the Jesuits, forgetful of their Spanish origin, occasionally preferred the advancement of the Lorraine princes to the extension of the power of the Catholic King.[2]

Henry of Navarre was now the most conspicuous person in France, scarcely excepting Henry of Valois himself; and upon him and his actions was seen to depend in the highest degree the future of the kingdom. The king was by no means unfriendly to his Bourbon cousin. For once he was clear-sighted. At the death of her youngest son, Catharine de' Medici seems to have devoted her energies to secure an end quite as chimerical as the fantastic design she cherished about this time on the crown of Portugal. She would use the Guises and the League to thwart the pretensions of Henry of Navarre. Indeed, she ridiculed these pretensions. A relationship so distant as his with the reigning monarch she regarded as about as close as with Adam and Eve; beyond the sixth degree of remove, she said, there is virtually no tie of blood.[3] But after securing her Huguenot son-in-law's

Henry of Valois recognizes Henry of Navarre as his successor.

---

[1] We shall see that the confidential correspondence of the Tuscan agents at the French court, a fresh and inestimable source of information, is full of references to the straits to which Philip's parsimony drove the Guises. The duke will not have peace on any terms, writes Cavriana, February 11, 1588, because so advised by the King of Spain, from whose bounty he gets just enough to keep him alive, but not enough to satisfy his hunger—"della grazia del quale egli vivotta piutosto che vive, non tirando di là tanto che si possa sfamare," etc. In the same letter, Cavriana estimates the debts of the Duke of Guise at more than one-third of his entire property, and the debts of his cousin, the Duke of Aumale, at more than one-half of his property. He predicts that one must become a Catiline, the other a Cethegus. Négociations avec la Toscane, iv. 750, 753.

[2] See Michelet, La Ligue et Henri IV., 100, 121.

[3] Lettres missives, i. 674.

rejection, she firmly intended to discard the instruments she had employed, and secure the coveted crown for the representative of the elder branch of the Lorraine family, for the duke who had married her daughter, and for her daughter's children.[1] Her son had no sympathy with this plan, and saw its utter impracticability. Before Anjou's death, but when the serious character of his disease left no room for doubt as to the issue, Henry the Third, as he stood one day before the fire after dinner, had been heard by Mayenne and many other gentlemen of the court to exclaim: "Now I recognize the King of Navarre for my sole and only heir. He is a prince of high birth and good parts. My disposition has always been to love him, and I know that he loves me. He is a little hasty in temper and sharp; but at bottom he is a good man. I am sure that my humors will please him, and that we shall get along well together." To the prévôt des marchands, Henry had expressed himself in a similar way: "I am greatly pleased with the actions of my cousin of Navarre. There are those that are trying to supplant him, but I shall take good care to prevent them from succeeding. I find it, moreover, a very strange thing that any dispute should arise as to who is to be my successor, as if that were a question admitting of doubt or discussion."[2] A little later, on hearing that old Cardinal Bourbon said that the King of Navarre was not his nephew but a bastard, and, moreover, a heretic, so that the succession would be his in case of Henry's death, his "Very Christian Majesty" contemptuously remarked that the cardinal was a fool.[3]

---

[1] "J'ay receu nouvelles certaines," writes the King of Navarre to the Protestant counsellors of the chamber of justice at L'Isle en Jourdain, July 13, 1584, "que la royne, mere du roy mon seigneur, avoit traicté et resolu avec messieurs de Guyse la revocation de l'eedict de pacification, et qu'elle y avoit faict condescendre le dict seigneur roy. Touteffois sa Majesté, ayant despuis receu une declaration que j'ay faicte, auroit suspendu la dicte revocquation et estoit après à prendre quelque aultre deliberation." Lettres missives, i. 674. The queen mother's action is explicable only on the ground stated in the text.

[2] Duplessis Mornay, Clervant and Chassincourt to the King of Navarre, Paris, April 14, 1584, Mémoires de Duplessis Mornay, ii 575, 576.

[3] Busini, June 25, 1584, Négociations avec la Toscane, iv. 515, 516. Compare Lestoile, September, 1584, ii. 176.

Meanwhile Henry of Navarre himself received from his faithful servants some candid advice. Duplessis Mornay and the other envoys sent by their master to warn the King of France of the plots against his eastern provinces, from the side of Savoy and Burgundy,[1] were still in Paris when the news of Anjou's approaching death arrived.

<small>Duplessis Mornay's sound advice to the King of Navarre.</small>

Too sincere friends to be consummate courtiers, the three Huguenots did not confine themselves to congratulating the Béarnais upon having obeyed the inspiration of God, and having from Pau sent messengers to Paris to give timely information, thus turning his majesty's heart toward him. They embraced the occasion to remind him that the eyes of all France, and of a good part of Christendom, would henceforth be upon him; that his court would be the resort of foreign nations, and especially of the afflicted, whether princes or peoples. Until now he had been content with the testimony of his own conscience or the care of his private concerns; he must henceforth live for others. And they added these significant sentences: "Pardon your faithful servants, sire, one word more. These love affairs which are so open, and to which you give so much time, seem no longer to be in season. It is time, sire, that you make love both to all Christendom and particularly to France, and that by all your actions you render yourself agreeable in her eyes. And, believe us, sire, you will not have thus spent many months, seeing what we read in her countenance, before you will have gained her good grace and have secured the honorable and lawful favors that are within your reach, to enjoy them at your ease and contentment, when God, justice, and order shall call you thereto."[2] This was sound advice for a prince before whose eyes a magnificent destiny was unfolding; it remained to be seen how far he would profit by it.

There was, in the view of the King of France, one way, and only one, whereby the Bearnese could, at a stroke, defeat the projects of his enemies. Let him renounce his Protestantism, and few would venture to contest his right to style himself

---

[1] See above, p. 234.

[2] Duplessis Mornay, Clervant and Chassincourt, Paris, April 14, 1584, Mémoires de Duplessis Mornay, ii. 574–578.

heir presumptive to the crown, even on the ground of apostasy after his forced conversion of Saint Bartholomew's Day. With the intention of inducing him to take this politic step, the Duke of Épernon, one of the king's principal minions, took occasion to visit Henry's court, then sojourning at Pamiers, in the county of Foix. But the duke's arguments availed nothing.[1] The son of Jeanne d'Albret had not yet forgotten his mother's instructions, and could not at present be persuaded to barter his convictions against temporary advantages. It was so that, a year before, he had met the solicitations of his cousin, the young Archbishop of Rouen,[2] when that stripling—the prelate was not yet twenty-one years of age—requested him to change his religion in order to win favor with the nobles. "Tell those who make such proposals, my cousin," said he, "that religion—should they chance to know what religion is—is not stripped off like a shirt; for it has its home in the heart, and, thank God, is so deeply impressed upon mine that it is as little in my power to rid myself of it as it was at the beginning to enter upon it, this grace being of God alone and coming from no other source. . . . Believe me, cousin, the course of your life will teach you that the only true plan is to commit one's self to God, who guides all things, and who never punishes anything more severely than He does the abuse of the name of religion."[3]

Navarre is entreated to abjure Protestantism.

His noble reply.

Much as the stout refusals of the King of Navarre to change his religion under the pressure of political expediency commended him to the esteem of every upright and intelligent observer, certain it is that his "obstinacy"—for such it was styled by the Roman Catholic clergy—contributed greatly to the rapid spread of the League. Care was taken to spread the new proofs of Henry's incorrigible

Reports of Navarre's incorrigible obstinacy.

---

[1] De Thou, vi. (book 80) 391, 392, as modified by Duplessis Mornay's note.
[2] Subsequently Cardinal of Vendôme, and, after his uncle's death, Cardinal of Bourbon.
[3] Henry of Navarre to the Archbishop of Rouen, March 6, 1583, Lettres missives, i. 502, 503; Mémoires de Duplessis Mornay, ii. 230, 231. The reader needs, however, continually to remember that this and similar letters really emanated from the pen of Duplessis Mornay.

heresy far and wide among the people. Every Frenchman, it was said, must now expect to see a detested Huguenot upon the throne. The anger of heaven, so clearly manifested in denying to the reigning king the long-desired boon of a son and heir, despite vows and prayers at the shrines of Our Lady of Cléry, the Virgin " parituræ " at Chartres, and elsewhere, despite all popular litanies and processions in every part of the realm, is now revealed even more unmistakably by this sure prospect of disaster. And lest this should not suffice to move the ignorant peasantry and the bigoted burgesses, the story of Ségur's mission, grossly exaggerated and perverted, was circulated as proof positive that nothing short of extermination was in store for the faithful Catholics. Similar rumors of bloody intentions on the part of the adherents of the Reformation had prevailed almost from the time of its birth. It was reported more than once in the reigns of Francis the First and Henry the Second that the Lutherans were deeply involved in conspiracies to cut the throats of their orthodox neighbors. The massacre of Saint Bartholomew's Day had been preceded, if not precipitated, by wild accounts of the approach of an overwhelming force of cavalry under Francis of Montmorency, which was to avenge Coligny's wound and destroy countless numbers of the Parisians. Three years later the capital had been terrified by another fiction of the same sort, in which Henry of Damville, now Marshal Montmorency, figured much as had his elder brother on the previous occasion.[1] But now the enemies of the Huguenots added forgery to calumny. A document was fabricated purporting to be a solemn compact entered into by a Protestant confederacy. It was represented that at Magdeburg —others said Middleburg in Zealand—a meeting had been held, on the sixteenth of December, 1584, at which there had been present the ambassadors of the Queen of England, the King of Navarre, the Protector of Scotland, the Count Palatine, Prince Casimir, the Duke of Pomerania, the Landgrave of Hesse, the Rhinegrave, the Duke of Würtemberg, the Prince of Orange, and the Swiss Cantons.

Hostile rumors.

A pretended Protestant confederacy.

---

[1] The matter is well put in Michelet, La Ligue et Henri IV., 71, 72.

In the paper adopted there was but one great object distinctly stated, namely, to summon the King of France to observe his last edict of pacification and require him not only to swear to it publicly, but to pledge the faith of his states and affix his own signature to the solemn declaration. In case of his refusal, war was to be proclaimed against him. It was even stipulated how large should be the contingent of troops to be furnished to the common army by each of the parties. Queen Elizabeth engaged to bring into the field five thousand reiters and four thousand Swiss, in addition to the twelve thousand Englishmen who were to make a landing upon the French coast. Navarre and Condé promised twenty-five thousand arquebusiers and fourteen thousand horse. The rest of the high contracting parties stood pledged for smaller numbers, down to the Rhinegrave and the Scotch Protector, against each of whom only two thousand men were put down. The entire force of eighty-three thousand five hundred men was to be ready by the fifteenth of the coming month of April, and no truce or peace was to be concluded without the consent of all the confederates.[1]

The paper was a clumsy fabrication, and could easily be exposed. Ségur, represented in the document as having appeared as Navarre's ambassador, was not in Germany at the time referred to. The Elector Palatine and the Prince of Orange, both of whom, forsooth, engaged, through their plenipotentiaries, to appear in the field at the head of their troops in the coming spring, had been in their graves, the one for more than a year, the other for five months. The Elector Palatine had left only a minor heir, and his dominions were in the hands of Casimir as administrator. Besides, there was an absurd disproportion between the contingents allotted to the several princes and their well-known resources; not to insist

A clumsy forgery.

---

[1] "Protestation des liguez, faicte en l'assemblée de Mildebourg, au mois de décembre dernier passé, 1585." Reprinted in Cimber et Danjou, Archives curieuses, xi. 1-6. Among the other stipulations of this paper is one providing that a demand be made at the next German diet for the reunion to the empire of the domain "détenue à faux de l'evesque de Rome et autres." See Recueil des choses mémorables, 607, 608.

upon the singular blunder of the forger in choosing Magdeburg for the seat of the fictitious meeting, and yet not representing the Elector of Brandenburg, within whose territories the city was situated, as having taken part in the adoption of the compact either in person or by deputy. Well might the King of Navarre allege the fabrication to be an imposture worthy of emanating from the bench of a charlatan, and point to the circumstance that its author set the month of May following for the assembling of the Protestant confederates at Basle as being a revelation of the purpose of the managers of the League to resort to arms, ostensibly for the purpose of meeting the invading force, before that date.[1]

Whether true or false, however, the stories circulated by the League met with abundant credence among the people, and produced the desired effect.

Respecting the history of the origin of the League in the capital we happen to have a few particulars, though by no means all the information that could be desired. Fragmentary as is the account, it deserves careful study; for, in the midst of much that is obscure or doubtful, it places beyond dispute the fact that, instead of having been in its beginnings a spontaneous, popular impulse, as it has sometimes been portrayed, the powerful movement with which not the Huguenots alone, but the crown itself, was soon to be called into conflict, was the result of a systematic and carefully laid plan, intelligently devised and patiently carried into operation. Such a scheme presupposed, indeed, as indispensable to its success, a very ignorant and bigoted populace, intense in its devotion to the name and the forms of the Roman Catholic Church, easily stirred to frenzy by plausible, if unfounded, rumors, and already, as I have said, much disturbed at the prospect of a Huguenot successor to the throne of the Very Christian King.

The League in Paris the result of a systematic plan.

---

[1] Henry of Navarre exhibited the inconsistencies of the supposed "concordat," in the 23d section of his important manifesto, dated Bergerac, June 10, 1585, entitled "Declaration du roy de Navarre contre les calomnies publiées contre luy es protestations de ceux de la Ligue, qui se sont eslevez en ce royaume." Reprinted in the Mémoires de la Ligue, i. 133-163, and Mémoires de Duplessis Mornay, iii. 89-126.

But it was in itself no offspring of the people's hate of heresy, and the secret of its appearance at this particular time must be sought not in the obscure homes of the Parisian rabble, but in ducal palaces, in ecclesiastical houses, and in the Escorial itself.

<small>The plan of Charles Hotman.</small> Realizing the importance of Paris in any such struggle as all saw was impending over France, the Guises are said to have chosen one Charles Hotoman or Hotman, known also as M. de la Roche-Blond, to organize the strongly Roman Catholic party and bring all its latent energies into play. A man of considerable means and great activity, a burgess of the city and boasting of a good pedigree, Hotman seemed to be just the instrument demanded by the emergency. His mind had been inflamed by artful diatribes against the misfortune of the times, the ambition of courtiers, the corruption of the judges, the dissoluteness of all ranks of society, and the utter indifference of the king to the religious welfare of his subjects evidenced by his concession of the cities now pledged to the Huguenots. Liberal promises of personal advancement were also added. At first Hotman called but three persons into his counsels. All three were ecclesiastics: Jean Prevost, curate of Saint Severin; Jean Boucher, curate of Saint Benoist; and Matthieu de Launoy, canon of Soissons. After mature consideration, the number of counsellors was increased, each one of the four naming one or two persons more whose zeal and prudence were beyond question. Next, others were gradually and cautiously admitted to a participation in the scheme—curates, advocates, maîtres de comptes, and the like. To prevent discovery, the management of affairs was at first confided to a small council of nine or ten members, partly ecclesiastics, partly laymen; and <small>The council and the "five."</small> five persons were intrusted with the duty of carrying out the decisions of this council in the sixteen quarters of the city and the faubourgs. Compans attended to the whole of the "Cité"—the island to which Paris was originally confined. Crucé was charged with oversight of the two quarters of the "Université"—or the southern part of the town—and its faubourgs of Saint Marcel, Saint Jacques, and Saint Germain. La Chapelle, Louchard, and Le Clerc Bussy had

similar functions in all the quarters of the "Ville"—as the growing portion of Paris on the northern bank of the Seine was popularly designated. Everything was done with an eye to secrecy, expedition, and safety. Not a living man was admitted by the "five" into the new society until his character and previous history had been thoroughly canvassed by the council, and his devotion to the Roman Catholic religion, or, as it was more succinctly expressed, his "zeal for the mass," had been fully established. By the same "five" everything that occurred in any part of the capital was daily reported to the council, and the decisions of the council were in turn communicated to all the faithful. The latter, for the most part, obeyed implicitly without seeking to discover the source whence the command emanated. From the obscure room of curate Boucher, first in the college of the Sorbonne, and afterward in the "collége de Forteret," true cradle of the League, issued mandates which even the king upon his throne soon learned to fear. So well was the affair managed that neither Henry nor his agents were able for a long time to obtain any trustworthy information respecting the secret organization, and could only conjecture the source of the marvellous power that thwarted their chosen designs. Among the members, carefully selected and trained to submit to arbitrary rule, a spirit of self-sacrifice supplied the place of military discipline, while even the money necessary for carrying on the League's operations was contributed by the wealthy families that privately countenanced the movement, until such time as the treasures of the Indies, supposed to repose in the coffers or to be subject to the drafts of the Catholic King, should be directed toward France. It would be anticipating too much the history of succeeding years, were I to record, in this place, the part taken by the Parisian League, especially the later "Council of the Sixteen," in the subsequent wars under Henry the Third and Henry the Fourth. For the present let it suffice to notice that the example of Paris was gradually imitated in the great provincial towns, and that an engine, originally contrived, it is said, for local purposes and for defensive operations, was found so well adapted to aggressive warfare that, in the end, the fortunes of the great nobles

THE HUGUENOT WORSHIP.

at whose instigation it had been constructed, indeed, the destinies of France itself, were dependent, to no inconsiderable extent, upon it.[1]

Florimond de Ræmond's account of the Huguenot worship. The usages of a people are often depicted most vividly by those to whom, by reason of novelty and contrast with their own customs, they appear strange or absurd. The unfriendly pen of Florimond de Ræmond, author of a virulent "History of the Origin, Progress, and Ruin of the Heresies of our Times," has drawn a sketch of the mode of conducting divine worship that was in vogue among the Huguenots (Latin edition, Cologne, 1614, ii. 589-626); and information derived from other and less inimical sources may enable us to fill in some of the details that have been omitted.

Rude barns had been among the earliest resorts of the persecuted Protestants, and it was a common reproach brought against their successors that they continued of choice to meet in barns, even after the necessity of consulting safety had passed away. The case was not, however, very different from that of the early Christians of Rome, for whom the dark recesses of the catacombs long possessed a singular fascination. Unlike the old parish churches, the Protestant places of worship were provided with benches, against which apparently no objection could be urged, save that they bore too close a resemblance to the forms of the schools. This was not the only particular wherein the Huguenots studied the comfort of the people, or set themselves against traditional practice. They went to the length of declining to kneel down in prayer on entering the hallowed precincts, and based the refusal upon a determination to avoid everything that savored of idolatry.

While the minister is expected, or while he is preparing for his sermon, says Ræmond, a plain man will come forward and, from the pulpit, read a chapter of the Holy Scriptures. If the minister be for any reason prevented from coming, the same person may, indeed, go on and read to the assembled hearers a sermon written by John Calvin himself. At least, this was frequently done until a synod put an end to the practice, for fear, as it said, lest Calvin's writings should seem to be substituted for the Word of God. The Roman Catholic writer, however, suggests, as the true reason, that the Protestant divines apprehended a diminution of the willingness of the laity to submit to the superfluous expense of supporting living teachers,

---

[1] The story of the institution of the League in Paris is told appreciatively by the "manant" in the famous "Dialogue du maheustre et du manant" (reprinted in full in the appendix to the Ratisbon edition of the Satyre menippée, iii. 434, etc., and in part in Cimber et Danjou, Archives curieuses, xiv. 30–89). It is told, for the most part in the same words, but from a royalist point of view, in the Mémoires de la Ligue, v. 641, etc. See Recueil des choses mémorables, 603, etc.

when the works of the dead could be turned to such good account. But if Florimond de Ræmond is shocked that a simple artisan be permitted, though merely a deacon or reader, to take so important a place, he is even more surprised at the occasional disregard of conventional usages by the minister himself, who next enters. Instead of the rich vestments of the priest, the Huguenot pastor is clothed in simple dress, differing little from that of every-day life. It may even be that, like M. de Fay, the chaplain of Henry the Fourth's sister, he will (in time of war), conduct the services wearing his sword, or possibly, like some others, with spurs and greaves on.

Even the most ornate "temples" of the Calvinists strike our Roman Catholic visitor as bare and unattractive. Moreover, he charges the Reformers with having turned into " a house of preaching" what Christ himself declared to be " a house of prayer."

On ascending the pulpit, the minister, having removed his hat, begins the service, if it be a Lord's day, by the repetition of the Confession of Sins: " Seigneur Dieu, Père éternal et tout puissant." On other days, he uses no set form, but composes his prayer according to his pleasure. The worshippers either stand or kneel, and many turn their backs to the minister. After a very brief prayer (which the Roman Catholic contrasts with the prayer without ceasing enjoined by St. Paul), a section of some one of the psalms, translated by Marot and Beza into the vernacular, is sung. Under the guidance of a leader, all join in this part of worship—men and women, old and young. In those vast assemblages that used to come together in the city of Paris, when all France seemed, as with one impulse, to be madly following the new teachers of religion, it sometimes happened that the most strenuous exertions of the minister or leader could not keep so many voices in harmony, and that in one part of the edifice the people were singing one verse, in another a different one. But, if there be only a few gathered, the clear, sweet voices of the girls are heard entrancing all that listen. "It may easily be conjectured," cynically remarks Ræmond, "whether the girls have their heart more fixed upon God than the young men have both heart and eyes fixed upon the girls." And then, this is all done in spite of St. Paul's words: "Let your women keep silence in the churches"!

Next, the minister in a few words invokes the aid of the Holy Spirit, and reads from the Holy Scriptures, which he always has at his hand, a text which he then proceeds to expound. The sermon is followed by a short prayer, this by the singing of the psalms, and then all retire from the church. Of the external manifestations of devotion upon which the Roman Catholics lay great stress there are none. No hands are stretched out toward heaven. Smiting upon the breast passes for pure idolatry. Nor is it only on Sunday that preaching is practised. On Thursday, too, the Huguenots flock to their places of worship with as great alacrity as on the Lord's Day, upon the latter of which days they not unfrequently fast.

The same simplicity, we are assured, characterizes other occasions of worship. In camp, when the soldiers are about to be assigned to their quarters for the night, a deacon standing before them utters a brief prayer. When the rite of Baptism is administered, which is always in church and at the principal service of the Lord's Day, the ceremony consists of an address, a prayer or admonition, and the sprinkling of a little water, with the use of the words, "I baptize thee," etc. Great latitude is allowed in the matter of godfathers and godmothers, even the parents themselves being permitted to present their children at the font.

The administration of the Lord's Supper is even more noteworthy for its contrast with the pompous ceremonial of the Romish Mass. It takes place only four times a year. That is at Easter, at Pentecost, on the first Lord's Day in September, and on the Lord's Day nearest to Christmas. (See the notice at the end of the various editions of the Huguenot psalter.) It was, however, the opinion of Calvin and Farel that the Lord's Supper ought to be celebrated far more frequently—if possible, on every Lord's Day. "Il seroyt bien à desirer que la communication de la Saincte Cène de Jesucrist fust tous les dimenches pour le moins en usage quant l'esglise est assemblée en multitude, veu la grand consolation que les fidèles en recoipvent, etc. . . . Mays pource que l'infirmité du peuple est encore telle qu'il y auroit dangier que ce sacré et tant excellent mistère ne vint en mespris s'il estoyt si souvent célébré, ayant esgard à cela, il nous a semblé bon que en attendant que le peuple qui est encores au cunement débile sera plus conferm é, ceste saincte Cène soyt visitée une foys chascung moys en l'ung des troys lieux où se font maintenant les prédications," etc. Mémoire de Calvin et Farel sur l'organisation de l'Église de Genève, 16 janvier, 1537, in Archives of Geneva, and printed in Gaberel, i., pièces justificatives, 103, 104. The bread used is leavened. There is no altar, but instead a simple table spread with a cloth. The minister comes down from the pulpit and breaks the bread, using, for the most part, these words from Calvin's liturgy, "The bread which we break is the communion of the body of Christ." He then gives a piece of the bread to the member of the consistory who stands nearest to him, saying, "Remember that Christ endured death and passion for thee," or, "This is the body that suffered for thee." The communicants successively come up, and to each the minister, as he gives him a piece of the bread, repeats a different verse from the Word of God. The communicant, says Ræmond, kisses the hand of the minister in token of honor, or, if the communicant be more honorable, the minister kisses, or makes as if he would kiss the bread he gives. At the other end of the table a deacon hands the cup—no jewelled chalice, but a plain vessel, even, it may be, of glass—to each communicant, with the words, "The cup of blessing which we bless is the communion of the blood of Christ," or, "Remember that the blood of Christ was shed for thee." In some places the civil magistrates, according to Ræmond, approach the table even before the consistory. Each communicant, on retiring, places a piece of money on a plate or upon the table, for the relief of the poor. The "cœna peripatetica," as the writer is pleased to style it, of the Huguenots is strikingly different, not only from the mode of communing practised in the Roman Catholic Church, but from the customs observed in the Reformed churches of other countries. In some of these the communicants kneel in their places, while the consecrated elements are brought to them by the minister and deacons, while in others, as in those of Scotland, Belgium, and Holland, the communicants observe the primitive usage of sitting down at the table.

Nothing impressed itself upon the adherents of the Romish Church as so remarkable as the great use of the psalms. The early Huguenots, we are told, carried their Bibles and psalm-books even to their meals, and brought them out at the end, as a sort of dessert, wherein persons of both sexes and every age vied in partaking. They chaunted them on the way to their places of worship. It was a pleasant sight to see ten or a dozen boats full of Huguenot men, women, and children gliding over the peaceful waters of some river toward the spot where the great assembly of worshippers was to meet, and filling the banks on either side with the melody of their song. Artisans made their work-rooms, merchants their shops, to resound with the music of their favorite hymns; nor were they deterred by the fact that priests and monks held up their hands in holy horror at the profanation of transferring the psalms of David from the church to the private house, or stopped their ears when they passed by the cobbler at his bench singing the divine *Miserere*, or caught the strains of the *De profundis* rising above the din of the smithy.

CHAPTER V.

THE "HOLY LEAGUE," AND THE EDICT OF NEMOURS.

If any conflict be more pitiful than a war sincerely waged for religion's sake, it is a conflict in which religion serves merely as a convenient pretext to cloak private and selfish ends. Of such a conflict the Huguenots were about to become the unwilling witnesses, without the ability, by taking an active part, to secure the triumph of the side upon which their interest lay.

Both Henry the Third and the Guises were by profession devout Roman Catholics. Between the two, if there were any question of relative sincerity, Henry was entitled to be regarded as the more sincere. The Guises might choose to dissemble. They had on occasion pretended to have leanings toward the Reformation. Even the bloody Cardinal of Lorraine had more than once made his orthodoxy suspicious in the eyes of rigid churchmen. But Henry of Valois, brought up to hate the Protestants with a perfect hatred, never feigned the slightest affection for them, even when most desirous of entrapping them in a false security. On the other hand, at a time when his heart might have been expected to be touched with gratitude for their signal fidelity to the crown, the king's assurances went no further than vague promises of peace and good treatment.[1] Meanwhile he gave the most practical proof of hearty detestation for the Huguenots and their faith. He rigidly excluded the adherents of the Reformed doctrines from all posts of trust, from all civil and military offices, from all judicial seats. The monarch set his

The king's cordial hatred of the Huguenots.

---

[1] "Je leur entretiondrai la paix, et leur monstrerai que je leur veulx du bien." Duplessis Mornay to the King of Navarre, Paris, February 20, 1584, Mémoires de Duplessis Mornay, ii. 528.

face resolutely against their preferment. Ambitious men among the Huguenots were privately informed by Henry's minions, Joyeuse and Épernon, that religious constancy was the only obstacle in the way of their obtaining the coveted prize. To such inducements to apostasy many an aspirant for power fell an easy prey. At the same time, if in any city of the kingdom a Protestant happened to have secured some magistracy, there were not wanting persons ready to avail themselves of the slightest pretext of irregularity in his appointment, or of error committed by him in an official capacity. It went hard with his enemies, enjoying, as they did, the all but open support of the king and his advisers, if they did not involve the Huguenot in costly litigation or even secure his removal.[1] So shrewdly devised, so systematically pursued, was the scheme of repression, that worldly wise men, politicians judging of others by themselves, and statisticians who had implicit faith in their arithmetical processes and were confident that the fate of the Protestants could be safely calculated according to the rule of simple proportion, predicted the speedy extinction of heresy in France. But for the interference of this meddlesome League, "Huguenotry," Cavriana positively affirms, would, in the course of four years, have become so obsolete as to leave no memory of itself, so complete would have been the effect of the determination of Henry the Third to tolerate no Huguenot near him or in any public office.[2]

His plan for the extinction of Protestantism.

---

[1] De Thou, vi. (book 81) 444, 445.

[2] Letter of Filippo Cavriana, August 4, 1585, Négociations avec la Toscane, iv. 619. The Venetian ambassador, Lorenzo Priuli, in his relation of June 5, 1582, maintained that the number of Huguenots in France had already diminished seventy per cent. Ranke, History of the Popes, bk. v., p. 204. The absurdity of such affirmations and prognostications lay in the fact that they made no account of the people. Instead of diminishing, the number of Protestants in France was steadily and even rapidly increasing at the very period of the civil wars, when political wiseacres, judging from the occasional defection of courtiers and men ambitious of place, were foretelling the annihilation of the Huguenot party. For instance, so soon as the peace of 1577 was signed, the Reformed religion received a notable impulse in the city of Pons in Saintonge, now that protection was secured by a Protestant garrison. The church, or "temple," erected in 1575, became too contracted for the multitude of Protestants flocking to it. As it was impracticable to erect a new church, the

Were the Guises desirous of such a consummation? The question may confidently be answered in the negative. The restoration of doctrinal unity to France would have removed the chief excuse of which an ambitious family could avail itself for taking up arms against the sovereign—an excuse which it would have been loath to renounce.

For many years the mind of Henry of Guise had been the receptacle of the wildest hopes, and had harbored the most extravagant schemes. Enjoying unlimited credit with the people as the self-constituted champion of Roman Catholicism, the idol of a clergy that viewed his advancement as a pledge of the overthrow of heresy, a prince still in his early prime, whose manly beauty was scarcely marred by the honorable scar securing him the epithet of "Le balafré," and an adept in all the arts that conciliate favor and confirm friendship, Guise was quick to discern the possibilities of his situation. Chafing under the fate that decreed him birth as a subject, he never for a single instant forgot that a king of Scotland married a daughter of Duke Claude of Guise, and that Mary Stuart, Queen of Scotland and of France, was his cousin. Nor did the voice of sycophantic followers tire of repeating the suggestion that to him, as a lineal descendant of Charlemagne, not to Henry of Valois, much less to his apostate cousin of Navarre, belonged of right the crown of France. True, the ducal House of Lorraine had, of necessity, a superior title to the succession; but the Guises gave themselves little solicitude on this score, well assured that ample grounds would in due time be discovered for setting aside the possible claim of a branch that made no pretence of being French in character or in past history.

Ambition of the Duke of Guise.

Pending an opportunity to put forth a serious effort to wrest the French sceptre from the grasp of a monarch confessedly one of the feeblest of his line, Henry of Guise had not resigned himself to inaction. Naturally the island of Great Britain, both because of its proximity to France and by reason of the

---

Huguenots converted the "halle du minage" into a place of worship. Here, too, they met on any emergency of a secular character, to discuss measures of self-defence. A. Crottet, Histoire des églises réformées de Pons, Gémozac et Mortagne en Saintonge (Bordeaux, 1841), 93.

religion professed by the ruler of the southern part, afforded the most attractive field for intrigue. A heretical queen was *ipso facto* a deposed queen, and when to the taint of heresy was added the express and formal excommunication of the pope, the dominions of Queen Elizabeth could be regarded by a devout servant of the "Holy See" only as a lawful prize for the first comer who might be of orthodox sentiments and of sufficient military prowess. In the city of Paris, at the house of the papal nuncio, or at the house of the Jesuits, or at the house of the ambassador Juan Baptista de Tassis, were held those grave deliberations respecting the best method of freeing the world from the presence and dominion of the indomitable princess whom all the conspirators joined in styling the English Jezebel. The Duke of Guise offered to lead an invading force, and to effect a landing of four thousand troops of his own on the coast of Northumberland; while his brother, Charles of Mayenne, should conduct as many more to Sussex; and Duke Albert of Bavaria, with five thousand Germans, should descend upon Norfolk. These scanty forces were to be supplemented by the retainers of the great Roman Catholic noblemen of England, who had pledged themselves to rise in mass and join the foreigners coming to effect their liberation. Happily, however, the projectors of this magnificent scheme were not altogether of one mind. The English Jesuits, jealous for the influence of Philip the Second, insisted that the conduct of the enterprise should be more distinctly confided to the Catholic king, and that, even if Guise were permitted to lead, the troops employed should not be Frenchmen but Spaniards. And as for Philip himself, although the details of the plot had been thoroughly discussed for months and even for years, that prudent monarch found, as the moment for action approached and everything turned upon prompt decision, fresh reasons for caution, and scrupled about trusting any French general with the chief command. Thus the last chance of success slipped through the fingers of the impatient captains and theologians who from Paris and Rheims had laid cunning plans for the overthrow and death of Elizabeth. The Spanish vessels essential for the transport of troops never arrived. Meanwhile the sagacious forethought of Walsingham, in providing her majesty with a legion of spies, who, in the garb of priests, or of members of the Order of Jesus, penetrated the inmost recesses of religious houses and communicated to the English secretary of state the most private resolutions of Romish conspirators before the ink was fairly dry upon the paper to which those resolutions were consigned, was rewarded by ample discoveries. At the right moment every feature of the plot against Protestant England and its queen was laid bare, and the precise part taken by Philip, by Gregory the Thirteenth, by the Jesuits, by Guise, by the minor instruments employed, lay open to the light of day. Francis Throkmorton—unworthy nephew of the eminent statesman, Sir Nicholas, whose invaluable correspondence furnishes a clew to the intricacies of French history at the time of the outbreak of the civil wars—disclosed, when extended on the rack, even the places on the English coast where the invading fleet was to land, and the names of the English Roman Catholics that had promised their co-operation. And William Parry, a few weeks later, described the manner in which the detestable plot to assassinate the English queen was concocted, and reluctantly informed Walsingham where he had hidden that remarkable letter in which the Cardinal of Como, in the pope's name, had conveyed his holiness's strong desire that Parry should persevere in his laudable purpose of murder, and had sent his pontifical blessing with a concession of plenary indulgence and remission of all his sins.[1]

Gregory and Philip were out of the reach of the English government, but upon one remarkable man the hand of the executioner might justly have been laid. Bernardino de Mendoza, Spanish ambassador at London,[2] stood clearly convicted

The plot laid bare.

---

[1] For the plot against England in which Guise was concerned the reader may consult, with profit, Froude, History of England, xi. (Reign of Elizabeth, chapter 31); Michelet, La Ligue et Henri IV., chapitre 10. The narrative of Parry's plot, translated into French, is the second of the numerous documents of the Mémoires de la Ligue, a collection of which the first volume appeared in 1587. The letter of the Cardinal of Como, dated Rome, January 30, 1584, is given, i. 34, in the original Italian, with trifling mistakes, and in French.

[2] "One Bernardin Mendoza," wrote Walsingham to Dr. Dale, July 17, 1574, "is sent from the King of Spain to use Spanish compliments to lull them

by the testimony of Throkmorton—corroborated in all its parts by the envoy's own correspondence with his master, first brought to light in our own days—of having stimulated and abetted the nefarious project. It was, of course, impossible to permit him to remain at the English court, but, fortunately for him, the royal council did not think fit to punish his breach of the law of nations by sending him to the scaffold. As it was, after having been unceremoniously expelled from England, in January, 1584, he was sent to France by Philip, a few months later, to condole with the king upon the death of his brother. Before the close of the year he had taken the place of Tassis as resident Spanish ambassador at Paris.

<small>Bernardino de Mendoza.</small>

Few Frenchmen were destined to play so important a part in the history of their own country, for the next ten years, as this intriguing Spaniard, whose house became at once the centre of all the sinister plots, directed not so much against the existence of the Huguenots in France as against the crown itself. It was not by accident that Mendoza had been assigned to so important a post. No man could have been found in Spain better qualified to discharge its responsible trusts. Of a family inferior in distinction to no other of the peninsula, and himself boasting of important military service in the Netherlands, he came to France rich in the experience of years spent mostly in attempting to deceive Queen Elizabeth respecting the intentions of Philip and the Roman Catholic powers. Proud and imperious by nature, he was no novice in the art of dissimulation, and few diplomatists could surpass him in the solemnity with which he was in the habit of asseverating the truth of statements false but profitable. Of regret that he was compelled to stoop to such dishonorable expedients his secret despatches betray not the faintest trace. On other points his sensibility was more keen. Threats of punishment for the treacherous plots which he had countenanced against the person of a friendly sovereign to whose court he had been deputed were hurled back with contempt. For the most part, however, he preferred the

---

to sleep, until they have compounded their troubles in Flanders, when all wise men think they will wake them." State Paper Office.

path of conciliation, and, while fomenting discord and devising the ruin of all with whose interests the policy of Spain was not coincident, he maintained a gracious exterior. His lavish expenditure of money both surprised and alarmed his fellow ambassadors, who knew well that neither the exchequer of their states nor their own private purses could furnish them the means of competing successfully with such magnificent but ruinous extravagance. "If it be the characteristic of a good ambassador," wrote Busbecq, "to make a great outlay of money, a better envoy than Don Bernardino could not easily be found."[1]

The arrival of Bernardino de Mendoza in France marks the date of the rapid development of the League, which, after a period of about seven years of suspended animation, now began to show signs that its capacity for mischief had not been destroyed, and only awaited the opportunity for a more terrible manifestation. Mendoza had come with the commission to employ this engine of war in the interests of the King of Spain and of the Roman Catholic Church.

We have already noticed the use to which the enemies of the Huguenots had turned the report of the efforts made by the King of Navarre to unite all Protestant princes and states in a common profession and in a defensive alliance. We have also witnessed the industry displayed in circulating the refusal of that prince to abandon his religion without previous instruction in a free and legitimate council, as proof that, unless the Roman Catholics of France should take decisive measures, they would find themselves, on the death of the present monarch, the subjects of a determined enemy of their faith. Fresh ground for misrepresentation was now found in the just concessions of Henry of Valois. The cities pledged to the Huguenots by the edict of pacification of 1577 had been intrusted to them for six years only, and the King of Navarre, the Prince of Condé, and twenty other Protestant gentlemen had taken a solemn oath, collectively and individually, to restore these places to the king at the expira-

The Huguenots and the cities of refuge.

---

[1] In proof of which he alleged the report that Mendoza intended to spend the enormous sum of sixteen thousand crowns a year upon his legation. Busbecq to the emperor, December 10, 1584, Epistolæ, fol. 82.

tion of the term of time agreed upon.¹ Since the edict bore date of September, 1577, the cities were to be given up in the corresponding month in 1583.²

As the time approached, however, for redeeming their promise, the Huguenots besought the king to prolong the period for which they were permitted to retain the cities. Nor was the demand altogether unreasonable. The eight cities had originally been conceded in view of the excited condition of France resulting from the long prevalence of war. While commanding the Protestants at once to evacuate all the cities, towns, and castles seized during the late hostilities, the edict gave a satisfactory reason for leaving a few places of refuge in their hands: "And nevertheless," said the king, "inasmuch as many private individuals have received and suffered, during the troubles, so much injury and damage in their property and persons, that hardly will they be able to lose the memory thereof so soon as would be requisite for the execution of our intentions; desiring to avoid all the inconveniences that might thereby arise, until such time as the existing feelings of rancor and enmity be allayed, we have committed to the custody of those of the said pretended reformed religion, for the term of six years, the following cities."

The conditions upon which the cities were given, said the Huguenots, have not been fulfilled; the object of the trust is yet unaccomplished. The edict of pacification has been executed in scarcely any of its articles, save such as depended on the obedience of the Protestants or the interests of the Roman Catholics. When the king spoke of six years, he evidently intended six proper or, in legal parlance, serviceable years—that is, years serviceable in allaying the existing rancor and enmity. The king ought, therefore, to imitate the intelligent physician who, although at first he ordered the plaster to be kept on the wound for but six days, afterward

Reasons for the retention of the cities.

---

¹ See above, chap. ii., p. 166.

² The king's reply to the Protestants, of December 10, 1584, referred to below, makes the precise date to be August 17, 1583. This is probably a mere clerical error. The "secret articles" of Bergerac bear date of September 17, 1577.

retains it as long as may be necessary. And, in this case, it is not the impatience of the sufferer that has aggravated the sore by meddling with it, but the inconsiderate temerity of the physician's assistant who, contrary to his master's will, has poisoned the wound and destroyed the efficiency of the remedy applied. When the results sought for by the edict shall be attained, it will be time enough to restore the cities originally given as safeguards to the Protestants. It is dangerous for them to restore them, as it would be cruel in the king to insist upon their restoration, so long as there are many important cities in France, such as Toulouse, Cahors, Castelnaudary, and others, that will not allow a single Protestant to live within their walls; so long as the prescriptions respecting schools and cemeteries, respecting patients in the public hospitals and worshippers in the churches, are suffered to remain inoperative; so long as some of the chambers of justice established by the edict exist only on paper, and the jurisdiction of others is impeded by vexatious restrictions; so long, above all, as, in spite of the prohibition of insulting and seditious preaching, the Roman Catholic pulpits everywhere resound with declarations that the time for the extirpation of the Protestant religion approaches, and some of the preachers are so audacious as to indulge in bloodthirsty threats from the sacred desk, lauding, in the hearing of your court, and even in your majesty's presence, the murders and massacres heretofore perpetrated, and instigating their hearers to fresh acts of the same kind, as if inviting them to a participation in a holy sacrifice.[1]

To say that Henry of Valois was convinced by the Huguenot arguments would be to assert too much. In fact, while pretending to redress the wrongs of which the King of Navarre and the Protestant churches complained, and making lavish professions of a desire to act fairly, he continued for months to

---

[1] "Cahier général dressé par M. Duplessis sur les Mémoires envoyés au roy de Navarre par les églises de France, et presenté au roy Henri III. par M. de Clervant" (July 3, 1583), Mémoires de Duplessis Mornay, ii. 320-344; "Raisons pour induire le roy à accorder la prolongation des places pour quelques ans à ses subjects de la relligion reformée" (August 12, 1583), ibid., ii. 358-362.

insist upon the letter of the compact, so far as his subjects of the other faith were concerned. It was only when a Huguenot assembly which, in answer to repeated requests, he had at length permitted to come together in the city of Montauban, in August and September, 1584, urgently renewed the petition, that he consented to prolong the term of the Protestant possession. Even then it is probable that the inability to secure their compliance with his summons for an instant surrender had much to do with the concession. However this may be, the king, in order, as he said, to show his desire to bring back his subjects to obedience rather by gentle than by harsh measures, consented that the cities heretofore granted to the Protestants be left in their guard for one or two years, as he should hereafter deem advisable.[1]

The king reluctantly prolongs the term of the Protestant possession.

The repeated refusals of Henry of Navarre to abjure his religion, the exaggerated story of a great Protestant confederacy, and the complaisance of the king toward heretics, evidenced by his granting to the Huguenots prolonged possession of the cities of refuge, were not the only sources of popular alarm for the safety of the faith. With rare skill the League summoned fresh spectres, unreal phantoms, the creation of a disordered imagination, to frighten the masses of the people into compliance with its suggestions. Living in a day when knowledge is so generously diffused, when the imponderable agents have been impressed into man's service, in order to secure the instantaneous transmission of accurate in-

The League circulates alarming rumors.

---

[1] A condition was exacted that the Huguenots should give up certain other towns which they had, it was alleged, seized of their own authority or by force. Upon this matter the most important documents to be consulted are: "Cahier général adressé par M. Duplessis sur les Mémoires envoyés au roy de Navarre par les églises de France, et presenté au roy Henry III. par M. de Clervant" (dated July 3, 1583), Mémoires de Duplessis Mornay, ii. 320–344 ; " Raisons pour induire le roy à accorder la prolongation des places pour quelques ans à ses subjects de la relligion reformée " (August 12, 1583), ibid., ii. 358–362 ; and the long " Cahier au roy " drawn up at Montauban by the assembly of the Protestant churches, September 7, 1584, and signed not only by all the delegates, but by Henry of Navarre, with the reply of Henry III. at the end of the separate articles and at the close of the whole document, ibid., ii. 606–667.

formation respecting events of the most recent occurrence at the most distant points on the surface of the globe, we find it well-nigh impossible to picture to ourselves the isolation and consequent ignorance of the people in the sixteenth century. Where communication between different parts of the country was sluggish, infrequent, and irregular, the wildest rumors could be set on foot with little immediate danger of detection and contradiction. The peasantry and the small tradesmen of the towns were the ready prey of designing men. Especially was this the case in matters directly or remotely affecting religion. The love of the marvellous, being re-enforced by the power of sectarian hate, secured to the inventor of pious falsehoods an immediate and almost unimpeded course for the most baseless of fabrications. To believe anything and everything asserted to the disadvantage of the enemies of the Roman Catholic Church was the fashion; while it was often as much as a man's life was worth to express the slightest incredulity respecting their actual or prospective misdeeds.

What wonderful fictions had been composed in order to raise the enthusiasm of the populace to fever heat, we learn from the narrative of one Nicholas Poulain, to which I shall have frequent occasion to refer hereafter. The heads of the League in Paris, whose origin was traced in a preceding chapter of this history, had set their hearts upon securing the co-operation of Poulain, because, as lieutenant of the provost of the province of Île de France (the provost himself being an old man and averse to labor), he had virtual command of a good part of the troops, within the walls of Paris, upon whom the king believed that he could count. The lieutenant had been vouched for by friends who had known him for more than a score of years, and was therefore accepted without apparent distrust. He was first informed that a fine opportunity now offered itself for him to gain a sum of money that would enable him to live at his ease, as well as to obtain the favor of certain lords and high personages of the city of Paris who had it in their power to give him rapid advancement. The only condition was fidelity to a cause which was no other than the preservation of the Catholic, Apostolic, and

The narrative of Nicholas Poulain.

Roman faith. Having given the necessary promise, and taken a solemn oath, Poulain was notified to come the next morning to the house of Master Jean Le Clerc, a "procureur" of the Parliament of Paris. Here he found assembled a number of the members of the Parisian League, together with a gentleman by the name of Mayneville, sent, as he was informed, by the Duke of Guise, to consult with them respecting their common enterprise.[1] Le Clerc himself initiated the new member into the secrets of the organization which he had joined. "The Catholic religion is lost," said he, "unless prompt measures be taken to succor it and forestall the preparations made for its ruin. There are upward of ten thousand Huguenots in the Faubourg Saint Germain intent on cutting the throats of the Catholics, in order to give the crown to the King of Navarre.[2] There are many others hired for the same purpose, as well in the city as in its suburbs, one-half of them Huguenots and the other half Politiques. A number of the members of the royal council and of parliament favor the King of Navarre; and provision must be made to meet this difficulty. At the same time the good Catholics must secretly take up arms, so as to get the upper hand and defeat the plots of their enemies. They have good princes and high noblemen ready to support them—the Dukes of Guise, Mayenne, and Aumale, with the entire house of Lorraine. The pope, the cardinals, bishops, abbots, and the whole body of the clergy, with the Sorbonne, will help them, and they will be backed by the King of Spain, the Prince of Parma, and the Duke of Savoy. The king, we know of a truth, favors the King of Navarre, and, for this reason, has sent to him the Duke of Épernon to give him, by way of loan or otherwise, the sum of two hundred thousand crowns, in

Pretended Huguenot conspiracy.

---

[1] Mayneville, or Mèneville, appears, from the Simancas MSS., to have been one of the most customary agents of Guise in his communications with Mendoza and with the Parisian League. See also De Thou, vi. 721.

[2] This was the standard formula. Elsewhere, referring to the recruits obtained from the various trades in the city, Poulain informs us: "à tous lesquels l'on faisoit entendre que les Huguenots vouloient couper la gorge aux Catholiques, et faire venir le roy de Navarre à la couronne." Mémoires de Henry III., 150, 151.

order that he may be in a position to wage war against the good Catholics. But there are already secured secretly in Paris a goodly number of men, all of whom have sworn to die rather than suffer this outrage to be perpetrated. Nor will they find any great difficulty in their way. They will only have to overcome the king's forces in Paris, which are feeble and small in number—some two or three hundred guards at the Louvre, the provost of the hôtel de ville and his archers, and the provost of the Îsle de France." The address ended with a few hints as to how Poulain might render the League good service, and himself derive great advantage, by playing into the hands of the conspirators.[1]

Such were the horrors upon which the imagination and fears of the "good Catholics" were fed. To "cut the throats of the good Catholics" of the city of Paris, forsooth, was a project very likely to enter the heads of the Huguenots. So seem their opponents to have thought, since the accusation recurs periodically—in 1572, in 1576, and now in 1584, not to speak of other occasions at an earlier date. And each time the credulous people swallows the absurd story without the least objection, and, when it can, sets itself to murdering the supposed plotters of so much mischief, never deigning or being able to consider the improbability that the hated sect, so insignificant in numbers in Northern France, should dream of getting the better of its antagonists in the populous capital of the realm.

Meantime, political considerations very vital to his own in-

---

[1] "Le procez verbal d'un nommé Nicholas Poulain, lieutenant de la prevosté de l'Isle de France, qui contient l'histoire de la Ligue, depuis le second Janvier 1585 jusques au jour des Barricades, escheues le 12 May 1588." Mémoires de Henry III., 145, etc. Also in Cimber et Danjou, Archives curieuses, xi. 289-323. Poulain, in disgust, revealed the secrets of the League to the king, from time to time, and was particularly serviceable in frustrating a scheme, matured in the house of the Jesuits near St. Paul's Church, for treacherously seizing Boulogne-sur-mer, "qu'ils disoient leur estre fort necessaire, pour faire aborder et descendre l'armée qu'ils attendoient d'Espagne." Mémoires de Henry III., 153. Latterly, if not from the first, Poulain was a spy in the king's pay, as appears from the extracts of the expense accounts of the monarch (1588), published in the Archives curieuses, x. 433.

terests warned Philip the Second that he must give the signal to his French allies and future stipendiaries to bestir themselves.

The States-General of the Netherlands had finally, in October, 1584, resolved to offer to Henry the Third the sovereignty of the United Provinces. Even Holland, long reluctant to take this step, had finally acquiesced in the action of the sister republics, and the last obstacle in the way of concerted action had been taken out of the way. Rarely has monarch received so rich a present as that which a deputation of Dutch statesmen was now commissioned to place in the hands of Henry of Valois; never has kingdom enjoyed the prospect of a more welcome accession to its territory and resources. Rich in her broad fields and manifold industries, France had now the promise of becoming the most commercial state upon the face of the earth by the annexation of the free provinces at the mouth of the Rhine, whose inhabitants, not content with wresting the lands they inhabited from the grasp of the ocean, had avenged the wrongs received at its hands by daring and untiring efforts to compel every part of the wide seas to render tribute to their growing wealth and power.

<small>Offer of the sovereignty of the Netherlands to Henry III.</small>

The hearty acceptance of the gift by the very Christian king, strong in the support of a united and patriotic people, there could be little doubt, would have placed the hardly contested war for Dutch independence beyond the possibility of failure. Unfortunately, it was not in the power of the last Valois to rally to his standard, even in a conflict appealing so strongly to national pride, the full resources of his kingdom, the first of Christian states. Not the most sanguine advocate of the acceptance of Holland's magnificent offer could delude himself into hoping that the "good Catholics" of Henry's dominions would, with unanimity, flock to their king's support. But it was of the utmost importance to Philip that the offer should not be entertained at all, or if entertained be peremptorily declined. To secure this result the surest plan seemed to be to set at once in operation that powerful enginery with which the League had furnished him, and again to plunge a land which had scarcely had time to breathe the invigorating air of peace into the horrors of civil war.

Just now King Henry was beginning to awake from his dream of security, and to realize that, after all, the chief danger was to be apprehended, not from liberty-loving Huguenots, but from Spanish-minded Leaguers. Tidings came to him of conferences between his subjects and those of Philip, obscure hints of compacts made by Frenchmen with the natural enemies of France, and of pledges of money for service yet to be rendered; vague accounts of associations formed in the heart of the kingdom, nominally for the defence of the Roman Catholic religion, but in reality for the overthrow of the royal authority. When all this became so apparent that no one but a person wilfully blind to the truth could be in doubt of the approach of serious trouble, Henry endeavored to conjure the storm with words and threats. On the eleventh of November, 1584, a declaration was signed by the king at Saint Germain en Laye, "against all persons making leagues, associations, enrolment of troops, intrigues and practices against the estate of the realm." It was carried in haste to parliament, and was registered the same day. On the morrow it was published by the crier on all the public squares of the capital. Henry set forth in this document the earnestness with which he had been laboring daily more and more to remove every occasion for the disturbance of the peace and tranquillity which he desired to be enjoyed by the subjects God had placed under his care. He declared that nothing could therefore be more displeasing to him than to hear, as he had heard, that "certain evil spirits, enemies of the public tranquillity of his kingdom," had been unable to restrain their propensity to work all the mischief in their power, and had begun to solicit the nobles, as well as members of the other orders in the state, to enter into a league or association and to sign certain papers not less prejudicial to the common welfare than insulting to the royal dignity. For this reason the king announced that all who solicited others to enter into such league or sign such paper were guilty of treason, and also affixed the penalties of treason to all compliance with their solicitations. At the same time

<small>A royal declaration against the League, November 11, 1584.</small>

he granted full and unconditional pardon to all persons who, before the first day of the new year, should renounce the disloyal engagements into which they might have entered.[1]

Had proclamations been sufficient to strike terror into the hearts of the secret conspirators against the peace of France, the threats of Henry of Valois would have put an effectual end to the League. As it was, the declaration, if it served any purpose, only hastened the catastrophe.

Late in December, a council met in the famous castle of Joinville, whose conclusions were to be fraught with as much misery and bloodshed for France as had been the Sunday's assault of Francis of Guise upon the Huguenot worshippers in the rude barn in the neighboring village of Vassy,[2] nearly twenty-three years before. As if in irony, the day chosen for signing a document so pregnant of disaster to crown and people was the last day of the year; the last day, also, of the period of grace allowed by the terms of the king's recent declaration.

Conference of the League at Joinville, December, 1584.

There were present at Joinville: first and foremost, Juan Baptista de Tassis, commander of the order of Saint James, late ambassador at the court of France, the skilful workman to whom had been intrusted by Philip the delicate task of arranging the parts of the fearful engine which was to bring glory and power to Spain and deal ruin and death to countless souls in France. His work done and well done, he was now, after giving the last finishing touches and setting it well under way on its destructive mission, to consign it to hands not less scrupulous and perhaps equally able, the hands of his successor Mendoza. Juan Moreo, commander of the Knights Hospitallers of Malta, was his assistant. Next came François de Mayneville, the representative of the old cardinal, Charles of Bourbon, now for the first time laying claim to the title of heir presumptive of the crown of France. The third place was held by the princes of Lorraine origin. Henry, Duke of Guise, and

---

[1] Text of the Declaration in Mémoires de Nevers, i. 633, 634. See De Thou, vi. (book 80) 393.

[2] Joinville and Vassy are not over ten or twelve miles apart.

his brother Charles, Duke of Mayenne, appeared in person. The former presented a paper giving him full power to act in behalf of his brother, the Cardinal Louis of Guise, and his cousins, the Dukes of Aumale and Elbeuf.

Between these few actors the terms of the definite alliance entered into by Philip and the League were soon settled. They were reduced to the following points:

The terms of alliance.

The Cardinal of Bourbon was recognized as heir to the crown, in case the present King of France should die childless, to the exclusion of all heretical or relapsed claimants.

The cardinal, on his accession to the throne, was to strengthen the present union by ratifying the Treaty of Cateau Cambrésis, made in 1559, and pledging himself by oath to observe it.

No other religion than the Roman Catholic and Apostolic would be tolerated in France, and all persons refusing to embrace it would be exterminated.

The decrees of the Council of Trent would be accepted and published in France.

The future king was to renounce for himself and his successors all alliance with the Turk.

No undertaking was to be permitted that might jeopard the Spanish navigation and trade with the Indies.

To defray the expense of the war which was to be waged by the princes of the League for the extirpation of the Huguenots, Philip engaged to advance to them monthly fifty thousand crowns of gold, beginning at the day on which war should be declared.

These advances were to be repaid by the cardinal-king at his accession.

The princes were to assist Philip in recovering the cities belonging to him, now unlawfully held by the French, and especially the city of Cambray.

For the mutual defence of France and of the Low Countries there was to be an eternal and inviolable alliance between Philip and his successors, on the one hand, and the Roman Catholic princes and their successors, on the other; and Philip, besides the stipulated monthly allowance above provided, was to send them as many men and as much money as they might need.

All Roman Catholic nobles, gentlemen, cities, and universities, and, in short, all Roman Catholics of whatever station that might ally themselves with the parties to this compact, were to be regarded as comprehended in it; provision being particularly made for the Dukes of Mercœur and Nevers, of whose sentiments, though they were absent, it was supposed that there could be no doubt, and for the insertion of whose signatures blanks were purposely left at the end of the document.

The compact was for the present to be kept a profound secret, in view of the trouble which the heretics might create were its contents to be divulged.

Such was the Treaty of Joinville, to which, consistently with the reputation of all the high contracting parties for sincerity, guilelessness, and disinterestedness, they prefixed a "protestation" to the effect that no one of them was moved in the premises by any other consideration than a pure desire to preserve the Roman Catholic religion, imperilled, as it was, by the open and covert attacks of heresy.[1] In point of fact, however, it may be doubted whether any two of the princes, present in person or represented at the conference by others, had the same ends in view, or cared very much for the interests of each other. So far as the King of Spain was concerned, Bourbon, Guise, and Mayenne were simply the convenient tools thrown in his way by fortune for sowing discord in a neighboring kingdom, for diverting attention and preventing interference with his Netherland provinces, and for furthering his ambitious designs upon England and England's queen; not to speak of those other and more distant plans of a world-monarchy in which France figured as an appendage of the Spanish peninsula. What matter to him whether Henry of Valois, or the decrepit voluptuary, Charles of Bourbon, or the ambitious Guise, claiming descent from Charlemagne, occupied the throne which he hoped would one day belong to

Designs of Philip II.

---

[1] De Thou, vi. (book 81) 445–447; Davila (Eng. trans. of 1678), bk. 7, 254, 255. The monthly receipts of the Duke of Guise, for 50,000 crowns, in the name of all "comprised in our common league," appear in the Simancas MSS.; see, for instance, the document in J. de Croze, Les Guises, les Valois, et Philippe II., i. 372.

him or to a child of his? What was said of the Spanish ambassador at Paris, a little later, by one of the cool lookers-on at the frightful tragedy enacted on French soil, was pre-eminently true of the ambassador's master, that crowned scribbler who, from his closet in the Escorial, issued in secret his orders to set on foot perfidious schemes of murder and rapine. His was the part of the devil who, with truly Satanic craft, lures men into danger and then abandons them to their fate and suffers them to perish.[1]

Of Henry of Guise it may be said with truth that a more perfect specimen of duplicity cannot be found, even in the annals of a family by no means deficient in examples of double-dealing. Not only had the mantle of his uncle, the Cardinal of Lorraine, fallen on his shoulders, but in the distribution of that worthy's mental and moral effects the eldest nephew had certainly secured fully the share to which he was entitled by birthright. It was characteristic of him that he worked by himself, confiding his inmost designs to not a living soul. Under a brilliant mask of affability and confidence he concealed the darkest plots. To everyone he had a different story to tell. He assured the common people and the world in general that he was laboring, in perfect consistency with his duty to his king, only for the preservation of the Roman Catholic faith. He filled Cardinal Bourbon's ears with stories of future greatness, and seriously proposed that he should obtain a dispensation from the pope to marry Guise's widowed sister, the Duchess of Montpensier. He privately told the queen mother that his sole design was the elevation of the son of the Duke of Lorraine to the throne of France; for, at best, Bourbon could last but a few years, and then a grandson of Catharine—the offspring of her own daughter—would succeed to the inheritance of her childless son, Henry. Meantime, he did not leave the King of Spain in ignorance respecting the insincerity of his professions both to the cardinal and to

Duplicity of the Duke of Guise.

---

[1] "Consigliato a ciò dall' ambasciatore di Spagna, il quale, a guisa del demonio, accompagna gli uomini al pericolo poi ne gli lascia perire." Letter of Filippo Cavriana, May 18, 1587, Négociations avec la Toscane, iv. 687.

the queen mother, hinting that the advancement of his own immediate family was naturally a matter of more concern to him than the aggrandizement of a more distant branch of the same house. But not even to his own brothers, the Duke of Mayenne and the Cardinal of Guise, much less to his cousins of Aumale and Elbeuf, did the Balafré intrust the dangerous secret of his designs upon the royal dignity.

It is needless to speak further of Cardinal Bourbon, who really had no longer perception enough to see that his senile aspirations were an object of covert ridicule to all his fellow-conspirators.[1]

Provision had, as I have said, been made in the Treaty of Joinville for the addition of the signature of Louis de Gonzagues, Duke of Nevers, a politic and cautious nobleman, who had doubtless been absent from the conference because he scarcely knew what to do. Half Italian and half French, the fiery advocate of the doctrine of the "one religion" at the states general of Blois, he was yet perplexed with doubts as to his duty, or, perhaps, rather his interests, when devotion to the Roman Catholic Church and loyalty to his king seemed to be drawing him in two opposite directions. He had lost none of his intolerance during the past eight years. He was as anxious as ever to proclaim a new crusade. To use the expression of the scoffing queen mother, he was quite ready to send the king off to Constantinople. But how about taking up arms against the king, or, as the supporters of monarchy never tired of styling him, in biblical phrase, "the Lord's anointed?" There seemed to be but one way out of the difficulty. The duke must send and get the pope's opinion as to whether he might with a clear conscience engage in the enterprises of the "Holy League." He found the Jesuit, Claude Matthieu—popularly known, from his frequent flittings between France and Rome, as the courier of the League—not averse to the task of sounding Gregory's sentiments. The pontiff readily complied with the Jesuit's request to give his opinion. Shortly before Matthieu's arrival, in November, 1584,

The Duke of Nevers resolves to consult the pope.

---

[1] Compare De Thou, vi. (book 81) 441, 442.

he had come to the resolution to declare, by public sentence, the King of Navarre and all other heretical princes of the blood incapable of succeeding to the throne of France. Only one thing still delayed him—his prudent counsellors, the cardinals, insisted that he must wait until the " good Catholics " should have gained the upper hand in the kingdom.[1] Of course, then, when consulted by Matthieu, Gregory highly approved the proposed action of the League, and, in answer to the request of the agent, did not hesitate to give him a memorandum of his words of praise and encouragement. Inasmuch as the first and principal end of the Catholic princes, in whose behalf he had been consulted, was to take up arms against the heretics of France, his holiness expressly relieved them of all scruples of conscience they might have on this account, and bade them God speed.[2] True, there was not a word in the minute about taking arms against the king. Gregory had been too prudent to put anything of the kind upon paper. But in his oral remarks to the Jesuit he was outspoken. "The pope," Matthieu reported to Nevers, " does not think it at all well that any attempt be made on the king's life; for that cannot be done with a good conscience. Yet if his person could be seized, and those removed from about him who are the cause of the ruin of the kingdom, and if other men could be assigned to keep him in check, and give him good counsel, and compel him to follow it—this the pope would approve. For, under his authority, all the cities and provinces of the kingdom could be secured, and everything that is good could be established. Thus countless evils might be avoided

Gregory's cautious as to committing his views to paper.

---

[1] " S'il n'eust esté empesché par la remonstrance d'aucuns Cardinaux, qui luy dirent, qu'il n'estoit aucunement expedient qu'il fist la susdite déclaration, jusques à ce que les Catholiques de ce Royaume fussent les plus forts, et eussent les armes en main pour executor la sentence du Pape." Deciphered letter of Claude Matthieu to the Duke of Nevers, February 11, 1585, Mémoires de Nevers, i. 655.

[2] " Consente e lauda che lo facianno, e leva loro ogni scrupolo di conscienza, che per tal conto potessero havere e instando ch'el regno havera anco esso per ben fatto: ma quando fosse altrimente, non per ciò havevanno a resistere, essendo l'animo loro, come è detto, di conseguire quello primo e principale fine." Ibid., ubi supra, i. 656.

which will come to pass should the king continue as he is and be so ill-advised as to take sides with the heretics in opposing the Catholic princes. This, apparently, he intends doing, in which case he will be followed by a good part of the Catholics." [1]

The Duke of Nevers, however, was not so well satisfied by these assurances as the pope evidently expected him to be. Three or four months later (March, 1585), he again sought relief for his oppressed conscience. He could not be at rest, so he said, unless the pontiff should grant him a bull or a brief expressly declaring the justice of the proposed course of the League. Now, this was precisely what Gregory had no idea of doing.[2] He replied that his verbal assurances were quite sufficient, and that the duke must content himself with them. He fell back upon his judicial character, and declined appearing to become a party in interest. Above all, he urged that, were he to follow the duke's suggestion, he might set all Europe by the ears; for he knew well enough the jealous humors of the German Protestants, of the Swiss, of the Dutch, and even of the French. He hinted that if Nevers would not rest satisfied with the pope's verbal statements, it was a great pity, but nothing more could be done. He even went so far as to suggest that the duke's squeamishness must be the offspring of his fears for his person and his possessions, or be the convenient excuse for his intention to desert the body of "so zealous and Catholic princes." [3] As to a trip which Nevers had talked of taking to Italy in person, Gregory promptly discouraged it as a very bad notion, and not likely to

The pope's displeasure at the duke's pertinacity.

---

[1] Mémoires de Nevers, ubi supra, i. 657.

[2] Lestoile, recording in his journal (i. 184) the arrival of the news of the death of Gregory XIII., under date of April 18, 1585, states that this pope had never favored the League, and that, a few days before his end, he had declared that the League should have no bull or brief from him until he saw more clearly into its designs. It will be seen from the text just how much of truth there was in Lestoile's representation of the pontiff's attitude. Sixtus certainly did not regard his predecessor in any other light than as a decided upholder of the seditious movement of Guise and his fellow-conspirators.

[3] It must be confessed that Gregory's impressions on this score were shared by many in France, especially when Nevers retracted his adhesion to the League. See De Thou, vi. (book 81) 460.

be productive of edification. The duke would do far better to remain in France and jeopard his life for the protection of the faith.

For this somewhat rough treatment, however, Gregory made amends by sending a notable consignment of rosaries blessed by his own hand, and intended for the special benefit of the Cardinal of Bourbon, by whom they were to be distributed among the Roman Catholic princes and chief men of the League. Evidently the duke was deemed an incorrigible grumbler if these consecrated trinkets would not pass current with him as the equivalent of an honest avowal of sentiment over the signature of the pontiff and authenticated by the impress of the seal of the fisherman.[1]

Consecrated rosaries in place of advice.

Precisely at this juncture, on the tenth of April, 1585, Gregory the Thirteenth died. It was fitting that a pope who had signalized the first year of his reign by an enthusiastic approval of the massacre of Saint Bartholomew's Day should illustrate the close of his pontificate by underhand efforts to encourage the rebellious subjects of the King of France in their traitorous projects.

Death of Pope Gregory.

Nevers had not renounced his intended visit to Italy, and now put his purpose into execution. Upon his arrival in Rome he found Sixtus the Fifth already seated in the chair vacated by Gregory. A marked change had come over the relations of the papacy to the French League. The new pope, to whom the very memory of his predecessor was repugnant,[2] had as little inclination to pursue Gregory's foreign policy as to imitate the laxity of his domestic administration. Of this Nevers had abundant proof in his first audience.

Nevers visits Rome.

After graciously welcoming the nobleman with the complimentary exclamation, "Behold an Israelite indeed, in whom is no guile!" Sixtus could scarcely wait to enter upon a discussion of French affairs. "I am convinced," said he, "that con-

---

[1] Letter signed "Jacques La Rue, alias Martelli," to the Duke of Nevers, March 30, 1585, with letters of Matthieu and Cardinal Pellevé on the same subject, Mémoires de Nevers, i. 651-654.
[2] Ranke, History of the Popes, 142.

science is your only rule of conduct, and that, in your connection with Cardinal Bourbon and the other princes of the Union, you have no regard for anything else than the glory of God and the preservation of the Catholic, Apostolic, and Roman religion. But, nevertheless, in what school did you learn that you must form parties against the will of your lawful prince?"

<small>Sixtus the Fifth censures the League.</small>

"Most holy father," broke in the astonished Nevers, in the heat of excitement rising from his knees, "whatever has taken place has been done with the king's consent."

"How now!" rejoined Sixtus. "You warm up very fast. I imagined that you came to me in order to hearken to the voice of your father, to take his advice and follow it. Instead of that, I see you have the same disposition as have all the members of your association. You cannot endure correction. You condemn all that do not agree with you. Believe me! The King of France has never cordially consented to your leagues and your assumption of arms. He regards them as assaults upon his authority. Although constrained to dissemble, through fear of greater evils, it must be that he accounts you his enemies—enemies more to be dreaded and more cruel than the Huguenots. I fear me that matters will be pressed so far, that at length the King of France, Catholic though he be, will be constrained to appeal to the heretics for aid that he may rid himself of the tyranny of the Catholics."

The pope waxed hot as he thus pursued the theme. "O Gregory the Thirteenth!" he exclaimed again and again. "O Gregory the Thirteenth! What desolation of all Christendom by fire and sword have you occasioned by approving and fomenting the League and the Union of the French Catholics!"[1] It was not the only time that Sixtus gave vent to his resentment against the guilty authors of the conspiracy which had involved France in bloodshed and

<small>He bitterly condemns his predecessor's course.</small>

---

[1] "De temps en temps il s'escrioit contre Gregoire XIII., et contre le cardinal de Cosme, et leur reprochoit d'avoir mis le feu et le sang dans toute la Chrestienté," etc. Nevers to Cardinal Bourbon, Rome, July 31, 1585, Mémoires de Nevers, i. 667. M. de Gomberville gives the exclamation of Sixtus in this form: "S'écria plusieurs fois, 'O Gregoire XIII! Qu'en voulant faire du bien,

laid waste her fair towns and villages. He held Gregory, above all others, responsible before the bar of God, and he gave out no obscure hints of his belief that the late occupant of Saint Peter's seat might at that moment be suffering the torments of another world for his complicity in the great crime that had been perpetrated. "I bear the authors of the League great ill-will," he said, a year later; "and I do not think that God will ever forgive them. Possibly the soul of Pope Gregory might have something to tell us about this."[1]

The fact was that the shrewd pontiff saw through the flimsy disguise of the Leaguers, and detected their real motives. He maintained that there had never been a more pernicious conspiracy. He was convinced that not a man among all that cried out so loudly against the heretics had the glory of God and the promotion of the true faith as the sincere object of his undertakings. "Each one of them," he said, "wishes to become not a better Christian, but a greater lord. A hundred ambitious men would like to be kings, and, since they cannot be kings of the whole of a mighty state like France, they try, at least, to rend it in pieces and find a fragment on which they may settle and make themselves mimic sovereigns." "Poor France!" Sixtus used to say, "everybody has designs upon her; everybody racks himself to secure her ruin. But I love France. The Holy See owes to her its splendor and defence, and the popes cannot be too watchful in seeing to it that the first crown of Christendom shall remain entire upon the head of those whom God has chosen to wear it." "Tell Cardinal Bourbon," he said, on one occasion, "that he ought to despise distinctions which it is beyond his power to enjoy, since he has reached an age at which, if he already possessed them, he should think of resigning them to others. Let

Ambition the motive power of the League.

---

vous avez fait du mal! Vostre ame respond aujourd'huy devant le trosne de Dieu, de la desolation de la France, et de l'effusion de tout le sang qui y sera répandu.' " Ibid., i. 662.

[1] "J'en veux grand mal aux autheurs, et je ne pense pas que Dieu leur pardonne jamais. Peut-estre que l'ame du pape Gregoire en sçauroit bien que dire." Pisani, French ambassador at Rome, to Henry III., September 11. 1586, ibid., i. 750.

him remember that he is a bishop, and that he will have to give an account before a judgment seat where a misimprovement of opportunities will never pass for a right use of them."[1]

Had the conspirators of Joinville been able to shroud their dark proceedings in secrecy so profound as to escape the notice of the king and his agents in every part of the realm, the attitude assumed by the Spanish ambassador on the occasion of the advent of the Dutch envoys might have given the alarm to a less suspicious prince.

It must be confessed that rarely have bearers of costly and precious gifts been so shabbily treated as were the unlucky deputies of the states bringing to Henry the proffer of the sovereignty of some of the fairest provinces of Europe. True, they were not, like their countrymen, when sent on a similar mission, immediately after the Duke of Anjou's death, peremptorily forbidden by the queen mother from proceeding to the capital, and detained at Rouen for an entire month, almost in the guise of prisoners, before the king deigned to give them a polite but none the less positive refusal. More fortunate than their predecessors in this ungracious work, Chancellor Leoninus and his grave companions were allowed, after landing at Boulogne-sur-mer, ultimately to go up to Paris, where no expense was spared to do them honor. Yet, though they set foot in France on the third day of January, it was not until more than six weeks had elapsed that, on Wednesday, the thirteenth of February, they were admitted into the royal presence in the Louvre. Incredible as such puerile indecision may appear to us, the king could not make up his mind exactly how to act in the premises. For this reason it was that when the patient envoys had gotten over five-sixths of their way, and hoped within a few hours to see the towers of Notre Dame de Paris, they were stopped by command of the monarch at the city of Senlis. Thence they were subsequently brought to the capital by a secret royal order.

Unworthy treatment of the Dutch envoys.

---

[1] Letter of Nevers to Cardinal Bourbon, without date, Mémoires de Nevers, i. 673, 674. The duke himself gave to the historian De Thou some account of his negotiations with the pope. Histoire universelle, vi. (book 81) 460, 461.

But no secret could be so well kept at the court of Henry the Third as not instantly to be reported to Bernardino de Mendoza. The irascible ambassador of Philip at once took fire, and made bold to protest against the reception of the envoys. Twice, it was reported, he applied for an audience, and twice Henry declined to see him. A third request, accompanied by a judicious expenditure of Spanish ducats upon members of the royal council, was successful.[1] What was said and done on this occasion only the king and the ambassador knew, for no others were present. It is not strange, therefore, that the accounts of the interview given by foreign diplomatists to their royal masters, and accepted by contemporary historians generally well informed, differ materially from the written statement of one of the parties to the conversation, found in a document to which a former age had no means of access.

Mendoza tries to prevent them from securing an audience.

It was generally reported that Mendoza was outspoken, even to insolence. He demanded, forsooth, that Henry should grant no ear to men abandoned of God, as well as of their fellows, proscribed by the Holy Inquisition, and with nothing to hope for from their lawful prince. He professed to feel no apprehension lest Henry should be so ill advised as to listen to the unjust propositions of the Netherlanders, and stated that, if he thus protested, it was only because of his official position and because the interests of all the crowned heads of Christendom were involved in the matter. The King of France, said Mendoza, ought not to give such monsters an asylum within his dominions, but forthwith expel them from the country without deigning to give them an audience; just as the King of Spain had uniformly shut his ears to every appeal addressed to him by the disloyal subjects of his very Christian majesty. He closed by somewhat jauntily informing Henry that, if he had thus spoken, it was not because

His reported insolence.

---

[1] Froude, xii. 91, who, basing his account upon the despatches of Sir Edward Stafford, English ambassador at Paris, notices that Mendoza went so far as to demand his passports, and that Catharine de' Medici recommended that they should be given to him.

he had any fear that the King of France would take the rebellious Dutch under his protection. Indeed, should any person be found so lost to conscience and honor as to venture upon such a course, he would soon discover that, instead of attacking, he must take measures for self-defence ; for he would learn, at his own cost, that time was not always left for repentance over foolhardy undertakings, especially when one had to do with so powerful and fortunate a monarch as the King of Spain, whom no one had thus far insulted with impunity.

Henry the Third could on occasion play the magnanimous prince. The reply to Mendoza, with which he has been traditionally credited, was worthy of a better man than the effeminate weakling with whom the Valois name was to become extinct. Briefly, but forcibly, even angrily, we are told, he reminded the haughty Castilian that the Dutch were not obstinate rebels against lawful authority, but oppressed subjects whose just complaints of maltreatment had not been listened to, and who were condemned to suffer the evils of war because of the malignity of certain persons who preferred commotion to peace. He declared his intention to grant the envoys an audience, and justified the act by the interest the French had always felt in a country so near and so closely allied to their own. No one, he said, ought to mistake for an insult what was in reality a simple deed of generosity. France had always enjoyed the reputation, above all other nations, of extending a kindly welcome to those who sought to escape from the yoke of unjust domination. As for himself, he would take good care that his kingdom should not see its most glorious distinction obscured by ceasing to be the refuge of the unfortunate. Accordingly, he was happy to tell him and all the world, that a king of France does not know what it is to tremble ; and that neither threats nor dangers can prevent him from exhibiting toward afflicted princes and peoples having recourse to his protection, even to his latest breath, the same generosity that earned such glory for his ancestors.[1]

Magnanimous reply ascribed to the king.

---

[1] De Thou, vi. (book 81) 447, 448. Walsingham in a letter to Davison, January $\frac{14}{24}$, 1585, based on Stafford's report, gives a very similar account of

It is an amazing pity that most of these good, blunt words seem only to have existed in the imagination of the writers or their informants. The letters of Henry himself to his ambassador in Spain, which an eminent historian of our own day ¹ has been the first to unearth, strip the monarch of all this borrowed finery. They show that Mendoza was, indeed, urgent in his demands, but scarcely insolent in demeanor; while Henry would seem to have made not the slightest allusion to any grand defence of France as the refuge of oppressed innocence. What he did say was, that he was determined to hear the Dutch envoys, because he could not abandon his mother, Catharine de' Medici, in her pretensions upon the crown of Portugal, not only for the filial obedience which he owed her, but because he was her only heir! That Henry said anything more than what he has himself recorded, anything approaching the disinterested sentiments ascribed to him by others, is in the highest degree improbable. And so we get at the true explanation of the whole matter—both the determination of the king and his mother that the envoys from the Netherlands should be heard, and their almost incredible neglect to profit by the offer the envoys brought. Insincerity reigned unbroken from the beginning to the end of the transaction. Neither Henry nor Catharine had a thought of compassion for the country that had so long been the theatre of war and carnage, and that now stretched out its arms toward France for relief and protection. They only hoped, by judiciously encouraging its advances, to compel Philip the Second to make some large pecuniary offer for the renunciation of Catharine's chimerical claim upon the throne of Portugal.

It was pitiful, but not strange, that the wretched monarch

Mendoza's reception: "He went presently to court and dealt very passionately with the king and queen mother to deny them audience, who being greatly offended with his presumptuous and malapert manner of proceeding, the king did in choler and with some sharp speeches, let him plainly understand that he was an absolute king, bound to yield account of his doings to no man, and that it was lawful for him to give access to any man within his own realm. The queen mother answered him likewise very roundly, whereupon he departed for the time, very much discontented." Quoted in Motley, United Netherlands, i. 100. ¹ Ibid., i. 100-106.

who, in a transaction calling for manliness and magnanimity, had in reality displayed none but the most sordid motives and the lowest aspirations, should have made such an exhibition of himself to the Dutch deputies, when at length they were brought to the Louvre, as disgusted everyone not accustomed to the mad fashions of the French court—dressed with elaborate care and an attention to details that might have done credit to a professional beauty; with hair as daintily curled and heavily perfumed as that of a maid of honor of Queen Louise; his neck encircled with the famous ruff that gave the wearer's head the appearance of the head of Saint John Baptist on the charger; and with a sash thrown over his shoulders, from which hung a basket full of diminutive puppies. It was still more pitiful that, after keeping the envoys of the Netherlands a month longer in Paris, Henry sent them home with a definite refusal of their magnificent gift.[1] France had missed an accession to her territory that would have given her the "natural boundaries" for which, after three centuries, she still longs, but with little prospect of ever attaining. Better than that accession of domain would have been the extension and perpetuation of religious liberty, which could not have failed to result from the union of the Low Countries to France, even had no actual incorporation of lands ensued. With Holland under the protection of the French king, a proscription of the Huguenots would have been impossible. Civil wars might, indeed, again have broken out, but they must have been conflicts in which all loyal Frenchmen would be found fighting for the integrity of a magnificent realm—conflicts necessarily of short duration, because honor, national pride, and the prospect of distinction would all be enlisted on the side of the legitimate monarch.

Failure of the embassy.

The loss to France.

---

[1] De Thou, vi. (book 81) 475. Compare Motley, United Netherlands, i. 98, 99, and Froude, xii. 91, etc., the latter of whom finds Queen Elizabeth and the Dutch respectively responsible for counselling the proffer and for offering less than that absolute sovereignty which Henry the Third and Catharine de' Medici presumably would have accepted. His view appears incorrect in the light of the correspondence which Motley has published, and to which reference has already been made in the text.

SOVEREIGNTY OF THE NETHERLANDS.

Henry the Third had never seriously entertained the thought of accepting the sovereignty of the Low Countries. With his constitutional sluggishness and a love of repose that had become with him a second nature, he instinctively shrank from a step immediately involving him in a war with the foremost prince of Christendom. That war might indeed be waged in the name of the queen mother as mistress of Cambray, bequeathed to her by the will of its late owner, the Duke of Alençon; none the less would it require for its successful prosecution all the resources of the Very Christian King himself. Besides, to render assistance to those that had revolted against their lord paramount, with however good excuse, might be esteemed a dangerous thing for a king who certainly had given to his own subjects sufficient reason for dissatisfaction. Worst of all, the monarch who prided himself on his immaculate orthodoxy, the hero of Jarnac and Moncontour, the idol of the Roman Catholic party at the time of the massacre of Saint Bartholomew's Day, could not, without infinite reluctance, bring himself to take up arms in behalf of Dutch heretics, who held precisely the sentiments of the Huguenots of his own dominions—the Huguenots whom he hated cordially, and whose very existence it was notorious that he tolerated only by constraint.[1]

Queen Elizabeth sends the Earl of Derby to France. The advent of the envoys from the Netherlands was not the sole incident calculated to alarm Philip of Spain, and to serve the purpose of the authors of the League by arousing a popular fear of the approaching triumph of Protestantism in France. A magnificent embassy arrived in France about the same time, sent by Queen Elizabeth to invest Henry with the insignia of the Order of the Garter which she had seen fit to confer upon him. The deputation was headed by the Earl of Derby,[2] who was met on his approach to Paris with

---

[1] Busbecq to the emperor, January 25, 1585, Epistolæ, fol. 83. If anyone was in earnest, this writer believed it was Catharine de' Medici: "Certum est regem non libenter in hanc causam descendere; atque etiam desiderare quædam in mandatis Belgarum. Sed mater urget, cujus in nomen Hispanum infinitum est odium." Ibid. (March 6, 1585), fol. 86.

[2] It is difficult to recognize Lord Derby's name under the strange Latin disguise of "Comiti de Herbei" with which Busbecq invests it, or the still more

unsurpassed pomp. A house was assigned to him, during his stay, in close proximity to the Louvre, and he and his suite were provided for in the most luxurious manner, at an expense, it was said, of two hundred crowns a day. A single masquerade in his honor cost the king not less than thirty thousand crowns. On the appointed day for the solemn reception of the decoration, the twenty-eighth of February, the king and his court attended the great shrine of Saint Augustine, where vespers were chanted. Every member of the Order of the Holy Ghost was invited. So also were the foreign ambassadors, among whom, much to Mendoza's disgust, were all the envoys from the Netherlands.[1] To the astonishment of all (except possibly those familiar with the singular faculty which the Papal See and its representatives has always displayed for adapting themselves to circumstances) the nuncio graced the grand ceremonial with his presence, not seeming to think that there was any incongruity in his participation in a celebration intended to lend dignity to the gift of the excommunicate queen of England, the princess with whom his pontifical master had forbidden all intercourse on pain of incurring the censures of the church, the Protestant Jezebel for whose assassination plots were daily laid.[2]

None the less, however, on account of the nuncio's complaisance, did the Leaguers take occasion from the honors paid to the ambassador of Queen Elizabeth to malign Henry of Valois. The respect shown to the English envoy, said they, proves that the king is an abetter of heresy. Under him or

Reported atrocities of the English persecutions. under his successor, should the Protestant Henry of Navarre be permitted to mount the throne, the old religion will be driven to the wall and the new errors of Luther and Calvin will take its place. Then will the good Catholics be forced to experience in their own persons all those horrible persecutions to which the good Catholics of England have been subjected within our own times, and at the hands of the very queen whose ambassadors the king has so magnificently

---

remarkable form "le comte Herbert" of his French translator. Cimber et Danjou, Archives curieuses, x. 125.

[1] Busbecq to the emperor, March 6, 1585, Epistolæ, fol. 85.
[2] Letter of Busini, March 5, 1585, Négociations avec la Toscane, iv. 548, etc.

welcomed, at whose hands he has been proud to receive the Order of the Garter. What those "horrible persecutions" were, there was an attempt to show in a pamphlet that shortly saw the light, emanating from the pen of a fiery lawyer, one Louis d'Orléans, whom we find among the originators of the League in Paris, and purporting to be a note of warning sounded by the English Catholics to their brethren across the channel.¹ The production was a dry and tedious one. Its falsehoods were refuted in an answer that presently appeared, composed by Duplessis Mornay, a master of dialectics and a vigorous and skilful writer as well in French as in Latin.² But it was more difficult to remove from the minds of the Parisian populace the impression produced by prints and paintings representing the atrocities inflicted by order of Queen Elizabeth upon the bodies of unoffending priests and "religious" of both sexes. No sooner had the rude placards been affixed to the walls of some house in the capital, than a Leaguer was ready to step forward, rod in hand, and point out to the gaping and horrified crowd that pressed about him every actor and every harrowing detail of the picture.³

A war of manifestoes and declarations ushered in, as usual, the more serious war of arms. First, the king hurled at the conspirators a fresh edict, in the vain expectation by such a missile to reduce the batteries which, too late, he discovered had been directed against him. Again his majesty sought to make capital of the marvellous pains at which, as he alleged, he and his highly honored mother had been, to restore quiet to his realm, and dwelt upon the re-

A new royal edict against the League, March 28, 1585.

---

¹ "Advertissement des Catholiques Anglois aux François Catholiques du danger où ils sont de perdre leur religion, et d'experimenter, comme en Angleterre, la cruauté des ministres, s'ils reçoyvent à la couronne un Roy qui soit Heretique, 1586." Reprinted in Cimber et Danjou, Archives curieuses, xi. 111-202. Well styled by De Thou, "un long et ennuyeux discours."

² Duplessis Mornay's reply, "Lettre d'un gentilhomme Catholique François contenant breve Response aux calomnies d'un certain pretendu Anglois," may be read in the Mémoires de la Ligue, i. 454-493, in the Mémoires de Duplessis Mornay, iii. 335, etc., and in Cimber et Danjou, xi. 203, etc.

³ De Thou, vi. (book 81) 443, 444, who himself had seen some of these works of art.

forms he had introduced with the view of lightening the burdens under which the people groaned. He emphasized, in particular, the fact that he had, this very year, taken advantage of the peaceful condition of France to relieve his subjects of taxes amounting in all to seven hundred thousand livres, besides repealing sundry ordinances of which he had discovered the pernicious results. Notwithstanding this, certain persons envious of the public tranquillity had set themselves about raising troops, ostensibly for the king's service, but in reality to foment discord. Against these disturbers of the peace the king commanded his faithful servants to proceed in a summary manner, by ringing the tocsin to call the well-affected together, and by cutting in pieces all that might be so bold as to venture upon resistance.[1]

It was but three days later that the secret compact of Joinville bore fruit in an open declaration of hostilities on the part of the League. The affairs of Philip would admit of no delay; the success of the Prince of Parma's siege of Antwerp depended upon the promptness of the diversion made in his favor by Spanish-minded Frenchmen. The document bore for its title the words: "Declaration of the causes that have moved my lord the Cardinal of Bourbon and the Catholic princes, peers, prelates, lords, cities, and communities of this kingdom of France to oppose those who are seeking by all means to subvert the Catholic religion and the entire state."[2]

<small>The declaration of Cardinal Bourbon and the League.</small> For four-and-twenty years has France been plagued with a sedition aiming to subvert the religion of our forefathers—strongest bond of the state. So wrote a pen more skilful than that of the lumpish prelate whose not unwilling hand subscribed the treasonable paper. The remedies applied, instead of curing, have only rendered the evil more formidable, while the peace secured has been only a name, which left undisturbed those alone that were

---

[1] Edict of Henry III., Paris, March 28, 1585, De Thou, vi. (book 81) 451; text in Mémoires de la Ligue, i. 70, 71.

[2] The declaration bears date of Péronne, March 31, 1585. Text in Mémoires de Nevers, i. 641-646; Mémoires de la Ligue, i. 61-69; Cimber et Danjou, Archives curieuses, xi. 7-19. See also Recueil des choses mémorables, 607-609; Lestoile, 182, 183; De Thou, vi. 454, etc.

causes of trouble. Despite the prayers of good men, there is now the prospect that the king will die childless. Since the death of the duke, his brother, the plans of those who have ever persecuted the Catholic Church have rapidly matured; witness their great preparations within the kingdom, and their levies outside of it, and their retention of the cities which they were in duty bound long since to restore to the king. Evidently they intend to overthrow the Catholic religion, in order to enrich themselves with the patrimony of the church, thus following the example set them in England. Moreover, certain persons, insinuating themselves into the confidence of the sovereign (whose majesty always has been and always will be sacred to us), have possessed themselves of his authority, to the extent of gaining sole access to his person and distancing not only the highest princes and nobles, but even those nearest of kin to him. They have engrossed the control of affairs. Governors of provinces, captains in charge of strong places, and others, have been constrained to part with their honorable trusts, contrary to their desire, in exchange for a sum of money paid to them; the novel example being thus set of purchasing back with silver the distinctions originally conferred as rewards of virtue. Meantime, the diversion of the public revenues to these favorites has inflicted intolerable burdens. The hopes raised by the convocation of the states general of Blois have been frustrated by the bad advice of certain persons who, feigning to be good political counsellors, were really possessed of evil intentions respecting the service of God and the good of the state; for they persuaded the king to renounce his holy and very useful determination, adopted at the request of all three orders, to reunite his subjects in one single Catholic, Apostolic, and Roman religion—a project which would, at that time, have been carried into effect without peril and almost without resistance. In place of which they have convinced his majesty that he must weaken and diminish the authority of those Catholic princes and lords who have often jeoparded life under his banner, fighting in defence of the faith and earning a claim to honor and not suspicion. So far have these abuses gone that every estate of the kingdom is well-nigh overwhelmed: the clergy is crushed by tithes and extraordinary subventions, the nobles are degraded, enslaved, and reduced to villanage, and the cities, the royal officers, and the common people are so hard pressed by the frequency of fresh impositions, known as "inventions," that there no longer remains anything to be invented, always excepting the means of applying a good remedy.

For these reasons, pursues the declaration, we, Charles of Bourbon, "first prince of the blood," and other princes, cardinals, governors, cities, etc., constituting the best and soundest part of the realm of France, have sworn and solemnly promised to take up arms for the restoration of the Holy Church of God to its pristine dignity, for the maintenance of the nobility in its rights, and for the relief of the people; to which end, all new impositions shall be abolished, all increased taxes reduced to the standard of the times of Charles the Ninth; parliaments shall once more be made sovereign, governors be maintained in office, the moneys raised from the people be employed for the defence of the kingdom and for the other purposes for which they were destined; while the states general shall henceforth be convened freely and without intrigue, so often as the needs of the realm require, and with liberty extended to all men to offer their complaints.

The accustomed protestations follow. The cardinal and his associates profess their perfect readiness to shed the last drop of their blood in defence of the king, and promise to disarm so soon as his majesty shall be pleased to put an end to the peril threatening the ruin of God's service and of so many good people. Although they might with propriety call upon Henry to name his successor, they abstain from so doing, "for fear," say they, "lest the wicked should take occasion from this to calumniate our actions, as if we, Cardinal of Bourbon, in our old age, were thinking of another kingdom than that whose enjoyment is better assured, more desirable, and of longer duration." The queen mother is entreated to use her influence with her son, and all nobles and cities are besought to prevent the enemy from gaining an advantage by seizing important places. It is only against armed forces, adds the declaration, that we intend hostilities, and we assure everybody that our holy and just armies will harass and oppress no one, either in their passage or in their abode in any place whatsoever, but will live in good discipline, and take nothing without paying therefor. Then, in a fine outburst of patriotism and piety, the confederates declare that they will never lay down their arms until the accomplishment of their ends, desiring rather to perish and to be buried in one common sepulchre devoted to the last Frenchmen dying in arms for the cause of God and their native land.[1] Finally, they beg all good Catholics to make sure of the Divine favor by amendment of life, by holy processions, and by public and private prayers.

Such were the reasons which the League saw fit to give to the world in justification of the enormous crime against humanity it was about to perpetrate, in plunging France in a civil war destined to be more disastrous to civilization, morality, and human happiness than any of the preceding conflicts. How sincere was the interest affected by its leaders in the welfare of the poor people, how truthful their professions of undying loyalty to the king, how profound their regard for the maintenance of the Roman Catholic religion, how trustworthy their assurances of a purpose to abstain from pillage, and to offer violence to none but those found in arms, are questions that can best be answered in the light of the events of the next ten years.

To the manifesto of the League Henry of Valois replied very shortly by a declaration of his own,[2] in which he endeavored, not without success, to destroy the force of the arguments of his rebellious subjects. So far as religion was concerned, it was no difficult matter for him to show that both before and since his accession to the throne he had given conclusive proof of unsurpassed devotion to the interests of the Roman Catholic faith by exposing life and state

<small>Henry of Valois replies by a counter-declaration.</small>

---

[1] "Avec desir d'estre amoncelez en une sépulture consacrée aux derniers François morts en armes pour la cause de Dieu et de leur patrie." For the proposed tomb, however, a witty Huguenot offered the epitaph: "Ce sont les premiers Espagnols François." Mémoires de la Ligue, i. 114.

[2] "Declaration de la volonté du roy sur les nouveaux troubles de ce royaume." Ibid., i. 72-82.

in its behalf. If he had not successfully carried out the proscriptive policy requested by the states general of Blois (in proffering which request the deputies had been prompted by his majesty's own fervent attachment to the Catholic religion),[1] the cause of the failure was to be found in the neglect of the states themselves, despite royal entreaties, to provide the means necessary for carrying on war against the heretics. The king declared that the peace so roundly denounced by the League was concluded with the advice of the Cardinal of Bourbon himself and other princes, and for the express purpose of seeing whether that might not be effected by mild measures which severity had been powerless to accomplish. In fact, under its beneficent rule, the exercise of the Roman Catholic faith had been reintroduced into many places from which it had been banished during the prevalence of war, and great progress had been made in the reformation of abuses in the administration of justice, and in other departments of church and state. He showed the unreasonableness of the fears expressed respecting the succession of a king yet in his prime, and with a youthful wife for his consort, and he ridiculed the hope of re-establishing the Roman Catholic religion by means of a war and the introduction of foreign troops. Strangers would then grow at the expense of France, and triumph in its misfortunes. As for the good discipline that was promised, the frightful excesses in which the troops already enlisted had indulged sufficiently demonstrated the futility of such expectations.

All this was very sound argument, and might under other circumstances have been convincing enough. The trouble was *An undignified answer.* that throughout his counter-declaration Henry betrayed a weakness of purpose even more deplorable than the feebleness of the resources at his command. Where he should have commanded, he condescended to argue. Although the names of the conspirators against the peace of France were matter of common notoriety, they were not men-

---

[1] "Que les députés y estans, auroyent requis sa Majesté (induits à ce faire de sa fervente affection à la Religion Catholique) prohiber du tout en ce Royaume l'exercise de la dite Religion pretendue reformée."

tioned in the royal counter-declaration. Even Henry of Guise, whose designs upon the crown of France were so little concealed, and in favor of whose claims written treatises had been industriously circulated, was not particularly referred to. So cautiously and even coldly had the king expressed himself, that the world at once compared his majesty to a poltroon who has been well beaten but, while complaining of his bruises, dares not tell who struck him.[1]

This does not mean, however, that Henry was not now in some degree sensible of the danger of his situation. Indeed, the violence of the blow by which he had been aroused from his accustomed torpor excited, in his yet drowsy faculties, irritation against those who had ventured to interfere with his sluggish repose, not unmingled with fear for his own person. While the old queen mother resorted again to her former arts—setting out, one March evening, in her litter, very weak in body, and suffering both with a severe attack of catarrh and with gout in one leg, that she might reach Épernay, where Guise was reported to be, and confer with him respecting the present condition of affairs—Henry, in a spasm of activity, gave himself up to a consideration of the best method of quelling the disturbance. A diligent search was made of every house in Paris, to find who had gone out to join the Duke of Guise; resulting, we are told, in the discovery that, within twenty days, of artisans alone more than six thousand persons had absented themselves, all going to swell the numbers of the insurgents. Steps were taken to keep the capital in check; the captains of the quarters being changed, and new men, men of property, who, the day before, had taken a solemn oath of

The king's spasmodic activity.

---

[1] "Pour toutes armes il print la plume et fit une declaration, encore si froidement, qu'on disoit qu'il n'avoit osé nommer son ennemi le duc de Guise chef de l'armée, et qu'il ressembloit un qui se plaind, sans dire qui l'a battu." Recueil des choses mémorables, 610. Henry, it is worthy of notice, was equally careful not to mention the name of the Duke of Guise in his conference with the Dutch envoys, even while muttering threats of vengeance, and these by no means obscure. "Je scay bien," said he, "qui est l'autheur de ces troubles, mais si Dieu me donne vie, je luy rendrai pareille et l'en ferai repentir." Report of Calvart, apud Motley, United Netherlands, i. 111.

allegiance to the king in the presence of the parliament, being substituted. Turning scribe, Henry wrote, it was said, with his own hand, to all the governors of the realm and to a great number of the gentlemen. Never had the Louvre presented a more animated appearance. Couriers were coming and going incessantly. One hundred and fifty or more were sent out within the brief compass of a week. It looked almost as though the king would at last summon resolution to act the man. He informed the nuncio of the pope that if, as was reported, his master had entered the League, he would himself be constrained to take measures to defend himself, and make such counter-demonstrations as might not at all please his holiness and the Sacred College. He professed the greatest indignation against the Duke of Mercœur, who, after having been permitted to marry the queen's sister, had displayed in return for countless favors shown him by his royal brother-in-law such signal ingratitude as to join hands with those who were in arms against him.[1]

But all Henry's resolution evaporated in complaints of ill usage. That he hated the Duke of Guise and his brother the cardinal, with undying hatred, was no secret to anyone, least of all to those who were the objects of that hatred.[2] But, in his desperate desire to relapse again into his wonted quiet, in his impatience once more to be pursuing those degraded pleasures in which he found the chief end of his creation, he soon made it evident to observing men about him that, rather than sacrifice his selfish ease, he would concede everything demanded of him.[3] The day of vengeance

His hatred of the Guises.

---

[1] The letters of Busini are full of interesting details respecting the movements day by day. Négociations avec la Toscane, iv. 554, and onward.

[2] The envoys of England and of Florence use, about this time, almost the very same words to describe Henry's feeling toward Guise and his brother. "He hated the Guises," Sir Edward Stafford said, "with a hatred which would never be quenched." Froude, xii. 104. "L'odio che ha il Re contro il duca di Guise e il suo cardinale è immortale, visto che aspirano alla corona." Letter of Cavriana, Négociations avec la Toscane, iv. 603.

[3] "È cosa certissima, che Sua Maestà vuole la pace, resoluta, per quello che intendo, di concedere quanto vogliono." Busini, May 13, 1585, ubi supra, iv. 573.

would come in the due course of events. When it should come, Henry of Valois would exact the full equivalent for the insults received at the hands of Henry of Guise. Other old scores would also be wiped off at the same time; among the rest, the reckoning against the wife of Marshal Retz, who, alluding to the possibility that the last Valois might end his days in a cloister, immured there by the Guises as Childeric had been compelled by Pepin to receive tonsure and enter the conventual walls of Saint Omer, had remarked that "the whole trouble could be settled with a pair of scissors." [1] The day of requital, however, had not yet dawned, the day when the Guises, intoxicated by past impunity and lured into the lion's den, would suddenly, but too late, discover that there were limits to the forbearance of the most inert of kings. Not that the monarch even now neglected precautions against such a catastrophe as that which Madame de Retz had hinted at. On the first of January, 1585, his majesty instituted a new and extraordinary guard, which the public were not slow in concluding to be a band of salaried assassins. "There is another order," wrote the English ambassador, "maketh men to fear a determination of a very tyrannical intention, for besides his ordinary guard of French in two sorts, Swissers and Scots, he hath erected Five and Forty, which they that are acquainted with Italian terms do term 'Taillagambi.' These must never go from his person. Whensoever he goeth out, they must be nearest to his person, every one a cuirass under his coat, and to look at nothing but the fulfilling of the king's will." [2] The world was to hear, before four years should have passed, of the murderous exploits of the "Forty-Five." Meanwhile, Henry of Valois, drowsy and apparently irritated only at being compelled to collect his wandering thoughts, did little to the purpose, and rather played into the hands of the enemy than seri-

His unconcern.

---

[1] "Ancora, per dire, tutto s'accomoderà poi con un paro forbici." Letter of Busini, June 11, 1585, Négociations avec la Toscane, iv. 581.

[2] Sir E. Stafford to Lord Burleigh, December 25, 1584, Murdin State Papers, 426. The Florentine agent Busini, under date of January 5, 1585, denominates the guard "Tagliagaretti" (*i.e.*, "coupe-jarrets"). Négociations avec la Toscane, iv. 545.

ously attempted to thwart them. Though compelled to take up arms, his inclinations were all for peace. The immediate present was all that he was concerned about, the more so that he had no child, legitimate or illegitimate, and expected none.[1] The last of his race, he cared nothing for the future of the kingdom which, " by the grace of God," had been confided to him, and from which his sole endeavor was to extract as much treasure as possible to lavish upon himself and his favorites. After him might come the deluge; let those who aspired to be his successors, and were ready to cut each other's throats to clutch the sceptre, see to that. Two months had not gone by, when a shrewd Italian at Paris wrote home that the king was living as unconcernedly as in time of peace, giving himself little solicitude for his troops. "These," said he, " are fresh levies, undisciplined, licentious, disaffected, and, what is worse, badly paid. You may judge what can be hoped from such sort of men."[2] Before the recent inopportune outbreak had come, disturbing all his calculations, Henry of Valois, it was well understood, had been meditating an entire retreat from the conduct of public affairs. The lessons of Catharine de' Medici, so sedulously instilled into the minds of all her children, had not been wasted upon this, her last surviving and best loved son. Henry, never destined to become a man, however long he might live, or a true king, however many the crowns that might be placed on his head, loved private life so much that he intended to transfer the whole burden of the state to the shoulders of his mother,[3] who, whatever else might be said of her, never shrank from assuming fresh responsibilities, though she might be weakened by approaching old age, racked by gout, harassed by occasional returns of her constitutional timidity and indecision, and haunted not infrequently by the ghosts of the tens of thousands of her

His desire to leave affairs of state to his mother.

---

[1] Letter of Cavriana, April 2, 1585, Négociations avec la Toscane, iv. 608.

[2] Letter of Cavriana, May 27, 1585, ibid., iv. 611.

[3] " È certo Sua Maestà andava a cammino di fare una ritirata da sè stesso dalle cose publiche, e lasciare la carica totale alla Reina Madre, amando egli sopra modo la vita privata." Cavriana, July 9, 1585, ibid., iv. 615.

victims in the Saint Bartholomew massacre. And what was the present course of that mother? Was she anxious to avert the disaster impending over her unfortunate son? Contemporary writers, on the contrary, represent her as co-operating with the Duke of Guise and furthering the design of the League, not indeed so much to render Guise great, as in order to introduce confusion and render it necessary that she should be called in to restore order.[1]

<small>General success of the League.</small> It is, happily, not needful that the story of the disgraceful scenes which followed should be recounted in these pages. The League concerns us here only so far as it affected the fortunes of the Huguenots, and a detailed account of the successive affronts it was able to put upon the King of France would be out of place. This dreary episode of French history must be read in the pages of the contemporary chroniclers, or, still better, in those letters and pamphlets in which the righteous indignation of an outraged people vented itself upon the miscreants who had dared, under cover of religion and piety, to plunge the nation into civil war; upon the traitors who, from cowardice or for money, surrendered the posts they had taken to defend, and upon the pusillanimous monarch who removed even the ordinary inducements which encourage subjects to be faithful to their trusts and loyal to their sovereign. Suffice it to say that almost everywhere the League struck promptly and effectually; scarcely resorting at all to the pen, save in a few pasquinades and libels, wherein the most infamous of the king's secret immoralities were held up to popular detestation.[2] In rapid succession all the towns of Picardy, save only Boulogne, fell under the power of the League. Guise's agents seized Verdun and Toul, but failed in securing Metz, the third and most important of the "Three Bishoprics." Lyons, under its notorious governor, Mandelot, expelled from its citadel the loyal commandant, and razed the citadel itself to the ground; the soldiers of the garrison exclaiming, we are told, for all answer to the remonstrances

---

[1] Recueil des choses mémorables, 613.
[2] Agrippa d'Aubigné, ii. (liv. 5, ch. 5) 424.

of the superior officer, that "they had no idea of being damned for the benefit of a favorer of heresy such as was the king, and, as for the oaths they had taken, they had received a dispensation from the Jesuit Fathers."[1] In short, throughout France the only serious rebuff encountered by the adherents of the League was experienced at Marseilles, where, after having obtained possession of the city, under the authority of one of the consuls, they were speedily expelled and their leader was hung, when the inhabitants came to their senses.[2] In general, to use the expressive words of Agrippa d'Aubigné, "none were seen arriving at the royal court except couriers coming from all parts to announce the capture of cities taken without a combat, and by means so shameful that history refrains from the recital, for all the stratagems employed are reduced to two categories, namely, great sums of money promised or paid, or else the declamations of the preachers, in public or in private, to move the people to the agreeable pretexts of their new party."[3]

In the midst of the general treachery, however, the fidelity of a few governors of cities shone out resplendent. Aymar de Clermont, Sieur de Chastes, who commanded at Dieppe, was among the king's trusty servants. Interested, as a knight of the order of Malta, in the prosperity of the established church, he was nevertheless a man of exemplary fairness, loving the people

---

[1] Agrippa d'Aubigné, ubi supra; De Thou, vi. (book 81) 477.

[2] The fullest account of the attempt upon Marseilles is contained in a pamphlet, reprinted in Cimber et Danjou, Archives curieuses, xi. 29–45, entitled "Lettres escrittes de Marseilles contenant au vray les choses qui s'y sont passées les 8, 9, et 10 du mois d'Avril dernier, 1585." There is a shorter account in Mémoires de la Ligue, i. 85, etc. One of the first acts of the Second Consul D'Aries was to throw all the Huguenots into the Tour Saint Jean, and to write inviting M. de Vins, commanding for the League in Provence, to come to the city. Subsequently two Huguenots were killed, and their bodies, as usual, dragged by little children through the streets. The Duke of Nevers was waiting at Avignon, on his way to Italy, for the welcome tidings of the capture of Marseilles.

[3] Histoire universelle, ii. 424. See De Thou, vi. 452–477. Busini sums up the triumphs of the League, in a letter of May 13, 1585: "Di maniera che, come vostra signoria può comprendere, questi della Lega hanno già la maggior parte del regno, cioè le principali terre, come Orleans, Bourges, Tours, Angers, Nantes, Lyon, etc." Négociations avec la Toscane, iv. 573.

committed to his charge, irrespectively of their religious tenets, and in turn beloved by them; determined to preserve the peace despite the confusion of the times and the severity of the royal edicts which he was called upon to execute. Reposing no confidence in the Roman Catholic inhabitants of Dieppe, his own fellow-believers, De Chastes summoned to his aid the Protestants, whose loyalty was unimpeachable. Nightly were these partisans of another faith quietly assembled, by the governor's orders, in various houses throughout the city, with distinct instructions as to their duty in case of tumult. For months—in fact, until the king's disgraceful surrender to the League, soon to be narrated—the Protestants, whose public worship was only tolerated outside of the walls, in the distant hamlet of Pallecheul, were intrusted with the guard of Dieppe, their citizen soldiers spending the day, we are told, in prayers, the night watches in reading the Word of God. Rarely had clearer testimony been given to Huguenot loyalty.[1]

While Henry of Valois was feebly defending himself, permitting his mother to negotiate with traitors who should have been pursued and cut to pieces without mercy, and suffering Mendoza to hoodwink him and convince him by letters of Philip the Second, which he showed him, that his Catholic majesty had no part at all in the League,[2] other spectators, scarcely less interested than he in the issue of the struggle, were curiously watching the course of events. Not Philip himself, kept as well informed of the occurrences at the French court as were the faithful servants of the crown in the command of armies,[3] scanned each item of news as it arrived

Philip the Second's attitude.

---

[1] Histoire de la Réformation à Dieppe par Guillaume et Jean Daval (published by the Société Rouennaise de Bibliophiles), i. 132, 133. The same writers inform us (ibid., i. 138) that Governor De Chastes, three or four years later, invited the Huguenot refugees home from England to defend Dieppe, and prevent the city from following the example of all the rest of Normandy, save Caen, by embracing the side of the Holy League, after the murder of the Guises at Blois.   [2] Busini, ubi supra, iv. 468.

[3] " Et se rejouissent fort [les Espagnols] des troubles de France, desquels ils sont si bien advertis que les nouvelles que jen ay de vostre court me sont mandées toutes pareilles d'Espaigne." Joyeuse to Henry III, Narbonne, April 23, 1585, Loutchitzky, Documents inédits, 169.

with half the intensity of anxiety felt by the impetuous Henry of Navarre from his far-distant domains at the foot of the Pyrenees.

<small>Henry of Valois writes to Henry of Navarre,</small> The death of the Duke of Anjou, removing the only person who stood between him and the king, had awakened in the Béarnais for the first time the full consciousness of the destiny for which he was reserved. The fact that he had been able, as mentioned in a previous chapter, to bring to the king's knowledge, and thus to thwart, the earlier plot of the League against the royal authority, seemed to give him an additional title to act in the present emergency as the most important ally and supporter of his cousin of Valois. Nor did the latter disallow the claim. As early as the twenty-third of March, Henry of Navarre received this brief note from the king.

"My brother, I notify you that I have not been able, whatever resistance I have made, to prevent the evil designs of the Duke of Guise. He is in arms. Be on your guard, and make no move. I have heard that you are at Castres for the purpose of conferring with my cousin the Duke of Montmorency. I am very glad of this, so that you may provide for your own affairs. I shall send you a gentleman to Montauban who will advise you of my will. Your good brother, HENRY."[1]

<small>but fails to call in his assistance.</small> Impatiently, and not without grave misgivings as to the fulfilment of the royal promise, did the King of Navarre await the word that was to permit him, the much-abused Gascon and Huguenot prince, to fly to the assistance of his hard-pressed sovereign. Past experience had made him doubtful of the favor in which he stood. Still, he renewed to Marshal Matignon his offer of service for the king as against the League, "although," he mournfully added, "on similar occasions that have presented themselves, within three or four years, his majesty has not deigned to see or listen to those whom I sent to him, and this through the artifice of his enemies."[2] The King of Navarre's forebodings were destined to be verified; the summons never came. Henry might advance

---

[1] Dom Vaissète, Histoire de Languedoc, v. 400, and Lettres missives de Henri IV., ii. 38, taken from the Mémoires de Gaches, 299.

[2] Henri of Navarre to Marshal Matignon, April, 1585. Lettres missives, ii. 26, 27.

to the banks of the Dordogne, in order to be near at hand in case of a sudden call; the Valois was unwilling or afraid to make a requisition upon him. In fact, it would seem that the French king felt both fear and aversion. Earlier in the year, before their departure for home, the Dutch envoys had despatched their secretary, Calvart by name, to confer secretly with Henry of Navarre. Calvart had found the great Protestant leader full of hope and sympathy. Not content with the cold assurance of words, Henry had promised to send a body of two thousand soldiers, at his own expense, to assist the states in the desperate struggle in which they were engaged. He had merely stipulated that the consent of the King of France should first be obtained for the passage of the Gascon troops over the border. But, much to Calvart's disappointment, Henry of Valois could not be induced to permit the Béarnais to aid an enterprise in which he had himself so recently declined to take part. Secretary Villeroy, acting as the king's mouthpiece, justified the refusal by the declaration that, should his majesty either openly or secretly assist the Netherlands, or allow them to be assisted, he would give all the Catholics now sustaining his party reason to go over to the Guise faction.[1]

Navarre's offer declined.

From the moment his keen eyes had descried the coming storm, the King of Navarre had been on the alert, ready to help with his own arm, anxious also to enlist in behalf of the unworthy monarch the co-operation and support of others. For this purpose the skilled pen of his faithful follower, Duplessis Mornay, was incessantly occupied. Everyone at court whom Navarre could hope to influence for good was plied with urgent letters. On a single day (the twenty-ninth of March) the secretary wrote from Montauban to M. d'Elbène, to Abbé Guadagny, to Bellièvre, to Villeroy, to Chancellor Chiverny, begging them, in view of the audacity of the League, to act promptly and prudently, and encouraging them with bright hopes of success. To each the language was the same: "You have acquired great reputation for prudence;

The King of Navarre's letters.

---

[1] Report of Calvart, Hague Archives, apud Motley, United Netherlands, i. 108, 111.

do not suffer the kingdom, committed to the keeping of your arms, to perish. Whatever the appearances may be, the patient can weather the disease, if only his strength and his blood be husbanded. Fevers that spend their force most quickly are wont to have the severest beginnings."[1]

In a letter to the Duke of Montmorency, toward whom Navarre now turned as an old and natural ally, his secretary, in his name, vividly sketched the present crisis. "In my estimation," he wrote, "this war will be the sieve to sift out true Frenchmen, for, while those that play upon the boards are dressed in French costumes, yet is it clear that the author of the tragedy is a Spaniard. If these actions depended upon the persons that seem to move, we might expect the actors to draw back; but, granting that they have a higher source, they will apparently proceed in their course. . . . My lord, in these great affairs there is no one that can help this prince more by his advice than you can. Preceding occurrences have only been play. Frenchmen were pitted against Frenchmen—men who had long since measured their strength against each other, and of whom the one party was as impatient and as likely to grow weary as the other. Now, French troops are indeed in the field, but marshalled and led by a Spanish intellect, which is so much the more willing to behold our sufferings, as we alone shall suffer, while it will gain all the advantage. God most frequently laughs at such devices, and makes the thunder end in smoke."[2]

The war to sift out true Frenchmen.

Meanwhile, the Béarnais did not cease to remind the king, by letter and by the mouth of his agents at court, that the person of his majesty could not be defended more faithfully than by a prince of his own blood, nor his state than by those who could hope to be saved only by its salvation.[3] At the same time, he advanced to the very northern borders of his government of Guyenne, keep-

Navarre's continued offers.

---

[1] Duplessis Mornay to Villeroy, March 29, 1585. Mémoires de Duplessis Mornay, iii. 8.

[2] Duplessis Mornay to the Duke of Montmorency, March 30, 1585. Ibid., iii. 11.

[3] "Ramentevés lui, M. de Chassincourt, que sa personne ne peult estre plus fidelement defendeue que par son sang propre, ni son estat que par ceulx qui

ing his soldiers busily at work repairing and fortifying the cities intrusted to Protestant hands, so as to keep them out of mischief until the moment when, by the permission of their sovereign, they should cross the broad provinces of Angoumois and Poitou, and hasten to meet him on the northern bank of the Loire.¹ His example was followed by his cousin the Prince of Condé, who, from the walls of Saint Jean d'Angely, begged to be allowed to enter the king's service with his company of Protestant gentlemen, all of whom had provided themselves with horses and arms, and only awaited the word of command.²

If Henry of Valois should follow the suicidal course suggested to him by traitors in the royal council, if he should make nominal friends of the enemies who had conspired against his crown and authority, by breaking his compacts with the Huguenots, dissolving the peace so often claimed as his own voluntary act, and proscribing the Protestant religion, it would be from no lack of wholesome advice either from within or from without, from no want of proffers of assistance. The historian De Thou has inserted in his great work the long, candid, and forcible plea for peace and toleration made by François de Noailles, Bishop of Acqs, a prelate who had acquired the greatest distinction as an ambassador to London, to Venice, and to Constantinople.³ From beyond

Forcible plea of the Bishop of Acqs.

---

ne peuvent estre conservés qu'en le conservant." Henry of Navarre to Chassincourt, ibid., iii. 15.

¹ Henry of Navarre to Henry III., April 13, 1585, Lettres missives, ii. 38–40; same to same, May 7, 1585, ibid., ii. 63–65. Mr. Motley makes Henry of Navarre to have been "resident at Chartres" when visited by Calvart on his secret mission (United Netherlands, i. 108). As the Béarnais never resided on the north side of the Loire after his flight from the French court, in February, 1576 (see above, i. 85), until he came to the aid of Henry III., at his invitation, thirteen years later, this is evidently a mistake. Probably, for "Chartres" we must read "Castres." The two cities are nearly three hundred and fifty miles apart in a straight line. Henry of Navarre had a conference with the Duke of Montmorency at Castres in March, 1585. See Mémoires de Gaches, 297–299.

² "Mais joze à cette heure men asseurer de tant plus qu'il est plus que jamais necessairo au service de vostre dite Majesté par l'outrecuydee license de ses ennemys." Henry of Condé to Henry III., May 22, 1585, Loutchitzky, Documents inédits, 132. ³ De Thou, vi. (book 81) 465–473.

the channel, Queen Elizabeth—not deterred by the unworthy treatment of her envoy Wade, assaulted and beaten by the Duke of Aumale, contrary to the law of nations, nor disgusted even by the treacherous conferences of Secretary Villeroy with Mendoza respecting a proposed invasion of England, which had been reported to her by Sir Edward Stafford[1]—wrote a letter of vigorous remonstrance. She expressed her amazement that a great king, contrary to all reason and honor, should sue for peace of traitors, instead of forcing them to submit to authority. She warned him that it was unlikely that the rebels would be content with ruling France under his name; for princes conquered by their subjects are rarely of long continuance. She offered her own assistance, and declared that should he be pleased to accept it, the Leaguers would be seen put to the greatest shame that ever rebels knew. She bade him encourage his loyal subjects, now disheartened by doubts engendered of his neglect to punish traitors. It were better to lose twenty thousand men than reign at the pleasure of rebels. "If a queen, in sixteen days, brought thirty thousand men into the field, to chastise the vagaries of two fools, excited thereto by another prince and not led by desire of private gain, what ought a king of France to do against such persons as claim descent in direct line (as they dream) from Charlemagne—a line taking the precedence of that of Valois—and, in order the better to palliate their deed, protest that they are the champions of the Catholic religion, to which you belong, taunting you with not being so faithful a servant of the church as they are! For the love of God, indulge no more in this too protracted sleep!"[2]

The remonstrances of Queen Elizabeth,

With this kind appeal came a substantial offer of four thousand foot-soldiers whom the queen had ready for service,[3] and of liberal advances of money.

---

[1] See Froude, xii. 99, 100, and Motley, United Netherlands, i. 124–127.

[2] Queen Elizabeth to Henry III. [May, 1585], Lettres missives, ii. 227, etc. Translated in Froude, xii. 101. The letter was much admired by Henry of Navarre, who wrote to the Countess of Grammont: "Vous y verrés un brave langage et un plaisant style." Lettres missives, ubi supra.

[3] Letter of Busini, May 28, 1585. Négociations avec la Toscane, iv. 574.

Other old and tried allies of the French crown sent envoys bearing similar remonstrances and similar offers of help. To Paris came in close succession the extraordinary embassies of the Electors of Saxony, Brandenburg, and the Palatinate, of the Landgrave of Hesse, and of the Dukes of Brunswick and Würtemberg. Among the members of these deputations appeared some of the most distinguished diplomatists of Germany.[1] Meanwhile, the German princes indicated unmistakably the drift of their sympathy, by strictly forbidding any troops from leaving their territories without license, and by threatening the Duke of Lorraine, both by the mouth of messengers and in writing, with their severe displeasure, should that nobleman venture to war against the Huguenots.[2]

<small>and of the German princes.</small>

But offers of assistance, protests, and entreaties were alike useless. Henry, openly menaced by the League, had the misfortune to have about him few faithful advisers. If a Marshal d'Aumont was found to advocate strenuous resistance to the demands of Guise and his associates, he stood almost alone. The queen mother played upon his fears, and exaggerated the perils of his situation. As for his other advisers, their attitude showed clearly that Spanish ducats had been judiciously expended upon them. And Henry of Valois had within himself no reserve of moral force to resist their importunities.

<small>The king's evil counsellors.</small>

It is always an unprofitable inquiry to ask why the coward refuses to adopt the manly course of conduct which, although attended with temporary discomfort and possible danger, infallibly leads to that very rest and security upon which he sets a value far transcending all considerations drawn from truth, honor, and integrity. There are problems in human nature beyond the power of men to solve. Above all, in the analysis of motives in a character so depraved as that of the man (scarcely worthy of the name of man) now seated upon the throne of France, are we confronted with difficulties

<small>His moral turpitude.</small>

---

[1] Agrippa d'Aubigné, ii. 459.
[2] Letter of Busini, June 11, 1585. Négociations avec la Toscane, iv. 580.

and contradictions so great as to defy satisfactory explanation. Some points, however, are sufficiently clear. Henry of Valois was the most purely selfish, as he was in morals the most despicable monarch that ever wore the French crown. For not a living soul did he sincerely care. Childless and without hope of begetting an heir to the throne; united in wedlock to a wife to whom he was habitually false, and toward whom he frequently did not pretend to offer even an outward show of respect;[1] cursed with a mother as faithless to her own children as she was treacherous to her kind and reckless of any higher Power; able to boast of no friends, of no comrades save the necessary companions and accessories of his vices—this prince gave himself no solicitude for the future, and plunged deeper and deeper in the abyss of sensuality. Excesses had destroyed the very tissue of his moral constitution, and left no room for the hope that nature, always more benignant than men deserve to find her, might reconstruct the original fabric. In so untoward a soil as Henry's mind no seed of magnanimous resolve could find a lodgement with the prospect of germinating and eventually bearing fruit in heroic accomplishment.[2]

Early in the progress of the struggle between the king and the League, Henry of Navarre had held a conference of his chief supporters to deliberate respecting the important question, what attitude the Protestants should take in this emergency. All the leaders of the party were there, and the hall of the priory of Guitres (not far from the field of Coutras, soon to attain world-wide fame) was crowded with a company of Huguenot warriors of various ages. Some were young men unused to scenes of conflict, others veterans in the military art, but all were flushed with expectation, and anxiously awaiting the decision of the Béarnais. There may have been sixty persons present in all.

Navarre consults the Huguenot chiefs.

A contemporary historian, who himself took a leading part in the discussion, has preserved for us a full and graphic ac-

---

[1] See Busini's letter of June 11, 1585, ubi supra, iv. 581.

[2] The disgusting story of Henry's depravity is told with a plainness of speech characteristic of the sixteenth century by Agrippa d'Aubigné, ii. 424, 439.

count of this momentous consultation. The picture well deserves to be reproduced here, so characteristic was the scene of the sturdy Huguenot chiefs whose strong right arms sustained an unpopular cause for a whole generation against all the attacks brought to bear upon them by a hostile king and an overwhelming majority of the French nation.

The proceedings began, according to the good old custom of the Huguenots, who, whatever their faults may have been, were at least a religious folk, with a solemn invocation of the presence and blessing of the Almighty. The name of the Protestant minister who officiated has not been transmitted to us, but it is not improbable that to Gabriel d'Amours, who offered prayer before the charge at Coutras, the honorable duty was committed. Then the King of Navarre addressed those present with that mixture of earnestness and cheerful good nature which he could command on every occasion. He assured them that, had the critical juncture in the affairs of France been likely to affect his own life and interests alone, he would not have troubled them to come to this conference. But now the preservation or the ruin of all the Reformed churches was in question, and the first point to be settled was a vital one. "Shall we sit still," said Henry, "with crossed arms, while our enemies are contending together, and shall we send all our warriors into the king's armies, as some maintain that we ought to do, without assuming a special name or setting up a distinct banner; or, shall we, according to the view advanced by others, arm ourselves, but stand aloof, ready at any moment to help the king or strike a blow to better our own condition? Here is the matter respecting which I beg each one to express his opinion freely and without passion."

The Huguenot chiefs had seated themselves around the room with little regard to form or precedence. The Viscount of Turenne, who chanced to be on the king's left hand, was the first to reply to the invitation. He espoused the policy of quiet inaction. "Our patience," said he, "will cut the throat of our enemies' reasons; our impatience would justify their arms and their plans. As respects success, I reason thus: If you take up arms, the king will fear you; if

Advice of the Viscount of Turenne.

he fear you, he will hate you; if he hate you, he will attack you; if he attack you, he will destroy you. My advice is that, by our endurance, we should heap coals of fire upon the heads of those who unjustly hate us. Let us permit our braves to enter the royal armies. The King of France will then owe his deliverance to our valor, and will sacrifice his past hatred to our humility. Should he hereafter come to an agreement with his adversaries and ours, our integrity will shine forth resplendent as the mid-day sun in the sight of all mankind."

So convincing did the viscount's arguments appear, that as man after man was called upon, each declared himself of the same mind, none venturing to do more than, perhaps, to add some historical illustration or parallel by way of corroboration. A score had spoken, and Turenne's opinion seemed about to be adopted as the unanimous sense of the meeting, when, the turn of Agrippa d'Aubigné coming, that ardent and blunt speaker turned the tide of feeling.

"It would be to trample under foot the ashes of our martyrs and the blood of our brave soldiers," said he; "it would be to erect the gallows over the tombs of our dead princes and great captains, and condemn to the like ignominy those who survive and have devoted their lives to the cause of their God, here to call in question the justice of their magnanimous course. It is not ours to look behind us, where we shall only see churches, cities, families, individual persons ruined, partly by the perfidy of the enemy, partly by that of men who sought excuses to exempt themselves from those labors and dangers to which God calls us whenever so it seems good to Him. 'If you take up arms, the king will fear you.' That is true. 'If the king fear you, he will hate you.' Would to God that this hatred on his part were yet to begin! 'If he hate you, he will attack and destroy you.' Would that we had not yet experienced the power of that hatred, but rather the power of that fear which prevents the effects of hatred! Happy those who by that fear forestall their ruin! Wretched he who shall draw down upon himself this ruin by making himself contemptible. I say, therefore, that we alone ought not to remain unarmed, when all France is in arms, nor permit our sol-

<small>Reply of Agrippa d'Aubigné.</small>

diers to take an oath to support captains who have taken an oath to exterminate us, nor compel them to show respect for the countenance of those whom they ought to slash with their cutlasses; much less force them to serve under the flag of the white cross, which has always been, and must still be, the target for our missiles. Shall we exhibit to our young nobles ignominy dwelling with us and honor with the other side? What will become of our princes of the blood and our great party leaders, when they shall have given over to their enemies both their followers and the credit purchased by so many benefits conferred? We must indeed manifest our humility, but let us see to it that there be no cowardice mingled with it. Let us remain in good condition, to be of service to the king in his need, and to help ourselves in our own. Then, when the right moment shall come, let us bend our knees before him fully armed, take our oath of allegiance to him, drawing our right hand from out of the knight's gauntlet, and bring our victories, not our amazement, to his feet. The pretext which our enemies have seized in order to escape from the authority of their sovereign, is that they might fly at our throats. It is necessary, since the royal sceptre cannot stop them, that respect for our swords should produce that effect. I conclude thus: If we disarm, the king will despise us; contempt for us will give him over to our enemies; joined with them, he will attack us and ruin us in our defenceless condition. On the other hand, if we take up arms, the king will respect us; respecting us, he will summon us to his assistance; united with him, we shall overthrow all our enemies."

Scarcely had D'Aubigné ended his earnest remonstrance when Henry of Navarre, forgetting, in his impatient ardor, the proprieties of the occasion, which dictated silence on his part until all his advisers should have been given an opportunity to express themselves, audibly exclaimed: "I am of his opinion!"—" Je suis à lui." The rest of the company was as much carried away by the fervid eloquence of D'Aubigné as was the king himself, and, as each was consulted, all, including the Prince of Condé and the prudent Duplessis Mornay, concurred in the view that the

<small>Henry of Navarre's decision.</small>

Protestants of France could not afford to stand by, unarmed spectators of the conflict now raging.¹

Meanwhile, the more timid Henry of Valois showed himself the more the courage and arrogance of the League increased. Cardinal Bourbon knew enough of religion at least to use pious phrases in his correspondence. So he wrote to the Duchess of Nevers, with no attempt to conceal his glee: "Our quarrel is for the honor of God, albeit the greater part of men think it to be for our ambition;" adding, "I will tell you that, if it please God, there will be seen the finest army that has ever been seen in this kingdom for five hundred years. The queen speaks to us of peace, but we demand so many things for the good of our religion, that I fear our demands will not be granted." ² Within a little more than a fortnight after this, the cardinal and his associates presented to the queen mother, one fine Sunday (the ninth of June, 1585), the modest requests they made of her son the king. The title of the paper stated its object to be "to show clearly that their intention is no other than the promotion and advancement of the glory and honor of God, and the extirpation of heresy, without making any attempt upon the State as the heretics falsely assert." The petition was not long, and after sundry protests of loyalty and pure intentions, went directly to the matter in hand. The League begged the king to issue an edict constraining all his subjects to make profession of the Catholic religion, all other worship being interdicted, and declaring heretics incapable of holding any public office or dignity. His majesty was to swear to observe this edict and require a similar oath of all others, from the peers of the realm down to the lowest officer of the crown. He was to demand and enforce the restoration of the cities now withheld by the Protestants, and, in particular, to cease from protecting the city of Geneva, "the fountain from which heresy flows forth into his kingdom and throughout all

Arrogance of the League.

It presents a petition to the king, June 9, 1585.

---

¹ Agrippa d'Aubigné, ii. 427–430 (liv. v., c. 5).
² Cardinal Bourbon to the Duchess of Nevers, May 23, 1585, Mémoires de Nevers, i. 648.

Christendom." Whereas they might with propriety demand some security for their own persons and property, the petitioners declare that they are quite ready to divest themselves of all safeguards, save those that depend upon his favor, their own innocence, and the good-will of all good men. In fact, they offer, if so it please the king, to resign into his hands all the charges conferred upon them by him or by his predecessors, and to retire into private life and end their days in their own houses, content with having, under his name and authority, aided so excellent a work.[1]

The sincerity of the offer, and, indeed, of the entire document to which Charles of Bourbon and Henry of Guise affixed their signatures, could be gauged by the fact that the accumulation of offices upon the Duke of Épernon and other royal favorites not of the family of Guise had been again and again avowed to be one of the standing grievances that had provoked and rendered necessary the present appeal to arms.

Insincerity of its offer.

It was but a single day after the Sunday which the League had chosen to desecrate at Châlons, by the presentation of a paper seeking to secure the undisturbed sway of religious persecution throughout France, that one of the most striking manifestoes ever published in that country saw the light in the city of Bergerac. Henry of Navarre had thus far kept silence. It was now time that he should publish to the world, and especially to the French people, the falsity of the accusations set forth by the League as a pretext for their treasonable acts.

Manifesto of Henry of Navarre, Bergerac, June 10, 1585.

The King of Navarre began by a distinct profession of his belief in the Christian religion. He held, he said, the Scriptures of the Old and New Testaments to be the infallible rule

---

[1] " Requeste au roy, et derniere resolution des princes, seigneurs, gentilshommes, villes et communautez Catholiques, presentée à la royne, mere de sa Majesté, le dimanche neufiesme juing, 1585. Pour montrer clairement que leur intention n'est autre que la promotion et avancement de la gloire, honneur de Dieu, et extirpation des heresies, sans rien attenter à l'etat, comme faussement imposent les heretiques malsentans de la foy, et leurs partizans." Mémoires de la Ligue, i. 184–7; Mémoires de Nevers, i. 681–3. See De Thou, vi. 483, etc. It may be noted that the date at the end of the paper is one day later; "faict à Chaalons, le dixiesme jour de juin."

of faith, he received the creeds of the early Church, and heartily anathematized all the errors condemned by the most ancient, celebrated, and lawful councils. As to the questions now in dispute, he was neither the first nor the only person that had insisted upon the necessity of reforming the abuses prevailing in the Church. That necessity had been the burden of all recent councils, the aspiration of all good men (who were not for that reason reputed heretics), and the demand of the Very Christian kings of France. The refusal to grant a general council for the purpose of reformation had led to a protest on the part of a number of princes and states, and to the schism which the writer now deplored. For himself, born since this schism began, and brought up at a time when the exercise of both religions was permitted by the king in the states general, as it had been since confirmed by several royal edicts, he had not only been taught from early infancy to believe that the Romish Church was corrupt and needed reformation, but had been confirmed in this opinion by the reading of God's Word and by converse with learned men. This conscientious belief had exposed him to many perils, and, to his great regret, deprived him, on the present occasion, of the favor of his majesty and of the opportunity to render him good service, as he might have done, could he, with a clear conscience, have embraced the same religious profession as the monarch. Nevertheless, in order to show that his course was dictated not by obstinacy but by constancy, not by ambition but by a single desire for his own salvation, he begged his majesty to convene a free and lawful council, such as had been promised in his edicts, and declared himself ready and resolved to receive instruction from it and to regulate his belief by what might there be decided on the religious questions of the day.[1] To the possible objection that the Council of Trent had rendered unnecessary such a council as he spoke of, he replied that no account could be taken of a body against which the ambassadors of the King of France

---

[1] "Estant ledit Seigneur Roy de Navarre tout prest et resolu de recevoir instruction par iceluy, et regler sa creance par ce qui en sera decidé sur les differents de la religion."

had been instructed to protest, and whose decrees neither they nor the Parliament of Paris could ever be prevailed upon to recognize and publish, even after Saint Bartholomew's Day, when everything seemed to favor the demand of those who urgently sought the acceptance.

It would, therefore, be as absurd to style the King of Navarre a heretic, before the settlement of the matters in dispute by a council to whose decisions he had offered to submit, as it would be to hold a man guilty upon whose case a court of justice has not yet passed. Nor was he contumacious or schismatic, since he stood ready to appear, to give an account, to learn, even to change for the better, so soon as the better should be taught him. He complained that, up to the present time, he had seen, through long years, an abundance of men zealous for his destruction, not one man zealous for his instruction. Nor could he be called a relapsed heretic, since he had never been converted from his alleged heresy. If, indeed, it was true that, after Saint Bartholomew's Day, he sent a messenger to the pope and embraced the mass, yet no argument was needed to prove the nullity of a conversion effected by such notorious injustice and violence.

Having thus vindicated his own religious attitude, Henry of Navarre proceeded to vindicate himself from the charge of being a persecutor of the Roman Catholic Church, and showed that not only had he in his own patrimonial estates of Béarn conceded the largest liberty to the adherents of that church, but even when, in other places, he might have been provoked by the rigorous proscription exercised against the Protestants of France to retaliate upon priests and monks, popularly believed to be the advocates of the persecution, he had, on the contrary, extended to them his full protection. For example, in Agen, his own ordinary residence, the Romish clergy had discharged their accustomed duties and the monks had freely preached in the churches, even at the very height of the troubles; while at the same time he had been satisfied that the Protestants should hold their services for preaching in houses whose use had been obtained for the purpose.

After protesting his own affection for the reigning monarch and sincere desire for his long life, Henry next exposed the absurdity of the League in demanding of a young king, married and in the flower of his age, that he should name a successor to the throne, in the person of a Cardinal of Bourbon, a prince sixty-six years of age, as unlikely to have posterity as he was to marry.[1]

It is needless, in view of the attention already given to these points in a previous chapter, to repeat the justification of the King of Navarre's course in the mission of Ségur to the Protestant princes of Germany, or to notice his reference to the pretended "Concordat" of Magdeburg, and his clear exposition of the motives of the Huguenots in seeking, as absolutely necessary to their self-preservation, the prolongation of the term for which they held the cities of refuge. Those cities he now offered to restore to the king, without awaiting the expiration of the two additional years for which his majesty had consented to leave them in Huguenot hands, provided the heads of the League would restore the cities they had seized. Nay, he made a similar offer with regard to the government of provinces with which the King of France had been pleased to honor him.

Navarre challenges Guise. He closed the long and important document by requesting the monarch not to be surprised at a further offer which he now made to the Duke of Guise, with a desire to stop the effusion of blood and prevent the extreme impoverishment and desolation of France certain to follow in the course of the war. This offer was that, without resorting to domestic or foreign troops, whose participation would only entail the ruin of the poor people, the Duke of Guise (who now commanded the army of the League) should settle the dispute by a combat with the King of Navarre—either singly, or with two on either side, or with ten, or twenty, or such other number as the duke might prefer. The arms would be such as were usual among honorable knights, and the place either such as his

---

[1] "Comme si le Roy n'avoit plus qu'un an ou deux à vivre, pour lui susciter semence, comme si d'un vieil estoc de celibat nous devoit plustost sortir lignée, que d'un marriage vigoureux et florissant de sa Majesté."

majesty might designate within the kingdom, or a spot beyond its borders of safe access to both sides. It is an honor, certainly, said Henry of Navarre, which, in view of the disparity between our persons and rank, known to all men, the Duke of Guise will certainly embrace; while, on the other hand, my cousin, the Prince of Condé, and I shall esteem it a piece of good fortune by our blood to redeem the king, our sovereign, from the toils and troubles which the League is plotting against him, his State from confusion, his nobles from ruin, and all his people from calamity and extreme misery.[1]

Such was Henry's famous Declaration—another of the masterly productions of the pen of Duplessis Mornay that have added to the renown of the brave King of Navarre. The paper was not meant for the royal court of Paris alone, nor even exclusively for France, but for the civilized world entire. Extraordinary pains were therefore taken to send copies to all the parliaments and other important bodies of the kingdom, while beyond its bounds every prince who might be supposed to sympathize with the Béarnais in the struggle upon which he was entering received a formal communication of the document that was to vindicate his course in the eyes of the world. Upon their minds and upon the public opinion of Christendom it exerted an influence which it would be difficult to exaggerate.[2] Nor was the favorable impression diminished when news arrived that the Duke of Guise had declined the single combat with the King of Navarre, and that the futile attempt had even been made to suppress the publication of a manifesto so damaging to the Roman Catholic side.[3]

Favorable impression produced by the paper.

Guise declines the challenge.

---

[1] "Declaration du Roy de Navarre contre les calomnies publiées contre luy," etc. Text in Mémoires de la Ligue, i. 133-163, and Mémoires de Duplessis Mornay, iii. 89-126. See also De Thou, vi. 479, etc.; Agrippa d'Aubigné, ii. 425, 426; Recueil des choses mémorables, 611-3; letters of Busini, June 25 and July 9, 1585, Négociations avec la Toscane, iv. 583, 586.

[2] Mémoires de Duplessis Mornay, iii. 87-89.

[3] Despite the king's prohibition, all the foreign ambassadors soon had printed copies of the manifesto in their possession. Letter of Busini, July 9, 1585, Négociations avec la Toscane, iv. 586.

In most of those that read it the conviction was deepened of Henry of Navarre's inflexible devotion to the Reformed faith. There were some, however, who interpreted it otherwise, and saw in the prince's profession of willingness to be instructed by a legitimate council of the Church only corroboration of their belief, based on other considerations, that he would yet be converted to the faith of the majority of the French nation. Henry of Navarre was ambitious. Catharine de' Medici was powerful and could procure the means of gratifying his ambition, were he but willing to sacrifice his religion. "Nothing is impossible to this princess," wrote an enthusiastic foreigner, "especially with the people here. If there is anything that influences men in this world, it is the longing to possess and to command. You may therefore hold it for a certainty that the King of Navarre, seeing himself obliged, as he will be, will become a Catholic. God grant that he may not be like those who from Jews have become Christians, very few of whom are ever found to be of any worth!"[1] Now that Henry had gone out of his way to asseverate his teachableness in matters of theology, it was not unnaturally concluded that it would be no difficult thing to induce him to return to the bosom of Mother Church. Much was looked for from the persuasions of the theologians, and of the Bishop of Auxerre in particular, who had been, or was soon to be despatched to hasten the much-desired consummation. Not to speak of other arguments, there was one thought to be whispered in his ear that would be likely to have great weight with him: "It is much better to be King of France, eating fish on Friday, than to be a poor Duke of Béarn, with liberty to eat meat when he pleases."[2] Should Henry take advantage of the propitious moment to proclaim himself converted to the Romish

Navarre's willingness to be instructed excites suspicion.

---

[1] "E voglia Dio che non rassomigli a coloro che di giudei si sono fatti cristiani, trovandosene molto pochi che buoni sieno." Letter of Cavriana, July 9, 1585, Négociations avec la Toscane, iv. 614.

[2] "E uno che li dira all' orecchio: 'ch' è molto meglio essere re di Francia mangiando pesce il venerdì che povero duca di Béarn con la licenza di mangiar carne a suo beneplacito.'" Letter of Cavriana, August 4, 1585, ibid., iv. 623.

faith, it was believed that he would reap all the advantages from the present commotion. The seizure of arms by the League had already raised the House of Bourbon from a position of comparative neglect to the first place in the public attention.[1] In case of Henry's conversion it would be found that the Dukes of Guise and Mayenne had been at the pains of furnishing the feast for the entertainment of the man whom of all men in France they hated most.[2]

How much significance ought to be attached to the King of Navarre's profession of willingness to be instructed, is a question which can be more correctly and dispassionately considered at a later stage of this history, when his words on the present occasion will naturally come into comparison with similar language employed at other critical junctures. It need only be observed that whatever latitude may have been allowed to Duplessis Mornay in shaping the declaration, there can be little or no doubt that the form in which the King of Navarre expressed himself in reference to the proposed instruction was prescribed by Henry himself.[3]

So long as there was any hope, and even when incontrovertible proofs came that the King of France had virtually surrendered his own convictions to the pressure of his unworthy mother, and the treacherous counsellors who surrounded him, Henry of Navarre continued his ungrateful task of remonstrance. So late as on the tenth of July, in a letter more full of compassion for the wretched weakling on the French throne than of apprehension for himself, he reminded the Valois that the edict he was about to break was his own cherished ordinance, and that the Guises and their confederates, with whom he was about to be reconciled, were the same persons whom he had proclaimed rebels, the same persons

_{Navarre's letter to the king, July 10, 1585.}

---

[1] "Credete che è miracolo di udire : 'Guise ha preso le armi contro il Re, e la famiglia di Bourbon, che era negletta e vilipesa, risorge.'" Ibid., ubi supra.

[2] Ibid., ubi supra.

[3] I do not find that the words gave any dissatisfaction to the king's fellow-Huguenots. They took the alarm only when they observed the studied repetition of the profession in subsequent papers and speeches.

whose nefarious intentions against his person and estate he had expressly recognized and denounced in his letters to Navarre himself. He called the monarch's attention to the writer's own offers of assistance which had been neglected, and to the challenge he had condescended to make to his inferiors in rank and men guilty of treason. "If," he added, "I shall have this misfortune (and I will not yet believe it) that your majesty proceed to the conclusion of this treaty, despite such conditions and submissions, breaking his edict, arming his rebels against his state, against his own blood, and against himself, I shall deplore with my whole heart your majesty's condition, seeing you forced (in consequence of your unwillingness to make use of my fidelity) to the entire ruin of your state. I shall deplore the calamities of this realm, of which an end will in vain be hoped for save in the end of the realm itself. But I shall console myself in my innocence, in my integrity, in my affection for your majesty and your state, which I would gladly have saved at my own peril from this shipwreck; but especially in God, the protector of my justice and loyalty, who will not abandon me in my need, nay, will redouble my courage and my resources against all my enemies, who are yours also."[1]

It was too late. Three days before the King of Navarre indited his last letter of remonstrance, the terms upon which the League would return to its allegiance had been agreed upon in a conference between the queen mother, on the one side, and the Cardinals of Bourbon and Guise and the Dukes of Guise and Mayenne, on the other, held in the little town of Nemours. From this circumstance the royal ordinance in which the results of the conference were legally set forth, although signed and published in Paris, on the eighteenth of July, 1585, has come down in history under the designation of "the Edict of Nemours."

The conference of Nemours, July 7, 1585.

In this fatal decree, fruitful source of misery and bloodshed, Henry was made to declare, by way of preamble, that the

---

[1] Henry of Navarre to Henry III., Nérac, July 9, 1585, Mémoires de la Ligue, i. 192-5; Mémoires de Duplessis Mornay, iii. 141-5, etc.; De Thou, vi. 484.

method of mildness which he had been trying had proved as ineffectual for the restoration of unity in religion and of a stable peace among his subjects, as the previous method of war and force; wherefore he recognized that, if human foresight is feeble in all matters, especially is it so in everything that concerns religion. The cardinal prescriptions of the edict were the following: That there should henceforth be no exercise of the "new so-called Reformed religion" in France, on pain of death and confiscation of property; that all preceding edicts of pacification be abrogated; that all Protestant ministers leave the kingdom within one month after the publication of this law; that all adherents of the "new" religion either embrace the Roman Catholic religion before the expiration of six months or leave the kingdom; that all offices and dignities be taken away from Protestants, the "chambres mi-parties" and "tri-parties" be abolished, and the cities of security be restored to the king. The edict forbade, however, any resort to violence. It forgave the members of the League all their recent acts of hostility, for the reason that those acts had been the fruits of their zeal and affection for the maintenance of the Catholic, Apostolic, and Roman religion. It prescribed that the present law should not only be published everywhere, but be indorsed by the solemn oath of all classes of royal officers and judges. The proscriptive ordinance was to be "a thing firm and stable forever," and, in unconscious irony, this latest of enactments in the rapid succession of the contradictory legislation of France was styled—as its predecessors had been styled—"a perpetual and irrevocable edict."[1]

The intolerant edict of Nemours, July 18, 1585.

The Guises and their confederates of the League had received plenary pardon and absolution from the king in his public edict, and all their deeds of very questionable piety and pretty distinct treason had been "avowed" and set down in the category of praiseworthy acts of zeal for the Roman Catholic faith. It was very convenient for conspirators of such known selfishness to appear in the eyes of the

The conduct of the Guises approved.

---

[1] The text of the Edict of Nemours is given in the Mémoires de Nevers, i, 689-692.

world as the most disinterested of patriots and as paragons of Christian self-abnegation; there was, therefore, no provision for any material advantage to be derived from the persecution inaugurated against the Protestants—at least in the document intended for the public eye. But forgiveness was not precisely what the heads of the League wanted, and substantial fruits would certainly give great zest to the victory just obtained.

Practical advantages secured by the League. These fruits were secured in the protocol which had been signed by Catharine de Medici and the Guises at Nemours eleven days before. Each of the princes who, a brief month earlier, had closed their "requeste" by offering the king to resign into his hands all the offices and dignities conferred upon them by him or his predecessors and to retire into private life, content with the consciousness of having contributed to an excellent work for France, now took good care to stipulate for a fresh accession of power and military protection. Cardinal Bourbon was to receive the City of Soissons for his security and a hundred men, horse and foot, as his body-guard. To Guise fell not less than four towns—Verdun, Toul, Saint Dizier, and Châlons; to Mayenne, Dijon and Beaune; to Aumale, Saint Esprit de Rue; and so on through the list. Moreover, the king assumed the payment of the sums expended by the heads of the League in bringing into France foreign troops to assist them (these sums amounted to two hundred thousand crowns), and released them from the obligation of restoring the sums they had taken from the general receipts of the kingdom, amounting to over one hundred thousand crowns more.[1] It was poor comfort to the king that these princes and noblemen who had complained so bitterly of the detention of the cities of refuge by the Huguenots and were now so ready to demand cities for themselves, faithfully promised to restore these cities to the king in five years.[2] True, the signataries pledged themselves at the same time to give up all leagues and associations within or without

The Guises renounce all leagues and associations.

---

[1] Recueil des choses mémorables, 615.

[2] "Articles accordez à Nemours, au nom du Roi, par la Roine sa mere, avec les Princes et Seigneurs de la Ligue, en présence du Duc de Lorraine." Mémoires de Nevers, i. 686-9.

the kingdom, if they had entered into any;[1] but the one engagement was as honestly assumed as the other. The sequel proved, at least, that no member of the League ever voluntarily surrendered a single city which he could by any means retain, and that the intrigues of Guise and his friends with each other, and of Guise, in behalf of all, with the King of Spain and his agents and governors in the Netherlands and elsewhere were pursued without intermission and with no apparent qualms of conscience.

On the eighteenth of July, the king proceeded in person to the " Palais," to enjoin upon the Parliament of Paris to enter upon its registers the new ordinance. " My uncle," said he to Cardinal Bourbon, who joyfully accompanied him on this welcome errand, " against my conscience,

The king orders the parliament to register the edict.

but very willingly, have I heretofore come to this place to publish the edicts of pacification, because they were to conduce to the relief of my people. Now, I am about to publish the edict revoking them, and, in so doing, I shall act in accordance with my conscience, but contrary to my will, inasmuch as upon the publication of it depends the ruin of my state and people."[2] Meantime of external manifestations of approval there was no lack. In the assembly of learned and prudent judges, it is true that more than one dared to raise his voice in fruitless opposition to an instrument which at one stroke completely changed the relations of a very important part of the population of France in the eyes of the law, and converted a religion until now tolerated, if not protected, into a proscribed faith.[3] But the populace, thoughtless of the con-

---

[1] "Et outre ce se sont departis et departent dès à present de toutes ligues et associations dedans et dehors le royaume, si aucunes y en ont." Ibid., ubi supra.

[2] Lestoile, i. 187 ; Letters d'Estienne Pasquier (Ed. of Lyons, 1607), fols. 423, 424.

[3] In the remonstrance which was offered, three months later, to the royal declaration of October 7, and to which attention will be given in the next chapter, the judges say : "S'il eust pleu à Dieu que les raisons qui furent discourues en vostre presence sur la publication de l'Edict de Juillet passé, eussent peu penetrer jusques à l'aureille de la patience et bonne affection que

sequences, and dreaming little of the torrents of blood which were to flow, as well in Paris as in the provinces, greeted the monarch on his return from the chambers of parliament with loud cries of "Vive le roi!"—cries to which his ears had not been of late much accustomed. Henry of Valois, on his part, succeeded tolerably well in dissembling. The day of sweet revenge would some time come. For the present he was content with having compelled the judges to come to the solemn pageant of the registry of the Edict of Nemours dressed, contrary to custom, in red gowns. It was no crazy man's freak. An act destined to be productive of the butchery of so many innocent men, women, and children could most appropriately be performed in clothing of the color of blood. Those were not mistaken who interpreted the royal command as an evil omen, and as indicative of settled animosity against the persons who had constrained the king to embrace a distasteful policy.[1]

---

vostre Majesté avoit accoustumée de reserver à la voix de ceste compagnie, nous ne serions maintenant en ceste extremité." Mémoires de la Ligue, i. 245.

[1] "Mémoire trouvé entre ceux de Monsieur de Nevers," Mémoires de Nevers, i. 639.

CHAPTER VI.

PROSCRIPTION OF THE HUGUENOTS, AND EXCOMMUNICATION OF HENRY OF NAVARRE.

THE repeal of the Edicts of Pacification was no child's play. Even should the Huguenots ultimately succeed in securing a renewal of these laws, or in extorting from the enemy the recognition of at least a part of their just claims, it could not be hoped that the goal of their desires would be reached without a protracted and bloody struggle. "If the king has consented to the revocation of our edict," Henry of Navarre exclaimed, on hearing a rumor of the approaching catastrophe, "he has certainly given us enough work to do for the rest of our lives."[1] However fully the Béarnais and his fellow Huguenots may have endeavored to prepare themselves for the impending blow, the news of the actual surrender of the French king to the exorbitant demands of the League produced a marvellous effect upon them. The story that, in the single night succeeding the announcement, the hair of the valiant King of Navarre turned half white, may not be sufficiently attested to claim our belief; but there is no doubt that the tidings appeared so terrible as to demand instantaneous action on his part.

A difficult problem confronts the Huguenots.

Happily the Huguenots were not destitute of powerful sympathy even within the kingdom. Their former ally, Henry of Montmorency, now completely reconciled, in view of the common danger threatening all true Frenchmen, had been more than once consulted during the past few weeks. Now a more formal conference took place between him and the King of Navarre, on the confines of their respective provinces of Languedoc and

---

[1] "Qui seroit bien nous tailler de la besogne pour le reste de nos vies." Henry of Navarre to Ségur, June 10, 1585, Lettres missives, ii. 75.

Guyenne, in the little town of Saint Paul de Cade-jours.[1] The result of their deliberations was given to the world in a "Declaration and Protestation," made in the name of the two noblemen and of the Prince of Condé, "respecting the peace made with the members of the House of Lorraine, heads and principal authors of the League, to the prejudice of the House of France."[2]

Whatever uncertainty might attend the arms of the Huguenots in the successive contests in which they were, for more than thirty years, compelled to take part, no such doubt invested the exploits of their pens in the discussions to which those contests incidentally gave rise. Here the Protestants, whether professed theologians or secular diplomatists, rarely failed to exhibit their remarkable intellectual superiority to the antagonists with whom they had to deal.

Never had the good fortune of Henry of Navarre, in possessing so able an advocate as Duplessis Mornay, been more conspicuous than upon the present occasion. The document drawn up by him in the name of the associated princes was one of that kind of papers which opponents generally deem it more prudent to ignore than attempt to answer. The intrigues of the ambitious family of Guise, which never could conceive of peace even in the time of the most profound external peace, were passed in review, from the reign of the second Francis down to the present moment. The sum and substance of their designs was shown to be the extinction of the royal House of France, and the appropriation of the crown by themselves; and, as means to this end, the division of the kingdom, the fostering of troubles, the enfeebling of the nobles, the abasement of the greatness and au-

Joint declaration of Navarre, Condé, and Montmorency.

---

[1] Saint Paul de Cade-jous, or Cap de Joux, is situated in the modern Department of Tarn, three leagues above Lavaur on the river Agout.

[2] "Declaration et protestation du Roi de Navarre, de monseigneur le Prince de Condé, et de Monsieur le Duc de Montmorency, sur la paix faicte avec ceux de la maison de Lorraine, chefs et principaux autheurs de la Ligue, au prejudice de la maison de France." Mémoires de la Ligue, i. 201-219 ; Memoires de Duplessis Mornay, iii. 159-182. See also De Thou, vi. 488, and Recueil des choses mémorables, 616.

thority of the princes. Meanwhile it was part of their plan to manage always to retain arms in their own hands for the purpose of gaining new partisans and oppressing their enemies. The inconsistency and absurdity of the attitude the Guises had assumed in the present crisis were particularly commented upon. They spoke of exterminating heresy, whereas the primitive Christians made war upon it by means of councils, and the King of Navarre offered to submit to a council, and declared his readiness to be instructed by it, and to acquiesce in its decisions. They demanded certain reforms in the government of the state, which, according to the ancient statutes of France, must be referred to the states general; and the King of Navarre had proclaimed his willingness to be bound by the result of the deliberations of the three orders when convened by his majesty. They demanded that the King of Navarre and the Huguenots should give up the cities of security, despite the prolongation of their term of tenure by express grant of the King of France; and the King of Navarre had replied, offering to restore the cities to his majesty, provided only that the Guises would surrender the cities unlawfully seized by them.

The King of Navarre and the Prince of Condé, for themselves, declared that they had no intention to interfere with the Roman Catholic religion or its professors, "having always been of the opinion that men's consciences ought to be free;"[1] while as to their own religion, they proclaimed that they were ready to submit to a council of the church. They therefore invited all good and true Frenchmen, both ecclesiastics and laymen, to join their standards, and particularly exhorted all members of the Roman Catholic Church to take as their guide and example the Duke of Montmorency, a peer of France and the first officer of the crown, himself a Roman Catholic, and a nobleman of known prudence. As for the heads of the League, the three associated princes held them for the enemies of the king, the royal house, and the commonwealth, denounced by the king himself in letters heretofore verified by the parliaments of the realm. "As such," said Navarre, Condé, and Montmorency,

---

[1] "Ayans tousjours esté d'opinion que les consciences devoyent estre libres."

"we shall wage war with them to the utmost, and shall exterminate them by all means in our power."[1]

Nor were these brave words spoken merely for effect. It is evident that, taking in the gravity of the situation and wearied by the length of the period of uncertainty to which the malice of their enemies condemned them, the King of Navarre, at least, was resolved to invoke the aid of all Protestant Christendom, and make one supreme effort for the settlement of the religious dispute in France upon some fair and equitable basis. In a remarkable letter which has come down to us, sent on the very day after the publication of the joint declaration, by Du Pin, secretary of the King of Navarre, to Ségur, who was still acting in his master's behalf in Germany, we have some significant hints. The words are the more striking because of the extraordinary pains taken to secure secrecy; the whole letter being written with sympathetic ink between the lines of another letter written with ordinary ink. The secretary, evidently writing at Henry's dictation, first bids Ségur to give no credit to any rumors that may reach him of the probability that peace may be concluded by deputies sent by the king, or even by the queen mother coming in person; "for," says he, "we are resolved with this blow to put an end to our toils and to the perfidy of our enemies, and never to lay down our arms until they shall have been exterminated, and to conclude no peace save by the advice of the Christian princes who shall join with us." Thereupon he proceeds to sketch a

Secret correspondence of the King of Navarre.

---

[1] "Leur feront la guerre à toute outrance et les extermineront par tous moyens." To this time belongs a letter of Henry of Navarre to Ségur, evidently written after the Edict of Nemours, to which the editor of the Lettres Missives (ii. 20) has erroneously given the date of March 25, 1585. "Je suys venu en ce lieu, où mon cousin, monsieur de Montmorency, m'est venu trouver, pour conférer ensemble de ce qu'il est besoing de faire sur ceste publication d'un nouveau et cruel edict revocatif de celui de pacification. . . . Ce qui est cause que mon dict cousin et moy avons prins ensemble une resolution de nous opposer à eux et de leur courir sus et exterminer, ou les reduire par la voye des armes, et pour ce faire, appeler à nostre secours tous les princes chrestiens . . . estant le dict edict une declaration de guerre ouvertement contre tous ceulx qui font profession de la Religion et couverte contre l'Estat et maison de France," etc.

most decided policy. "They must be induced to embark in the undertaking as fully as possible, and colonies must be settled in this kingdom of those who shall consent to come, in order that they may be rewarded and advantaged.[1] We shall have Catholic princes, our relations, to join us. There are many Catholics, that have perceived the designs of our enemies and their ambition and false dealings, who will help us. But our trust is in God, who will bless our labors, and will favor the justice of our cause."[2]

Great at this moment was the contrast between the courts of the two kings. In the little court of the Béarnais, barren of external pomp and poor in money, all was promptness and decision. From Navarre himself down to the humblest retainer, not a man but was resolved to win a way to victory though suffering and blood might lie between. A common danger, impending over all, inspired all with a courage which was a true presage of ultimate success. At Paris, bitter hatred glowed beneath the surface, and a slight accident might at any instant bring the burning embers into open view. Henry of Valois could scarcely conceal his anger. A second time he had been compelled to act in a manner diametrically opposed to his purpose and desires. Once—nine years ago—the Huguenots had forced him to grant them a peace on conditions which he regarded as insupportable. Now it was the professed friends of the Roman Catholic Church who had, in the eyes of the whole world, imposed upon him a war of extermination to be waged against the Huguenots, from which he looked for no fruits but humiliation or ruin. Were success to crown the royal arms, what could be expected but that all the glory should be appropriated by Henry of Guise and his ambitious house; if defeat, what but the complete ruin of the royal family and the shameful loss of the last vestiges of a once glorious patrimony? If the king had never rested until the

Contrast between the two kings.

---

[1] "Il les y fault embarquer le plus qu'on pourra et faire des colonies en ce royaulme de ceux qui y voudront venir, afin qu'ilz soient recompensez et accommodez."

[2] Du Pin to Ségur, August 11, 1585, Lettres missives de Henri IV., ii. 116.

hateful provisions of the Peace of Monsieur were recalled, it was certainly unlikely that he would forget the contempt with which he had been treated by the heads of the Holy League.

Upon the very day on which the secretary of the King of Navarre recorded the unalterable determination of the Huguenots, once for all to make an end of the perfidy of their treacherous enemies, and suggested as possible the extreme resort to a system of colonization on French soil, the King of France invited three or four representative men to meet him in the palace of the Louvre. They were the Prévôt des marchands, the principal municipal officer of Paris, the first and second presidents of the parliament, the Prévôt de Notre Dame, and the Cardinal of Guise. The cardinal had been specially requested to be present. The royal guests were not long left in doubt respecting the reason of the summons. Henry began by expressing to them his great satisfaction with the step he had so recently taken, by the advice of all his servants, and, in particular, of those present, in repealing his edict of pacification. If he had been slow to come to this decision, he confessed it was only because he had entertained grave doubts whether the present determination could be carried into effect with any more ease than the previous attempt of the same kind. Now, however, seeing himself assisted by so many persons, from whose fidelity he felt the assurance that they would persevere in the execution, he rejoiced with them and begged them all to co-operate with him in devising the best methods of carrying forward to a happy issue the counsel which they themselves had given him. He would lay before them his plan and his forces. He designed to set on foot three armies, one for Guyenne, a second to retain near himself, and the third to prevent the entrance of the foreign auxiliaries of the Huguenots, whom, whatever might be said to the contrary, he knew to be in readiness to march. It was no time to think of the means of war when one had the enemy upon one's hands, nor of making peace when one was the stronger. He reminded them that it would be too late to cry for peace when the windmills about Paris should be in flames, and declared that, having accepted the advice of others

The king demands money from the Parisians and the clergy.

contrary to his own judgment, he intended not to spare himself, as he had in fact sufficiently proved already, by stripping himself almost to his very shirt. Since they had not believed him in the matter of maintaining the peace, it was only reasonable that they should help him in maintaining the war. Next, addressing each of the persons before him, he began with the first president of parliament, whom he praised for the excellence of the long harangue which he had recently delivered in favor of the revocation of the edict, and calmly informed him that, under the extraordinary circumstances in which France was placed, the judges must expect no payment of their salaries, as such a thing would be quite out of the question so long as the war continued. Next the provost was quietly reminded that the city of Paris, having exhibited unusual demonstrations of joy at the repeal, would be expected at once to furnish two hundred thousand crowns; and the provost was commanded to call a meeting of the municipality, on the morrow, for the imposition of this sum. The expenses of the war would, the king calculated, amount to four hundred thousand crowns monthly. For the first month, he informed Cardinal Guise, to whom he now turned with an expression indicative of anger, he proposed to provide with the help of the purses of private individuals. Hereafter he would look to the clergy to aid him every month from the resources of the Church. In taking this course he did not think that he did anything contrary to his conscience, nor did he intend to wait for the authorization or consent of the pope. It was the heads of the clergy that had been most active in pushing him to undertake this war, and it was necessary that they should bear a part of the expense. He had no mind to ruin himself alone in its prosecution.

Here Henry paused to listen to the replies of his guests, who, as may be imagined, were not slow in offering objections to the demands made upon the classes they represented. In the end, the king lost his assumed patience, and, with more frankness than a due regard to policy might have dictated, exclaimed: "It would, then, have been better to believe me. I fear much that, in striving to ruin the 'Prêche'

The king's significant observation.

(meaning Protestantism), we shall greatly imperil the 'Mass.'"
And he added, "It would be better to make peace; and yet I
do not know whether the Huguenots will be willing to accept
it when we choose to make the offer."[1]

Ordinarily the king was not so imprudent in his expressions,
and seemed resolved to derive the greatest advantage possible
from the position into which he had been forced against
his will. "I am resolved in every way," said he, "to
destroy the Huguenots; else they will have to destroy
me." And the royal determination was strengthened by the papal
nuncio's promises of money to be furnished by his master to help
carry on the war. Not content with this, Sixtus the Fifth had
furnished the League with a brief, absolving the confederates
from the obligation of any oath which they might have taken;
and it was reported that, by a second brief, sentence of excommunication was pronounced upon all persons that favored the
Huguenots, and the offer of plenary indulgence was made to
every man who should give the new enterprise his countenance
and support.[2]

The King of France and the pope.

Although war had now been formally declared, and the
Huguenots were to be destroyed from the face of the earth,
the solicitations of the court addressed to the King of
Navarre did not cease. On the twenty-fifth of August
there appeared at Nérac ambassadors from Paris—
Lenoncourt, formerly a favorite of Antoine of Bourbon, Henry's father, and soon to be made a cardinal by Sixtus the Fifth,
and two or three laymen of good standing and repute. The
arguments they offered and the replies of the Béarnais need
not here be recorded. They were much the same as those that

Royal embassy to seek Navarre's conversion.

---

[1] "Il s'escria, 'Il eust doncques mieulx valu me croire. J'ay grand peur qu'en voulant perdre le Presche nous ne hazardions fort la Messe'; adjoustant, 'Il vaudroit mieux faire la paix; encores ne sçay-je s'ils la voudront recepvoir à nostre heure.'" Harangue du roy faicte à Messieurs de Paris, l'onziesme d'Aoust mil cinq cents quatre vingts cinq, in Mémoires de la Ligue, i. 219-21. See, also, Recueil des choses mémorables, 616, 617, and De Thou, vi. (book 81) 489-91.

[2] Letter of Busini, September 30, 1585, Négociations avec la Toscane, iv. 594.

had come from the lips of Roman Catholics and Huguenots respectively at previous junctures, and were likely to be repeated in future as occasion might require. There was the same profuse assurance of the singular good-will of Henry of Valois toward his cousin of Navarre, and the same anxiety that the latter should remove all obstacles in the way of the re-establishment of peace by becoming a Roman Catholic. On the other hand, there were declarations of the usual kind to the effect that it would be unseemly in Henry of Navarre to abandon the Reformed religion, in which he had been born and brought up, and for the defence of which so much time had been consumed, so much blood freely poured out, without having as yet learned that he was in error on any point. Coupled with this assertion came also the customary assurance of the prince that he would always, in matters concerning his conscience, place in the background all considerations of honor, wealth, or possible favor which the world might hold in prospect ; but that, nevertheless, he was ready to have his errors pointed out to him and to submit to a free council of the Church. However, when the envoys asked for a suspension of Protestant worship during the six months covered by the prescriptions of the royal edict, and requested that the cities of security be given up and the foreign troops of the Huguenots be countermanded, they met with a distinct refusal. The King of Navarre said that he neither could nor would dampen the ardor of the good friends who, at a time of his so great need, had hastened to his assistance. Among other things, the deputies brought an offer on the part of the queen mother to meet the King of Navarre for a conference at Champigny in Touraine, and meanwhile to have the royal armies recalled to the northern bank of the Loire; but the Huguenot prince fell in with Catharine's proposal only so far as to consent to come to Bergerac. Doubtless he deemed it, in the circumstances, the part of prudence to make no unnecessary venture ; Catharine de' Medici could better afford to come one hundred and fifty miles farther in her litter, old and racked with gout though she was, than could Henry of Navarre leave the safer confines of Guyenne and put the broad prov-

Henry's readiness to submit to a Council.

inces of Poitou and Angoumois between him and his place of retreat.[1]

Precisely the same attitude did the King of Navarre assume in his more private communications with those who begged him from motives of prudence, and certainly much more sincerely, to avoid impending ruin by reconciliation with Rome. When Navarre's proposals of this kind were made to him by the Duke message to of Montpensier—a prince whose father eight years the Duke of Montpensier. before was a principal cause of the temporary failure of the proscriptive policy indorsed by the first states general of Blois, and who himself now showed great disinclination to lead a royal army against the southern Protestants—Henry of Navarre answered courteously but firmly. He instructed his envoy to tell the duke that a king who believed everything contained in the Old and New Testaments, and held the primitive faith as enunciated by the first four general councils, besides professing willingness to receive instruction from a free and general council to be held in the future, was no heretic, and that any papal excommunication that might be fulminated against him would be a direct violation of the liberties of the Gallican Church. Having imbibed the Reformed religion with his mother's milk, and professing that religion in conformity with the established laws of the realm, it would be good and honorable neither for himself, nor for his friends and relatives, nor for the king's subjects, that he should lightly renounce it, whether from hope, or from fear and constraint. He therefore pronounced the true object of the League and conspiracy of the present year to be, not the promotion of religion, but the overturning of the state and the usurpation of the crown, or, to say the very least, the appropriation of the greater part of the French dominions.[2]

---

[1] "Propositions des deputez du Roy, envoyez au Roy de Navarre, avec la responce de leur legation," in Mémoires de la Ligue, i. 233–5; De Thou, vi. 491–3.—Champigny, not far from Chinon, in the present Department of Indre et Loire, is not over a dozen miles south of the river Loire; Bergerac, in the Department of Dordogne, is in the same latitude as Bordeaux, and about sixty miles east of that port.

[2] Despatch of the King of Navarre to M. de Pecheré, his ambassador to the Duke of Montpensier, Lectoure, October 30, 1585, published for the first time

It is time, however, that we should turn to the conspirators whose persistent efforts to involve in war a kingdom that had enjoyed a brief respite from the horrors of carnage and desolating hostilities had at length been crowned with success. It will be remembered that the Guises and their associated nobles had pledged themselves to the king, in the secret articles of Nemours, thenceforth to renounce any leagues or associations, either within or without the realm, into which they might have entered.[1] It is worth while to notice how far these champions of orthodoxy and paragons of Catholic virtue observed their promise, or, indeed, intended from the beginning to observe it.

Not a moment did Henry of Guise desist from his disloyal intercourse with Philip the Second, carried on through the instrumentality of Bernardino de Mendoza, resident ambassador at Paris. Not for a single instant did he dream of suspending the operation of a compact that recognized his relation as that of a stipendiary of the King of Spain. Upon the very day on which Lenoncourt was endeavoring to influence the Béarnais to renounce his religion, the Duke of Guise was inditing a letter to the Spanish ambassador. His object was to convey a piece of news and to proffer a request. The news was stated in these words: "I have written a despatch to Rome to Cardinal Pellevé and Father Claude (Matthieu) to solicit with diligence the completion of the trial, already far advanced, of the Prince of Béarn"—so these patriotic Frenchmen always studiously designated the King of Navarre in their correspondence with the Spaniard—"as a relapsed heretic, and his proscription. It is a thing that is of marvellous importance for the continuation of our designs, to complete what we have begun for the extermination of their religion and to prevent the designs of a deceitful peace."[2] The

Intrigues of Guise with the Spanish ambassador.

---

in the Bulletin de la Société de l'histoire du Protestantisme français, i. 153, 154.

[1] See above, chapter v., p. 346.

[2] "Chose qui importe merveilleusement pour continuer noz desseings, pour mectre à fin ce que nous avons commencé pour l'exterminacion de leur religion," etc.

request was for fifty thousand crowns to be sent in all haste to the "Princess of Béarn"—Margaret of Valois—who was ex-pected to attract the war into Gascony and thus add to the perplexities of the unfortunate brother-in-law of the King of France.¹ This last device seemed too promising to be lost sight of; so thought Guise. Accordingly, three weeks later, he wrote to Philip the Second himself, extolling the prowess of Margaret, who, from the very commencement of the troubles, had joined the League, with a goodly number of gentlemen, and had opposed her husband's plans. It was this peculiar position of the princess, in the very midst of the "heretics," which had suggested to Guise, so he said, the plan of pursuing, under cover of her name, the realization of the original designs of the League. He had therefore, until now, borne all the expense, with the help of his associates, hoping that his majesty the King of Spain would deign to carry into execution the plan laid down in his last instructions to Juan Baptista de Tassis.² Happily, however, for the Huguenots of Guyenne and for the quiet of Margaret's husband, Philip the Second, or his ministers imitating his illustrious example, displayed so much of the wonted Spanish dilatoriness that the princess found herself bereft of men and of money, and was compelled to retreat from Agen. In fact, in their impatience to get rid of her, the sturdy burghers came near throwing her over the walls. Thereupon great was the grief of Guise and his associates, for now Guyenne was left to the mercy of "those of the religion" who could boast that there was no one within the bounds of the province to check any of their enterprises.³ Meantime, Guise did not neglect to remind his correspondents of the immense burden of indebtedness under which he and his friends were groaning. The levy and support of three thousand reiters, three thousand lansquenets,

Margaret of Valois an ally of the League.

---

¹ Mucius (Henry of Guise) to Bernardino de Mendoza, Châlons, August 25, 1585, apud De Croze, i. 349, 350.

² Mucius to Philip II., September 14, 1585, De Croze, i. 350, 351.

³ Mucius to Mendoza, Châlons, October 17, 1585, De Croze, i. 360; Lestoile, October, 1585, i. 191.

and eight thousand Swiss, in addition to an army of thirty-five or forty thousand French troops, had entailed an expenditure of more than nine hundred thousand crowns. There was no hope that any part of this vast sum would ever be reimbursed; or if repaid, the time would be so distant that the interest alone would consume the whole payment.[1]

As time passed, and Guise heard nothing more of the publication of the proposed brief or bull against Henry of Navarre —the brief had, however, been published, although the tidings of the glad event had not reached the city of Rheims, where the duke was—he became more and more impatient. He wrote to Mendoza on the first of October, begging that Philip the Second should use his influence with Sixtus to have "the Prince of Béarn" and his sister, together with the Prince of Condé, pronounced "heretics, relapsed persons, incapable and unworthy of possessing any lands, with excommunication of those who might favor or treat with them," and indulgence promised to all who, in order to exterminate them, should attack them or contribute funds for the purpose.[2] By this brilliant stroke of policy all hope of reconciliation with the heretic was to be removed. All Roman Catholics would be deterred from entering into the service of a prince excommunicated by the head of their Church, and be constrained, through fear of incurring ecclesiastical censures, to wage war upon him. Then, in case the King of France should be so ill-advised as to repeal the late edict against the heretics, in contempt of the pope's declaration, there would be just occasion given for openly taking up arms to resist him. Then, too, Philip the Second would, it was hoped, help in the extinction of heresy, and indemnify himself for the trouble and expense by seizing what little remained of the former kingdom of Navarre. So did Guise purpose that the troubles of France should contribute to the aggrandizement of Spain, and that Philip should gain a footing on the northern slope of the Pyrenees.[3]

---

[1] Mucius to Mendoza, September 14, 1585, De Croze, i. 352, 353.
[2] De Croze, i. 357. [3] Ibid., i. 358.

To the success of these designs but one thing more was necessary: the Duke of Montmorency must, if possible, be detached from the party of the Huguenots, where he did not belong, and be converted from a friend into an enemy of his old associate, the King of Navarre. Hence, it happened that the Guises, ancestral and natural rivals and foes of the house of the great constable, suddenly appear playing a new part, and actually pleading the cause of him whose greatness they had for years been attempting to pull down. Lest a more direct effort to gain Montmorency over should arouse suspicion, we find Henry of Guise, in his secret correspondence with the Spanish ambassador, entreating that worthy to induce his master, the Duke of Savoy, and the pope to unite in bringing about this much-desired consummation. Philip's activity was, apparently, to be limited to a strenuous effort to persuade Sixtus and Charles Emmanuel to intercede with Henry of Valois to make such generous concessions to Montmorency that the marshal would renounce the alliance with the Huguenots. As for Philip, it was probably deemed more prudent that his hand in the proceedings should not be perceived.[1] On this plan Guise counted much. With Montmorency on the side of the League, its leaders " would be strong enough to give the law to others," and could prevent any other road than the right one from being taken against heresy. That road they would pursue to the end in spite of everybody. They would never permit any enterprise to be undertaken against the lands of any Catholic prince, and especially against any possession of his Catholic Majesty the King of Spain. " From him," significantly remarked Guise, " we should receive our commands, and we should cause them to be executed."[2] Meantime, while awaiting the results of the pope's expected advocacy of Montmorency's interests, Guise was determined that nothing

---

[1] Mucius to Mendoza, Rheims, October 1, 1585, in De Croze, i. 358.

[2] " Et ne permettrions que l'on entreprist jamais chose contre aulcun catolique, mesmement portant toute seureté qu'on ne oseroit regarder rien qui fust au roy catolique, duquel nous recevrions le commandement et le ferions executer." Mucius to Mendoza, November 28, 1585, De Croze, i. 365, 366.

should be done by himself or by any other member of the Lorraine family that might imbitter the mind of the marshal.

Guise bids Mayenne avoid attacking Montmorency.
Toward the close of the year the king gave orders to the Duke of Mayenne to proceed at once against Montmorency's possessions in southern France. Let it not be supposed for an instant that any junior member of the family ever felt at liberty to obey the king, especially in so important a matter, without consulting or receiving instructions from its head and leading spirit. "You have been notified," the Duke of Guise wrote to Mendoza, "that the king sent word to my brother to be pleased to take up his journey without delay toward Languedoc. This was the reason that in all diligence I despatched this courier to him, in order that he might not in anywise, or whatever command were given him, accept this charge, so that he should not offend Marshal Montmorency. At once, if possible, he is to sit down before some place in Guyenne, so as not to lose time; and then he is to invent objections based upon the difficulty of obtaining provisions, the season of the year, the strongholds, the roads—in short, on all the impediments experienced by those previously sent in that direction. While these difficulties are alleged, we shall, if possible, slip into Auxonne. Then Mayenne will demand his congé outright, and he will certainly not go to Languedoc. Of that you may assure the King of Spain, and his Highness the Prince of Parma."[1]

Here again the sluggishness of Philip the Second would seem to have been the best ally of Henry of Navarre and the Huguenots.
Philip of Spain procrastinates.
Not an inch would that prudent monarch move without due deliberation, and, happily for those against whose peace he was daily conspiring, events did not tarry for his delay. Guise might repeat his petition to Mendoza, week after week, month after month, till the duke's patience was quite exhausted, and his appeal became almost pathetic. He had begged "so often"! A year had

---

[1] "Puis tout à plat il demandera son congé, et certainement il n'y ira, de quoy vous pouvez advertir Sa Majesté et Son Altesse." Mucius to Mendoza, Châlons, November 15, 1585, De Croze, i. 362, 363.

passed since the matter was first proposed and agreed upon. He had until now prevented his brother from attacking Montmorency, upon the assurances which he had received that the Duke of Savoy, by means of his Catholic Majesty, would induce the marshal to make common cause with the League and the Catholic party. It was out of respect for this understanding that Mayenne had delayed his approach to the city of Toulouse, foreseeing that this would involve some encounter with the marshal. But, as ill-luck would have it, he had not yet heard that the slightest thing had been done. The King of Spain had left the whole matter to the Duke of Savoy, the latter had procrastinated, and there it had ended. Not a point of Guise's just requests had been provided for, and so the danger was great, not only for him, but for all Christendom. At last came news that other powerful allies had thrown in their lot with the King of Navarre, and now Montmorency, with this new accession of strength, would be able " infinitely to traverse all the affairs " of the League.[1]

Meantime the marshal himself showed no symptoms of any disposition to abandon his allies, and it is quite possible that his constancy might have stood the test of all the temptations which the united ingenuity of the pope, the King of Spain, and the Duke of Savoy, reinforced by the cunning of the Guises, could have brought to bear upon him. Be this as it may, the "Protestation" which he sent forth in his individual name was as decided in tone as any Huguenot could have wished it to be. The marshal therein strengthened his own position as an advocate of religious toleration by quoting the death-bed counsel of his late father, Anne de Montmorency. The constable, in the vigor of health, and at the beginning of the civil wars, had certainly been no friend of the Huguenots, and it had fared ill with such of them as had the misfortune to fall into his hands. But we have his son's word for it that, after the fatal wound received in the battle of Saint Denis, he gave Charles the Ninth and his mother the sound ad-

Protestation of Marshal Montmorency.

---

[1] "Peult infiniment traverser noz afayres." See letters of Mucius to Mendoza, January 29, and February 3, 1586, in De Croze, i. 368–371.

vice to compose existing troubles by a peace between the two religions, while awaiting the convocation of a council of the Church; and that he tersely expressed his sentiments upon the subject by the remark, which may well have come from his lips, "that the shortest follies are the best, and an end must be put to them as quickly as possible."[1] In view of the disasters resulting from the conspiracy of the foreign family of Lorraine, who, failing in their object, the seizure of the king's person, had brought into France troops paid by the King of Spain, and reduced Henry to such perplexity that they had wrung from him a peace deplorable to all good subjects of the realm, by which war was diverted from rebels and directed against obedient servants of the monarch—Montmorency demanded that a council should be called, and declared his own intention to maintain by force of arms the Edict of 1577, as being the expression of the king's own will, and to hold the authors of its pretended revocation to be enemies of the public tranquillity.[2]

The importunity of the Guises at last proved successful at Rome. Sixtus the Fifth was brought to the decisive measure of hurling the Church's thunderbolt at the devoted head of Henry of Navarre. The pontiff had not ceased to watch with deep interest the progress of the conflict of the King of France and the League, and had expressed great satisfaction when an apparent reconciliation was effected between the parties. His only fear seemed to be that trouble might again break out, and the Very Christian King be compelled by the very perversity of the champions of orthodoxy to make an arrangement with the King of Navarre and the Prince of Condé; as a consequence of which France would be deluged with Lutherans and Calvinists. He therefore

The pope still opposes the League.

---

[1] "Qui conseilla tres bien à leurs majestés, au lict mesmes de la mort, et mourant toutesfois des fruicts de ceste guerre, de composer ces troubles par une paix des deux religions, attendant ung Concile, en ces mots, que les plus courtes folies estoient les meilleures, et qu'il estoit necessaire d'y mettre tost une fin."

[2] "Protestation de M. le duc de Montmorency," in Mémoires de Duplessis Mornay, iii. 186-196.

begged the heads of the League to join Henry of Valois in good faith, and help him to devise plans for the extermination of heresy. "I have had some experience in affairs," said Sixtus, "and I think that I can see clearly enough into the future to make a bold but true prophecy: the Huguenot will never be undone till the League shall have been." Whereupon his holiness broke down in tears over the prospective misfortunes of that kingdom which was the flower of Christendom—tears which his politic hearer took good care to accompany with some show of emotion of his own.[1] None the less did the lachrymose pontiff pour out the vials of his wrath unsparingly on the Huguenot Prince of Navarre.

The bull from which Henry of Guise looked for such excellent results for the cause of Roman Catholicism in France was dated the ninth of September. It began with a clear and unmistakable enunciation of the rights of the Holy See.

<small>Sixtus excommunicates and deposes the King of Navarre.</small> The authority given to Saint Peter and his successors by the infinite power of the Eternal King surpasses all the powers of earthly kings and princes, and the Holy See being founded upon the firm rock, and being never shaken by any winds or storms, whether adverse or favorable, it pronounces irrevocable decisions and judgments. With all diligence does it watch over the observance of the divine laws, and, when it finds any persons contravening the ordinance of God, punishes them with grievous punishment, depriving them, however great they may be, of their seats, and casting them down as ministers of Satan. Such was the arrogant preamble; after which Sixtus proceeded to state that, in the discharge of the care that had been confided to him over all churches and nations, it became his duty to purge Christendom, and in particular the flourishing realm of France, of wicked and detestable monsters, and to restore peace to a country whose monarchs, by their great piety and signal good services to the Roman Church, had justly earned the title of Very Christian. In order, therefore, never to be accused before God of contempt of

---

[1] The Duke of Nevers to the Cardinal of Bourbon, Rome, August 20, 1585, Mémoires de Nevers, i. 672, 673.

duty, the pope declared himself to be constrained to use the arms of his warfare, which were not carnal, and proceeded not from him, but from Almighty God, for the overthrow of the power of the enemy, chiefly against two children of wrath— against Henry, of Bourbon, formerly King of Navarre, and against Henry also of Bourbon, formerly Prince of Condé. Next were given in considerable detail the misdeeds of the two cousins, especial emphasis being laid upon their conversion from the heresy in which they were brought up to the true faith, and upon their more recent apostasy, with all the hostile acts since perpetrated by them. The conclusion of the whole matter was that Pope Sixtus pronounced the King of Navarre and the Prince of Condé to be relapsed heretics, guilty of treason against heaven, and therefore to have forfeited all their goods, honors, and dignities, and to be incapable, themselves and their posterity, of succeeding to any principality or kingdom, especially to the kingdom of France. The subjects of the King of Navarre were pronounced to be absolved from their oaths of allegiance, and the King of France was enjoined to fulfil the engagement publicly taken at his coronation, and to labor to carry into effect the present just sentence, as a deed agreeable to God and a means of cancelling his obligations to mother Holy Church. Twenty-five cardinals appended their signatures, below the signature of the pope, to the terrible document which was to annihilate the leaders of the Huguenot party in France.[1]

The pretensions first put forth by Gregory the Seventh, and more vigorously and successfully asserted by Innocent the Third, were never more distinctly enunciated. But, for some reason or other, the thunderbolt did not vindicate its traditional effectiveness. Neither the Bourbons, at whom it was aimed, nor the adherents of the Roman Catholic Church in France, who were expected to prostrate themselves in fear at the mighty sound of the apostolic artil-

The Excommunication calls forth indignation and ridicule.

---

[1] The bull may be found, in the French garb under which it was circulated in France, in the Mémoires de la Ligue, i. 236-242, and Cimber et Danjou, Archives curieuses, xi. 47-55, with the title: "La declaration de Nostre

lery, were seriously disturbed. In fact, the day of terror seemed to have passed away, and fear of priestly excommunication to have given place to indignation at priestly assumption. Henry of Valois, it is true, felt obliged to use moderation and hide his displeasure when the papal nuncio requested an audience, and placed in his hands the bull of excommunication, with the request that he should publish it and see to its execution. But the moment the prelate had left the room, Henry scoffingly exclaimed to his courtiers as they stood about him: "It seems that the pope would like to have me act as his provost marshal in France!"[1]

As for Henry of Navarre, that cheerful prince made little of the pope's impotent threats, but thought it not amiss to turn the whole affair into ridicule. Under his name, and Navarre challenges Sixtus to appear before a general council. doubtless with his consent, a pungent reply was put forth, and not only put forth, but actually carried to Rome, and as sedulously posted in all the public places of the eternal city as the pontifical excommunication had been. From the mutilated statue of Pasquin and elsewhere, the astonished ecclesiastics of Rome read the sentences in which Henry, by the grace of God King of Navarre and Sovereign Prince of Béarn, appealed from the bull, as abusive, to the Court of Peers of France, of whom he had the honor to be the first, and maintained that Mr. Sixtus, styling himself pope (saving his holiness), had falsely and maliciously lied, and was himself a heretic. This statement, the placard went on to say, the king was ready to prove in a free and lawfully assembled council of the Church, to which, if Sixtus refused to submit, he denounced him as Antichrist. Meantime, he would proceed

---

Sainct Pere le Pape Sixtus cinquiesme, à l'encontre de Henry de Bourbon, soy disant Roy de Navarre, et Henry semblablement de Bourbon pretendu Prince de Condé, heretiques, contre leurs posteritez et successeurs : par laquelle tous leurs sujects sont declarez absous de tous serments qu'ils leur auroyent juré, faict ou promis." See also Recueil des choses mémorables, 617-620, and De Thou, vi. 514-516.

[1] "Subito che detto nunzio si partì, dicono che Sua Maestà dicesse : ' Il Papa vuole pare ch' io serva per suo prevosto in Francia.' " Letter of Busini, October 29, 1585, Négociations avec la Toscane, iv. 594.

against him, in vindication of the honor of his house, as occasion might offer, and would show himself not inferior to the princes and kings, his predecessors, who had known full well how to chastise the insolence of such gallants as this pretended Pope Sixtus. For this end he called to his aid all Christian princes and communities against the usurpation of the pope and the conspirators of the League inimical to God, to the king, and to the general peace of Christendom.[1]

Pope Sixtus, who always appreciated a brave action, made, indeed, a strict but useless search for the persons who had had the audacity to bring the King of Navarre's cartel; but, failing in this, ever after expressed warm admiration for the prince who had challenged him to combat in the sight of the whole world. He used to say that he knew but two persons—a man and a woman—who, apart from religion, deserved the throne, and to whom he felt inclined to confide his own great designs; and that man and that woman were Henry of Navarre and Elizabeth of England.[2]

Other pens than that of Lestoile busied themselves in holding up to the light of day the absurdities of Sixtus's bull, and, in particular, the "Brutum Fulmen" of Francis Hotman added to the author's popularity in his own age, and to his celebrity in ages to come.[3] For the purposes of the present history, however, it is important only to notice the calm and dignified attitude assumed by the Parliament of Paris.

Hotman's "Brutum Fulmen."

About the same time that the papal bull was received in France the king signed a second edict or declaration respecting the Huguenots, at the dictation of the League. In the edict of

---

[1] "Coppie de l'Opposition faite par le Roy de Navarre et Monseigneur le Prince de Condé, contre l'Excommunication du Pape Sixte cinquiesme, à luy envoyee et affichee par les cantons de la ville de Rome." Posted in Rome, November 6, 1585. Mémoires de la Ligue, i. 268, 269; Cimber et Danjou, Archives curieuses, xi. 59-61; Lestoile, i. 190, who claims to have composed the reply: "fait par l'aucteur des presens mémoires."

[2] De Thou, vi. 521.

[3] Bayle, in his dictionary, has corrected the misapprehensions to which De Thou's statements respecting the "Brutum Fulmen" have given rise.

July—the so-called Edict of Nemours—the term of six months had been set within which all Protestants were commanded either to become Roman Catholics or to leave the kingdom. It now appeared that, instead of employing the time of grace for the purpose intended, many of the Huguenots had availed themselves of the opportunity to take the field or to render assistance to their companions in arms. For this reason the king declared the property of such persons to be forfeited to the state treasury, and ordered the proceeds of its sale to be applied exclusively to the maintenance of the present war. Moreover, he diminished the time for which unoffending Protestants were suffered to remain in France, from six months to fifteen days.[1]

Royal declaration of October 7, 1585.

To the king's new edict, and to the papal bull which the monarch sent to them for registry, the parliament made reply in a remonstrance creditable alike to the intelligence and to the conscience of the judges. They confessed that they had little hope, in view of their late ill success, of securing a favorable hearing from his majesty; but they must discharge their duty, and with the more boldness, as they saw the license displayed by the enemies of the state to take advantage of the king's piety and devotion in order to cover their own impiety and rebellion. If the king had listened to their remonstrances, made on occasion of the Edict of July, he would have recognized the fact that the designs of the League tended only to disunion among his subjects, and that, however great and redoubtable its forces, in view of the ills they inflicted on the people, past experience taught that they were too weak to accomplish their purpose. Even could they accomplish it, his majesty ought not to make use of them, inasmuch as the crime which he wished to punish is fixed in the consciences of men. Now, man's conscience is beyond the power of chains and of fire, and can be reached by

The remonstrance of the Parliament of Paris.

A forcible plea for liberty of conscience.

---

[1] "Declaration du Roy sur son Edict du mois de Juillet dernier, touchant la Reunion de tous ses sujectz à l'Eglise Catholique, Apostolique et Romaine," October 7, 1585. Mémoires de la Ligue, i. 251-6. The example of France was followed by the Duke of Lorraine, who also commanded all Huguenots to

other means more befitting a king's affection for his subjects.[1] Kings are but shepherds, edicts are but the staff wherewith they guide the flock. The name of edict scarcely belongs to a bloody proscription decreeing in express terms the massacre of the flock, and the consequent destruction of the shepherd's authority. "Were the entire Huguenot party reduced to a single person, there is not among us one judge," said parliament, "that would dare to render a sentence of death against it, unless its solemn trial had first been held. And, therefore, were it not duly attainted and convicted of a capital and enormous crime, in condemning the malefactor we should lament the loss of a good citizen. Who, then, shall dare, without any form of justice whatsoever, to depopulate so many cities, destroy so many provinces, and convert this entire kingdom into a tomb? Who shall dare to utter the word that is to expose so many millions of men, women, and children to death, and that, too, without apparent cause or reason; seeing that no crime is imputed to them save heresy, heresy as yet unknown, or, at least, undecided, heresy which they have sustained in your presence, against the most famous theologians of your kingdom, in which they have been born and brought up for the past thirty years by permission of your majesty and of the late king, your brother of happy memory, and which they refer to the judgment of a council, general or national."

The crime of proscription.

What affection for the king's service can those entertain, what loyalty to an old and decrepit state, who draw from it the little of strength and vigor which remains, by so excessive a bleeding, that those who perform the operation will run the risk of being themselves drowned? Thirty or forty thousand Huguenots, fighting in defence of their lives and of everything most dear to them, cannot be routed, but as many Catholics be left on the field. Who will venture to promise himself the

leave his dominions within a fortnight. Mucius to Mendoza, Châlons, November 18, 1585, De Croze, i. 363.

[1] "Le crime que vous voulez chastier est attaché aux consciences lesquelles sont exemptes de la puissance du fer et du feu, et se peuvent manier par autres moyens plus convenables à l'affection paternelle que vostre peuple a tousjours trouvee en vous."

victory after so wholesale a destruction as may be expected; or, rather, what will be left for Pestilence and for Famine, which even now dispute with War the honor of effecting the final ruin of his majesty's realm?

From the royal edict, parliament turned to the consideration of the papal bull, the style of which was so novel, so far removed from the modesty of former popes, that the judges failed in any way to recognize the voice of a successor of the Apostles. And inasmuch as they found neither from their registers nor from past history that the provinces of France had ever been subject to the jurisdiction of the pope, or that subjects had the right to take cognizance of the religion of their princes, parliament refused to deliberate respecting this document "until the pope" said they, "shall first have shown upon what rights he bases his claim to transfer kingdoms established and ordered of God before the name of 'pope' was known in the world—until he shall have told us on what ground he meddles with the succession of a prince, young and vigorous, from whom offspring may naturally be looked for—until he shall have informed us with what show of justice or equity he refuses the common rights of man to persons accused of heresy—until he shall have taught us with what sort of piety and holiness he gives away what does not belong to him, takes from his neighbor what is lawfully his, incites vassals and subjects to rebellion against their lords and sovereign princes, and overthrows the foundations of all justice and political order.

"Inasmuch," added the judges, "as the new pope, instead of instruction, breathes in his bull nothing but destruction, and changes his pastoral crook into a frightful torch to serve for the entire ruin of those whom he ought to lead back to the fold of the Church, if they have strayed from it, the court cannot further deliberate respecting the publication of a bull of such a kind, so pernicious to the interests of all Christendom and the sovereignty of your crown. For it judges from this moment that the bull deserves no other reward than that which one of your predecessors made us give to a similar bull which a predecessor of this pope had sent to him, namely, to throw it into the fire in the presence of the whole Gallican Church, while enjoining your 'procureur-géneral' to make diligent search for those who had urged the issue of it in the court of Rome, for the purpose of inflicting such good and speedy justice as should serve as an example to all future generations."

The judges therefore begged the king not to require them to promulgate the bull of Pope Sixtus, and brought their remonstrance to a close with this suggestion: "It is therefore more expedient for your majesty to be without a court of parliament than to see it so useless as we now are; and it is also far more honorable for us to retire into private life in our houses and weep over the public calamities in common with our fellow-citizens, than to bring the dignity of your charges into slavery to the mischievous inventions of the enemies of your crown." [1]

These were brave words, worthy of the best days of the Parliament of Paris, when Séguier, and Anne du Bourg, and others like them, sat upon the benches in the "palais de justice." But unfortunately the patriotic chancellor Michel de l'Hospital no longer stood near the throne, to repel with righteous indignation all attempts of the papacy to usurp powers which the Gallican Church had always denied to it. So it has happened that, whereas the bull of Pius the Fourth, threatening Jeanne d'Albret with excommunication and deposition, was, through very shame, dropped from the pontifical constitutions and has left no trace of its existence, the document hurled by Sixtus the Fifth against the son of Jeanne has been audaciously permitted to occupy a place among the authoritative declarations of the Church of Rome.[2]

Yet the discontent with the pope's action was almost universal. Even the queen-mother was outspoken in condemnation. It does not indeed appear that she sent word to Sixtus, as she had to Pius, twenty-two years before, "that he had no authority and jurisdiction over those who bear the title of king or of queen, and that it was not for him to give their states and kingdoms as a prey to the first con-

Displeasure of Catharine de' Medici.

---

[1] "Remonstrance au Roy par la Cour de Parlement," in Mémoires de la Ligue, i. 244-250.

[2] See the just remarks of De Thou, vi. (book 82) 519, 520.

queror."[1] But none the less was she vexed and astonished that her relative, the Cardinal de' Medici, had consented to sign the obnoxious document.[2] In the end some decisive steps were taken to suppress the bull and prevent its circulation among the people. It was forbidden to print it; and, greatly to the disgust of the nuncio and the League, one adventurous man who had contravened the order was promptly thrown into prison.[3]

The printer of the bull imprisoned.

Meanwhile the Huguenots had not been inactive. To the Edict of Nemours and the Declaration of October Henry of Navarre answered by a Declaration of his own, wherein, after rehearsing the motives that had induced him to wait so long before a resort to arms, he ordered that all the goods and chattels belonging to the inhabitants of cities or towns in which the proscriptive edict and declaration had been published, should be seized and sold to the highest bidder.[4] War had broken out in good earnest, and the West had witnessed some successes for the Protestant arms. Most notable, however, was the enterprise of Angers, the romantic history of which seems to carry one back to the days of mediæval knighthood, while the perils with which it was accompanied nearly involved the death of a prince, next to Henry of Navarre, most essential to the Protestant cause.

Henry of Navarre retaliates.

The important city of Angers, situated upon the river Maine, about two miles below the spot where that stream is formed by the confluence of the Sarthe and the Mayenne, and five miles above the place where, having run its short course, the Maine empties into the Loire, was the former capital of the dukes of Anjou. The city extended to a small island, and there was a considerable quarter on the right bank; but the larger part was built upon the left or eastern side of

The Castle of Angers.

---

[1] Catharine de' Medici to Bochetel, December 13, 1563, Le Laboureur, i. 783. See Rise of the Huguenots, ii. 143.

[2] Letter of Busini, November 12, 1585, Négociations avec la Toscane, iv. 599.

[3] Letter of Busini, November 25, 1585, ibid., iv. 600.

[4] "Declaration du Roy de Navarre sur les moyens qu'on doibt tenir pour la saisie des biens des fauteurs de la Ligue et leurs adherens." Bergerac, November 30, 1585; Mémoires de la Ligue, i. 298-300.

the Maine. Here, on a commanding elevation, overlooking the surrounding country and frowning upon the humbler homes of the burghers, stood a massive castle, long the residence and safe retreat of the princes of the Angevine line. It was a gloomy pile in the shape of a vast parallelogram. The walls, strengthened at intervals by eighteen formidable round towers jutting out from the general work, rose full one hundred feet in height above the neighboring Maine, built of solid slate, of which the blackness was rather intensified than relieved by contrast with layers of a lighter stone running like ribbons around the entire building. The castle was protected by a moat cut out of the solid rock, thirty-five feet in depth and nearly thrice as broad as deep. The original builder was unknown. There were those that made it to be the happy thought of a queen of Sicily who had it constructed in the absence and without the knowledge of her husband. Others ascribed it to the English. Moderns affirm that it was begun in the reign of Philip Augustus and completed in that of his grandson, Louis the Ninth. Whoever the builders may have been, however, it was certain that they did their task well. Though often besieged, the Castle of Angers had never been captured, and was justly deemed, so far as force was concerned, quite impregnable. Ample provision had been made against treacherous surprise. There was but a single entrance to the keep, and this was so well guarded, that, what with successive gates and draw-bridges, the stealthy admission of an enemy might well have seemed impossible.[1]

During the lifetime of Francis of Anjou, the king's brother, his favorite Bussy d'Amboise had been intrusted with the guard of Angers, and had placed one Captain Du Halot in command of the castle. Brissac, an undisguised partisan of the League, who had succeeded Bussy d'Amboise, upon the death of the duke, had dismissed Du Halot and given the post to one Captain Grec. Du Halot was not the only officer whose enmity Brissac had gained. A second captain,

A plot to surprise it.

---

[1] Jodocus Sincerus, writing about thirty years after the events here described (the dedication of his "Itinerarium Galliæ" is dated July 15, 1616),

Fresne, had served under his colors so long as the League was in open war with the king, but had been ignominiously turned adrift as soon as the Edict of Nemours was signed. Both Du Halot and Fresne swore that they would be revenged. It was under these circumstances that the two Roman Catholics met, in the neighboring town of Beaufort, a Huguenot soldier of the same grade, who happened to have come north of the Loire with a few men of the same religion, under command of one of Henry of Navarre's followers, a Protestant nobleman named M. de Clermont. The three agreed to make a common attempt to seize the Castle of Angers; yet each had his own ulterior views. Du Halot intended, so he said, to hand over the castle when gained to the king, from whom he maintained that he had a commission. Fresne would have used the possession of the castle to secure better terms from the League. Both believed that after taking advantage of what help in men the Huguenot Rochemorte might bring them, it would be an easy matter to get rid of him, should he prove a troublesome associate. The joint plot was speedily executed. Captain Fresne, who was on terms of intimacy with the commander of the small garrison of scarce a dozen men, called upon him one day and was hospitably invited to remain and dine with him. When he pretended to excuse himself on the ground that he had asked some friends of his own to dinner, Captain Grec urged him to return to his house and bring them with him. Fresne desired no better pretext, and came back in company with his fellow-conspirators, attended by some of the Huguenot soldiers of Rochemorte. The first guards met had been gained over and easily let them pass, and when the second body of guards demurred at the entrance of so many armed men, the pretended guests fell upon them and killed them. Fresne himself stabbed his unfortunate host, when the latter came to the door of his room to ascertain the cause of the uproar. In a word, almost before the occupants were aware that they were threatened, the

---

says, p. 106: "In arcem exteris facilior est aditus quam indigenis. Transeundæ aliquot portæ et pontes antequam intus sis. Cumque unum pontem superaris, illum elevant atque egressum obserant, antequam ulterius intromittaris."

castle was taken. Meanwhile, however, Du Halot, intoxicated by success, at the very moment when he might have safely shut himself in with his companions, was so ill advised as to turn aside into the town in order to try to get the citizens to espouse his side as against the League; but instead of persuading them he was himself taken prisoner. Toward evening the townsmen proposed a parley, and Du Halot was put forward to entice the enemy into their hands. Under cover of the gathering darkness, a body of thirty or forty arquebusiers had been posted near the grating, to seize the person of Fresne when he should come to the conference, or make themselves masters of the draw-bridge before there should be an opportunity to raise it. The imprudent discharge of one of the arquebuses gave premature warning of the plot, and the entrance was instantly closed. Unhappily there was not time for Fresne himself to retreat before the bridge had risen. In his despair he caught the chains, but the enemy promptly using their swords cut off his hands and he fell defenceless into the dry moat. Here a deer, kept by the city for the amusement of the people, inflicted such wounds upon him with its horns that he soon died. Du Halot also was now executed. By a singular series of events one of the strongest castles in France, in a region altogether Roman Catholic, had come into the hands of a follower of the King of Navarre. Unfortunately he had but seven Huguenots with him, out of a total garrison of sixteen men all told; and the King of Navarre was far away in Southern France. The nearest Huguenot general, the Prince of Condé, then occupied with the siege of the seaport of Brouage, was not less than one hundred miles distant.

The castle in Huguenot hands.

The tidings were speedily carried to all the Roman Catholic generals on the north of the Loire, and troops gathered from every quarter. More tardily the news reached Condé, who, at first incredulous of the truth of so strange an incident, was led by bad advice to come too slowly to the rescue.[1] The expedition, in truth, was sufficiently hazardous,

Condé advances to Anjou.

---

[1] According to Agrippa d'Aubigné (ii. 442, 443), who was at first to command the expedition for the relief of Rochemorte and the Huguenot handful in

for the Huguenots held not an inch of ground north of the Loire, outside of the castle of Angers; if, indeed, venturesome Rochemorte perchance still held out against such odds. And the Loire was a dangerous river, first to cross, and still more to have between one's self and one's companions in arms. Still Condé pushed forward with a force of seven or eight hundred horse and ten or twelve hundred foot, and at Les Rosiers, between Saumur and Angers, effected a crossing to the northern bank. But when he reached the neighborhood of Angers, and skirmished even in the suburbs of the place, he found that he had come too late. No friendly signal was held forth from the castle, in answer to the clarion's inspiring notes. Weeks had elapsed, and Rochemorte had been compelled at length to surrender to the enemy, in sheer despair of receiving any reinforcement or provisions from his brethren in the faith. And now the question pressed upon Condé and his army, How should they extricate themselves from the net into which they had been so eager to plunge? Laval, indeed, and a part of the troops were so fortunate as to cross safely again to the southern bank of the Loire at the same place where Condé had a few days before been ferried over the river; but before the remainder of the army could follow their example, two large covered boats made their appearance, laden with cannon and armed men, and it was deemed too foolhardy an undertaking to brave this fresh danger. While, therefore, Laval pressed on southward toward Poitou, the prince was compelled to turn in the opposite direction, and, leaving his perilous position in the contracted tongue of land between the Loire and the Authion, to make his way to the Loire, which he crossed with difficulty at Le Lude. But an advance in this direction was not promising. In front Épernon, Biron, and other nobles from the court, and troops of horse and regiments of foot, were coming to meet the Huguenots, and had proceeded as far as Bonneval, midway from Paris. From Orleans came the alarming news that the Duke of Mayenne had crossed the Loire at

<small>Peril and escape of his army.</small>

---

the castle of Angers, the prince made a fatal delay of eleven days before leaving Brouage.

that point with fifteen hundred reiters and French horse, ready to cut off the retreat of Condé should he succeed in reaching the southern bank. Lest, however, he should have the opportunity to do so, La Chastre had seen to it that the Huguenots should find no bridge, boat, or mill to serve their purpose. The Duke of Joyeuse was behind the Huguenots. In every direction the towns and villages were on the lookout, ready at the first sound of the tocsin, to meet and aid in harassing them.

Under these discouraging circumstances, the prince was spared the necessity of choice between the desperate alternative of making a stand against a far larger number of the enemy, and permitting his army to break up into small bodies, each of which should seek safety as best it could. The Huguenots had quietly adopted the latter course of their own accord, and nothing remained but to acquiesce in their decision. It speaks well for the valor of these heroes of many past engagements that their very name had spread such consternation among their foes that none seemed anxious to come near enough to watch their movements very closely. And so with a uniformity which would scarcely be credited but for the unimpeachable evidence by which it is sustained, the Huguenots, although by the most various routes, succeeded, with scarcely the loss of a man by the way, in reaching some point of safety. The Duke of Rohan escaped to his great domains in Brittany, and was out of danger among his ancestral retainers. The Prince of Condé managed to reach the shores of the English Channel, whence he sailed to the island of Guernsey, and soon after accepted the hospitality of Queen Elizabeth of England. Some of the minor chiefs owed their salvation to boldness and the unexpected paths they chose. Thus Agrippa d'Aubigné, with a band of thirty Protestant horsemen, first struck boldly far in the direction of the capital, then suddenly turned, and, reaching the Loire at Saint Dié, between Blois and Beaugency, succeeded, almost against hope, in crossing. Next following the course of the river Cher for twenty-five leagues to Saint Florent, in the neighborhood of Bourges, the little company, although much farther from Brouage than when they first started from the walls of Angers, easily made their way to the sea. Other captains rescued their followers by almost equally circuitous routes, and met with adventures not less romantic. The safe deliverance of the whole of Condé's army has scarcely a parallel in history.[1]

The failure and dispersion of Condé's army thus proved less serious in their consequences than might have been apprehended. In fact, the Huguenots were probably better off than they would have been had they succeeded in throwing themselves into the castle of Angers and thus obtaining a foothold on the north of the Loire; since, but for the return of Laval to Saint Jean d'Angely, the Protestants of the provinces of Aunis and Saintonge would scarcely have had a competent leader or sufficient troops to ward off the attacks of the enemy. There was another respect, however, in which the result was less favorable to the cause for which they were fighting. Exaggerated reports, for some time left uncontradicted, magnified disappointment into disaster, and timid men, already a prey to extreme fear, could hardly be expected to look for the speedy reassembling of the prince's army apparently scattered to the four winds of heaven.

Bravely as had the King of Navarre and his followers entered upon the war, strong as was the confidence they expressed of ultimately achieving success, with the blessing of Heaven ever vouchsafed to oppressed innocence, the autumn of the year of grace 1585 was certainly one of the darkest hours of their history. In the prospect before them there were few gleams of light. The most hopeful of

<small>General discouragement of the Huguenots.</small>

---

[1] For the history of the enterprise of Angers see the detailed account entitled " Discours du premier passage de Monsieur le Duc de Mercure (Mercœur) au bas Poictou, de sa deroute et fuitte. Du siege de Brouage par Monseigneur le Prince de Condé et de son voyage d'Angers," reprinted in Mémoires de la Ligue, ii. 1–53. Also, the admirable narrative in the Recueil des choses mémorables, 628–633; De Thou, vi. (book 82) 523–536; Agrippa d'Aubigné, who was not only an eye-witness, but an active participant, ii. 440–452. Busini, who had no love for the Huguenots, in his letter of November 4, 1585, expresses admiration of Condé's boldness, and repeats a remark ascribed to the prince when remonstrated with : " I poltroni non mi seguiranno, come so farà che arà cuore." Négociations avec la Toscane, iv. 595. Busbecq, in his letter of November 15, 1585 (fol. 97 verso), is less accurate in

Huguenots could scarcely regard as extravagant the statement of their leader, already referred to, that their enemies had, by the infamous compact of Nemours, prepared them enough trouble to last an entire lifetime. Protestantism had often before been threatened with annihilation; but never had the plan been so calmly and resolutely laid, never had its projectors adopted such precautions against the possibility that the king's determination might give way, never before had his majesty been so distinctly warned that an attempt to make peace with or to spare heretics would infallibly cost him his crown. No wonder that dejection fell like a pall upon great numbers of the Protestants. And now when, in the very first months of the war, came tidings, false though they subsequently proved, of the complete destruction of Condé's army, even those seemed for the moment dazed who until now had retained full possession of their senses. Their opponents took good care not to let the opportunity pass by unimproved. Many of them believed that the hopes of Protestantism were buried in the same grave with its most daring champion.[1] Nothing was therefore spared to hasten the return of the Huguenots to the Romish Church. The king's second edict "of reunion," shortening the term within which all Protestants must either abjure or leave the kingdom, from six months to a fortnight, and menacing all that refused with dire punishment, came in good time to add to the general dismay.

Jesuit preachers, parish priests, and monks thundered from every pulpit and every confessional in France against the Calvinistic heretics. If they failed to persuade the Protestant to abjure, they either excited the people to attack them or pressed the civil magistrates, already more than usually inclined to rigorous measures against the Huguenots, to pursue them with the full

---

describing Condé's movements, but adds an interesting rumor that the king had ordered the destruction of the castle of Angers.

[1] "La fureur se renflamma par tout universellement contre ceux de la Religion : car ceux du party contraire estimans Monsieur le Prince perdu (pource qu'on fut un fort long temps sans sçavoir qu'il estoit devenu), jugeoient que la foy et esperance de tous ceux de la Religion estoit aussi avec luy ensevelie." Mémoires de la Ligue, ii. 174, 175.

terrors of the law. Men and women who had, on some previous occasion, apostatized from the Protestant faith, and persons suspected of favoring that faith, were naturally distinguished for the persecuting zeal which they exhibited, and whereby they strove to prove their unimpeachable orthodoxy. To the threats and malicious exertions of enemies were added the more insidious and powerful suggestions of friends and relatives, of parents and children, of brothers and sisters, all reinforcing the natural instinct for self-preservation, and urging weak believers to the cowardly but profitable step of submission to the authority of a hated ecclesiastical system. Such is the picture of the deplorable state and of the mental conflict of great numbers of the Protestants of France drawn by a contemporary writer.[1] That it is a faithful delineation, neither distorted by exaggeration nor disfigured by excess of color, appears from the confirmatory representations of Agrippa d'Aubigné, who assures us that the terror inspired by the proscriptive edicts of Henry the Third drove three times as many Huguenots to mass as the massacre of Saint Bartholomew's Day had driven.[2]

<small>A great number of apostasies.</small>

Happily for the future of Protestantism in France, the timid and wavering did not constitute the majority, nor, in fact, anything but a comparatively unimportant part of those upon whom the King of Navarre and the Prince of Condé relied. Not to speak of the Huguenots who, while remaining in their homes and exposed both to the assaults of hatred and the seductions of friendship, successfully resisted the most strenuous efforts to move them from their religious convictions, there were many that early deemed it the part of prudence to seek some safe refuge. Entire families temporarily forsook their native land. From the northern provinces Huguenots fled in great numbers to the principality of Sedan or to contiguous parts of Protestant Germany. To the

<small>Flight into foreign lands.</small>

---

[1] Mémoires de la Ligue, ii. 175.

[2] "Ce coup non attendu, et bien tost redoublé par un second Edit qui accourcissoit les termes de moitié, donna un tel effroi par toutes les parts du Royaume, qu'il fit aller à la messe trois fois plus de Refformez que n'avoit fait la journée de S. Barthelemi." Agrippa d'Aubigné, ii. 484.

inhabitants of the east, Switzerland, as usual, threw wide open its hospitable doors. The Huguenots of the western seaboard either pressed into La Rochelle and Saint Jean d'Angely or, taking ship, passed over into England, to swell the already considerable colony of French Protestant refugees that worshipped, according to their accustomed rites, in the chapel in Threadneedle Street, London, given to them by Edward the Sixth, or with the Walloons in the crypt of Canterbury Cathedral.[1] Dieppe, in Normandy, being specially favored by its situation on the British Channel, within a few hours' sail of the southern shores of England, witnessed the exodus of nearly its entire Protestant population. Its Huguenot church, with the pastors, Cartault and de Licques, passed over almost in a body to Rye, in Sussex, where it resumed its interrupted services, and maintained its worship until the advent of better times permitted a return to France. Other Norman Huguenots, including some from Dieppe, founded a new French Protestant church at Winchelsea, a few miles from Rye, with M. de la Touche as pastor. It was a characteristic circumstance that the refugees from Dieppe did not forget their fellow-believers who had remained behind—even those who, to save their property, had been so weak as to go to mass—but in the famine that visited France in 1586, sent them not only grain, but even bread straight from their ovens in a strange land.[2] Nor were the Huguenot fugitives treated with harshness untempered by humanity, even in some quarters where little kindness was to be anticipated.

The Huguenots in Savoy. About the middle of November, the Duke of Savoy, having learned that divers French Protestants had come to the city of Nice, with the intention of settling there or in the vicinity, felt compelled to refuse them permission to remain,

---

[1] See Ch. Weiss, Histoire des Refugiés protestants, i. 257-265.

[2] See the interesting account given in the Histoire de la Réformation à Dieppe, par Guillaume et Jean Daval, first published by the Société Rouennaise de Bibliophiles (Rouen, 1878), i. 135, 136. The editor has erroneously read Winchester instead of Winchelsea. A glance at the map would have shown him that the description, "distante de la Rye d'environ deux mille," would hardly apply to the city of Winchester, which is not far from one hundred miles distant in a straight line.

but accompanied his refusal with kindly instructions. "Our council of state," wrote the duke to the governor, "has learned that his majesty the King of France has ordered the adherents of the new religion to leave his realm. We know, moreover, that some of them have crossed the borders and are preparing to sojourn in our states. It seems proper for me to give you some directions on this score. I desire you to see them, and to tell them quietly, with all gentleness and modesty, that, for very grave reasons, and through motives worthy of respect, we cannot allow them to remain long in our dominions. They must leave in three days; but we command that not only they be subjected to no annoyances while crossing our lands, but be treated with all favor and receive all convenient help by the way. You will see to the faithful execution of these instructions, in so far as concerns you, and thus doing will have our approval."[1]

Meanwhile the clergy did not neglect the advantage which the wide-spread fear of the Protestants put into their hands. The king was induced to resort to measures more and more decided. A new order, issued just before Christmas, strictly enjoined upon all bailiffs and seneschals throughout the kingdom to draw up a general roll of the Protestants within their respective jurisdictions. On this roll five classes were to be carefully distinguished: all persons, of whatever profession, at present in arms against his majesty; all that, having borne arms, had consented to submit and be converted; all who had retired from France in obedience to the edict; such as had remained in their homes and had declared their intention to live in a Catholic fashion; and, lastly, such as stayed at home but still persisted in their old opinions. Against the first and last of these classes the procedure by confiscation of property was laid down with great precision, while as for those who professed a willingness to embrace the Roman Catholic religion, it was declared that their abjuration of Protestantism must be made, not before simple curates who had no power

A general roll of Protestants made.

---

[1] Charles Emmanuel to the Count of Boglio, November 13, 1585, French translation given by Gaberel, Histoire de l'Église de Genève, i. 483, 484.

to grant them absolution, but solely before bishops, archbishops, or their vicars.[1] The king's proclamation was industriously circulated in every part of France, accompanied by episcopal rescripts and formulas of abjuration.

The authors and instruments of religious persecution can never rid themselves of one formidable difficulty. The human intellect is proof against violence; it will yield only to persuasion. Men may be forced to make a profession of faith, but it is always at the risk and often with the certainty of transforming them into hypocrites. Between the ardent desire to gain proselytes and the honest dread of multiplying insincere members of their communion, conscientious persecutors have frequently found themselves involved in hopeless embarrassment.

Such a dilemma confronted the bishops of France, and vainly did they strive to escape it. "We have been duly informed," says Bishop Ruse, of Angers, in his preamble, "that certain persons of our diocese, following the new opinions of the heretics of our times, and being unwilling to abjure in their souls, nevertheless intend to avail themselves of the king's edict, and, contrary to his majesty's intention, to profess with the mouth, and not from the heart, the articles proposed by our holy Mother the Catholic, Apostolic, and Roman Church, reserving for themselves in their assemblies this excuse, that they conformed to the times, and obeyed the king's edicts, in order to live in accordance with law. In proof whereof they employ in their protestations these words, 'since it is the king's pleasure,' etc., thinking by this means to cover their professions which are altogether contrary." Thereupon the bishop declares that such is not his majesty's purpose—his desire being to invite those that have gone astray to come back to the right way, not to furnish a mask for hypocrites. The gift of such holy things as the sacraments of the Church to false brethren not only redounds to the dishonor of God and is

Perplexity of the Roman Catholic bishops.

---

[1] "Reglement que le Roy veut estre observé par les Baillifs et Seneschaux ou leurs lieutenans, pour l'execution de l'edict de sa Majesté sur la reunion de ses sujects à l'Église Catholique," etc., Paris, December 23, 1585. Mémoires de la Ligue, i. 301-306.

expressly forbidden by the Lord, but involves the perdition of the unworthy recipients, who by lying against the Holy Ghost incur the curse pronounced upon Ananias and Sapphira.

The confession of faith, which the bishop next laid down as an indispensable prerequisite for the absolution of the new convert, was certainly comprehensive enough to satisfy the most scrupulous Roman Catholic, though it might be hard to see what precaution it afforded against insincere profession. In addition to the entire Nicene creed, it comprehended a distinct recognition of the authority of tradition, of the Church as the sole interpreter of the Holy Scriptures, of the seven sacraments, of transubstantiation, of purgatory, of the worship of saints and images, of indulgences, of the Church of Rome as the mother and mistress of all churches, of the pope as true successor of Saint Peter and vicar of Jesus Christ on earth, and of the authority of the Council of Trent. The whole concluded with a formal rendering of thanks to the king for his sovereign goodness in granting a term of grace within which the subscriber might recognize his errors and return to the good path from which he had gone astray. And (apparently lest the thanksgiving should be suspected of insincerity) the unfortunate Huguenot was required to make the following additional guarantee :

A confession of faith imposed on converts.

" I protest that herein I am not forced nor compelled by the edict of the king or otherwise, but purely and frankly induced and brought back by a desire to emerge from the error in which I have until now been plunged, and henceforth to pursue the path which I must follow for the salvation of my soul. This I protest, with heart as well as with mouth, praying God that if I dissemble in this matter, and have aught in my heart but what I have said with my mouth, He may put forth His vengeance upon me to the everlasting damnation of my soul."[1]

Additional guarantee of sincerity.

In so puerile a fashion was the incongruous attempt made to

---

[1] "Maniere de profession de foy que doivent tenir ceux du dioceze d'Angers, qui se voudront remettre au giron de nostre S. Mere l'Église Catolique, Apostolique, et Romaine. Laquelle maniere a este presque suyvie par tout le Royaume." Mémoires de la Ligue, i. 306–310.

force the Huguenots to a sincere and voluntary acceptance of every tenet of the Roman Catholic Church.

That a certain amount of apparent success rewarded the efforts of the clergy, in securing at least an external conformity with the practices of that church, is seen from letters, still preserved, in which Protestant pastors strove to recall to the path of duty the numerous members of their flocks who had gone astray. Themselves forbidden by the Edict of Nemours to hold any religious exercises, on pain of death, and allowed but a single month to leave the kingdom, these faithful ministers had for the most part sought some nearer refuge than a foreign land would have afforded them. From the sea-girt walls of La Rochelle or from Saint Jean d'Angely—that plague-stricken Huguenot city which owed its safety less to its strength than to the fear entertained by its enemies of the contagion raging within—they raised loud voices of remonstrance, and exerted themselves strenuously to resist a current of apostasy which, if too strong for the moment to be successfully resisted, was fortunately destined soon to spend its strength.[1]

<small>Pastoral remonstrances.</small>

It would have been well had weakness and dissension been confined to the inferior ranks in the Huguenot party. Unfortunately they reached even the leaders, and the King of Navarre and his cousin, the Prince of Condé, began to betray symptoms of mutual jealousy. The courtiers of the Béarnais are said not to have been ashamed to make the misadventure of Angers a subject for their ill-timed jesting. Never before had Henry so distinctly shown that selfish motives were more potent with him than religious considerations. To those who saw him from near at hand he

<small>Jealousy among the Huguenot leaders.</small>

---

[1] See the letter of L. Blachière to the Church of Niort and Saint Gelais, from La Rochelle, December 20, 1585, Mémoires de la Ligue, i. 311–323; and that of Jean de l'Espine to the Church of Angers, from Saint Jean d'Angely, February 25, 1586, ibid., i. 323–330. The former writes: "J'entens que le nombre est tres-grand entre vous de ceux qui ont apostaté et renoncé la verité de l'Evangile;" the latter: "De jour en jour nous n'avons aucunes nouvelles de vous, sinon que la plus part se revoltent et se departent de la Religion, laquelle ils ne peuvent ignorer estre la vraye." Both expressions should probably be taken with some allowance for the excitement under which the writers labored.

appeared in an entirely new light. He seemed, said they, to have forgotten the sufferings of the Huguenots whose defence against an unjust proscription he had espoused, and prated only of the necessity of preserving the state and making himself indispensable to the King of France.[1] Evidently some of Henry's most intimate friends began to fear, as the Florentine Cavriana began to hope, that sooner or later the great Protestant leader would subordinate his personal predilections in matters of faith to supposed political exigencies, and would infallibly abandon the doctrines which, in his own words, he had imbibed with his mother's milk, rather than forfeit a possible claim to the crown of the Very Christian King. And yet, it must not be forgotten that the expressions of Huguenot distrust, though assigned to the period now under investigation, were not recorded until long after, at a date subsequent to the formal abjuration of 1593, and probably receive a very decided coloring from events that were yet to come. For the present, if less inclined to look at the situation in which the Huguenots were placed from the stand-point of the "consistorial" party, Henry of Navarre displayed to the world no hesitation in the maintenance of the good cause.

Of this the papers he published on the first day of the new year sufficiently testified. Three were letters addressed respectively to the three orders of the kingdom; the fourth was a letter to the City of Paris in particular. In all he spoke in the tone of one who is well convinced of the perfect justice of his position and the unrighteousness of his opponents. In fact, Henry of Valois had spared him the necessity of much argument on that score, by his solemn and reiterated declarations to the world, not a year since, to the effect that the authors of the League were enemies of the crown and disturbers of the public peace and tranquillity. After that, it was self-evident that any contrary declarations of his majesty could only be the result of com-

Henry of Navarre writes to the City of Paris and to the three orders.

---

[1] "Joint que le roi de Navarre jouoit un personnage nouveau, ne parlant plus que de conserver l'Estat, et aiant mis les passions Huguenottes en crouppe," etc. Agrippa d'Aubigné, ii. 453.

pulsion or fear. Under these circumstances, Henry adapted each of his letters with great art to the character and attitude of each of the estates. To the clergy he spoke with mingled kindness and decision. He begged God to open their eyes to the hypocrisy of the authors of the League, who had not scrupled to light a fire at the four corners of the kingdom, nor hesitated to seek private revenge for fancied insults by originating a universal calamity. But he added : " I do not fear (and God knows it) the evil that may befall me, either from your money or from their arms. Both the one and the other have already been employed often enough in vain. I commiserate the poor, innocent people which suffers almost alone from these acts of folly. I commiserate even a goodly number of yourselves, who contribute to the ambition of these disturbers—you giving of your poverty, they scarce from their abundance. I bewail chiefly the fault you are all committing, some from one motive, others from another, who will one day have to answer to this kingdom and to your native land for the misery into which you are plunging them." He remonstrated with the clergy for neglecting the offers he had made in his declaration, and assured them that the bolts hurled at him by the pope gave him no solicitude. " It is God," said he, " that disposes both of kings and of kingdoms, and your predecessors, who were better Christians and better Frenchmen than the promoters of this bull, have taught us sufficiently that the popes have no supervision over this state." The writer did not hold the entire body of the clergy responsible for the malicious persecution set on foot against him, preferring to believe it to be " the plot of a few persons instigated from abroad, perhaps by the inspiration of certain Jesuits, the seed of Spain, enemies of the welfare of this kingdom. May God grant that they be as prompt in abstaining from mischief in future, as I now feel myself ready to pardon them." " What remains for me to say," added the Béarnais, by way of conclusion, " is this: God has given me my birth as a Christian prince. I desire the strengthening, growth and peace of the Christian religion. We believe in one God ; we acknowledge one Jesus Christ ; we receive one and the same Gospel. If in the interpretation of the same

<small>His appeal to the clergy.</small>

passages we have differed, I believe that the gentle means which I proposed might have brought us to an agreement. I believe the war you are so ardently prosecuting to be unworthy of Christians, unworthy among Christians, unworthy above all of those who pretend to be teachers of the Gospel. If war pleases you so much, if a battle delights you more than a dispute, a sanguinary conspiracy more than a council, I wash my hands of it. The blood that may be spilled in it be upon your heads! I know that the curses of those who will be the sufferers cannot fall upon me; for my patience, my obedience, and my reasons are well known. I look for the blessing of God upon my just defence, Whom I entreat, gentlemen, to give you the spirit of peace and union, for the peace of this state and the union of His church."

There is less necessity that we should pause to examine in detail the other documents. To the nobles he appealed as men of honor and as Frenchmen, protesting his love to them all, and a regret, into the poignancy of which no stranger could enter, when their blood was shed.

His remonstrances addressed to the nobles and commons.

"Do not think, gentlemen, that I fear the authors of the League. I know what violence can do against me. My enemies will sooner be weary of assailing me, than I shall be of defending myself." To the commons, Henry reiterated his deep sympathy with them, amid the disasters into which they were hurried against their will. He ridiculed the pretence of the Leaguers that they sought to lighten financial burdens, and bring back the taxes to the scale of the time of Louis the Twelfth.[1] He called attention to the circumstance that the gift of two hundred thousand crowns, or thereabouts, by the clergy, was only a bait offered for the purpose of inducing France to begin a war in which the poor people would be involved to the amount of millions. Addressing himself to the City of Paris, he spoke in more confident terms, reminding the municipal authorities of their recent answer when appealed to

---

[1] There was a touch of quiet sarcasm in the remark which he threw in: "Et desja, qui leur eust voulu croire, ils se faisoyent surnommer *Peres du Peuple.*"

for money, that these troubles had not arisen through their advice, and that it was for those who had caused the war, and not for them, to bear the burden of it. "Such a reply," said he, " you are not accustomed to make when you think the king's service or the good of the kingdom to be in question; for never have subjects been more generous in this respect than you. It is the answer you give when you perceive that your money goes, not for the restoration of the kingdom, as you are told, but for its ruin; when you clearly see that your jewels are demanded, not to furnish the ransom of a King Francis, or his children, nor of a King John, but in order to extinguish the blood and posterity of the House of France, and to reduce your king to slavery and imprisonment."[1]

Public documents of the kind we have been examining are chiefly valuable as an index of the prevailing sentiments of parties; for, however cogent their reasoning, they are wont either not to be read at all by the persons whom they should influence, or to be robbed of their weight by the passions and prejudices of those who peruse them. Unfortunately the appeals of Henry of Navarre were little heard or heeded amid the tumult of active warfare.

As yet, however, though there was an abundance of local conflicts, nothing significant or decisive had been done in arms. Navarre was busily seeking recruits for the Protestant cause in Germany, whither Clervant, Ségur, Guitry, and Montmarin had been sent, to take advantage of the gathering of Casimir and many of the Protestant princes and noblemen at Durlach, at the nuptials of the Margrave Ernest of Baden and the daughter of the late elector palatine.[2] Henry of Valois, indeed, despatched the Duke of Mayenne in the direction of his namesake of Navarre, but, what with the impediment of heavy rains and the nameless ter-

Indecisive warfare.

---

[1] The four letters, all dated at Montauban, January 1, 1586, are printed in Mémoires de la Ligue, i. 331-342; Mémoires de Duplessis Mornay, iii. 286, etc.; Lettres missives de Henri IV., ii. 165, etc. There can be no doubt that they were composed by Duplessis Mornay. See Recueil des choses mémorables, 621, and De Thou, vi. 659, etc.

[2] Mucius to Mendoza, November 28, 1585, De Croze, i. 364.

rors of the plague, he had as yet no victories to report. The king had little inclination to trouble himself about the war into which he had so reluctantly entered. Again foreign ambassadors wrote home that his majesty was wholly given up to his new ceremonies and to a life of seclusion, so that men feared lest his health might suffer, and, at any rate, lest he would plunge into some new sort of hateful superstition.[1] Guise, indeed, was so importunate in his demands that the king had at last despatched Schomberg for the levy of eight or nine thousand "reiters" and six thousand Swiss. As for the duke himself, his own letters paint a very vivid picture of his mental perturbation and unrest. Constant were his fears lest the boon of peace so longed for by bleeding France might by some mischance be obtained by her; harrowing his complaints of the disastrous effects of the dilatoriness of the foreign prince upon whose bounty he was a dependent. Notwithstanding his success in wringing from the king the promise of a German levy, he was in deep distress in view of what might happen. Frenchmen pitted against Frenchmen might possibly remember that one and the same blood coursed in their veins, and thereupon stop to consider whether they should engage in the unprofitable work of cutting each other's throats. Such was the dreadful contingency which the pious duke prayed that heaven might in mercy forefend. "Yet," writes he to the Spanish ambassador, "I do not cease from fearing lest, the forces of both parties being in the field, some union may be made, by means of which, coming to a general peace, which I know is desired above all things, the whole may be made to fall upon his Catholic Majesty (Philip the Second), and we be constrained by force to do what we do not wish to do and never shall do of our own accord."[2] What was deplorable was that, had the Spanish king only sent help

The king's levies in Germany and Switzerland.

Guise's anxiety lest peace should ensue.

---

[1] Letter of Busbecq, December 6, 1585, fol. 99.

[2] "Mais pourtant je ne laisse à craindre que les forces des uns et des autres estans aux champs, il ne se fasse quelque union moyennant laquelle venant à une paix générale, que je sçay que l'on désire sur toutes choses, on ne fasse fondre le tout sur le bras de Sa Magesté catholique," etc., Mucius to Mendoza, November 28, 1585, De Croze, i. 364.

in time, and as he was asked to do, there would have been no cause of solicitude. Instead of which, the prudent Philip permitted four whole months—and we know not how much more —to pass without vouchsafing an answer to the imploring call of his good friends in France, and the League was at its wits' end to discover upon what it could hereafter count.[1]

It was not long after this time that Henry of Guise resolved to visit Paris, with the view of strengthening the power of the League over the populace of that seditious city. His entry resembled a triumph. Great was the desire of the Parisians to see the nobleman who, forsooth, had become the principal champion of orthodoxy, and had forced the Very Christian King to engage in the work of destroying heresy. Crowds of men, women, and children flocked to the street through which he was to come, and on his appearance greeted him with loud acclamations. The duke's hat was in his hand almost all the while from the moment he entered the gate until he reached his stately mansion. The nobles looked on with little satisfaction at this popular demonstration, while the judges could scarcely disguise their want of sympathy. "They perceive," wrote an observing stranger, "that this infamous League is ruinous to France, and that, under the pretext of the propagation of the Catholic faith, every man is seeking to satisfy his greedy desires." Once within the walls of the capital, Guise betrayed unmistakable signs of the anxiety preying upon him. He went about with a body-guard of nearly two hundred men. The cheerful and contented looks he formerly wore had disappeared from his countenance. It was remarked that, although he was only thirty-five years of age, the front part of his hair had turned altogether white. "I know not what has caused it to change," says our informant; "whether it be mental regret for the offence he has done to his king, or annoyance at not having succeeded in the accomplishment of all his designs, or, possibly, he may be meditating some new revolution." Meanwhile Catharine de' Medici was profuse in her demonstrations of favor. She could not have lavished more caresses upon him

The duke's entry into Paris.

---

[1] Mucius to Tassis, December 31, 1585, De Croze, i. 366, 367.

had he been her son; in fact, she assured him that she loved him as much as if he had been her own offspring. It was the current impression that this extraordinary kindness was proof positive that the queen mother had been Guise's accomplice in his conspiracy against Henry of Valois. The physician Cavriana—who, as a compatriot, better understood the character of the great Florentine family—came to an entirely opposite conclusion, and regarded the story as a base calumny.[1] The Duke of Guise prolonged his sojourn in the capital for full three months, busily employing his time and energies in the congenial work of undermining the royal authority and destroying the last vestiges of the good-will once entertained for the king by the city which, above all his predecessors, Henry had made his favorite residence.[2]

The military exploits of the general who takes the field reluctantly, and only after interposing all manner of objections, are not wont to prove very brilliant. Charles of Mayenne, as we have seen, had been ordered to command in the south of France, and to co-operate with Marshal Matignon. Certainly no duty could have been more congenial to a zealous Roman Catholic and a leader of the League second in authority only to his brother, the Duke of Guise himself. Here was a fine chance to display enthusiasm and energy in suppressing heresy, by the overthrow of the King of Navarre and his confederate, the Duke of Montmorency. But unfortunately there was an object nearer to the heart of the adherents of the League than even the destruction of heresy, and that was the destruction of the authority of Henry of Valois. It was highly undesirable to defeat the Béarnais with the king's arms, and indeed to do anything that might conduce to the restoration of his majesty to public esteem and confidence. Above all, Mayenne must not furnish the slightest help toward bringing about that dreaded consummation, the return of a peace which, if a priceless boon to the wretched people, would sound the death-

The Duke of Mayenne purposely procrastinates.

---

[1] Letter of Cavriana, March 3, 1586, Négociations avec la Toscane, iv. 634–636.
[2] Lestoile, under date of May 18, 1586, i. 202.

knell of the ambitious hopes of the Guises, and might be little less fatal to the interests of their employer, Philip the Second, in the Netherlands. Thus it happened that the Duke of Mayenne delayed his departure as long as he could, and, when at length he did start, received his orders from his brother, not from the king. Setting off about the month of November, he executed to the letter the instructions which the Duke of Guise, in a letter to the Spanish ambassador, written on the fifteenth of November, represents himself as having issued to him.[1] He sat down before Castillon and one or two other places of minor importance in Guyenne. He "invented objections based upon the difficulty of obtaining provisions, the season of the year, the strongholds, the roads—in short, on all the impediments experienced by those previously sent in that direction." So neatly was the programme carried out that all he had to show for his year's work was the capture of a few insignificant towns. The only exploit of the campaign was one inuring to his own advantage: he managed to carry off by force young Mademoiselle de Caumont, daughter of the Maréchale de Saint André, a girl of twelve years of age, hitherto brought up as a Protestant, intending, on account of her great wealth, to give the heiress in marriage to his own son, a boy of ten.[2] It was sorry fruit to show from an expedition whose achievements had been so boastfully set forth in advance that one might almost have been pardoned for looking to see all the walls of the strongholds in Guyenne shivered to pieces or crumbling into dust at its approach.[3]

It was natural that the valorous duke should close his dilatory warfare by publishing to the world a glowing account of the great deeds he had accomplished; while ascribing the failure to

---

[1] See above, p. 309. [2] Lestoile (under October, 1586), i. 209.

[3] "Et si vous voulez vous souvenir ou de leurs vanteries ou mesmes de vos imaginations d'alors, toutes les murailles de Guyenne alloyent en esclas, ou s'envoloyent en poudre." Remonstrance aux Trois Estats de France sur la guerre de la Ligue; reprinted in Mémoires de la Ligue, i. 361. On the military operations of the year 1586, "full of exceeding great machinations, but of very few and weak executions touching the war," see Davila (book 8), 292, etc.; De Thou, vi. (book 85), 667-676; Agrippa d'Aubigné, iii. 24, etc.

do still more than he had done partly to the want of co-operation of Marshal Matignon, partly to the neglect of the king to furnish him more money. Whereupon a Huguenot commentator remarked with scathing sarcasm that the intention of the writer of Mayenne's "Declaration" was plainly to give the duke by the pen that honor which he had not been able to acquire by his arms. And he called attention to the fact that the "small means" of which the duke complained were the entire wealth of the clergy placed at his disposal; the "small forces," an army of fifteen thousand soldiers at his command; the "annoyances and inconveniences," a few cold mornings. As to the duke's assurances that the Huguenots were now so scattered and astonished that, if his majesty should be pleased to furnish the means promptly to make a second charge, they could be brought to such a pass as never again to be able to rise and make another war, the Huguenot writer replies: "I see not whence comes this astonishment. I see that they were never so strong in Dauphiny. They give battle in Provence. They are the masters in Languedoc, and have lost nothing in Guyenne. I fear me that these Leaguers easily find fright, because they carry fear along with themselves. . . . If the Duke of Mayenne take only three towns a year, we have work enough for many a long day. If Castillon made his army disband, I believe that he will not tarry long before fifty places in Guyenne which are stronger than Castillon."[1]

Meanwhile the Huguenots held their own in other parts of France. The Prince of Condé had returned in safety to France after his perilous adventure of Angers. Queen Elizabeth had not only entertained him very handsomely in England, but had sent him back to La Rochelle, escorted by a goodly number of noblemen and soldiers, in well equipped vessels. Nothing could exceed the joy of the Huguenots, great and small, at his coming; never were there more

---

[1] "Fidele exposition sur la declaration du duc de Mayenne, contenant les exploits de guerre qu'il a fait en Guyenne;" reprinted in Mémoires de la Ligue, i. 493–515. The Huguenot expositor, who scarcely disguises his identity, answers the duke's Declaration, paragraph by paragraph. See also Recueil des choses mémorables, 622–625; De Thou, vi. 676, 677; Agrippa d'Aubigné, iii. 17.

sincere congratulations than those that accompanied him when, not long after, he contracted, at Taillebourg, his ill-fated marriage with Catharine Charlotte de la Trémouille.¹ One inauspicious event, however, marred the rejoicing over this event and over the general success attending the Protestant arms in the West. By a strange coincidence the Sieur de Laval and three of his brothers fell victims to the pitiless ravages of war—one of Laval's brothers dying of disease, the others of the wounds they had received; while that distinguished nobleman himself, unable to survive the loss of his kindred, fell a prey to inconsolable grief and died after a brief illness of scarcely a week. Within the compass of a few days almost the entire family of the brave D'Andelot, "the fearless knight," Admiral Coligny's youngest brother, had been cut off.²

Death of D'Andelot's sons.

But while Mayenne and other generals of the king justly or unjustly complained that they were insufficiently supplied with money for the successful prosecution of their plans, his majesty himself was in sore straits to meet the demands made upon his purse. Not that the war alone claimed his attention. His puerile fondness for collecting dogs of choice breeds was unabated. The sums of money expended upon these animals, and upon birds of prey, parrots, monkeys, and the like, almost baffle computation. Year after year more than one hundred thousand crowns were required for the purchase of little dogs of the Lyons breed, and the maintenance of a large force of men and women whose sole occupation was to take care of them. To add to the expense, Henry would from time to time become tired of his pets and give them

Henry of Valois's diversions.

---

¹ See the minute account of the events in the West given in the "Advertissement au lecteur par lequel est sommairement discouru ce qui se passa en divers lieux de France, apres la rupture de l'armee de Monsieur le Prince de Condé de la Loire, à la fin de l'an mil cinq cens octantecinq et en l'an suyvant 1586," Mémoires de la Ligue, ii. 173–199; and the brief statements in Recueil des choses mémorables, 632, 636, etc. Condé landed at La Rochelle, Friday, January 3, and was married, Sunday, March 16.

² See the "Advertissement" above referred to, Mémoires de la Ligue, ii. 191, 192; De Thou, vi. 664, 665-; Recueil des choses mémorables, 638, etc. These events occurred in April, 1586. The four brothers were known respectively by their seigniorial designations of Laval, Rieux, Tanlay, and Sailly.

all away, then, as capriciously, conceive the desire for them again, and send out his agents in every direction to get together a similar collection, whatever the price demanded by the owners might be.[1] Much of the people's hard-earned treasure was lavished upon the purchase of costly manuscripts, which he accumulated not because of the beauty of the handwriting, much less that he might master their contents, but simply for the sake of the miniature illustrations, often the work of skilful artists, with which they were embellished. Nor did this childish prince hesitate for a moment to mutilate the rarest relics of a past age, in order to have material wherewith to gratify a passing whim, and decorate the walls of his chapels and oratories.[2] The Edict of Nemours and the subsequent declarative ordinances had brought little or nothing into the public treasury. Pretended creditors, for the most part, contrived by their claims to forestall any possible funds to be derived from the confiscation of the property of Huguenots.[3] It may be doubted whether a new and sharper prescription, contained in royal letters patent of the twenty-sixth of April, 1586, produced much more tangible results. Money, however, was necessary and must be had, if not with his subjects' consent, the king thought, then without it, and in defiance of their remonstrances. Especially was this the case when his favorite, the Duke of Épernon, lately appointed governor of Provence, wished to raise an army in his new command. It was useless to ask the Parliament of Paris to sanction fresh taxes. That body had of late persistently refused to register the monarch's iniquitous imposts. Accordingly, Henry of Valois, provoked beyond endurance, resolved to take the matter into his own hands, and, going in person to the Palais de Justice, on the sixteenth of June, delivered to the astonished counsellors not less than twenty-seven fresh edicts, all relating to the levy of extraordinary taxes, which he compelled them to enter upon their records without any deliberation as to the contents.

His injudicious financial edicts.

---

[1] De Thou, vi. 681, 682.   [2] De Thou, vi. (book 85) 682.

[3] See the preamble of the Letters patent of April 26, 1586, in Mémoires de la Ligue, i. 343, etc.

The ill-advised act of arbitrary power bore speedy fruit in the undisguised dissatisfaction and murmurs of all classes of the population.[1]

The Protestants of the surrounding countries had not remained unsympathetic witnesses of the new struggle forced upon the Huguenots of France by the enemies of their common faith. The question with them was whether to resort first to diplomacy or to arms; and on all hands the former course was deemed most proper.

The earliest envoys to arrive were those of the Protestant cantons of Switzerland. As soon as on the seventh of February, 1586, at the solicitation of Berne, they had resolved to send an embassy to France, with the view of helping to negotiate a peace between the crown and the Huguenots. This they determined to do without waiting to see whether the German princes would join them, well assured, as they said, that both the king and the nobles of France would look with a more friendly eye upon their intercessions than upon those of the Germans, because of the close alliance between Switzerland and the French crown. They were persuaded that, should their exertions prove fruitless, they would, at least, have adopted the most honorable course in interesting themselves in behalf of the kingdom of France, and have given some consolation and encouragement to the Protestants of that country.[2] The ambassadors were instructed to assume a position of neutrality, and not to act as though their kind offices had been asked by the King of Navarre. While urging a general peace rather than a peace for the Church alone, they were to remind the king that there could be no thorough tranquillity without provision for religious liberty. To force human consciences, said the Swiss, is to aim at making hypocrites of them, or to drive a great number to despair or atheism. The king will never succeed in having but one religion in his realm; he will not be able to prevent his subjects from following the path

---

[1] De Thou, vi. 679, 680.
[2] J. C. Mœrikofer, Histoire des réfugiés de la reforme en Suisse, 115. I have made use of the French translation by G. Roux of the German work.

that suits them. This has been the experience of the Swiss confederates. The Reformed cantons are therefore of the opinion that they will find it impossible to prevent a good part of their population from lending help to the Protestants of France, so much the more as it is generally believed among them that these troubles and seditions tend to the extermination of the first princes of the royal house of France.[1]

So kindly a remonstrance, accompanied, it is said, by the exhibition of a letter of Francis the First, in which that prince, the reigning monarch's own grandfather, had urged the Swiss, at that time in arms, Roman Catholic warring against Protestant, to come to terms of amity, was well calculated, if it did not secure its object, at least to avoid irritating Henry of Valois. The Swiss ambassadors were honorably dismissed after a very gracious reception.[2]

It was quite otherwise with the German deputation.

In response to the urgent solicitations of the King of Navarre, through Ségur and others, and in deference to the appeals of the aged Theodore Beza, a large and influential body of German rulers had agreed to send delegates to France to plead for the restoration of the rights of conscience and worship to the Huguenots, and, should those rights be denied, had consented to a new resort to arms in their behalf. True, every scheme hitherto proposed with the intention of a doctrinal reconciliation between the adherents of the views of Calvin and the supporters of the Lutheran tenets had signally failed. The most recent instance was seen in the issue of the conference held in March, 1586, in the city of Montbéliard, in consequence of the exertions of Count Frederick of Würtemberg, himself not a little disposed to favor the doctrines of the Swiss reformers. Beza came in person, and labored patiently and perseveringly to find common ground upon which to stand with the German theologians. But he was again met by Andreæ, tried champion of Lutheran orthodoxy, in no conciliatory mood. The long and earnest discussion has been preserved in the *ex parte* statements

Appeal of the German princes.

Conference of Montbéliard, March, 1586.

---

[1] Mœrikofer, ubi supra.   [2] De Thou, vi. 680.

of both of the able theologians; for the Germans, in apparent violation of the common understanding, gave to the world their version of the proceedings, and claimed that Andreæ had won a notable victory over Beza—a pretension which the latter could disprove only by himself resorting to the printing press. But what concerns us here is not the comparative merit of Beza and Andreæ as dialecticians, nor the particular methods by which they attempted to vindicate the belief of their respective churches on the person of Christ or the elect for whom our Saviour died. These things have been well related elsewhere.[1] All that we need record is the fact that, at the conclusion of the debates, Lutherans and Calvinists were farther away from each other than at the beginning. It was indeed evident to everybody that both were practically at one in their views upon essential points, as opposed to the Roman Catholics, and Beza was anxious to do away with all bitterness and party names. But when the Genevese reformer was about to leave, and, in token of cordial affection and trust, offered his hand to Andreæ, the latter repelled the advance. He could, he said, as little see how Beza could regard him and the Würtemberg theologians, to whom he had ascribed all sorts of errors, as brethren, as he himself could recognize fraternal communion with Beza, who had given evidence that he held the imaginations of men above the Word of God. While, however, he could not greet him as a brother, Andreæ kindly offered to give Beza his hand as a mark of his love toward him as a fellow-man—a condescension which, not unnaturally, the Genevese reformer at once declined.[2]

Despite the failure of this new attempt to bring the two branches of the Protestant Church into harmony of profession, the Germans seemed disposed to make common cause with the French Huguenots against the aggressive policy of the Roman Catholics and the League. The embassy now sent to Henry of Valois appeared in the name of the three

The embassy reaches Paris.

---

[1] See F. C. Schlosser, Leben des Theodor de Beza, 253-267, and especially H. Heppe, Theodor Beza, 267-287.
[2] Heppe, 287. Compare De Thou, vi. 687.

Protestant Electors of the Palatinate, Saxony, and Brandenburg, of Marquis Joachim Frederick of Brandenburg, Julius Duke of Brunswick and Lüneburg, of the three brothers, William, Lewis, and George, of Hesse, of Prince Joachim Ernest, and of the four imperial cities of Strasbourg, Ulm, Nuremburg, and Frankfort. To give more influence and effect to the deputation, Frederick of Würtemberg, Count of Montbéliard, and Wolfgang Count of Isenburg, had been placed at its head. But the King of France was in no mood to listen to them, and doubtless thought it a shrewd trick, the moment he heard that they were well under way, to slip off to Lyons, leaving word for the ambassadors to wait in Paris until his return. If the worst should come to pass, the delay would secure him one year's immunity from Protestant auxiliaries from beyond the Rhine. On the other hand, the Germans, though chafing under their enforced inactivity, had no resource but to tarry as patiently as they might in the French capital, whose marvels, architectural and of other kinds, were little to their taste. The two counts, indeed, thinking it beneath their dignity to be so put off, returned to their homes without seeing the king. But the remaining envoys, when at length Henry of Valois was pleased to direct his steps northward once more, discharged their duty with all the dignity which even the ostentatious Count of Montbéliard could have assumed. Casimir's deputy was their spokesman.

Speech of Duke Casimir's envoy. They assured the king of the very great affection entertained for him by the German princes in whose name they appeared, and of the regret with which the princes had watched the progress of the new war. "As the king's faithful friends and good neighbors," said they, "our masters have been moved with Christian compassion toward your majesty; especially in view of the fact that those who have set on foot this injurious scheme have so far forgotten themselves as to plot against the crown and the administration of government, pressing you, nay, even constraining you by force of arms to make war against and persecute with violence your obedient subjects, and even those so nearly bound to you by the ties of relationship, and breaking the Edict of Pacification so solemnly made and resting upon the faith and word of your majesty, a singular ornament and the most precious jewel of all princes and potentates in the estimation of all peoples." Much that followed was of the same frank character. The ambassadors contrasted the king's more recent attempts to throw the blame upon the Huguenots with his declarations of a few brief days before, in which he had explicitly acknowledged them as faithful and obedient subjects. They professed themselves unable to see what advantage could accrue to Henry from lending an ear to those who would turn him aside from his royal promises, and from his faith and word pledged in the edict which the king himself had been wont to style his own peace. They warned him of the ruin of himself, and of his kingdom, certain to arise from a breach of faith instigated by the pope, which would of necessity inure merely to the benefit of the pope and of the authors of these troubles. Not only would the king's conscience be laden with a heavy responsibility in God's sight, but his reign would be defiled with blood; while, in place of confidence, distrust would be engendered between the kings of France and the princes, electors, and other states of the Holy Empire.[1]

This was plain speech, but Henry of Valois, for the moment, concealed his annoyance under an exterior of patient and courteous attention. In reply he confined himself to a few general declarations of his constant solicitude to prove himself a good king toward his subjects, and of his earnest affection, as very Christian prince, for the preservation of the Catholic religion. He claimed for himself the sole right to modify the laws and ordinances of his realm according to the exigencies of the times, leaving to all other sovereign princes of Christendom the care of governing their subjects as they might judge reasonable. He was competent of himself, he said, to decide what would be best for the interests of the nation which the Almighty had committed to his charge by making him king of the first realm of Christendom.[2]

---

[1] "Harangue des Ambassadeurs des Princes Protestans d'Allemagne faicte au Roy." Mémoires de la Ligue, i. 352-358.

[2] "Response du Roy aux Ambassadeurs." Mémoires de la Ligue, i. 358, 359. At the end: "Faict à Sainct Germain en Laye, l'onziesme jour d'Octobre, 1586."

Thus far Henry had maintained his apparent equanimity. But in the evening, when, the interview being over, he was left alone, the words of the Germans began to rankle in his breast. He then remembered with indignation that again and again he had been accused, by implication, if not in so many words, of faithlessness, falsehood, and perjury. At the thought of the insult his anger knew no bounds. He was disgraced forever in the eyes of the world, should he let the accusation pass unchallenged. In his inconsiderate fury, he adopted, as usual with him, of all courses the most impolitic. Snatching a scrap of paper from the table, he wrote a few lines upon it; then told an officer of the bedchamber to take it to the room where the German ambassadors were gathered together. The words were to this effect: "Whoever has said that, in revoking his Edict of Pacification, the king has violated his faith or stained his honor, has lied." It was well on in the night when the astonished envoys saw the royal officer enter with his supplementary answer. As soon as they had somewhat recovered from the first effects of the undiplomatic announcement, they requested the messenger to furnish a copy of it. The Frenchman, however, refused. He had been bidden to read the paper and then destroy it. He told the Germans that this was to be taken as their dismissal; his majesty would have nothing further to do with them.'

<small>The king's rough answer.</small>

The envoys of the King of Denmark and of the Queen of England were scarcely better treated by the French monarch, when they came to remonstrate against the war waged with the Huguenots. "As the Queen of England will have but one religion in her dominions, so I will have only one religion in my kingdom," was the surly answer of the angry prince.²

<small>Action of Denmark and England.</small>

Henry of Valois could have taken no step better calculated to provoke the strong Protestant princes beyond the Rhine to increase the number of the troops sent to the help of the King

---

¹ De Thou, vi. 690; Davila (book 8), 299, 300; Journal d'un curé ligueur (Jehan de la Fosse), 200.

² Lestoile, under date of April 24, 1586, i. 202; Jehan de la Fosse, 200.

of Navarre, none more certain to hasten the departure of the auxiliary army. At the same time, if he had hoped by his conduct to win the Guises back to their allegiance, he failed signally. Never were they more busy with plots for the purpose of thwarting him in every way, and of diminishing his authority. A conference was held by the duke and his chief adherents during the course of the very month in which Henry returned his rough answer to the German electors. The place was the ancient abbey of Ourcamp near Noyon, Calvin's birthplace. One of the complaints brought forward was that the king secretly favored the Protestants. One of the points settled was to call upon his majesty to observe the Edict of Union in every particular; and, in case he should make any agreement with the Huguenots, to oppose him as all true Christians ought to do. Moreover, the conspirators agreed upon the seizure of Sedan and Jametz, important places belonging to the Duke of Bouillon.[1] After the close of the conference, whose conclusions were duly reported by Guise to the ambassador of the king whose true liege man he was, the duke pursued unremittingly the policy marked out for him. He laid his plans so as always to have as many pretexts as possible for remaining in arms.[2] When he must choose between loyal obedience to Henry of Valois and fidelity to Philip the Second, he unhesitatingly chose the latter. "Six days ago," he sent word to Bernardino de Mendoza in Paris, "the king wrote to me that he was informed of certain preparations going on in Luxemburg against Jametz, and ordered and very expressly commanded me to resist them in every way, even in person. I openly replied to him that I was a Catholic, that he could not disapprove of an enterprise of this kind unless by reason of a little pardonable ambition, and that if my charge obliged me to obey such commands, I had much rather resign it than, by op-

The Guises determined not to lay down their arms.

Conference of Ourcamp.

---

[1] De Croze, i. 321.
[2] "Ay choisi de ceste façon de traicter afin que me soit occasion et moyen de demeurer armé le plus longtemps que faire se pourra, et que durant le séjour de mon frère à la court, il puysse estre asseuré de ces forces," etc. Mucius to Mendoza, December 30, 1586, ibid., i. 407.

posing the destruction of the heretics, offend Catholics; that I was unwilling in any wise to stand in their way, and had rather be dead than draw my sword for so detestable a cause. This reply I am sure that he will consider a very bad one; as all my actions are odious to him. But if only the truth be recognized by good and honorable men, to whom I am willing to give an account, I shall endure his displeasure gladly and patiently."[1]

Troublesome commands from Henry, which had to be disregarded, were not the only causes of vexation to the Duke of Guise. The queen mother's old fondness for negotiating with the Huguenots gave him infinite uneasiness. It would never do to let poor France regain the blessing of peace. What, then, would become of the fine plan that was to secure the crown of England to Mary Queen of Scots, with Philip the Second as her adopted heir, in case of James's obstinate refusal to become a Roman Catholic? Of what use the proposed invasion of Britain by the Duke of Parma, to be put into instant execution the moment the welcome news of the assassination of Queen Elizabeth should be received, in case that, the dissensions of France being healed, Henry of Navarre, or even Henry of Valois, or possibly both these princes, supported by all loyal Frenchmen, were to interfere with the accomplishment of the first decisive move of the Catholic king in the direction of a world-monarchy?[2] "I am constantly in alarm because of the designs of the queen mother," said Guise to Mendoza. "Within a few days she is to have an interview with the King of Navarre. I fear lest by what is there concluded she means to disturb the peace of the Catholics of these two crowns, which consists in union." Against such a con-

The League apprehensive.

---

[1] Mucius to Mendoza, February 6, 1587, De Croze, i. 417.

[2] De Croze, i. 312. Besides the Guises, the papal nuncio protested against the contemplated negotiations with Navarre, and the populace of Paris openly murmured at what was represented as a betrayal of the cause of religion. Davila, bk. 8, 397. According to Davila and others, Catharine seriously contemplated tempting Henry of Navarre by the prospect of a divorce to be obtained for him from her daughter Margaret of Valois and a marriage to Christina, daughter of Margaret's sister, the Duchess of Lorraine.

tingency he thought it necessary not only to hasten to secure his control of Eastern France by the seizure of Lyons, but to urge the Spaniard to be prepared for every emergency and to make ready the English expedition before Catharine could by any possibility conclude a peace.[1]

Nor did the queen mother, on her part, find it altogether an easy matter to bring the Béarnais to a conference with her. It is almost needless to say that the Huguenots had seen enough of Medicean diplomacy to repose little confidence in its good faith. It would have been no new or strange thing had the Roman Catholics taken advantage of a conference to attempt some surprise. At one time a hostile fleet hung out at sea opposite La Rochelle, and Henry would have nothing to do with Catharine while the Huguenot capital was threatened. At another, some Huguenot troops were attacked not without suspicion of treachery. The King of Navarre was fully determined to do nothing without consulting his associates, and to let every advance come from the other side.[2]

It was the thirteenth of December when Catharine de' Medici, having overcome a host of difficulties, at last succeeded in effecting a meeting with her distrustful son-in-law at the castle of Saint Bris, not far from Cognac.[3] Henry, who had been careful to come with a powerful retinue of Huguenot nobles, as a precaution against a treacherous surprise, was received by the queen mother in the presence of her ladies of honor, at the first interview, with even more

Conference between Catharine and Navarre, at Saint Bris, December.

---

[1] "J'escris à mon frère, que devant qu'elle puisse prendre conclusion, il s'en revienne en diligence en son gouvernement, qui depuis Auxonne est tout nostre, et qu'il s'asseure de Lyon, afin que nous soyons prests à empescher l'effect de telles menées." Mucius to Mendoza, September 22, 1586, De Croze, i. 319, 320.

[2] See the contemporary account "Lettre d'un gentilhomme françois à un sien ami estant à Rome, contenant le discours du voyage de la Royne Mere du Roy," in Mémoires de la Ligue, ii. 85-98.

[3] Saint Bris, Saint Brix, or Saint Brice as the name appears upon some maps, is on the northern bank of the Charente, between Cognac and Jarnac, in the present Department of Charente. Catharine de' Medici had come to Cognac attended by Nevers, Retz, Lansac, and other noblemen. The King of Navarre had advanced to Jarnac, with Turenne, La Force, and other Huguenot chiefs

than her customary demonstrations of good will. After a lavish display of embraces and caresses, however, the serious business in hand was promptly entered upon, and a lively conversation arose.

"Well, my son," said Catharine, "shall we accomplish anything of advantage?"

"It will not be my fault if we do not," answered Henry.

"That is what I wish."

"You must tell me, then, what you desire for that end."

"My desires, madam, are only the desires of your majesty."

"Let us drop this ceremony; tell me what you demand."

"Madam, I demand nothing. I am come only to receive your commands."

"So! So! Make some opening."

"Madam, there is no opening here for me." [1]

"What! Do you wish to be the cause of the ruin of this kingdom? Do you not consider that, after the king, there is no other person more interested in its preservation than you?"

"Madam, neither you nor the king has believed this to be the case; for eight armies have been set on foot with the purpose of ruining me."

"What armies, my son? You deceive yourself. Do you think that, had the king wished to ruin you, he would not have done it? The ability has not been wanting, but he has never had the will."

---

and a body of eight hundred horse and nearly two thousand foot—an escort of such strength that the queen mother is said to have been somewhat apprehensive lest her son-in-law intended to carry her off a prisoner to La Rochelle. When the interview took place at Saint Bris, about midway between the two towns, a company of fifty Roman Catholics and a company of the same number of Huguenots stood on guard at the gates, while squadrons of horse of both parties kept the field. Davila, bk. 8, p. 305. Of the nobles in Henry's suite, one or more uniformly remained outside for fear of some plot. We are not informed as to which of Catharine's ladies attended her; but we may conclude that they were neither better nor worse than those who graced the Conference of Nérac with their presence.

[1] "'Madame, il n'y a point icy d'ouverture pour moy.' Cet équivoque fut incontinent remarqué par les dames, pour un traict de la galanterie de ce prince, qui en tout temps et en toute sorte de discours, faisoit voir la vivacité de ses reparties."

"Pardon me, madam, my ruin does not depend upon men. It is neither in the king's power nor in yours."

"Are you ignorant of the king's power, and of what he can do?"

"Madam, I know well what he can do, and still better what he could not do."

"What! Will you not obey your king?"

"I have always had the will to obey him, I have desired to testify to him its effects, and I have often begged him to honor me with his commands, in order that I might, under his authority, oppose the adherents of the League, who had risen up in his kingdom, in spite of his edicts, to disturb his rest and the public tranquillity."

At this Catharine flew into a passion.

"Do not deceive yourself, my son. They are not in a league against the kingdom. They are Frenchmen. They are all the best Catholics of France, who are apprehensive of the domination of the Huguenots; and to tell you the whole matter in one word, the king knows their intentions and approves all they have done. But let us drop that subject. Talk only about your own concerns. Ask all you want; the king will grant it."

"Madam, I ask you for nothing; but if you ask anything of me, I will submit it to my friends and to those to whom I have promised to do nothing and treat of nothing without their participation."

"Very well, my son, since you will have it so, I shall say nothing farther, but that the king loves and honors you, and wishes to see you by his side, and to greet you as his good brother."

"Madam, I thank him very humbly, and I assure you that never shall I be wanting in the duty I owe him."

"But what! Will you not say anything more than that?"

"Is that not saying much?"

"Do you, then, wish to continue to be the cause of the wretchedness and, in the end, the destruction of this realm?"

"Madam, I am sure that it will never be so completely ruined but that there will always remain some little corner for me."

"But will you not obey the king? Are you not afraid that his anger may be enkindled against you?"

"Madam, I must tell you the truth: it will soon be eighteen months since I ceased obeying the king."

"Do not say that, my son!"

"Madam, I may say so; for the king, who is, as it were, my father, instead of cherishing me as his child, has waged war with me as a wolf, and as to you, madam, you have waged war against me as a lioness."

"What! Have I not always been a good mother to you?"

"Yes, madam, but that was only in my childhood; for the past six years I have noticed that your disposition is greatly changed."

"Believe me, my son, the king and I seek only your good."

"Pardon me, madam, I perceive quite the contrary."

"Let that pass, my son. Do you wish that the trouble I have taken during the past six months or thereabouts should prove fruitless, after having so long kept trifling with me?"

"Madam, I am not to blame for this. On the contrary, it is you yourself. I do not prevent you from resting in your bed, but it is you that for eighteen months have prevented me from sleeping in mine."

"What! Shall I always be put to this trouble—I who ask only for rest?"

"Madam, this trouble pleases you, and is your very food. If you were at rest, you could not live long."

"How now? Formerly I used to see you so gentle and tractable; and now I see your ire flash from your eyes, and I hear it in your words."

"Madam, it is true that repeated crosses and the annoying treatment to which you have subjected me have induced a change in me, and have made me lose my native disposition."

"Well, since you can do nothing of yourself, let us make a short truce, during which you may confer with your associates, so as to facilitate a good peace, under valid passports which will be sent to you for this purpose."

"Well, madam, I will do so."

"Do not deceive yourself, my son; you expect to have some reiters, but you will have none."

"Madam, I did not come here to receive intelligence from you."[1]

Such were the first words of Catharine and Navarre, apparently taken down at the time by someone that was present at the singular interview. They show that the Gascon prince was the equal of the cunning Italian woman in shrewdness, and not much inferior to her in prompt repartee. Of his ready wit the Duke of Nevers also had experience, when, at this same conference, he ventured to tell Henry of Navarre that he would find it to his advantage to court the favor of the King of France rather than of a mayor of La Rochelle, a city in which he had not influence enough to make an impost of a single penny in his necessity. "We understand nothing as to imposts," was the swift retort; "for we have not an Italian among us. Yet I do what I will at La Rochelle, because I will to do only what I ought."[2]

But it was not for an opportunity to display his mother-wit that the Huguenot leader had come to Saint Bris. He sought,

Catharine refuses to grant religious liberty. with little prospect of obtaining it, some way of restoring to his fellow-believers the civil and religious rights unjustly denied to them by the compact of Nemours. This, however, Catharine had not the slightest idea of conceding. She prated only of the absolute necessity of Navarre's conversion to the Roman Catholic Church, as the sole means of putting an end to the miserable conflict now raging; and she was very properly informed that she might well have spared herself, ill with the gout as she was, the trouble

---

[1] This interesting dialogue, given by Matthieu, Histoire de France soubs les regnes de François I., etc., ii. 518, etc., and reproduced by the editor of the Lettres missives de Henri IV., ii. 251-253, note, bears every mark of authenticity. The account given by Mézeray, iii. 625, which Stähelin has made use of (Der Übertritt König Heinrichs des Vierten, 95, note), is drawn from this source, but loses in vividness through the attempt to give a more modern form to the phraseology.

[2] Agrippa d'Aubigné, iii. 23. "Le Duc de Nevers osa dire, 'Sire, vous seriez mieux à faire la cour au Roi qu'au maire de la Rochelle, où vous n'avez pas le credit d'imposer un sol en vos necessitez.' La response fut, 'Nous n'entendons rien aux impositions, car il n'y a pas un Italien parmi nous; je fai à la Rochelle ce que je veux, en n'y voulant que ce que je doi.'"

of journeying so far in order to suggest an impossible solution to the problem. It was trying to remove a difficulty by means of a difficulty. "How," exclaimed the indignant king, "with so much intelligence as you possess, have you come from so great a distance to propose a thing so detested, and one respecting which I can deliberate with conscience and honor only by means of a legitimate council, to which I and my followers will submit?"[1]

There was no danger that the Huguenot king would at present make any imprudent concessions, least of all to Catharine de' Medici. In fact, it is only by remembering the strange fatuity oftentimes displayed by the most cunning of cheats, that we can account for the almost childish simplicity of the queen mother in her notion that she could again entrap the Protestants into relaxing their military preparations and countermanding levies in Germany and Switzerland, the fruit of so much patient toil. But Henry of Navarre was, as he declared himself to be, resolved to do nothing that was not for the good of the Protestant churches, and that was not by their advice and consent.[2] Smarting under the consciousness of the dishonorable manner in which the king had treated him, not without his mother's connivance and persuasions; remembering how he had remained inactive for long months in obedience to the monarch's command, and ready to fly to his assistance, and this only to be rewarded by being made the victim of a treacherous union between that monarch and the deadly enemies of the Huguenots, he could not resist the temptation to tell Catharine some sober truths. She apparently expected the peace of the state to be restored by a proscribed person, the prosperity of his native land by a man driven into banishment![3] "Madam," said he, with pardonable bitterness, "you can accuse me of no fault but an excess of fidelity. As for myself, I do not com-

---

[1] "De laquelle je ne puis deliberer avec conscience et honneur, que par un legitime Concile, auquel nous nous soumettrons moi et les miens." Agrippa d'Aubigné, iii. 23.

[2] Henry of Navarre to M. de Scorbiac, December 27, 1586. Lettres missives, ii. 251.

[3] Agrippa d'Aubigné, ubi supra.

plain of your faith, but I do bewail your age, which, by weakening your memory, makes you forget easily your promises to me."[1]

Despite the King of Navarre's firm attitude with regard to a change of religion, it cannot, however, be denied that he left the impression upon Catharine de' Medici and upon others that, but for certain difficulties in the way, the Huguenot leader would very cheerfully make the change demanded of him. It may well be that the sentiments now to be recorded were really opinions gained from Catharine herself; for the writer, Filippo Cavriana, of Mantua, besides being a secret agent of the Medicis, was a physician, apparently in attendance upon the queen mother during her last illness, two years after the period now under consideration.[2] However this may be, the observing writer, within sixty days from the interviews at Saint Bris, wrote thus for the benefit of the Florentine government: "The King of Navarre would like to be a Catholic; but he fears that, situated as he is, the Catholics would ridicule his conversion, and that he would have to work miracles before they would believe him to be a Catholic in very deed. If then the present king were to die in this interval, Navarre would not become king, and would find himself deprived of the support of many by means of whom he can now render himself formidable to his enemies. This is the most

The possibility of Navarre's conversion.

---

[1] "Lettre d'un gentilhomme françois," Mémoires de la Ligue, ii. 90. Besides the authorities already quoted, see the Mémoires de Sully, c. 22 ; Péréfixe, Histoire du Roy Henry le Grand (ed. of 1662), 61–63 ; Matthieu, Histoire des derniers troubles, fols. 33, 34 ; Davila, bk. 8, 305–307 ; the articles of the truce of fifteen days (December 19, 1586), Mémoires de la Ligue, ii. 209, 210; Henry of Navarre's circular account sent out to the Huguenots in the different provinces, dated La Rochelle, December 29, 1586, ibid., ii. 211–215. Whether Catharine was better pleased than most women would have been, to be reminded of her advancing years, does not appear. It will be remembered that, having been born April 13, 1519, the queen mother was now in her sixty-eighth year. See Comte de la Ferrière, Lettres de Catherine de Médicis (Paris, 1880), i., introd., pp. i., ii.

[2] Négociations avec la Toscane (remarks of the editor, M. Desjardins), iv. 602. Compare Cavriana's own account of Henry III.'s visit to his mother's apartments after the murder of the Duke of Guise, ibid., iv. 842.

powerful reason that tends to make him hard and obstinate in his opinion."¹

Even such writers as applaud the subsequent defection of the Béarnais from the faith in which he was reared, and style his signal act of hypocrisy " a satisfaction given to France and the earnest of a new compact between the nation and his race," are compelled to agree with the Florentine Cavriana that had Henry yielded to the persuasions of the King of France, either at this time or when, a year or two earlier, Épernon was sent to solicit his conversion, that conversion would have been ill-timed and perilous. And one of Navarre's own descendants, who, in our own days, has given to the world a history of the princes of Condé, does not conceal his opinion that, if his great ancestor had been induced by Henry the Third's threats abruptly and prematurely to accomplish the great act that was hereafter, forsooth, to put an end to the long prevailing discord in France, he would only have reaped ruin and dishonor for his reward. No disturbance would have been quieted, no hatred allayed, not a soldier of his small army would have remained with him.²

The heroic struggle in which the Huguenots were engaged was well fitted to throw into bold relief a self-devotion that knew no bounds to its sacrifices save the demands of the great cause of religious liberty to which they had consecrated all their power and all their material resources. It must not, however, be forgotten that the followers of the holiest of standards are after all but men, upon whose conduct, conscientious as may be their motives, the circumstances of birth, station, and education are wont to exert a notable influence. The Protestant soldier looked upon the course of events from a very different point of observation from the civilian, and the inhabitants of the southern towns, bred to suspicion of their neighbors, and taught by

---

¹ "Il re di Navarre vorebbe essere cattolico; ma teme che, come egli lo sia, questi altri non se ne burlino, e che convenga far miracoli innanzi che si creda da loro che lo sia da dovero; e se in questo mentre il Re morisse, egli non sarebbe re, e si troverebbe privo dell' appoggio di molti, coi quali può dare da fare ai suoi nemici." Letter of Cavriana, February 16, 1587, ibid., iv. 675.

² Duc d'Aumale, Histoire des Princes de Condé, ii. 141-143.

the fortunes of war to look for protection mainly to their own strong arms and to the massiveness of their fortifications, entertained a distrust, which was far from being unnatural, of garrisons composed even of soldiers of their own party. The experience of François de Châtillon, at Milhau, throws light upon the divergent views and the prejudices that might be entertained by fellow-combatants equally interested in a common warfare.

<small>Huguenot distrust of garrisons.</small>

No city of France was more thoroughly Protestant than Milhau-en-Rouergue, situated on the upper waters of the river Tarn. It was the same place which had declared, at the close of the first civil war, that there was not a man, woman, or child within its walls desirous of the restoration of the papal mass—the same Milhau that boasted that, were the churches to be restored to the Roman Catholics, in accordance with the terms of the Edict of Amboise, no one could be found to take possession of them.[1] More than once had the political assemblies of the Huguenots been convened within its friendly and hospitable enclosure. Such honors, and, perhaps, a natural pride arising from the prolonged enjoyment of security in the midst of prevailing disorder and violence, engendered a feeling of self-sufficiency, and fostered a sensitiveness that would have been more appropriate in the case of an independent republic. It is true that the citizens were deeply moved by the tidings of the approach of the king's forces, and urgently called upon Châtillon to grant them the services of an engineer well versed in the important art of building and strengthening fortifications. The consuls and other leading inhabitants went even farther, and thrice despatched envoys to beg the brave son of Admiral Coligny to accept the post of governor of Rouergue, and to assure him of their hearty esteem and confidence. But when once Châtillon had come in the capacity of lieutenant-general of the King of Navarre, and had brought with him the force of arquebusiers they had themselves solicited, the citizens speedily changed their minds. The Huguenot soldier was a less inviting object near at hand than

<small>François de Châtillon and Milhau-en-Rouergue.</small>

---

[1] Rise of the Huguenots, ii. 147.

when seen at a distance. As this soldier, moreover, had to be fed and lodged, enthusiasm gave place to coldness, and gratitude to disgust. Just in proportion to his wealth, the burgher was reluctant to open his door to the unwelcome guest, and it was said that the well-to-do were quite willing that the heaviest part of the burden of entertainment should be borne by the poor. To Châtillon's suggestion that, in view of the scarcity of provisions, the citizens should be required to make a common store of the wheat in their private granaries, the consuls returned an answer savoring strongly of insolence. They informed him that they were no minor wards in need of a guardian, but could manage their own affairs without his assistance. But most was their ire aroused when Châtillon, being unable to spare so large a part of his forces for Milhau, now out of actual danger, undertook to put the royal castle which stood in the place in a condition to resist, with a diminished garrison, any sudden attack of the enemy. The cry was heard on all sides that Châtillon was erecting a "citadel"—that very instrument of tyranny against whose erection in other cities the Protestants of France had again and again protested. Conjecture made way for certainty in the minds of the people, when Châtillon politely declined, as a lieutenant acting in Navarre's name, to intrust the guard of the stronghold to a company of citizen soldiers, who, as he shrewdly suspected, would be likely to take advantage of the first opportunity afforded by the temporary absence of the arquebusiers on duty elsewhere, to close the gates of the city against their return. At length, the popular ferment ran so high that one winter's morning (the third of January, 1587), Châtillon himself being away, the tocsin was violently rung. At the preconcerted signal the whole city rose as one man. Workmen rushed into the streets armed with what tools they could lay hands on. Women brandished spits and other domestic utensils. Even children provided themselves, as best they could, with sticks and stones. In a moment the few straggling soldiers found in the public thoroughfares were overpowered. The mob, surging on toward the obnoxious castle, then demanded its surrender. The single officer in command and his followers, numbering scarcely more than seven or eight, and without store of provisions or hope of speedy relief, dared not attempt to hold out. The evacuation was effected, however, with as much formality as if the parties to the transaction had been deadly enemies, instead of Huguenots battling for the same great principles. Many hands now made light work of the destruction of all Châtillon's new works, and that night the satisfied citizens of Milhau went to their beds proud of the fact that no " citadel " any longer menaced their freedom. A day or two later, a town meeting, called, according to custom, by the ringing of the bells, resolved, after due deliberation, that inasmuch as the thing had been accomplished, the King of Navarre should be requested to approve of the result and restore matters to their old condition. The consuls of Milhau took great pains to impress upon Henry and their fellow Protestants throughout the kingdom the justice of their cause and the magnitude of the insults to which they had been subjected. They failed, however, to convince impartial men that the son of the great martyr of Saint Bartholomew's Day had grievously erred; and an assembly of the churches of Languedoc, which met soon after in Nismes, gravely censured the fault committed by the citizens of Milhau.[1]

The "citadel" demolished.

---

[1] See "Discours veritable des actions et comportemens de M. de Chastillon pendant le temps qu'il a esté à Milhau-en-Rouergue, et de la sedition que les consuls et habitans auroient esmeue à l'encontre de lui," in Mémoires de Duplessis Mornay, iii. 434–452. This account, which is altogether favorable to Châtillon, may profitably be compared with a number of documents recently brought to light by Loutchitzky, and printed in his Documents inédits pour servir à l'histoire de la Réforme et de la Ligue, 195–216. These papers present the strongest points of the case for the citizens. In particular, the document entitled "Articles presentés par les consuls de Millau aux Estats de Rouergue convoqués par Mr. de Chastillon, gouverneur du pais pour le Roy de Navarre, sur la citadelle qu'il faisoit faire en ladite ville, 1586," denounced the building of the citadel as a mark of dishonor, since it reduced the burghers to a servile condition, and as an evidence of Châtillon's disregard of the oath he had taken to preserve their privileges, prerogatives, and accustomed liberties under all preceding kings. See, also, Count Jules Delaborde's monograph, François de Chastillon, 255, 256.

CHAPTER VII.

THE BATTLE OF COUTRAS, AND THE ARMY OF THE REITERS.

THE first eighteen months of the war had been barren enough of stirring incident. The great military demonstrations of Henry and the League had come to nothing. The Huguenots were fully as strong as they had been when the unrighteous Edict of Nemours was promulgated, and certainly much less dispirited. Having lost by apostasy the timid and wavering, those who remained constant were more than ever determined to accept no peace save one that recognized their religion and permitted its exercise. On the other hand, had resolutions to the effect that there should be but one religion in France been of any avail, the fate of Protestantism would have been finally settled. At the beginning of the new year, the knights of the Order of the Holy Ghost went through the farce of passing such a resolution, prompted thereto by the king, who himself promised to take horse and lead against the heretics. Instead of which, for the present, his Very Christian majesty confined his activity to making a round of the various monasteries and other religious houses, in the course of which the public was astonished, if, indeed, any puerile action on Henry's part had longer the power to excite surprise, at seeing him successively donning the costume of each community.[1] Not to the

The war accomplishes nothing.

---

[1] Journal d'un curé ligueur (Jehan de la Fosse), 204, under the date of January 9, 1587. Davila, 308, concedes that the king's declaration appeared to many persons, then and subsequently, absurd and contradictory, as coming from a prince who, by means of the queen mother, was, or had been only a few days before, treating with these same "heretics" that were to be exterminated; but the Italian historian will have it that the declaration was opportune, since thereby "he at once beat down all the complaints and calumnies of the heads of the League, and appeased in great part, at least for a time, the minds of

knights of the order alone did the king give pious assurances. Again he assembled in the Louvre a select company of some of the presidents of parliament, the prévôt des marchands, and other officials, whom he informed of his intention to push the war against the Protestants to the direst extremity, and of his expectation to be able to crush them within the next two years. His sentiments of loyalty to the Roman Catholic faith were duly applauded by his hearers, who, despite their previous experiences of the same kind, may not have been prepared on the instant for the modest demand which the king proceeded at once to make, of six hundred thousand livres for the purpose of prosecuting the war.[1]

Meantime his majesty had gained nothing in the esteem and confidence of the adherents of the League, who were convinced —and they were quite right—that he was very willing to have the power of his rebellious subjects broken, even if this had to be done by means of an army of reiters such as John Casimir was known to be getting ready in Germany for the benefit of the Huguenots of France. In Paris the turbulent Roman Catholics were prepared to adopt the most desperate measures;

The zeal of the League at Paris.

and, much to the annoyance of the Duke of Guise, his brother, the Duke of Mayenne, encouraged them in these inopportune and premature ventures. At one time it was proposed to surprise the king as he should ride through the Rue Saint Antoine, on his way from the Bois de Vincennes to the Louvre. At another, the scene of the execution of the conspiracy was to be the dining-hall of the abbey in the faubourg of Saint Germain, when the monarch should have repaired thither to attend the fair. What was to be done with him when his person should be secured, was the next question, and it was answered in various ways. A king is a troublesome prisoner to have in one's possession, and some were in favor of at once falling upon him and killing him; while others would have

---

the Parisians." Davila seems to have forgotten that, within the next sixty days, the Parisians were, as we shall see presently, conspiring against the king's liberty, if not against his life.

[1] Lestoile, under date of January 10, 1587, i. 214; Mémoires de Henry III., 98.

been content to shut him up in a monastery. But the conspirators were, happily or unhappily, spared the trouble of deciding; for Henry's trusty spy, Nicholas Poulain, reported each plot in ample time for his majesty to guard against it.[1] As for Mayenne and his fellow-conspirators, they found it no easy matter to excuse themselves to Guise for their breach of faith in not remaining quiet according to their engagement to him; and were only too glad to beg his pardon and give renewed assurances of their undying confidence in his leadership, and of their hope of success under so brave a captain.[2]

<small>Annoyance of the Duke of Guise.</small>

The year opened well for the Huguenot arms. Success attended the enterprises of the King of Navarre in the west, not less than those of Lesdiguières in the east. The former, overcoming the timid counsels of the burghers of La Rochelle—satisfied, for the most part, if they could hold the neighborhood of their own walls—did not rest content till he had extended the boundaries of the district in which the Huguenots had the upper hand by the capture of such important towns of Poitou as Fontenay-le-Comte, Saint Maixent, and Talmont, not to speak of other places of less note.[3] In Dauphiny, on the other hand, brave Lesdiguières added yet more to his well-earned laurels by a series of captures stretching with little interruption through the summer, the natural result of the pains taken by that careful general in spending the first three months of the year in a personal inspection of the province.[4] It is true that no vigilance of his

<small>Huguenot successes in Poitou.</small>

<small>Lesdiguières in Dauphiny.</small>

---

[1] "Le Procez verbal d'un nommé Nicolas Poulain," in Mémoires de Henry III., 155-165; Letter of Cavriana, March 3, 1587, in Négociations avec la Toscane, iv. 676, etc.; Lestoile, i. 215, 216. See De Thou, vi. 727, etc.; De Croze, ii. 3, etc.

[2] "Monsieur de Guise," says Poulain (ubi supra, 165), " estant averty de l'entreprise du Duc de Mayenne, en fut fort courroucé contre ceux de la Ligue : de fait il leur envoya le Sieur de Mayneville, pour sçavoir qui les avoit meus de ce faire . . . qu'ils sçavoient ce qu'il leur avoit promis, s'ils ne s'asseuroient pas assez sur sa foi ; et finalement qu'ils eussent à dire, s'ils estoient entrez en quelque soupçon et defiance de luy."

[3] Lestoile, i. 225 ; Agrippa d'Aubigné, iii. 37-40.

[4] Agrippa d'Aubigné, iii. 33, etc.; De Thou, vii. 53, 54. See, especially, the report sent to Henry of Navarre, entitled "Mémoires de ce qui s'est passé en Daulphiné, depuis le mois d'Avril, jusques au vingtiesme de Decembre,

could prevent the surprise of the important city of Montélimart, on the left bank of the Rhône below Valence, one Sunday morning in August; but the Huguenots held the castle of the place, and, instead of abandoning hope, promptly took measures to recover what they had lost. On Wednesday morning of the same week, a little force of two hundred Protestant cuirassiers, and perhaps a thousand men carrying the arquebuse, who had been gathered from far and near, at the news of the disaster, made a furious assault upon the barricades of the enemy. Nor did they prove unequal to the perilous enterprise. The works were carried, and the Huguenots did not stay their impetuous valor before they had slain of their antagonists almost twice their own number. The hero in this action, if, indeed, all that took part were not entitled to be termed heroes, was the Baron du Poët, to whose sagacious planning and bold execution was due the success of the enterprise, with the capture of a large number of noblemen of distinction, at the loss of scarcely more than a score of killed and one hundred and twenty wounded.[1] But if the adventure

---

1587," reprinted in Mémoires de la Ligue, ii. 221-227 ; as well as a royalist account printed at Paris, by Guillaume Linocier, with privilege of the king, September 21, 1587, ibid., ii. 227-229.

[1] "Veritablement ce fut un œuvre de Dieu, et toutesfois ne peut estre desnié à la valleur, diligence, et sage conduitte du sieur du Poet, gouverneur de laditte place (comme à l'instrument principal) cest heureux exploit : ayant avec si petit nombre de gens de guerre (à sçavoir environ douze cens hommes), forcé plus de trois mil hommes de combat, preparez et logez avantageusement dedans leurs barricades, flanquées et deffendues en front par trois pieces de canon." Mémoires de ce qui s'est passé en Daulphiné, etc., ubi supra, ii. 224. Du Poët, a noted Protestant leader of Dauphiny, during the greater part of the second half of the sixteenth century, is a personage the more interesting as the nobleman to whom are addressed two letters purporting to come from the pen of the reformer Calvin, which, after having been quoted without question as genuine originals by Voltaire, Audin, Capefigue, and others, M. Jules Bonnet (Lettres françaises de Calvin, ii. 588-595) has proved to be the most patent of forgeries. The handwriting is not Calvin's, nor that of his secretary ; the style is as harsh and turgid as the style of the Genevese reformer was graceful and forcible, and anachronisms abound. In short, these productions have nothing to commend them to the acceptance of the most partial enemy of Calvin, save that they represent him as truculently uttering the sentiment respecting perverse Roman Catholic preachers that "such monsters ought

of Montélimart proved that a small army of Huguenots might, under good leaders, overcome and destroy a force of Roman Catholics far superior in numbers, an incident, which is said to have occurred on the very day of the recapture of the town, demonstrated with equal clearness that a handful of Roman Catholic soldiers might rout and cut to pieces an entire battalion of Protestants. The scene of the defeat was in Dauphiny, and the victims were a body of Swiss, variously stated at three or at four thousand men, accompanied by an escort of four or five hundred French troops, whom Vezins and Cugy were bringing to the help of Lesdiguières. The instruments in their destruction were Bernard de la Valette, brother of the Duke of Épernon, and not more than five hundred arquebusiers, supported by four companies of cavalry. Twelve hundred prisoners sent to work on the fortifications of Valence, and nine or ten standards forwarded to the king at Paris, testified to the reality of the exploit of the royal troops, at a period when many a victory loudly proclaimed at the capital existed only in the imagination of romancers.[1] What rendered the defeat of the Swiss the more remarkable was that it took place on a spot in every way favorable for infantry, and where the enemy could scarcely have approached them with any more serious intent than to reconnoitre. "Surely," writes the pious chronicler, "God makes numbers and arms to be good for just so much as it pleases Him."[2]

Rout of Swiss auxiliaries.

Meanwhile the condition of things at Paris was such as to

to be smothered (étouffés) as I have done here, in the execution of Michael Servetus, a Spaniard!"

[1] The Protestant and Roman Catholic accounts agree remarkably well, although there is some discrepancy in figures. See Mémoires de la Ligue, ii. 224, 228. De Thou, vii. (book 88) 55, displays his usual impartiality. Agrippa d'Aubigné's account (iii. 34) is too brief to be satisfactory.

[2] "Dieu fait comme il lui plaist valoir le nombre et les armes." Mémoires de la Ligue, ii. 225. The defeat of the Swiss took place, according to Agrippa d'Aubigné, iii. 34, "près d'Uriage;" or, according to De Thou, following the account in the Mémoires de la Ligue, on the banks of the Isère and Drac—that is, at the confluence of these two streams—near the city of Grenoble (Isère). St. Martin d'Uriage is a village of over two thousand inhabitants five miles east of Grenoble, and Uriage is at present a station upon the Lyons and Chambéry railway.

perplex the most clear-headed of statesmen; not that they were in doubt as to what ought to be done, but that they could not divine what would be done. The great difficulty was that the king did not know his own mind for twenty-four hours together. Whatever qualities of his mother he had failed to inherit, there was no question that her vacillation had been fully transmitted to him. With two such unstable characters at the helm of state, it became a matter of perfect uncertainty toward which point of the compass the course would next be directed. To this it must be added that Catharine was strongly suspected of perfidy to the king, and of being as untrue to him as she was to the Guises. "There are those that believe," wrote the Italian Cavriana, employing an expressive proverb of his countrymen, "that in her eagerness to have the control of affairs, the queen mother slyly gives a blow now to the cask, now to the hoop."[1] Under these circumstances men knew not what to do. Those who would have preferred to follow his service faithfully, seeing so much irresolution in Henry of Valois, feared that when they should have rendered themselves hateful to the Guises by some open act of loyalty, they might be abandoned to the mercy of these pitiless enemies by the shifting policy of the monarch. And yet, had Henry chosen to pursue a manly course, he had still a following strong enough to defeat the intrigues of the League. As the picture is painted by a contemporary, the king could count upon the support of three Bourbon princes—Soissons, Conty, and Montpensier; upon such great nobles as Nevers, Longueville, Biron, Aumont, Matignon, and Épernon; upon the public magistrates, the parliaments, the wealthy holders of lands, the old military captains, the men of ripe thought and experience, and even a part of the clergy—possibly a few among the Jesuits themselves, who began to recognize the fact that the League was likely to prove disastrous to France. On the other hand, Guise had at his devotion the inferior people—the mob—the

---

[1] "Anzi c'è chi crede ch'ella, per avere il maneggio delle cose, dia un colpo alla botte e l'altro al cerchio."

needy part of the population and outlaws from society, the inhabitants of the towns, some governors of strongholds, and, as was believed, the king's mother and his wife, together with almost the entire clergy. It was needless to add the Spanish ambassador, who was the prime mover and counsellor of the plot. What might not have been expected, was that it included Brûlart, one of the king's own secretaries of state, Villequier, his former tutor, and René de Birague, L'Hospital's unworthy successor in the office of chancellor. Such was the depth of meanness to which some of the highest functionaries of state had descended, encouraged thereto doubtless by the example of Catharine. But there was good reason to expect that this princess, if not the imitators of her double-dealing, would come to grief. She had lost none of her assurance; she was just as confident as ever that she would be able by her intrigues to make Huguenots and Leaguers take up arms and lay them down again at her pleasure. "But the Huguenots, already cheated three or four times by her words and artifices, are no longer willing to believe her in any wise, and it is precisely so also with Guise."[1]

Indeed, the duke had recently given conclusive proof of the fact that he had passed beyond the reach of the influence both of Catharine de' Medici and of her promising son and pupil in the art of dissimulation.

One Saturday, toward the end of May, the queen mother had had an interview with Guise at Fère-en-Tardenois.[2] Catharine began with her accustomed blandishments. Feigning ignorance of the reasons of the duke's discontent, she assured him that her son the king was very strongly disposed to advance him more than ever, knowing that he had not a more faithful subject nor one that was more worthy of being intrusted with great offices of state. "In short," says the account which Guise sent to Mendoza, "she

The queen mother's interview with Guise. May, 1587.

---

[1] See the instructive letters of Cavriana of June 24 and July 5, 1587, in Négociations avec la Toscane, iv. 693-699.

[2] In the southern part of the present department of Aisne, between Château-Thierry and Rheims.

thrice addressed to him such language, and thrice resorted to such artifices as are represented to us in the Gospel: 'Hæc omnia tibi dabo '—' All these things will I give thee, if thou wilt fall down and worship me.' " The faithful chronicler does not tell us that the redoubtable duke answered his tempter, " Get thee hence, Satan;" but none the less was he proof against her seductions. " Madam," said he, " I have always been honored by the favors and gifts of the king. I have always tried to respect his commands and employ my life in their execution. I have no cause of discontent for myself individually. But let us come to the public interests, to which I protest I have altogether devoted myself." When, however, the concerns of state were taken up, an irreconcilable diversity of opinion was developed. The seizure of the king's cities in Picardy and elsewhere, which Catharine complained of, demanding their restitution, the duke justified as a meritorious act which he stood ready to defend with his own life. In fact, the queen mother had nothing for her pains but the sorry privilege of listening to a repetition of the old story of the grievances to which the good Catholics of France were subjected, and the indignities shown to their religion.[1]

About a month later, the queen mother procured a meeting between Henry of Valois and Henry of Guise, at Meaux. The king met his rival very graciously, and even condescended to entreat him to turn his mind only to peace, and to prevent the kingdom from becoming a prey to the devastations of war. He told him that he was himself resolved to tolerate but one religion in France, and yet that, under the present necessity, he hoped to buy a good peace and turn aside the foreign troops from entering his dominions. But Guise would hear of no peace, and begged his majesty to remember only that religion was in its death-throes. He complained of the maltreatment of good Catholic cities and leaders. The king was able to meet these statements by counter reproaches of the usurpation of the royal prerogative and other

Meeting between the king and the Duke of Guise.

---

[1] " Entrevue de la Reine Mère avec le Duc de Guise à Reims," dated May 25, 1587; being an account drawn up at Guise's command, sent by him to Mendoza, and by Mendoza to Philip II. in a despatch of June 9. De Croze, ii. 284-286.

acts of insubordination. When the duke undertook to reply, the king cut him short, and led him into another room, where the farce ended with a pretended reconciliation between Guise and Épernon, who embraced each other so affectionately that they might have been mistaken for the best friends in the world.[1] Nor was it wonderful that Henry of Guise would not listen to the suggestion of peace. Overwhelmed with debt, and every month becoming more and more involved, it was out of the question for him to pause in the work upon which he had been incited by Philip the Second to enter, but for the prosecution of which that penurious monarch, through his ambassador, furnished him very scantily the needful funds.[2] The treasuries of Venice and Florence, with the treasury of the pope superadded, would scarcely have been sufficient to free the good duke from his load of obligations.[3]

The duke's debts.

Meanwhile the war both in the east and in the west gave signs of becoming more decisive than it had hitherto been. Early in the spring the Duke of Joyeuse led a large army in the direction of the King of Navarre, and the latter prudently retreated before the superior force to the walls of La Rochelle. The duke thereupon proceeded to retake certain places which had fallen into Huguenot hands—Saint Maixent, Tonnay Charente, and Maillezais, but distinguished himself less by the brilliancy of his exploits than by the ferocity in which he permitted his soldiers to indulge. A Protestant minister, M. de la Jarrière, who was discovered among the soldiers of the garrison of Saint Maixent, as they were leaving the place after the capitulation, was by his orders ignominiously executed—a needless act of cruelty toward a person of recognized excellence of character, which was far from conciliating the favor of the Protestants to whom he had long been a faithful

Joyeuse marches toward Guyenne.

---

[1] Lestoile, i. 226, 227, gives the date of July 2 to the interview of Meaux; Cavriana, in his letter of July 5, makes it to have been held two days later, ubi supra, iv. 703. See Guise to Mendoza, July 4, 1587, De Croze, ii. 295.

[2] Mendoza gave him "danari assai scarsamente per intertenere il fuoco acceso già in Francia." Ibid., iv. 691.

[3] "Il buon duca di Guise è talmente indebitato, che l'erario di Venezia, del Papa e il vostro insieme gli sarebbe necessario." Ibid., ubi supra.

pastor, or from commending itself to the approval of the Roman Catholics who heard his firm and Christian profession of his faith and the touching prayer he offered before his death. Nor was this all. On one occasion two hundred Huguenot soldiers who, with their comrades, had been compelled to surrender, were ruthlessly put to the sword; on another, a number of prisoners were stripped naked, after the capture of the town they had bravely defended, that the troops of Joyeuse might have the exquisite pleasure of slashing their unprotected bodies with sword and cutlass. It is by no means certain, in the conflict of statements, that in either case there was a direct breach of faith on the part of the victors; there is, unfortunately, however, no doubt that the massacre was in both cases without excuse and perpetrated in cold blood. The incidents were not forgotten by the Huguenot soldiers a few months later on the field of Coutras.[1] It is true that the duke justified his savage action, when asked by a Huguenot somewhat later for his reasons, by referring to the demands of the times; but most readers will consider the justification as bad as the offence. "The object of as many of us as want to have our share in the ruins of the kingdom," said Joyeuse, " is, above all things, to be preached about in the pulpits of Paris, and in other notable quarters in which the Duke of Guise manages his business. Now this act, which I acknowledge to you pained my heart, suits the taste of our preachers more than a battle won with great peril in which some gentleness might have been practised."[2]

[1] "Ce fut un article qui ne servit guère au duc à Coutras." Recueil des choses mémorables, 640. See the account in the Mémoires de la Ligue, ii. 72, 73; Agrippa d'Aubigné, iii. 41, 43; De Thou, vii. (book 87) 4-6. It is Agrippa d'Aubigné (who always exhibits a soldier's unwillingness to give credit to stories of treachery in war) that denies that there had been given to the garrison of La Mothe Saint Heray, any promise that their lives would be spared, and implies the same with reference to the band of Protestant soldiers at Croix Chapeaux. The first-named place is not, as Browning erroneously states (ii. 139), the same as La Mothe Achard, in Vendée, but a small town near Saint Maixent. The distance between the two places is fully seventy miles. Croix Chapeaux is situated close to La Rochelle. See the map of the neighborhood of La Rochelle in Arcère, Histoire de La Rochelle.

[2] The authority for this strange admission is D'Aubigné (iii. 44), to whom it was made.

With such ignoble victories to boast of, Joyeuse thought it best to hurry back to the capital, fearing lest too long an absence from the monarch over whose mind he had gained such ascendancy might endanger the permanence of his influence. A month or two later, however, convinced that only by some exploit could he make good his position at court, he returned to the southwest, resolved, so he said, to bring on a general engagement with the King of Navarre, and either conquer or die.[1]

The Béarnais had left the walls of La Rochelle and advanced to the southern bank of the Loire. The movement was made for the purpose of facilitating the escape of the Count of Soissons. This nobleman and the Prince of Conty were younger brothers of Condé, but, unlike Condé,

<small>The Count of Soissons and the Prince of Conty join Navarre.</small>

had been brought up in the Roman Catholic faith, and had long resided at court. Dissatisfied as they now were with the course of events, their cousin, the King of Navarre, had found it easy to induce them to abandon a side whose success would inevitably lead to the ruin of the head of their house. Conty, the elder but feebler of the two, contrived to make his way to Strasbourg, where he was to discharge the important functions formerly so well discharged by Condé; while Soissons, who wished to serve under Navarre's standard in the approaching conflict, had advanced as far as Montsoreau, on the Loire. Here, with the help of Turenne, he was able to cross the stream and to bring a considerable body of Huguenots from the north to re-enforce the King of Navarre's army.

It was the purpose of the Huguenot leader, after having formed this union, to turn his face once more toward Gascony, there to strengthen himself by gathering fresh troops, and then to march boldly in the direction of the great auxiliary army of Germans and Swiss, whose adventures will soon have to be considered in detail. Marshal Matignon, commanding for the King of France in the neighborhood of Bordeaux, had correctly read the Huguenot scheme, and, in order to prevent its execution, entreated the Duke of Joyeuse to press rapidly forward. He promised to meet him on the

<small>Navarre marches toward the Dordogne.</small>

---

[1] De Thou, vii. (book 87) 8, 9.

banks of the Dordogne with an additional body of four thousand men. The united forces would greatly outnumber the army of Navarre, and effectually block his return to Gascony. The duke, having accepted the plan, hastened forward to put it into execution. Thus it happened that while the King of Navarre, after tarrying at La Rochelle to mount the two cannon that constituted his entire artillery, was pushing southward through Archiac and Montlieu, the Duke of Joyeuse, leaving Poitiers far in the rear, found himself but a few miles east of the Huguenot king, at Barbezieux and Chalais. The objective point of both generals was the same. Both wished to arrive first at Coutras, a small town between the little rivers Dronne and Isle, just above their junction, through which Henry must almost of necessity pass in order to reach Bergerac and the rendezvous of the Gascon Huguenots.

Either because of its more compact form and smaller numbers, or because of the superior energy and sagacity of its leader, the Protestant army outstripped its rival, and late on the afternoon of the nineteenth of October reached the northern bank of the Dronne. Before night had set in, all Henry's troops, with the exception of a part of his infantry, had safely crossed, and were quartered in the town. Meanwhile Joyeuse had leisurely crossed the river higher up, and stopped for the night at La Roche Chalais, in profound ignorance that Navarre had placed himself in front of him with the intention of disputing his advance. Indeed, the duke, somewhat to the surprise of his own officers, openly expressed his contempt for Navarre and Condé, whose forces he expected to swallow up in the first encounter. It was, therefore, with peculiar satisfaction that, having surprised a body of four Huguenot guards, he received from one of the men, who was taken alive, the following reply to his inquiries: "The King of Navarre is so determined to fight that he will await an engagement with firm foot; and he is not far distant now." "Give me your hand," said the duke to the Huguenot soldier. "You have brought me such welcome tidings that I cannot thank you sufficiently save by giving you your liberty, as I now do." Whereupon he dismissed him, but not before he had

He takes position at Coutras.

made him sit down and eat with him, and had given him a small sum of money.[1]

That night the Huguenots slept undisturbed in Coutras, or encamped about it; while the Duke of Joyeuse, apparently fearing lest the heretics might steal away before affording him a chance to attack them, set his army in motion at eleven o'clock, having despatched his cavalry an hour earlier. The distance to be traversed was about twelve miles; the darkness prevented the column from advancing except by the highway, and the road was muddy. It was daybreak before the Roman Catholic troops appeared before Coutras, worn with a night march upon which they had been harassed by the small body of light horse which Navarre had thrown forward about five miles, to the hamlet of Les Pointures, to skirmish and fall back slowly upon the main force.

After rejecting the spot which Turenne at first selected for the engagement, Henry had assumed another somewhat nearer Coutras. No position could have been more happily chosen. Across a plain that might measure six or seven hundred paces in breadth the Huguenot line was drawn in the form of a crescent, the centre somewhat in advance of the two wings. On the left was the Dronne and a small wood marking the course of a tributary brook, the Pallard. On the right were the park and warren of a stately castle built by Marshal Lautrec, that brave but unfortunate general of Francis the First who had lost his life before Naples almost sixty years before. Navarre himself held the centre with a body of three hundred men-at-arms, with Condé on his right and Soissons on his left in command of squadrons of nearly equal size. Beyond Condé was the Gascon cavalry under Turenne and the light horse of Trémouille. The infantry was posted chiefly on the wings; but in every gap between the different squadrons of horse stood a square of twenty-five arquebusiers, with strict orders on no account to fire until the enemy should come within twenty paces of them. The whole

The Huguenot line.

---

[1] I take this incident from Cavriana's long and interesting letter of November 1, 1587, in Négociations avec la Toscane, iv. 725, 726.

Huguenot army might number about five thousand five hundred men. The army of the Duke of Joyeuse was seven thousand strong. Here, too, the infantry occupied the wings, while opposite to the three Bourbon princes were marshalled the twelve hundred lancers of the duke himself and the five hundred men-at-arms of Montigny—together constituting the flower of the Roman Catholic nobles. Never, said an eye-witness, had there been seen in France a body so resplendent with ornaments of gold and glittering tinsel. Lavardin's four hundred light horse stood next, opposite to Turenne's position.

The action began with the artillery. Strange to say, the pieces of the Huguenots, so contemptible in number, did great execution, mowing down whole lines of bedizened knights, while the seven cannon of the enemy were so badly situated that upon the Protestant side scarcely a man was struck. Then it was that, unable to keep his troops steady under the murderous fire, Joyeuse gave Lavardin permission to charge. The attack was successful. Turenne's Gascon cavalry were broken in a moment, and the victorious Roman Catholics pursued their course unchecked even into the very streets of Coutras. The infantry on their left was not so fortunate in an assault upon the regiments of Protestant foot posted in the castle's grounds, and was easily repulsed. This was, however, but the prelude of the main action. The Gascons, so far as they could be rallied, and the troopers of Trémouille took position behind Condé. What the day would accomplish was evidently going to depend upon the reception which the Bourbon princes should give to Joyeuse and Montigny.

Battle of Coutras, October 20, 1587.

As the signal was sounded for the Roman Catholic lancers to advance, the King of Navarre called upon the Huguenot ministers who accompanied his army—Gabriel d'Amours, his own favorite preacher, and the not less distinguished La Roche Chandieu—to offer up a prayer for the blessing of Heaven upon the royal cause. D'Amours stood near the Béarnais. At the sound of his voice, raised in fervent petition according to the simple fashion of the Church of Geneva, every soldier prostrated himself with as much devotion as if he had been worshipping in the quiet of

Gabriel d'Amours offers prayer.

his own home, or with the company of his fellow Protestants in the crowded "temple," and not upon the open field and in full view of the scoffing enemies of his faith. The trooper had leaped from the saddle and, with bridle in hand, knelt side by side with the arquebusier. To the noblemen in the opposed ranks, men who, for the most part, had known little of Huguenot prayer or of Huguenot warfare, the spectacle was novel, and admitted but of one explanation : it must be that the Protestants, overcome with fright, were preparing for craven submission or for flight. "Par la mort Dieu!" cried some of the knights about Joyeuse. "The cowards are trembling! They are making their confession!" "Monsieur," interposed one of their own number who had enjoyed better opportunities for becoming acquainted with the characteristics of the foe, addressing his warning to the Duke of Joyeuse, "Monsieur, when the Huguenots act after that fashion, they are prepared to fight hard." The assertion was fully borne out by the sequel, and the survivors of Coutras, flying to other parts of France, carried with them wonderful stories of the magical effect produced by Gabriel d'Amours' potent petitions. Years afterward, when Henry of Navarre was seated upon the throne of France, and when many of those who had fought against him at Coutras were arrayed on his side in opposition to the League, some of the loyal Roman Catholics desired to experience for themselves the advantage of the charm employed to their detriment on the banks of the Dronne. "Sire," said Montigny to Henry the Fourth on the eve of the battle of Ivry, "permit us to have at the head of your army to-morrow that minister who cast a spell of enchantment over us on the day of Coutras, and over the army of the League at Arques. We desire to hear his prayer when in sight of the enemy."[1]

---

[1] "Sire, aions demain à vostre teste ce Ministre qui nous charma à la journée de Coutras, et l'armée de la Ligue à Arques. Nous desirons d'ouir sa priere à la veue des ennemis." Agrippa d'Aubigné, iii. 229 (liv. iii., c. v.). Von Polenz, iv. 667, has noticed this interesting little incident, but, strangely enough, has misunderstood the word "charma," which he incorrectly renders by "erfreute," instead of "bezauberte." It is probable that Montigny, in

Their devotions ended, the Huguenot men-at-arms threw themselves upon their horses, ready to meet the fierce onslaught of the opposed battalion. Then from many throats, as from the throat of one man, rose the solemn chant of one of the grandest of exultant hymns—a part of Clément Marot's quaint version of the one hundred and eighteenth Psalm :[1]

A Huguenot battle-psalm.

"La voici l'heureuse journée
Que Dieu a faite à plein desir :
Par nous soit joye demenée,
Et prenons en elle plaisir.

"O Dieu Eternel, je te prie,
Je te prie, ton Roi maintien :
O Dieu, je te prie et reprie,
Sauve ton Roi, et l'entretien."

With the words still upon their lips, of gratitude that they had at last been permitted to meet their enemies in a free and open encounter, and of prayer for a prosperous issue, the Huguenots met the charge of the Duke of Joyeuse.

The eager lancers, well mounted and resplendent in their costly armor, had dashed madly forward, as if to take part in some holiday parade. Never had there been a pleasanter sight. The ground seemed positively shaded by the profusion of banners and streamers with which they and their weapons were adorned. But the intervening space was considerable. Before long the break-neck ride introduced confusion in the ranks; here a horseman was a length ahead of his companions, there one lagged as much behind. The first ardor diminished before the foot of the gentle elevation occupied by Navarre was reached, and as the horses began the ascent they fell from a gallop into a brisk trot. To add to the disorder, the duke's troops now for the first time perceived that they were opposed, not by a single corps, but by the three distinct detachments under the command of the three Bourbons, and a portion of the right and left diverged

---

command of the gendarmes on Joyeuse's left, was as little " delighted " with D' Amours' performance at Coutras as were the partisans of the League, two years later, at Arques.
[1] Verses 24 and 25.

in the direction of Soissons and Condé. A wide gap was thus created on either side of Joyeuse, which the Huguenots were not slow in turning to good account, and, a few minutes later, attacked the combatants in flank.

Meantime Navarre's arquebusiers restrained their impatience until the duke's lancers were within the prescribed distance, Rout and death of Joyeuse. then fired with fatal precision, and sent many a rider reeling from his seat. Just then the Huguenot men-at-arms, who had been well held in hand, advanced, quickening their pace as they came, and discharging with murderous effect their pistols loaded with pieces of steel and other destructive material. The struggle was soon decided. The Huguenots bore down with terrific force; the Roman Catholics, out of breath from their long run, could scarcely deliver with their lances a thrust sufficiently vigorous to do execution. Entangled by the very excess of the silken pennons they carried, with scant room to use their weapons, they fought bravely but hopelessly, and fell an easy prey to their enemies. The Duke of Joyeuse himself, discovering the extent of the disaster in which he had involved his army, after vainly imploring a friend to kill him,[1] found death at the hands of a Huguenot, who disdained the ransom of one hundred thousand crowns he offered, and remembered only the butchery the duke had permitted, a few months since, at La Mothe Saint Héray. On all sides there were prodigies of valor. Soissons fought as bravely as if he were a born Huguenot, and had been bred to no other profession than that of arms. Condé was not less determined, despite his being so unfortunate as to be unhorsed by Saint Luc, who then judiciously embraced the opportunity to surrender himself a prisoner to the prostrate prince. But of all the combatants the King of Navarre was undoubtedly entitled, on this occasion, to bear off the palm for superior prowess. His brave speeches before and Navarre's bravery. during the conflict were repeated from mouth to mouth. To Condé and Soissons he remarked, as the action was about to begin: "I shall say nothing to you but that you are of the House of Bourbon, and I shall show you that I

---

[1] Letter of Cavriana, November 1, 1587, Négociations avec la Toscane, iv. 727.

am your elder;" to which Condé and Soissons replied: "And we shall show you that we are your juniors." And when about to plunge into the thickest of the fight, "My companions," he exclaimed, " the glory of God, honor, and life are at stake. Whether to save ourselves or to conquer, the way lies before us. Forward in the name of God, for whom we are fighting!" Beset by Roman Catholic knights, Henry contended with several single-handed, and when he had shot one with his pistol, closed in with another, at the same time crying out, "Yield thee, Philistine!"[1]

It was nine o'clock when the battle began; within an hour the enemy were routed. The pursuit lasted for three hours, the fugitives being followed almost to the very entrance of Chalais. The Huguenot horse scoured the plain and cut to pieces, with little show of mercy, the unfortunate regiments of foot that had incurred their special enmity through participation in the butchery of the Protestants at La Mothe Saint Héray and Croix Chapeaux.

As for Navarre and his cousins, they soon desisted from following the retreating foe. Even before the conflict was fully over, the Béarnais had halted for a moment beneath a tree on the battle-ground, and had asked that a prayer of thanksgiving be offered to God for His mercy. Now that the enemy were routed, the king returned to the scene of the beginning of the engagement, and bade the same Huguenot minister—Gabriel d'Amours—conduct a more deliberate service of praise, who so short a time before had raised a supplication to Heaven for assistance, and who, sword in hand, had been among the most active of the combatants. Navarre himself designated the psalm to be sung on this joyful occasion.[2]

The prayer and psalm after battle.

---

[1] The addresses to Condé and Soissons and to the captains and soldiers, as given by Bap. Legrain in his "Decade contenant la vie et gestes de Henry le Grand" (Paris, 1614), and reproduced in the Lettres missives, ii. 308, differ altogether from the speeches given in the text, but are, to say the least, of suspicious authenticity.

[2] "N'estoy-je pas près de vous lorsque vous poursuiviez vos ennemis, que vous me fictes faire la premiere action de grâce soubs ung arbre, et, au retour de la pourçuite, la seconde au champs de batailles entre les mortz, que vous choisistes le ps. 'Or peut bien dire Israel maintenant,' etc." Gabriel d'Amours to Henry IV., June 20, 1593, ubi infra, i. 281.

Right heartily did the Huguenot soldiers, dust-begrimed and worn with the fierce encounter, sing in Beza's translation the sacred poem so appropriate to their own case:

> "If it had not been the Lord who was on our side,
> Now may Israel say;
> If it had not been the Lord who was on our side,
> When men rose up against us :
> Then they had swallowed us up quick."

The losses of the two sides were out of all proportion. The Roman Catholic army left upon the field four hundred noblemen, many of them of high rank, including their general and his brother, M. de Saint Sauveur, and two or three thousand foot soldiers. So considerable a number of nobles had not been cut off in three of the most bloody battles of the century taken together. The King of Navarre, on the other hand, mourned the loss of but twenty-five men in all.[1]

It was the first time, in a warfare extending over a quarter of a century, that the Huguenots had gained a pitched battle. Hitherto their enemies had been successful in every considerable engagement; but the Huguenots had contrived to neutralize the effects of defeat at Dreux, at Jarnac, and at Moncontour, by that practical sagacity which often avails quite as much as the most brilliant generalship in

The first pitched battle gained by the Huguenots.

---

[1] The best account of the battle of Coutras is unquestionably that of Agrippa d'Aubigné, in his Histoire universelle, iii. 48–58 (book iii., cs. xiii., xiv.). D'Aubigné, who was one of Navarre's squires, took place among the "maréchaux de camp" previously to the battle, and was intrusted with the honorable commission of marking out the field. After receiving a sword wound in the action, he led ten gentlemen in pursuit of the fugitives to the distance of three leagues, and prevented the troops of Joyeuse from rallying. Mémoires de D'Aubigné, 499. Other valuable accounts are those given in the Mémoires de la Ligue, ii. 262–270 ; in Cimber et Danjou, Archives curieuses, xi. 257–265, and, in great part verbatim, in Recueil des choses mémorables, 641–645 ; Mémoires de Sully, c. 23 (i. 194, etc.) ; De Thou, vii. (book 87) 10, etc. ; Davila, 320, etc. ; Lestoile, i. 232 ; Péréfixe, Histoire de Henry le Grand, 66, etc. ; the letter of Cavriana of November 1, 1587, ubi supra, iv. 725–731 ; the remarkable letter of Gabriel d'Amours, of June 20, 1593, first published in the Bulletin de la Société de l'histoire du Protestantisme français, i. 280–285. On D'Amours consult Haag, La France protestante, i. 175–179. The description of the battle in the Duc d'Aumale's Histoire des princes de Condé, ii. 163, etc., based on Agrippa d'Aubigné, is admirably clear and intelligible.

harvesting the fruits of military campaigns. It remained to be seen whether Henry of Navarre would prove equal to the task of securing as marked advantages from "the most signal victory gained in France for the defence of the Reformed religion" as Gaspard de Coligny had wrung from uniform defeat—in short, whether the conqueror of Coutras would show to the world a march to meet his German allies that would eclipse the glory of the raid through one-half of France by means of which the admiral, on the morrow of his defeat at Moncontour, carried terror to the royal court and made Paris itself tremble at the prospect of seeing the heretic at the gates of the capital.

There was no doubt of the surprise and sorrow with which the intelligence of the loss of the flower of the royalist nobles was received at court. Henry of Valois, however little he regretted in his heart the loss of a favorite whom he had lately learned to distrust as a secret partisan of the League, was conspicuous as a mourner. He gave to the dead Duke of Joyeuse such a pompous burial as was customary only in the case of princes of the blood—then turned and conferred upon the Duke of Épernon the office of admiral and the government of Normandy, the two most important trusts the late favorite had held.[1] As for the Cardinal of Bourbon, he disgusted even his majesty by volunteering the expression of a characteristic wish, that it had been his nephew that had lost his life in place of Joyeuse.[2]

It was for the purpose of preventing Henry of Navarre from obtaining in Gascony those re-enforcements with which he should march to the Loire and effect a junction with the German army, that Joyeuse had been despatched with such pressing orders on the expedition to which he owed his death. Now that Joyeuse had been killed and his army routed, it was to be expected that the Béarnais would pursue with vigor and alacrity the plan previously laid down. Instead of this, no sooner was the battle well over than he hurried off to Pau, to lay the ensigns taken from the enemy at the feet of his mistress, Corisande d'Andouins, Countess of Gram-

The fruits of victory lost.

---

[1] Cayet, Chronologie novenaire, 42.   [2] Lestoile, i. 232.

mont. Such were the strange inconsistencies in the character of this remarkable prince, that the same man who one day was imperilling his life at the head of a religious party, in arms for the defence of what it deemed the truth, the same man who craved the public recognition of the sovereignty of the God of battles before and after the bloody conflict, was seen, a few days after, bringing the trophies of victory to gratify the vanity of a woman whom he loved adulterously.

While there can be no question as to the flagrant indecency of his action, views widely divergent have been entertained respecting the military expediency of the course which the King of Navarre adopted on this occasion.

The "Army of the Reiters" was known to be on its way. It would require the best guidance and all the help the Huguenots of France could afford, to conduct the foreign troops across the wide intervening spaces. The inhabitants of the regions to be traversed were, almost to a man, Roman Catholics. The rivers were numerous, and some of them deep. The bridges were all in the hands of the enemy. Above all, should the reiters conclude to take the shortest path from Germany to Gascony, they must of necessity come within easy striking distance of Paris.

Why did not Henry of Navarre instantly press forward to prevent the occurrence of such a calamity as might well befall an army freshly recruited, in a strange land of whose geography it was scarcely less ignorant than of the language of the people? It is by no means easy to attain certainty upon this point. On the one hand, the king himself and such a trusty and conscientious a servant of his as Duplessis Mornay assert that it was impracticable for the victor of Coutras to do otherwise than as he did. To use their own expression, the troops of Navarre had been "borrowed" for a few days only. They had left home with little provision for a longer absence, and must be allowed time to refit themselves. They were now, moreover, encumbered by the very weight of the rich booty which they had taken, and which they must deposit in their houses before entering upon a long and perilous march. Besides, where and how were they to meet and join their German allies,

Navarre's justification.

who, in place of coming toward the Upper Loire, had, it was now known, contrary to the understanding which they had with them, deflected their course toward Beauce and Chartres—with what object in view it was difficult to surmise. How could either Henry of Navarre reach them or they reach Henry of Navarre, with the bridges and fords all in the enemy's hands? In fact, should the Huguenots of the south venture to start out in quest of the auxiliary army respecting whose plans since they left the German borders they had been left in complete ignorance, it was less likely that they would succeed in their endeavor than that they would, before reaching them, be overwhelmed by the army of the King of France. "Consider," wrote Duplessis Mornay, soon after the battle of Coutras, "that the king will have the option of bringing on a combat with whichever army he may please, and that his preference will be to attack us rather than the reiters. Hence, we must act cautiously; hence, too, it is very reasonable that for every two steps we take in the direction of our foreign army, it shall take three steps toward us."[1]

Unfortunately the plausible excuses of the King of Navarre, and of his conscientious but too partial advocate, are more than counterbalanced by the candid admissions of other followers of the Huguenot cause equally devoted and enjoying scarcely inferior opportunities for the formation of a correct judgment. Sully and Agrippa d'Aubigné, however much they may differ on other points, agree in deploring the signal mistake which in a brief week caused all the expected fruits of a great and signal victory to vanish into thin air. Both unite in ascribing

---

[1] "Au moins auront ils bien apperceu que nous n'espargnons rien pour aller à eulx." Duplessis Mornay to Morlas, November, 1587, Mémoires de Duplessis Mornay, iv. 34. See, also, "Mémoire envoyé par le roy de Navarre en l'armee estrangere qui le dobvoit venir joindre au commencement de Novembre, 1587, faict par M. Duplessis," ibid., iv. 39-43; and "Instruction au sieur de Monglat, retournant de la part du roi de Navarre vers l'armee estrangere," ibid., iv. 43-47. In the latter, p. 44, Henry expresses his surprise at seeing the reiters "descendre vers le bas, où il cognoissoit, en la saison d'hyver, et veu la grossesse de la riviere, une impossibilité de parvenir à eulx." Compare, also, "Instruction à M. des Reaux, allant de la part du roy de Navarre vers MM. des cantons de Suisse," iv. 47-54.

Henry's failure to march in all haste to extend a helping hand to the reiters on the banks of the Loire, or, if that was impossible, at least to strengthen the Protestant cause by the capture of all the important towns of Poitou and Saintonge, to the unfortunate sacrifice of duty at the altar of vanity or love.[1] And, if this testimony of sagacious captains be deemed insufficient, we have the direct statements of one of the chief actors in the drama of Coutras—no other than the brave Huguenot minister, Gabriel d'Amours—to the effect that, even immediately after the battle, the King of Navarre had not been left without faithful warning against the suicidal course which he seemed resolved to take. " The next day, in the morning," writes this frankest of servants to his royal master, " did not Monsieur de Chandieu and I go and entreat your majesty to pursue your victory and to make the most of it, as being the person who had had this honor from God to be elected Protector of the Churches in so notable an assembly as that of Montauban? Did we not tell you that if you should do otherwise, the victory which God had given you would prove to be of no account in future? You broke up your army, you went into Béarn ; you understand me well."[2]

Queen Elizabeth renders assistance. Meanwhile the great auxiliary army, from which the Huguenots anticipated so great advantage, and of whose advent their enemies stood in undisguised fear, had for some weeks been actually upon the march. Queen Elizabeth of England, having been persuaded to lend the Huguenots the material support of which they stood in need, had advanced at Frankfort a sum of over thirty thousand pounds sterling to be expended in the levy of German soldiers.[3]

---

[1] Sully, c. 24 ; Agrippa d'Aubigné, iii. 58, 59.

[2] " Le lendemain au matin Monsr. de Chandieu et moy n'allasmes-nous pas supplier V. M. de pourçuivre votre victoire et la faire valoir comme celuy qui avoit eu cest honneur de Dieu d'avoir esté esleu protecteur des Eglises en une assemblee si notable qu'estoit celle de Montauban ? Que si vous faisiès aultrement, la victoire que Dieu vous avoit donnée seroit comme de nul effect à l'advenir ? Vous rompistes vostre armée, vous alastes en Béarn ; vous m'entendez bien." Gabriel d'Amours to Henry IV., June 20, 1593.

[3] " Memoire des sommes de deniers que la Reyne d'Angleterre a prestez ou desboursez pour le Roy Treschrestien," submitted to the Council of Henry

Eight thousand reiters, or German horse, and twenty thousand Swiss foot soldiers[1] constituted a force which, added to the French troops at the disposal of Henry of Navarre, would perhaps enable the Huguenots to dictate terms of peace.

The Army of the reiters.

The old ally of the French Protestants, Duke John Casimir, had engaged either to lead the expedition in person or to furnish it with a competent head. In a document of great length he had promised never to lay down his arms until the Huguenots should have secured all the rights for which they were contending—the repeal of the entire body of unfriendly legislation enacted since the death of Henry the Second, complete equality of Protestants and Roman Catholics in the sight of the law, free admission to all offices, the "chambres mi-parties," three places of security in every province; in short, all that the most sanguine adherent of the Reformed Church could desire. At the same time the rights of Navarre as the legitimate heir to the crown of France were not forgotten.[2]

John Casimir's compact.

IV., May 21, 1599, O. S. The first item is: "An. 1587. Desbourse par les mains du Seignieur Horace Pallavicini pour la levee de l'armee Allemande, conduicte par le Baron d'D'aunau pour laquelle somme il y a obligation des Ambassadeurs du Roy datée à Francfort, Lib. Sterl. 30,468 ; Scud. Franc. 101,560." Edmund Sawyer, Memorials of Affairs of State (London, 1725), i. 29.

[1] These are De Thou's figures, vii. 17 (book 87) ; but other accounts differ widely. Guise, in a letter to the king, August 27, 1587, makes the army to consist of 5,000 reiters (instead of the 9,000 expected), 4,000 or 5,000 lansquenets, 12,000 Swiss, and 2,000 or 3,000 French troops under the Duke of Bouillon. See De Croze, ii. 23. The Recueil des choses mémorables, 646, agrees very nearly with the Duke of Guise, making the army consist of 5,000 reiters, 5,000 lansquenets, 12,000 to 15,000 Swiss, 2,000 French arquebusiers, and 400 to 500 horse. Duplessis Mornay, in a letter to Morlas, January, 1588, also makes one cause of failure to have been that but 4,000 reiters were sent. Mémoires, iv. 135. The account in the Mémoires de la Ligue, ii. 233, does not differ greatly from the above, but makes the total strength of the army, after the union with Châtillon's troops, to have been about 35,000 men, with nineteen pieces of artillery of various sizes.

[2] "Accord et capitulation faicte entre le roy de Navarre et le duc de Cazimir, pour la levee de l'armee des Reysters veneus en France en l'an 1587," dated "Fridelsheim, le 11ᵉ jour de janvier, l'an 1587." Mémoires de Duplessis Mornay, iv. 56–81. Casimir is here styled "Count Palatine of the Rhine, Administrator of the electorate and palatinate, Duke of Bavaria."

Unfortunately for the Huguenots, Casimir, who by this time was certainly familiar, by reason of past expeditions, with the French territory to be traversed, could not or would not go in person,[1] and deputed his authority to a nobleman far inferior to himself in birth, and scarcely more than a simple gentleman, the Baron Dohna—brave, upright, and conscientious, but utterly unacquainted with the affairs of the country. Destitute of the influence which high rank frequently confers, he was equally lacking in that mysterious faculty which enables some men sprung even from the lowliest station to control great bodies of soldiers. It was only to be expected that such a person should expose himself to misinformation, and fall a prey to the evil counsels of injudicious or corrupt counsellors.[2]

<small>Baron Dohna.</small>

It was late in August before the army started from its rendezvous in Alsace; and the reiters, who had been re-enforced by a small French contingent, would gladly have delayed further until the arrival of Châtillon, known to be on his way from Gascony. From the first, dissension prevailed in the ranks. The French were dissatisfied with the general assigned to the joint force, and insisted that, in default of a German prince, the supreme control should be intrusted to a French prince. It was only after much controversy and some hard feeling that the nominal command was reluctantly conceded to the Duke of Bouillon, whom youth and inexperience prevented from being adequate to discharge with credit the thankless and onerous duty. The Duchy of Lorraine was reached after a toilsome march through the woody passes of the Vosges near Pfalzburg, and the army, experienced at once the inconvenience of having neither authoritative leader nor settled plan of action. The Duke of

<small>The reiters enter Lorraine.</small>

---

[1] "Le duc Casimir ne pouvant, à cause de ses occupations domestiques, ou ne voulant, pour l'experience des peines passees, se faire chef de l'armee," etc. Agrippa d'Aubigné, iii. 77. This author's estimate of the Baron Dohna's qualifications is fair and moderate: "homme de quelque experience, de grand courage, parmi les reistres mestres (maïtres) d'heureuse reputation."

[2] "Le baron de Dono, son domestique, gentilhomme peu auctorisé parmi eulx." Duplessis Mornay to Morlas, Mémoires, iv. 135.

Bouillon and the French insisted upon the importance of taking advantage of the present opportunity to lay waste the possessions of the House of Lorraine, which, after having in previous wars pretended to be neutral, had now openly espoused the cause of the League. There was no more certain method of putting a speedy end to the present struggle, than by reducing the Duke of Lorraine and his kinsman the Duke of Guise to the necessity of begging the King of France to negotiate a peace with the Huguenots and their German allies. On the other hand, nothing could be more ill-advised than to spare the lands of the prime enemies of the Protestants, lying on the very road between Germany and France, and leave Sedan, Jametz, and the rest of the friendly Duchy of Bouillon exposed to the attacks of its implacable neighbors. It was then suspected, as it is now known, that Henry of Valois secretly hoped that the invading army would take this course; for that prince had no desire to cross swords with the Germans, and only longed for the quiet that must follow the humiliation of the League. Moreover, the French declared that in carrying fire and sword throughout Lorraine the army would only be executing the instructions of the King of Navarre himself.[1]

For a moment it seemed that this plan would be pursued; but suddenly Dohna and his council of war declared for another. They would march without delay to meet the King of Navarre, and therefore direct their course toward the river Loire. Dohna maintained that these were his instructions from Casimir.[2] His countrymen supported him from consid-

---

[1] Duplessis Mornay expressly states that it had been ordered that the army should occupy itself for a time in Lorraine, "et y prendroit quelque pied, afin d'y laisser une espine à ceulx de la Ligue, et de monstrer à la France qu'on se prenoit aulx aucteurs de ses malheurs." " Au contraire," he adds, "on dispute pour l'espargner; on declare qu'on ne souffrira poinct que la guerre s'y fasse; on se bande pour la Lorraine contro tous." Mémoires, iv. 135.

[2] Nor was this improbable in itself. Casimir and the Duke of Lorraine were closely connected by marriage, and both had been brought up together in the court of Henry the Second. It was at that time that Constable Montmorency remarked of the young German prince : " That little fox will in his youth find the hens of France so good, that he may very possibly return to eat them some future time, with a much larger company." Mémoires de la Huguerye, iii. 3–5.

erations of prudence. It was evidently safer for Germany to have the friendship than the hostility of the border land of Lorraine. As for the Duke of Bouillon, he deemed it best to yield the point without too much opposition. What had induced Dohna to adopt a decision which was the first of a long series of blunders in which the "Army of the Reiters" was destined to involve itself? Contemporaries for the most part ascribe it to the pernicious suggestions of one Michel de la Huguerye, who had been given to the baron, partly as counsellor, partly, from his familiarity with both German and French, as a convenient medium of communication between the troops of the two nations. So uniformly bad was the advice given by this person, that the story, whether true or a baseless surmise, gained currency that he was a paid agent of the House of Lorraine.[1]

It was a long and tedious journey that confronted the reiters, even before the formidable stream of the Loire could be reached. Numerous rivers intervened—the Meurthe, the Moselle, the Meuse, the Marne, the Aube, the Seine, the Armançon, the Serein, the Cure, the Yonne. Upon the banks of any one of these their progress might be disputed. The population of the region was hostile,

Route taken by the Germans.

---

[1] "Un nommé la Huguerie fut suspect deslors et depuis à plusieurs, d'avoir porté grand nuisance à toute l'armee, et rompu beaucoup de desseins tant contre le duc de Lorraine que contre ceux de Guise. Il essaya de s'en excuser: neantmoins long temps depuis a esté en reputation d'avoir empli ses cofres en ceste guerre." Recueil des choses mémorables, 647. See Agrippa d'Aubigné, iii. 63, and Duplessis Mornay, ubi supra, iv. 136. Respecting La Huguerye's calumnious statements about Jeanne d'Albret, etc., in his Mémoires, see the Rise of the Huguenots, ii. 424. De Thou (vii. 17) had seen the man and weighed his character: "Cet homme, qui avoit appris à ne rougir de rien, avoit autrefois été précepteur à Paris, où je l'avois vû pendant ma jeunesse. Du reste il étoit vendu à la Ligue, et s'étoit, dit-on, laissé corrompre par le Duc de Lorraine, pour trahir ses alliés." It is only just, however, to say that this was not the opinion of François de Châtillon, who, in a letter to Casimir, February 17, 1588, after deploring the unfortunate issue of the expedition, remarks: "Quoi qu'on dise, M. de la Huguerye s'y est comporté en homme de bien et en bonne conscience, pour le moins en tout ce que j'ay vu et apperçu de luy." See Count Delaborde, 324, and Baron de Ruble, in the admirable introduction to the third volume of his edition of the Mémoires de la Huguerye, xxi., etc.

and in the Duke of Guise and other leaders the German army had watchful antagonists who did not, indeed, venture upon general engagements, but who harassed it continually, and more than once inflicted considerable loss. Meanwhile the generalship of the Germans was too incompetent to take advantage of such opportunities as the reckless audacity of the other side sometimes afforded. On the long march one notable accession of strength was gained, when, at the abbey of Saint Urbain, not far from Joinville, François de Châtillon came in, having safely accomplished, with the troops intrusted to him by the King of Navarre, a long, difficult, and perilous circuit from the neighborhood of the Garonne, through the whole length of Languedoc, Dauphiny, and Savoy, to Geneva, and thence through Switzerland and the Spanish Franche Comté to Lorraine. Fresh dangers awaited the little band of scarcely one hundred men-at-arms and twelve hundred mounted arquebusiers, at the very end of its pilgrimage ; for a superior force of the enemy, having enveloped Châtillon and his troops in the village of Grésille (Grizelle), compelled him to retire for safety into the castle. Happily he was rescued within a few hours by the timely arrival of friendly troops.[1]

They are joined by François de Châtillon.

The gain of Châtillon's troops was more than counterbalanced by the losses sustained by the undisciplined army, which, after the common fashion of the German soldiers of the period, was more intent upon plundering such towns and villages as fell in its way, and exacting a ransom from wealthy abbeys like that of Clairvaux, than careful of health and life. Many of the reiters died because of their imprudence in feeding upon unripe and unwholesome fruit, and many who lagged behind, half dead with disease, were despatched by the peasants. Yet it must be confessed that the Duke of Guise makes too great a draft upon our faith when, in his letters to the King of France, he swears that on a single day

Want of discipline, and losses.

---

[1] See the very full account of this expedition given by Count Jules Delaborde, in his life of Châtillon, pp. 264-283, based upon the letters of Châtillon himself and the Mémoires of his lieutenant, M. de Saint Auban. These Mémoires may also themselves be consulted with profit (Petitot Collection. vol. 43, pp. 472-482).

he has seen, in following them, more than eight hundred dead bodies left in the wake of the army.¹

Harassed by the Duke of Guise, who hung on their right, and by his brother, the Duke of Mayenne, who was never far from their left, the Germans and their allies at length found themselves approaching the centre of the kingdom. But, what with the self-will of the troops and the weakness of their superiors, little advantage was to be hoped from their coming. Scarcely had the army crossed the river Yonne when it was met by a messenger sent by the King of Navarre— Louis de Harlay, Sieur de Monglas. He bade Baron Dohna, in his master's name, to discontinue his advance, and take the road to the left which, at this spot, branches off in the direction of the upper waters of the Loire. In vain, however, did the envoy insist; the Germans were in no mood to engage in a toilsome and circuitous march through the Morvan and other mountain districts, such as those through which François de Châtillon had lately made his way and which he was so soon again to traverse. It seemed much more pleasant to push on to the Loire, where they were informed that a bridge might easily be secured by the seizure of the town of La Charité. This hope was destined soon to be crushed. The troops sent forward to make themselves masters of La Charité arrived before the place twenty-four hours too late. Another and a more serious disappointment befell the Germans about the same time. Knowing that the war with the Huguenots had been undertaken by the king sorely against his will, the Baron Dohna had confidently expected that his majesty would seize the advent of the reiters as a pretext for promptly concluding a peace with Henry of Navarre; in which event he might have returned to the Rhine with little loss, and with all the substantial fruits of a victorious campaign. Instead of this, he discovered

The Germans disregard Navarre's orders, and push on to the Loire.

---

¹ De Croze, ii. 27-29. The course taken by the Army of the Reiters may be traced on the map, from Pfalzburg, through or near Saarbruck, Blamont, Lunéville, Bayon, Pont Saint Vincent, Saint Urbain, Chaumont en Bassigny, Clairvaux, Château Vilain, Châtillon sur Seine, Laignes, Ancy le Franc, Tanlay, Noyers, Vermanton, Mailly la Ville, to Neuvy, etc., on the river Loire.

that the only practical result of the German irruption had thus far been to shame Henry of Valois into taking the field in person, and thus bringing about an apparent community of purpose between the royalists and the League. In fact, he found that, to the two merciless enemies who still hung upon his flanks, leaving him no rest by day or by night, he must now add a third enemy in the king's own forces posted in his front at Gien and guarding every crossing of the Loire.

Here again Monglas gave the Germans good but fruitless advice. Since they had been unwilling to obey the Béarnais's commands by taking the route of the Upper Loire, let them at least not shrink from making a vigorous attempt to cross the stream where they were. This, he assured them, was quite practicable, for the fords were numerous and the forces of the enemy would not be likely to offer any insurmountable obstacle. But Navarre's envoy was as unsuccessful in persuading his intractable allies now as he had been in the first instance. The reiters absolutely refused to make the venture. Either they would turn westward along the northern bank of the Loire, or they would go home by the road they had come.

<small>They insist on going westward.</small>

There was no help for it. The headstrong Germans must be permitted to have their own way, plunging still farther into the most populous districts of France, with no visible plan, and with little likelihood of being able ultimately to extricate themselves from the pitfalls lying in their path. The Frenchmen in their company, not being able to lead, were fain to content themselves with following their unruly associates, and diminishing, if possible, the effects of the inevitable disaster in store for them.

The Duke of Guise, as has been seen, had never been far away from the army of the reiters since it entered France. Determined to inflict the utmost damage possible upon the intruders, he was no less resolute that the King of France should receive little assistance and no glory at his hands. To the Spanish ambassador, with whom he maintained an unbroken correspondence, he revealed the intensity of the hatred he entertained toward his lawful sovereign, and the profound distrust with which he viewed every action of the

<small>Guise's correspondence with the Spaniards.</small>

Valois prince. It was to Philip of Spain that he turned for help, pleading for the payment of those sums of money without which he declared himself unable to meet his necessary expenses. He could not see, he said, what difference there was between the present condition of things and that contemplated by the treaty of Joinville. If the house of Guise remained under arms, it would compel the King of France to continue the war, and so the tranquillity of the Netherlands and of Philip's affairs, so far as the French were concerned, would be assured. "So long as we keep the king thus busily employed," added the duke, with undisguised satisfaction, "it will not be in his power to turn his thoughts elsewhere."[1] Meantime, if Philip should withhold his promised aid, save in case of the declaration of open war between Henry of Valois and the League, that wily prince would continue to conduct his hostilities in so covert a manner that the latter would never be able to break the public peace without apparent injustice, and when abandoned by all its supporters; or else he would wait until six times as large a sum of money would not raise the forces at its command to their present degree of effectiveness.

But while thus patiently holding forth his hand for the alms which his Catholic Majesty might be pleased to dole out to his very humble petitioner and pensioner, the Duke of Guise took good care to earn Philip's esteem and confidence by sedulously disobeying Henry's commands. "The king," he wrote to Mendoza, a few days before the events which we are next to consider, "has sent me word to annoy the enemy as much as possible, and to make ready to join him. In order to find an excuse for not doing so, therefore, I place the enemy between him and myself; and I have sent to hasten the Duke of Lorraine. If he succeed in coming, we shall have an army stronger than his and than that of the enemy. To-day I shall effect a junction with my brother and cousins, so as to continue to do them damage. After that I shall see what is to be done."[2]

---

[1] "Tant que nous tiendrons le roy en ces exercices, il n'est possible qu'il puisse penser ailleurs."

[2] Guise to Mendoza, from camp at Joigny, October 20, 1587, De Croze, Appendix, ii. 296-298.

Just one week after the date of this remarkable letter, which casts a flood of light upon the attitude of the parties in the war that was desolating France, the first serious encounter of arms occurred. The scene was the village of Vimory, not far from Montargis, former abode of Renée of France, Duchess of Ferrara, where, in previous wars, a hospitality worthy of the daughter of Louis the Twelfth had been dispensed to the poor Huguenots. Faithful to his policy of keeping the enemy between himself and the monarch whom he wished to avoid, Guise had advanced to Courtenay, and thence to the vicinity of Montargis. The little river Loing intervened between him and the reiters, protecting him from any surprise on their part, but offering no impediment to him, commanding as he did all the passages. The Germans were barely through their supper one evening—it was about seven o'clock and already quite dark—when the Duke of Guise and his brother, with a strong band of horse, suddenly dashed in among them, confidently expecting to cut to pieces one of the divisions of the Protestant army. But though there was some terror for the moment and much loss of baggage, the Baron Dohna speedily rallied his men and repulsed the assailants, with whom it might have gone hard had not a violent rain and the consequent darkness, together with the lack of familiarity of the strangers with their surroundings, effectually prevented the pursuit. As it was, the German general and Mayenne came into a personal combat, in which the former received a sabre cut upon the forehead that might well have proved serious, while the latter was stunned by two well-aimed pistol-shots that struck the chinpiece of his helmet. It was clearly a very indecisive action,[1] as Guise virtually admitted on the morrow by sending the baron an offer to exchange the dead, and the prisoners and banners taken on both sides. None the less did the Lorraine prince, with whom neither modesty nor verac-

---

[1] "Au reste cette attaque fut très-sanglante, et ne couta pas moins cher au Duc de Mayenne qu'aux ennemis." De Thou, vii. (book 87) 34. Cayet makes Guise and Mayenne lose 240 men and the reiters but 150. Chronologie Novenaire, 41.

ity was a virtue held in high repute, publish far and wide stories of a signal victory. To Mendoza, in particular, who was dispenser of Philip the Second's bounty, he reported, in a letter written three days later, a marvellous success. Contrary to the advice of everybody, he said, he had attacked a quarter of the enemy containing twenty-two cornets of reiters, whom he had defeated, cutting to pieces more than seven hundred of their number, not to speak of the wounded, and capturing the principal colonels and captains, and more than twelve hundred horse, with an infinite quantity of booty and "chariots." [1] However idle the boast, it accomplished its end in inflaming still more the enthusiastic devotion of the silly populace of Paris to the House of Guise, while sensible men, able to make a liberal discount from the claims of the lying League, shook their heads and felt sure of only one thing—that, whichever side might gain, the king was sure to lose.[2]

As the army advanced farther, the difficulties from within and from without multiplied from day to day. Bad as were the roads through a district converted by copious rains into a quagmire, so deep that the Swiss and German foot soldiers lost their shoes, and even the horses of the reiters,[3] if we may believe the chronicles, were at every step liable to suffer a similar disaster, the divisions and dis-

The Germans involved in increasing difficulty.

---

[1] Guise to Mendoza, from camp on the Loire, October 30, 1587, De Croze, ii., pièces justificatives, 299.

[2] Letter of Cavriana (who styles the affair a puny victory—"una vittorietta"), November 1, 1587. Négociations avec la Toscane, iv. 731. See the accounts in the Mémoires de la Ligue, ii. 241, 242; Recueil des choses mémorables, 649; Agrippa d'Aubigné, iii. 63, 64; De Thou, ubi supra; "Sommaire discours de toutes les deffaictes des Reistres," etc., in Cimber et Danjou, Archives curieuses, xi. 267-275. Lestoile, i. 233, caustically observes that more reiters by nearly two thousand were reported to have been routed at Vimory than had entered France altogether. As for Etienne Pasquier's panegyrical letter (Ed. Feugère, ii. 300, 301), it is only less inaccurate than Davila's account (324, 325), which makes Guise's gain in horses captured more than twice as large as that claimed by the duke himself. Almost the only loss of the German general on which all parties were agreed, was of the strange present of two camels and two kettledrums (such, says Cayet, as the Turkish bashaws are accustomed to have carried in front of them when in command of armies), intended by Dohna for the King of Navarre.

[3] Cayet, ubi supra.

sensions prevailing among the troops were still worse. Not inaptly does Sully liken the ponderous army in its uncertain progress to some huge hulk of a vessel left to drift at the mercy of the waves.[1] The Swiss, no such dullards as to be blind to the ruin in which the incompetency of their leaders must infallibly end, had early taken the alarm. Under the circumstances it is not altogether to be wondered at that, even before the incident at Vimory, they fell in with an artful suggestion that they should send deputies to the King of France, to inform his majesty of the reasons for which they had entered his dominions. This step having been taken, the Duke of Nevers and others had an opportunity for intrigue which they were not slow in improving. The issue could not be doubtful. It was not difficult to induce the Swiss to believe that they had been enlisted under false pretences. Was not the very monarch who, they had been assured, had been compelled by the rebellious League, contrary to his will, to take up arms against his Huguenot subjects, now himself at the head of his forces, opposing the advance of the very army that had come to espouse the Huguenot cause? Was he not contending for the same objects as Guise and Mayenne? Henry of Valois himself, much as he would certainly have been delighted had his old Swiss allies been employed in humbling the power of Lorraine and the League, on the outskirts of France, could not, save at the risk of manifest dishonor, treat as friends the perverse invaders who had ill-advisedly penetrated to the very neighborhood of his capital. It is not surprising that, when the envoys were admitted to his presence, the king showed them "a very bad countenance," or that he reproached them with some bitterness for violating their oath and taking arms against him. "I am King of France," said he; "I wear on my head the crown. I am not a mere shadow." In short, after a fortnight or more, during which messengers went to and fro between the royal camp and the quarters of the Swiss, the latter adopted a resolution, which the joint remonstrances of the Baron Dohna and of the French

The Swiss send deputies to the king.

They determine to return to Switzerland.

---

[1] Œconomies royales, i. 201.

Protestants were unable to shake, to return to Switzerland under the guarantee of the king's protection during the march.

The defection of the Swiss has naturally met on all sides with severe and merited animadversion, as bearing unmistakable marks of fickleness, if not of positive cowardice. Yet some weight ought certainly to be given to the remark of the historian Agrippa d'Aubigné, who, with all the facts of the case before him, and fully understanding the difficulties of their situation, charitably concedes that never had any Swiss mercenaries so nearly a justification of their course in coming to a separate arrangement with the enemy.[1]

Through the whole autumn the army of the reiters had been aimlessly pushing westward. Now, near the end of November, it found itself only two leagues short of the city of Chartres, with what ulterior destination no one seemed to know. The new resolution adopted by the Swiss, together with the evident folly of persisting in a course that only took them farther from all hope of meeting the friendly forces of the King of Navarre, at length determined the Germans to retrace their steps, with the possible purpose of seeking by the Upper Loire a passage into Southern France. Even now, however, this unfortunate army was not suffered to go unharmed.

The Germans begin a retreat.

Barely had it turned its face eastward when a new disaster befell it. Baron Dohna lodged his guards in the little walled town of Auneau, ten or twelve miles east of Chartres. The peasants of the neighborhood had shut themselves up in the castle overlooking the town, and had not been molested, on their engagement to furnish the reiters with the provisions the latter might require. Dohna was a careless general. He had not informed himself of the fact that the Duke of Guise, having marched all day toward Auneau, had secretly thrown into the castle a body of arquebusiers, while he himself

---

[1] "Je dirai pourtant à la descharge de cette nation, qu'aiant ouï alleguer leurs raisons dans le conseil des Princes, estant bien connu combien ils estoient mal conduits, jamais les Suisses n'ont fait capitulation à part (comme il leur est arrivé quelques fois) de laquelle ils puissent monstrer plus justifiantes raisons." Histoire universelle, iii. 65. The most full contemporary account of the Swiss episode is found in the Mémoires de la Ligue, ii. 239-245, 247, 248-250.

waited outside of the town ready to fall on the Germans at daybreak. His bold plan succeeded in every point. Early on the morning of the twenty-fifth of November, a simultaneous attack was made from the castle and from the country side. The gates were found open and unprotected, for no thought had been given to them at a moment when the army was about to march out. The ponderous "chariots" or wagons of the Germans encumbered the narrow streets; the reiters themselves were engaged in bringing out of the houses the troublesome effects without which they never deigned to go to war. When they had hastily thrown themselves into the saddle, they knew not whither to go for combat or escape. Dohna and seven or eight of his men, fortunate in reaching a gate early, fought their way through and reached the open country. A few others clambered to the walls, and thence threw themselves into the moat. All the rest of the detachment of reiters that had passed the night at Auneau were either killed or taken prisoners. The loss of the Germans was considerable, but it was not irretrievable. Had the conduct of the army been even passably fair, the disaster might have been forgotten in the glory of subsequent successes. As it was, the Germans lost all heart. It is doubtful, indeed, whether had the king desired to effect the utter destruction of the foreigners from the other side of the Rhine, he might not have virtually accomplished it. But he was too shrewd to press an advantage of which the glory would inure altogether to the Duke of Guise and the League. As for Guise, his secret correspondence with the Spanish ambassador sufficiently testifies to the bitterness with which he chafed at the impediments thrown in his way by his royal master. To Mendoza he declared that what induced him so promptly to resolve on making the attack at Auneau was the certain advice he had received of the intention of the King of France, "which was to pursue and conclude treaties with the strangers, and bring under immediate consideration a peace which this happy enterprise now averted."[1]

They are surprised by Guise at Auneau.

Guise accuses the king of throwing obstacles in his way.

---

[1] "Et faire parler à l'instant d'une paix que j'ay divertie par ceste heureuse entreprise."

He assured him that he had lost but four of his men, while the enemy had lost the choicest part, the very soul of their army, and the remainder had not dared even to come to the rescue. Their flight had been disorderly, but the Duke of Épernon, commanding the king's forces, though following them day by day, and never more than from two to four leagues distant, had not suffered an arquebuse to be fired or a lance to be broken. Indignant at such evident cowardice and treachery, whole companies of Épernon's soldiers had forsaken him with standards flying and without leave. When the Dukes of Mercœur and Nemours offered to join him with five or six hundred lances, Épernon resolutely declined their assistance, and induced the king to recall them; and, on learning that Mandelot and other friends of Guise were about to attack the retreating Germans, the perfidious favorite of the king at once began to treat with the enemy to prevent their entire discomfiture. "I rejoice," truculently added the Duke of Guise, "that if they pass through my government (Champagne) or through Lorraine, I shall attack them, at any cost, and without regard for any promise which may have been given to them, and that I shall put an end to them."[1]

The reiters accept a safe-conduct to Germany. The tidings conveyed by the duke to Philip the Second's ambassador in Paris were only too true. Disheartened by the mismanagement of their leaders and by the desertion of the Swiss, the reiters were not long in resolving to avail themselves of the liberal offer of a safe-conduct made to them in the king's name, provided they would return to Germany.[2] Thus did the great "Army of the Reiters," upon which such magnificent hopes had been founded, come to an impotent conclusion.[3] As an anonymous chronicler of the

---

[1] See the instructive letters of Guise to Mendoza of December 5 and 11, 1587. De Croze (documents inédits), ii. 300–303. In the second letter Guise significantly remarks: "Le roi pense que ces reistres dehors, il nous manquera beaucoup de subject d'entreprendre."

[2] It is unnecessary to give in detail the articles of the "capitulation," which the curious may read in the Mémoires de la Ligue, ii. 260, 261. It is dated December 8, 1587.

[3] "La susdite armée s'estant ruinee," pithily observes brave François de la Noue, Bras-de-fer, "plus par elle mesme que par l'effort de ses contraires."

period piously remarks: "This army was in France the terror of some and the hope of others; howbeit, both parties were deceived in their expectation. God made use of it as an example to teach man, on the one hand, that He has many means of chastising him when He pleases, and, on the other, that he is ill-assured who trusts in man and makes an arm of flesh his strength."[1]

The disappointment of the Huguenots was only less than the indignation of Guise. "Not merely," he wrote to Mendoza, "has Épernon placed himself between the reiters and me, in order to favor them during the fine treaty he has concluded with them, but he has given them money, so as to maintain the credit of the heretics with the strangers, and a thousand arquebusiers of the king's own guard and ten companies of gendarmes to accompany their retreat. It is strange that the forces of the Catholics must be employed to recompense the heretics for the evils they have inflicted upon France. Every good Frenchman and true Catholic must feel himself offended."[2] To these words the Duke of Guise added, in the letter just quoted, the statement, which, but for the sequel, might have appeared unimportant enough: "I have joined the Marquis du Pont, as a simple soldier, having dismissed my troops. But for the king's strange declaration, I should have attacked the heretics and those who wished to preserve them."

Indignation of the League.

Attended by the royal troops, and effectually guarded from the assaults of the followers of the League, the remains of the army that had marched so boldly into France, three or four months before, made an ignominious exit by way of the territories of the Duke of Savoy and of the free city of Geneva. Balked of his prey, the Duke of Guise looked around for some unprotected district upon which to vent his anger and disappointment. Such a district he found close at hand, in the county of Montbéliard, which at the period now under consideration had not as yet been incorporated in the kingdom of France. No better excuse was needed than that the cousin

Guise and Du Pont lay waste the county of Montbéliard.

Declaration de Monsieur de la Noue, sur la prise des armes pour la juste defense des villes de Sedan, etc. Mémoires de la Ligue, ii. 320.

[1] Mémoires de la Ligue, ii. 233.

[2] Mucius (Guise) to Mendoza, December 16, 1587, De Croze, ii. 303.

of the Duke of Würtemberg, to whom Montbéliard belonged, was in alliance with the Huguenots and had favored their enterprise. Guise's troopers and those of his kinsman, the Marquis of Pont à Mousson,[1] had not received their pay; it was convenient, and, it would seem, not contrary to the religious or humane instincts of their princely leaders, to sacrifice to them an unoffending population in lieu of wages. What atrocities they perpetrated I cannot here undertake to narrate; and the reader curious of such things must be referred to the contemporary account, in which the recital fills more than a score of closely printed pages.[2] Suffice it to say that no savage device for extracting money from reluctant peasants already burdened by oppressive taxation, was wanting; while of all the most repulsive forms of lewdness and unnatural crime that history has unfortunately been compelled from time to time to chronicle, scarcely one can be imagined of which instances are not here recorded. "It was necessary," wrote a Huguenot, some years later, by way of apology for committing to paper so disgraceful a story, "that our posterity should know how insane the adherents of the League have been to desire for king one of a family that has in so many different ways declared itself the sworn enemy of honor, humanity, nature, and every form of religion."

There was one Frenchman who, indignant beyond measure at the course of events, had absolutely refused to have anything to do with the offers of the Duke of Épernon, and disdained to take refuge beyond the Rhine from an enemy at whose hands

---

[1] Henry II., Marquis of Pont à Mousson, afterward Duke of Lorraine and of Bar, was the eldest son of Charles III., reigning Duke of Lorraine. He was born November 20, 1563. He married, January 31, 1599, Catharine of Bourbon, only sister of Henry IV. of France. On the present occasion he appears as a merciless patron of murder and rapine. On a subsequent page of this history he will be seen a slave of superstition and bigotry. The two phases of his character were not inconsistent with each other.

[2] "Histoire tragique des cruautez et meschancetez horribles commises en la Comté de Montbéliard sur la fin de l'an 1587 et commencement de l'an 1588, par les troupes des sieurs de Guise et Marquis de Pont, fils aisné du Duc de Lorraine. Nouvellement mise en lumiere." (Comprised in the Mémoires de la Ligue, iii. 705–732.)

[3] Mémoires de la Ligue, iii. 704.

he asked no favors. Châtillon had come many a mile to join the auxiliary army, despising alike the dangers thrown in his way by nature and the greater perils that might await him from watchful enemies. He now prepared to return to Languedoc by a not less adventurous path. So long as there had been any hope of bringing the Germans to a manly course, he had remained with them. At Lancié, not far from Mâcon, he made a last attempt to overcome their repugnance against striking southward in the direction of the King of Navarre. He pointed in the distance to the hills of Vivarais, and pledged to them his life that in four days, if they would but follow his lead, he would place them beyond the reach of harm.[1] He assured them that, acquainted as he was with the forces at the disposal of the governor of Lyons and other neighboring royal officers, they had nothing to fear from any attempts to hinder their progress. But finding remonstrance and persuasion alike fruitless, and the Germans determined to conclude the compact with the Duke of Épernon, to which allusion has already been made, Châtillon promptly retired from the camp of his timid associates. It was quite another thing for a slender troop of horse to elude Mandelot and his associates from what it would have been to march through the same territories with an overwhelming force of Germans and French combined; yet Châtillon accomplished the feat. In five days from his parting with the reiters, he found himself safe and sound in a castle in Vivarais held by a friendly garrison of Protestants.[2]

Magnanimity of François de Châtillon.

His daring retreat to Languedoc.

With Châtillon's safe arrival in Languedoc the story of the Army of the Reiters reached its natural though unexpected conclusion. Most of the French nobles who had accompanied the Germans had managed to escape, in various directions. The young Duke of Bouillon had taken refuge in the city of Geneva

---

[1] The details of his plan are given in the Mémoires de la Ligue, ii. 257.

[2] It is the judgment of competent military critics that Châtillon's retreat was one of the most brilliant affairs of the kind known in history. Count Jules Delaborde, in his life of Châtillon, 310-320, reproduces the whole of Saint Auban's interesting account of the entire movement.

only to die within a few days of disease brought on by fatigue and exposure.[1]

---

[1] On the Army of the Reiters, the following authorities, among others, may be consulted with profit: Recueil des choses mémorables, 646-654; De Thou, vii. (book 87) 17-46; Pasquier's letter " sur l'arrivée des reiters," etc., Œuvres choisies (Feugère), ii. 300; Sommaire discours, in Cimber et Danjou, Archives curieuses, xi. 267-275; Mémoires de la Ligue, ii. 232-262; Agrippa d'Aubigné, iii. 62-68; Davila, 318-328; Mémoires inédits de Michel de la Huguerye, publiés d'après les MSS. autographes, par le Baron A. de Ruble (vol. iii. 1880); Count Jules Delaborde, "François de Chastillon, Comte de Coligny" (Paris, 1886). The last gives, in an appendix, 469-491, the original narrative of the expedition sent by Châtillon to Henry of Navarre, under date of Montpellier, December 31, 1587, from the MS. in the National Library at Paris. It had already been noticed by Baron de Ruble that the account in the Mémoires de la Ligue is in fact only a copy of this narrative, which the editor (probably Simon Goulart) used without giving any clue as to the source whence he derived his information.

END OF VOLUME I.

www.ingramcontent.com/pod-product-compliance
Lightning Source LLC
Chambersburg PA
CBHW071136300426
44113CB00009B/991